Counseling and Psychotherapy

A Practical Guidebook for Students, Trainees, and New Professionals

Salvatore Cullari

Lebanon Valley College

Allyn and Bacon

Boston ▪ London ▪ Toronto ▪ Sydney ▪ Tokyo ▪ Singapore

Executive Editor: *Rebecca Pascal*
Editorial Assistant: *Whitney Brown*
Marketing Manager: *Caroline Croley*
Editorial-Production Administrator: *Annette Joseph*
Editorial-Production Coordinator: *Holly Crawford*
Editorial-Production Service: *Omegatype Typography, Inc.*
Composition Buyer: *Linda Cox*
Electronic Art and Composition: *Omegatype Typography, Inc.*
Manufacturing Buyer: *Megan Cochran*
Cover Administrator: *Brian Gogolin*
Cover Designer: *Jenny Hart*

A Pearson Education Company
160 Gould Street
Needham Heights, MA 02494

Internet: www.abacon.com

Between the time Website information is gathered and then published, it is not unusual for some sites to have closed. Also, the transcription of URLs can result in unintended typographical errors. The publisher would appreciate notification where these occur so that they may be corrected in subsequent editions. Thank you.

Library of Congress Cataloging-in-Publication Data

Cullari, Salvatore.
Counseling and psychotherapy : a practical guidebook for students, trainees, and new professionals / Salvatore Cullari.
p. cm.
Includes bibliographical references and index.
ISBN 0-205-29425-1 (alk. paper)
1. Psychotherapy. 2. Counseling. I. Title.
RC465.5 .C855 2001
616.89'14—dc21

00-036231

Printed in the United States of America

10 9 8 7 6 5 4 3 2 1 RRD-VA 05 04 03 02 01 00

This book is dedicated to my good friend and cousin, Paolino Falduto, who made learning a lifelong activity. He was taken away from us prematurely and unexpectedly on the day this book was completed.

CONTENTS

PREFACE

Even for experienced therapists, providing effective psychological services in our society is often a daunting task. For the newcomer to this field, this responsibility may at times appear to be overwhelming. There just seems to be too much to read, too much to learn, and too much to do. One of the goals of *Counseling and Psychotherapy: A Practical Guidebook for Students, Trainees, and New Professionals* is to make this task a bit easier. This book provides a comprehensive and practical examination of the major topic areas of clinical and counseling psychology. Rather than being based on any one orientation, it takes an integrationist approach to psychotherapy, so it should be applicable to a wide audience. It is designed to be a practical "how to" guide for beginning psychotherapists and counselors. As such, it is written for advanced graduate students in the areas of psychotherapy and counseling and for new professionals. It is also an excellent guide for those who are starting a professional internship. It will be useful for students and professionals in related disciplines such as psychiatry, social work, and psychiatric nursing as well.

Counseling and Psychotherapy is unique in a number of ways. Rather than being written by a single person, the book is written by a collection of individuals who are experienced experts in various subfields of clinical and counseling psychology. It is difficult for any one person to keep pace with the ever changing world of counseling and psychotherapy. The group of experts who have written the chapters in this book are recognized leaders in their respective fields; all of these authors have extensive "real world" experience as opposed to having solely academic or research backgrounds. The wide diversity of these authors' ideas and suggestions should further develop and complement your emerging intrinsic theories of psychotherapy.

Edited books are often criticized for having chapters that are too different or inconsistent with each other. While this may, in fact, be a problem at times, I believe that differences in the ideas, orientations, or even writing styles between authors can also be an asset. One of the persons I admire most in my career is Gregory Bateson. In many of his writings, Bateson talked about the importance of differences for the process of learning (what he called the "difference that makes a difference"). According to Bateson, without differences, learning would be impossible. Often we arrive at our most useful insights when we are exposed to information that is new or unlike any we have experienced before. I believe that by having a number of diverse but highly experienced individuals write this book, the reader's prospect of achieving new insights and understanding is enhanced.

On the other hand, this does not mean that theories, techniques, facts, and information can be just thrown together haphazardly. In an earlier publication, I stated that eclecticism at its *worst* is frameless and somewhat chaotic. Psychotherapy integration at its *best* is like a well-orchestrated concert with each separate piece fitting snugly together like a puzzle. This is what separates an experienced psychotherapist from a novice. An experienced therapist knows what to do, when to do it, and, perhaps more importantly, when to stop doing it. One of the goals of this book is to *help* the reader develop a personally integrated and effective system of psychotherapy. I say "help" here because no single textbook or course will be able to accomplish this single-handedly. Like anything that is worthwhile, this process will take a lot of time and a lot of hard work.

Counseling and Psychotherapy has several goals and objectives. First, it is designed to help prepare the reader for the challenging but rewarding field of psychotherapy (please note that the terms *counseling* and *psychotherapy* are generally used interchangeably throughout the text). Second, it is meant to decrease the common fears and anxieties that all new therapists face upon entering this career. Third, it is intended to serve as a road map for future learning. No textbook can be completely comprehensive, and this is especially true in the field of psychotherapy. This book offers many additional sources of information that you can use to further your knowledge of the topics that are presented. In a related manner, at the close of this Preface, I offer a list of Internet sites related to clinical and counseling psychology, which should further enhance your knowledge. Most of these sites have additional links that should be useful as well. I will maintain an updated and expanded version of this list, which will be available free of charge to any reader who requests it (Cullari@lvc.edu).

Another goal of this book is to help bridge the gap of the critical period between advanced student and new professional. As far as I can tell, this is the only book on the market that attempts to do so. In this case, it offers chapters on material that is often not found in other similar textbooks: opening a professional office, consulting, outcome evaluation, integrating psychotherapy with psychotropic medications, working with clients with serious mental illnesses, and other often neglected topics. Following this plan, Part One of this book is written mainly for students who are still in graduate school, and Part Two is designed for the immediate postgraduate time period.

For those of you who are just starting out in the helping profession, a more basic coverage of some of the material presented in this book is included in the companion textbook *Foundations of Clinical Psychology* (edited by S. Cullari and published by Allyn and Bacon). Together, these two guidebooks cover virtually every aspect of clinical and counseling psychology. In addition, I would recommend that all beginning therapists read the following classic works, which I consider to be essential readings for everyone in the helping professions. Please note this is not in any way an exhaustive list, nor are the books in any particular order of importance.

Thomas Szasz, *The Myth of Mental Illness*
Jay Haley, *How to Be a Failure as a Therapist*
Jay Haley, *Strategies of Psychotherapy*
Paul Wachel, *Psychoanalysis and Behavior Change: Toward an Integration*
James Bugenthal, *The Search for Authenticity*
Thomas Kuhn, *The Structure of Scientific Revolutions*
Joanne Greenburg, *I Never Promised You a Rose Garden*
Sigmund Freud, *The Interpretation of Dreams*
B. F. Skinner, *Walden II*
B. F. Skinner, *Science and Human Behavior*
Alfred Adler, *The Practice and Theory of Individual Psychology*
Gregory Bateson, *Mind and Nature*
Gregory Bateson, *Steps to an Ecology of the Mind*
Carl Rogers, *Client-Centered Therapy*

Eric Berne, *Games People Play*
Oliver Sacks, *The Man Who Mistook His Wife for a Hat*
Albert Bandura, *Self-Efficacy: Toward a Unifying Theory of Behavior Change*
Paul Meehl, *Clinical versus Statistical Prediction*
Elizabeth Loftus, *Eyewitness Testimony*
Aaron Beck, *Cognitive Therapy and the Emotional Disorders*
Albert Ellis, *Reason and Emotion in Psychotherapy*
Alan Watts, *Psychotherapy East and West*
M. Scott Peck, *The Road Less Traveled*
Paul Watzlawick, *How Real Is Real?*
Robert Lindner, *The Fifty Minute Hour*
R. D. Laing, *The Politics of Experience*
Elisabeth Kubler-Ross, *On Death and Dying*
Carl G. Jung, *Modern Man in Search of a Soul*
Frederick Perls, Ralph Hefferline, and Paul Goodman, *Gestalt Therapy*
Michael Kahn, *Between Therapist and Client*

Every journey must begin with the first step. Many of you have already taken a number of steps toward becoming effective therapists. I hope this book will bring you much closer to this goal.

Acknowledgments

I first want to thank all of the clients I have worked with over the years for imparting their wisdom to me. I would like to thank the many clients and psychotherapists who participated in the questionnaire study that formed the basis for my chapter in this book. I would like to thank my wife Kathi and children Dante and Catherine for putting up with yet another writing project. I would like to thank the students, staff, and administrators at Lebanon Valley College for their help and support of this project. I would like to thank the staff at Allyn and Bacon, especially Susan Hutchinson, Becky Pascal, and Mylan Jaixen for their help and support in this and other projects. I would like to thank the individuals who reviewed this book for their thoughtful insights and suggestions: James Guinee, University of Central Arkansas; Dana Hardy, Vanderbilt University; Jan Hinsen, Gannon University; and Lynne Kellner, Fitchburg State College. I would especially like to thank the other authors of this book for all of their dedicated work in helping to put this book together. Finally, I would like to thank my now deceased grandfather Salvatore for immigrating to the United States from Italy in 1923, which helped make all of this possible.

Useful Internet Sites Related to Clinical and Counseling Psychology

Teaching clinical psychology: <http://www.rider.edu/users/suler/tcp.html>

Clinical psychology problems: <http://govan.cent.gla.ac.uk/Acad/Psychology/APPLIEDP/sld058.htm>

Clinical psychology: <http://www.ndonline.com/TribWebPage/askapro/psych.html>

Division of clinical psychology: <http://www.bps.org.uk/sub-syst/division/dcp/dcp.htm>

American schools of professional psychology: <http://www.aspp.edu/acad_masclin.html>

Links to other sites related to every aspect of psychology: <http://www.psychweb.com>

The original home of Psych Central, Dr. John Grohol's Mental Health Page: <http://www.psychcentral.com>

Psychopharmacy and drug references: <http://mentalhelp.net/guide/pro22.htm>

Mental health net: <http://mentalhelp.net/prof.htm>

A comprehensive information service for professionals (pay site): <http://onlinepsych.com/aboutpro.htm>

American Psychological Society: <http://psych.hanover.edu:80/APS/>

American Psychological Association: <http://www.apa.org/>

Academy of Counseling Psychology: <http://academyofabpps.org/>

Science of psychology resource site: <http://stange.simplenet.com/psycsite/>

Clinical psychology resources: <http://www.psychologie.uni-bonn.de/kap/links_20.htm>

Information about professional counseling, psychotherapy, and conflict resolution: <http://www.counselorlink.com/>

Online dictionary of mental health (gives links instead of definitions): <http://www.shef.ac.uk/~psysc/psychotherapy/index.html>

Non-Mainstream psychotherapy and counseling resources: <http://ourworld.compuserve.com/homepages/selfheal/nonmain.htm>

ERIC test locator: <http://ericae.net/testcol.htm>

International Association for Cognitive Psychotherapy: <http://iacp.asu.edu/>

Beck Institute for Cognitive Therapy and Research: <http://www.beckinstitute.org/>

Links to online journals: <http://www.psychwatch.com/journalpage.htm>

Healthcare organizations on the Web: <http://www.healthgate.com/>

Resources for graduate students in psychology: <http://www.sinc.sunysb.edu/stu/pjeffrie/index.html>

A collection of tips, guides, and resources for new professionals: <http://members.aol.com/drhord/>

Behavior on-line, the gathering place for Mental Health and Applied Behavioral Science Professionals: <http://www.behavior.net/>

CHAPTER

1 Ethics for Psychotherapists

SAMUEL KNAPP

Example One
A psychologist conducted a custody evaluation on a family and recommended custody to the mother. Because the psychologist got along so well with the children, the mother's attorney asks her to see the children in therapy. Upon hearing of this recommendation, the father threatens to bring a complaint before the state psychology licensing board for professional misconduct if the psychologist goes ahead and becomes the therapist for the children.

Example Two
The patient of a psychiatrist threatens to kill his ex-girlfriend. The psychiatrist wonders if the legal requirement of confidentiality will prevent him from warning the intended victim.

Example Three
After undergoing hypnosis with a social worker, a young woman becomes convinced that her father abused her when she was a child. The patient takes her father to court and sues for damages. Some time later the patient becomes convinced that the recovered memories were not accurate and sues the social worker for malpractice.

Example Four
The patient of a licensed mental health counselor is moving to another city. On their last session, the patient asks her counselor if they could go out to get coffee together and become friends. The counselor wonders if this social contact would be in the best interests of the patient.

Introduction

The purpose of this chapter is to help mental health professionals perform at a higher level of care by attending to the ethical issues that arise in their practices. Otherwise competent psychotherapists can harm patients if they ignore the cumulative wisdom about patient/client relationships found in the ethics code. Otherwise successful psychotherapists can feel themselves in great distress because they could not discern the ethical implications of a given clinical intervention until it was too late, they did not know the ethics code, they did not know how to engage in ethical decision making, or they did not have a source to fall back on when faced with a difficult ethical situation. The four examples at the beginning of this chapter represent some of the ethical and legal dilemmas that may confront psychotherapists. Fortunately, the ethics codes of the mental health professions offer solutions to the problems found in these examples or at least a methodology by which the ethical implications of the situations can be thought through.

Conversely, psychotherapists who are attuned to the moral implications of their professional work and the ethical codes of their professions are better able to fulfill their professional obligations. Not only are they less likely to violate the mandatory portions of the ethics code, but also they are more likely to fulfill the highest aspirational goals of the profession. They are more likely to accept the limits of their professional competence, self-monitor their physical and mental health, and engage in ongoing professional development.

Indeed, the practice analysis of psychologists commissioned by the Association of State and Provincial Psychology Boards (ASPPB) (Association of State and Provincial Psychology Boards, 1996) found that professional psychologists rated ethical and legal issues as the second most important domain of knowledge used in their daily practices. Only direct intervention skills were rated slightly higher. The operational definition of ethics used by ASPPB can be broadly classified into three large categories: intellectual content (ethics codes; relevant guidelines and standards; and state, provincial, or federal laws and regulations), ethical decision making, and self-care.

Although the ASPPB practice analysis was done only with psychologists, the operational definition of ethics used in the analysis appears relevant to the work of other mental health professionals. This chapter covers the three broad areas of ethics identified in the ASPPB practice analysis. Within the domain of intellectual content, the chapter covers the common ethical issues faced by psychotherapists and reviews some risk management strategies. Relevant sections from the Ethical Principles of Psychologists and Code of Conduct of the American Psychological Association (APA) (American Psychological Association, 1992) are cited and comments made, when appropriate, if the ethical codes of the other mental health professions vary from the APA standards. Readers will find many of the salient ethical and risk management principles summarized in the appendix at the end of this chapter. Although the preponderance of commentary will be given in the general area of intellectual content, the reader will quickly note that it is impossible to divorce ethics decision making and self-care from the day-to-day implementation of the ethical principles.

The reader will also note the overlap between ethical and legal issues. At times malpractice courts, applying the standards of reasonable competence, will consider psychotherapists to have fallen below the minimum standards required in their profession. Although the opinion was formed in the context of a legal proceeding, the failure to adhere to minimal standards of competence is a violation of ethical principles as well.

Intellectual Content

The content of the ethics is reflected by the codes of ethics psychologists (American Psychological Association, 1992) and the other mental health professions (American Counseling Association, 1997; American Psychiatric Association, 1998; National Association of

Social Workers, 1996). In addition, ethical principles of these mental health professionals may also be reflected in relevant professional guidelines and standards and pertinent state, provincial, or federal laws and regulations. However, learning the ethics codes is essential, but not sufficient. Ethics codes are one of several mechanisms, along with licensing board laws and regulations, miscellaneous state laws, and malpractice court precedents that regulate the practice of the mental health professions. These different regulatory mechanisms may overlap. For example, many state licensing boards adopt the ethics code of the profession or a highly similar version of it. Or a disciplinary action by a state licensing board may be used as evidence of misconduct in a malpractice suit.

Psychotherapists need to understand these regulatory mechanisms to practice effectively, legally, and ethically. For example, licensing laws usually specify the scope of the practice of the mental health profession, exemptions to the licensing law, standards for supervisors, and other issues directly relevant to the practice of their profession. Other state laws specify the criteria for reporting suspected child abuse, the standards and procedures for involuntary civil commitments, age of consent for minors, standards for expert witnesses, and more. Psychotherapists who are ignorant of these laws could easily find themselves out of compliance with their statutory responsibilities. For sources of the state and federal laws governing the practice of psychotherapy, mental health professionals can look to their national, state, or provincial professional association, which usually provides references or guidance for members on these issues.

For example, psychologists can rely on practice guidelines including the APA Guidelines for Child Custody Evaluations in Divorce Proceedings (American Psychological Association, 1994) when dealing with custody issues. Although these guidelines are not enforceable documents, many courts or licensing boards refer to them when adjudicating allegations of misconduct on the part of psychologists. Other professions often have similar documents.

The Regulation of Professional Psychotherapy

The mental health professions are regulated through before-the-fact controls (training programs, licensing, continuing education) and after-the-fact controls (malpractice suits, ethics charges, disciplinary actions by the state licensing boards, and various other statutes). Before-the-fact controls are those that are designed to prevent abuses from occurring. After-the-fact controls are those that are designed to punish offenders after an abuse has already occurred. Before-the-fact controls are preferred because they prevent harm from occurring in the first place.

Before-the-Fact Controls. Before-the-fact controls include training programs, licensing boards, and continuing education programs. Training programs select candidates who have adequate academic credentials, good character, and demonstrate social responsibility. Training programs weed out candidates who fail to demonstrate competence as future psychotherapists. However, graduation from a training program does not guarantee the right to practice a mental health profession. It is only the first hurdle that must be met.

The regulation of health care rests with the state government and is conducted primarily through licensing boards. No person has a right to practice a profession (although once a profession is officially recognized, there is a right to be treated fairly and impartially by the state). The practice of a profession is a privilege conferred by the state to promote the public welfare. State agencies, such as the state boards of Psychology, Medicine, Social Work, Nursing, or Counseling establish minimal entry level credentials based on acceptable academic backgrounds, supervised experience, and knowledge of basic information on the licensing examination.

In addition, state licensing boards may also require evidence of continued competency through mandatory continuing education. Many state and provincial licensing boards require continuing education as a condition of licensure renewal.

After-the-Fact Controls. After-the-fact controls include malpractice cases, charges by ethics committees of professional associations, disciplinary actions by state licensing boards, and various other governmental statutes. Malpractice refers to acts conducted in the context of a professional relationship that fall below the minimal standard of competence and directly harm the patient. A good mnemonic device is to think of four Ds: Duty to provide treatment, Deviation from standard of care, behavior Directly related to harm, and Damage to the patient. As a regulator of professional practice, malpractice has its limitations. Although malpractice suits do provide redress for harmed patients, most patients who are harmed do not file complaints. Furthermore, jury awards are capricious, leaving many patients overcompensated or undercompensated.

Complaints before ethics committees or state licensing boards require only that the ethics code of the professional association (or the state licensing board) was violated. The patient need not prove personal harm. Consequently, patients who proved that a psychotherapist had, for example, violated professional boundaries and entered into a dual relationship, would have grounds for an ethics complaint even if they could not prove that they were harmed by the behavior. However, those patients would not have grounds for a malpractice suit, unless they could prove that they suffered actual harm.

Complaints against psychotherapists before ethics committees or state licensing boards are easy to file. Any aggrieved person can complete the necessary form and submit it to the ethics committee or the state licensing board. Ethics committees do not require complainants to have an attorney. If the attorneys for the licensing board believe that the complaint has merit, then they will handle the complaint, sparing the plaintiff the litigation costs. The burdens of ethics complaints on the providers are increased by the fact that licensing boards and ethics committees may have different rules, procedures, time lines, and elements of due process.

Ethics committees of professional associations can issue letters of reprimand, censure, or, in extreme cases, revoke the membership of the practitioner. Very often ethics committees also add supervision or educational requirements that attempt to rehabilitate the professional. At first consideration, the removal of a practitioner or a disciplinary note from a professional association may seem minor to the aggrieved patient; however, the very existence of a sanction from a professional association may label the practitioner as a high risk for malpractice insurance or for managed care panels, which almost always ask the applicants if they have been investigated or disciplined by an ethics committee or a licensing board.

State licensing boards have typically adopted codes of ethics identical or similar to those used by professional associations. Nevertheless, state licensing boards have more authority to regulate psychotherapists. Because of their authority as licensing boards, they can mandate supervision or further education as a condition of continued licensure. If circumstances warrant, they can also restrict or revoke the practitioner's authority to practice. As with ethics committees, even "minor" sanctions, such as a reprimand or censure, can make it difficult for the practitioner to purchase malpractice insurance or be accepted onto a managed care panel.

A variety of criminal laws apply to psychologists and other mental health professionals including the willful failure to report child abuse, and fraud against insurance companies. In some states, sexual contact between patients and psychologists is a crime.

Specific Ethical Issues

All psychotherapists need to know a wide range of information. A short chapter of this nature can be considered only an introduction or a sampler on these ethical issues. Consequently, this chapter focuses on the major topics that come to the attention of disciplinary bodies: multiple relationships, breaches of confidentiality and privileged communications, treatment of patients who endanger themselves or others (including those suspected of child abuse), treating adults who may have memories of being abused as children, and working in the area of child custody evaluations.

Multiple Relationships. Multiple relationships refers to the existence of a social or business relationship with a patient, in addition to the professional therapeutic relationship. There is considerable concern that the mere presence of a multiple relationship will harm the objectivity and confidence necessary to have a sound therapeutic relationship with a patient. The ability to form good personal relationships is essential to the practice of a professional psychotherapist.

A multiple relationship is characterized by a boundary violation wherein the psychotherapist steps out of the role of psychotherapist or evaluator and engages in a nontherapeutic (business or social) relationship with the patient. Boundary violations include the blatantly exploitative, such as social or sexual relationships with patients, and the subtle, in which the boundaries are weakened by just-noticeable gradients of behavior. Sometimes the boundary violations occur when psychotherapists willfully place their welfare above that of their patients. For example, psychotherapists who encourage a social relationship with a patient are placing their own social needs above the therapeutic needs of the patient. At other times, psychotherapists who act with the purest of motives can violate the norm of psychotherapeutic neutrality by using the psychotherapist-patient relationship to promote a social cause (such as stamping out childhood abuse). Although this cause is commendable, it is a boundary violation to make it a higher priority than the welfare of the patient.

Example One at the beginning of this chapter represents the temptation to engage in a boundary violation. The role of an evaluator in a court-ordered custody evaluation is to provide disinterested and factual information to the court. A psychologist who acts as both a psychotherapist and as an evaluator may not have the objectivity necessary to do an impartial evaluation. Even if the evaluation is already completed, the psychologist cannot rule out the possibility that she may be called on later to testify about her evaluation in court.

Nonsexual boundary violations include developing social or business relationships with patients. Examples include having patients over for dinner, soliciting patients to join one's church, or becoming friends with a patient. However, not every contact with a patient outside the office is necessarily an ethical violation. It could be appropriate for psychotherapists to conduct some therapeutic techniques, such as in vivo desensitization, outside the office. Also, the APA Code of Conduct (American Psychological Association, 1992) acknowledges that some incidental or unavoidable contacts with patients may occur outside the office. Furthermore, some boundary modifications or crossings may be acceptable, such as attending special events such as the funeral of the spouse of a patient or visiting the house of a small child/patient who is moving to another city (Guthiel & Gabbard, 1993). Example Four is a possible boundary violation and is discussed in more detail in the section on ethics decision making.

Some boundary modifications present a high risk of being violations. These include, but are not restricted to, initiating a social, business, or nonprofessional contact; giving patients a ride home; any use of physical touch or massage as a therapeutic technique; allowing debts to mount in the absence of a pro bono or delayed payment agreement; conducting therapy during lunch; accepting favors such as returning library books or picking up the psychotherapist's lunch; or accepting valuable gifts. In the examples at the beginning of the chapter, the boundary modifications could conceivably be acceptable given a particular set of circumstances. However, these modifications present a risk of violating boundaries.

Even conscientious and scrupulous psychotherapists need to watch certain behaviors that, in and of themselves, are harmless. Even if the psychotherapist is capable of reaching the theoretical goal of having a completely objective attitude toward the patient, the patient probably can't maintain that attitude toward the psychologist. For example, the psychotherapist risks having the patient view the favor of returning the book as representing a social or friendship relationship instead of a professional one, thus complicating the progress of therapy. Other patients may construe their favors as a form of bartering and expect reciprocity in terms of fee reductions or other special favors.

Other behaviors that could be misconstrued include, but are not limited to the following: scheduling patients for last appointment of the day; extending sessions beyond scheduled time (even if it appears therapeutically indicated); self-disclosure (even if minor and intended as therapeutic); telephone conversations with patients between sessions; lax fee collection practices; use of sexually explicit language; receiving or giving gifts; or touching or hugging.

The treatment of patients in wraparound (home-based) or residential facilities often involves grey boundary areas. The direct care staff is around the patients at least eight hours a day and are involved in their day-to-day living. Psychotherapists working in these facilities may be invited to birthday parties for their patients at the home or treatment facility; they may be called upon to transport patients in an emergency or urgent need situation or to be otherwise involved with patients in nontherapeutic settings. Although these nontherapeutic relationships may be unavoidable for home-based or residential psychotherapists, caution should be used to evaluate the impact of the nontherapeutic contact on the patients and the other residents.

The APA Code of Conduct acknowledges that some multiple relationships with patients or former patients are unavoidable.

> In many communities and situations, it may not be feasible or reasonable for psychologists to avoid social or other nonprofessional contacts with persons such as patients, clients, students, supervisees, or research participants. Psychologists must always be sensitive to the potential harmful effects of other contacts on their work and on those persons with whom they deal. . . . If a psychologist finds that, due to unforeseen factors, a potentially harmful multiple relationship has arisen, the psychologist attempts to resolve it with due regard for the best interests of the affected person and maximal compliance with the Ethics Code. (Principle 1.17)

Psychotherapists (especially in small towns or rural areas) may have chance encounters with patients. Some of the chance meetings could involve passing contact with patients in stores or other public places, or through common affiliations (such as common membership in a country club or church), ordinary business transactions (the son of the patient delivers your pizza, your patient arrives at your yard sale, and so forth), or familial contacts (a family member encounters one of your patients in any of the above situations). Psychotherapists who anticipate random meetings with their patients can notify the patients of their right to privacy and assure them that they may choose not to recognize them in these nontherapeutic contexts. This is sometimes called the "you first" rule because it allows the patients to introduce themselves first ensuring that they can control the situation depending on their companions and settings and whether or not they want to be acknowledged.

Sexual Exploitation of Patients. The minor boundary violations, in addition to being potentially harmful in and of themselves, may be the first steps toward more serious sexual boundary violations. Typically the allegation of sexual contact involves no other evidence than the patient's word against that of the psychotherapist. However, often the ethics committee will reach a judgment on the basis of other boundary violations. Sexual contact often occurs in the context of multiple nonsexual violations whereby the interaction between the psychotherapist and patient gradually moves away from a focus on the patient and onto a focus on the needs of the psychotherapist (Pope, 1994).

Sexual contact with patients is prohibited by the ethics codes of all mental health professions. Despite its universal condemnation, it continues, albeit at a low rate, causing great harm to individual patients and embarrassment to the profession. The reported rate of sexual contact between psychiatrists, psychologists, and social workers and patients ranges between .02 and 3.0 percent for woman psychotherapists and .09 and 12.1 percent for male psychotherapists (Pope, 1994). Although different surveys each have some methodological limitations, several generalizations can be made. Typically, older male psychotherapists have sexual relations with younger female patients. Sexual contact with former patients is more frequent than sexual contact with current patients. The number of civil suits, licensure complaints, and ethics complaints related to sexual exploitation has increased in recent years, probably reflecting greater public awareness of the issue and not to any increase in the number of exploitative episodes (Pope, Sonne, & Holroyd, 1993).

Sexual Exploitation of Former Patients. Although the prohibition with patients has been in effect for many years, some controversy has occurred over sexual relationships with former patients. The Code of Conduct of the APA (1992) clarifies that sexual relationships with former patients are prohibited absolutely for two years after the termination of treatment. After two years, however, they may occur in unusual circumstances after appropriate steps are taken to protect the former patient and maintain objectivity. The psychologist has the responsibility of demonstrating that there is no exploitation after considering relevant factors such as

> (1) the amount of time that has passed since therapy terminated, (2) the nature and duration of therapy, (3) the circumstances of termination, (4) the patient's or client's personal history, (5) the patient's or client's current mental status, (6) the likelihood of adverse impact on the patient or client and others, and (7) any statement or actions made by the therapist during the course of therapy suggesting or inviting the possibility of a posttermination sexual or romantic relationship with the patient or client. (Principle 4.07)

This principle means "Two Years and a Flashing Red Light." The burden is on the psychologist to demonstrate that exploitation did not occur according to the standards listed above. Sexual contact with former patients is viewed as a rare exception.

Also, it would not be acceptable for a psychologist to terminate treatment with the patient only for the purpose of initiating a romantic relationship. Although therapy has ended, the relationship still gives a disproportionate amount of power to the former therapist who can use influence and information to keep the relationship going. Even before the APA prohibited sexual relationships with former patients (for at least two years), the APA's and other organizations' ethics committees commonly disciplined psychologists who initiated romantic relationships with patients shortly after termination. The American Counseling Association has a similar two-year standard. However, the American Medical Association and the National Association of Social Workers do not permit sexual contact with former patients under any circumstances.

In addition to problems developing with sexual contact with patients and former patients, problems can also occur if a psychotherapist initiated a romantic relationship with a close relative or friend of a patient. An example could occur if a psychologist, for example, initiated a romantic relationship with the mother of a child/patient.

Sexual Relationships with Supervisees. Sexual relationships between supervisors and supervisees are prohibited by the ethics codes of all of the mental health professions. The educator or supervisor does not typically have the same degree of interpersonal influence over the supervisee as the psychologist has over the patient. Nevertheless, the educator or supervisor has some control over grades, work conditions, and letters of recommendation (and subsequent professional future). Furthermore, some supervisors have a style that requires substantial interpersonal disclosure of emotions, background, and personal experience that approximate the disclosure found in psychotherapy.

Sexual exploitation occurs for many reasons. Sometimes the exploiting psychotherapists or supervisors have long-standing personality disorders or have serious sexual disorders (for example, pedophilia, sexual sadism). However, other psychotherapists have impairment either through the abuse of substances or from a serious mental illness. Other psychotherapists may have recently had a major loss, such as a divorce or career reversal, and feel particularly lonely and vulnerable. During this time, they may let their personal needs overshadow their normal judgment. Often they are mainly "lovesick," believe themselves in love, and block out their role as psychotherapist. Finally, some psychotherapists are poorly trained and have not learned to recognize and handle transference, countertransference, or boundary issues in psychotherapy. Although it is very difficult, if not impossible, to prevent sexual exploitation by psychotherapists with long-standing personality or sexual disorders, the profession can do more to prevent misconduct by psychotherapists who are temporarily impaired or undertrained.

Confidentiality. Confidentiality is a general term for the promise of psychologists to keep information about patients private. Confidentiality rules were originally found in the code of ethics of the mental health professions. However, they are now embodied in legislation and case law. Psychotherapists can be found guilty for breaches of confidentiality under many state statutes and could be liable for damages as a result of a malpractice suit.

Confidentiality is the cornerstone of effective psychotherapy. In addition to refraining from gossiping about patients, psychotherapists are also required to keep patient records secure (usually in a locked file in a locked room). Also, psychotherapists have to get the signature of patients before they are allowed to release the records of the patient.

The most egregious examples of breach of confidentiality would include gossiping about patients in public places. Fortunately, these types of complaints against psychotherapists are rare and psychotherapists tend to take their responsibilities to protect patient privacy very seriously. Of course, confidentiality is not always absolute and, at times, must be balanced by other ethical or legal requirements, such as the obligation to report suspected child abuse (see discussion on exceptions to confidentiality with life-endangering patients in the next section).

The ethics codes of mental health professions permit psychotherapists to discuss their patients in professional consultations without their consent as long as there is no identifying information given in the consultation. When it is necessary to give identifying information, then the consent of the patient should be acquired (APA, 1992, Standard 5.06). Information received from consulting relationships has to be kept confidential by the consultant.

Confidentiality in Family Therapy. Confidentiality issues can be especially important in family therapy or when treating adolescents. In family therapy, the failure to address confidentiality early could lead to considerable problems. Sometimes one family member may reveal a confidence "in secret" with an unspoken expectation that it will be kept as a secret with the psychotherapist, only to find it discussed openly later on. Or, some family members may want to disclose a secret because they want to develop an alliance between themselves and the therapist at the expense of the other family members. Keeping secrets can become therapeutically burdensome because it is often difficult to know which bit of information is secret, to whom secrecy is promised, and so on.

The optimal response is to define the policy regarding family secrets at the beginning of therapy. Some psychotherapists state that they will not guarantee to keep any secrets at all, including extramarital affairs. Others may not disclose the information, but insist on discussing the resistance to sharing the information. Regardless of the particular position taken, the policy toward family secrets should be discussed as early in treatment as feasible. Unless they are a major focus of treatment or necessary to justify a diagnosis, family secrets and other gratuitous embarrassing information should not be included in the records.

Confidentiality with Adolescents. Some states permit adolescents to seek psychotherapy without parental consent in limited circumstances. In most other states, however, children must have parental consent before they can seek psychotherapy on their own. The traditional assumption is that the ability to seek psychotherapy implies the ability to control information generated in psychotherapy. This rule does not apply in life-endangering circumstances in which health care providers may provide treatment in emergency situations without the consent of the parents.

Psychotherapists need to balance the legitimate needs of their adolescent patients for privacy with the understandable interest of their parents to know what is going on in therapy. Typically, adolescents have no legal right to keep information confidential from their parents. Although it may not be stated explicitly in any state statute or regulation, an argument is often made that the ability to authorize or consent to treatment implies the ability to access or control the information generated from such treatment. Consequently, if parental consent is needed to institute treatment, the parents would also have a right to obtain information generated from such treatment, whether it be psychotherapy or psychological testing. Sometimes, it may be clinically indicated to get an adolescent to sign a release of information form ahead of time, although it is not required and would be legally meaningless.

The optimal manner for psychotherapists to handle this issue is to discuss it openly at the start of psychotherapy. At times, psychotherapists may be able to persuade the parents to withhold their requests for complete information to allow the adolescent a greater sense of privacy, and thus encourage a stronger therapeutic alliance. When discussing this issue with parents, psychotherapists need to be candid and note that the information generated (and withheld from the parents) may include highly sensitive information, such as the use of drugs or sexual activity. Nonetheless, in situations where parental consent to treatment is required, the parents may continue to insist on obtaining the information generated within the therapeutic setting.

Privileged Communications. Privileged communication is a legal term barring patient information, under circumstances, from being introduced into courtroom proceedings. The U.S. Supreme Court in *Jaffee* v. *Redmond* (1996) recognized a privileged communication rule for psychotherapy in cases coming before federal courts. In this case, the court ruled that a social worker/psychotherapist could not be compelled to reveal the content of psychotherapy in a court proceeding without the consent of her patient. However, the Supreme Court recognized that lower federal courts would define future exceptions to that privilege.

In reality, most cases in which psychotherapists are involved are heard in state courts. Almost every state has an attorney/client, clergy/communicant, and psychologist/patient privilege. Most have a social worker/client privilege. Some states have privileged communication laws for mental health counselors and sexual abuse or domestic abuse counselors as well.

Privileged communications statutes, as they apply to psychotherapists, are a recent statutory development. Privileged communications statutes run counter to the common law principles to admit all evidence into court. Consequently, most courts will interpret them narrowly because they are reluctant to restrict evidence or testimony that can shed light on the issues before the court.

The privileged communication statute only applies if a professional relationship exists between a psychotherapist and a patient. Casual conversations between acquaintances, business contacts, or friends are not privileged. Furthermore, the privilege belongs to the patient, not the psychotherapist. The patient, or the patient's legal representative, decides when to invoke or waive the privilege. Psychotherapists do not have the standing to invoke or waive the privilege against the wishes of their patients.

Patients or their representatives may waive their privilege whenever they want. In addition, patients automatically waive the privilege if they enter their mental health into the issue, such as through a psychological malpractice claim, personal injury case with emotional damage, or an insanity plea. For example, patients alleging emotional damage as a result of an industrial accident could not proceed with their cases unless they presented their mental health records before the court so they could be scrutinized as to the accuracy of the patients' claim of harm. The privilege does not apply to court-ordered examinations; patients are advised prior to evaluation that if they participate in the examination, then results will be disclosed to their attorney and may be admitted into court.

Once the privilege is waived, it is waived completely. In a malpractice suit against a psychotherapist, for example, patients may not enter selected facts about their mental health treatment that would help their case, but then try to withhold other facts that would hurt their case. In legal parlance, the privilege cannot be used as both a shield and a sword (Knapp & VandeCreek, 1987).

The Treatment of Life-Endangering Patients. As illustrated in Example Two at the beginning of this chapter, some of the most difficult situations for mental health professionals occur when they are treating a patient who threatens to harm themselves or others. Also, psychotherapists often deal with parents or other caregivers who have harmed, or are at risk to harm, children. Under these circumstances, it is important for psychotherapists to pay close attention to ethical and legal precedents. This section will review the ethical and legal responsibilities of psychotherapists when treating patients who threaten to harm others or themselves or who are suspected of child abuse.

Treating Patients Who Threaten Others. Over the years case law has developed concerning the responsibilities of psychotherapists to protect identifiable victims of patient violence. The legal implications of these issues can best be understood by looking in detail at the tragic case of Tatiana (Tanya) Tarasoff (*Tarasoff* v. *Regents of the University of California,* 1976).

A student at the University of California at Berkeley, Prosenjit Poddar met Tatiana Tarasoff at a New Year's Eve party and became infatuated with her. However, he became depressed when she did not return his affection. Tanya told him that she was involved with other men and did not want an intimate relationship with him. After being rebuffed by Tanya, Poddar underwent a severe emotional crisis and became preoccupied with Tatiana. During the summer of 1969, Poddar sought mental health treatment at the Cowell Memorial Hospital, an affiliate of the University of California at Berkeley. During one of his therapy sessions, Poddar confided to his treating psychologist that he intended to kill Tanya.

The psychologist took the threats seriously and notified the campus police that Poddar should be committed involuntarily to a psychiatric hospital. However, when the campus police officers talked to Poddar, he appeared rational and promised to avoid Tanya Tarasoff. The police did not follow through with taking Poddar to the psychiatric hospital. Subsequently, the psychiatrists who were supervisors of the treating psychologist learned of the failed arrangements to commit Poddar and ordered the psychologist to destroy his therapy notes and take no further action to commit Poddar. After the commitment attempt failed, Poddar discontinued therapy. That fall, Tanya returned to campus unaware of the danger to her. In October 1969, Poddar went to Tanya's house and killed her.

Tanya's parents initiated a wrongful death suit against the Regents of the University of California, the psychologist and supervising psychiatrists, and the police officers who were involved in the treatment or abortive commitment attempt with Poddar. The suit prompted a national debate concerning the limits of confidentiality with life-endangering patients.

Although the *Tarasoff* case was decided by the California Supreme Court and was binding only on courts in California, supreme courts in numerous other states have followed suit and adopted the *Tarasoff* standards for their states as well. Consequently, it is important for psychologists to know what the *Tarasoff* ruling did and did not say.

Tarasoff said that psychotherapists have a duty to act to protect identifiable targets from imminent danger coming from their patients. According to *Tarasoff,* "discharge of such duty may require the therapist to take one or more of various steps, depending on the nature of the case, including warning the intended victim. . . ." (551 P. 2d at 334). These steps include, but are not limited to, notifying the intended victim, notifying someone who will notify the intended victim, notifying the police, and insisting on voluntary or involuntary hospitalization. Other interventions may be effective, but are less dramatic: increasing the frequency of therapy, involving the targeted victim in psychotherapy (especially if the targeted victim is a family member), referring the patient to a more structured program (such as a partial hospitalization program), or getting the patient on psychotropic medications.

Because the *Tarasoff* decision has been subject to many misinterpretations, it is equally important to know what *Tarasoff* did *not* say. The court did not require psychotherapists to issue a warning every time a patient made an idle comment or had a fleeting thought about harming others. On the contrary, the court stated that "a therapist should not be encouraged routinely to reveal such threats . . . unless such disclosure is necessary to avert danger to others" (551 P. 2d 347).

The court does not require psychotherapists to interrogate their clients or to conduct independent investigations when the identity of the victim is unknown. Rather, the duty to protect arises only when the victim has been identified or could be identified upon a "moment's reflection" (551 P. 2d at 345). However, at least one subsequent court has held a psychotherapist liable for failing to warn when there was an identifiable *class* of victims.

Finally, the court did not see warning the intended victim as the only therapeutic response when danger arises. On the contrary, the court stated that the "discharge of such duty may require the therapist to take one or more of various steps, depending on the nature of the case, including warning the intended victim . . ." (551 P. 2d at 334). The psychologist may attempt an involuntary commitment, notify the police, or take another step to deter the violence.

The decision was based on an affirmative duty to act, which arises out of the fiduciary or "special relationship" between a psychotherapist and patient. According to the common law (the judge-made law that establishes precedents for future courts), an individual usually has no duty to control the behavior of another to protect a third party. Nevertheless, once a "special relationship" has been established, the law may require affirmative obligations. These socially recognized relationships, such as parent to child, innkeeper to guest, or physician to society, implied a legal duty to attempt to protect others from harm or to warn them of harm. Parents must protect their children, innkeepers must notify guests of reasonably foreseeable dangers, and physicians must protect the public by reporting a contagious disease.

Furthermore, custodians of psychiatric or similar institutions have a duty to protect or warn third persons about dangerous patients. In several cases, hospitals or doctors in their employ were liable for failure to warn murdered victims of the dangerousness of released mental patients. In this regard, *Tarasoff* provided nothing new in the area of tort liability. It merely took the rules that had been established with inpatient tort law and applied them to an outpatient setting (VandeCreek & Knapp, 1993).

Current statutory solutions to these *Tarasoff*-related problems have been found in several states. Although the wordings of these laws vary from state to state, they typically require or permit psychotherapists to warn identifiable third parties when patients threaten identifiable third parties (although in at least two states psychotherapists are specifically prohibited from such warnings). Immunity is specifically granted for any allegation of breach of confidentiality, although some states and provinces also permit discharge of the duty through an involuntary hospitalization. However, here, as in other cases, it is essential for psychotherapists to know the law in their particular state or province.

Emerich v. *Philadelphia Center for Human Development* (1998) provides an example of how courts apply the standards of liability in duty to warn or duty to protect cases. In *Emerich,* a patient had made a serious threat to kill his girlfriend. The mental health counselor took the threats seriously and warned the intended victim. The intended victim ignored the warnings to avoid her boyfriend and was subsequently murdered by him. In reviewing the case, the Pennsylvania Supreme Court opined that the mental health counselor had followed the standards expected of his profession and would not be held liable. Even though a tragedy had occurred, the psychotherapist had followed the standards of his profession in assessing the dangerousness accurately and acting to try to prevent a tragedy.

Treating Patients Who Threaten Suicide. The suicide of a patient can jar the confidence of the most competent psychotherapist. Often they have become quite fond of their patients. They may have lost a person for whom they felt affection and a sense of responsibility, and they wonder if they might have done something differently to prevent the tragedy. Many psychotherapists become depressed after the suicide of a patient (Kleespies, Penk, & Forsyth, 1993).

The reactions of the family members may vary considerably. Some readily acknowledge the efforts of the psychotherapists and thank them for their efforts. Other family members display extreme and irrational hostility. In addition to their personal discomfort, psychologists may experience legal problems as well. Any time a patient dies of a suicide, the risk of a malpractice suit increases substantially. Litigious plaintiffs may try to sue as many entities as possible, including a hospital, outpatient clinic, and whatever providers are involved.

Over the years, the therapeutic standards regarding the treatment of suicidal patients have changed. Recognizing that some of the traditional restrictive practices impaired the patients' ability to recover, courts recognize that the effective treatment of depressed and suicidal patients may involve some short-term risks. Psychotherapists must balance the benefits of treatment against the risks of freedom.

Psychotherapists must use reasonable professional judgment in assessing the therapeutic risks of freedom. They must carefully assess the decision to reduce the supervision of suicidal patients, whether it involves a transfer to a less restrictive ward or a discharge out of the hospital. Of course, when the patient is dangerously suicidal, the psychotherapist may be expected to seek a hospitalization.

Treating Patients Suspected of Abusing Children. Every state has a law that requires professionals to report any suspected child abuse they encounter in their professional duties. Psychotherapists should know how their state defines child abuse, the conditions that activate the duty to report, and the definition of a perpetrator of child abuse. The exact wording of the law varies from state to state, but most include nonaccidental injuries, neglect, emotional abuse, or sexual abuse within their definitions. Other states include promotion of prostitution and participation in pornography in their definition of child abuse.

In many states, the duty to report under the child protective services law only applies when the child comes before the professionals in their professional capacity. In other words, the professional may not have a duty to report under the child protective services law if only the alleged perpetrator has come before them in therapy. Nevertheless, in situations where the psychotherapist sees the perpetrator alone, it is conceivable that they could be sued on the basis of the *Tarasoff* doctrine (the duty to protect) if the perpetrator reveals a credible intent to inflict serious harm on an identifiable child in the imminent future.

Most states require that reporters only need to suspect or believe that a child was abused. The intent is that the child welfare agency and not the psychotherapist should have the responsibility to determine whether the abuse actually did occur.

The child protective service laws provide sanctions against mandated reporters who fail to make the reports as required by law. Psychotherapists could suffer because state laws provide criminal penalties for mandated reporters who fail to make a report. It was intended, however, that these penalties would rarely be invoked and that they would be reserved for those who willfully disregard the law. Nonetheless, most states have provisions within their licensing laws that the failure to fulfill a statutorily required duty is grounds for suspension or revocation of a license to practice their profession. The willful or knowing failure to report suspected child abuse would qualify under this provision of failing to fulfill a statutorily required duty. In addition to the criminal penalties, civil suits have been initiated against mandated reporters who failed to report child abuse.

Adult Survivors of Childhood Abuse. Recent years have seen the development of a lively and sometimes acrimonious debate concerning the veracity of memories of childhood abuse that are lost from memory and subsequently retrieved into consciousness. On the one hand, some survivors of childhood abuse claim that they lost the memories from conscious awareness until they became adults. In some cases, they have relied on their memories to sue or confront their alleged perpetrators. Their critics claim that recovered memories are highly unreliable and, especially if they were recalled through the use of hypnosis or other suggestive techniques, may lead to false accusations of innocent persons. In these cases, some alleged perpetrators have sought to sue the psychotherapists they perceive to be responsible for implanting false memories. Example Three at the beginning of this chapter illustrates the conundrum sometimes faced by patients who are questioning whether or not they experienced abuse earlier in their lives.

Some psychotherapists are becoming reluctant to treat adult survivors of childhood abuse because they fear litigation from former patients or the parents of their patients who may claim that the therapists implanted false memories of childhood abuse. However, the liability risks of treating adult survivors of childhood abuse are low if psychotherapists adhere to the ethical code of their profession and refrain from using unscientific "memory recovery" techniques. This section will review the liability issues in more detail.

From the standpoint of the psychotherapists, the liability risks are minimal when treating patients who always knew that they were abused as children, who retrieved the memories spontaneously, or who have valid corroborating evidence. Liability risks are slightly higher when the patient retrieves memories through talk therapy. Even in these situations, however, the liability risks are relatively low as long as the psychotherapist has not used memory retrieval techniques and has otherwise used good ethical and clinical judgment. However, liability risks are high when the psychotherapist uses questionable memory retrieval techniques or crosses therapeutic boundaries. Techniques commonly associated with the allegations of implanted memories include age regression, body work (the recovery of memories that are allegedly stored within body tissues), trance writing, narcoanalysis (sodium amytal), or the improper use of hypnosis, guided imagery, journaling, or dream interpretation. In reality, none of these techniques has been proven reliable in identifying the accuracy of past memories. All of these techniques have been suspected of creating false memories.

In addition, some recanters have described harmful boundary crossings, such as a patient promoting a workshop for her psychotherapist, a psychotherapist attending a party at a patient's house, or a psychotherapist inviting a patient over for coffee and taking her for rides in the country. Other alleged boundary violations were more subtle and have included prohibiting adult children from receiving letters from their parents, forbidding patients to talk to family members, and pressuring patients to write angry letters to their parents (see the review of recanter literature in Knapp & VandeCreek, 1997). While the accuracy of these boundary violation accusations has not been independently confirmed, they would, if true, represent breaches in the ethical standards and fiduciary relationships to which psychotherapists are held.

The case of *Hamanne* v. *Humenansky* (1995) provides an example of a psychotherapist who fell below the minimal standards of conduct expected of psychotherapists. In this case, it was alleged that the psychiatrist had implanted memories of abuse through coercive group influence and hypnosis. In addition, it was alleged that the psychiatrist had engaged in multiple boundary violations including disclosure of her own serious emotional problems and using the patient and her husband to do office chores.

Encouraging detachments from, confrontations with, or lawsuits against alleged perpetrators violates the standards of psychotherapeutic neutrality. Unfortunately, a few psychotherapists appear to believe that they have a social responsibility—out of a concern for the "silent victims" who are afraid to come forth—to encourage confrontations with alleged perpetrators. However, the encouragement of confrontations risks a boundary violation where the therapist's allegiance shifts from the patient to nonpatients. Although it is highly desirable for all persons to work to reduce childhood abuse, using the dependence engendered in psychotherapy to enlist a patient to help redress this social wrong violates appropriate boundaries.

As the media popularizes the possibility of recovering memories through hypnosis and other techniques, prospective patients may ask psychotherapists to "diagnose" them as survivors of childhood abuse by helping them to retrieve memories of childhood events or to verify their vague recollections or feelings of abuse. Although the attribution of such power is flattering, prudent psychotherapists will disavow any such skill, noting that memory is a reconstructive process and that no "truth serum" exists, be it hypnosis or drugs.

Patients may become angry with a psychotherapist who disavows the ability to provide a truth serum, or who expresses uncertainty about the literal truth of the childhood impressions or memories that they might have retrieved. Nevertheless, the patients are better off with a psychotherapist who honestly holds judgment in abeyance. Clinical skill is required to balance the patients' need for emotional support with the need to remain open to alternative explanations in the presence of ambiguous or conflicting evidence.

Psychotherapists should not be afraid to express uncertainty about the etiology of a particular problem. Symptomatology can be multidetermined, and it should not be presumed that similar symptoms in different patients have the same etiology. Patients who are not able to confirm their inklings or impressions of past abuse may be better off living with uncertainty and ambiguity, rather than rushing to an ill-conceived conclusion about their past. Treatment may help these patients adjust to this unresolved area of their lives.

Recently, some parents have initiated lawsuits against the psychotherapists who treated their adult children (Knapp & VandeCreek, 1998). Often their suits are initiated after patients file suits against their parents for abuse based on lost and recovered memories of abuse, or after patients confront their family members with memories of past abuse. Several years ago lawsuits against psychotherapists by third parties of adult patients were unheard of, but now they are increasingly common.

Except for the *Tarasoff* decision discussed in the previous section, a legal duty ordinarily exists only between psychotherapists and their patients, and not to any outside party such as the patients' parents. Nevertheless, some aggrieved parents have argued that the duty of the psychotherapists to third parties should extend to them as well.

Generally, courts have not granted third parties standing to sue for the alleged negligent treatment of their adult children. However, in *Ramona* v. *Ramona* a parent was given standing to sue the psychotherapists of his adult daughter on the grounds of negligence. The court allowed the suit to proceed by relying on a California precedent that allows third parties limited status to sue when they are harmed by the behavior of a health professional. The father in *Ramona* alleged that the psychotherapists had implanted false memories of sexual abuse in his daughter. Although the daughter testified on behalf of her psychotherapists, the court ruled in favor of the father (Knapp & VandeCreek, 1997). Since the Ramona case, the courts in other scattered cases have allowed third parties standing to sue psychotherapists. Mostly they have involved bizarre circumstances with little relevance to the day-to-day practice of most psychotherapists. However, it is too soon to tell whether these cases represent aberrations or an emerging area of case law of importance to psychotherapists.

Child Custody Evaluations. Psychotherapists who conduct child custody evaluations are at high risk of being charged with negligence. In some cases, the aggrieved parent may file a complaint against naive and well-meaning psychologists who violated an ethical standard because they did not understand the unique features of custody evaluations. Psychotherapy patients are typically quite forgiving of the mistakes of their psychologists. However, an aggrieved parent in a custody case typically lacks the positive feeling that commonly occurs in psychotherapy. Consequently, an ethical error by a mental health professional conducting psychotherapy will often be forgiven, but an identical error by a mental health professional conducting a child custody evaluation will more likely result in an ethics complaint or a malpractice suit.

A full discussion of the ethical issues involved in child custody evaluations is beyond the purview of this introductory chapter. However, suffice it to say that psychotherapists doing custody evaluations should develop the necessary competencies, consider mediation as an alternative to an adversary court decision, minimize the possibility of fee disputes, inform parents ahead of time of the limits of confidentiality and other parameters of treatment, avoid multiple relationships, and document findings properly. Psychotherapists who scrupulously attend to these issues can greatly reduce their legal risks (Knapp & Keller, 1993).

The first example given at the beginning of this chapter presents one possible way in which multiple relationships could occur. It is quite clear that a psychotherapist should seldom, if ever, conduct a child custody evaluation in a case where he or she has been a therapist. However, in the scenario in Example One, the situation is reversed. Here a psychologist who had conducted a custody evaluation on a child was subsequently asked to become the therapist for that child. An astute mental health professional would know, however, that custody disputes often continue for years and it cannot be assumed that the custody report will not come under scrutiny again sometime in the future. Furthermore, the attorney who requested that the psychologist conduct therapy did not consider that the father, who lost the custody battle, might have a difficult time trusting or cooperating with the psychologist who recommend against his having custody. It may be better for the children to be seen by a psychotherapist who is viewed as neutral by all of the parties involved in the children's lives—although it is not per se unethical for psychotherapists to conduct therapy with children on whom they have conducted an evaluation. Indeed, there may be rural or other underserved areas in the United States where there are no other psychotherapists reasonably available to see the children in therapy. Such arrangements are fraught with difficulty, however, and should generally be avoided. *The Guidelines for Child Custody Evaluations in Divorce Proceedings* of the APA (American Psychological Association, 1994) states that "therapeutic contact with the child or involved participants following a child custody evaluation is undertaken with caution" (p. 678).

Risk Management Strategies. Psychotherapists can do much to reduce their personal risk for liability and to increase their adherence to the letter and spirit of the ethics code by following several basic procedures automatically. These include proper use of consultation and supervision, adherence to areas of competency, sensitivity about the need for informed consent, and maintenance of adequate records.

Consultation and Supervision. Consultation and supervision need to be distinguished. During consultation, the psychotherapist receiving the consultation is acting independently and retains the authority to accept or reject the opinion of the consultant. In supervision, however, the psychotherapist receiving the supervision has no independent authority to treat the patient and the supervisor retains ultimate authority over the patient's care. Supervision arrangements are common for recent graduates who are receiving supervised experience before they are allowed to sit for the licensing examination of their profession, for unlicensed employees of licensed professionals, or for psychotherapists who work in institutions or agencies.

Practitioners, even if they are licensed and legally able to provide services independently, should consult with other psychotherapists as part of the larger process of self-monitoring and self-improvement of their professional behavior. Consultation should be ongoing for all clinicians. "Peer consultation" or "mutual consultation" groups are effective ways to share information about treatment plans and techniques with patients. These groups also provide emotional support for clinicians who have, by the very nature of their profession, demanding work.

Unlike a psychotherapist receiving consultation, a psychotherapist (or psychotherapist-in-training) who is receiving supervision is not an independent provider and may not accept or reject the opinions of the supervising psychotherapist. In clinical supervision, the supervisors assume professional control and responsibility for the work product of others. In a supervisory relationship, the supervisee becomes an extension (hands and arms, so to speak) of the supervisor. Psychotherapists who are providing supervision need to take their responsibilities seriously and recognize that they are ultimately responsible for the work product of their supervisees. Supervisees are required to inform their patients of their supervisee status, including how to contact the supervisor in the event of a problem.

Ascertaining Competence. According to the APA Code of Conduct, psychologists are required to restrict their practice to their area of competence or expertise. Principle 1.04 (a) states that "Psychologists provide services, teach, and conduct research only within the boundaries of their competence, based on their education, training, supervised experience, or appropriate professional experience." Furthermore, consistent with the moral value of responsible caring, all psychotherapists should try to do their best in whatever they are doing. All of the mental health professions have similar competency requirements in their ethics codes. However, competence is sometimes difficult to define.

The question of competence may refer to the use of a technique (neuropsychology, hypnosis, biofeedback, and so forth), a particular problem area (martial therapy, child management, and so forth), working with a particular population (children, geriatrics, African Americans, and so forth), or some combination of these (pediatric neuropsychologist, for instance). The general rule is that persons can best ascertain their proficiency in a certain skill after submitting themselves to external feedback. The most obvious example of external feedback is when a person attends a graduate program and submits his or her learning and experience to the feedback of faculty and clinical supervisors. However, some competent psychotherapists may feel a need to develop expertise in a different or emerging area of professional practice. It is not always feasible or even necessary for them to return to graduate school.

In some areas, psychotherapists may work for a proficiency credential, such as biofeedback certifications. In other areas, no such credential exists. Moreover, there may be no uniformly agreed on course of study (set of readings, workshops, or classes) or examination for psychologists to become proficient in other areas, such as family therapy, child therapy, or competency with African Americans. The issue of cultural competence is especially important. Psychotherapists are becoming increasingly aware of the impact of cultural factors on the presentation of symptoms, expectations of benefits from mental health treatment, and ability of the patient and psychotherapist to form a working therapeutic relationship.

Psychotherapists who want to retrain themselves can submit themselves to external feedback. Although these psychotherapists may undergo a self-prescribed course of readings and continuing education programs, the most important action for them to take is to submit their actual work product to the detailed and routine evaluation of another psychotherapist who is an expert in that field. This could be done through the submission of tapes, copies of reports, or other work products that the supervisor can evaluate to determine if the required level of competency has been reached.

Informed Consent. Informed consent means the full and active participation of patients in treatment decisions. According to the APA Code of Conduct, "Psychologists obtain appropriate informed consent to therapy or related procedures, using language that is reasonably understandable to participants" (Principle 4.02 (a)). All of the mental health professions have a similar informed consent requirement in their ethics codes. The nature of the specific communication should vary according to the sophistication and needs of the patient, but a general rule is to ask, "What would the average patient undergoing this procedure want to know about the procedure?"

Informed consent is an ongoing process. Patients may develop questions and need more information about treatment as it progresses. Informed consent is not a pro forma statement given to all patients at the beginning of psychotherapy. Rather, it is an integral part of the dialogue with the patient and means, among other things, informing patients of relevant limits to confidentiality, information about fees and payment, and other relevant office practices. Finally, it may mean informing other involved parties, such as family members, of their role, if any, in the treatment decisions.

The underlying moral value behind the informed consent doctrine is that psychotherapists should respect patients and their ability to make their own decisions. Except for highly unusual situations, such as when the patient is in extreme distress, psychologists trust the ability of patients to decide which treatment under which conditions would be helpful to them.

In several states, psychotherapists are required to use informed consent forms. Unfortunately, some of the forms used are highly legalistic and do little to help inform the patients. Although psychotherapists in most states or provinces are not required to use these forms, it may be prudent to give patients a brochure, consent form, or handout that explains the basic nature of the treatment relationship and the office practices. This brochure could include professional information on the psychotherapists or their associates (degrees, areas of competence or specialties, and so forth), fees, what services incur charges (including court appearances, collateral contacts, between session phone calls, and so forth), regular office hours, the availability of emergency services, general statements on confidentiality, and the like.

Record Keeping. Good clinical records are an integral part of acceptable clinical practice. Patient records help psychotherapists to monitor the quality of the treatment, recall important patient details, justify treatment to third party payers, and ensure continuity of treatment if a patient receives subsequent services from another provider. Furthermore, a well-written document recording treatment decisions and procedures is a powerful defense against any accusation of negligence. An axiom among malpractice defense attorneys is "If it isn't written down, it didn't occur."

State or provincial licensing laws or regulations may provide information on the minimum requirements for record keeping. The exact requirements allow for considerable variety in records, depending on the needs of the patient, the nature of therapy, and the theoretical orientation of the psychotherapists. Very often institutions have specific record-keeping requirements beyond the minimum established by the state law or the ethics codes of the profession. Nevertheless, any future mental health professional reading the records should be able to understand the presenting problem and treatment. Receiving past records is also a necessity when developing a treatment plan (VandeCreek & Knapp, 1997).

Patients may have access to their records depending on the circumstances involved or the particular laws of the state or province. Often the laws permit psychotherapists to withhold records from patients if there is content in them that would be therapeutically contraindicated for them to see. Nevertheless, psychotherapists should not assume that their patients will never, under any circumstances, see their records. Consequently, care should be taken in the creation of the records. Records should be written as if the patient is expected to see them sometime in the future. Pejorative remarks, if seen by the patient, may provoke anger and create a perception of the psychologist as insensitive and uncaring. Comments about family members or other third parties should be included only if relevant and necessary to the diagnosis or treatment of the patient.

As much as possible, the record should be objective. The psychotherapeutic process is, in and of itself, subjective. Psychotherapists necessarily relate to their patients as other human beings with feelings and emotions. Nevertheless, remarks in the chart should be as objective as possible. Psychotherapists are advised to use behavioral descriptions whenever possible and should only record statements relevant to the treatment or diagnosis of the patient.

For example, writing that "the patient stated that she was upset because her boyfriend failed to call her" is more helpful than saying "the patient has unresolved dependency needs." Or writing that "the patient arrived 20 minutes late for therapy for the second time this month" is more helpful than "the patient continues to show resistance." Although writing the interpretations about dependency needs or resistance may be clinically indicated, such brief descriptions can be more helpful if they are placed in the context of more specific information.

When there is a high risk situation, such as when there is suspected child abuse, threats of violence toward others, or transference problems, it may be necessary to increase the level of documentation so that there is no doubt about the process of decision making involved.

State and provincial laws typically specify the minimum length of time that records have to be kept. Psychotherapists also have a responsibility to make certain that their records are reasonably retrievable. Electronic storage of records is permitted, but there is no excuse if the records are somehow destroyed through electronic failures. Psychotherapists also have a responsibility to ensure that the records are kept secure (see section on confidentiality).

Ethical Decision Making

Professional ethics codes and standards and government laws and regulations cannot guide psychotherapists in every ethical situation. Instead, psychotherapists must often balance two or more competing moral principles to ascertain the most appropriate course of conduct. This can be seen readily in the APA Code of Conduct, which contains qualifiers, such as "usually," "in most situations," or "generally speaking." These highlight the fact that the ethics code does not contain algorithms that can neatly direct psychotherapists in all situations (Bersoff, 1994).

For example, the ethics code states that psychotherapists should inform patients of the nature of fees as "early as is feasible" in the treatment relationship. The goal of this wording is to give sufficient leeway so that psychotherapists do not feel compelled to engage in therapeutically contraindicated informed consent procedures with a patient in an acute and possibly suicidal crisis. On the other hand, it does express the expectation that psychotherapists will routinely tell patients about fees as soon as professional contact is made or as soon as it is clinically possible after professional services are initiated. Consequently, the ethics code requires discretion on the part of the psychotherapist to know when it is feasible to talk about fees.

Furthermore, in many emerging areas of professional practice (such as therapy by teleconferencing, e-mail, or Internet), professional standards have not yet emerged. Nevertheless, psychotherapists may have to make decisions about their participation in these media. Also, the APA ethics code was written more for individual psychotherapy and less for family, couples, or "wraparound" (home-based) treatments, which are seldom addressed directly in the code (Marsh & Magee, 1997). Finally, difficult ethical dilemmas may emerge due to a highly unusual set of circumstances that no ethics code could anticipate.

One prerequisite for ethical decision making is to understand the assumptions underlying ethical principles. Despite differences in the degree of specificity in individual steps of different ethical decision-making formulas, all require an understanding of the moral assumptions on which ethics code are based.

Moral Principles Underlying Professional Ethics

Although there are several different ways to conceptualize the moral principles underlying the ethics of psychotherapists, this chapter emphasizes three that were identified by Beauchamp and Childress (1994) (respect for patient autonomy, nonmaleficence, beneficence) and a fourth identified by Kitchener (1984) and Bersoff and Koeppl (1993) (fidelity).

Autonomy means the freedom to think or choose as long as these do not infringe on the rights of others. "To respect an autonomous agent is, at a minimum, to acknowledge that person's right to hold views, to make choices, and to take actions based on personal values and beliefs" (Beauchamp and Childress, 1994, p. 125). Psychotherapists should treat patients as autonomous and independent agents who can participate as full partners in determining the treatment goals and methods.

Other moral principles are nonmaleficence (avoiding harm) and beneficence (working to help others). The obligations of nonmaleficence can be summarized in the phrase *primum non nocere*—above all, do no harm. Beneficence, the close cousin of nonmaleficence, is the moral aspect that is commonly assumed to occur in the helping professions: working to help others. "Morality requires not only that we treat persons autonomously and refrain from harming them, but also that we contribute to their welfare" (Beauchamp & Childress, 1994, p. 259). In addition to the primary directive of doing no harm, psychotherapists have a positive obligation to help patients by selecting and conscientiously implementing an appropriate treatment for them.

The principle of fidelity means that psychotherapists should be faithful to their primary obligation to serve their patients. According to Kitchener, it means "truthfulness, promise keeping, and loyalty" (1984, p. 51). In other words, psychotherapists will give primary allegiance to their therapeutic role, protect patient privacy, and when potential conflicts of interests exist, place the welfare of their patients first.

Balancing Ethical Principles

According to rules of prima facie ethics, the general rule is that psychotherapists and other moral agents should follow these moral principles. However, isolated moral principles are not absolute guides to human behavior and may be superseded by other moral principles in some situations. "A prima facie obligation indicates an obligation that must be fulfilled unless it conflicts on a particular occasion with an equal or stronger obligation" (Beauchamp & Childress, 1994, p. 33). If it is necessary to infringe one moral principle in an effort to adhere to another one, then efforts should be made to minimize the harm to the offended moral principle.

For example, psychotherapists generally show full respect for the autonomy of patients by acknowledging their control over the direction and major events of psychotherapy. However, under rare circumstances, such as when a patient presents an imminent danger of harm to him- or herself, psychologists may temporarily invoke the principle of beneficence to override the principle of respect for patient autonomy. Even in those situations, it is highly desirable to minimize the infringement of patient autonomy and to involve him or her as much as possible in deciding on the intervention designed to reduce the likelihood of self-harm (VandeCreek & Knapp, 1993). For example, if the desired intervention requires notifying the spouse of the patient, then the psychotherapist can ask the patient, "How should we go about informing your spouse? Do you want to be present when I share the information about your needs?"

In the next paragraphs, the fourth ethical dilemma found at the beginning of this chapter will be analyzed according to the prima facie moral principles just delineated. In grey areas, counselors can follow a sequential series of problem-solving steps. Although different authors have proposed slightly different decision-making processes, the one presented here is an abbreviated version of the one proposed in the Preamble to the Code of Ethics of the Canadian Psychological Association (1986). The problem-solving model requires psychologists to (1) identify the relevant ethical issues; (2) consider the alternative sources of action; (3) evaluate the short-term and long-term outcome of the actions; (4) chose the appropriate source of action, and (5) evaluate and/or modify those actions, if necessary.

Step One: Identify Relevant Ethical Issues. The salient moral principles here appear to be nonmaleficence and fidelity. In this case the counselor needs to consider whether the patient would be harmed (nonmaleficence) by developing a social relationship with her. The moral responsibility of counselors to refrain from harming their patients is the primary directive. Also, the question arises as to whether the counselor needs to retain fidelity to the professional relationship now that it is ending and, because the patient is moving to another city, will never exist in the future.

Step Two: Consider Alternative Sources of Action. The two potential courses of action would be to accept or reject the offer of a social relationship. In weighing these options, the counselor needs to consider whether she has missed anything clinically in the patient. For example, is the request for friendship indicative of a pathological trait that the counselor, desiring the friendship herself, has missed? Or are there issues that would make the social relationship clinically contraindicated?

The counselor also needs to consider whether she is placing her own desire for friendship above the welfare for the patient or letting it cloud her clinical judgment. Because it is often difficult for persons to appreciate their own emotional needs and reactions, getting feedback from a trusted colleague may be indicated.

Step Three: Evaluate the Short-Term and Long-Term Outcome of the Action. Although the patient may feel short-term pleasure at the development of the desired relationship, it is not clear that the long-term outcome will be desirable. Of course, the present counselor would be lost to the patient as a source of treatment. This is not a relevant issue in this case because the patient is moving out of town anyway. Nevertheless, in this situation the counselor needs to consider whether the social relationship with the patient will create special transference issues if the patient enters psychotherapy with another therapist sometime in the future. That is, will the patient immediately begin to see the future counselor or psychotherapist as a potential friend, thus creating an obstacle to effective psychotherapy.

Step Four/Step Five: Act and Evaluate Outcomes and/or Modify Actions. In this particular situation, it would be difficult to establish a social relationship with a patient, and then to terminate it because it appears pathological or clinically contraindicated. However, if the counselor decides to establish a social relationship, and then finds there are clinical features of the patient she had missed that made the relationship countertherapeutic, she should advise the former patient accordingly and decide whether or not to continue the social relationship.

In this brief example, it is possible for readers to add more details that would make the social relationship with the former patient more acceptable or to add details that would make it less acceptable. When in doubt, however, it is recommended that the psychotherapist err on the side of protecting the patient and follow the principle of nonmaleficence: First of all, do no harm.

Self-Care Strategies

The ASPPB practice analysis also included a self-care domain composed of professional education, self-monitoring, and personal self-care. It is important for psychologists to appreciate the need for self-care. Many students entering the mental health field come from dysfunctional families of origin (Feldman-Summers & Pope, 1994), although many may have already resolved personal issues that could impair professional performance. Also, many psychologists report mental illnesses and addictions to alcohol and other psychotropics (Thoreson, Miller, & Krauskopf, 1989), although the rates are probably no higher than those found in the population in general. Nevertheless, distress and impairment do occur among psychologists, and a degree in psychology provides no vaccination against mental disturbances. Psychologists need to care for themselves and show concern for their fellow psychologists-in-training.

Furthermore, regardless of their personal mental health when they enter the field, mental health professionals are in a field in which certain negative life events or life stressors are probable. Throughout their careers, psychotherapists can expect to encounter suicides or attempted suicides of their patients, assaults and threats of assaults from patients, patient threats to third persons, boundary challenges by patients, and excessive workloads. Psychotherapists need to be prepared for these challenges. All experienced psychotherapists can give long discussions about their own "patient from hell" who taxed their mental, emotional, and physical resources to the limit.

Although these stressful life events and life circumstances are difficult to manage, properly prepared psychotherapists have been handling them adequately for many years. Psychotherapists who have strong social support systems, continually engage in professional development, and have a sense of obligation beyond their own personal careers are better prepared to withstand the trials associated with being a psychotherapist.

Few resources can help psychotherapists as much as a strong social support network. In difficult situations, it is important to "share the burden" or involve others in the critical decision making. Proper self-regulation can include a systematic continuing education program, peer consultation groups, working in a supportive institutional setting, and the like. The major goal is to embed oneself in a social structure that provides continual feedback and monitoring. Indeed, social support was rated as one of the key components of success among psychologists who were nominated by their peers as "well-functioning" (Coster & Schwebel, 1997).

As professionals in a field with an ever expanding knowledge base, psychotherapists need continual training and retraining. Although many state licensing boards now require continuing education as a condition of licensure renewal, these requirements represent only the bare minimum of professional education that psychotherapists should receive. Conscientious psychotherapists will go beyond that minimum and continually seek ways to improve their skills and competencies through readings, professional seminars, discussions with their colleagues, and formal supervisory relationships.

Finally, psychotherapists who are best at caring for themselves are those who are best at caring for others. They know that, as professionals, they have specialized training and knowledge that can benefit society, and they take proactive efforts to ensure that their knowledge gets translated into public policy. The aspirational obligations of psychotherapists include an obligation to work in sustained and meaningful ways to ensure that institutions develop policies consistent with scientific evidence and humane moral principles. This advocacy is not limited to the individual third-party reimbursement concerns of the psychotherapist, but also includes efforts to redress any systematic policy that negatively impacts on the quality of human life. Although some advocacy efforts can be done individually, they can usually be best accomplished organizationally through their respective professional associations at a national, state, provincial, or local level.

REFERENCES

American Counseling Association. (1997). *Code of ethics and standards of practice.* Alexandria, VA: Author.

American Psychiatric Association. (1998). *The principles of medical ethics with annotations especially applicable to psychiatry.* Washington, DC: Author.

American Psychological Association. (1992). Ethical principles of psychologists and code of conduct. *American Psychologist, 47,* 1597–1611.

American Psychological Association. (1994). Guidelines for child custody evaluations in divorce proceedings. *American Psychologist, 49,* 677–680.

Association of State and Provincial Psychology Boards. (1996). *Study of the practice of licensed psychologists in the United States and Canada.* Montgomery, AL: Association of State and Provincial Psychology Boards.

Beauchamp, T., & Childress, J. (1994). *Principles of biomedical ethics* (4th edition). New York: Oxford University Press.

Bersoff, D. (1994). Explicit ambiguity: The 1992 ethics code as an oxymoron. *Professional Psychology: Research and Practice , 25,* 382–387.

Bersoff, D., & Koeppl, P. M. (1993). The relation between ethical codes and moral principles. *Ethics and Behaviors, 3,* 345–357.

Canadian Psychological Association. (1986). *Code of ethics.* Ottawa, ON: Author.

Coster, J., & Schwebel, M. (1997). Well-functioning in professional psychologists: as program heads see it. *Professional Psychology: Research and Practice, 29,* 5–13.

Emerich v. *Philadelphia Center for Human Development,* 720 A 2d 1032 (Pa. 1998).

Feldman-Summers, S., & Pope, K. (1994). The experience of "forgetting" childhood abuse: A national survey of psychologists. *Journal of Consulting and Clinical Psychology, 62,* 636–639.

Guthiel, T., & Gabbard, G. (1993). The concept of boundaries in clinical practice: Theoretical and risk management dimensions. *American Journal of Psychiatry, 150,* 188–196.

Hamanne v. *Humenansky,* Second Judicial District, Minnesota, C4–94–203 (1995).

Jaffee v. *Redmond,* 116 S. Ct. 1923 (1996).

Kitchener, K. S. (1984). Intuition, critical evaluation and ethical principles: The foundation for ethical decisions in counseling psychology. *The Counseling Psychologist, 12* , 43–55.

Kleespies, P., Penk, W., & Forsyth, J. (1993). The stress of patient suicidal behavior during clinical training: Incidence, impact, and recovery. *Professional Psychology, 24,* 293–303.

Knapp, S., & Keller, P. (1993). Ethical issues in child custody evaluations. In L. VandeCreek, S. Knapp, & T. Jackson (Eds.), *Innovations in Clinical Practice,* Vol. 12, (pp. 257–262). Sarasota, FL: Professional Resource Press.

Knapp, S., & VandeCreek, L. (1987). *Privileged communications in the mental health professions.* NY: Van Nostrand/Reinhold.

Knapp, S., & VandeCreek, L. (1997). *Treating adults with memories of abuse: Legal and ethical issues.* Washington, DC: American Psychological Association.

Marsh, D., & Magee, R. (1997). *Ethical and legal issues in professional practice with families.* New York: Wiley.

National Association of Social Workers. (1996). *Code of ethics.* Washington, DC: Author.

Pope, K. (1994). *Sexual involvement with therapists.* Washington, DC: American Psychological Association.

Pope, K., Sonne, J., & Holroyd, J. (1993). *Sexual feelings in psychotherapy.* Washington, DC: American Psychological Association.

Stromberg, C., Haggarty, D., Leibenluft, R., McMillian, M., Mishkin, B., Rubin, B., & Trilling, H. (1988). *The psychologist's legal handbook.* Washington, DC: The Council for the National Register of Health Service Providers in Psychology.

Tarasoff v. *Regents of the University of California,* 551 P. 2d 334 (1976).

Thoreson, R., Miller, M., & Krauskopf, C. (1989). The distressed psychologist: Prevalence and treatment considerations. *Professional Psychology: Research and Practice, 20,* 153–158.

VandeCreek, L., & Knapp, S. (1993). *Tarasoff and beyond* (Rev. Ed.). Sarasota, FL: Professional Resource Press.

VandeCreek, L., & Knapp, S. (1997). Record keeping. In J. Matthews & C. E. Walker (Eds.), *Basic skills and professional issues in clinical psychology* (pp. 155–172). Boston: Allyn & Bacon.

FOR FURTHER READING

Beauchamp, T., & Childress, J. (1994). *Principles of biomedical ethics* (4th edition). NY: Oxford University Press.

Although many of the issues are more appropriate for medical practitioners, Beauchamp and Childress provide a good introduction to the moral principles underlying professional ethics.

Bennett, B., Bryant, B., VandenBos, G., & Greenwood, A. (1990). *Professional liability and risk management.* Washington, DC: American Psychological Association.

This is a thorough review of the ways in which psychologists can reduce their legal liability and, at the same time, provide high quality care to their patients.

Bersoff, D. (1999). *Ethical conflicts in psychology* (2nd. ed.). Washington, DC: American Psychological Association.

Dr. Bersoff does a fine job of identifying the relevant legal and ethical principles applying to the practice of psychology. In addition, he identifies situations in which psychologists have to consider problems with no clear moral directives.

Canadian Psychological Association. (1986). *Code of ethics.* Ottawa, ON: Author.

The Code of Ethics of the Canadian Psychological Association is explicitly a teaching document. Although many of the principles are nearly identical to those of the APA, it differs from the APA Code by the explicit identification of moral principles that underlie the code and in the exposition of a decision-making format.

Haas, L., & Malouf, J. (1989). *Keeping up the good work: A practitioners guide to mental health ethics.* Sarasota, FL: Professional Resource Exchange.

A good basic introduction to ethical principles for psychologists and other mental health professionals.

Knapp, S., & VandeCreek, L. (1997). *Treating adults with memories of abuse: Legal and ethical issues.* Washington, DC: American Psychological Association.

A review of the ethical and legal issues underlying the "repressed/false memory" controversy. Include a good review of risk management strategies.

Marsh, D., & Magee, R. (1997). *Ethical and legal issues in professional practice with families.* New York: Wiley.

The editors have compiled numerous commentaries on the unique ethical issues that arise in family or martial therapy.

APPENDIX 1.A
Sources Checklist

1. Copy of your state or provincial licensing law and regulations for your respective profession including:
   a. Scope of practice
   b. Record keeping
   c. Rules on advertisements and other public pronouncements
   d. Exceptions to confidentiality
   e. Supervision of trainees or employees
   f. Other relevant ethics codes
2. Copy of your state or provincial laws concerning the reporting laws (if any, in your state or province) for
   a. Child abuse (including definitions of child abuse and the circumstances of mandated reporting)
   b. Older adult abuse
   c. Impaired drivers
   d. Domestic abuse
   e. Impaired colleagues
   f. Sexual misconduct by health care providers
   g. Imminent danger of substantial physical harm to an identifiable third person or class of persons
3. Copy of your state or provincial laws concerning
   a. Age of consent for minors
   b. Bill collection (fee disputes)
   c. Testimony by expert witnesses
   d. Privileged communications
   e. Duty to protect
   f. Involuntary hospitalization
   g. Other rules regarding forensic work by psychologists
4. Copy of documents from your professional association including the
   a. Ethics code
   b. Guidelines on record keeping (if any)
   c. Guidelines on child custody evaluations (if any)
   d. Other relevant standards and documents
5. Working relationships with professional associations or other sources able to provide guidance on ethical and legal issues

APPENDIX 1.B

Risk Management Questions

1. Are you careful about informing your patients about the nature of therapy, fees, and other relevant office practices?
2. Do you focus on a good relationship with your patients, and are you meticulous about maintaining appropriate therapeutic boundaries?
3. Do you rely on scientifically derived or professionally supported techniques for intervention and diagnosis?
4. Are you aware of the limits of your expertise, and refer or seek consultation when appropriate?
5. Do you continually seek to upgrade your skills through proctorships, readings, continuing education programs, and other professional development activities?
6. Do you monitor your mental and physical health? As part of this self-monitoring, do you belong to a supportive professional consultation network, or are you otherwise embedded in a professionally supportive environment?
7. Are you aware of the state and federal laws and regulations governing your practice?
8. Are you able to discern the ethical issues implicit or explicit in your daily clinical practice?
9. Do you seek appropriate ethical or legal consultation when indicated?
10. Do you document your interventions carefully?

CHAPTER

2 Getting Started

JANET P. MOURSUND

Beginning to Begin

In the year 1900, Sigmund Freud's *The Interpretation of Dreams* was published, and the era of the "talking cure" began. Of course, this statement reveals a certain ethnocentrism: "Talking cures" of various sorts have existed, and continue to exist, in many cultures other than our own, and are practiced by people who never heard of Freud. Nevertheless, the statement is accurate for Western versions of psychotherapy. We began with, and have our roots in, the work of Freud and his associates. And surely 1900 is an appropriately memorable date to mark the beginning of our profession.

So, in the beginning, there was Freud: psychoanalysis, lying on a couch, five days a week, excavating one's earliest memories. If you had emotional problems (and enough money), this was virtually the only treatment available. It was to be several decades before an alternative to psychoanalysis would emerge.

Actually, not just one but two alternatives eventually became available. One of these, generally known as "behavioral therapy," came from academia, from the scientific study of learning. More specifically, it was based on the work of Ivan Pavlov in Russia and of B. F. Skinner, Albert Bandura, Joseph Wolpe, and others in the United States. The development of behavioral therapy is a fascinating story in itself, and it is a pity we do not have the space here to say more about it. Generally, though, it involves using experimentally derived principles of learning to help people learn new behaviors—to exchange their old, self-defeating and pain-producing behaviors for new ones that will work better for them (Kanfer & Goldstein, 1991).

Behavioral therapy began to come into its own during the late 1940s. In the years following World War II, there was a great demand for efficient ways of treating the GIs who suffered from what we would now call PTSD (post-traumatic stress disorder), and behavioral therapy promised to do just that. There was, however, a young professor at the University of Chicago who thought that the behavioral approach was missing something. Just changing a behavior—applying some set reinforcement schedule or learning a new pattern by rote—didn't really help people to grow and develop their highest potential. And wasn't that what psychotherapy ought to do, help people become the very best they could be?

So argued Carl Rogers, and in so doing he began the third major movement in the world of psychotherapy. Rogers believed that people, like animals and plants and all living things, naturally do what they are biologically intended to do. It is only when something gets in the way—when they are deprived of some necessary support or nutrient—that their growth is stunted or their behaviors become maladaptive. It seems reasonable, then, that when a living thing is *not* doing well, we should find out what need is not being satisfied, and meet the need. The organism itself will take care of things after that.

Rogers further came to believe that people have three basic psychological needs; when these needs are met, people will do well. The three needs are (1) unconditional positive regard—feeling respected and valued as a unique individual; (2) congruence—that others be open and honest in their dealings with you; and (3) accurate empathy—that others understand your feelings and experiences, and convey that understanding to you. Rogers deemed these three to be the "necessary and sufficient conditions" for psychological healing and growth. His whole approach to psychotherapy involved providing clients with the three "conditions"; he believed that nothing more was needed (Rogers, 1951). This was "client-centered therapy," and it has had an enormous influence on the way in which psychotherapy is practiced today. Indeed, it is probably safe to say that *all* modern psychotherapy training begins with learning the attitudes and techniques of client-centered (or "person-centered," as it came to be called) therapy.

Learning to be a psychotherapist can be divided into three main segments: acquiring the fundamental knowledge base of your particular profession (each of the professions—psychologist, psychiatrist, social worker, psychiatric nurse practitioner, or pastoral counselor—rests on a somewhat different set of knowledge, assumptions, and values); learning the generic skills of the "talking cure" (learning to provide Rogers's necessary and sufficient conditions is a major part of this segment); and learning the techniques and skills relevant to your specific theory of counseling. The chapters in this book focus on the second of these three segments. These are the behaviors that are relevant to all varieties of the counseling/psychotherapy profession, the things that everyone who works with emotionally troubled clients needs to know.

We shall assume, in these chapters, that you have already acquired your professional knowledge base—such as an understanding of personality and human learning (for psychologists and counselors), how to diagnose and treat physical illnesses (psychiatrists and nurses), or the philosophy and credo of your chosen faith (pastors). Learning to be a counselor or a psychotherapist comes after you have acquired this first level of competence—though, obviously, you will continue to add to those learnings throughout your professional life. And, at the other end of the spectrum, we will not be discussing the tools and techniques of specific psychotherapeutic schools. This book will not teach you how to be a psychoanalyst, a gestalt therapist, or a behavioral therapist. It will, however, introduce you to the concepts and skills that *every* counselor and psychotherapist, regardless of theoretical orientation, must build on. We'll start, in this chapter, with the elements that should be in place before you set up your first appointment with your first client.

Before we begin, I would like to ask *you* a question: Are counseling and psychotherapy basically the same thing? Or, if they are different, what *is* the difference? Like most other important questions in this field, there are a number of viewpoints about this topic. One is that there is no difference, and therefore the two terms are equivalent. This viewpoint is very popular and supported by Kirman (1977) who states: "When we perceive the helping process from the point of view of the counselee, the differentiation between counseling and psychotherapy becomes meaningless" (p. 22). Currently, this position appears to be accepted in many training institutions, and the two terms are used synonymously in the current text.

Another opinion is that there are, in fact, differences and that these stem from the theoretical, philosophical, and historical foundations of each approach. The assumption here is that these dissimilarities are expressed in practice as well. For example, psychotherapy originates from the medical model and tends to focus on the client's previous history and abnormality whereas counseling traces its roots to humanistic philosophy, which takes a holistic and teleological approach to treatment. Some individuals point out that traditional psychotherapy tends to be more authoritarian and accentuates differences in power between therapist and patient, while counseling attempts to be more egalitarian by emphasizing the client's individuality, potential, and uniqueness. A common assumption with this position is that psychotherapists work with individuals who are more dysfunctional and thus in need of intense behavioral or personality changes, while counselors work mainly with persons who are essentially normal and thus the treatment is viewed as more superficial and guidance oriented. Often implicit in this latter position is the idea that psychotherapy carries with it a sense of higher prestige and expertise than does counseling. Although it may seem like a simple matter of semantics, I urge you to think carefully about your own views of counseling and psychotherapy. After all, assuming that state laws have not already done so, at some point you will have to decide what you are going to call yourself after you finish your training.

Theoretical Base

We cannot, in these few pages, discuss all the possible theoretical bases from which counseling and psychotherapy can develop. By the time you read these words, you should already have been exposed to a number of them and will have realized that what you do (or try to do) with clients will be strongly influenced by which theory you choose to follow. But wait—what's this "choose to" business? Isn't there a right way, a valid and proven set of rules that will allow you to understand and work with your clients? Unfortunately, there is not. Many physicians of Freud's day—and, back then, anyone who attempted to cure "sick" people was a physician—scoffed at his methods, and the psychotherapeutic bickering continues to this day. Behaviorists argue with transactional analysts; neo-Freudians take issue with behaviorists; humanists disagree with the object-relations folks. Thousands upon thousands of research hours have been spent trying to determine who is right and which approach works best; significant efforts have even been made to demonstrate that *no* psychotherapy is useful at all! (The best-known of these is probably Eysenck's 1952 paper, "The Effects of Psychotherapy.") To date, none of these research efforts has come up with a definitive answer. Some methods tend to work better with some clients in the hands of some therapists.

The clearest conclusions that can be drawn from all the pages of psychotherapy research are that (1) psychotherapy does seem to help many people deal with their emotional problems and pains; (2) the basic, generic people-skills of the counselor or therapist are probably more important than his or her specific theoretical orientation (Smith & Glass, 1977; Luborsky, Singer, & Luborsky, 1975; Luborsky, 1995; see also Chapter 4); and (3) the therapist's belief in and comfort with his or her own theoretical orientation is a significant factor in determining his or her effectiveness with clients (Frank, 1961).

Using the technique of meta-analysis, some recent studies suggest that the average effect size for psychotherapy is large. For example, psychotherapy is found to have an effect size that is twice as great as placebo and three times that of no treatment. In fact, many studies show that psychotherapy is more effective than medication in treating disorders such as depression (Lambert & Bergin, 1994). Despite these findings, not all therapy is therapeutic. As pointed out in Chapter 4, sometimes psychotherapy can have detrimental effects. An important rule that all new therapists should keep in mind is the principle of nonmaleficence: "Above all, do no harm." (For more information about psychotherapy outcome research, see Chapter 13. For the interested reader, the *Journal of Clinical Psychology* [Volume 55, 1999] devotes an entire issue to this subject.)

Before we take another step, I want to assert that every single therapist and every single student of therapy has a "theoretical orientation." Your very choice to enter the profession demonstrates that you believe, first of all, that counseling or psychotherapy can make a difference—that people can change as a function of some sort of verbal interaction with a professional helper. Moreover, you probably have some (perhaps unexamined or out-of-awareness) assumptions about what sorts of verbal interaction are most helpful to people. To get a handle on these assumptions, I invite you to pause here and write down your answers to the following questions:

1. How do people get to be the way they are? Why do different people respond very differently to similar sets of circumstances?
2. Why do people often continue to do the very sorts of things that cause discomfort to themselves or others?
3. How do some people manage to change patterns of behavior that they have been engaging in for months or years?
4. How can counseling or psychotherapy facilitate the kinds of changes people want to make in their lives?
5. Are some people unlikely to benefit from counseling or psychotherapy? If so, who are they?

The answers you have written are your current theoretical orientation. You have developed it out of your life experiences—including your formal studies of human behavior. To the extent that a given theory of therapy is consistent with your own orientation, you will be comfortable with it and are likely to use it effectively. If a theory is inconsistent with your own beliefs, you will have to change those beliefs or modify the theory before you will find it particularly helpful.

The process of becoming a competent psychotherapist involves working back and forth between your own belief system and the assertions of the various theories that you encounter. The ideas propounded by theories (based on the wisdom and experience of our psychological ancestors) will and should prompt you to question your personal assumptions. And, in turn, you will and should find yourself adapting the formal theories you encounter so as to fit your personal style and belief system.

All of this back-and-forth-ing is part of the normal developmental process. Jean Piaget, who gave us much of our understanding of cognitive development, based much of his theory on the twin processes of *assimilation* (reshaping new information so as to fit with what we already know) and *accommodation* (changing what we believe on the basis of new information). Children do both of these as they learn how to get along in the world, and adults (successful ones, anyhow) do it whenever they enter an arena that is new and different for them. Indeed, an inability to assimilate and accommodate to one's life situation may well be a primary distinguishing factor for people who seek psychotherapy. The process is, and will continue to be, a necessary part of your professional development.

Which brings us (finally) to the point I wanted to make: Your ability to engage in a continuing dialog between your own theoretical base and the assumptions/suggestions/assertions of others requires that you be aware of what you believe and knowledgeable about the beliefs and theories of others. Self-examination—no less than formal exposure to the models of psychotherapy—is a vital part of your training and of your ongoing professional activity. Knowing what you believe, why you believe it, and how it is similar to and different from the beliefs of your colleagues is vital to the practice of psychotherapy.

Mentoring

Some competencies can be acquired from reading books, listening to lectures, watching demonstrations, or probing the Internet. Others can only be acquired through practice, supervised and monitored by an adept professional. Apprenticeships, in which a beginner in the craft works under the tutelage of a more experienced practitioner, are common in many trades. Learning to be a counselor or psychotherapist is a kind of apprenticeship; but instead of a single supervisor, the beginning counselor/therapist is likely to work under the direction of a series of supervisors or even of several at the same time. The best of these supervisors become mentors: people whose skills you respect, whose support you trust, with whom you want to learn and grow.

No one should consider beginning to work in a helping profession until providing for ongoing supervision and/or consultation. Fortunately, in virtually all formal training programs such supervision is an integral part of the educational experience. Often beginning with role-play work between pairs or triads of students and then moving on to closely monitored work with actual clients, supervised practice is usually the centerpiece of counselor training and is given nearly equal emphasis in the training of other helping professionals.

Sometimes, though, one may find oneself thrust into a counselor role without such formal training. An example is that of a pastor or priest, who has probably had some rudimentary coursework in "pastoral counseling" but not supervised practice and who finds him- or herself working with troubled parishioners. In such a situation, there is only one allowable solution: Find your own mentor, a colleague experienced in the kind of counseling that you are facing, and arrange for regular consultation. There is no substitute for the mentoring process, reviewing and critiquing your day-to-day work with clients under the guidance of a competent and experienced psychotherapist. To take on any sort of counselor role without such help is unethical, because it does not provide proper protection for your client; it is also impractical, because it does not promote the most efficient learning on your part.

Using mentoring is an active, not a passive, process. You will learn little (and your clients will benefit little) if you simply present yourself to your mentor and wait for him or her to critique your work. Rather, supervision sessions are a time for you to bring up the problems you have encountered with clients, the things you were not sure of, the interventions that did not quite go as you expected—all the things you would probably rather not talk about! Showing someone else your professional deficiencies can be pretty embarrassing, rather like undressing for your doctor. In both cases, though, the problem needs to be seen before it can be treated. Your mentor can spot some problem areas without your help, but certainly won't notice everything that you might or should be concerned about. Your job here is not to look good; it is to get your mentor to help you to *be* good.

At the close of every session, while things are still fresh in your mind, jot down a set of questions to bring up with your supervisor or consultant. If you are fortunate, you will have been able to make a video (or at least an audio) recording of your work and will be able actually to show your mentor the segment that you have questions about. Recordings are especially valuable because they frequently reveal something that you are doing (or not doing) that is outside your own awareness—something you cannot ask about because you do not know it is happening. Nevertheless, the most profitable mentoring sessions are almost invariably those that begin with a question initiated by you: "Help me with . . ." or "I don't know what happened . . ." or "Why did the client . . . ?"

It is especially important, of course, to seek supervision or consultation when things are not going well with a client. "Stuck places" happen often in the course of counseling. Sometimes clients seem to be stuck when, in fact, they just need time to integrate and assimilate what they have done before moving to the next chapter. Sometimes they need something from the therapist that is not being provided. And sometimes the therapist is doing something that is getting in the way of the work. One of the most useful aspects of mentoring is that the mentor can help differentiate among these different kinds of "stuckness" and make suggestions about what to do.

Even when things are moving nicely, though, mentoring is important. It helps you to continue to improve, to go from "pretty good" to "even better." It helps you to learn to be constructively critical of your own work. And—too often overlooked!—it gives you the opportunity to celebrate your successes and to have your competence affirmed.

Mentoring does not end at some well-delineated "graduation" point. It does not even end when you are competent to become a mentor yourself. Regularly scheduled peer supervision and/or consultation can and should be a continuing part of your professional practice. The very fact that we call it a "practice" is significant: We continue to practice, to learn from our errors, as long as we work with clients. Supervision and consultation are an essential adjunct to such learning. They should be scheduled and in place before you see a single client.

Motivation

Knowing what you need to know, having the entry-level skills to put that knowledge to use, and setting up ongoing professional consultation are your base. What else is needed for your therapeutic practice? The final piece is harder to talk about, because it's harder to measure. It has to do with feelings, with attitude, with your private, internal reasons for doing this sort of work. For me, this internal state can be summed up in the phrase "therapeutic intent."

Every counselor or therapist has a whole constellation of motivations for entering the profession. It is more than just "wanting to help people," although most practitioners certainly care about making a difference in clients' lives. Some of us have been clients ourselves, have found that experience transforming, and want to share it with others—and, perhaps, want to re-experience vicariously what we found so meaningful. The therapeutic relationship can involve an intense sort of closeness, and we may enjoy being with someone at that level of intimacy. And we may enjoy being the confidant, the trusted Other, the sharer-of-secrets. There's nothing wrong with these motivations as long as they don't take center stage. That center stage position must be held by our therapeutic intent: our desire to be competent and effective in the exercise of our profession.

This notion of therapeutic intent is not a simple thing. It requires a balance between caring too much, on the one hand, and not caring enough, on the other. If we care too much about the client, become too personally involved in his or her doing well, we risk rescuing, caretaking, overprotecting and overdirecting. If we care too little, we may become technicians, going through the motions of the relationship but without ever being truly involved in the process. Maintaining a balance between the two extremes is one of the most important reasons for ongoing supervision and consultation; it is often easier for someone outside the therapeutic relationship to notice a swing too far one way or the other.

Another important factor in keeping your motivational balance is to have your own emotional house in order. Any unfinished business that you bring to the therapy session is likely to interfere with your ability to maintain an appropriate therapeutic intent. This is as true of ongoing, here-and-now problems as it is of old "stuff" from the past. If you find it hard to deal with a client's issue because it is similar to one you don't want to face in your own life, you won't be able to be fully available for that client. Being aware of your own psychological sore spots, and keeping them separate from those of the client, is essential to maintaining the therapeutic balance. In order to do this, many therapists need to enter into therapy occasionally. In fact, I don't personally know *any* good therapists who have not been in therapy themselves at one time or another. There may be some, of course, but most therapists can benefit from some professional help now and then. Therapists' personal sensitivity is our most important tool, and keeping that sensitivity sharp and clear is as important for us as sharp and sterile instruments are for a surgeon.

Our motivation—our therapeutic intent—is not always going to be steady and unchanging. We, too, will have our ups and downs. We will have days when we would rather not see a particular client or rather not have to go to work at all. We will find ourselves enjoying some clients more than others. We will get tired, impatient, or bored, just like any other human beings. Again, supervision and consultation will help us know when these fluctuations are too great and when we need to make some changes or get some help in order to regain our full effectiveness. Maintaining appropriate therapeutic intent does not mean always doing it right—it means knowing when we are *not* on track, and doing something about it.

Preparing for the First Session

In this section, a number of issues that need to be dealt with as you begin to work with clients will be described. Remember, though, that counseling and psychotherapy are practiced over a wide range of settings by professionals who utilize a host of different models and methods. Therapists work with children and with adults, with individuals and with couples, and with families and with groups. Therapists practice in schools, in agencies, in psychiatric hospitals, and in office buildings. Some work for a salary, and some are in private practice.

Therapists may be part of a group practice, with colleagues and secretarial staff readily available, while others work alone with only an answering machine for support. As you read the rest of this chapter, be aware that some of the issues and some of the suggestions may not be relevant to the setting in which you find yourself right now. But don't skip over a section completely—remember, professional settings can change, and being aware of some of the issues that your colleagues are dealing with may help you decide what kind of career you want to build.

Appointments

How do you want to handle your first contact with a client? In the vast majority of cases, that contact will be made by telephone: The client will call your agency or your office to make an appointment. If you are working in an agency—particularly if you are a beginner—you will have little to say about how that first contact is handled. The agency will have its own procedures, and nearly always those procedures will be carried out by someone other than yourself. The client will be screened for appropriateness in some way, some information will be gathered, and an appointment with you will be scheduled.

Those agency procedures are not neutral for the client. They leave an impression; the client feels welcomed, discounted, understood, or "treated like a number" depending on what happened during the first contact. While you may not be able to change the procedures, or the way they are carried out, you should certainly know what they are—and, if possible, how the client seemed to respond to them—so that you can anticipate the expectations that the client will bring to that first appointment. It goes without saying that you should also familiarize yourself with whatever information the client gave in setting up the appointment.

In some settings, the appointment will not be scheduled for you. "Will you talk to Tommy Henderson? I think he needs some help," a teacher may say to a school counselor. As a psychiatric social worker, you may find a new client form in your mail box, with the client's name and phone number and some initial information; you are expected to take it from there. Many therapists in private practice schedule their own appointments, either because they prefer to do so or because they cannot yet afford the luxury of a secretary. When you schedule your own appointments, you will need to decide how much information to collect from the client over the telephone. Some therapists like to do a fairly extensive initial screening during the first phone contact, while others prefer to keep the scheduling call as brief as possible. Even in a brief contact, though, some information exchange is essential. You need to know enough about a client to decide whether you are an appropriate therapist for him or her: Are you competent to deal with a person of this age/gender/culture, and do you know how to treat the kind of problem being presented? Do your respective schedules match well enough to find a time to meet? If you have no openings in the next few days, should the client be referred to someone who can see him or her sooner?

Clients, too, will need to get some information over the phone. Obviously, they need to know when their appointment will be and how to get to your office. They need to know about how long the appointment will last. You may want to talk briefly about your approach to therapy, so they will have an idea of what to expect of you—whether that first session will be primarily information-gathering and different from subsequent sessions, for instance. You should inform them of how much they will be charged for the session and how much of that charge will be covered by their insurance.

If you are in private practice, the insurance issue is particularly important. You will need to find out what kind of insurance the client has and whether your services can be covered under the client's policy. Many people have only a hazy idea about their mental health coverage and know even less about how provider panels work. It is your responsibility to insist that clients inform themselves about their insurance coverage, so that they know clearly what therapy will cost them. Before they set foot in your office, you and they both should know whether you can be reimbursed by their insurance, the amount of that reimbursement, and what their co-payment will be.

Whatever the procedure your office uses and whatever the degree of your involvement, remember that the appointment-setting contact creates your client's first impressions about what it will be like to work with you. Your job begins with doing your best to ensure that the first impressions are favorable ones, since those first impressions set the tone for everything that follows.

Intake Interviews

Will you handle the first session with your client? This question is not as silly as it may sound: Many agencies have intake workers whose job it is to interview a prospective client, obtain a history, do an initial diagnosis, and then pass the client on to a therapist or refer the client elsewhere. In such agencies, the therapist generally receives a detailed report from the intake worker, summarizing the information that was obtained.

Using a specialized intake worker is intended to save time for both therapist and client (theoretically, such a procedure ensures a good therapist–client match, as well as giving the therapist the most relevant information about the client before the first true therapy session). It also allows an agency to assign workers to the kind of jobs they do best: initial assessment interviewing or longer-term actual therapy. And, finally, it makes clear the distinction between information gathering and therapy.

There is a down side of separating intake and therapy functions, though. It creates an additional disjoint for the client, who often comes away from the intake session wishing to do his or her therapy with that interviewer and must then form yet another relationship with a different therapist. It also forces the therapist to either get the client's story secondhand, or make the client tell it all over again—neither of which is particularly desirable. On balance, I would rather conduct my own intake sessions than have them done by an intake worker. I have found, though, that it is important to tell the client that this first session will be primarily concerned with gathering information, that I will be asking a lot of questions and taking notes of the answers, and that my style once we get started in therapy will probably be quite different. I don't want the intake session to set up an expectation in the client that being in therapy means sitting passively, answering my questions, and letting me figure out what to do next.

Finances

Handling fees and payment is often the most difficult part of being a counselor or therapist, at least early on. Dealing with a client's anxiety or depression can be a breeze, compared with asking him or her for money! If you work in a public or private agency, this issue probably won't come up; billing is handled for you, and you simply draw your salary. If you are in private practice, though, be prepared for some discomfort around this issue. You will need to know what to do about requests for reduced fees (the "sliding scale"), about late payments, and about charging for missed sessions. You will find it much easier to do all this if you've thought through, well ahead of time, what your rules are about payment.

An ex-student of mine, newly set up in private practice, told me, "It's so hard to ask people to pay me money—lots of money!—when just a few months ago they would have been doing me a favor just to let me work with them in the training clinic!" Another colleague said to me, "I don't think I'll ever get over feeling guilty when I insist on full payment from a client who needs the money so much more than I do." Most of us have had little or no experience in making a direct request for payment, and even less in deciding how much our services are worth. I don't know of any way to make it easy to get past this problem, but talking it over with colleagues certainly helps—as does the knowledge that it does get better as time goes on, and that eventually you will be able to discuss your fees with your clients without feeling queasy about it.

My advice to beginning counselors and therapists is to find out how much other professionals in your area are charging and to set your own fees near the middle of that range. If possible, avoid using a sliding scale: Sliding scales tend to set up an unnecessary issue for you and the client to deal with, and can leak into and contaminate the therapeutic work. It is better for you to see a few clients *pro bono* (completely without charge) and keep your actual fees the same for everyone else, than to have to haggle and worry over how much to charge each individual client. Decide what your rules will be about missed sessions and late payments, make sure the client knows these rules, and then stick with them.

Physical Arrangements

Your office, the place where you see your clients, is an extension of you. Accurately or inaccurately, the client will experience that office as *yours,* as reflecting your tastes and preferences. Even if you must share an office with someone else, or (as is often the case in a training clinic) do your work in common treatment rooms, there are still things you can do to personalize your space and make it work better for both you and the client. Let's take a look at what we want an office space to do, and how to make that happen.

What You Need. Your office space is, first and foremost, a place for you to do your therapeutic work. It needs to be large enough to see families (if your practice includes family therapy), yet small enough that you and an individual client don't feel lost in it. Many therapists use a different room for group work, since an office large enough for groups often feels too big for individual therapy; another solution is to use furniture arrangement to divide your office so that one end or side is partially closed off and comfortable for just two or three people.

You also need an area in which to do your paperwork: writing case notes, reading files, and preparing reports. If possible, this area should be physically separated from the therapy space; minimally, there should be enough distance between your "paperwork space" and your therapy setting so that clients cannot see any papers or files that you may have left lying out. (Don't just assume that you will always keep your work space cleared and all client materials put away; we all get busy, or forget, and one error can result in a serious breach of confidentiality. How would *you* feel, as a client, if you thought that information about you might be left out where others could see it?)

Speaking of paperwork, you also need a place to keep all those records. Your files must be kept locked, but they should be close by—you may need information from them when you prepare reports, handle phone calls, and occasionally even during a session. More and more, files are being prepared and stored electronically, and software now exists that can save significant amounts of time and file space. If you keep your records on your computer, you'll still need hard copies of some documents, though; it will be a while before filing cabinets disappear completely. Whatever kind of record storage you use, make sure that a trusted colleague has a key and/or knows the password that will access your electronic records. If some sort of personal emergency makes it impossible for you to see clients for a while, whoever takes over for you will need to be able to find your files.

In addition to all of these practice activities, you need to plan your working space so that it can be used for reading, reflecting, or conferring with a colleague. Which brings us to the issue of comfort. Make sure that this place where you will be spending so much of your time is the kind of place you like. Your chair (and the client's, as well!) should be comfortable, and your desk arranged to fit your needs. The colors and decorations should fit your personality. Don't shortchange yourself here: Spending a little extra time and a little more money making your office feel right for you will help you relax and focus on the work at hand.

Finally, you will need a waiting area separate from your therapy space. In the ideal situation, clients enter the waiting area by one door and leave by another, so they don't have to pass (and possibly recognize) each other. Frankly, I have not encountered this arrangement outside of books and movies, though; most of us make do with the same sort of waiting rooms used by doctors and dentists. Several therapists (or other professionals) who work in the same general area may share a waiting room. The more you can arrange things for your clients' convenience, the better—but we make do with what we can afford.

What if you do not have the luxury of an office all your own? What if you must share waiting and office space with other therapists? You can still insist that your chair be comfortable and that you have a private area in which you can prepare and store records. You can bring something uniquely yours—a throw rug, a picture, a small bit of statuary, a jug of flowers—into the room where you will see a client. I have, for instance, a bowl of polished rocks that I put on a low table in my therapy office, and even when I must see clients away from my own office, that bowl of rocks goes with me. It provides continuity for both the client and myself; it reminds me of who I am as a therapist, and it is something that clients come to recognize and enjoy each time we meet.

What the Client Needs. One of the most important needs that clients have is the need for privacy. It is hard enough to talk about one's thoughts and feelings to a therapist; doing so while worried that someone else might overhear is even more difficult. Your office should be as soundproof as possible, and most especially, sounds from your sessions should not drift out into your waiting room area. A good quality stereo or CD player can provide soft music that will help to cover any sounds that do leak out.

Notice that I said *soft* music. The furnishings, sounds, and decor of both waiting room and office should be gentle. They are a background to therapy, supporting and surrounding the work. They shouldn't call attention to themselves. Furniture should be comfortable, decorations should be pleasing, lighting should be moderate. Tissues should be close at hand; a clock should be visible but unobtrusive.

Clients get to know their therapist's office very well. They expect it to be the same from one session to the next; they notice when something is changed. When things are difficult, when the pain and problems seem overwhelming, the therapist's office is a place of refuge and comfort. It provides a holding environment (Winnicott, 1971), a space where clients can let go of the ordinary rules and subterfuges of social relationships, where they can be and feel what would not be safe to be and feel anywhere else. To the degree that your office provides such a space, the work will be facilitated.

Again, if you don't have complete control over your therapy space (sharing with another therapist, or being assigned to whatever therapy room is free for a given appointment), you can still take a few moments before your session begins to personalize the room. Move the furniture a bit, throw an afghan over a chair or a pillow onto the floor, adjust the lighting. For this hour, this is *your* place—claim it. And, if you doubt the significance of that claim, try it both ways (with, and without, your personal touches) and notice the difference in the work!

Before the First Session

So here you are, with the name of a client and a time pencilled into your calendar. You may have spoken to this person on the phone, setting up the appointment, or you may have been given a note scribbled by a secretary. It doesn't matter; tomorrow at 2:00 you will walk into your treatment room with this as-yet-unknown person. What needs to happen between now and then?

How Much to Know?

One of the first issues to be faced is that of prior knowledge. Just how much do you want to know before you begin about this client and what brings him or her to treatment? There are lots of varying opinions about this; different practitioners do it different ways. Some want to know as much as possible; they peruse all available files, hope that an exhaustive intake interview will have been done, or ask clients to come early to fill out information questionnaires. They believe that the more they know, the less time is likely to be wasted chasing down blind alleys.

At the other extreme are the therapists who want to know nothing at all secondhand. If they had their way, there would be no screening interview, no specialized intake workers. If there is an intake report in the file, they may not even read it; in fact, they may not open the file at all. They want to get their information about the client *from* the client, uncluttered by someone else's possibly inaccurate interpretations.

If I am to be perfectly honest, I must confess that I lean toward this second point of view. Getting the information directly from the client not only eliminates middleman interpretations, but also allows you to pick up a wealth of secondary impressions. It lets you follow up those impressions by asking questions that aren't generated by the standard intake format. And it provides a semistructured task to carry both you and the client through the somewhat awkward getting-acquainted period.

There are, though, at least two drawbacks to this scenario. First, if the client *has* gone through an intake interview or filled out a questionnaire as a part of your agency's routine procedures, he or she may be confused or annoyed that you didn't read it and are now asking those same questions all over again. "If you weren't going to pay attention to it, why did I have to bother doing it?" This is a reasonable question and not very easy to answer.

The second, and even more critical, drawback has to do with the kinds of expectations that may be set up during an initial information-gathering session. In such a session, the therapist or counselor is going to be fairly directive. Certain questions need answers, certain data must be collected, and the therapist is responsible for getting this information. You'll ask lots of questions, take notes, and make sure the client stays on track. In other words, *you* will determine what happens in the session. This is not the way most therapists want to operate when the actual therapy begins. At that point, you want the client to take charge, to decide what to talk about, and to have a sense of what he or she wants to accomplish during the therapy hour. If you've trained the client, during that first hour, to wait for your guidance, it may be an uphill battle to undo that training. This is especially true for clients who already expect that counselors and therapists act much like physicians: They listen to your problems, and then tell you what to do about them. It is hard enough to get clients to let go of this expectation without having reinforced it during an initial session.

So how can this dilemma be resolved? In the usual way, by finding a middle course. If an intake interview is done, it seems only courteous to read it; make notes of the answers you want to follow up on, and do so when the occasion arises. If you do your own intake interview, tell the client that this is a different kind of session than the ones that will follow, and how and why it is different.

An intake report, of course, is not the only source of information about a prospective client. Your referral source may have told you about the client and why he or she was referred. A client's relative may have made the appointment (especially if the client is a child) and may have wanted to talk with you about the situation. Or you may already know this client, or know about him or her, in another context. With regard to this latter kind of information, information that is incidental to the actual therapy context, my rule-of-thumb is clear: The less I know, the better. Unless there is some specific reason to do so, I do not get information about my clients from colleagues, from other professionals, and especially from friends or family members. I would not want other folks talking to my therapist about me, and I extend that courtesy to my own clients.

The primary exception to this rule is that of danger to self or others. If you have reason to believe that a client may be suicidal or about to hurt someone else, you will need to do whatever you can to protect the person or persons at risk—and that may mean talking about your client with a variety of people, including family members, friends, or public officials. Clients need to know that this is a possibility, and they should be told so during your first session. A simple statement, "If I should ever have reason to believe that you might hurt yourself or somebody else, I'll do whatever is needed to protect you," generally suffices, and I've yet to meet a client who objects to that warning. Under some (relatively rare, thank goodness) conditions, you may even need to take action before your first session. If someone calls for an appointment, for instance, and sounds suicidal or psychotic, it may not be wise to simply make an appointment for a few days hence. Your first duty is to act in your client's best interest, and doing so requires that you know when your client is at risk and what you can do about it.

Paperwork

Oh, that paperwork! You didn't sign up to be a secretary; you are a therapist. Why should you spend so much time dealing with records and forms and reports? Unfortunately (for most of us), record keeping and report writing are a necessary evil; they come with the psychotherapeutic territory. And the paperwork begins before you even set eyes on the client.

The more care you take with your records, from the very outset, the less time and trouble you will have with them later on. A client file should be prepared for each client *before* that client is seen. Files need to be stiff enough to be easily handled, with pronged paper-fasteners inside so that your records can't sift out onto the floor when you pick up the file. The most common organizing system is to put your notes from each session, in reverse chronological order, on the right; all other information (correspondence, testing reports, release of information forms, and so forth) on the left.

If the client is to fill out or sign any forms, put the client's name on them and have them ready before the client arrives. Along with the intake summary (if there is one), these will be the first items in the client file.

A note should be made of every contact with or about your client, even if it's just a short phone call. Most especially, you'll need to write notes about each session; this will be described more fully later in the chapter.

Feelings

Few of us have not experienced a rush of feelings as we wait for our first client to arrive. Primary among those feelings is likely to be anxiety: Will I be able to do this? Will the client like me? What if the client won't talk? What if the client gets really upset and I don't know what to do? These are normal worries, and the first step in dealing with them is to recognize how normal they are. In fact, if you didn't feel any anxiety at all, you probably wouldn't do as good a job.

Gestalt therapists tell us that anxiety is often disguised excitement: excitement without enough oxygen to support it. So the next step in dealing with anxiety is to breathe deeply—get that oxygen in there—and allow your sense of excitement to emerge.

The likelihood that anything will go seriously wrong in your first sessions is very, very small; most of your fears are unfounded. On the other hand, the likelihood that you will make mistakes is just about 100 percent. Okay, so you're going to do some things wrong. So what? The client is at least as anxious as you are, at least afraid of "doing it wrong." If you focus on his or her experience, story, and feelings, your concerns about yourself will melt away. You may have an occasional twinge of "that was a dumb thing to say" or "I think I missed the point here," but—as in any conversation—you can always backtrack and repair your error.

One last, but important, precaution: In the unlikely event that your client *should* become very upset, or get into some other emotional space that you don't know how to handle, know how to call in a backup. There should be another therapist near, or at least available by phone, who can come in to help in case of emergency. Even experienced therapists occasionally need help when the unexpected occurs; just knowing that someone else is available can be very reassuring.

I've spent a lot of time talking about anxiety. What about all the other feelings you may be experiencing? Happiness, to be finally getting started. A sense of being ready, of eagerness. And most useful of all: curiosity. What is this client going to be like? What is his or her story? What wonderful, complex patterns will unfold between us as we begin our journey together? Curiosity is the best possible complement to competence and therapeutic intent; together, they are the triad of attitudes that will guide your professional behavior throughout your career.

The Session Itself

As mentioned already, first sessions are different from later ones. Even if you do not do your own intake, the first session still involves the getting-acquainted process, the awkwardness of new beginnings. The client doesn't know you, doesn't know what you expect, and (usually) wants your approval. You don't know the client, don't know what he or she expects, and (usually) want his or her approval. If you are a beginning therapist, you don't even know yourself yet, in this role; you don't know exactly what you will be like or how you will respond to this person. All of these things will emerge as the therapeutic relationship comes into being.

If you conduct your own intake interviews, the difference between the first session and later ones will be even more marked. The purpose of an intake interview is to get enough information to make decisions about this person: Can he or she benefit from working with you? If so, where will you start? What will be your focus? What sort of approach is most likely to be helpful? If not, what referral should you make?

Kinds of Information

Two kinds of information are to be gathered in any session, intake or otherwise: what you need to know and what the client needs to tell you. In most instances, the client's needs come first; allowing clients to begin with what they think is important not only will help you to understand their point of view, but also conveys respect. Moreover, you will find it much easier to get clients to answer your own questions after you have attended to their story.

This doesn't mean, though, that you should sit passively and let the client ramble all over the map. Part of your job is to help clients sort out their stories, put them in order, and make sense of them. For me, the best way to do that is to be actively engaged in trying to get it straight myself. *I* need to understand what is going on, how it came about, and what the client feels about it; making me understand all that will help the client understand it, too. Don't pretend that you understand when you don't; don't assume or fill in the blanks when the client skips over something. If some part of the client's story seems fuzzy to you, it may well be fuzzy for him or her as well.

Being willing to say that you do not quite get it—asking for clarification and for details—has another advantage. It makes the client a collaborator, perhaps even a teacher, in the therapeutic adventure. You can't read the client's mind (you might be surprised how many clients think you can); you don't know what he or she should do; you don't have magic answers. The two of you will work *together* on the problems, and you are *both* responsible for solving them.

Have you ever done river rafting or watched someone else do it? Good rafters work with the current, steering around rocks and snags and moving into the best channel to get where they want to go. They let the river do most of the work, yet they are always alert to what is coming next, to the obstacles and opportunities on all sides. Good therapists do the same thing: They let the client's concerns carry the session along, but are alert to steer into useful channels and to avoid snags and dead-ends. And, like a river rafter, when they do get hung up, they unsnag themselves, set the boat back into the current, and keep on going.

The First Five Minutes and Beyond

The two most important questions to be dealt with in your initial session are "How are you?" and "What do you want?" "How are you?" is more than a polite, almost ritual question: It is a serious inquiry into the client's state of being. You need to know what this client is bringing to his or her meeting with you, what sort of physical condition he or she is in, what his or her emotional state is, and what he or she believes about seeking professional help. You need to know what sort of help the client is looking for, and what his or her goals are in therapy, and what kinds of things he or she wants to change. Attending to these questions during the first session, underlining them so that your client recognizes their importance, will set the tone for the rest of your work with that person. I teach my students to begin every session with them. I suppose I teach my clients the same thing. It is not unusual for a client to arrive at my office, sit down, and say "Well, you want to know how I am and what I want today."

But I'm getting ahead of myself—we are still at the very beginning of the very first session. Just as the way you conduct that first session tends to set the tone for future work, so the first few minutes of the session tends to set the tone for the rest of your time together. Let's take a look at that important first few minutes, what needs to happen in it, and what you should avoid.

You walk into your waiting room, looking for someone you've never seen before. "Mary Smith?" you ask. She nods, and you introduce yourself. "I'm Jan Moursund. Will you come in?" And you both go into your office. What happens next? You won't open your mouth and say "How are you? What do you want?"; that would be preposterous. Yet those are the questions you should be asking inside your head. How *is* this person? What's going on for her? What's it like to be Mary Smith, at this particular moment in her life? And what *does* she want? What does she hope will happen here? What does she expect of me? How has she gotten tangled up in her life, and what does she think she needs in order to get untangled?

There is much to think about, so many questions you could ask—and the best way to start is not to ask any of them. Instead, use your eyes. *Notice.* There is a lot going on, without words, and you need to pay attention if you are to catch all of it. How does Mary Smith look? What sort of clothes is she wearing, and does she seem comfortable in them? The way people choose and wear clothing, and the way they groom themselves, can provide useful hypotheses about their state of mind. Many therapists have commented on how their clients seem to use dress as an unspoken comment on how they are feeling. Notice her demeanor. Does she seem nervous? Composed? Embarassed? Does she wait to be invited to sit down, or does she take a chair without being asked? Where does she choose to sit? If she carries a purse or packages, where does she put them? What does she do with her hands? Mary Smith's appearance and her nonverbal behaviors are all communications—communications that she may not yet be able to put into words.

When talking begins, who will begin it? Does Mary Smith wait for you to speak, or does she launch right into her story? If she does wait, is the pause uncomfortable and tense, or does it seem natural? In a first session, before the client knows you or your therapy, it is both rude and unkind to draw that initial silence out; nevertheless, busying yourself with your chair or a notepad for a few seconds will give her a chance to settle in, and you a chance to observe, before words become foreground for you both.

There are a number of ways to structure an initial session. If you prefer to let the client warm up by dealing with (probably) neutral questions first, you may begin by asking for her full name, address, phone number, insurance company, and general demographic information. The problem with this approach is that it sets a kind of "therapist-ask-and-client-answer" rhythm that may be hard to break out of. For that reason, I prefer to have clients fill out a general information sheet the first time they come to my office, so that we don't have to deal with that sort of thing during our time together. We can use our together time to talk about the important stuff: Who are you, really, and what do you really want?

Most clients need to be "primed" to begin their story: They need some sort of question, some sort of suggestion about how to jump in. Even if they have rehearsed what they are going to tell you (and many will have done so), it can still be hard to get started. I've found that "How can I be of help to you?" is a wonderfully neutral question that allows clients to begin wherever they want to, yet gives them a sense of direction. And having them start where they want to is useful because it tells you what's important to them. Does Mary Smith begin by giving you some past history, or does she move right into a list of symptoms? Does she flounder, jumping from one topic to another, or is her story organized and coherent? Does she know clearly what her problem is, or is she simply confused and hurting and wanting help?

After the First Five Minutes

If the first few minutes of your session is used to ask "How are you?" and "What do you want?" then the rest of the session can be devoted to exploring the answers to those two questions. Obviously, the answers will be more complex than "Fine" and "To feel better." Exploring the complexity of the client's answers is where your own curiosity and creativity can be your best friend. If you allow yourself to wonder what lies beyond the answer your client gives you—what beliefs, expectations, and memories are just around the corner—you will always have another avenue of inquiry to pursue. Take the "How are you?" question, for instance. How are you, physically? How are you, emotionally? What do you think about how you've been feeling? How are you different now from how you were before you decided to seek help? How long have you been feeling as you are now? What happened that helped you get to where you are? How are your feelings different from other people's? And so on, and so on. "What do you want?" has the same virtually endless set of branches: What do you want right now? When, in the past, did you have it, or something like it? How did you come to lose it? What sorts of things have you tried to get it (or get it back)? What happened when you tried them?

All of these questions have two important characteristics: They are all open-ended, and none of them uses the word "why." It may be necessary, in an intake session, to ask some closed-ended questions; if you want to know a person's age or marital status, a closed-ended question is the best way to find out. Once those necessary-for-the-record items have been dealt with, though, closed-ended questions should be avoided. Keeping questions open-ended allows clients to convey their sense of what's important in the answer, to elaborate on a theme, and to tell their story in their own words. It encourages them to be active participants in the therapy process, rather than passive givers-of-answers. Similarly, simply repeating a client's phrase can act as an open-ended question, an unspoken "tell me more about it." "I've been feeling really rotten for about three months," says your client. Your response of "About three months . . ." says that you're interested in more details; the client will decide whether to tell you about the rottenness of the three months, or about what happened three months ago, or about how different his or her life was before then.

So much for open-ended questions; you'll read more about this topic in later chapters. Let's turn, for a moment, to the absence of "why" in those lists of questions. In my experience, "why" is seldom a helpful word and can be actually hurtful. For one thing, it carries an underlying quality of criticism. "Why did you do that?" *What a stupid thing to do . . .* "Why do you feel that way?" *Normal people wouldn't . . .* "Why do you think that strategy didn't work?" *Either the strategy, or your effort to carry it out, must have been pretty pitiful . . .* It is useless to say that you would not intend these meanings; if your client believes that you intend them, that's all that counts. And even beyond that accusatory tilt, "why" questions generally don't yield useful information. Remember when you were a kid, and some grown-up asked you "Why did you xxx?" or "Why don't you want to yyy?" or "Why do you care about zzz?" There really wasn't any answer to those questions. If the grown-up had asked "How were you feeling when you did xxx?" or "What do you think would happen if you yyy'd?" or "What is it like for you when zzz happens?" you might have been able to answer. The same thing is true for adults: Questions that take you inside—into your self-observable internal experiencing—are more useful than abstract "why" questions. Moreover, when someone does manage to answer a "why," the effort nearly always sends him or her into some realm of cognitive generalization and away from direct experience. And direct experience is, most often, where clients will find their answers.

Most experienced therapists have a kind of road map in their head, a sense of what topics they want to cover, or at least touch upon, in a first session with a client. Knowing the map well, they don't have to follow it strictly; they can let the client take the lead, and double back later to fill in the gaps. Or, if the client takes them in some quite unexpected direction, they may decide to leave their own map (temporarily) and let the client decide what to explore. Depending on your own theoretical orientation (and, if you are a student, on the demands of your supervisor), you may or may not be free to follow the client's lead. Even if you have a well-delineated set of information to gather, though, it is still very important to attend to what is foreground for the client. Not only is this useful information—helpful for you in understanding this client's beliefs and concerns—but also the process of attending to and being guided by the client conveys your expectation that the client will be an active partner in the therapeutic process.

Ending

Surprisingly soon, your time is up. The hour is over, and you must figure out a way to say good-bye. Actually, if it happens this way, you've made an error: You need to be aware of the clock, so that you can begin winding up the session with 10 or 15 minutes to spare. Beginning to stop before it's time to stop allows space for tucking in the loose ends, answering the client's questions, and making decisions about where to go from here.

Tucking in the loose ends involves creating some sort of closure to the client's story. Often this can best be done by summarizing the high points of what the client has told you. Here the questions "How are you?" and "What do you want?" can be a helpful outline. "We only have a few minutes left, Roger, and I'd like to see if I'm understanding what you've been telling me. You say that you began feeling pretty depressed about three months ago, and that up until then your life had been reasonably pleasant. You want to get past the depression and have the kind of life you had before—going out with the guys, enjoying school, being kind of happy-go-lucky, instead of sitting around home feeling bad. . . ."

This kind of quick summary can be followed by the request, "Now, tell me what I've missed." Notice, not "Have I missed anything?" That question invites the polite fiction, "No, that's about it. . . ." Requesting that the client tell you what you've missed carries with it the assumption that of course you *have* missed something, and the client is expected to do his or her share by filling in the missing parts.

Clients nearly always have questions at the end of a first session, and it's only reasonable that they should ask them. If you are willing to give a straight, honest answer to these questions and if answering them is in the client's best interest, then answer. If you aren't willing to answer them, either because you don't know the answer or don't feel it would be appropriate to give one, say that. Above all, don't try to deceive the client; don't pretend to give an answer while not actually doing so. Clients can sniff out this kind of dishonesty with remarkable accuracy, and it's hard to think of anything that could do more to derail the kind of trust and rapport you are trying to build.

One question your client will certainly have in mind is "What happens next?" Will you continue to work together, and, if so, what will that work be like? If not, will you send him or her elsewhere? And why would you make that decision? Let's look at these possibilities in turn.

The decision to work together is, of course, a joint one; both client and therapist must make it. If you believe that working with you may be helpful to the client, say so. The client still has the option of declining the offer, or of taking some time to think about it. In fact, it is often a good idea to tell the client what you think would be most helpful, and then suggest that he or she think it over for a day or two and let you know what he or she has decided.

In order to make an informed decision, clients must know what your work together will be like. They've learned something of that in the time you've already spent together—but, as we've said several times, first sessions can be quite different from later ones. Give the client your best guess as to how many sessions his or her treatment will require and how often those sessions will be scheduled. If you typically give clients some sort of homework assignment, talk about that. If you have a sense of what the focus of the work will be, say so (and find out if the client agrees or disagrees). Warn clients that they may experience some temporary worsening of symptoms at the beginning of treatment and that they may find some of their sessions disquieting or uncomfortable.

Some of the information a client needs in order to make an informed decision about continuing with you is "generic"—it has to do with standard practices, the same for everyone. Many therapists use an informed consent document, in which these standard practices are described; the client is asked to read and sign it before proceeding with treatment. Using this kind of document saves time during the actual session and also protects you legally. A sample informed consent document can be found in the appendix at the end of this chapter. Even if the clients read and sign such a document, though, you should give them an opportunity to ask questions about it.

The client may be quite clear that he or she wants to continue with you and need no more time to think it over. Well and good—go ahead and schedule the next appointment. You're almost done; there's just one more piece. But first, what about the client who *doesn't* continue?

If the decision not to continue with you is the client's, your job is easy (even though your ego may feel a bit bruised). You simply wish the client well, offer to provide names of other therapists, and acknowledge that you respect both the decision and the courage it took to tell you about it.

If you are the one who is deciding not to continue, you need to find a constructive way to give that information to the client. People seeking therapy are likely to be sensitive. They are probably in emotional pain when they come to you. If you decide not to work with them, they may create even more painful fantasies about being rejected: "This therapist doesn't like me"; "I must be really sick"; "There's no hope, and I'll never feel any better." Stating the reasons for your decision clearly and unambiguously will go a long way toward avoiding such negative self-talk. You may feel that psychotherapy is not what the client most needs at this point (for instance, a person who is abusing drugs may need to enter a drug treatment program and get clean and sober before he or she can benefit from working with you) or that a different therapist (with a different area of specialization) would be a better fit. Whatever your reasons, don't simply send the client away empty-handed. Let him or her know what resources are available and what action you recommend next.

Every person who walks out of your office, whether or not they expect to walk in again another time, needs to leave with two things: a plan of action and a sense of hope. That's your last task, the last bit of therapeutic business for you to conduct. Simply having talked through problems with a sympathetic and competent therapist often brings some relief and hopefulness in and of itself. Having a plan of action—a task to complete—is also beneficial because it increases the client's sense of self-efficacy. The client is doing something, taking steps on his or her own behalf, not just passively waiting or hopelessly struggling and getting nowhere. If you won't be seeing the client again, your recommendations for other kinds of treatment and your suggestions about where such treatment is available are a potential plan of action. If you will be meeting again, you may want to give some concrete "homework" assignment to be brought back to the next session; at the very least, suggest that the client attend to some aspect of internal or external behavior that will be discussed when you next meet.

Forewarned Is Forearmed

It's good advice: The more you know about what might happen, and the more you have thought about how you will deal with it, the better prepared you will be to help your clients. This is as true in the first session as it will be later on—even more so, perhaps, because therapeutic effects cumulate. Eric Berne (1961) used the analogy of a stack of coins to describe the effects of events throughout a person's life; a bent coin near the bottom of the stack (trauma early in one's life) will do more to unbalance the stack than a bent coin toward the top. Similarly, a critical event early in therapy will do much more to influence the overall course of that therapy than will such an event later on. So let's look at some of the more common concerns that can arise during your early sessions and at some strategies for handling them.

Client Requests for Information

We've already talked a bit about this issue: Clients often want information and often ask for it. Their first concern, appropriately, is for themselves. "What's wrong with me?" "Will I ever get any better?" "Is there any hope?" A client who is paying for your professional help, who has spent an hour telling you his or her story, and who may have spent additional time with an intake worker or have filled out an extensive questionnaire, certainly has a right to expect that you will be able to make some sort of a diagnosis based on all that information.

The diagnosis, though, should be in terms that are understandable and make sense to the client. DSM-IV (1994) terminology tends to be frightening and often misleading; few clients feel reassured by being told that they have an "adjustment disorder with mixed emotional features," even though you may know that this diagnosis refers to conditions that usually respond well to treatment. I have found that the "What's wrong with me?" question can usually be addressed by simply summarizing the symptoms that the client has been describing: "It sounds like you've been feeling pretty depressed for several months, that your sleeping and eating patterns have become disturbed, and that your anxiety about all of these problems is making things even worse." Having thus demonstrated to the client that you truly have heard and understood what he or she has been telling you, you can move on to the more important question: "Can I get better?"

Clients need believable reassurance—not a wishy-washy, "Don't worry, everything will work out," but a clear, solid assessment of their prognosis. What they would really like, of course, is a guarantee that things will improve, preferably one that involves no hard therapeutic work on their part. A pill, maybe, or a way to make someone else change so that their own lives will be more comfortable. And that is exactly what they can't have. We therapists don't have magic bullets; we can't be absolutely sure that a client will respond to treatment or make a guaranteed prediction of how long that treatment will take. What we can usually say is that most people with these sorts of problems find therapy helpful, that the usual length of treatment is xxx weeks or months or sessions, and that the effectiveness of treatment will be partly determined by how much effort and energy the client is willing to put into the process. I tell my clients that coming to therapy is similar to joining a health club: If you just come in every other week and sit and look at the exercise machines, you are not likely to benefit much from your membership. In order to get trim and slim, you need actually to use the machines and work up a sweat; and you'd progress much faster if you did exercises at home as well.

Sometimes clients ask questions about you, the therapist. They may want to know about your professional background—your therapeutic orientation, where you were trained, how much experience you have. Questions of this sort should be treated as evidence that the client is a good and careful consumer, making sure that he or she is getting the best treatment possible. Even if this isn't the case, even if the questions have some other, less benign motivation, taking them at face value is appropriate at this early stage. Answer them honestly and succinctly. Clients don't need a ten-minute discussion of theory, or a detailed personal resumé; they just need to know that you are competent to help them.

Somewhat more problematical are personal questions: Are you married? Do you have children? Have you ever had these sorts of symptoms yourself? Depending on your theory of therapy, you may or may not want to give the client this kind of information. If you do choose to give it, do so briefly. This is not a chatting time, not the beginning of a friendship, and your personal business will not be a focus of your work with this client. Whether or not you give answers to personal questions, it will almost certainly be useful to ask about the client's reasons for asking them. "How is that important to you?" or "What difference might my answers make in our work together?" can help both you and the client understand his or her belief structure and ways of relating to others.

When all is said and done, there are two basic guidelines in dealing with client questions. First, don't lie or evade. Be straightforward, be clear, speak in language the client can understand. If you don't want to answer, say so and give an honest reason for your refusal. Second, attend to the thoughts and feelings that underlie the question. Questions don't come out of nowhere; they're asked for a reason. The beliefs, fears, hopes, and past experiences that prompt a client's question may be the most important things you could possibly be talking about with this person.

The Client Who Won't Stop

Although it is valuable to follow the clients' lead—to let them tell their stories in their own way—it is also necessary to guide them out of dead ends and to keep the storytelling productive. There is seldom an advantage to allowing a client to carry on a tirade against a resented partner, to discuss in detail the menu of a dinner party attended last week, or to tell you at length about the problems that his or her married children are experiencing. In this initial session, your task is to find the balance between encouraging clients to talk about what is important to them, and at the same time making sure that you cover the topics *you* believe will be relevant.

Your first move in this direction is likely to be a simple question or directive that changes the focus of the conversation: "Tell me about your family, the people you live with now." "How have things been going at work in the last few weeks?" "What sorts of things do you like to do in your spare time?" "Have you ever been hospitalized for these kinds of problems?" If the client ignores your question, or answers it briefly and then returns to the (seemingly) nonproductive theme, note what has happened and then ask your question again. "It sounds like those fights between your son and daughter-in-law have upset you a lot. Let's come back to that later, if we have time; right now, though, I need to know some other things about you. . . ." If the client still perseveres, you can be reasonably sure that the theme isn't trivial or a side issue at all, but is a disguised way of talking about something very important indeed. Think—and ask—about what underlies the client's focus, what beliefs, reactions, and feelings are tied up in it.

Talking about oneself, to a sympathetic and understanding listener who is truly interested in what one has to say, is a rare experience for most of us. It feels good. It is wonderful to be taken seriously, to be the focus of attention, to be treated as worthy of respect and caring. No wonder some people don't want the experience to end! Even though the time is up, and another person may be waiting, some clients will keep talking as long as you are willing to listen. Here, again, it is the therapist's job to set appropriate limits. Even though you have probably been trained that it is rude to interrupt, you may need to do so. This will be more comfortable, and less abrupt, if you have given the client some warning that time is getting short. It's much easier to interrupt with a "I'm sorry to have to end this, but our time is up" when the client has been told some time earlier that the session is nearly over. You may want to let the client know that you really are interested in what he or she is saying, and suggest that you can continue to talk about it at your next session. But don't let the hour drag on past the agreed-upon ending point. To do so sets a precedent and may encourage the client to talk in circles for much of the session, saving the really important issues for the very end.

One of the most frustrating ways for a session to end is with a "doorknob transaction": the time is up and the client, about to leave, tosses out a critical and often ambiguous bit of information. "By the way, I'm getting married on Wednesday." "Oh, and I wanted to be sure to tell you that I've quit my job." "Is it important that I sometimes cut on myself?" Saving such a remark for the very end of the session is not accidental. It is most often a bid for extra time, an attempt (often out of awareness) to hook the therapist back into further interaction. Only in the case of serious danger to self or others should this kind of maneuver be responded to. Ordinarily, it is appropriate to say something like "I really wish we had time to talk about that, because it sounds very important. Let's start there next session," and continue to escort the client out. And be sure that you *do* start there at your next session, dealing with both the overt content and the client's choice of timing.

The Noncooperative Client

Most people come to counseling or psychotherapy because they want help. They are willing—or at least think they are—to do whatever they have to do in order to feel better and get their lives in order. Occasionally, though, someone will show up in your office who really doesn't want to be there at all. An oppositional child or a rebellious adolescent is dragged in by a parent; a spouse comes because of an ultimatum from his or her partner; or an offender is mandated by the court to get therapy as a condition of probation or parole.

Clients of this sort will generally answer direct questions, will go through the motions, but aren't likely to see themselves as partners in the therapeutic enterprise. They don't particularly want to change, they have no therapeutic goals, and they are likely to expect you to be on the side of the "enemy" who insisted that they work with you.

In a first session with a mandated or otherwise noncooperative client, there are two primary objectives. First, as with any other client, you need to gather some basic information about what is going on and why this person has come to see you. It's essential, as you inquire about these things, that you maintain a middle ground, neither taking the part of adversary and trying to argue with your client's perceptions, nor trying to be an advocate who will side with him or her against the world. Either of these positions will damage whatever chance there may be of forming a working relationship—arguing will prove that you really are one of the enemy, and moving too quickly into advocacy is likely to be seen as unauthentic and phony.

Don't pretend that mandated clients have chosen to come of their own volition, and don't try to sidestep the issue of their not wanting to be with you. If you have prior information about the client, say so and say where you got it. If not, be clear about that. "Your parents asked me to talk with you, but I don't know anything about what's going on. I've told them that I want to hear your version of things first, before I talk to them." Or, "Your wife told me something about what she sees as problems at home. How do you see those problems?" It can also be useful to ask the client to speak for the other side: "Your parole officer thinks it's important for you to be here. What do you think she would like you to get out of meeting with me?"

Questions of this sort lead into the second objective of a first session with an unwilling client: finding some common ground. If there is to be any significant therapeutic work, there must be some goal, some sort of change, that both you and the client can subscribe to. Often, that common ground will involve getting the significant other to change. The teenager wants his parents off his back, the wife wants her husband to be more understanding, the parolee simply wants to be left alone. Framing this goal in terms of figuring out what the client will need to do in order to get the other person to change will usually allow you to enter into such a contract honestly.[1]

That word *honestly* needs some examination. There can be an element of deceitfulness in this sort of therapeutic agreement; after all, you do suspect that the kinds of things the client will need to do in order to get that Other to change are precisely the changes that the Other wanted in the first place. Moreover, you may thoroughly agree with the Other's point of view—parents wanting their children to go to school, husbands wanting their wives to stop binge shopping, or parole officers wanting their clients to learn to control their rage are generally positions with which most people easily identify. But before dismissing it all as a sort of therapeutic hoax, be aware of one critical fact: *Nobody* acts in isolation. The "lazy" child or the "spendthrift" wife or the "rageful" offender live within a web of relationships, and it is in untangling this web that we are likely to find the "how" (not the "why," although that may come as an added bonus) of change for both clients and the others in their lives.

[1] A team of family therapists in my community does a masterful job of eliciting information about family dynamics from teenagers, and concluding that people (usually parents) in the family don't treat the teenager as if he/she were as old as he/she really is. They then ask the teenager if he/she would like their help in getting the parents to allow the teenager to grow up. It's a rare adolescent who refuses this proposition.

The Seductive Client

So much has been written lately about sex between client and therapist that it is hardly necessary to repeat the obvious: Sexual behavior with a client is never, under any circumstances, to be condoned. You will probably have clients whom you find sexually attractive, and with whom, under other circumstances, you might well begin a romantic relationship. Regardless of those feelings, such a relationship is simply not an option for you and your client—not before, during, or after therapy has terminated. The American Psychological Association's ethical standards state that it is unethical to enter into a sexual relationship with a former client for at least two years after termination, but an increasing number of therapists are recognizing that even after years have passed, relationships between therapist and ex-clients are still unlikely to be in the client's (or the therapist's!) best interest. Much better, much safer, and much more ethical to simply declare all clients off limits, period (see Chapter 1 for more information about this topic).

Even more likely than your feeling attracted to an occasional client is the client's feeling attracted to you. You have at least been trained to function in a therapeutic milieu; you understand the nature of transference and counter-transference; you know that the emotional intimacy of therapy need not be an invitation to physical intimacy. Clients frequently don't know these things; they only know that you are really interested in them, that you seem to care what happens to them, that you take them seriously, that they feel a kind of closeness with you that they may never have felt before. It's hardly surprising that many clients become confused about their own feelings, or that they misunderstand those of the therapist.

Some clients use their sexuality as a defense, a way of protecting themselves against danger from others or from their own feelings. For these clients, establishing a sexual relationship is a way to stay in control, to keep things predictable, to avoid the acute discomfort of changing their beliefs about self and others. These clients are often quite overt in their sexual approach to a therapist, behaving seductively over and over again.

Whether the seductiveness is subtle or overt, whether the client is using sexuality as a means of control or is honestly confused about his or her feelings, the therapist's response is the same: Set, talk about, and maintain clear limits. The "talk about" is particularly important. It's a great temptation, out of our concern for the client's embarassment or our fear of making fools of ourselves, to just ignore the client's signals. "Maybe if I pay no attention, my client will get the message that I'm not interested and back off . . ." we tell ourselves. But ignoring the signals may send the precisely wrong message: The client may conclude that you are tacitly encouraging his or her tentative advances.

But wait, you may be saying—we're talking about the first session here! Isn't this the sort of thing that crops up later in therapy, if at all? And you are right; clients seldom make overtly sexual advances or innuendos during the first session. But occasionally they do, and you will handle such situations much better if you've thought in advance about what you might say and do with them. Moreover, thinking about these issues now gives you a chance to set your own internal radar screen, to be sensitive to your own feelings and to the out-of-awareness messages you may be sending to an attractive client. Do you feel sexual attraction? Of course, you're human. Is it all right to fantasize a little, and just enjoy the feelings? Not a good idea; it's far too likely to interfere with your therapeutic effectiveness. Act on those feelings? Under no circumstances.

The Frightening Client

Most clients aren't frightening. They may be confusing or leave the therapist feeling inadequate or depressed, but they aren't usually scary. On the rare occasion when you do find yourself confronted by a frightening client, you need to know what to do and how to do it. Such knowledge is the best antidote to your fear, as well as providing the best protection for the client.

I have found myself, over the years, frightened by clients in two ways. One involves fear for the client. Clients who are in physical danger, either from their own behavior or from the violence of others, scare me. I'm afraid of what might happen to them, and I'm tempted to become overprotective. When this happens, I need to pull myself back, remind myself of my own limitations, and then calmly and realistically ask the client about his or her perceptions of the danger, and what he or she is willing to do to take care of himself or herself. Clients who may be in danger from someone else (most often, a potentially violent spouse) need to have contingency plans: an escape route, a safe place to go, a means of getting help. It is the therapist's responsibility to help them make these plans and support their following through. Clients who are in danger from themselves need to talk about their self-harming impulses, make a firm decision not to yield to them (often referred to as a "no-suicide contract"), and again set up contingency plans for what they will do when those feelings begin to strengthen. Having a list of people to call (including a 24-hour crisis line, if one is available in your community) is an important part of such plans; the list should be kept near the telephone. The client's no-suicide contract may, in fact, include a promise to "Pick up the phone instead of the pills/gun/car keys." You cannot protect your clients completely—you aren't in control of what happens to them or what they do once they leave your office—but you can and must help them to protect themselves. Knowing that you have done so in a responsible and professional manner will go a long way to relieve your sense of scare about them.

The other kind of scare around clients involves fear for yourself, for your own physical safety. Again, it is rare for a client to threaten violence toward his or her therapist—but it does happen occasionally. Your bottom line: You cannot do good work when you are afraid of your client, and your client does not have permission to threaten you. There are some elementary precautions that any prudent therapist takes: making sure that there are other people in the vicinity when you have a scheduled appointment with a potentially violent client and arranging the furniture in your office so that the client's chair is not between you and the door. The most effective precaution, however, is discussing the issue with the client and being clear about your expectations and your limits.

The Three Ingredients of Successful Psychotherapy

As I read over these pages, I find that I've referred rather often to the notion that initial therapy sessions tend to be different from subsequent sessions. They involve a first-time-getting-acquainted process, they usually require more information gathering and may be more therapist-directed, and they also may involve more information giving than subsequent sessions. There's a paradox here: part of what you are doing during your first session with a client is teaching that client how to *be* a client—what to expect of you, and what to expect of him- or herself—but in the very teaching and learning of those behaviors, you are both doing something different from what you will be doing later on.

Underlying the differences, though, there is a fundamental and essential consistency to therapeutic behavior. Your interest in the client, your therapeutic intent, and the skills of observation and communication that you bring to the interchange are present throughout therapy, from first session to last. It is these qualities, much more than the mechanics of who talks when and about what, that set the tone of the relationship and differentiate counseling and therapy from other sorts of interpersonal situations.

Just as Rogers posited empathy, congruence, and positive regard as the three necessary and sufficient conditions for personal growth, I believe that three ingredients are essential to being an effective psychotherapist. I have spoken at length about these three ingredients in the book *Beyond Empathy* (Erskine, Moursund, & Trautmann, 1999). These ingredients are as important in the initial session as they are anywhere else in therapy. It seems fitting to end this chapter by describing them.

First, *inquiry*. Whatever else we are doing, we are always *inquiring* of our clients. We inquire directly, with questions, and we inquire indirectly by inflection, body language, the whole thrust of what we do and say. We inquire about the client's behaviors, thoughts, feelings, wants, needs, hopes, and fears. We inquire about past, present, and possible futures. We inquire about relationships—including the relationship between this client and ourself. In a very real sense, therapy *is* inquiry: it is the process of inquiry that helps clients explore their worlds, internal and external, and discover the solutions that they need in order to grow and change.

Second, *attunement*. Being attuned to the client makes sensitive inquiry possible; it allows us to follow not only the client's words, but also his or her internal process. We attune ourselves to the way the client thinks, to what he or she is feeling, to the rhythm of his or her speech. To the degree that we are truly attuned in these ways, we can craft our inquiry so as to stay right at the growing edge of the client's experience, pointing always in the direction of new awareness yet not so far ahead that the client will be jarred, confused, or frightened into retreat. We are also attuned to ourselves, to our own reactions to the client, to the associations, ideas, and emotions that his or her presence calls forth in us.

The notion of self-attunement brings us to the third ingredient of effective therapy, *involvement*. We therapists do have associations, ideas, and emotions about what is going on in the session; we are involved in the process. We are not therapy machines, producing responses and interventions mechanically. We are living, breathing human beings, *involved* in a relationship with this other person who is our client. Our interest is genuine and our caring is real. The genuineness of our involvement, our willingness to enter into a relationship in which we, too, have feelings, creates a living substrate that supports and nourishes the therapeutic process.

Clients know when their therapists fail to inquire, to be attuned, and to be involved. They sense the absence of inquiry as a lack of interest and/or respect: Therapists who do not inquire will either be silent or will give opinions and advice rather than help the client to find his or her own wisdom. Failures in attunement feel to the client as if the therapist is always slightly off-target, not getting it just right, not quite in synch with the client's process. And a lack of involvement will generally be understood by the client to mean that the therapist isn't truly interested, doesn't like that client, or would rather be somewhere else. All of these outcomes, of course, are the antithesis of what the therapeutic relationship is intended to be.

In the rest of this book, you will find detailed discussions of how to do counseling and therapy, how to survive as a therapist, how to meet the expectations of clients, colleagues, and community. Throughout all of these discussions, I hope that you will keep in mind those three basic ingredients—inquiry, attunement, and involvement. They are as important in the middle and at the end of therapy as they are at the beginning.

REFERENCES

American Psychiatric Association. (1994). *Diagnostic and statistical manual of mental disorders* (4th ed). Washington, DC: Author.

Berne, E. (1961). *Transactional analysis in psychotherapy.* New York: Grove Press.

Erskine, R., Moursund, J., & Trautmann, R. (1999). *Beyond empathy.* Washington, DC: Brunner-Mazel.

Eysenck, H. J. (1952). The effects of psychotherapy. *Journal of Consulting Psychology, 16,* 319–324.

Frank, J. (1961). *Persuasion and healing.* Baltimore: Johns Hopkins University Press.

Kanfer, F. H., & Goldstein, A. P. (Eds.). (1991). *Helping people change: A textbook of methods.* Boston: Allyn & Bacon.

Kirman, W. (1977). *Modern psychoanalysis in the schools.* Dubuque, IA: Kendall/Hunt.

Lambert, M., & Bergin, A. E. (1994). The effectiveness of psychotherapy. In A. E. Bergin & S. L. Garfield (Eds.), *Handbook of psychotherapy and behavior change.* (4th ed., pp. 143–819). New York: Wiley.

Luborsky, L., Singer, B., & Luborsky, L. (1975). Comparative studies of psychotherapies: Is it true that "Everyone has won and all must have prizes"? *Archives of General Psychiatry, 32,* 995–1008.

Luborsky, L. (1995). Are common factors across different psychotherapies the main explanation for the dodo bird verdict that "Everyone has won so all shall have prizes?" *Clinical Psychology: Science and Practice, 2,* 106–109.

Piaget, J. (1971). *Biology and knowledge.* Chicago: University of Chicago Press.

Rogers, C. R. (1951). Client-centered therapy. Boston: Houghton Mifflin.

Smith, M. L., & Glass, G. V. (1977). Meta-analysis of psychotherapy outcome studies. *American Psychologist, 32,* 752–760.

Winnicott, D. W. (1971). *The maturational processes and the facilitating environment.* New York: International Universities Press.

FOR FURTHER READING

Erskine, R., Moursund, J., & Trautmann, R. (1999). *Beyond empathy.* (See References.)

This book goes beyond the basics of conducting therapy, and I recommend it for anyone who is studying to be a counselor or psychotherapist.

J. Moursand. (1993). *The process of counseling and therapy* (3rd Ed.). Englewood Cliffs, NJ: Prentice-Hall.

With all modesty aside, this is a very readable and practical book for new students. It focuses not just on clients but also on the experiences of students undergoing training.

Corey, M. S., & Corey, G. (1998). *Becoming a helper.* Pacific Grove, CA: Brooks/Cole.

This is useful and practical book for anyone considering a career in the helping professions.

APPENDIX 2.A

Sample of a Disclosure and Informed Consent Form

Therapist's Education, Background and Specialty Areas. In this section, indicate your terminal degree(s), name of institution, and the area in which you received your degree (e.g., clinical psychology, counseling psychology, etc.). In addition, list any specific areas of special training or certification such as neuropsychological testing, Marriage and Family Therapy, and so on. You may also want to indicate that you are not licensed to prescribe medications and that if these are needed the client will be referred to a physician or psychiatrist.

A Brief Description of Therapy. In this section, describe the therapeutic process in general terms and give concrete examples of what the client can expect from treatment. Examples of areas that may be covered are self-disclosure, the assessment process, goal setting, collaboration, and an approximation of the length of treatment. You may also want to briefly describe the general process of change, signs of progress, and relapse issues.

Confidentiality. In this section, describe the boundaries and exceptions to confidentiality. For example, a statement such as this one can be used.

All of the information obtained during our sessions will be held confidential and will not be disclosed to anyone or any agency without your prior written consent. By law, there are certain exceptions to confidentiality which you should know about. These exceptions include the following conditions:

1. *I have reason to suspect that you may be at risk of harming yourself or others.*
2. *There is an indication that child abuse or neglect has occurred.*
3. *Under some special circumstances, the court may order the release of information regarding your treatment.*

Client Rights.

As a client, you have a right to:

1. *Terminate therapy at any time. In the event that this occurs, you will be provided with a list of referral sources and possible alternatives for meeting your treatment goals.*
2. *Actively participate in the treatment process, including the development and modification of treatment goals.*
3. *Confidentiality as outlined above.*
4. *Be informed of treatment fees and payment policies and other office procedures.*
5. *Ask any questions about the treatment process and procedures at any time.*

General Office Procedures. In this section you should describe the typical session length and how often the client will meet with you. In addition, provide the procedure for canceling a session, who to call and deadlines for notification (e.g., at least 24 hours before the scheduled appointment). Indicate any penalties for missed appointments (such as having to pay the full or partial rate of the treatment session), and valid exceptions to this rule (such as emergency situations). Indicate your hourly fee, when payment is expected (e.g., at the end of each session), and acceptable payment methods (e.g., cash, personal checks, credit cards). Indicate how your office handles insurance claims.

(continued)

APPENDIX 2.A (Continued)

Informed Consent.
My signature below indicates that I have read and understand the above information and that my questions have been adequately answered at this time. I understand that I may terminate therapy at any time. My signature below indicates that I am giving ________________________ (fill-in your name and title) *permission to treat me at this time.*

Client Signature and Date

Therapist Signature and Date

CHAPTER

3 Hear This

Sharpening Your Communication and Listening Skills

PATRICIA A. FARRELL

A good listener is very much like a good dancer; each knows how to follow their partner in the "dance" whether it is literal or one of communicating thoughts and feelings. If good dancers are born and not trained, then there is little hope for the lead-footed, but listening skills can be taught and practice will only make you more adept at it. Think about how you listen. The first problem is that most of us find ourselves listening only half-heartedly even when we know we need to listen intently.

Second, we think we are "hearing" everything that is said, but that is inaccurate. The habit of *believing* that we are actually hearing what is said becomes fixed in us at an early age, and as psychologists or counselors, we need to begin to exercise other ways of listening. Above all, we need to have ways of checking our *knowing* what is being said. The checking is where active listening comes into play.

When I am not involved in my private practice or my consulting work, I teach psychology to undergraduates, graduate students and medical students. Helping the medical students, especially, understand that they can develop other listening skills is one of my most challenging tasks. The future physicians, I find, are ill prepared for dealing with real-life patients. These students seek refuge in the "safe" medical symptoms of illness. Instead of trying to draw a patient out, they will ask questions (Evans, Stanley, & Burrows, 1993) about feelings, but only feelings related to physical symptoms rather than the emotions attached to them. Physicians (Beckman, Markakis, Suchman, & Frankel, 1994) and others in the health care professions have found a need to hone their skills and "cut to the chase" as it were in order to optimize their time and the material they can gather.

The skill most needed is multidimensional and involves listening, experiencing, and expressing empathy. When we speak of multidimensional aspects of listening, we also need to include the idea of cultural intentionality (Ivey & Ivey, 1999), a lifelong process of expanding on our current repertoire of responses, problem-solving techniques, and alternatives within a multicultural context.

I can see my students struggling to figure out where the path to understanding lies and feeling frustrated in their attempts to find it. It is a good example of wanting to reach a destination and hacking away at the thick forest ahead of you in an aimless fashion.

Where are the maps they should have constructed before the journey? How did they study the terrain in advance? Your maps and your terrain inspection are the chart on the unit or the questionnaire, which the patient has provided to you. From these you begin to formulate a plan of action, but remember that this plan is always in flux. You continue to refine the plan as you continue to receive new information to confirm or negate assumptions you make regarding the illness, the causes, or the wishes of the patient.

Multidimensional Skills

The multidimensional aspect of listening contains the component of expressing empathy. The question of empathy and how it fits into our professional lives is that it is an important communication and listening skill. Some people, of course, believe that empathy doesn't actually exist but that it is a façade that we present to our patients. We call them jaded or burned out. Most of us do want to help. We care so much that we sometimes forget to care for ourselves and there lies the path to burnout.

Try an exercise to illustrate to yourself that you can develop skills that you never knew you had. I call it my "ear wiggling for science" experiment, and I do it whenever I want to teach my students something about selective attention.

Selective attention is a developed skill that we use when we want to *isolate* something in the environment, such as a voice or a conversation in a crowded room. The literature also refers to it as the "Cocktail Party Phenomenon" (Broadbent, 1956) because we frequently use it at social gatherings whenever we hear our name or the name of someone in whom we are interested or another of those ear-catching buzzwords, sex. Mention sex and ears all around the room will attend to that conversation. Good thing we do not actually see those ears move as we do in animals. It would be straight out of a Mel Brooks movie.

Back to our experiment. Wiggle your ears. Go ahead, wiggle your ears. Not able to do it? What is the reason? You obviously have muscles that control your ears and you can dampen down your hearing in a noisy environment, so why is it difficult for you to wiggle your ears? I can. I have, of course, perfected the technique by examining myself in the mirror and watching for the slightest movement of my eyeglasses. A vigorous back-and-forth movement of the frames signals success.

Practice this bit of party trickery in your spare time and you will impress your friends with it once you have managed to do it more fluidly. The obvious thing that I am illustrating here is that you can wiggle your ears although we do not have much call for it, but you also need to monitor yourself to know when you've gotten it.

Self-monitoring is something we do in much of our daily lives as we take great care not to offend the rules of our culture. Monitoring ourselves in our professional lives, where we begin to interact with patients and peers, is also an area in which we need practice. We can begin to practice in our personal lives the skills that we need to apply to our professional lives.

Self-Monitoring for Effectiveness

Before we go any further, read the following statements and see which of them apply to you. Much of what you read about here contributes to the barriers to effective communication. It is your job to recognize them in yourself, to remediate them just as you would symptoms or maladaptive patterns in your patients, and to help plan strategies for the future.

Listening Self-Test. Test yourself on your current listening skills by completing this self-test. Mark these statements according to whether you engage in them R (rarely), S (sometimes) or A (always):

_____ I allow speakers to complete sentences.
_____ I make sure I understand the other person's point of view before responding.
_____ I listen for the important points.
_____ I try to understand the speaker's feelings.
_____ I visualize my response before speaking and think of alternative phrasing.
_____ I try to think of a solution before speaking, if one seems called for.
_____ I am relaxed and calm when listening.
_____ I use affirming sounds ("um," "yes," "I see," "oh") when listening.
_____ I look at the person who is speaking.
_____ I am patient when listening.
_____ I ask clarifying questions when someone speaks.
_____ I try not to show by my body language how I feel about the discussion.

What was your grade? If you rated yourself as an "A" (always) on four of the statements, you are not a good listener. An "A" rating on 5–9 would be fair, on 10–12 is an excellent listener.

Improve your rating by becoming more aware of your body language and your choice of words. The process of improving on listening skills also involves utilizing your *third ear.*

Physical Barriers to Effective Listening. A major barrier to listening is a physical one involving your feelings and your body's reaction to them. Feelings about the situation may begin to well up and affect your body language (Van der Merwe, 1991). This type of situation will arise whenever you are confronted by something that you find personally very distressing, such as child abuse, sexual assault, or a natural disaster.

You can liberate yourself from this bodily restriction by taking slow, deep breaths. Concentrate on the position of your shoulders and your chest as you breathe in and out five times. The exercise helps to slow you down; it can be helpful with your clients, as well.

The Third Ear. What we do not do very often, if at all, is to listen with our third ear (Waldinger, 1997). The third ear is the one you can't wiggle, no matter how hard you try. It is the ear that we use for filtering content in a conversation and making sense out of the unsaid or latent comments. Frequently, the most fruitful part of any therapy session or conversation with a peer or friend will be the unsaid portion. It is like being on a Hollywood movie set. You see a huge white Colonial house with shrubs, drapes, and window shades, but when you open the front door and look inside, all you see are two-by-fours holding up the front. You find that there is no house, but you believed there was one. What questions should you have asked to clarify the exact nature of the situation?

You are becoming a professional listener. Language is your tool and your "medicine," if you will. Language takes on a whole new level of gravity in this way, and it requires your most intense scrutiny.

The Basic Elements of Active Listening

Active listening is a system that incorporates several techniques that can help you follow a conversation, make relevant contributions, and ask pertinent questions or probes. The basic elements are focusing/following, empathizing, effective inquiry, reflecting, and shadowing.

Focusing/Following

This component involves three basics: eye contact, nonverbal behavior, and verbal expressions of interest. Eye contact is valuable because it indicates that you are not hiding from interaction with this person. The only time you might alter your eye contact would be in the case of cultural, religious, or psychiatric constraints.

In some cultures, it is considered impolite to look directly at the other person, especially if they are of higher status than the client (Ivey & Ivey, 1999). Psychiatric clients with paranoid delusions would find a direct gaze to be threatening; it might cause them to include you in their delusions. Usually, looking directly at the client encourages the client to continue speaking, and with subtle moves of your head, leaning forward or smiling, you can offer additional encouragement.

Eye-contact breaks occur when you or the client look away from each other. What does it say about the content of the conversation or the person's reaction to something he or she is telling you? Avoiding eye contact can indicate fear, anxiety, or delusional thinking.

Following also means staying on-topic and bringing the interview back to the business at hand. Often, clients will wander off to other topics perhaps to avoid something or perhaps because they are easily distracted. Individuals with bipolar disorder, traumatic brain injury, geriatric depression, or attention deficit hyperactivity disorder are the most likely to get off-topic frequently.

Any time a client begins to go off onto another topic, you can bring the client back with, "I find that very interesting, but right now we have to finish this (interview, assessment, or the like)." The gentle nudge back provides a sense of respect for the client, while maintaining the level of control required by the situation.

Empathizing

Empathizing is different from sympathizing. The former involves a sense of feeling the client's pain or emotional suffering, and the latter is one of feeling sorry for the client. There is a qualitative difference. Gibb (1961) suggested that nonverbal facial and body expressions were the most effective means of communicating a sense of empathy.

Effective Inquiry

Effective inquiry involves your making, beforehand, decisions about the *types of questioning* that will be used, the information you require, how best to complete your task, and what forms and types of encouragement to use.

Reflecting

Reflection is one of the most basic of listening skills and entails your providing feedback by repeating the client's own words in order to elicit more information without asking for it. The basics are reflecting content and emotion. Here's an example of each:

Example One.

CLIENT: "I am really anxious and I think most of my problems and my anxiety are caused by the stress I feel at work."

COUNSELOR (CONTENT): "You think that most of your problems are caused by your stress at work."

COUNSELOR (EMOTION): "You are depressed, and your anxiety is coming from your work stress."

Example Two. Ann has been having problems with her husband. She believes that he's seeing another woman.

> I know he's seeing someone else because he comes home smiling and the first thing he does is take a shower. It is disgusting to me. When we go to bed, he rolls over and goes to sleep. I've been following him and I see him at the business talking and smiling to these young girls. I want a divorce.

Write down what you would reflect to Ann, exactly. How many things could you reflect back and how much of it would be important? Remember to avoid the use of any comment that would be a cliché, ignoring the issues, giving advice, blaming, or joking about a serious matter.

Example Three. An example of inappropriate joviality, in a college counseling center, is shown by the following illustration involving a doctoral student.

> The student called to inquire about her registration for a particular seminar that was needed in order for her to graduate on time. The young woman who answered the telephone showed a lack of sensitivity by laughing and responding, "Well, I guess that means we have you for another year at least. Better get that student loan application in to us." The student, after an initial moment of panic, wanted to argue with the young woman on the telephone, but didn't tell her. She went away feeling disrespected and resentful toward the school and the counselor.

Shadowing

Shadowing is repeating, in your own words, what the client has just said. It can be a valuable means of reinforcement to help you retain information. It is a good means of keeping your attention focused on the session and helps the client see that you are following what he or she is saying.

Easing into Listening

At first, you may feel a bit like the person who is attempting to bowl. The bowler has been told how many steps to take, which foot to start on, how to swing back the bowling arm, and how to "spot" the pins or look at the lane. Try not to be too critical of yourself or you will get tongue-tied and reinforce your feeling of foolishness or ineptness.

Effect a philosophy that is based on what I call a good-from-bad orientation, which is also called *reframing*. Making a mistake helps you affirm your resolve to improve and to avoid those pitfalls the next time. Each of your clinical placements will afford this opportunity as you and your colleagues process group therapy or community meetings or individual sessions. The experience can also be a humbling one, but that is good, too. Truly seasoned therapists are therapists who realize that they will never be finished learning and who eagerly look to learn even more.

Types of Listeners

Overall, there are three distinct types of listeners, the overly concerned, the less-than-interested, and the actively-focused ones.

Overly concerned listeners are those who are swept away by the emotional content of the communication. These listeners are not able to sort through the information. They fail to formulate helpful responses and are unable to frame helpful questions to aid the speaker in a constructive way.

The less-than-interested listener allows his or her mind to wander. For this type of listener, the conversation is a series of bits of information that do not provide a cohesive picture of the content. It is as though a video camera were switched on and off. What the listener takes in is colored by self-interest and lack of attention.

Actively-focused listeners are "in the moment" with the speaker. They note discrepancies or ask for verification of their understanding of what is being said. The communication is one of a give-and-take dialogue and neither person is left with unanswered questions about the content.

What We Reveal or Hide

Active self-discovery leads to better communication. One of the best-known methods for self-discovery and for evaluating your self-image is the Johari Window (Van der Merwe, 1991). A rectangle is divided into four squares. The panes of the window are labeled to diagram how you and others perceive you in terms of what you know, what you do not know, and what you hide. See Figure 3.1.

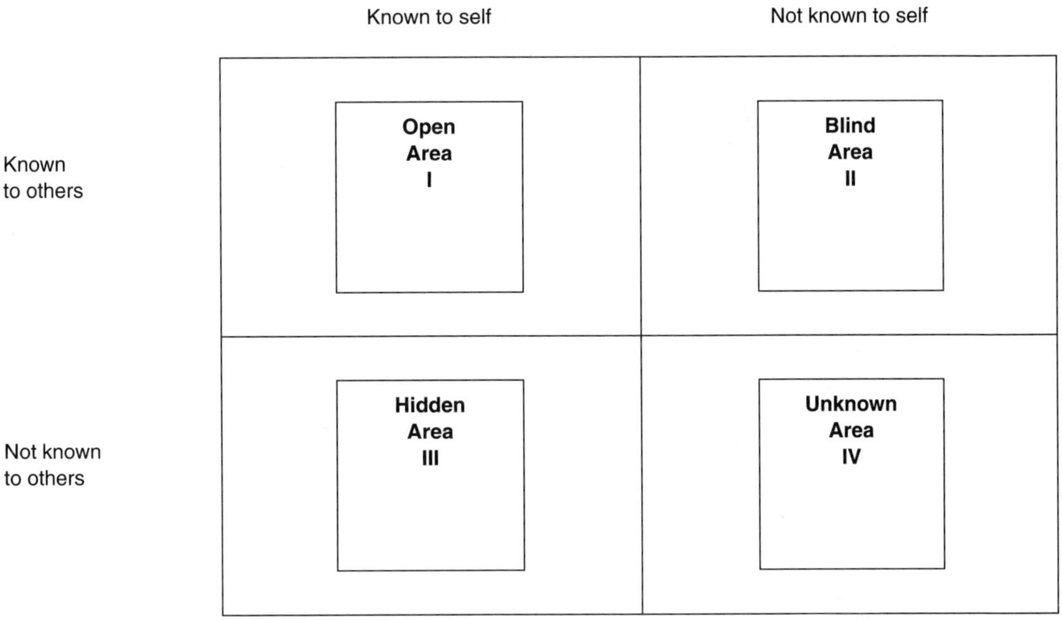

FIGURE 3.1 The Johari Window

Note: The Johari Window is used to illustrate how feedback from others about our behavior affects our sense of self-image. It also maps out aspects of ourselves that are unknown and unavailable to us until revealed.

In many ways, it resembles a graphic representation of Jung's concept of archetypes (Hall & Nordby, 1973) that we use to protect or present ourselves as we wish.

The squares in the Johari Window represent the following:

I. What you know about yourself and what is known to others (open area)

II. What you do not "know" or realize about yourself that is known to others (blind area)

III. What is not known to others that you consciously keep hidden from them (hidden area)

IV. Aspects of yourself of which you are unaware that are also not known by others (unknown area)

Feedback from others provides the means to open the blind and unknown areas to you and to help you realize your abilities and work on your shortcomings.

Types of Climates

An additional tool for listening has been found in the work of Gibb (Gibb, 1961; Van Der Merwe, 1991) who provided important guidelines regarding listening and responding styles in terms of *climates* we create. Gibb suggested six examples of how to cultivate defensive or supportive climates.

Defensive Climates

Defensive climates are fostered through the use of communication that fits into one of the following: evaluation, control, strategy, neutrality, superiority, or certainty.

Evaluation is your attempting to label, usually in a negative fashion, something the person has said or to interpret without waiting for sufficient information. For example, if you were to interpret a client's comments as "I do not think you have a clear idea of . . ." you've made an evaluation and put the individual on notice that he or she is inept.

Control is your attempting to direct the individual to your way of thinking about the situation, problem, and so forth. It is as though the client is there only to follow what you indicate as the appropriate course of action. A climate of control is much like that of a parent who orders children around instead of facilitating independence and problem-solving skills.

Strategy is your giving the client detailed instructions on what to do and when to do it. It is also a means of control and establishes an unequal power differential. The client is not actively engaged in laying out any plan of action; you provide it fully formed.

Neutrality shows a lack of sensitivity about a situation. You maintain an emotional distance and, in effect, dismiss the topic as not worth consideration.

Superiority involves your indicating that you are above the client's types of situation and, possibly through self-disclosure, that you do not understand the reason for the client to be distressed.

Certainty shows a lack of acceptance of another's viewpoint as being as valid as your own.

Supportive Climates

These are developed through a *description* of the situation and a *problem orientation*. You show a genuine interest in the client (*spontaneity*), verbalize your understanding (*empathy*), and engage with the client as an *equal*.

Provisionalism can be demonstrated as you temper your comments to show that you appreciate the difficulty the client is experiencing and that there is always a need to learn and to use new information. You also affirm the need to consider other viewpoints. Words you can use to indicate this openness are "perhaps," or "I may not know," or "to the best of my knowledge."

Remember that it is a process where the use of "I" and "you" language (Brownell, 1996) can be a determining factor in facilitating the dialogue. "I" language is shown when you are the central focus and your feelings, plans, or whatever are seen as paramount. The other person *has done something* that has inconvenienced or caused a problem for you and is being blamed for his or her actions.

"You" language is a more considerate stance whereby you express your emotions or feelings about the reason something upset you. You explain the reason it caused you difficulty or loss, or how it was emotional.

Defensive stances are countered by the supportive ones and for each defensive/negative comment, you can develop a more helpful, encouraging statement. A counterpoint graphic (Figure 3.2) is offered to help visualize which negative statements are balanced by which

FIGURE 3.2 Creating Climates

Defensive Climate	Supportive Climate
Evaluation	***Description of the Situation***
"You seem incapable of . . ."	"That must have been difficult because . . ."
Control	***Problem Orientation***
"You need to . . ."	"What would your choices be in . . ."
Strategy	***Spontaneity***
"First you need to . . ."	"I can understand you don't know where to begin."
Neutrality	***Empathy***
"Well, that's over so . . ."	"The hurt hasn't stopped because it's over, so how are you feeling now?"
Superiority	***Equality***
"I've never had a problem with anything like that."	"It's something that's been a problem for me, too."
Certainty	***Provisionalism***
"You can't say . . ."	"I've often felt that . . ."

supportive ones. Examples of both the negative listening environment and its counterpart positive environment are provided here. See how you might incorporate these elements into your communication style.

Creating a Comfortable Climate

Therapy, interviewing, or active listening can be accomplished anywhere—from a wood-paneled office to an outdoor picnic table. The climate is set more by your tone of voice and physical presentation and your use of active listening than by the physical setup. Much of this climate of comfort is established in the first few minutes when you approach your client and utter your first few words.

Depending on the age of your client among other factors, you will want to be sensitive to your use of address.

"Hello, I am . . . and I'll be interviewing (or working with) you today."

You may extend your hand or not. Next comes an all-important query that is directly related to self-esteem and respect.

"How do you prefer I address you? (Mr., Mrs., Ms.) or by your first name?"

I find it very disturbing and disrespectful for a younger person to call an elderly patient by their first name unless they have received permission to do so. It is an initial sign of respect and sensitivity on your part. Some clients will take exception *if you do not* use their first name, so it is always best to inquire.

Another point to consider is whether or not you should shake hands with your patient. You might wait for the client to extend a hand first.

A few religious groups do not allow men and women to shake hands. I remember a patient who refused to look at anyone, much less allow him or her to shake hands with him. He believed that if he looked at or touched you, you would die and he was trying to protect you. The obsession became so difficult that, in time, he found it uncomfortable to allow even his own fingers to touch and he would keep a small piece of paper between his thumb and index fingers. If you met him, how would you respond to such actions?

Prepare for your session before you go into the room. Once you are in the room, look at the nonverbal communication and cues, seeking information from clothing, hair styles, eye contact, body positioning, and movement.

Listening Chart

Whether or not you fit one or the other, the following descriptions of types of listeners will help you to begin strengthening your existing skills while you work on developing new ones. Think about your actions over the past 24 hours and see if you've engaged in any of these poor listening behaviors.

Just as you would with a client who had a particularly problematic behavior, chart your behavior relative to listening and communications skills. Items on your chart should include the following:

- When the behavior took place
- What type of client
- The diagnostic category
- Your emotional state
- Your response
- The outcome

The chart provides you with a pattern of your behavior that will sensitize you to situations in the future. It also points toward listening types that are counterproductive.

Listening Types

Everyone listens. We might say that is true, but there there are certain listening types that are truly revealing in what they indicate about a person and that person's needs or concerns (Adler & Towne, 1978). We've outlined just a few of them for your review. See if you know anyone who might fit into these categories and then ask yourself what this says about that person. Again, it is the third ear that you are using here.

Defensive Listeners. These listeners tend to turn everything into a personal attack or something that is directed at them. They suspect everyone's motives and seek hidden snide remarks in conversations.

Insensitive Listeners. Listeners who are insensitive fail to appreciate the subtleties of a conversation where not everything is to be taken literally.

Insulated Listeners. Closely related to those who pay attention exclusively to only things that interest them—that is, selective attenders—insulated listeners avoid things that are painful, problematic, or with which they *must* deal. They just nod and forget what you just said.

Pseudolisteners. Watch for their eyes to glaze over or go out of focus as you speak.

Selective Attenders. These listeners pull out only those statements that they find interesting or useful. In the process, they fail to appreciate the full message and often act on only "information bits" of the conversation.

Stage hogs. People who behave as though they feel that two people together, facing each other, means they can talk incessantly about their ideas and feelings exclusively are stage hogs. It is not a conversation but a diatribe. Very often their statements will be little more than "chest beating" about their own accomplishments, knowledge, or power.

Listening Exercises

The old joke about how you get to Carnegie Hall applies here, too. Yes, it is practice, practice, and practice. Here are a few brief exercises for your practice. Try them out whenever the opportunity presents itself:

1. Sit silently for an hour.
2. While in a small group, let others talk and just listen.
3. If you go to a party, talk as little as possible.
4. Do not be the first one to speak in a group and try to hold off for at least a half-hour before you do.
5. Watch how others express themselves or how they show interest in what is being said. Are there any tips you have picked up?
6. Find someone who is involved in a field about which you know nothing—say medicine or chemistry or computer programming. Begin a conversation about that person's specialty. This is a great way to learn how to be an active listener. The process that enables you to "follow" the conversation, ask appropriate, targeted questions and obtain feedback, is exactly what you need to use in counseling or other interviewing situations.

Much of our monitoring has to do with *containing our comments* regarding our peers or skillfully handling questions we can't answer or that might be counter-therapeutic to answer. "What is the master gland?" Is it the pituitary or the hypothalamus?

Our ears hear the question, process it, and try to answer. What we have done is tried to answer the question, we *believed,* was asked. Does the person really want to know which is the master gland or are they trying to determine something else?

The One Process Brain Concept

Listening to a client with the intensity needed to retrieve and retain important facts requires that you remember what has been described as the "one process brain concept" (Shea, 1998). The concept contains the following ideas and acronyms (Brownell, 1996):

DDOT—do not do other tasks
DMP—do not make plans
DD—do not daydream

Undoubtedly, you have found yourself with wandering attention during a conversation or a lecture. You began thinking about other things you needed to do that day, you were making plans, or you just daydreamed. Once you caught yourself, you found that you had missed part of the conversation or lecture. A therapy session or interview cannot tolerate these instances of "zoning out."

Whenever you find that you are having problems with your concentration or the session, change your body position a bit. You may find that your client is shadowing your body movements unconsciously and that is not a bad thing because it may also signal they are following your communication closely.

Active listening gives your client a sense of being heard and understood. There is a delicate interplay that moves the communication along a predetermined continuum, leading you to your desired destination. Much of what you learn to do is to use effective questioning or probing techniques or restatements of what you believed was said.

While a variety of techniques are used, it is the third ear, again, that enables you to pull back from the situation and see it in a different light. What appears to be said and what you will come to see is actually said is deciphered with the third ear. This is where self-monitoring comes into play again.

Probes

Probes are either verbal or nonverbal responses you make to something the client has said that smacks of problems with relevance, clarity, or completeness. The purpose of a probe is to remove doubt and help you understand what the client means.

It is not a confrontation or question of veracity necessarily. One of the objectives, aside from your understanding what is being said, is to provide the client with an opportunity to more fully explore what he or she means. The problem for the neophyte therapist is in failing to use probes more frequently because of a belief that the client has answered the question posed.

Forensic work or court evaluations for child abuse can require that you be insistent in your probing, but in a manner that is respectful and produces information. If you were asked to evaluate a mother for possible Munchausen's Syndrome by Proxy abuse, what would you need to know and how would you proceed? These clients rarely admit they have committed the acts alleged and are seen by many therapists as especially difficult in terms of interventions (Leonard & Farrell, 1992).

At the end of the interview, will you be asking yourself how well the woman answered your questions? Ask yourself if you've ever listened to someone and truly believed that you understood what that person was saying and then walked away and tried to provide someone else with a brief summary. The person to whom you are providing the summary begins to ask questions, and it is then that you realize you didn't truly get all the information. In forensic work, this is a luxury you cannot afford.

Using the case of Ann, outlined previously, do the following:

List a series of probes you would use regarding her feelings about herself, her marriage, and her suspicions.

Marriage probes
Self-esteem probes
Suspicion probes
How would you show that you were empathic to her situation?

Even if you think you have gotten all the information, use a few probes to allow the client more time to go over the information again. Clients sometimes have a tendency to proceed without thoughtfully lingering on a subject. Probes will give them that opportunity.

How are probes framed? Begin with a clear idea of what you hope to accomplish and then rework the phrasing in your mind before you give voice to them.

Now that you have completed this exercise, see how else you can frame your probes to pinpoint the information you want. Here are a few examples using Ann in the case outlined:

Topic Control

Explore many aspects of a theme. You might use this when you want as complete a description of something as possible. In the case of Ann, after she offered some information—for instance, the fact that her husband showers when he comes home—you would respond with something like "And then what happened?" This can be used several times until a thorough inspection of the facts is completed.

Silent Probes

Use a pause of three or four seconds, and wait for the client to continue. Very often, silence can be both comforting and uncomfortable, and both will prompt discussion.

Focusing Probes

Zero in on some aspect of the situation where the client may have experienced something or seen something. You are trying to help the client look at the behavior or cognition that he or she exhibited at the time of the event. Ann's husband was seen smiling and joking with his young workers. Ann observed them and thinks it is reason to believe he is having an affair. Frame a probe that will delve into her reasons for thinking this way.

What focusing probes could you use to

1. Help Ann examine her feelings at the time?
2. Look at the situation and determine what suggested an affair?
3. Examine Ann's beliefs about, possibly, her age or attractiveness?

Neutral Probes

Encourage elaboration and do not contain any inference of what is being sought from the client. A neutral probe is a means of continuing whatever is being discussed. In its simplest form, it is a motivator and is usually accomplished via facial expressions, body language, or saying, *"Humm," "Uh huh," or "I see."*

Interpretive Probes

This probe is characterized (Gordon, 1975) by the use of a combination of the client's words and the additional element of reflection of the client's feelings. Ann said, "I know he's having an affair because he takes a shower every night when he comes home."

You might say, "He takes a shower every night when he comes home and you feel somehow less important to him or that there's some sort of distance between the two of you? What does his taking a shower at that time mean to you?" In this way, you are avoiding a close-ended question, providing some interpretation of her feelings, and also following her train of thought while getting additional clarification.

A counseling session with someone who is experiencing vocational problems would be similar.

CLIENT: The office manager got the promotion to vice president because he used my plan for the reorganization.

COUNSELOR: The office manager got the promotion because he used your plan for the reorganization, and you felt that wasn't right, that you hadn't been recognized for your contribution. Tell me how that felt for you.

Immediate versus Retrospective Probes

Refer back to some other item that came up earlier and that, based on information you just received, needs clarification. Probe about the prior information and then return to the present topic once you have satisfied yourself that you have sufficiently clarified your view.

While we are discussing probes, a word needs to be said against their overuse. Remember that once you begin to stop the flow of the session or interview, you gamble that you will not distract the client or interrupt their train of thought. Too frequently asking questions can have a counterproductive effect. One way to handle this, if you feel you truly need to ask many questions, is to make a note of the current topic in order to jog the client's memory back to the original thought.

Extremely upset clients can have a very difficult time focusing their thoughts. Probing can lead down many avenues that will not help bring your interview or session to some reasonable conclusion.

The watchwords here would be to *use probes prudently.*

Confronting

Etiquette has taught us to live by a set of rules that do not work to our advantage when we are involved in psychotherapy or interviewing therapy clients. The psychological/psychiatric interview depends on asking questions of a highly personal nature and questioning inconsistencies or illogical thoughts. One of the prime areas where you will find yourself confronting, possibly more than you had intended, will be in sessions with clients who are substance abusers and families of substance abusers (Stevens-Smith & Smith, 1998). Another instance will be in forensic or abuse cases.

The stage is set for confrontation when you inquire about how much of the abused substance the person uses each day or each week. I have found that it takes a bit of creativity to come to an understanding of how much is too much for the client.

> ***Example of Probing and Confronting a Substance-Abusing Client***
> John has come in for an intake interview after having been referred by the local BAC (Bureau of Alcohol Countermeasures) force. He was stopped for speeding while driving his car from the train station to his home, and he was under the influence of alcohol. John indicates that he only had one drink on the train; he says the local police do not like him because he would not give to their annual fundraiser.

You have familiarized yourself with the local laws about drunk driving and who is referred for DWI offenses. Now you begin to probe and confront John regarding the specifics of his situation. John stated he only had one drink on the train and he isn't a heavy drinker.

> **COUNSELOR:** "When you really want to get drunk, how much would you have to drink?"

I've had clients say anything from 2 six-packs to 36 bottles of beer. The answer gives me a much better idea of their capacity and from that I can extrapolate to their daily or usual use. It also prevents any hint of disbelief on my part and leaves me in a therapeutic communication mode rather than a detective one.

I have some question regarding John's "one drink" on the train, so I might continue to probe.

> **COUNSELOR:** "Did you have one drink on the train? What was it and how big was the glass? How many drinks did you have before you got on the train?"

Then I would continue as follows:

COUNSELOR: "John, you had only one drink and yet you were seen driving in an erratic fashion and then you failed a Breathalizer test at the scene. Now tell me how that could have happened, if you weren't drinking?"

I know that the BAC only refers clients to us when they have had at least two DWI offenses. My confrontation continues:

COUNSELOR: "John, I know that the BAC only sends people to us after they have two DWI offenses, so I know you've had more than just this one. The other offense was in a different town, so I cannot understand how that police force, too, would want to harm you."

John may not like it, but he knows I know he has a problem with alcohol and the one-drink-on-the-train story is not being accepted.

The client can now begin to talk about the drinking because it is a fait accompli and has been recognized.

Reframing

A method of helping the client see the other side of a problem or situation is known as reframing. It places the problem in a different context. The problem becomes an opportunity. While this may sound a bit like a Pollyanna approach, it is intended to encourage more cognitive flexibility and instill that all-important element of hope in our clients. It is, in effect, seeing the glass as half-full rather than half-empty.

Example: Your client has come in telling you that he has just caused a major problem in his corporation's computer network. He was responsible for maintaining the network and made a mistake that prevented everyone's access to e-mail, including the corporate vice president's. He reported, "I worked through my lunch hour and I had to call the consultants and I got it up again. I think this is the end. They are going to fire me for this one. I do not want to go back tomorrow."

You might reflect and reframe and then say what? Remember that in reflecting you restate exactly what the client has said and in reframing you look for a different perspective to help provide some degree of hope and a sense of the client's resourcefulness. What would you say to reflect the content of his thoughts? How would you reframe this?

Self-Disclosure

What is an appropriate degree of counselor self-disclosure? Experienced and neophyte practitioners alike struggle with this question as they try to provide feedback that indicates they truly do understand the client's problems. It is an area where there are many points of view. Is it better to provide the patient with a sense of sharing a common experience with the therapist (Wachtel, 1993), or is it better not to think of the relationship as one of similarity?

In discussing his teaching, Wachtel indicated he has continued to wrestle with the problem and encourages his students to do likewise. Clients will continue to ask personal questions and to expect civil answers rather than the retort "How does that make you feel?"

The psychoanalytic practitioner will find the question a new avenue for exploration while the cognitive therapist may give it a momentary thought and go on to the work that has been outlined for the sessions to be contracted. Perhaps managed care has helped in redirecting our attention to a clear idea of the problems and the solutions that we have devised to resolve them. It is, therefore, in great part, a question of your theoretical orientation.

Questions from clients and your answering them can also distract you from your goals, and if you allow your ego to take over to the point where you are waxing enthusiastic about yourself, the session quickly is less-than-satisfactory and is over. What do you want? Do you want to do the work or to sit and talk about common experiences?

Freud (Roazen, 1974) would have argued against self-disclosure because of its "contaminating" effect on the work to be done. His methods have been well detailed, as has his habit of sitting behind his patients to avoid their disquieting view.

The avoidance of questions, no matter how benign, may be appropriate with patients who are given to obsessiveness or who may be paranoid about you and your intentions. When you consider what you will do in any given situation, remember that Freud, as quoted in Roazen (p. 112), felt that whatever results in recovery is good.

Others (Evans, 1979) believe that a counselor or therapist provides whatever is necessary to facilitate the relationship and help the client. Again, you are the final authority regarding what will "help" your client. How much information (Craig, 1997) would be helpful? You may frame your answer to show that you share similar experiences and to provide a sense of your humanity.

The question of self-disclosure can arise at any time. It may be at the first interview that you are asked to provide some bit of personal information such as your marital status or whether or not you have children or live alone. The client may want reassurance (Morrison, 1995) or may be looking for information on which to plan some strategy in the therapeutic relationship. The latter is especially true when working with court-referred clients (Daum, 1994; Lissner, Gilmore, & Pompi, 1976) or those you know to be sociopathic, such as child molesters, petty criminals, or those with personality disorders. There may also be an effort to intimidate you in the future by bringing up this seemingly innocently offered information in another context.

I have worked with forensic and court-referred clients and have had colleagues who have been confronted by this dilemma. The statement "I know what kind of car you drive" or "I know where you live" has made many therapists guard almost all information regarding their personal lives. Patients who later become stalkers of therapists depend on information they have gleaned in sessions over weeks, months, or even years. The purpose here is not to foster paranoia in you, but to encourage caution.

The initial interview, at any rate, is not the appropriate time to reveal information about yourself because you know little about your client. Some clients may bristle and see you as not willing to reveal yourself. If you are a new therapist in an outpatient or inpatient setting, you can always indicate it is against policy or it is not something you do.

You can also indicate that you have limited time and must complete all the questions on your interview or that you want to make the most of the time in the session.

Dual relationships (Peterson, 1992), do not forget, can begin by innocent sharing of information. While not necessarily a boundary violation, it is a path in that direction unless you proceed with care. The suggestion for careful scrutiny (Bersoff, 1996) has been made and you should ask yourself your reason for disclosing. Do you want to be liked? Is the interview or session not flowing smoothly and that is making you feel uncomfortable? What statement, action, or question caused you to become uncomfortable? Is the client attempting to control the interview?

The temptation always exists to fill those anxiety-ridden, empty voids (Waldinger, 1997) that come up in a session. These intervals are important, so do not give in to the wish to rush quickly to help the client out. The client needs time to formulate thoughts coherently and to express himself or herself. It is a time for their reflection.

Beginning psychotherapists and medical psychiatry residents (Davis & Nicholaou, 1992; Evans, Stanley, & Burrows, 1993) must hone their skills through experience, discussion with their supervisors and colleagues, and careful self-examination of their motives and shortcomings. A skilled therapist is one who understands and accepts his or her own vulnerability, strengths, and weaknesses.

Is there an absolute answer to how much disclosure is good and how much is "bad"? Each counselor looks at the individual case and comes to his or her own decision.

Facilitating Communication: The Do's and Don'ts

What about questioning? Listening and checking on what you're hearing requires one additional thing—questioning or querying, if you prefer—and it is here that you can facilitate or stop the flow of information.

There is one word that you should avoid using at all costs. The word? *Why.* Avoid its use as you would avoid the plague. Suppose you came into my office and sat down on the floor, and I asked you, "Why did you do that?" How would you respond? Most probably, you would take offense or feel defensive, and it would not be in a good-natured spirit that we would begin communicating. Chances are you would bark something back at me or try to ask a question that you felt was either threatening or somehow a put-down. Good? No, not good, so do not ever ask "Why?"

Avoiding the use of the word *why* is not all that difficult, and you will quickly become adept at it. Try my simple rephrasing technique with a few friends, co-workers, or fellow students.

Avoiding the Use of Why

The secret here is to take a few moments in any conversation when you find you want to know the reason someone did something and you know you can't ask why. Remember that "why" is an invitation to your listener to become defensive. Try rephrasing questions. Here are a few scenarios to practice:

Mom and Dinner. Your mother invited you to dinner and made turnips, your least favorite food, and your mother knows it. You are steaming as you ask, "What was it that made you select turnips for dinner tonight?" Of course, you are thinking, ". . . unless you wanted to kill me," but you do not say it. How else can you phrase your question?

Your Friend. A friend borrows your car on a snowy day and returns it with a dent in the fender. The friend took it down a steep hill that was rather icy and you are dying to use that little three-letter word, but you ask, "How did you decide to take that hill?" Give one or two more ways you can rephrase your question.

A Psychotherapy Client. A therapy patient calls to tell you, one hour before your weekly scheduled appointment, that he will not be coming today. You have a 24-hour cancellation policy. The patient is offering no reason for not coming, and you know it might be important to the therapy. You ask . . . ? Try to rephrase a few more ways of stating your concern.

Alternatives to Asking Why

- "How did you arrive at that decision?"
- "What were you thinking at that time?"
- "What was it about that (whatever) which made you do that?"
- "What did you hope to accomplish by doing that?"
- "Help me to understand your thinking about this."
- "Go over your thinking on this for me."
- "Take me over your actions on this and use a step-by-step method, so I can understand better."
- "You were thinking that *what* would happen if you did that?"
- "Tell me how this has worked for you before."

What other ways of asking why, without using the word, can you suggest? Remember to begin immediately to use this rephrasing technique in your everyday life. It is not something you save for use in therapy sessions. Before asking any question, stop for a moment and see if it will be one that will facilitate communication.

You might keep a "defensiveness diary" to help you track particular situations in which you have a problem with this. Your communications may need work in this regard in interactions with peers, relatives, and loved ones or in learning situations. Note to whom you were insensitive sufficiently to make them defensive, where you did it, how you felt at the time, what the outcome was.

Tone of Voice

Tone of voice and body language, of course, are always part of the communication. A good way to really hear yourself is to have a tape recorder, but there is a more rudimentary way to hear your voice. Try taking each hand and cupping it behind each of your ears. Now begin reading a passage aloud, in your natural tone of voice. Never thought you sounded like that before? It can be a bit of a shock.

Your literal voice has become so important that researchers (Brown & Gilligan, 1992) are now looking at it as a very potent force in therapy. The belief is that the voice we use is not our own, but one we have learned (Zuckerman & Driver, 1989) to use in our various environments. Voice, therefore, is an important tool for measuring comfort level, status considerations, anxiety, and even social role.

Practice the above avoiding-why-remarks with a tape recorder. Play your remarks back and see how you would respond to your own statements. Do you sound sincere? Perhaps a bit aloof or condescending? Do you sound like an adult? The idea is to avoid a judgmental tone or approach. Research backs up the idea of your voice and how you use it (Street & Buller, 1987; Street & Wiemann, 1987; Zuckerman, 1993) as extremely important in establishing a working relationship with your clients.

The Three Types of Questions

Questioning is an important part of active listening. There are three ways you can inquire—by using closed-ended, open-ended, or leading questions.

Open-Ended Questions

Allow the client to answer fully. This type of question also affirms that you are listening and involved in the dialogue with the client. You might inquire, "What was it like in the hospital?" rather than "Did you like it at the hospital?" Practice turning your questions into open-ended ones. Open-ended questions cannot be answered with either "yes" or "no."

Closed-Ended Questions

Closed-ended questions force a yes or no response, cutting off an opportunity for more information that would have allowed the conversation to flow. Lawyers and other individuals in the legal system use closed-ended questions to interrogate persons. A therapist would not usually use this type of question unless they were filling in a forced-choice questionnaire or other instrument. This type might also be used with a client who is being evasive about something; you might directly ask, "Were you there on that night, yes or no?"

Leading Questions

Because they contain an inherent bias and redirect the client toward a predetermined end, leading questions are usually the least productive. I have seen a young psychiatric resident, trying to complete a mental status exam, look at the patient and, while shaking his head in a side-to-side fashion, ask, "You are not really good at math, are you?" The patient, dutifully, answered, "No."

Certain circumstances, however, do exist in which leading questions are very useful. You can use a leading question effectively when the client has just related some information about an action in which they engaged. You may feel that they can add more to your understanding of the situation, so you say, "and then what happened?" This can be used several times in a row to continue getting more information. In effect, you are getting the client to provide, in a step-by-step fashion, the series of events that transpired.

It is always a good idea, when you are first beginning to work with patients, to ask if you may tape-record at least part of the session. A videotape is very useful because it allows you to view your nonverbal behavior in addition to critiquing your verbal communication skills. Later, play it back with your supervisor or for yourself and see how the session flowed and what your visual sense of the session is. How can you improve? Did you have a plan, or were you just asking hit-or-miss questions and hoping to strike gold?

Nonverbal Communication

What signals to the client that you are actively listening (Brownell, 1996), rather than indifferent to what is being said? The obvious answer is your eye positioning. Look directly at the client, who will usually look directly back at you unless there is a cultural constraint against doing so or some underlying pathology or malingering.

Are you across from the client at a desk or table? What expression is on your face? Smiling isn't unacceptable, if the situation calls for it. Deadly serious behavior on your part will inhibit developing a warm, trusting interaction and may make the client very uncomfortable.

Physical distance is something that will be important to you in terms of personal space. Personal space is a culturally determined factor. American and European cultures consider three feet to be adequate, but other cultures consider it usual to be closer. In some situations, however, closer might be called for, if it is a situation of extreme distress. Even a touch of the hand or the arm might be in order.

Nodding in response to something being said is also helpful, as is leaning slightly forward. It goes without saying that yawning or becoming glassy-eyed is to be avoided at all costs. I have had clients tell me that they had therapists who actually nodded off during a session. I wondered what type of power differential could have kept someone going to a therapist who fell asleep while listening to him or her.

I prefer to have clients seated so that I can see most of their bodies because I want to see if there is any motoric restlessness, any tics or twitches. If there is a situation of risk, such as on an inpatient admissions or forensic unit, I take a seat by the door and have the client sit across from me. Some situations may call for your not closing the door in order to preserve your safety.

Sessions are time limited, but you do not want to keep looking at your watch or a clock on your desk, nor would I want an alarm going off at the end of the session. The effect will reinforce the client's feeling that you are not really interested. Position the clock across the room where you can see it unobtrusively over the client's shoulder.

Interview Preparation and Planning

Depending on whether you are preparing for an intake interview or an initial therapy session, you will need some preparation. One of the decisions to be made—most probably by the agency for which you are working—will be whether you will use a predetermined format or a more open-ended one. You will use, therefore, either a structured or an unstructured interview.

Structured or Unstructured Interview

A structured interview is one in which you follow a predetermined format of questions, perhaps a checklist, and go in sequence. Unstructured interviews have a broad outline of topic areas to include in your interview. The areas generally include the presenting problem, the current symptoms, a history of recent events, some family history, any prior treatment or medical illness, and medications being taken. A way to find several formats for structured interviews is to search the Internet, where colleagues will make them available for you to download.

Whether or not your interview will be structured or unstructured, you will need to note the appearance of the client including their grooming and form of dress, their posture and gait, any physical characteristics that are of note, facial expression, eye contact, motor activity, and any unusual mannerisms. Prepare a checklist that will help guide you through the process and eliminate your failure to note all of these.

I have always been very careful to note facial scars or deformities as well as tattoos or unusual body decoration or jewelry. Scars, especially on the face or head, can indicate head trauma or an impulsive or aggressive nature or even substance abuse. Tattoos tell me about relationships, peer groups, or, perhaps, insecurities.

How did the client get to the interview? Was the client driven, did he or she take public transportation or did a counselor bring the client? Disability determinations, which I do, use that information as an indicator of memory, motivation, attention, and the ability to make decisions. In essence, if the person came alone via public transportation or drove, they are not seen as suffering from major depression or a memory problem. Very often, clients will allege poor memory. How they came to the interview as well as what they do at home in terms of their ADLs (activities of daily living), their children, paying bills, going to religious services, or reading are all valued as indicators mitigating against memory impairment.

The volume, speed, and quality of speech are noted in terms of pitch, clarity and abnormalities. Substance abuse can often be noted by speech difficulty known as dysarthria or thickness of speech. Neurologic disorders as well as medication side effects, too, may be noted in speech problems (Adams, Parsons, Culbertson, & Nixon, 1996, pp. 32–34) as well as eye movements such as rapid eye darting from side to side known as nystagmus. The elderly frequently have medical problems (Farrell, 1997) or medication side effects that can present as psychological syndromes, and it is expected that you will familiarize yourself with them.

One brief note on the lack of understanding regarding medical illness and the overlap with seemingly apparent psychological problems seems called for here. Let me give you an illustration of what I mean.

Example

A woman came to a mental health center with her family for therapy. The interviewer made a detailed note regarding all the items needed for the development of a treatment plan and a diagnosis. The areas she neglected to explore included medical problems, medications, and extended-family physical health history.

Her decision was that the woman was histrionic, and the therapy was predicated on that diagnosis.

The family sessions involved encouragement to confront the woman regarding her hysterical symptoms related to periods of dizziness and problems with eyesight. The therapy went on for several months until finally, the family dropped out of therapy, having made little progress. The therapist saw the woman as dependent, angry, and resistant and felt she needed to come to terms with her internal conflicts.

Several years later, the woman again presented to the center for an intake and was directed to a psychologist for the initial interview. The symptoms, which had formerly been seen as hysterical, were explored in terms of longevity, duration of episode, and medical interventions. Over the years, the problems with vision had worsened, and she had consulted a neurologist.

The diagnosis was made, multiple sclerosis, a difficult-to-diagnose neurologic disorder with waxing and waning symptoms. It had been present for a number of years and had caused the original problems with balance and vision.

Exploration of medical history, therefore, is vital. Your medical knowledge needn't be very extensive, but you need to inquire. Medications that are used for many of the immune-system problems as well as those related to respiratory problems in both adults and children can cause clients to appear hyperactive or hypomanic. Closely noting both prescription and over-the-counter medications will prove helpful in ruling out such problems. Again, it is imperative that you identify Internet sites that will keep you up-to-date on medications that can cause psychological symptoms.

The client's mood and the content of the interaction with you—affect as well as thought processes—are all noted. Depression often presents as hyperactivity and irritability, not psychomotor retardation and paucity of verbalization.

Delusions, obsessions, ideas of reference as well as somatic concerns, or any thoughts of violence toward themselves or others are noted. At this point, you are following a path, which leads to diagnosis, and you question along the lines of psychiatric diagnostic decision trees (American Psychiatric Association, 1994). Questions of duty to protect (Beck, 1988; Ferris, Sandercock, Hoffman, Silverman, Barkun, Carlisle, & Katz, 1997; Mason, 1998) as well as your understanding are topics that will be left for you to explore with your supervisors and colleagues.

Delusions are noted and probed to help you understand them better. I once had a highly somatic patient in a psychiatric hospital. He was about to be discharged, and he continued to believe that he had an enormous tapeworm in his body. He wanted me to understand that it was "real" and that it was actually visible from his mouth. Opening his mouth extremely wide, he told me, "Look, look at the back of my mouth. See it?" It was his uvula.

Querying Diverse Populations

Therapeutic situations are not clear-cut and frequently require that you come to them with more than clinical skills. You will need to constantly keep yourself apprised of changes in culture, as well as looking backward to a time when there was no television, no air conditioning, and no plastic.

I remember one graduate student who had an interview with an elderly woman who told her of the time she sold Marvin watches. The young student thought little of it, as she failed to think much of the woman proudly telling her of their Atwater Kent radio. Was she interested in trading stories or in telling her something else? Did the woman's cultural background have anything to do with the telling of these seemingly irrelevant stories?

What would your third ear tell you? It told me that the woman wanted the student to know that her family had a better-than-average income in the 1930s and that they were people of taste. The student never picked up on the clues because she did not understand what the names meant and had not noted them in order to discuss them with her supervisor later. Knowing about the past can be a valuable aid in developing that all-important comfortable climate as you establish rapport with clients.

Who was Vaughn Monroe, anyway? Remember that band called Wings and the guy who was the lead singer? Who is the "girl singer" relative of that guy who used to be on the *ER* TV series? Do you know the answers to these questions?

Multiculturalism and Mental Health

The erroneous assumption has been made (Sue, 1994) that Asian Americans have fared well in terms of adjustment within the greater American culture and that they are relatively free from mental health problems. The truth, according to multiple authors (Atkinson, Kim, & Caldwell, 1998; Mezzich, Ruiz, & Munoz, 1999; Sue, 1994; Sue, 1998; Zayas et al., 1996) is that Asian American as well as other minority groups in the United States are not immune to the stresses of American society. These groups need counseling services to handle family, finance, and interpersonal problems, but their use of these services may require the clinician to rethink how to provide interventions and how to best communicate. Considerations of family, community, and transportation all play a role in understanding a minority client's approach to entering into and maintaining a therapeutic relationship.

Rethinking interventions and questioning techniques (Gergen, Gulerce, Lock, & Misra, 1996) also entails rethinking our own psychology and its presumptive application to that of people from other-than-Western cultures. The interpretation of psychopathology and personality characteristics (McCrae, Yik, Trapnell, Bond, & Paulhus, 1997) across cultures remains problematic. Ingrained cultural norms may present as problems unless viewed in terms of the larger culture and its values, and the DSM-IV (American Psychiatric Association, 1994) has made note of this in the section on culture-bound syndromes.

Even dating can be a culturally determined activity. A study of Asian American dating (Mok, 1999) attempted to tease out factors related to cultural constraints on dating both within the Asian American community and outside it—for instance, Asian Americans dating Whites—and acculturation. One of the findings was that there was a marked difference in acculturation between Asian American women and men. Men were slower than women to acculturate. Women, on the other hand, were more responsive to parental influence in their lives despite their quicker acculturation.

Two other important findings were that a family may disown a member for dating a non-Asian, and adolescents receive little encouragement to date. The tensions potentially brought on by parental concerns, acculturation, and divergent Western influences to date early are areas to explore in your interviews with Asian American clients.

Parental actions toward children were the focus of Chavajay and Rogoff (1999) who examined child-rearing patterns and attentional processes in two samples, Guatemalan Mayans and European-descent families. The Mayan mothers maintained an attentional process toward their children and surrounding events that was characterized as similar to what the researchers called "air traffic controller." These mothers followed their children's actions and the events surrounding them in a simultaneous fashion. In other words, both caregivers and children were likely to attend to competing events simultaneously. In contrast, European-descent mothers were apt to attend to only one activity at a time (for example, talking to other mothers *or* observing their child), thus giving the impression that they were more acutely aware of what their child was doing than the Mayan mothers. Mayan mothers, therefore presented a markedly different interactional style that could be interpreted as being less attentive to the untrained eye.

Culture and emotional expression provide another area of concern. One of the prime problems that arises when a member of the Puerto Rican community seeks psychological services (Malgady, Rogler, & Cortes, 1996) is that the current criteria listed in the DSM-IV (APA, 1994) for disorders is misinterpreted. For example, in the continental United States, a frequently seen culture-bound disorder is *ataque de nervios,* or sometimes referred to as the *Puerto Rican syndrome.* This affliction typically presents as a trancelike state accompanied by seizure-like episodes and hallucinations. It often develops after the loss or termination of important relationships. The challenge for clinicians is to neither over-estimate the degree of disturbance nor, in the other extreme, to dismiss the symptoms entirely to culture (Draguns, 1998).

Malgady et al. (1996) pointed out "although it is reasonable to suppose that different cultures have much in common . . . not all symptoms are culturally invariant." The researchers found that cultural expression of symptomatology may indicate different states of mind and that "anger" is not always anger, but may be an example of depression or anxiety. The suggestion, therefore, is to explore the differences in the culture. A similar note was struck by Zayas, Torres, Malcolm, and DesRosiers (1996) who researched clinicians' definitions of ethnically sensitive therapy. Clinicians, they found, were in agreement about their willingness to delve into cultural differences and learn how to utilize them in therapy.

Therapeutic communication style and ethnicity may be another important determining factor with some clients. An investigation of ethnic matching of therapist and client uncovered instances in which it was germane to the outcome and others where it was not. A study of Asian Americans who were unacculturated illustrated they stayed in treatment longer and had more favorable outcomes when they were matched with a therapist of the *same* ethnicity (Sue, 1998). When the therapist was White and the client African American, there appeared to be no effect on either the length of the therapeutic treatment or its outcome.

Asians (Sue, 1994) may not seek services because of "traditional Asian cultural values or negative experiences with inappropriate Western mental health services rather than . . . a mentally healthier population." The tradition of maintaining family honor and reputation would prevent the therapist from confronting these clients as might be done with other clients.

Exploring and using probes for somatic complaints with these clients rather than delving into emotional distress might be a productive route to uncovering problems. One of the major problems (Lin, 1994, 1998) found in the literature was that, while therapists were becoming culturally sensitive, they had a tendency to see all Asians as alike, forgetting the cultural differences between the many groups.

What are the key areas where a counselor needs to increase awareness? The primary focus of concern for nonminority mental health personnel is increasing the therapist's awareness of differences, obtaining knowledge of the client's culture, differentiating between pathology and cultural differences in assessment, and utilizing culture in the therapy (Zayas, Torres, Malcolm, & Des Rosiers, 1996).

The research indicated that it is helpful not only to recognize the cultural differences between the therapist and the client, but also to bring it up during the interview or session. An exploration of differences and similarities can provide insight for both participants, and it is here that your probing skills will prove most beneficial.

Example of Asian American Therapist-Client Interaction

A young, married woman came in for therapy because she felt her brother-in-law was ungrateful, and she was angry. The husband, the oldest son of a Korean family who still had family members living in Korea, was providing his brother with financial support for college. The husband was also actively looking for a suitable wife for the young man and was purchasing expensive engagement presents for the young woman and her family. The wife felt the brother-in-law was ungrateful, and this was a source of anger.

THERAPIST: What is the problem with your brother-in-law getting a part-time job and providing his own engagement gifts?

CLIENT: It would be wrong for us to do that. Our family would be seen as lacking in etiquette and my husband, as the eldest son, must help the others to make suitable marriages and give expensive gifts.

THERAPIST: So, the matter of money isn't the problem? The problem is you feel he is ungrateful?

CLIENT: Yes, but we can't say that because it would upset my husband and his family.

The primary problem is not that the young man may be a financial drain on this couple. The wife, who has become more acculturated, still accepts some of the old traditions, but finds others unacceptable and feels her husband is being exploited. Should the husband be brought into the sessions? What about the brother-in-law? If the family learns that the wife is in therapy, will this be seen as shameful? These are all areas to be explored.

Asian American families frequently do not seek mental health services because of their concern regarding family, friends, and neighbors. I live in a community where there has been a great influx of Japanese and Korean families in the past 20 years. The strong sense of status within the Japanese group led to isolation of the young women, who spoke little English and had no friends for support. The result was multiple suicides by jumping off the high-rise apartment buildings.

Status, therefore, is a further concern when dealing with any ethnic group. The power of the authority figure, the clinician, is increased, and questions or statements may be seen as mandates rather than ideas to consider.

Therapists who have not had much or any exposure to cultures other than their own can misunderstand behaviors that are not only acceptable, but also expected in other cultures. For example, eye contact is expected in psychotherapy, but in African American cultures (Ivey, Ivey, & Simek-Morgan, 1997) people use patterns that are directly opposite. More eye contact is maintained during the listening phase of a conversation than the talking phase. Much of our training has told us that when a client fails to look at us while they are speaking, it is a sign that they are trying to be evasive or they might be paranoid.

Therapy clients usually sit across from the therapist, but Eskimo and Inuit sit side-by-side when speaking about personal issues. In other cultures, such as in the Middle East, personal space is at a distance of only six to twelve inches. If one of your clients were to come this close, how would you interpret it?

Self-disclosure, which is the lynchpin on which therapy depends, is difficult for Asian Americans because of their cultural prohibition regarding revealing family problems (Dana, 1998).

Words, symbols, and possessions will all provide you with important leads that will enhance the richness of your search for meaning. Our own culture and language has regional traits of which we may not be aware. Let me provide a personal example.

> One problem I encountered involved a national major research project in which I was involved. The national research protocol required that we measure cognitive abilities of an elderly cohort on a biweekly basis. A psychometric instrument, which had been validated for this purpose, was to be used and appeared to fit all our needs.
>
> One portion of the test required subjects to name common items that they were shown as well as naming several of their fingers. Once the research was running in the South and the West, I became aware of a problem. Our subjects were consistently missing a certain item that they had to name as well as incorrectly naming one of their fingers.
>
> The item on which they were "wrong" was a black Lone Ranger mask and the finger that was consistently missed by many Hispanics was the middle finger. The problem was that the test constructors had standardized and validated the test on an East Coast sample and hadn't considered that in the South, the West, and the Midwest, the mask could be called a "door face" or a "false face."
>
> Hispanic subjects called the middle finger the "heart finger" because of the belief that there was a direct nerve connection from it to the heart. In our wisdom, we had been blind because of our own lack of knowledge of regional cultural differences within the United States.
>
> We had to allow for alternate answers that we hadn't originally considered. Once we did, it was amazing how our non-Eastern seaboard sample improved on the test. How many interviewers, do you suppose, missed a regional subtlety and let useful information pass unseen?

Another commonly missed piece of cultural information is of medical as well as psychological significance. If I were to tell you that a patient had come in and told me that she enjoyed eating crunchy laundry starch from the box, what would you think? Would you believe she had some organic brain syndrome, or that she was on drugs or psychotic? Suppose I told you that laundry starch (Rainville, 1998; Roselle, 1970) is eaten by women in certain areas of the country as a candy-like substance, how would that seem to you? It is not good for them and it causes very serious blood problems, but they are not psychotic, nor do they have brain damage nor are they drug abusers.

You will find that you need to adjust your techniques to the needs of the client and the demands of the situation.

Interview Vignettes

The acquisition of interviewing skills can best be accomplished by frequent use in your daily life. Communication is, after all, something you use every day, and in your life away from the therapeutic environment, you will have the greatest opportunity for practice. The additional benefit is that it will improve your relationships because anyone to whom you speak will have a new appreciation for your interest in them and what they have to say.

Subjects for practice can be found as you walk around malls or in offices or classrooms. Pick out a person, listen to them, and see how you have to form your questions to learn some special thing about them. Friends, family, and coworkers will benefit from your listening skills, as you become a better friend, a more responsive relative, and a facilitating coworker.

We have provided a few vignettes as an illustration of what you might find if you look.

> ***Scenario 1: Geriatric Patient, Mrs. R***
> Mrs. R is a 95-year-old widow who has lived in an upscale nursing home for the past five years. Her medical problems include near-blindness, a severe cardiac condition, and, for the past 30 years, addiction to prescription medication.
>
> Each day she sits at a table just inside the French doors, separated from the other residents. No one shares her perch, and she always eats in silence. Today, you meet her at breakfast and she is crying. "They stole my heart," she cries.

Play out the scene in your mind and do the following:

1. Use your probing skill to elicit more information. What would you ask first?
2. What are you attempting in your dialogue with her?
3. How are you going to display empathy toward her?

This scene actually took place in a nursing home where I was providing consultation services and I have given you more of the details in the next paragraph. See if you would have arrived at the conclusion I did. Again, what would you first say to her?

The Facts. Mrs. R had received a heavy, solid gold, etched heart on a gold chain from her husband, a wealthy businessman, for Valentine's Day on her 50th birthday. She wore it every day and cherished the memories associated with it. A widow, with no children and no relatives, she saw the heart as more than a bit of expensive jewelry. One of her favorite dresses was a two-piece knitted top and skirt. One day, while she was being helped to dress, the aide pulled at the top that had become snagged by the chain. The chain broke and the heart flew across the room. The aide looked on the floor but could not find it, and Mrs. R was told it had been lost. She insisted that they did find it and had stolen it. One month later, Mrs. R died in her sleep. Someone, it seems, had stolen her heart.

> ***Scenario 2: The Late Client, Mrs. M***
> Mrs. M is a 23-year-old, married woman with a high school education. She remains in the home to care for her three children and her husband, and lately she has been experiencing a condition that was originally thought to be symptomatic of cardiac problems. Her children's pediatrician suggested she needed a cardiac workup, which proved to be negative. The probable diagnosis is panic attacks, and she has been sent to you for treatment.
>
> You have given her a weekly 11 A.M. appointment, and from the first intake interview, she has consistently been late. When she comes to the session, there is a great deal of questioning about how you are and how your family is. You feel she is being resistant. Much of the time for the session is spent in this cordial interaction that always has a faint histrionic quality.
>
> You confront her on her failure to want to work in therapy, and she appears both shocked and hurt. After the session, she fails to keep her next appointment and is soon lost to contact by your agency.
>
> What is the problem? What should you have considered might have been the reasons for her behavior?

Mrs. M is a Hispanic woman acting within the guidelines of her culture in terms of etiquette. She does not wish to appear insensitive to your needs to talk, nor is there an overriding need to appear for her session exactly on time. The tone that you see as histrionic is merely a culturally accepted manner of speaking that is in sharp contrast to what is considered the American, unemotional, and flat style of speech.

You would have diagnosed her cultural differences as pathology.

> ***Scenario 3: Medical Patient, Mrs. B***
> Mrs. B is having problems leaving her home. She used to go to Atlantic City with her friends, driving down in her car. She had a standing appointment each Thursday for her hairdresser. Now, she cannot leave her home to get her mail in the mailbox at the street and the letter carrier has to slip the mail inside her screen door.
>
> Her heart pounds, she feels faint, and she begins to sweat. Mrs. B has panic disorder, or does she? What would you want to ask?

The Facts. Mrs. B has hypertension and, after years of being on the same medications, her internist changed her to a new one. A week into taking the new medication, she began to have these attacks. Her internist referred her to a psychologist for therapy. The internist believed that Mrs. B was having difficulty because her only child had recently moved away, and she saw her grandchildren only once a month.

Mrs. B was not able to come to the office, so the psychologist went to her home where they had therapy in the kitchen. Probes quickly revealed that the "attacks" were closely related, in time, to the new medication. A review of the medication side effects showed that some patients who had just begun taking it experienced panic and anxiety attacks.

The physician was consulted about this information, changed the medication and the "attacks" left within three days. Mrs. B was on her way to the hairdresser, the supermarket, and Atlantic City. She had her life back.

> ***Scenario 4: The Secret Divorcee, Ms. A***
>
> The young woman, Ms. A, came to her first session dressed in a stylish business suit, wearing expensive jewelry, and carrying a leather briefcase. She began filling out the forms and stopped, looked at the therapist and said, "I have insurance, but I want to pay cash. Is that all right? And I do not want anything going to my home." She explained that she didn't even live in this state, but had a home in a neighboring state in an upscale neighborhood. The two requests were somewhat unusual, and the therapist wondered why she would not be using her insurance and why the emphasis on nothing going to her home.
>
> What was the presenting problem? "I don't know what to do about my ex-husband," she said. "We have been divorced for two years, but I haven't told my family because they will not understand. He is a nice enough fellow, but he is not a professional man. I thought he was going to finish graduate school and things would be fine, but that never happened."
>
> During the marriage, the husband had depended on his wife earning a six-figure salary from the business she had set up. She was in international importing of jewelry and stated openly, "I love money. It is the only thing that makes me happy." The ex-husband did not tell his family, either, that he was divorced.
>
> "My family will never understand," she said, "especially my grandmother. She is very traditional, and I have been raised in the United States. I did not want to marry when I did, but I did it to keep the family happy." Now the young woman was thinking about remarrying her ex-husband in order to keep the family from experiencing any shame. Love was not a consideration; only the family mattered.

What course of action would you take with this young Asian American client? Dana (1998) recommended a solution-oriented approach that is sensitive to a woman's needs within the context of her culture. The family is central in this woman's life, and it is that power structure that must be recognized. Divorce, she has told you, is intolerable, and remarriage is a viable option. Does she want to change or to come to terms with her cultural conflicts? The social context within which this woman lives (Ivey, Ivey, & Simek-Morgan, 1997) is a paramount concern for her.

"I can't speak to anyone about this," she said. What was her purpose in coming to you? Living in both an American and an Asian culture at the same time was, obviously, creating tension, and her American education had led her to seek out someone to whom she could talk openly.

The Competent Counselor of the Future

Communication and listening skills, as you have seen in this chapter, can be learned. With practice, you can easily incorporate new methods of obtaining information into your counseling and your personal life. Probing, active listening, and using appropriate questions will enrich your interactions with your clients and help you to make better use of the time allotted in therapy sessions or intake interviews.

The real challenge for the future is for all mental health professionals to remain current with the needs of the clients and the community. Although the idea of the American melting pot has been one that we have accepted as reality, the mixture of our culture is changing and will continue to do so.

Ask yourself what steps you have taken within the past year to better prepare yourself for the challenges of the future. Not only do all of us need to know how to work with clients from many cultural backgrounds, but also we need to understand that within each of these groups there are subgroups. Childrearing practices, relationships, religious matters, and the basics of living life within a specific culture may be in contrast to our own backgrounds. Actively engaging in introspective probing can be a great benefit in your continuing professional development.

REFERENCES

Adams, R. L., Parsons, O. A., Culbertson, J. L., & Nixon, S. J. (Eds.). (1996). *Neuropsychology for clinical practice: Etiology, assessment, and treatment of common neurological disorders.* (pp. 32–34). Washington, DC: American Psychological Association.

Adler, R., & Towne, N. (1978). *Looking out/looking in: Interpersonal communication.* (2nd ed.). New York: Holt, Rinehart & Winston.

American Psychiatric Association. (1994). *Diagnostic and statistical manual of mental disorders: DSM-IV.* (4th ed.). Washington, DC: Author

Atkinson, D. R., Kim, B. S. K., & Caldwell, R. (1998). Ratings of helper roles by multicultural psychologists and Asian American students initial support for the three-dimensional model of multicultural counseling. *Journal of Counseling Psychology, 45*(4), 414–423.

Beck, J. C. (1988). The therapist's legal duty when the patient may be violent. *Psychiatric Clinics of North America, 11*(4), 665–679.

Beckman, H., Markakis, K., Suchman, A., & Frankel, R. (1994). Getting the most from a 20-minute visit. *American Journal of Gastroenterology, 89*(5), 662–664.

Bersoff, D. N. (1996). *Ethical conflicts in psychology.* Washington, DC: American Psychological Association.

Broadbent, U. E. (1956). Listening between and during practiced auditory distractions. *Journal of Experimental Psychology, 47,* 51–60.

Brown, L. M., & Gilligan, C. (1992). *Meeting at the crossroads: Women's psychological and girls' development.* Cambridge: Harvard University Press.

Brownell, J. (1996). *Listening attitudes, principles, and skills.* Boston: Allyn & Bacon.

Chavajay, P., & Rogoff, B. (1999). Cultural variation in management of attention by children and their caregivers. *Developmental Psychology, 35*(4), 1079–1090.

Craig, R. J. E. (1997). *Clinical and diagnostic interviewing.* Northvale, NJ: Jason Aronson.

Dana, R. H. (1998). *Understanding cultural identity in intervention and assessment.* Thousand Oaks, CA: Sage.

Daum, A. L. (1994). The disruptive antisocial patient: Management strategies. *Nursing Management, 25*(8), 46–51.

Davis, H., & Nicholaou, T. (1992). A comparison of the interviewing skills of first- and final-year medical students. *Medical Education, 26*(6), 441–447.

Draguns, J. G. (1998). Transcultural psychology and the delivery of clinical psychological services. In S. Cullari (Ed.), *Foundations of clinical psychology.* Boston: Allyn & Bacon.

Evans, B. J., Stanley, R. O., & Burrows, G. O. (1993). Measuring medical students' empathy skills. *British Journal of Medical Psychology, 66* (Pt 2), 121–133.

Evans, U. R. (1979). *Essential interviewing.* Belmont, CA: Wadsworth.

Farrell, P. A. (1997). Psychological disorders and medical illness in the elderly: A double-edged sword. In L. Vandecreek, S. Knapp, & T. L. Jackson (Eds.), *Innovations in clinical practice: A source book (Vol. 15,* pp. 283–309). Sarasota, FL: Professional Resource Press.

Ferris, L. E., Sandercock, J., Hoffman, B., Silverman, M., Barkun, H., Carlisle, J., & Katz, C. (1997). Risk assessments for acute violence to third parties: A review of the literature. *Canadian Journal of Psychiatry, 42*(10), 1051–1060.

Gergen, K. J., Gulerce, A., Lock, A., & Misra, G. (1996). Psychological science in cultural context. *American Psychologist, 51*(5), 496–503.

Gibb, J. R. (1961). Defensive communication. *The Journal of Communication, 11*(3), 141–148.

Gordon, R. L. (1975). *Interviewing: Strategy, techniques and tactics.* Homewood, IL: Dorsey Press.

Hall, C. S., & Nordby, V. J. (1973). *A primer of Jungian psychology.* New York: New American Library.

Ivey, A. E., & Ivey, M. B. (1999). *Intentional interviewing and counseling: Facilitating client development in a multicultural society* (4th ed.). Pacific Grove, CA: Brooks/Cole.

Ivey, A. E., Ivey, M. B., & Simek-Morgan, L. (1997). *Counseling and psychotherapy: A multicultural perspective.* (4th ed.). Boston: Allyn & Bacon.

Leonard, K., & Farrell, P. A. (1992). Munchausen's Syndrome by Proxy: A little-known aspect of abuse. *Postgraduate Medicine, 91*(5), 197–204.

Lin, J. C. H. (1994). How long do Chinese Americans stay in psychotherapy? *Journal of Counseling Psychology, 41*(3), 288–291.

Lin, J. C. H. (1998). Descriptive characteristics and length of psychotherapy of Chinese American clients seen in private practice. *Professional Psychology: Research and Practice, 29*(6), 571–573.

Lissner, A. R., Gilmore, J., & Pompi, K. F. (1976). The dilemma of coordinating treatment with criminal justice. *American Journal of Drug & Alcohol Abuse, 3*(4), 621–628.

Malgady, R. G., Rogler, L. H., & Cortes, D. (1996). Cultural expression of psychiatric symptoms: Idioms of anger among Puerto Ricans. *Psychological Assessment, 8*(3), 265–268.

Mason, T. (1998). Tarasoff liability: Its impact for working with patients who threaten others. *International Journal of Nursing Students, 35*(1–2), 109–114.

McCrae, R. R., Yik, M. S. M., Trapnell, P. D., Bond, M. H., & Paulhus, D. L. (1997). Interpreting personality profiles across cultures: Bilingual, acculturation, and peer rating studies of Chinese undergraduates. *Journal of Personality and Social Psychology, 74*(4), 1041–1055.

Mezzich, J. E., Ruiz, P., & Munoz, R. A. (1999). Mental health care for Hispanic Americans: A current perspective. *Cultural Diversity and Ethnic Minority Psychology, 5*(2), 91–102.

Mok, T. A. (1999). Asian American dating: Important factors in partner choice. *Cultural Diversity and Ethnic Minority Psychology, 5*(2), 103–117.

Morrison, J. R. (1995). *The first interview: Revised for DSM-IV.* New York: Guilford Press.

Peterson, M. R. (1992). *At personal risk: Boundary violations in professional-client relationships.* New York: W. W. Norton.

Rainville, A. J. (1998). Pica practices of pregnant women are associated with lower maternal hemoglobin level at delivery. *Journal of the American Dietetic Association, 98*(3), 293–296.

Roazen, P. (1974). *Freud and his followers.* New York: Random House.

Roselle, H. A. (1970). Association of laundry starch and clay ingestion with anemia in New York City. *Archives of Internal Medicine, 125*(1), 57–61.

Shea, S. C. (1998). *Psychiatric interviewing: The art of understanding.* Philadelphia: W. B. Saunders.

Stevens-Smith, P. S., & Smith, R. L. (1998). *Substance abuse counseling.* Upper Saddle River, NJ: Simon & Schuster.

Street, R. L., & Buller, U. B. (1987). Nonverbal response patterns in physician-patient interactions: A functional analysis. *Journal of Nonverbal Behavior, 11,* 234–253.

Street, R. L., & Wiemann, J. (1987). Patients' satisfaction with physicians' interpersonal involvement, expressiveness, and dominance. *Communication Yearbook, 10,* 591–612.

Sue, D. W. (1994). Asian-American mental health and help-seeking behavior comment on Solberg et al. (1994), Tata & Leong (1994), and Lin (1994). *Journal of Counseling Psychology, 41*(3), 292–295.

Sue, S. (1998). In search of cultural competence in psychotherapy and counseling. *American Psychologist, 53*(4), 440–448.

Van der Merwe, N. (1991). *Listening: A skill for everyone.* Capetown, SA: Arrow Publishers.

Wachtel, P. L. (1993). *Therapeutic communication: Principles and effective practice.* New York: Guilford Press.

Waldinger, R. J. (1997). *Psychiatry for medical students.* (3rd ed.). Washington, DC: American Psychiatric Press.

Zayas, L. H., Torres, L. R., Malcolm, J., & DesRosiers, F. S. (1996). Clinicians' definitions of ethnically sensitive therapy. *Professional Psychology: Research and Practice, 27*(1), 78–82.

Zuckerman, M., & Driver, J. B. (1989). What sounds beautiful is good: The vocal attractiveness stereotype. *Journal of Nonverbal Behavior, 13,* 67–82.

Zuckerman, M. M. K. (1993). The attractive voice: What makes it so? *Journal of Nonverbal Behavior, 17,* 119–130.

FOR FURTHER READING

Brownell, J. (1996). *Listening attitudes, principles, and skills.* Boston: Allyn & Bacon. (Cited in References.)

Dana, R. H. (1998). *Understanding cultural identity in intervention and assessment.* Thousand Oaks, CA: Sage. (Cited in References.)

Gopaul-McNicol, S., & Thomas-Presswood, T. (1998). *Working with linguistically and culturally different children: Innovative clinical and educational approaches.* Boston: Allyn & Bacon.

The book's underlying philosophy is that to intervene successfully with a culturally diverse child, a therapist must understand the values and beliefs inherent in the child's cultural upbringing and must utilize intervention strategies that are culturally sensitive. The book is based on years of cross-cultural practice and research with children of various linguistic and cultural backgrounds.

Herring, R. D. (1999). *Counseling with native American Indians and Alaska natives: Strategies for helping professionals.* Thousand Oaks, CA: Sage.

A thorough background on the developmental, cultural, and special mental health needs of native American Indian and Alaska native clients is provided in this volume. The author has included guidance in the establishment of rapport when working with these client groups. Topics include assessment, terminology, demographic distinctions, and implications for training and practice.

Ivey, A. E., & Ivey, M. B. (1999). *Intentional interviewing and counseling: Facilitating client development in a multicultural society.* Pacific Grove, CA: Brooks/Cole. (Cited in References.)

CHAPTER

4 The Client's Perspective of Psychotherapy

SALVATORE CULLARI

In the last one hundred years, there has been a progressive accumulation of knowledge about psychotherapy. Literally thousands of books and articles have been written about various psychotherapeutic theories, interventions, and techniques. Only relatively recently, however, has much research attention been paid to psychotherapy clients themselves. This chapter looks at psychotherapy from the perspective of persons who are undergoing psychotherapy. Part of this discussion is based on a questionnaire that was completed by 98 clients who were currently undergoing psychotherapy. The chapter begins with a review of previous research in this area and ends with an analysis of what clients actually want and expect from their therapists and from the process of psychotherapy itself. Throughout the chapter, the implications of these findings for client satisfaction and treatment outcome will be explored.

Previous Research

Carl Rogers was one of the pioneers of research into how clients experience psychotherapy. In his classic book *Client-Centered Therapy,* published in 1951, he commented on how little this area had been explored. "The way in which the client perceives or experiences the interviews is a field of inquiry which is new and in which the data are very limited. . . . It is an area which appears to have great future significance however" (1951, p. 65). Fifty years later, in spite of the fact that we have made some significant progress, I am tempted to make essentially the same remarks.

Although consumers of psychotherapy have become more sophisticated and vocal over the last few decades, research in this area has continued to play a relatively minor role as compared to other psychotherapy investigations. There are many reasons for this (see McLead, 1990). First of all, psychotherapists in full-time private practice actually carry out and publish relatively little research (Morrow-Bradley & Elliott, 1986; Cullari, 1996a). Most psychotherapy research is done by academicians who may or may not have their own practice. Thus a potentially rich source of subjects and data is lost. Secondly, research investigating how clients view their therapy is difficult to carry out. Many practical and ethical stumbling blocks must be overcome. A major problem is finding therapists who are willing to participate in such studies. It should come as no surprise that psychotherapists may be leery about letting a "stranger" collect data about their clients. For example, such studies may interfere with the client-therapist relationship. Also, the therapist may be apprehensive about the feedback the client may give about him or her. Other issues include those of maintaining client confidentiality and getting clients to agree to participate in an interview or complete questionnaires that may be time-consuming and embarrassing.

Aside from these practical problems, because of their subjective nature, survey and questionnaire data are often not accepted by professionals and scientists at the same level of confidence as more objective studies that use more formal experimental designs. At the same time, traditional treatment orientations such as psychoanalysis tend to downplay or question the value of possibly distorted treatment experiences of clients, and radical behaviorists complain that such data may not be directly observable, measurable, or reliable.

Despite these drawbacks, some important information about client experiences in psychotherapy has been collected over recent years. In addition to Rogers, a pioneer of this type of consumer research was Strupp and his colleagues from the University of North Carolina. Among his many findings, Strupp noted that the positive attitudes a therapist has toward the client (such as interest and caring) must be communicated. In other words, the more uncertainty clients have about the therapist's attitude toward them, the less likely they are to cooperate in the change process (Strupp, Fox, & Lessler, 1969). This is especially true during the initial stages of therapy. For example, some new clients report that they have no friends or that "no one likes them." By having the therapist communicate a sense of warmth, the client's self-esteem is likely to improve as well as his or her sense of isolation. These simple beginnings are often the first steps in increasing the client's level of self-efficacy and instilling a sense of hope for improvement.

In a related manner, Strupp found that the treatment conditions clients most desire from psychotherapy include liking and being liked by the therapist, having a sense of mutual trust, and having the perception that the therapist is dependable and will be there to support and encourage them. These types of factors were identified by Strupp and his colleagues as being the *sine qua non* for successful psychotherapy (Strupp, Fox, & Lessler, 1969, p. 17; Howe, 1993; Wright & Davis, 1994).

Many of the diverse studies concerning the experiences of clients in psychotherapy have been done outside of the United States. One large scale study was conducted by Mayer and Timms (1970), who interviewed 46 clients of social workers in London, England. These investigators broke down the collection of interviewees into two groups of satisfied and dissatisfied clients. The satisfied clients perceived their social worker as someone who was easy to talk to, who was interested in them (e.g., someone who seemed to care and wanted to help), someone who trusted the client, and someone who lessened feelings of shame. As with Strupp's findings, an important aspect of the treatment process was that the therapist communicated, in some fashion, positive feelings for the client. The authors summarized that the most positive aspects of therapy reported by clients fell into four categories: emotional relief through self-disclosure, support, guidance, and enlightenment.

Not surprisingly, the dissatisfied clients had treatment experiences that lacked these positive aspects of therapy. Many of the clients who were dissatisfied reported that their worker just seemed to be doing a job and were not really personally interested in the client. Also, these clients reported that their workers didn't really seem to understand them or their problems well, or did not seem to trust them. Additionally, the dissatisfied clients reported that their workers dwelt on topics that they (the clients) thought were irrelevant to their problems and needs. For example, some clients complained that the workers kept returning to the same topics and asking the same questions over and over again. Lastly, another important theme reported by these authors was that clients who were dissatisfied with their specific therapists were looking for specific advice, recommendations, and actions to overcome their problems, and perceived their therapists as being too passive or inadequate in providing these types of support services.

In the United States, Maluccio (1979) reported very similar findings. His results were based on 33 post-therapy interviews with a random group of former clients and therapists from a Catholic counseling service. His findings suggest that the first impressions clients have of their therapists are very important in terms of forming a positive working relationship and deciding to continue with treatment or not. Along the same lines, it appears that the initial sessions of therapy are the most vivid for clients. As you will see, these findings are replicated in other studies as well.

Maluccio noted that although clients were satisfied with having the opportunity to talk with someone, many of them were not sure how this particular psychotherapy technique could help them solve their problems. Similar to the Mayer and Timms (1970) study, many clients expected more active interventions from their therapists, such as specific suggestions and advice. Maluccio (1979) summarized the positive qualities that clients most desire from their therapists: The therapist should be a person with whom it is easy to communicate; who has the ability to put the client at ease; who shows genuine concern and interest about the client; who is tuned in to client needs and feelings; who is a good listener; who makes clients feel comfortable; who understands them; and who gives clients enough time to talk about themselves. In a similar vein, Sloane, Staples, Cristol, Yorkston, and Whipple (1975) found that about 70 percent of clients who had successful treatment believed that the personal characteristics of the therapist contributed significantly to their improvement. These factors included the therapist's personality, ability to help clients understand and face their problems, being an easy person to talk to, and ability to provide encouragement.

In discussing the major themes of his findings, Maluccio was most impressed with some of the striking discrepancies between the perceptions of the clients and their therapists. These tended to be the greatest at the beginning and the end of therapy. For example, in the early sessions of treatment, therapists tend to be concerned mainly with assessment, while clients are focused on their levels of distress. Maluccio also found that clients tended to see termination as being due to their own initiative, while the therapists viewed it as a mutual decision. He stated: "In a sense, client and worker start with divergent perspectives, gradually converge as their engagement proceeds, and again move in different directions as it comes to a close" (pp. 184–185).

Maluccio was not the first to report discrepancies between client and therapist perceptions in psychotherapy. For example, in an early study, Feifel and Eells (1963) suggested that many clients attribute the effectiveness of therapy to being able to talk over their problems with a sympathetic person, while therapists tended to attribute it to their own specific treatment techniques or interventions. For the interested reader, McLeod (1990) and Herman (1998) have reviewed a number of other studies that have investigated the differences in the perceptions between clients and therapists. Maluccio suggested that much of psychotherapy involves reducing the discrepancy between the client and therapist in terms of goals and expectations and that consistency between these is necessary for successful outcome. In support of this, Maluccio recommended that in addition to the role induction of clients into therapy, we should be concerned similarly with the therapists' role induction into the clients' ways of thinking and perceiving.

Oldfield (1983) conducted a similar large scale study in England, which surveyed 52 clients in an Oxford community mental health program called the Isis Centre. She found that client expectations for psychotherapy fell into four major response groups: a change in feelings; achieving greater self-understanding; regaining an ability to cope with life; and an improvement in personal relationships. Responses involving a change in feelings usually referred to a reduction of distress or relief from symptoms, such as depression and anxiety. Responses related to the client's self-understanding were typically associated with greater self-awareness and an increased ability to comprehend the causes of their personal problems, motives, and behaviors. The topic of clients regaining the ability to cope with life revolved around "getting back to normal." Such factors included learning to cope with their problems, increasing their self-esteem, getting back to work, or similar outcomes. The fourth area of improving relationships usually had to do with getting along better with people in general, or improving affiliations with parents or partners.

In the same study, Oldfield asked clients how they expected treatment to help them. These responses were grouped into five areas: not sure or uncertain; having someone to talk to; gaining psychological insight into their problems; getting specific advice; and receiving support. The factors that clients reported were most helpful in therapy were interpersonal characteristics such as the therapist showing true concern, his or her trustworthiness, his or her being a good listener, and perceived competence. Clients wanted their therapists to be intelligent, perceptive, honest, and sensible—someone they could respect. Other positive aspects of therapy included the client-therapist relationship, feeling "safe," being able to admit to flaws and weaknesses without being judged by the therapist, and talking to someone who could remain objective.

In looking at the responses concerning client disappointments with therapy, the main themes centered around not getting enough advice or specific recommendations, being with a therapist who was too "professional," and factors related to the therapist's inappropriate use of techniques. The latter included dwelling too much on childhood experiences or the client's past and using interventions without clearly explaining their purpose or rationale.

The issue of clients not getting enough specific advice from their therapists is one that is consistent with many other studies as well. In an early study by Goin, Yamamoto, and Silverman (1965), the authors reported that a large proportion of the clients in their group, especially those from the lower socioeconomic areas, expected to receive specific advice from their therapists and that clients who received advice were more satisfied with their treatment. In addition, Murphy, Cramer, and Lillie (1984) found that (1) clients perceive receiving advice from their therapist as having therapeutic value and (2) receiving advice was positively correlated with two objective measures of outcome. Despite these findings, Oldfield made the important distinction that many clients probably do not really want their therapist to tell them what to do, but rather want the therapist to help them understand and manage their problems so that they can eventually solve them on their own.

In summarizing the significant contributions of her study, Oldfield pointed out the importance that clients placed on their feelings. While this was not an unexpected finding, she suggested that the emotional feelings of clients should be a major focus of all psychotherapy: "Again and again, they describe their feelings as the dominant aspect of their problems; as the decisive factor in their choosing to seek help; as an essential part of their experience in counseling; as an area of significant change in the outcome" (Oldfield, 1983, p. 171).

The importance of the feelings of psychotherapy clients has been explored elsewhere. For example, Strupp et al. (1969) found a positive relationship between the amount of therapeutic change that clients perceived had occurred and the extent to which they thought the therapist had understood their true feelings. More recently, Strupp (1999) expanded this theme. He stated that "to immerse oneself as completely as possible in that other person's inner world and to try to understand and make sense of his or her experience in a way that one can only dimly glimpse is one of the greatest gifts one person can bestow on another" (Strupp, 1999, p. 34). In a related fashion, Murphy, Cramer, and Lillie (1984) found that aside from receiving advice, the ingredient that clients perceived as being most therapeutic was talking to a therapist who understood their feelings. These authors found that both of these factors were positively related to measures of treatment outcome. This is an area that I will return to again when discussing the results of my own study.

In a book that seems to be at least partially inspired by Oldfield's publication, France (1988) presented a fascinating account of her six and a half years of experiences as a patient undergoing psychoanalysis (see also Allen, 1990; Grierson, 1990; and Conran & Love, 1993 for similar accounts). Her reflections underscore many of the points made by clients in these other studies. For example, from her point of view, the personal aspects of her three therapists and the quality of the client-therapist relationship were the most significant and helpful aspects of her treatment. I recommend this book to all therapists-in-training because it illuminates many of the nuances of psychotherapy from a client's point of view—nuances that are not always apparent to beginners or that perhaps are simply glossed over. These include a vivid account of the awkwardness of the first few treatment sessions and how many clients really need a lot of support, encouragement, and concrete information during this period in order to help them get through it. For example, clients are often very anxious and tense during the first session, but may not trust the therapist well enough at this point to share these feelings. Thus therapists need to be aware of nonverbal cues that communicate these feelings and be willing to provide a lot of "hand-holding" during this time.

France also depicted the struggle of preparing topics to discuss at treatment sessions and some of the other artificiality of the treatment process itself. She described one aspect of psychotherapy in this way, "A problem experienced by many . . . is the difficulty of attending at a specific time and day for the purpose of discussing highly emotionally charged subjects for which one might not feel at all in the mood, or which, conversely, one had desperately wanted to discuss between sessions, but had by now lost sight of" (France, 1988, p. 155). In addition to these, France discussed at great length some of the potential negative outcomes of psychotherapy, which in her case included a protracted period of depression, which she attributed to her treatment experiences. She then described from her own viewpoint how some of these counterproductive consequences might have been avoided. Lastly, France discussed some of the fears that clients bring to therapy. In her own case, these included the fear of becoming too dependent on the therapist and the fear that her defenses would be destroyed. Unfortunately, both of these turned to fruition, and she explored how these might have been avoided as well.

Client Fears

Pipes and Davenport (1990) also discussed at some length the issue of potential client fears. An important point that these authors make is that many clients enter therapy because of failed relationships. Thus, many of their fears center on the unknown client–therapist relationship, which they are about to begin. This inevitably brings us to the issue of transference.

Although it can be a very complicated feature of psychotherapy, transference can be defined in very simple terms as the repetition of previously learned feelings, attitudes, impulses, or desires in relation to the therapist. Suffice to say that the consequences of transference are often the basis for what a client says and does in treatment, and frequently these behaviors offer a window to their personality styles and nuances of their interpersonal interactions. Although my own view of transference is somewhat different and less central than how it is typically viewed or explained by classical psychoanalysts, I believe it remains a critical element of psychotherapy. Contrary to classical psychoanalysis, I see transference operating similarly to our other pre-established cognitive schemes. For example, in terms of new clients, at least some and perhaps many of the fears or expectations that they have of their therapist are likely to be based on their previous important relationships. Thus a female client who has been repeatedly betrayed or abandoned by the men in her life is likely to hold some of these same expectations of a male therapist. Obviously these issues must be addressed and resolved if any progress is to be made in therapy. Unfortunately, the interest in transference issues has declined rapidly with the demise of Freudian theory (at least in its classical sense) and the advent of newer forms of therapy. A thorough discussion of transference is beyond the scope of this chapter. For these reasons, I encourage the reader to further explore this potentially useful subject matter (see Freud, 1912; Stone, 1995; Strean, 1990; Storr, 1979; France, 1988; Pipes & Davenport, 1990; Cullari, 1996b).

Based on their own psychotherapy experiences, Pipes and Davenport (1990) discussed a number of potential fears that clients may bring to their first few sessions or that may emerge as therapy progresses. Many of these are related to the client's perceived expectations of psychotherapy or the therapist. Some of the common questions clients bring to therapy include:

1. Will I be treated more like a case than a person?
2. Will the therapist be honest with me?
3. Will my problems be taken seriously?
4. Will the therapist share their own values with me?
5. Will the therapist truly understand my problems?
6. Will the therapist be competent?
7. Will I be pressured to say or do certain things?
8. Will I become dependent on the therapist and then later be abandoned?
9. Will I become engulfed by the therapist?
10. Will the sessions be confidential?
11. Will my self-disclosures lead the therapist to think that I am a bad person?
12. Will the therapist think that I'm more disturbed than I really am?
13. Will the therapist find out things that I really do not want to know?
14. Will I lose control of my emotions?
15. Will the therapy process disrupt my other personal relationships?

Pipes and Davenport give an extensive account of how these potential fears can be managed by new therapists, and I urge the interested reader to carefully review their suggestions. In general, depending on the specific situation, client fears can be handled in a number of ways, such as using a pretherapy orientation or perhaps by simply explaining the general process of psychotherapy. However, therapists need to be aware of what specific types of concerns the client has about the psychotherapy process before these can be addressed. Often, clients may be unlikely to divulge these spontaneously, so the therapist may need to make direct inquiries. For example, some of the more common fears can be described and the client can provide feedback to the therapist about whether these are pertinent. In situations in which the client seems overly anxious or apprehensive, the point can be made that the fact that they have decided to begin therapy is a sign that they are ready to explore some of their important fears and concerns. By addressing and resolving these issues, as well as other treatment stumbling blocks, early, many potential dropouts may be avoided.

Important Qualities of Therapists

Moving beyond client fears, one of the most exhaustive books dealing with the treatment experience of clients was published by Mearns and Dryden (1990). In the first chapter of this book, McLeod (1990) described the results of a comprehensive literature review and summarized the findings of a large number of studies related to client experiences, including some of the studies that have already been described (a similar review with comparable findings was completed by Elliott and James, 1989). Taken as a whole, the factors that clients found most useful in therapy are consistent with what has already been reported. These include increasing clients' ability to solve problems; having someone to talk to who is interested in them; having a therapist who offers encouragement and reassurance; and having a therapist who understands, instills hope, and promotes self-understanding.

The major conditions identified by clients as hindering therapy are their own inclinations to maintain silence and avoid talking about certain areas; their inability to cooperate with the therapist or make a connection with the therapist; and their perceptions that the therapist used the wrong interventions or said things that were inconsistent with the clients' real feelings. McLeod suggested that clients generally view the *process* of therapy (having someone to talk to, being able to trust the therapist, and so on) as being more important than the specific therapeutic techniques (for example, systematic desensitization) that are used (see also Drozd & Goldfried, 1996; Gershefski, Arnkoff, & Glass, 1996). McLeod's review also corroborated previous studies that suggested that clients want more specific advice and recommendations from therapy than they actually receive.

Most of the studies reviewed thus far suggest that it is unlikely that clients begin treatment with explicit expectations of therapists or expectations for particular interventions. In fact, many clients come to therapy not really knowing what to expect. It appears that the more crucial question facing the client is this: Can this particular therapist help me at this particular time? Whether justified or not, clients tend to resolve this issue relatively early in the treatment process, and their conclusions often become the steering points of therapy from then on. In addressing this concern, Mearns and Dryden (1990) suggested that from a client's perspective, four qualities of therapists seem to be especially important. These are transparency, commitment, engagement, and containment. While there is considerable overlap among these four qualities, each will be discussed separately.

Of the four, transparency seems to be most important in terms of client satisfaction and, perhaps, outcome. The transparency of the therapist relates to the client's being able to see beyond the role of the counselor to the real person underneath. This includes coming across as "real" or natural, as opposed to someone who simply knows and uses a number of therapeutic techniques. Therapists who are too abstract or technical tend to increase rather than reduce the anxiety level of new clients, who often view such persons as cold, detached, and uncaring. In short, clients want a therapist who is human. It should be obvious by now that although treatment techniques are important, most clients find the personal touch more significant. In this regard, I do not think that therapists have to worry too much about being replaced by robots or computers any time soon. It would not be an overstatement to say that to a large extent, therapeutic success depends a great deal on the interpersonal connectiveness between client and therapist. Of course, sometimes this requires the therapist to show his or her own warts and wrinkles. In commenting about this, Mearns and Dryden (1990) proposed that by letting the client view them as a real human being, therapists may lose some of their inferred social power, but simultaneously gain the more important client's respect for them as people. In my opinion, this underlying referent power is what cements the client–therapist relationship and becomes the driving force of successful psychotherapy.

In terms of commitment, clients need to be assured that the therapist will be there when they need them the most and will remain available over the long haul. My own experience suggests that this is especially true of clients with serious mental illnesses, such as schizophrenia and borderline personality disorders. Again, many times this need is born out of the client's prior experiences of failed relationships or history of abandonment. There are a number of ways that the therapist can communicate this sense of commitment to the client, such as the personal involvement just described, being available between sessions, and making sure that the client understands that this commitment continues even after treatment has terminated. Naturally, one needs to be a bit careful about this accessibility, but most clients will not abuse these opportunities. Commitment also means that therapists must be flexible and be willing to negotiate boundaries. In my opinion, flexible boundaries are not an option for successful psychotherapy, they are an absolute necessity (Gold & Cherry, 1997). I believe that at times our interpretations of the ethical codes of psychologists and other mental health professionals are even more rigid than they were designed to be, and that psychotherapists need to be less paranoid about following these to the exact letter.

The third quality of engagement is defined by Mearns and Dryden (1990) as the willingness of therapists to work within the frame of reference of the client rather than their own. Of course, readers may recognize this as being similar to Carl Rogers's definition of "accurate empathy" (Rogers, 1951, pp. 28–29). Briefly, this implies that therapists must minimize their own biases, remain as open and flexible as possible and try to experience the world as the client does. This does not simply refer to clarification or reflection of feelings, but rather to trying to understand the client's universe without confounding your own thoughts, biases, and idiosyncrasies within this interpretation. This again underscores the importance of fully understanding the feelings of clients, which has already been mentioned. Unfortunately, this tends to be among the most difficult aspects of psychotherapy to learn and carry out effectively.

The last quality of containment has been described the least in the psychotherapy literature outside of psychoanalytic studies. It implies a client's sense of safety, protection, and being "held" in a therapeutic alliance. However this "holding" environment also includes the consistency and stability of the therapist and the treatment process itself. Sometimes this containment may be as simple as meeting with the client at the same day, at the same time, and in the same treatment room each week, but often it involves the art of knowing how to structure the entire treatment process itself and when to tighten or loosen the process.

From the clients' perspective, containment also includes the sense that they can express their thoughts and feelings without fear. This is one of the factors that differentiates psychotherapy from just talking with a friend. Psychotherapy offers the opportunity to divulge information in an environment that is theoretically safe and eliminates the chance that the information will be revealed to persons whom we do not want to have it. This, in turn, contributes to the clients' sense of security. In the ideal therapeutic setting, clients can say (and to some extent do) whatever they want without risking ridicule and without the fear of being rejected. This sense of security seems to be linked to favorable outcome as well. For example, Orlinsky, Grawe, and Parks (1994) noted that "the quality of the patient's participation in therapy stands out as the most important determinant of outcome" (p. 361).

Consequently, it appears that clients' ability to trust the therapist and their ability to "open up" is a key ingredient of what clients eventually come to expect from treatment and probably of successful therapy itself. I say "eventually" here because I do not think this expectation is typically in the client's awareness before actually beginning therapy. For example, in the current study, only a small percentage of clients reported a fear of trusting the therapist before initiating therapy. However, as France (1988) pointed out, this often presents a dilemma because many people go to psychotherapy precisely because they have problems trusting anyone. For many clients, their life experiences have taught them to expect rejection or betrayal, and opening up to someone they hardly know can be very difficult. Thus, as Storr (1979) noted, clients only reveal their most intimate feelings to therapists if they can sincerely trust that person, and when no doubts, suspicions, or fears remain. In this case, even though self-disclosure is a key ingredient of therapy, we should not expect clients to automatically feel comfortable confiding in us.

Of course, the next logical question becomes, How can we as therapists instill a sense of trust between ourselves and our clients? My own experience suggests that getting clients to trust us is based almost entirely on the therapist's promotion of nontechnical aspects of therapy such as honesty and spontaneity, communicating warmth and respect, showing genuine interest, and using appropriate self-disclosures. I also believe that it is important at times for both client and therapist just to be themselves. Likewise, I agree with Strupp (1999) that the positive feeling we have for our clients needs to be communicated to them, but this does not necessarily always have to be done verbally. Often it is our nonverbal behavior, or the seemingly unimportant things we do, that promotes this trust. For example, one of my clients once commented that one of the most significant aspects of my treatment with her was that I always seemed to be in a good mood. This apparently allowed her to be much more open and less defensive in our sessions. Typically, when a mutual trust between client and therapist is achieved, it is usually salient and discernible to both parties, and, of course, it is often the factor that cements the client–therapist relationship.

Recent Developments

More recently, Howe (1993) discussed a number of important issues related to these four qualities in a book devoted entirely to what clients have to say about their experiences in psychotherapy. Howe concluded that clients' experiences with psychotherapy can be summarized by three principal themes: accept me, understand me, and talk with me. A section of his book is devoted to each of these. Most of the material he presented has already been addressed in one way or another in this narrative and thus will not be repeated. However, I do encourage the reader to obtain and examine this interesting and extensive account of clients' experiences.

The interest in how clients experience psychotherapy has continued to the present. While the following is not an exhaustive list, other relatively recent studies of client experiences in psychotherapy have been published by Rennie (1992), Conran and Love (1993), Zukowski (1995), Stalikas and Fitzpatrick (1995), Conte, Ratto, Clutz, and Karasu (1995), and McClintock (1999). With the exception of David Rennie's study, these reports have basically used the same research techniques (e.g., client questionnaires, written reports, or posttherapy client interviews), and found results similar to what has already been discussed. In Rennie's study, the client replayed an audio or videotaped session of therapy that was just completed in order to facilitate his or her experiences with this encounter. This novel technique resulted in some very interesting findings. First, Rennie reported that clients may be much more in control of the therapy session than therapists perceive. Secondly, much of the "process" of psychotherapy seems to involve a dialogue that the client is having with him- or herself, of which the therapist is often not cognizant. Furthermore, it appears that clients usually have plans for therapy and strategies for achieving them that may or may not be consistent with those of the therapist.

Rennie gave the label *reflexivity* to the quality of the client's self-awareness and self-control of topics explored in therapy. He pointed out that much of what occurs in therapy (at least in terms of the client) is covert and thus difficult to study objectively or understand. This holds some obvious implications for psychotherapy research. Related to this, much of what clients say in the therapy hour may not be what they are really thinking. Perhaps a more important finding is that even with direct questioning, clients are not likely to disclose their discontent with the therapy process or therapist. This is especially true in cases where there is a weak client/therapist alliance and again underscores the importance of fostering a trusting relationship between client and therapist. Of course, ultimately, the role of reflexivity is significant because it is likely to have a major impact on outcome. Rennie's illuminating research strategy is likely to produce further practical findings in the future.

Current Survey

Although the various studies cited teach us a great deal, they tend to have several drawbacks. First, many of the studies are dated, and virtually all of them were done before managed care became a major force in this profession. Secondly, many of the studies had relatively small sample sizes or were done retrospectively. In addition, many of the major studies were done outside the United States, which may lessen some of the generalizability of the findings. For these reasons, the current study was designed and carried out. The general results of the survey are presented in Appendix 4.A. The following sections will present a summary of the findings and the implications of these for psychotherapy practice.

The Sample

Ninety-eight psychotherapy clients completed the questionnaire. A look at the demographics of this sample of respondents shows that about three-quarters of them were female. The average age was 42, and about 60 percent of them were married or currently living with a significant other. As a group, the sample was well educated with about half of them either having a college degree or at least some undergraduate training. In addition, about 25 percent of them had graduate training or a graduate degree. The average length of treatment was about five months, and most of these clients had attended at least 12 sessions. Almost 60 percent of these clients had previously been in treatment, so as a whole these were persons who had some fairly extensive experience with psychotherapy. It was interesting that 17 percent of these clients had not told their friends about being in therapy; it appears that the stigma associated with psychotherapy still remains. It was also noteworthy that about 10 percent of this sample did not know the terminal educational degrees of their therapists.

In 25 percent of the cases, the main condition that brought the client to therapy was depression. Marital problems were the second leading reason for treatment, followed by the existence of a family member with a mental or physical disorder. Anxiety disorders accounted for only 7 percent of the cases despite the fact that many studies show that these are the most common mental health conditions in the general population. A chi square showed significant differences between men and women in terms of their presenting problems. The percentage of men and women who presented with depression, anxiety, or marital problems was very similar. However, men made up all of the cases of sexual disorders, while women made up all the cases for eating disorders, physical disorders, or relationship problems. In addition, women were more likely to be in therapy due to the existence of a mental or physical illness of a family member.

In the majority of the cases, the client had had the presenting condition or problem for about a year before actually starting treatment. This was despite the fact that virtually all the subjects said that this condition was causing a moderate or extreme amount of emotional distress and over 80 percent said that this condition was interfering with their normal functioning level. The two major factors that delayed the subjects from starting therapy sooner were (1) the cost of therapy (25 percent) and (2) embarrassment about their problems (20 percent). Some of the other common responses were that the subjects did not think the problem was serious, they thought that they could handle the problem alone, or they did not think psychotherapy could help them with the problem.

When asked about any fears they had before starting therapy, only about one-quarter said they had none. Of those who did have some fears, the most frequent answers were fear that the treatment would not be successful (19 percent) fear of self-disclosure or reporting personal information to a stranger (19 percent), and fear of the stigma associated with treatment (11 percent). However, virtually none of the subjects said that these fears were actually experienced during the treatment process. The important point here is that most clients do have some fears upon entering therapy. As discussed, the therapist should inquire about and process these during the first session. In addition, it may comfort the individual to know that the majority of clients find these fears to be unfounded.

The Results

In terms of the usefulness of psychotherapy, 92 percent of the subjects said that their treatment was either extremely or moderately helpful, and 97 percent said that they would recommend psychotherapy to their friends or family members. Clients who believed that psychotherapy was useful for them were asked to rate on a 1 to 10 point scale the various components of therapy that they perceived were most useful. The categories with the highest ratings were the therapists' ability to understand their problem (mean rating of 9.5), the therapists' willingness to listen to them (9.2), and the therapists' communication skills (9.2). The categories with the lowest ratings were the therapists' being the same gender as the client (5.5), the therapists' training level (6.3), and therapists' theoretical orientation (6.5). When asked to select only one category that was the most important, almost half of the sample chose the therapist's ability to understand their problem. This is consistent with the results of previous studies reported above and underscores the importance of trainees learning generic counseling skills, such as listening, clarification, and empathy. It also reinforces the idea that most clients find these processes to be more important that specific treatment interventions.

Clients were also asked how many therapy sessions it took before they noticed a real improvement in their condition. The overwhelming response was one (93 percent). This is interesting in light of research that shows that the modal number of treatment sessions for all psychotherapy clients as a whole is one and has implications for brief therapy as well (Talmon, 1990; Cooper, 1998). As many people have pointed out recently, with the advent of managed care, brief therapy is no longer simply an option—it is often mandated. On the other hand, when asked how many treatment meetings they would like to have if insurance or money were not an issue, the most frequent response was 20 sessions. In looking at the other responses to this question, no client selected one to three sessions and only four clients selected a number of sessions below ten. On the other hand, about 10 percent of the clients would like to have between 90 and 100 sessions! (See Lowry and Ross, 1997, for therapist perceptions of this issue). Of course, it is difficult to make any conclusions here because information from clients who dropped out of therapy is lacking.

One if the major goals of this questionnaire was to find out what expectations clients have from therapy and whether these are being met. The most frequent responses to the question of clients' expectations from psychotherapy were the following: receiving specific advice on how to change or improve their problem (96 percent); gaining greater self-understanding (87 percent); helping the client cope with life (87 percent); and having someone to talk to about their problem or condition (82 percent). Seventy-five percent of the clients also expected a reduction in symptoms, and this expectation had the highest rating in terms of having the greatest importance to the client (a rating of 9 on a 1 to 10 scale). This was followed by the expectations of getting specific advice (importance rating of 8.9), gaining greater self-understanding (8.8), and having someone to talk to about their problems (8.8).

FIGURE 4.1 What Clients Expect and Want Most from Psychotherapy

- Acceptance
- A feeling of safety and security
- Support
- Guidance
- Consistency
- A therapist who understands them
- The chance to talk to someone in a safe environment and without fear of repercussion
- A therapist who is warm and friendly
- A therapist whom they can trust and rely on in times of greatest need
- A flexible treatment program
- A therapist who likes them
- A therapist who is encouraging and reassuring
- A therapist who is competent but "human"
- A therapist who treats the client with respect
- A therapist who treats the client as a real person and as an important individual
- A therapist who gives pertinent and timely feedback
- Suggestions to help solve or cope with problems
- A good client–therapist fit

The expectations that were perceived to have been met most by the majority of the clients were gaining support and reassurance (89 percent), having someone to talk to (88 percent), and helping the client cope with life (69 percent). The greatest percentage of unmet expectations were a change in personality (42 percent unmet, although this was not a common expectation), an improvement in relationships (42 percent unmet), a reduction in symptoms (36 percent unmet), and receiving specific advice (30 percent unmet). The responses to this question were interesting in that although the majority of the clients found psychotherapy very helpful, a large percentage of their most important expectations were unmet even after an average of 12 sessions. On the other hand, this is not to say that treatment expectations are unimportant. It is likely that many clients who drop out of therapy (who are not represented on this survey) do so at least partly because their expectations are not being met.

FIGURE 4.2 Client Perceptions of the Most Positive Aspects or Effects of Psychotherapy

- A therapist who understands my true feelings and my problem
- Improving my self-esteem
- Learning to cope with my problems
- Feeling better
- Gaining a sense of hope
- Obtaining an objective point of view
- Simply talking to someone about my problem
- Gaining insight
- Receiving encouragement and reassurance
- Having someone to listen to me
- Helping me restore important relationships
- Achieving emotional relief (catharsis)
- Receiving guidance and support
- Helping me set realistic goals and expectations

In response to the open-ended question of what clients thought were the most positive aspects of therapy, there were many diverse responses. Many clients gave more than one answer. However, the most frequent response, which was given by about one-fourth of the sample, was a better understanding of themselves and their problem. The other most frequent responses were an improvement in their self-esteem, learning how to cope with their problem, relief from symptoms, and having someone to listen to them. Each of these were cited by about 20 percent of the clients and were generally consistent with their expectations for psychotherapy. These factors were similar to the findings of Elliott and James (1989), who conducted a review of the literature of clients' experiences of psychotherapy.

In terms of the most negative aspects of psychotherapy, the most frequent responses were the time involved in the process, having to deal with the past, the periods of no perceived progress, cost or insurance hassles, and having to share personal information with others. In the related question of what were the most difficult aspects of therapy, the most common response given by 35 percent of the sample was reliving old memories. The second most frequent response was that of the clients' talking about themselves or their condition (23 percent). The responses to these questions tend to highlight some of the paradoxical aspects of psychotherapy. In achieving some of the most positive aspects of psychotherapy, such as clients understanding their problems or having someone to talk to, they must often relive the past or self-disclose a lot of personal information to someone who initially is a stranger. Yet I believe an important point here for new therapists is not to rush clients into divulging a lot of personal information or reliving painful memories too soon, but rather to phase these in slowly. My own experience with training new therapists is that often beginners try to collect too much information too quickly.

Another frequently cited negative aspect of therapy was its cost. Recall from a previous question that one-quarter of the subjects said that money was also the primary factor in delaying the onset of their therapy. Previous studies on the effects of the cost of treatment

FIGURE 4.3 Client Perceptions of the Most Negative Aspects of Psychotherapy

- Time involvement
- Dealing with the past
- Periods of no progress
- Having to share personal or painful information with someone new
- Cost of treatment
- Making changes
- Not having enough time in sessions
- Facing personal shortcomings
- An inflexible therapist
- Having to be in therapy when you really do not feel like being there
- Having a therapist who is "just doing their job"
- Having a therapist who is too passive or too nondirective
- Having a therapist who talks too much and does not really listen
- Having a therapist use interventions without clearly explaining their rationale
- Having to accept the fact that psychotherapy is a long and arduous process
- Therapists who appear to be uninterested, distant, critical, hostile, or too authoritarian

on various aspects of psychotherapy are inconsistent and inconclusive (see Cullari, 1996b, Chapter 4 for a review). In the current sample, only 16 percent of the clients paid entirely out of pocket for their treatment. Interestingly, these clients were more likely to rate their treatment as extremely useful (80 percent) than other clients (60 percent each for those whose treatment was paid by insurance or insurance and co-pay, and only 28 percent for those who had other payment arrangements).

Despite some of the negative aspects of managed care, it has probably allowed many clients to utilize psychotherapy who otherwise would not have done so because of cost. In the current sample, 57 percent of the clients were covered by a managed care company. Almost the same percentage of clients rated their service as highly positive or positive (34 percent) as those who rated it negative or highly negative (38 percent). The factor they liked best about managed care was the low co-pay (50 percent) or lower overall costs of coverage compared to other insurance plans (21 percent). About half of the sample cited the factors they liked least about managed care as the restrictions in selecting providers and limits on the number of treatment sessions. When asked whether their current insurance coverage provided adequate mental health benefits, 44 percent replied yes and 50 percent said no. Of those who said no, the most frequently cited problems were insufficient coverage or restrictions in the number of treatment sessions. It is clear from this and some of the other responses to this questionnaire that if money were no object, many clients would prefer to attend more sessions than the commonly reported average of 4 to 8 meetings.

It may be reassuring to our profession that the most frequent response to the question of recommendations for how their therapy sessions should be changed was "none" (60 percent of responses). The second most frequent answer to this question was adjusting the time and number of treatment sessions to suit the client's needs (14 percent). In this and some of the other open-ended questions, some clients commented on the rigid boundaries of psychotherapy that many therapists follow. This is, of course, a very controversial issue in the field. With my own students, I often argue that beginning therapists should be very conservative about boundary issues, at least in the first few years. Later, with adequate experience, all good therapists will discover which areas they can become more flexible with and which ones they cannot. Often this depends on the characteristics of the client and the presenting problem. As already stated, I believe that because of the threat of lawsuits and other legal concerns, many therapists are too rigid about boundaries. On the other hand, loose boundaries have the potential to place the therapist on a slippery slope. This is an issue that should be thoroughly addressed in supervision.

There were many other responses to this question, such as suggestions about the therapist's being less concerned with time or reviewing the last session before starting a new one, but none of these were cited frequently. As a general rule, it appears that the clients in this sample were satisfied with the treatment they were receiving.

In response to the open-ended question of designing the "perfect" therapist, the most frequent response was someone who is a good listener (41 percent). This response is a theme that was repeated throughout this questionnaire. Other common responses were a therapist who is empathetic, understanding, and has expertise in the client's presenting problem. Other responses to this question are given in Figure 4.4. In general, the replies to this question are consistent with the idea that clients find the personal characteristics of the therapist much more important than technical or professional ones.

FIGURE 4.4 Client Perceptions of the Characteristics of the Perfect Therapist

Good listener	Easy to talk to
Empathetic	"Human"
Understanding	Easy going
Compassionate	Trustworthy
Broad knowledge base	Kind
Honest and open	Caring
Truthful	Spontaneous
Intelligent	Good communicator
Reliable	Perceptive
Concerned	Varied life experiences
Competent	Has the ability to steer the treatment sessions into pertinent topics or issues
Self-confident	Has the ability to put the client at ease
Good sense of humor	Shows true concern for the client
Objective	Provides straightforward feedback
Nonjudgmental	Avoids psychological jargon
Supportive	Has the ability to understand the client's true feelings
Dependable	Interested in me as a person
Friendly	Takes time to explain the process of psychotherapy

Clients were also asked to describe anything that the therapist said or did that was most significant for them in their treatment. There were many responses to this question, and there was no single major pattern or theme. The most frequent responses were providing positive feedback about the client or their progress, providing reassurance, helping the client get to the root of problems, validating the client's feelings, and acceptance. There were almost as many different responses to this question as there were subjects. My own experience suggests that on an individual basis it is difficult or impossible to predict what exactly will have the greatest impact with a particular client. With some cases, a spontaneous and seemingly trivial remark will be significant, and, at the same time, more carefully planned interventions may have little or no effect. This is one of the reasons I do not generally support the notion of manualized psychotherapy. (See Gold & Stricker, 1998 and Drozd & Goldfried, 1996 for a review.) While this type of treatment holds some advantages, unless it is done well, it holds the potential to be perceived as rigid and artificial by clients. The overwhelming responses to this questionnaire and the other studies reviewed in this chapter suggest that clients usually do not want this type of intervention. This is not to suggest that structured techniques are not useful in psychotherapy, but that their use has to be tempered. See Chapter 6 for a further discussion of this issue.

The chapter concludes with a set of general recommendations for new therapists (Figure 4.5). These are based on the previous studies discussed in the chapter, the findings of the questionnaire, and the author's own treatment experiences.

FIGURE 4.5 Simple Recommendations for New Therapists

Be human.

Instill trust.

Demonstrate in some obvious way your commitment to the client.

Be flexible. Do not be totally fettered by professional boundary issues.

Instill hope in the client and communicate this sense of hope in the first session.

Listen to the client.

Treat the client with respect.

Give the client timely feedback.

Go slowly. Be sure you have a good understanding of your client and his or her problems before you proceed.

When in doubt, just be yourself.

Show the client that you are interested in him or her as a person.

Be realistic. You will not be successful with every client you treat.

Make sure that your treatment goals and those of the client are compatible.

Above all, maintain your humility. You should consider the practice of psychotherapy to be a privilege rather than just a job.

Make sure you pay close attention to the client's feelings and emotional distress.

Be sure to explain to the client what you are doing and why you are doing it.

REFERENCES

Allen, L. (1990). A client's experience of failure. In D. Mearns and W. Dryden (Eds.), *Experiences of counseling in action*. London: Sage.

Conran, T., & Love, J. (1993). Client voices. Unspeakable theories and unknowable experiences. *Journal of Systemic Therapies, 12,* 1–19.

Conte, H. R., Ratto, R., Clutz, K., & Karasu, T. B. (1995). Determinants of outpatients' satisfaction with therapists: Relation to outcome. *Journal of Psychotherapy Research and Practice, 4*(1), 43–51.

Cooper, J. F. (1998). Brief therapy in clinical practice. In S. Cullari (Ed.), *Foundations of clinical psychology.* Boston: Allyn & Bacon.

Cullari, S. (1996a). Psychotherapy practice questionnaire. *The Independent Practitioner, 16*(3), 140–142.

Cullari, S. (1996b). *Treatment resistance: A guide for practitioners.* Boston: Allyn & Bacon.

Drozd, J. F., & Goldfried, M. R. (1996). A critical evaluation of the state-of-the-art in psychotherapy outcome research. *Psychotherapy, 33*(2), 171–180.

Elliott, R., & James, E. (1989). Varieties of client experiences in psychotherapy: A review of the literature. *Clinical Psychology Review, 9,* 443–467.

Feifel, H., & Eells, J. (1963). Patients and therapists assess the same psychotherapy. *Journal of Consulting Psychology, 27,* 310–318.

France, A. (1988). *Consuming psychotherapy.* London: Free Association Books.

Freud, S. (1912). The dynamics of transference. In J. Strachey (Ed.), *The standard edition* (Vol. 12). London: Hogarth Press.

Gershefski, J. J., Arnkoff, D. B., Glass, C. R., & Elkin, I. (1996). Clients' perceptions of treatment for depression: I. Helpful aspects. *Psychotherapy Research. 6*(4), 233–247.

Goin, M. K., Yamamoto, J., & Silverman, J. (1965). Therapy congruent with class-linked expectations. *Archives of General Psychiatry, 13,* 133–137.

Gold, J. R., & Stricker, G. (1998). Treating the individual. In S. Cullari (Ed.), *Foundations of clinical psychology.* Boston: Allyn & Bacon.

Gold, S. N., & Cherry, E. W. (1997). The therapeutic frame: On the need for flexibility. *Journal of Contemporary Psychotherapy, 27,* 147–155.

Grierson, M. (1990). A client's experience of success. In D. Mearns and W. Dryden (Eds.), *Experiences of counseling in action.* London: Sage.

Herman, S. M. (1998). The relationship between therapist-client modality similarity and psychotherapy outcome. *Journal of Psychotherapy Practice and Outcome, 7*(1), 56–64.

Howe, D. (1993). *On being a client.* London: Sage.

Lowry, J. L., & Ross, M. J. (1997). Expectations of psychotherapy duration: How long should psychotherapy last? *Psychotherapy, 34*(3), 272–277.

Maluccio, A. N. (1979). *Learning from clients.* New York: Free Press.

Mayer, J. E., & Timms, N. (1970). *The client speaks.* New York: Atherton Press.

McClintock, E. (1999). *Room for change. Empowering possibilities for therapists and clients.* Boston: Allyn and Bacon.

McLeod, J. (1990). The client's experience of counselling and psychotherapy: A review of the research literature. In D. Mearns and W. Dryden (Eds.), *Experiences of counseling in action.* London: Sage.

Mearns, D., & Dryden, W. (1990). *Experiences of counseling in action.* London: Sage.

Morrow-Bradley, C., & Elliott, R. (1986). Utilization of psychotherapy research by practicing psychotherapists. *American Psychologist, 41*(2), 188–197.

Murphy, P., Cramer, D., & Lillie, F. J. (1984). The relationship between curative factors perceived by patients in their psychotherapy and treatment outcome: An exploratory study. *British Journal of Medical Psychology, 57,* 187–192.

Oldfield, S. (1983). *The counseling relationship: A study of the client's experience.* London: Routledge & Kegan Paul.

Orlinsky, D. E., Grawe, K., & Parks, B. K. (1994). Process and outcome in psychotherapy: Noch einmal. In A. E. Bergin & S. L. Garfield (Eds.), *Handbook of psychotherapy and behavior change.* New York: Wiley.

Pipes, R. B., & Davenport, D. S. (1990). *Introduction to psychotherapy.* Englewood Cliffs, NJ: Prentice Hall.

Rennie, D. L. (1992). Qualitative analysis of the client's experience of psychotherapy: The unfolding of reflexivity. In S. G. Toukmanian and D. L. Rennie (Eds.), *Psychotherapy process research: Paradigmatic and narrative approaches.* Newbury Park, CA. Sage.

Rogers, C. R. (1951). *Client-centered therapy.* Boston: Houghton Mifflin.

Stalikas, A., & Fitzpatrick, M. (1995). Client good moments: An intensive analysis of a single session. *Canadian Journal of Counselling, 29*(2), 160–175.

Sloane, R. B., Staples, F. R., Cristol, A. H., Yorkson, N. J., & Whipple, K. (1975). *Psychotherapy versus behavior therapy.* Cambridge, MA: Harvard University Press.

Stone, L. (1995). Transference. In B. E. Moore & B. D. Fine (Eds.), *Psychoanalysis: The major concepts.* New Haven: Yale University Press.

Storr, A. (1979). *The art of psychotherapy.* London: Secker & Warburg and William Heinemann Medical Books.

Strean, H. S. (1990). *Resolving resistances in psychotherapy.* New York: Brunner/Mazel.

Strupp, H. H., Fox, R. E., & Lessler, K. (1969). *Patients view their psychotherapy.* Baltimore: Johns Hopkins Press.

Strupp, H. H. (1999). Essential ingredients of a helpful therapist. *Psychotherapy Bulletin, 34*(1), 34–36.

Talmon, M. (1990). *Single-session therapy.* San Francisco: Jossey-Bass.

Wright, J. H., & Davis, D. (1994). The therapeutic relationship in cognitive-behavioral therapy: Patient perceptions and therapist responses. *Cognitive and Behavioral Practice, 1,* 25–45.

Zukowski, E. M. (1995). The aesthetic experience of the client in psychotherapy. *Journal of Humanistic Psychology, 35*(1), 42–56.

FOR FURTHER READING

Kottler, J. A. (1992). *Compassionate therapy.* San Francisco: Jossey-Bass.

A very readable book describing many useful aspects of psychotherapy including how to deal with difficult clients.

Meichenbaum, D., & Turk, D. C. (1987). *Facilitating treatment resistance.* New York: Plenum Press.

A comprehensive look at the whole issue of adherence and compliance in psychotherapy as it relates to both client and therapist.

Zaro, J. S., Barach, R., Nedelman, D. J., & Dreiblatt, I. S. (1977). *A guide for beginning psychotherapists.* New York: Cambridge University Press.

Although somewhat dated, this book covers the basics of what every new therapist should know.

The Journal of Clinical Psychology devotes an entire issue on the research of psychotherapy (Volume *55,* No. 12, December, 1999.)

This issue addresses many important aspects of doing research about psychotherapy, including many factors related to the client.

APPENDIX **4.A**

Survey of Clients' Attitudes toward Their Therapy and Their Therapists

The following is a copy of the questionnaire that was completed by the psychotherapy clients accompanied by the general results. The responses to the open-ended questions are given in the order of highest frequency of responses to lowest. In order to save space on the following summary, only the most frequent responses are given to the open-ended questions. Note that where listed, *m* stands for the mean.

Purpose of the Questionnaire and Directions

Dear Client:

Thank you for agreeing to complete this form. The purpose of this questionnaire is to evaluate the general process of psychotherapy and to get information about what clients want most from psychotherapy. In order to do this, we would like to get feedback concerning your experience with psychotherapy. The information you provide will be used for a research project and may ultimately help us improve the whole psychotherapy process. This study is being conducted by Salvatore Cullari, Ph.D., who is a clinical psychologist and Chairman of the Psychology Department at Lebanon Valley College. Dr. Cullari is not formally associated with your therapist or this psychotherapy practice and the information you provide will *not* be used to evaluate your therapist or this practice. In fact, your therapist will not have access to this form. Although the information you provide will be summarized and possibly published at a later time, no identifying information will be revealed.

Please read each question carefully and answer as best as you can. Please be as honest as possible. Please do not skip any questions. **Do not put your name on this or any form that you return to Dr. Cullari.** After you have completed the questionnaire, please enclose it in the self-addressed envelope that was provided and drop in any mailbox. No postage is necessary. **DO NOT RETURN THE QUESTIONNAIRE TO YOUR THERAPIST OR OFFICE STAFF.** The information you provide *will not* be disclosed to your therapist or office staff member. If you have any questions about this study, please contact Dr. Cullari at 717-867-6197 or Cullari@lvc.edu (e-mail).

BASIC INFORMATION ABOUT YOURSELF

Gender: male 24% female 76%

Marital status: single 26% married 46% separated 14% divorced 8%
widow 2% not married but living with someone 3%

Age: m=42 (range from 14-66); there was only one subject below age 18.

Number of children: m=1

Education: less than high school 2% High school grad 19%
some college 22% college grad 33% graduate training 5%
Masters Degree 15% Doctoral Degree 3%

How long have you been in psychotherapy/counseling? (Specify number, for example, 0 years, 2 months, 2 weeks) years ____ months ____ weeks ____. m=5 months

How many total number of therapy sessions have you attended thus far? mode=12

Were you previously in psychotherapy/counseling?
(e.g., prior to seeing your current therapist) yes 59% no 41%

Are you currently taking any medications for emotional issues? yes 45% no 55%

If yes, please list the names of all *current* medications that are used for emotional issues.
majority (over 90%) taking SSRIs

Was this medication use first recommended by your current therapist?
yes 37% no 63% (I was taking medication prior to starting this therapy.)

Have you told your friends that you are undergoing psychotherapy? yes 83% no 17%

If no, please explain why. Most frequent response: stigma/shame

Have you ever been hospitalized for any emotional problems? yes 15% no 85%

If yes, how many times? mode=1

What is your current living situation? live with husband/wife 46%
live with parents 6% live with child/children 9% live alone 25%
live in boarding home 0% other (please specify below)
12% with significant other

I live in (check one): a city 36% a town 34%
rural area 20% other (specify) 9% (suburbs)

Is your therapy on a voluntary basis 99% or required by another agency 1% (e.g., court, etc.)?

Is your therapist a psychologist 93% social worker 5% professional counselor ____
marriage & family counselor ____ other (specify)? 2%

Does your therapist have a Doctoral Degree 78% Masters Degree 10%
other? 1% don't know 10%

(continued)

INFORMATION ABOUT YOUR THERAPY SESSIONS

1. What was the *main* problem or condition that brought you to psychotherapy? (please check only one) a. depression 25% b. anxiety 7%
   c. recent death of a loved one 3% d. sexual issues 6%
   e. drug or alcohol addiction 0% f. eating disorder 2%
   g. marital problems 19% h. relationship problems with other family members (parents/children) 3% i. occupational (work) issues 6%
   j. recent psychological trauma 2% k. physical illness 4% l. accident 3%
   m. other issue (please specify) 19% (family member's mental or physical disorder)
2. This problem or condition began:
   a. one week prior to starting psychotherapy 3%
   b. within the last month prior to starting psychotherapy 17%
   c. within six months of starting psychotherapy 22%
   d. within one year of starting psychotherapy 13%
   e. more than one year prior to starting psychotherapy 45%
3. This problem or condition has caused me: a slight 6% moderate 40% or extreme amount of emotional distress 54%.
4. To what degree was this problem interfering with your normal everyday functioning: slightly 19% moderately 45% extremely 36%
5. Did this problem prevent you from working or going to school? yes 29% no 71%
6. Before starting psychotherapy, how did you try to handle or solve this problem on your own? (check only *one,* the most important support)
   a. with help from my family members 6% b. with help from friends 6%
   c. both family & friends 18% d. on my own 40%
   e. with help from spiritual leaders 3% f. by ignoring the problem 14%
   g. other (please specify) 12%
   Other responses: worked more hours, religion, medication
7. What factors (if any) prevented or delayed you from starting therapy sooner? (*check all that apply*) a. financial concerns (e.g., cost of therapy) 25%
   b. time 4% c. embarrassed talking about my problem 20%
   d. work or scheduling problems 6% e. didn't know how to get into therapy 2%
   f. transportation 0% g. other (please specify) 42%
   Other most common responses: 1. I thought I could do it alone (6%)
   2. I didn't think my problem was serious (4%)
   3. I didn't think psychotherapy could help me (3%)

8. What specific fears did you have about therapy before starting your sessions?
   There were 101 responses to this question:
   1. none (24%)
   2. would not be successful (19%)
   3. stigma (11%)
   4. talking about myself to a stranger (10%)
   5. disclosing personal information (19%)
   6. I will be mismatched with therapist (8%)
   7. trusting therapist (7%)
   8. financial concerns (5%)

   Which, if any, of these turned out to be true? ____________
   Most frequent answer was: none
   Seven clients wrote one of the following: financial concerns
   overly emotional sessions
   had trouble finding the right therapist

9. In general, how would you rate your current therapy process?
   a. extremely helpful 59% b. moderately helpful 32%
   c. slightly helpful 8% d. not useful 0%

10. Would you recommend this or any other type of psychotherapy to your friends or family? yes 97% no 3%
    If no, why? ____________

11. If psychotherapy was useful for you, using a 1 to 10 scale (1 being low and 10 being high), please rate how important you think the following therapist characteristics were for your improvement in therapy:
    (Please rate all of these. If psychotherapy was not useful for you check here ______ and move to Question 14).
    a. number of years in school or training 6.3 b. experience as a therapist 8.3
    c. technical knowledge (e.g., use of specific treatment techniques) 7.1
    d. same gender as you 5.5 e. therapist's personality 8.5
    f. therapist's theoretical orientation 6.5 g. intelligence level 8.3
    h. therapist's ability to put you at ease 8.8 i. therapist's communication skills 9.0
    j. therapist's ability to understand your problem/condition 9.5
    k. willingness to listen to you 9.2 l. therapist's ability to establish a relationship with you 8.8 m. therapist's self-disclosure 6.1
    n. other (specify): religion of therapist
    Which of these do you think was MOST important (list one *letter* only)? ______
    j=46%, h=21%, i=13%, e=11% (c, d, k, l, m = 0%)

(continued)

12. On a 1 to 10 scale (1 being low and 10 being high), please rate how important these other aspects of therapy are (were) in terms of promoting improvement in your condition:
    a. your relationship with therapist 8.4 b. your similarity to the therapist 5.5
    c. attitude/behavior of office staff 4.8
    d. flexibility with appointment time or scheduling 6.5
    e. liking the therapist "as a person" rather than as a professional 7.1
    f. other (specify): kindness, showing he is human, gave straightforward feedback, knowledge of disorder
13. How many psychotherapy sessions did it take before you noticed a real improvement in your condition? 1=93%, 2=5%, 3=1%
14. If money or insurance coverage were not a problem, what is the *total number* of individual therapy sessions that you would like to have (or think you need) with your therapist? mode=20
15. Expectations for therapy: In the following section, using a check mark (✔), please indicate which expectations you had for psychotherapy (check all that apply). Then in the second column, on a 1 to 10 scale (1 being low and 10 being high), please rate how important these expectations were for you. Finally, on the last column, please indicate if these expectations were generally met in your therapy sessions:

Expectations:	✔	1 to 10 ratings	Expectations met? (yes, no, not yet)
a. specific advice on how to change/improve problem	96%	8.9	Y 67%, N 30%
b. gain greater self-understanding	87%	8.8	Y 69%, N 27%
c. improvement in relationships	76%	8.6	Y 58%, N 42%
d. reduction in symptoms	75%	9.0	Y 62%, N 36%
e. have someone to talk to about problem/condition	82%	8.8	Y 88%, N 8%
f. gain support and reassurance	71%	8.7	Y 89%, N 9%
g. change my personality	23%	7.0	Y 58%, N 42%
h. change my way of thinking	57%	8.4	Y 69%, N 29%
i. help me cope with life	87%	8.7	Y 65%, N 29%

16. How do you spend most of the time in the therapy sessions? (please check only *one*)
    a. talking about myself or condition 23% b. listening to the therapist 1%
    c. about equal time for both a and b 71%
    d. other (specify) 5%, depends on issue

17. What are (were) the most difficult aspects of therapy? (check *all* that apply)
    a. talking about myself or my condition 23% b. trusting the therapist 10%
    c. getting to appointments 5% d. not knowing what to expect 10%
    e. fear that the therapist will get me to do things that I don't really want to do 7%
    f. fear that the therapist will try to change my values 0%
    g. reliving old memories 35%
    h. other (specify) 9%, fear I could not be helped
    Are any of these still a problem for you? yes 53% no 47%
18. What are the most positive aspects (benefits) of psychotherapy for you?
    understanding myself and my problem (23%), improving my self-esteem (17%), learning to cope with problem (16%), relief from symptoms (15%), ability to talk about the problem—having someone to listen (10%)
19. What are the most negative aspects of psychotherapy for you?
    time involvement (14%), dealing with the past (13%), periods of no progress (12%), having to share personal information (11%), cost (11%)
20. What recommendations do you have for changing the way the therapy sessions are conducted?
    most frequent response=none (61%), adjustment of time and number of sessions according to client's needs (15%), less emphasis on time, review last session before starting new one.
21. If you could design the "perfect" therapist, what would be his or her main characteristics?
    (Most gave more than one answer)
    good listener (41%), empathetic (23%), broad knowledge of problem (21%), understanding (21%), honest and straightforward (14%), other answers: intelligent, good sense of humor, makes good suggestions, compassionate, objective, ability to put client at ease
22. If you had to pick only one thing that the therapist said or did in any of your sessions that was the most important or significant for you, what would it be?
    A wide range of answers was given. In order of frequency, the answers follow: provided positive feedback, told me my feelings are valid, gave me reassurance, helped me get to the root of the problem, told me my problem was not my fault, helped me to understand myself, helped me set realistic goals, helped me trust others, encouraged me to express myself
23. How do you pay for the therapy sessions? (Check only one.)
    a. out of pocket (no insurance) 16% b. insurance (or managed care) 18%
    c. both out of pocket (co-pay) and insurance 60%
    d. other (please specify) 7% (church or other source)

(continued)

24. Are you covered by a managed care company (e.g., HMO)? yes 57% no 40% don't know 3%
    If yes, how would you rate your experience with managed care?
    Highly positive 7% positive 27% neutral 27%
    negative 22% highly negative 16%
25. What aspects do you like *most* about managed care?
    low co-pay (50%), usually less cost overall than other insurance (20%), nothing (16%), coverage (12%)
26. What aspects do you like *least* about managed care? (55 responses)
    limits in selection of providers and number of treatment sessions (50%), hassle of getting approvals (13%), not a good idea for mental health treatment/conflict of interests (12%)
27. In your own words, what do you think the purpose of managed care is?
    low cost insurance and control costs (50%), save insurance companies money (30%)
28. Do you think you understand the difference between managed care and other types of insurance? yes 74% no 26%
    If yes, in your own words, what is the difference?
    Managed care has much more restrictions (75%)
29. Do you think managed care companies should be more carefully regulated by the state or federal government? yes 59% no 9% don't know 35%
30. Do you think you should have the right to sue managed care companies if they are negligent in any manner? yes 89% no 5%
    yes, but only for the following reasons (specify) 5%.
    Responses: if they refuse necessary care or if they are negligent; if they are careless; if they do not reimburse correctly
31. Do you think that your current insurance or managed care company provides adequate mental health benefits for you? yes 44% no 50%
    other (specify) 6% If no, please explain why not.
    a. insufficient coverage or payment (33%) b. costs too much out of pocket (17%) c. should not restrict number of treatment sessions (17%) d. coverage should be the same for mental conditions as physical conditions (17%)
    Please list any other comments you have about any of the questions.

CHAPTER

5 The Process of Psychotherapy

DAVID M. GONZALEZ

I. DAVID WELCH

Becoming a Psychotherapist

Becoming a psychotherapist is a unique endeavor. It does not consist of merely going to school, gaining a knowledge base and learning particular techniques or methods. Even though therapists are taught proven techniques and methods for helping others, such knowledge alone is not what makes an effective psychotherapist. The process extends far beyond the training needed for most occupations. "It calls for the very personal construction of a complex system of beliefs capable of providing trustworthy guidelines to professional thought and practice" (Combs & Gonzalez, 1994, p. 203). Becoming a psychotherapist requires a commitment to a process of change in the therapist. Hence, the word *becoming* is important. An ongoing process is implied by the word. A therapist who is unwilling to change or *become* is unlikely to be an effective helper. It is doubtful that therapists can be helpful to clients' growth processes if they are unwilling or unable to participate in their own growth process. Therapists must be willing to face themselves squarely if they are to have any consistent hope of being able to help clients do the same.

Thus, psychotherapists need to have an accurate, realistic view of themselves. They need to recognize who they are with all their strengths and weaknesses. If psychotherapists do not have an accurate conception of themselves, they are in danger of reenacting their own unresolved issues in the therapy process.

Therapy for the Therapist

In the journey of becoming therapists, it is sometimes advisable for therapists to seek therapy for themselves. Often therapists are reluctant to participate in the therapeutic process from the client's chair. There is a feeling that somehow they should be above needing help, and seeking therapy may be experienced as some sort of weakness. Or, perhaps they define themselves as helpers and have difficulty making the shift to asking for help for themselves, even when asking would be in their own best interest. Such a stance is akin to a physician who says that he or she would never go to a doctor. Yet, somehow it can be difficult for therapists to seek help for themselves. When considering the prospect of therapy for themselves, therapists are faced with the challenge of demonstrating faith or a lack of faith in the process they wish to offer others. Also, the experience of being a client has the potential of enhancing the therapist's understanding of the process and therefore increasing the therapist's effectiveness. A question in this regard is, If therapists somehow see themselves as beyond ordinary persons, how are they to remain in touch with the needs of people and therefore be able to help them? For example, how can therapists help someone who is frightened or depressed, if they deny experiencing these emotional states? Later in this chapter, the concept of the "wounded healer" is examined and makes the point that psychotherapists do not have to be perfect human beings in order to be effective therapists.

Setting Limits

Those who see themselves as helpers may struggle with being able to say no. No matter how much is asked of them, they keep saying yes rather than feel guilty for saying no to someone in need. Agreeing to appointment times that are extremely inconvenient or taking on more clients than can reasonably be tended to are just some of the ways this happens. An even more complicated situation can occur in small towns where most people know one another and a therapist may be expected to fulfill that role even in social situations. Learning to take care of their own needs is critical for psychotherapists. Those who do not, risk travelling the road to early burnout. In taking care of their own needs, therapists are more likely to be available to their clients in terms of health and vitality. Clients can learn vicariously to set limits based on interacting with therapists who demonstrate such a capacity.

Others' Discomfort with Therapists

Socially, being a psychotherapist is a two-edged sword. One edge gives therapists a degree of recognition and status. The other edge carries a degree of suspicion and rejection. Psychotherapists can tell endless stories of innocent conversations coming to a screeching halt once the other person asks, "What do you do for a living?" By admitting one is a psychotherapist, one risks a strong negative reaction from others who may fear that they have been "analyzed." Some mental health professionals avoid letting others know what they do for a living because of the reaction that so often follows. Some say that they usually go to social gatherings that are comprised of mostly mental health professionals to avoid the problem. Some may even go so far as to give a false answer as to their occupation rather than see people go through the contortions of discomfort that come with imagining that they may have said all sorts of things that the mental health professional must be analyzing. Regardless of how therapists deal with this problem, it is real and something with which psychotherapists have to find a way to cope.

Becoming a psychotherapist is an enormous challenge. The process of becoming a skilled helper takes time, commitment, and a willingness to participate in an ongoing process of growing as a person and as a helper. It is not possible to become a skilled helping professional and not come face to face with one's own struggles along the way. Thus, the process of becoming a psychotherapist is not one of merely mastering a set of techniques or skills but rather of coming to terms with who one is as a person and learning to use that self as an instrument of help for others. The training of a psychotherapist includes not only the mastery of skills but also of facing oneself and developing the attitudes and personal knowledge necessary to strive to understand others, enter the relationship honestly and without guile, and suspend moralistic judgment. The challenges to doing so are daunting, and along the way therapists may find themselves adopting roles or facades that interfere with their effectiveness.

Masks versus Genuineness

Why is it so difficult to be simply and plainly who we are? That is a question with which all psychotherapists wrestle from the time of meeting their first client and throughout their lives as professionals. It is often the very question many clients struggle with as well. What keeps us from showing others who we are? Resistance and the processes of defense are the explanations we have given for clients. We have been unwilling to use the same explanations when, as psychotherapists, we mask ourselves, yet this explanation may be the source of some common, and mistaken, roles psychotherapists adopt in striving to be of service.

A cornerstone of effective psychotherapy is the ability of psychotherapists to present themselves without guile, or deception. Psychotherapists must enable clients to see them as persons without withholding the essence of the self. A profound and potent psychotherapist is one who is present in the relationship without reticence. As it is with empathy and respect, so it must be with genuineness. Each psychotherapist must be present in the encounter for exploration, understanding, and change to occur most effectively and permanently. Most psychotherapists manage the transition from perplexity to congruence, but some make common therapeutic mistakes that plague them throughout their practice. Often the struggle to come to terms with the rigors of psychotherapy results in common and identifiable roles. The trials of personal genuineness prove too much for some individuals, and they adopt masks or roles by which some image of a psychotherapist is presented. These roles represent both self-doubt and a fundamental lack of faith in people. Each, in its own way, separates the psychotherapist from the client. Each lessens the depth of involvement, reduces the risks, and dilutes the experience of psychotherapy. In the common human struggle to discover and create who we are, those psychotherapists who hide themselves from their clients damage two lives: their own and the client's.

The Mask of the Pundit

One way some psychotherapists reduce involvement is to remain aloof from the relationship. They adopt the mask of the pundit. They might listen to the story with rapt attention and gather information. They might ask penetrating questions. When the listening, gathering, and questioning are completed, they do what pundits do. They analyze, arrive at conclusions, and provide opinions. A good illustration of this problem can be seen in the recovered memories controversy. Therapists have listened to symptoms and arrived at a conclusion and a diagnosis. A short story might make the point. While living in an agricultural community, one of us once saw a man standing on the side of the road holding a bridle. While passing the man, the realization came that it could be that he had found a bridle or he had lost a horse. Behavior is like that; it has a thousand parents. Making a diagnosis on the basis of symptoms alone is a serious psychotherapeutic mistake. Yet, because they are learned and possess the facts, pundits shift the focus of the psychotherapy from the person to the psychotherapist. The period of listening is over, and now the issue belongs to the psychotherapist. The psychotherapist does the talking now and explains the origins of the problem, what is transpiring inside the head of the person, how it may be illogical and irrational, and what to do about it. And in all of this, the pundit has not gotten dirty, has not become involved in the fray, and has failed to understand in any heartfelt way the life of the other person. Such an aloof approach to psychotherapy protects the psychotherapist from emotional material that can be personally frightening. It is an approach that leaves out the emotional aspects of life's problems and is dangerous because the client may be led to believe that this asymmetrical explanation can provide actual respite from life's predicaments.

A merely intellectual understanding may give the appearance of resolution. Sometimes antiseptic answers do resolve life issues, especially in those situations in which any answer will do. This is particularly so if given by someone considered an authority; but any resolution to life issues given in the absence of empathetic understanding can be helpful only by chance. Psychotherapists who are aloof from the experiences of their clients stand little chance of genuine understanding.

The Mask of the Wizard

Wizards heal by magic. They see themselves as possessing unique qualities and knowledge that result in astounding cures that baffle the professional community. Their practice includes special methods, devices, formalities, or strategies that other practitioners have failed to discover or do not use because of "narrow-mindedness" or "scientific snobbishness." They may present themselves as gifted or as unrecognized geniuses and may be charismatic enough to attract disciples through the sheer force of their persona. They may invoke the power of the supernatural. They may imply the endorsement of science. In all of this, magical psychotherapists are untouched by the human experience. In their presentation, they send the message that the resolution to life's quandaries lies in some technique or mysterious technology. Their message suggests that people should seek answers to a power outside the self either in the practice of some ritual or by surrendering the self to the power of the magician. Perhaps the most famous example of a "wizard" is Anton Mesmer, the founder of mesmerism. Mesmer manufactured an atmosphere of mystery. Adorned in costume, he would surround people with paraphernalia, load them up with laxatives, sink them in warm water, create an atmosphere of the mysterious, and make a show of moving magnets around them. Many became hysterical, crying out as if in pain or in the throes of some powerful struggle. In this intense climate of suggestion, and in highly charged emotional states, illnesses disappeared, paralyses lifted, and ailments vanished. Mesmer claimed that these cures were the result of an unrecognized force in the universe only he had discovered called "animal magnetism." He controlled its forces and used its power for good—and profit. Ultimately discredited, animal magnetism took its place in the annals of human foibles.

Mesmer was not and is not alone in his treachery. Charlatans throughout history have made their larcenous way by healing the unsick. They assign mysterious explanations to ordinary human experience. They take credit for the natural power of the body and the mind and, in so doing, demean people. They betray their implied loyalty to their patrons. They are among the most reprehensible of psychotherapists.

The Mask of the Priest

In this context, the term *priest* is used in its metaphoric and disparaging form to mean one who moralizes or makes sermons about some a priori, presupposed good. Such a person pontificates as to how things are supposed to be. Usually the word *priest* conjures up an image of religion, but there are preachers in the psychotherapy community, too, especially on the subject of self-help. Self-help is important and necessary, but it has also achieved a prominence in which the promise of simple answers and easy solutions has created a market for psychological priests. In this context, the solution is not necessarily a religious or spiritual good, but rather some assumption of psychological good. Such priests provide formulas for happy living and the end of suffering. They promise that those who are willing to follow the formula rigorously and faithfully will have the confusion and pain of life lifted from them. This involves a judgment that people are primarily unhealthy, in a state of iniquity, and therefore in need of salvation and forgiveness.

This position is grounded on three erroneous dimensions: The first is arrogance, the second is distortion, and the third is destructiveness. Arrogance is present because the psychotherapists involved in such a practice have elevated themselves to a position of moral superiority, assuming for themselves alone the knowledge of what is righteous and orthodox. Their position is also arrogant because they have made themselves teachers of righteousness. Distortion is involved because people are asked to learn or think in particular ways, adjust their bodies, eat certain foods, reflect in a disciplined fashion, or behave in prescribed ways. In each case, the power presumably lies in the method or practice, with the psychotherapist functioning as the mentor/intermediary through whom the person must learn. To clarify what constitutes the distortion, consider this example: You cannot hypnotize a rock because a rock does not have the capacity to benefit from the treatment. Thus, regardless of how powerful we consider a treatment or how elegant the philosophy, *the power to change lies in the person seeking change.* This truth is fundamental in biology, in medicine, and in the environment. We often forget that it is also fundamental in psychotherapy.

The destructiveness lies in the reasons people seek psychotherapy. They come because they have not learned or have lost touch with their own capacity to cope with the enigmas, quandaries, complications, and tragedies of life. They may be, and in all likelihood are, vulnerable and confused. They find reassurance in an opportunity to explore their vulnerability and confusion, to seek the sources and reasons for them, and, ultimately, to discover what to do about them. The destructive element is the exploitation of this vulnerability in leading clients to solutions, philosophies, practices, or life decisions that are more important and central to the psychotherapist than to any self-discovered, self-initiated personal resolutions. These introjected outcomes weaken clients and prepare them poorly for their continuing life outside the confines of the psychotherapeutic relationship. To replace the turmoil of a person's life with some philosophy or system of behavior may help for a time—time enough to propagandize new converts—but experience has taught us that imposed and introjected systems deteriorate and the person is left with not only the continuing original turmoil but also the crisis of new concerns over who may now be trusted as a source of help. One "psychological priest" can taint an entire profession.

There is, of course, a place for judging or moralizing, a time for the consideration of moral philosophy, a time for evaluating right and wrong. Any person and any society must make moral decisions. Psychotherapy is both a process and a time in which persons can and do make moral decisions. They do so with the assistance, and, perhaps, support of a psychotherapist but most importantly, it is *they* who do it. Any psychotherapist who presumes to make decisions for others distorts and loses sight of the purpose of psychotherapy.

The Mask of the Clerk

A clerk is one who gathers information, keeps records, and compiles reports. In psychotherapy, these practices may take the form of testing, assessment, and diagnosis. These processes represent a part of the psychotherapeutic enterprise, but stopping with such procedures is analogous in medicine to conducting an examination, blood tests, and analyses, concluding that the patient has an illness, and doing nothing further. Such behavior constitutes the pretense of care but, in reality, nothing is actually accomplished. The purpose of assessment and diagnosis is to inform the psychotherapy. Assessment and diagnosis are not psychotherapy itself. Psychotherapists who stop at these procedures are uninvolved in the lives and understandings of the people they have sworn to serve. Just as surely as testing, assessment, and diagnosis are meant to inform psychotherapy, psychotherapy can inform testing, assessment, and diagnosis. In plain fact, to separate one from the other represents yet another distortion of the psychotherapeutic process. To believe that people may be understood through the application of testing procedures alone slights human experience. Psychotherapy is not a process of external observation, evaluation, interpretation, and explanation. It is not an impersonal endeavor. It is subjective in the sense that to comprehend other persons, psychotherapists must understand the meanings that each person gives to his or her answers and behavior in any assessment. To do otherwise confuses appearance with substance. That is the primary mistake of the clerk.

The Role without a Role

If effective psychotherapists are not pundits, wizards, priests, or clerks, then who or what are they? The problem in each of these roles is exactly that: Each is a role. And, when psychotherapists mask themselves, they prevent a genuine relationship from forming. The role of a psychotherapist is to have no role. At the risk of sounding Zen-like, the phrase means to be truly who you are. To be your true self means to avoid phoniness and playing a role. Any attempt to wear the coats of Sigmund Freud or Carl Rogers is antithetical to effectiveness. Being an effective helper means not presenting yourself as a preconceived image of what you think you should be, but rather who you really are.

Years ago, one of the dominant training principles and metaphors for psychotherapists was known as "suspension of the self." In essence, it meant that psychotherapists were in the therapeutic relationship for the other person and that psychotherapists should not bring their personal issues into the session or introduce their personal lives into the psychotherapy. This practice even extended to how therapists dealt with a headache or a cold. We were instructed to "leave the headache at the door." This approach implied a passive sort of psychotherapy in which psychotherapists were wholly dedicated to the needs of their clients and left their own persons out of the room. This principle is, of course, stated in its extreme to make the point.

This concept gradually gave way to another training metaphor labeled the "self as instrument" approach. For this, psychotherapists are taught to use their personal qualities as a vehicle to help others. If a psychotherapist is by nature quiet, the training task is to develop that tendency so that it serves the therapeutic relationship. If he or she is by nature active, the training task is to develop that tendency to serve a therapeutic purpose. With a dramatic nature, the psychotherapist would use more dramatic interventions to facilitate the relationship. This understanding of psychotherapy espouses no one proper way to enter the psychotherapeutic relationship. How an individual practices psychotherapy is, instead, a personal and unique process guided by research into effective psychotherapy and tempered by the therapist's individual qualities. In this chemistry of the common, blended with the unique, the personal qualities of the psychotherapist can be present in the therapeutic relationship as psychotherapeutic tools. Any role that hides the unique qualities of the psychotherapist does a disservice to the therapeutic relationship. Psychotherapists struggle through study and practice to present an undistorted image. In so doing, they free each client from a burden he or she did not bring to therapy. The client does not have to second guess or speculate about the relationship with the psychotherapist. Other aspects of the client's life may be clouded, but the person of the psychotherapist, at least, will be clear.

On Giftedness, Intuition, and Sensitivity

Myths have a way of persisting even in the presence of solid evidence to the contrary. They may have their origins in some thread of truth, but myths are false beliefs. The danger of myths lies in the tendency of people often to be guided more in terms of such beliefs rather than by what they know. One of the destructive myths that lingers in the field of psychotherapy is the myth of giftedness. Newspaper articles, books, television, and the movies all labor diligently to perpetuate the myth of the gifted psychotherapist. To describe a familiar scene, picture a billionaire's son who has endured some unnamed trauma. Perhaps he was captured in some far-off land and tormented by a group of villains. After he is rescued, he is returned home only to face a life of mental anguish. The billionaire seeks the advice of his equally wealthy friend who tells him that years earlier his wife, whom everyone thought was travelling around the world, was, in actuality, in treatment with a famous and brilliant psychotherapist. She experienced a full recovery because of the revolutionary treatment she received from the brilliant and extraordinarily gifted psychotherapist. You've heard this story. In less financially gifted families, a worried father may talk to his wife who recommends Aunt Mary. Aunt Mary is the recognized therapeutic relative. Others may endorse the family physician or pastors, who have no more training in psychotherapy than Aunt Mary, but who do have distinct sets of myths and credentials surrounding them.

No disparagement is meant to Aunt Mary, physicians, or pastors. Indeed, there are people in the world who are helpful to others because they are compassionate. And, they have learned to reserve judgment and not to leap readily to condemnation. Though such persons can be helpful, it is important to recognize the limits of their ability to help. Consider this: You are in need of legal help, so we recommend Aunt Mary because she is naturally gifted in the law! Or you have broken your leg, so we recommend an accountant we know because accountants are schooled and must know about healing, too. Uncle Jim is a gifted toothpuller. These examples are, of course, exaggerated. Who believes any longer that physicians, attorneys, dentists, or accountants come by their skills and knowledge "naturally"? Some seem to believe that people trained in one field accrue the competencies of another through some automatic process, but this is not so. Yet, strangely, there are those who believe that some people have the skills and knowledge of psychotherapy "naturally." For one reason or another, through belief in a gift of intuition or extraordinary sensitivity, some people decide they have the natural abilities that qualify them to be psychotherapists. They may believe they are more sensitive than others or may have been told by their friends that they seem to feel more deeply than others. They may believe they are more caring than others and therefore can be of help. The myth is that understanding comes from sensitivity rather than training. Many people care; they simply do not know what to do. Consider the families and loved ones of any person who comes to psychotherapy. Should we conclude that they are insensitive and uncaring? More likely, they do care, but their ability to suggest solutions and resolutions has been exhausted, and the troubled person is now seeking help outside the ordinary networks.

Some people believe they can know the inner motivations and concerns of others without the conscious use of reason. They might even succumb to the seductive notion that they are more knowledgeable of other persons than the persons themselves. They are gifted with intuition. Thus, they may prescribe courses of action to others. For psychotherapists to believe that they are somehow able to sense what others are missing is arrogant and dangerous. It invites the misuse of power. It separates psychotherapists from the humanity they share with the persons who come to them for help.

In one of its other manifestations, this myth of the naturally gifted therapist takes the form of the "weekend wonder." In addition to believing themselves gifted with sensitivity or intuition, these people believe another myth: that all they need in addition to their natural intuition is the proper method. They know they lack training and skill, so off they go to weekend training workshops in Mental Somaticism or the Zauberhaft Method or Bilateral Neurodynamic Cybernetics or some other academic or esoteric-sounding technique professing to be psychotherapy. After a short period of instruction and some form of certification, they set up practice using a title that bypasses the laws governing the practice of psychotherapy. Competent practitioners in any field of study struggle, practice, and refine their work, yet the belief endures that some "natural ability," coupled with minimal training, qualifies a person to be a psychotherapist. To hold that the weekend study of anything qualifies anyone as competent in any field is a false and potentially dangerous belief. The people who come for help in psychotherapy are vulnerable. They deserve a practitioner who has taken time for education and training. There is honor in it. There is dishonor and potential danger in the overvaluation of "giftedness."

Wounded Healers

Another myth that plagues psychotherapy is the belief that the emotional health of psychotherapists ranges from "crazy" to "perfect." The professional literature is unclear as to the actual emotional state of psychotherapists compared to other professionals, but the myth of the crazy psychotherapist is one that is frequently repeated. Newspaper reporters seem to delight in reporting the clay feet of psychotherapists, and any scandal or failing is published with a subtle, but discernable, clucking of the tongue. Perhaps that is appropriate, since there may be special obligations for certain occupations. Psychotherapists themselves are not immune from back-fence gossiping, and a social gathering of psychotherapists is likely to buzz in some private corner of the party with rumors of the moral and ethical lapses of colleagues. Psychotherapy is a dangerous profession for those whose hold on emotional stability is slippery and may be overwhelmed by the profession, but persons such as these are not representative of the norm.

At the opposite end of the spectrum, there is the myth that psychotherapists are emotionally unflappable and somehow impervious to the struggles that most others experience. Because psychotherapists are typically seen only at work, a narrow perception or image is given, which contributes to the creation and maintenance of this myth. Also, since part of the training of psychotherapists involves the appearance of being unshakeable, it only follows that such a perception gets formed. This is a complex issue and deserves a bit of explanation. The research and experience of psychotherapists over the years have affirmed the concept of genuineness as an important component of effective psychotherapy. An effective psychotherapist is not a phony. Still, such genuineness has to be "therapeutic." In each response they give, psychotherapists have to make a judgment about whether a particular intervention is therapeutic or not. Is the response both genuine and therapeutic? Thus, from the many responses and interventions open at any given moment in psychotherapy, some internal selection must be made.

Take a situation in which a person reports something that may be bizarre or even unthinkable. If we take an extreme example, a professional might be working with a murderer who reports a particularly gruesome killing in graphic and appalling detail. Perhaps, the murderer eats part of the victim. On the inside, the psychotherapist might be thinking, "Wow, this is really bizarre," and, in fact, it is outside the range of ordinary, understandable human behavior. Psychotherapists, however, are trained not to respond with the ordinary and typical responses one might expect. Instead, they provide calm and collected response. The psychotherapist might say, "So even though most people see that as shocking and perverse, the way you see it is the way anthropologists have described some hunters? You gain power that way." It is a response that asks, "Am I understanding you accurately?" Of course, most psychotherapists would not encounter such graphic and shocking behavior in their clients. Nevertheless, the principle remains, and we must face the reality that there is much that is shocking in our world.

One of the primary purposes of psychotherapy is to understand. It is sometimes difficult for many in our society to understand that the purpose does not change in psychotherapy even when the subject is a criminal accused or convicted of vile acts. In more sympathetic but equally dramatic situations, such a calm and understanding response can allow people to feel more hopeful and less victimized. Understanding is aided when therapists suspend judgment and resist moralizing. Suspending judgment can give the appearance of unflappability and lead people to think that, even in the face of what they consider to be their most shameful behavior, psychotherapists are such wonderfully understanding and uncondemning people that they must be perfect: the pinnacles of humanity; saints; people without problems. Psychotherapists are in a dangerous position if they start to believe this themselves.

There is yet a third myth: the myth of perfection, or the unsuitability of the less-than-perfect or wounded healer. Some might believe that anyone who has suffered some physical or psychological injury cannot be a psychotherapist. Others hold a diametrically opposing view. Some believe that only those who have suffered can understand the suffering of another. The most provocative statement would be that only one who has suffered a particular shock should treat those who have experienced a similar trauma. One might find an advocate who argues, for example, that only combat veterans should do psychotherapy with other combat veterans. Another might argue that only recovering alcoholics should treat alcoholics. Another form of the argument is that one must come from some particular group to understand members of that group. Some insist, for example, that to provide effective psychotherapy for a gay or lesbian person requires that the helper also be gay or lesbian. Still others contend that culture is of such importance that only a psychotherapist who is African American, Asian, Hispanic, or Native American can understand someone fitting those descriptors. Some feminist thinkers assert that males cannot understand and therefore should not be psychotherapists for women. Each of these beliefs is a myth—they are plagued by overgeneralizations. Being an effective psychotherapist does not depend on leading a blameless or trauma-free life. Understanding does not depend on having experienced a particular form of suffering or belonging to some specific demographic group. Here is the dilemma. Each of these myths holds within it a small portion of validity. Some psychotherapists have been, and presumably some are, diagnostically disturbed. In fact, some of the most famous psychotherapists have experienced major mental illness. Further, while psychotherapists need not be perfect, they do need to be sufficiently free of damaging psychopathology or present personal problems that they can understand and be of service to others. Also, it is not necessary to have suffered some emotionally damaging episode in life or to identify with a certain group to understand what others have gone through or are going through, but it may help. Let us take the example of a psychotherapist who comes from a psychologically healthy environment and who has led a life of relative security. The individual has experienced no abuse as a child or as an adult; has not been victimized by violence or drugs; has maintained a stable marriage; and has experienced death only in its normal, natural, and expected role in life—the death of grandparents or parents at the end of long lives. How can such a person understand battering, incest, rape, war, or other life-disrupting incidents that hamper a person's effective living?

The question itself is formed in a misconception. First, the perception of a "life without problems" is false. All of us face difficult issues, problems, and dilemmas throughout our lives. We may see people who appear to have good lives and conclude that they do not have problems. Perhaps they are people who cope effectively. Perhaps our judgment is based on appearance, and we fail to see the internal struggle. Whatever the case, each of us has faced personal crises. Each of us has enough tragedy in our lives to be able to understand the pain of others. What precedes understanding is the willingness and the compassion to expend the effort to understand. True, human tragedy is not meted out in equal measure. Some are blessedly spared from ravaging anguish and sorrow. Some are not, and thus may become embittered and devastated.

We can understand other people through at least two different routes. One is by way of personal experience. For example, we can understand the pain of a father whose son has died because we know how deeply we love our children. Experience alone, however, necessarily limits understanding. That is, each of us cannot experience the total range of human thought, emotion, and behavior from zenith to nadir. The other route to understanding is by seeking knowledge of the human condition. We can be taught, in psychotherapy itself, by people who confide in us and share their experiences. We can read the accounts of those who tell others of their experiences, pains, and coping strategies. We can read works of other psychotherapists as they seek to tell us of their struggles to understand and work with people with damaging life experiences. We can immerse ourselves in the study of human experience and by so doing, come to understand what we have not experienced. We do not mean to imply that study and experience are the same or that understanding and emotion are similar. We mean only that by study we can comprehend the meaning and importance of the experience for the person. It is a false belief that any human being can do more than that. Even those of us who have lived through the same experience bring to it our unique perceptions. We are left to explore with one another how closely our experiences correspond. Our shared experience still demands our understanding and the comprehension of our unique meanings.

Sometimes we are pierced, leaving deep and jagged wounds. The scars remain. Some people prosper in spite of their scars. Ernest Hemingway is given credit for having said that we are strongest in our broken places, and Nietzsche thought that what does not kill a person makes that person stronger.

This brings us to the concept of the wounded healer—one who has been emotionally injured and has turned to help others similarly injured. These people use their own experience of psychological trauma to be of service to others. The important principle is not the wound, however, but the process of surviving the wound. Note that most people do not seek the help of a psychotherapist because of the background of the therapist. What they are seeking is knowledge, competence, and understanding to bring their lives to a place where they can live with themselves. Surviving psychological trauma alone is not sufficient. Many of us know the tragedy of the cycle of abuse. Perpetrators are often victims, and victims become perpetrators. It is a vicious cycle and reveals the inadequacy of survival alone. A therapist who has been hurt in some way needs survival that does not result in callousness, cynicism, or cruelty. For such therapists, painful emotional trauma, at some time in their lives, has been followed by painful personal healing. From their own personal experiences and their ultimate resolution, these individuals have arrived at feelings of compassion for people who, like themselves, have had their lives battered by inhumane treatment or its dreadful opposite, emotional indifference. Their compassion becomes the starting place for the study and development of skills that will let them be of service to others. These qualities are represented in self-help support groups such as Alcoholics Anonymous, Compassionate Friends (for parents whose children have died), Heartbeat (for the surviving family members of suicide victims), SHARE (for parents whose infants have died), or CanSupport (for persons diagnosed with cancer).

Sigmund Freud, no stranger to personal flaws, was a psychotherapist of remarkable courage. Maeder (1989) recalled Freud's "scrutiny of his deeply buried memories and then heroic confrontations with the painful things he found." Freud's willingness to search himself and then to "put his flaws at the service of the empathic process"' is the best and wisest use of hurt transformed into a healing capacity. The lie in the myth of the wounded healer is that the wounding is the significant element. It is not. Surviving in such a way that pain is transformed into compassion is the essential part. Someone has said that the best revenge is a good life—to survive and, out of the pain and a forecast of ruin, to construct a life of decency and strength. One form of the good life is to be of service to others.

The Problem of Power

The power that comes with the role of psychotherapist can entice the unaware and unprepared into amazing impropriety. Those who seek out psychotherapists often do so from a vulnerable position and may regard themselves as weak or less capable. In the psychotherapist, they seek a person who is calm and more capable. Whether the psychotherapist actually embodies those characteristics or not, clients project an image of their own making and attach various expectations to this image. The skill of psychotherapists is to make themselves clearly known so that these preconceptions can be overcome. If psychotherapists do not diligently strive for genuineness in the psychotherapeutic relationship, then they can easily fall prey to a subtle illusion—an illusion that the psychotherapist is responsible for healing the people who come for help. Seduced by power, psychotherapists may become manipulative and exploitive. Psychotherapy may become a province in which the psychotherapist rules and becomes a ruler in a domain where the ultimate failing of our profession is practiced with arrogant self-aggrandizement. Such psychotherapists diminish people who come for help. Their clients remain less than they could be as their ability to become autonomous human beings is usurped. This is a considerable error. Psychotherapy is no exception to the dangers of power that has corrupted many professions. The perplexing thing about power in psychotherapy is that using it is not necessarily wrong.

Power has its uses; however, the exercise of power is a delicate proposition and must be performed nimbly and humbly to avoid its many traps. One trap is the appearance that it is more useful than it really is. The uses of power are limited, and yet we may believe that power is useful any time and anywhere—that all we need to do is try harder. Arthur Combs (1989), an educator and psychotherapist, said that nothing is more dangerous than a partly right idea. People are not stupid. If something is wrong—clearly and definitively wrong—it will not work and people will abandon it; but if something works occasionally or to some extent, people's inclination is to try even harder. Because it seems to work a little bit, we might not ever stop trying to fix it. That is why a partly right idea is dangerous. We are lured into trying harder at something that is not working optimally. We might pour good money after bad. If one glass of wine is relaxing, then a bottle will reduce stress entirely. In psychotherapy, if the people who seek our help regard us as psychologically strong, as intellectually superior, as emotionally together, and as socially insightful, then perhaps we should give them the benefit of our perceptions. Surely, if they follow the recommendations of people as insightful as we are, their lives will improve. Such is the temptation of flattery and power. The difficulty of power in psychotherapy is to avoid exploiting the vulnerability of clients in the name of helping them. Genuine psychotherapeutic help is movement in the direction of self-help. Anything done in psychotherapy that interferes with this is a sham no matter how well intended.

In the delicate use of power, a psychotherapist might well help people develop a capacity for self-help. Just as in any other field of endeavor, power may be used or abused. Power, in a sense, is neutral. The user determines whether or not its use is positive or negative. Taoists have a concept that energy or power in the universe is neutral and can be used in constructive or destructive ways. The difference is in the user. Power may be exercised in several different ways. Some ways are more helpful than others. One use of power that is not helpful is "power against." It is the sort of power in which the aim is to diminish or harm. A good example of this form of abuse of power can be found in *One Flew over the Cuckoo's Nest.* Nurse Rachett uses her power against a group of patients in a psychiatric hospital to crush their spirit. She is damaging to her patients as she actively uses her position, will, and personality to repress and devalue the people she is charged with helping. Whether the exercise of power involves sex, religion, money, or submission, using it against clients in psychotherapy lacks redeeming value.

A useful way power may be used by psychotherapists is in gaining access to services otherwise restricted to the client. This can be straightforward and simple. A physician may not have appointments available unless someone is referred. For therapists to use their influence to secure an appointment for a client is appropriate. Using power to intervene between people and institutions, agencies, and other powerful individuals is proper and helpful. A man came to psychotherapy because of pain he was suffering after an implant operation. He had spoken to his surgeon and was assured that the pain was a normal part of the healing process and that perhaps seeing a psychotherapist could be helpful. The implication, of course, was that the pain was in his head and not in his groin. He could not get an appointment with his physician, who assumed that the operation was a success and there were no complications. After listening to the man's complaints, the psychotherapist called the surgeon. He suggested that although psychological issues might be involved, there could be physical ones as well; that perhaps, while attending to the psychological issues, it might be wise to do a more thorough physical examination. You know where this story is going of course. The physical examination did reveal some complication and the implant was replaced. The pain subsided. The psychotherapy consisted of listening and using power to obtain an appointment and more than a hurried examination. This sort of power is helpful. It empowers people. It reassures them that they are in touch with reality, that their pains are not illusionary, and that concrete steps can be taken to deal with their suffering.

In training, psychotherapists are cautioned again and again not to abuse power. Equally important for them to learn is the value of using power for people. People come to psychotherapists because they believe we have the competence, skill, and knowledge to help them. This is the authority that accompanies knowledge. This is the power that comes with skill. We are expected to use this power in the service of the person seeking help. We convey this strength through assurance and straightforwardness. For example, if the therapist believes it is therapeutic to use a technique or counseling strategy, then a short declarative sentence is appropriate. "You said, 'I know I can do it.' Say it again. . . . And again, with even more conviction." This is using power for the person. It is reaffirming a felt sense of internal strength. A psychotherapist might say, "Let's take some time in the session today to talk to your boss. Let's bring your boss into the session. Have him sit in this chair. Say, 'Boss, I have something I want to say to you.'" These directions are clear and direct, yet not directive. That is, the issue has not been taken away from the person and has not been created for the person. Instead, the psychotherapist deals directly with an issue the person has identified. This is an important distinction. The psychotherapist may give homework. "I want you to write down the angry thoughts you have and when and what caused them. Record them and bring them with you to the next session. We will talk about them then." Because the person believes in the authority of the psychotherapist, he or she will do what is asked. Sometimes, a person does not, of course, but that becomes an issue of a different sort.

In therapy, a person wants understanding, information, and solutions to problems. A psychotherapist can use power for change. A person with many acquaintances but few friends might be instructed to have coffee with at least two acquaintances during the week. By making contact, the opportunity for a friendship becomes possible through association. An angry person may be asked to keep a journal of his or her angry thoughts during the day. The journal begins the process of bringing the anger under control. Brought into awareness, recorded, and reported, the anger can be discussed concretely and specifically with respect to when and in what situations it comes. Tasks such as these will often be completed because people believe in the power and authority of the psychotherapist. The psychotherapist can be of help because power is used for the person. Psychotherapists can use power with a person so that his or her fears and anxieties do not have to be faced alone. In fantasy or in fact, a psychotherapist can accompany a person in confronting those fears. People who are afraid of enclosed places can step into an elevator with their psychotherapist. They may go into their past and confront old anxieties and not have to do it alone. They have someone to accompany them on their journey into their own fears. People can increase their own sense of power from the support they feel from the psychotherapist. There is a world of difference between confronting demons alone and confronting them with an ally. It is the difference between loneliness and companionship—between a line and a circle. A single line is vulnerable from every angle; a circle is protected from every side. It is the difference between being able to carry a burden and being weighed down by it. There is a saying that a burden shared is a burden halved.

Power with a person means that two people are stronger than one. What might be overwhelming for a person alone can be withstood with the support of another. The psychotherapist can say clearly and without reservation, "I will stay with you during your struggle. I will not waver, and I will not turn away. I will not abandon you. We can face this. We can endure this together." To use power with a person demands courage from the psychotherapist. Such courage can help clients to use power for themselves.

Power in psychotherapy is a matter of influence used as an advocate for the psychological self. It does not mean necessarily that the specific goals or behaviors of a person are buttressed through the power of the psychotherapist. To argue in extremes for a moment, say a man is so angry with a coworker that he wants to just "knock his head clean off." Obviously, using the power of psychotherapy to help the person bash his coworker would be a mistake. The correct use would be to hear, acknowledge, and accept the person's feelings as genuine. Using power to influence means to address directly, if possible, the anger itself. It does not mean to honor the typical cultural or societal responses to anger. To be an advocate for the psychological self means to seek understanding and solutions that empower the person. It means seeking solutions that will, when utilized, enable the person to feel pride, respect, and dignity. To be an advocate for the psychological self means helping clients see through "solutions" that may endanger themselves or others. To acknowledge anger does not mean to advocate violence. To be an advocate for the psychological self does not mean to endure mistreatment passively. Rather, it means to empower people creatively to discover within themselves the resources they need to cope effectively with the tumult of their lives.

Diversity and Effectiveness

As we further our skills in dealing with different peoples, few would argue that it is important to be sensitive to clients. In fact, the people in our profession depend on being sensitive to other human beings. It has become increasingly important in our multidimensional society to understand the societal, cultural, ethnic, gender, and lifestyle forces that contribute to the unique person who seeks us out for personal and emotional understanding. Developing a greater sensitivity to the variety of worlds in which people live can help psychotherapists respond more adequately and accurately to clients from backgrounds different than their own.

Part of understanding other cultures and their worldviews involves understanding *our own* cultural views and values. If psychotherapists are going to be empathic in working with clients from diverse backgrounds, we must be aware of the dominant cultural values that have shaped our expectations and worldviews. Similarly, therapists have to become acquainted with their own prejudices and biases. Often these can be unconscious or so much a part of us that we are not aware of them. While the temptation may be to claim that we are not prejudiced, we must recognize that such a declaration is akin to saying that we have no history. Society, media, or other experiences have conditioned all of us in some way. Our biases can result in unconscious cultural clashes with those to whom we want to be of service. Such can be the case whether we are talking about differences in culture, ethnicity, gender, sexual orientation, or other lifestyle differences. Psychotherapists need to educate themselves about the realities of their clientele and engage in a careful examination of personal attitudes that may affect their capacity to be helpful to clients whose background or culture may be different from their own.

Empathy permits all other aspects of therapy to occur and move forward in a helpful and skillful fashion. Providing an atmosphere of deep and *accurate* understanding of our clients' worlds can be challenging since there are a variety of potential barriers to connecting at an empathic level. Mere knowledge can be cold, even manipulative. Empathy, the very attitude of seeking to understand, is an appropriate path to cultural sensitivity. Allowing clients to instruct us as we build a relationship is a respectable twin to seeking intellectual knowledge. Cultural and other background differences can create enormous challenges to the empathy process. The authors are not implying that it is necessary to be of the same cultural background in order to be helpful to clients. Increasingly, there is a necessity to take cultural factors into consideration when trying to make sense of another's behavior (Castillo, 1997). As discussed earlier, we can increase our understanding of others through education, contact with others, consultation, reading, and empathic relationships with clients.

The Role of Theory in Psychotherapy

Psychotherapy is not a trial and error process. "Therapists must understand very specifically what they are trying to do in therapy—where they are going and why—in order to be consistently helpful to clients. Without a conceptual framework as a guide, decisions about intervention strategies and case management are too arbitrary to be trustworthy" (Teyber, 1997, p. 4). Combs (1989) provided similar but more personally directed advice: "To assure that counselor behavior is truly responsible and effective requires a comprehensive, accurate, and internally consistent personal theory" (p. 62).

Theory as a Guide

What is the role of theory in psychotherapy? From time to time, we hear someone ask psychotherapists early in their training how they would handle a particular case. They might answer with, "I'll do anything that works." There are two problems with this response. First, the implication is that they will try different approaches until they hit upon one that "works." Even a blind squirrel will occasionally find an acorn, but is likely to be the skinniest squirrel in the woods. The point of this old axiom is that sometimes good things may happen serendipitously. Positive outcomes can come about through trial and error. People, however, do not come to psychotherapy to be experimented on. Clients rightfully expect a knowledgeable and competent practitioner. Effective psychotherapists are ones who know beforehand that the methods they use are effective. They know so because the methods and practices have already been proven effective, and it is the methods and practices themselves for which psychotherapists are accountable. This is the place to point out that psychotherapists are not accountable for outcomes—they are the clients' responsibility. Psychotherapists are accountable for their methods. Effective psychotherapists do not attempt anything with clients that they do not already know is an effective and sound intervention in psychotherapy. Psychotherapy is a purposeful activity, and the purposes come from sound personality and counseling theories. Second, without a comprehensive understanding of human behavior, there is no guiding theory to inform psychotherapists that the therapy has "worked." The story of an art teacher who worked with young children will illustrate this point. She was known for helping children create truly wonderful hand paintings. She was asked once how she was able to teach children how to create such beautiful paintings. She said, "I know when to tell them to stop." The children did not know about composition, design, balance, or symmetry. The children did not have a theory of art. The teacher did. In psychotherapy, aside from symptom relief, it is often the therapist who knows that the therapy is finished.

Personality and counseling theory serve different purposes for psychotherapists. Let us discuss the role of personality theory first. Theories of personality are meant to answer a specific question: Why do human beings behave the way we do? Some personality theories also address another question: When does human behavior develop? How does it come about? Personality theory answers two questions for psychotherapists—why we do what we do and when that behavior developed. Perhaps, in your study of psychotherapy, you have read or been instructed that "why" is a question not often asked in a counseling session. "Ask why and get a lie." This little rhyme is often used by trainers with beginning therapists to stop them from asking the "why" question. There are at least two reasons for restricting therapists from asking "why." First, it is an accusatory question and will likely put clients in a defensive frame of mind. Their answer will be an expected and socially accepted reason for the behavior. Second, effective psychotherapists already know the answer before it is asked! Their personality theory has already answered the why question. That is the purpose of personality theory—to explain human behavior. For psychotherapists grounded in personality theory, there is no need to ask "why" because their theory has already addressed the question. Let us add to this discussion the difference between "why" for psychotherapists and "why" for clients. When psychotherapists address the question of "why," what they are asking is the underlying motivation for behavior. That is what personality theories address. When clients, however, ask "why" they are asking for an explanation that is acceptable enough for them so that they can live their lives. It is for this reason that the exploration of "why" is important in psychotherapy and one of the reasons for which it is so important that clients be active participants in that exploration. They are the ones who must live with their explanations.

Competing Theories

A bewildering number of competing personality theories provide apparently contradictory explanations of human behavior. Psychoanalytic theories point to the importance of an inner psychological world in constant conflict between the demands of psychic impulses and societal rules. Ego psychology, another form of psychoanalytic theory, emphasizes the importance of very early human relationships. One form of behaviorism maintains that behavior that is reinforced will likely be repeated. Cognitive theory stresses the role thoughts themselves play in influencing behavior. Humanistic theory accents the biological tendency toward organismic completeness or self-actualization and the development of a central organizing concept labeled the *self.* These theories hold contradictory assumptions regarding such important questions as the role of genetics versus environmental conditions—the role of biology versus the role of the mind. Other assumptions include whether behavior is a matter of choice or determined by forces that lie outside the person. Personality theorists differ on whether motivation must be stimulated from outside persons, or whether human beings have the capacity to resist strong outside pressures and through the force of personal will follow their own path. These are important questions, and ones that every psychotherapist faces.

Theory and Genuineness

For many, especially psychotherapists early in their careers, however, a difficult question is which of the many theories should be accepted and followed. It is not a question of which one is right but more a matter of which one is "right for me." This is a personal matter and one that requires study and time. To some extent, it does not matter which theory a psychotherapist follows. What seems more important is the concept of genuineness. This has to do with the correspondence between one's personal beliefs and values and the personality theory one embraces. It seems evident that all of us act on assumptions regarding human behavior whether we are aware of those assumptions or not. Each of us will explain to ourselves the meaning of another person's behavior based on the assumptions we hold dear.

The task of psychotherapists is to explore, examine, and study personality theories until one is found that fits, in the main, one's basic assumptions. Cormier and Hackney (1993) proposed that our assumptions regarding human behavior "may be crystallized into four broad categories: theories that emphasize feelings and affective states; theories that emphasize thought and conceptual processes; theories that emphasize behavior and how it shapes our reality; and theories that emphasize relationships and how they interact to manifest and support feelings, thoughts, and behaviors" (p. 124).

A personality theory is for the psychotherapist. Clients are not likely to have much interest in the theoretical orientation of the therapist. Psychotherapy is not meant to be a classroom where clients are lectured on the theoretical explanation of their behavior. Theory guides the therapist; it does not necessarily guide the client. That brings us to the importance and understanding of a counseling theory.

Personality theory addresses the question of "why." Cormier and Hackney (1993) suggested that "Counseling theories can serve a number of functions. They serve as a set of guidelines to explain how human beings learn, change, and develop; they also propose a model for normal human functioning (and ways in which human dysfunction may be manifested); and they suggest what should transpire in the counseling process and what the outcomes of counseling should be" (p. 4). Thus, counseling theory addresses the question of "how"—how to deal with the issues, problems, or dilemmas presented by clients. A counseling theory provides psychotherapists with a plan of action, a structure, or a model within which to begin the therapy. We have said that psychotherapy is not a trial and error process and that a counseling theory provides a purposeful approach to clients' narratives. Naturally, counseling theories are typically associated with a personality theory, although it is possible to have a counseling theory without a personality theory. While all personality theories are based in science, not all counseling theories are scientifically based. Some counseling theories, for example, may have a religious origin. Whatever its origin, a counseling theory provides the psychotherapist with guidelines regarding how to proceed in therapy. Clearly, all psychotherapy must begin in empathy, and to attempt to be of help to anyone without understanding is, at best, fishing without a hook. You might possibly catch a fish but it would be a hungry fish indeed to bite a string and hold on long enough for you to get it out of the water. How an empathic relationship is formed and how clients' stories are managed need to be guided by counseling theory. Some psychotherapists believe, in accordance with their personality theory, that early childhood experiences of clients are important and collect a detailed and elaborate history in order to understand their clients' difficulties. Others do not place so much emphasis on history and instead concentrate on clients' explanations for their behavior. They listen for the cognitive reasoning underlying the clients' reported behavior. Others isolate symptoms quickly and move to treat these identifiable behaviors concretely and expeditiously. Still others believe that the dream life of clients is important and instruct clients to begin a record of their dreams. Some therapists want to know and understand the family and present living arrangements of clients. Others emphasize a relationship characterized by empathy, genuineness, and respect in a structure of exploration, understanding, and resolution. Other therapists with other counseling theories have different emphases.

Eclecticism

Let us just take a moment here to discuss the issue of eclecticism. Suppose you were a well-informed client and approached a psychotherapist to ask his or her theoretical orientation. The psychotherapist replies, "I am basically psychoanalytical but I use cognitive behaviorism when it is appropriate." Well, this is just nonsense. To illustrate the inherent problem, suppose our response regarding a client was "I believe the client is suffering from an obvious Oedipal complex and has not been properly reinforced for his acceptable behavior toward authority figures. He is in an existential crises and filled with despair. He has a poor self-concept and clearly has not come to terms with the shadow part of his personality." This is nothing more than jargon strung together and reflects a mindless mishmash of hot words from various theories. This form of eclecticism is unacceptable and, perhaps, even dangerous, if not for psychotherapists, at least for their clients. In the realm of personality theory, one should "stay close to home." Let us also say that we do not mean to imply that every psychotherapist must subscribe to a single theory of personality (for instance, Freudian, Rogerian, Adlerian, or Jungian). Another form of eclecticism is one in which compatible elements of different theories may be systematically combined into a coherent personal theory. It is likely, however, that such a combination would still fit into one of the major theoretical families (that is, cognitive, behavioral, phenomenological, or psychoanalytical). In the explanation of human behavior, it is more helpful to stick to a comprehensive theory than to attempt to jump from theory to theory depending upon the diagnoses. It would be a hollow psychotherapist, for example, who said, "Well, I use humanistic theory for problems of the self. But, for depression I find that cognitive theory is best. If a client has some form of spiritual crises, I like existentialism and for anxiety, I use behaviorism." This is a counselor who has mistaken methods for the process. Combs (1989) warned us that "What therapists do, or do not do, in the counseling process is not a mechanical matter of applying the right method to the right client at the right instant. Instead, the behavior of counselors depends upon the counselor's beliefs, values, goals, and understandings applied to the problem of helping the client in the most effective ways possible" (p. 62).

There is, of course, no point in bouncing from theory to theory to deal with different symptoms since a thorough study of any one theory reveals that it has a theoretical explanation in place for symptoms. Intellectual laziness is revealed when psychotherapists hop from theory to theory in explaining symptoms. It reveals that they have not spent the time for in-depth study of a particular theory. While unsystematic eclecticism in personality theory is not helpful, using a variety of therapeutic strategies becomes a matter of practicality. While personality theories differ widely, there is much overlap in what psychotherapists actually do. For example, it is possible to make a statement like "All psychotherapy begins in empathy" (Welch, 1998) because, in practice, it is virtually impossible to be of help to someone unless we understand that person regardless of our orientation. Psychotherapists are, largely, compassionate people who want to be of help. It is no surprise then that, in practice, psychotherapists seek to understand what clients need help with. It follows that practitioners of one theory borrow from one another. A strategy or technique may be suggested by a variety of personality theories. Let us give you one example: In Victor Frankl's logotherapy, there is a technique he calls "paradoxical intention." In behaviorism, there is a strategy called "negative practice." In Gestalt practice, there is "exaggeration." In each of these techniques, clients are asked to do something that seems just the opposite of what they say they want. An example would be fingernail biting. In negative practice, clients would be asked to practice biting their fingernails! This method of dealing with human behaviors has even found its way into "commonsense" advise in what is called "reverse psychology." Throughout years of practice, psychotherapists from different theoretical orientations have discovered similar interventions that are effective in similar circumstances. "Practicing the problem" is one way to sensitize the self to a piece of behavior so that it may be brought under conscious control. Many theories can account for why this works, and the fact that one theory may be credited with the discovery or creation of a strategy does not preclude others from using it. In this sense, a practitioner may be technically eclectic while remaining congruent within a personality theory.

Being Grounded

When psychotherapists are well grounded in a personality and counseling theory, they are able to offer psychotherapy that is notable for several reasons. Remember that psychotherapy is purposeful. Theoretically grounded psychotherapists are not stumbling blindly around in the lives of clients. They are doing what they are doing for the practical benefit of clients. Their work is systematic, orderly, and precise. While the world may appear in shambles to clients, that is not the case for the purposeful activity of psychotherapists. Consider for a moment a ship at sea. Storms come up, and the craft may be buffeted and assailed by the elements. Tossed and shaken by wind and water, it may seem to be mere debris at the mercy of a chaotic storm. Yet, more often than not, the ship weathers the storm to sail more comfortably to its final destination. Its survival is not a chance event. The ship survived because the sailors performed their duties purposefully and skillfully. Psychotherapy can be a stormy time, but, precisely because the psychotherapist has purpose, knowledge, and skill, the turmoil can be navigated and weathered.

Another advantage theoretically well-grounded psychotherapists enjoy is a sense of confidence even in the face of the unknown. The great disadvantage of relying only on experience is that it does not teach us what to do outside our experience. Teyber (1997) pointed out that "Many therapists become exceedingly anxious in their early counseling work because they lack a coherent and practical conceptual framework. Uncertainty over how to conceptualize client problems and ambiguous guidelines for how to proceed in the therapy session heighten their insecurity and preoccupation with their counseling performance" (p. 4). A person may learn to run one machine efficiently but be totally lost with another piece of equipment. A mechanical engineer, however, may know nothing at all about a new piece of machinery and learn its secrets quickly because of an understanding of mechanics. Psychotherapists who are well grounded in theory can be faced with unusual and previously unexperienced human behavior and yet respond effectively and sensibly. Thus, they can be confident when they greet clients even though they have no idea what clients are going to bring to therapy.

In this way, psychotherapy can be spontaneous and creative. Theory does not provide practitioners with a map but with an understanding of climate, land forms, spatial patterns, soils, vegetation, and erosion, for example. In this analogy, explorers/therapists may not fully know where they are but they may be able to find water, tell direction, detect danger, and find food. They may respond creatively to necessity precisely because they have an understanding of principles in the absence of specifics. We need to say a bit more about spontaneity and creativity because we said earlier that clients do not come to therapy to be experimented on. Clients are people who are in a vulnerable state, and therefore an intervention cannot be risked that does not have a high prediction of success. Having said that, however, how can psychotherapy be spontaneous and creative without risk? There are two answers to this question. First, when psychotherapists experiment or risk a new intervention, it is not clients who are subjects. Psychotherapists are. Psychotherapists try interventions that are new to them not to see if they work on clients but to see if they can use the intervention effectively. Psychotherapists know that the new intervention should work because they found it in a book or have had it recommended by a colleague. The spontaneous use of a new intervention is an experiment by psychotherapists not to see if it works with clients but to see whether they can use the technique effectively themselves. Does it fit for them? It becomes a matter of congruence. The second answer is that psychotherapists do create interventions "on the spur of the moment." They creatively respond to a new situation with something they have never done before. They can creatively respond because they already know that the new intervention should work because they are guided by theory. It is not blind intervention.

Let us give you an example: In an episode of the original popular television series *Star Trek,* members of the crew are mysteriously spirited away from their spaceship to an unknown place and presented with challenges to test their skills. They are caught up in the experience when one of the crew, Mr. Spock, a highly cognitive and nonemotional character, conducts a simple experiment. It does not turn out the way it should. From this, Mr. Spock determines that what the crew is experiencing is an illusion. The crew questions his conclusion and doubts that their experiences are an illusion just because the experiment did not work out. Mr. Spock replies, "That is precisely why I know this is an illusion. The experiment *should have* worked as I predicted. It did not, therefore, the ordinary laws have been suspended. This is not real." Theory then becomes the sure ground from which to approach the unknown. It is not enough to "fly by the seat of your pants off the top of your head" (Martin, 1983). Creativity and spontaneity are guided by a theoretical understanding of human behavior. This theoretical knowledge contributes to the courage to explore what is unfamiliar, foreign, and even bizarre.

Identifying and Developing a Personal Theory

As you move forward in your development as a psychotherapist, it is important to have a personally meaningful conceptual framework in your work with clients. Combs (1989) identified this important task and stated clearly that "what makes an effective therapist is the acquisition of a comprehensive, internally congruent system of beliefs—development of a personal theory. Information and experience provide the raw materials; but it is the personal exploration and discovery of meaning which puts it all together into a system capable of providing trustworthy guidelines for professional practice" (p. 159). This approach to psychotherapy has been labeled the "self as instrument" approach by Combs and Gonzalez (1994) and leads to the conclusion that "how well helpers are able to use themselves as effective instruments is dependent on the quality of their belief systems" (p. 19). Study, time, and commitment are the necessary ingredients for developing one's personal theory.

The Process of Change in Psychotherapy

The Client

If the therapist is able to achieve the attitudinal and atmospheric climate described earlier and the relationship is characterized by a collaborative, trusting, and challenging nature, then what is hoped for, and even expected, is change for the client. Psychotherapy represents a step in the process of change. Sometimes it is painfully slow and tedious for both the client and the therapist. At other times, change can occur at a dramatic pace.

What follows is our attempt at describing the process of change as we have seen it in our clinical experience. We do not intend to imply that this is the only possible way in which one could conceptualize the change process, and, in fact, a number of others have identified the process and stated in both theoretical and research terms other descriptions of the change process in psychotherapy (Beitman, 1987; McConnaughy, Prochaska, & Velicer, 1983; McConnaughy, DiClemente, Prochaska, & Velicer, 1989; Steenbarger, 1992; Strong & Claiborn, 1982; Tracey & Ray, 1984; Welch, 1998).

Change begins in the recognition that something is not working in one's life. Combs and Gonzalez (1994) noted that change begins in acceptance. What clients are signaling to us is that the process for change actually begins before they enter psychotherapy. Clients have identified within themselves a need to change. We have labeled that process *admission.* In order to begin the process of change, a person has to *admit* (or accept) that something is so. The word *admit* means to "permit to enter, to let in." It means to concede a fact, not necessarily to agree or like it. The motivation for change is driven by discontent. What is being admitted is not that one likes or dislikes the behavior or life situation but rather that one's behavior or life situation has something that needs to be changed. It is an act of intrapersonal honesty that precedes any effective meeting with a psychotherapist. *Admission is made to the self.* It does not involve other people in any direct sense.

Next, change must, to some extent, involve others. Usually, in order for change to occur, the facts have to be *acknowledged* to others. A qualitatively different experience exists between admitting to oneself that change is needed and acknowledging it to others. Acknowledgment recognizes that change is possible, that one needs help, and that others can help. However, in order for others to be of help, they have to know what is needed. In order for them to know what is needed, they must be told. This step may involve already trusted friends and relatives, and a network of personal support is often sufficient to support the changes needed in persons' lives. In such cases, the involvement of professional helpers may not be needed. In therapy, the psychotherapist is the other person who hears the client's story. *Acknowledgment* is a significant step in the change process and one that we believe is dependent on the counselor attitudes and relationship characteristics described previously. Just as in any process, acknowledgment might unfold in layers, degrees, or stages. Clients typically come to therapy with a *presenting problem.* If the therapist proves to be empathic and respectful and is able to create a collaborative and trusting climate, then the presenting problem might give way to more intensely experienced issues or problems.

Change requires change. This seemingly redundant statement lies at the core of many deeply wished for, but not acted upon, life changes. Exploration and understanding are not sufficient. It is necessary to act. Change requires *accommodation.* Accommodation means the gradual process of giving up old ways of being and doing, and introducing new ones in their place. Yet, as clearly as this change process can be stated and as deeply as it may be understood, the process is often stalled at the point of actual change. What stalls change at this point, we believe, is threat. Psychological defenses are fierce opponents and do not willingly give up entrenched styles of coping. If the relationship between the therapist and the client develops well, then threat may be reduced in psychotherapy and the way may be opened not only for exploration and understanding but for lasting change as well.

Accommodation means altering the self to the demands of change. In the collaborative relationship, the external world's demands may be identified, understood, and to the degree necessary and possible, accommodated. At this point in the change process, clients have done all that can be expected of them. They have *admitted* the need for change; they have *ac-*

knowledged the facts and needed changes to others; and they have begun the process of *accommodating* their lives to realistic life demands. They have, in truth, done all that can reasonably be asked of them. Psychotherapy frequently ends at this point. Issues have been clarified and understood; options have been explored; and courses of action have been identified and pursued. While the psychotherapy may end, the process of change should continue.

The word *adapt* implies modifying the surroundings, circumstances, situations, or context. One has changed the self; now the world must adapt to the person. Development does not stop when psychotherapy ends. People *advance*. The word *advance* means to move forward. Years ago, interestingly enough, it meant *to lift up*. Tragedy may lead to strength. People do live through, overcome, and even transcend life circumstances (*ad astra per aspera*—to the stars through difficulties). In psychological theory such development is labeled *actualization*.

Change leads to a process of life involvement and possible fulfillment. This is the hoped for positive outcome of psychotherapy. Therapists who are empathic, authentic, and respectful, as well as holding a belief system that promotes empowerment and change can create climates that are characterized by such words as collaborative, trusting, and challenging. Clients who come to therapy and experience such a relationship are freed to walk the path of change, which makes its way from an initial personal admission of the need to change to a life in which they are more likely to be able to cope on more equal terms.

Ending: Completing the Psychotherapeutic Relationship

Few beginnings anticipate their endings quite so carefully as psychotherapy. Experienced psychotherapists know even in the midst of building the relationship that its end promises greater success than its continuation. New therapists may struggle with conceptualizing a process that seeks its own end, yet psychotherapy, perhaps more than any other enterprise, is a process devoted to its own dissolution.

Even as we begin this section, let us introduce a caution. The termination session is not something different from psychotherapy; it is an integral part of psychotherapy. Psychotherapists who understand that doing an intake form is a part of psychotherapy and that termination is also a part of psychotherapy are able to flow from one moment to the next without jarring transitions. The experience from beginning to end is of a single cloth without tears in the fabric. The process of ending is attended to with the same concern with which all other phases and processes of psychotherapy are governed. It is a time for summary, cementing gains, planning ahead, review, and, perhaps, referral.

The Ethics of Termination

Psychotherapists are not in the business of "stringing people along" for monetary or power needs. An ethical guideline for psychotherapists is that therapy be as time efficient as possible without a slavish commitment to brevity. Our task is to enter the relationship without guile and move toward a collaborative end as smoothly and expeditiously as possible. Ethically, counselors do not "abandon" clients because they are difficult or troublesome. Much of the help we are able to provide stems from our willingness to "stick it out" when others might have quit. Equally important is the recognition that if we are unable to be of help, for whatever reason (competence, personal conflicts, intrapersonally experienced dilemmas), then therapy should be ended. There are a number of appropriate ethical reasons for bringing therapy to a close. For example, if the client is no longer benefiting or no longer needs therapy, termination is appropriate. Also, it could be that the client is not invested in the process or needs a different therapist.

Practical Considerations

In a review of goals, accomplishments, and unfinished business, remember that perfection is not the goal. In the review process, it is not necessary to "dot every 'i' or cross every 't'." Consider Winnecott's advice to parents—you don't have to be perfect, you just have to be "good enough." The task of psychotherapy is not to send a perfect human being into the world but merely to do our best to send that human being out of therapy more able to cope than when he or she came in. We should, of course, do what we can to ensure that the client's newly discovered or newly created coping strategies have a reasonable chance of succeeding in the world. Given that, then we have done our job.

Preparing for Termination

As it becomes clear that the clients' abilities to cope with their lives are growing and approaching the point where they no longer need to be in therapy, it is important to begin the process of bringing therapy to an end. In so doing, it can be useful to review the intake session, treatment plan, and progress notes to get a firmer grasp on the evolution of change as it has occurred in therapy. Make a note of gains and plan an opportunity for a discussion of how those gains can be maintained once therapy ends. Also plan with the client on identifying work that still needs to be done—what might be called "unfinished business." Be prepared to reassure clients that while therapy is ending that the possibility of future contact is open, and, if necessary, be prepared to offer appropriate referrals.

When all things go well, the therapist and client mutually decide that the time has come to end the therapeutic relationship. Frequently, however, all things do not go well and rather than a planned and timely end, the therapy might begin to sputter. Clues might begin to be dropped that the therapy is no longer fully serving the needs of the client but the client might not feel comfortable bringing up these concerns directly. It appears to us that termination in psychotherapy falls into two types—planned and unplanned. When things go well, then termination conforms to our expectations and can be structured and managed. When things slip outside our expectations, then termination may be quick or not occur at all, both unsatisfying to therapists.

Planned Termination

Even when the therapy is proceeding well, it is sometimes difficult to appropriately determine when to end. This is especially true if the client's problems or dilemmas are vague and undifferentiated. In such a case, considerable time may have to be devoted to exploration, and determining clear and precise outcome goals may be difficult. Therapists may consider factors such as whether or not the presenting problem has been sufficiently addressed or the degree to which any crippling stress has been alleviated. Other factors to consider are such things as the quality of the person's relationships at home and work.

Time-Limited Termination. Limiting psychotherapy happens for several reasons. One, of course, is that the practitioner uses a form of psychotherapy that is intentionally brief. Such a solution-focused approach is explained to the client in the beginning and termination is included in the planned number of sessions. It might also be the case that the client is employed by a company with an Employee Assistance Program (EAP), which permits a contracted number of sessions. After those sessions, the client might be referred to another psychotherapist outside the EAP. Each of these time-limited models plans a closing session into the counseling experience, and both the therapist and the client know the number of sessions and the ending date from the beginning.

Natural Termination. When the process of psychotherapy moves along at a good and effective clip and both the therapist and client mutually decide that the therapy has served its purpose, then termination can be anticipated and planned in a collaborative way. By this, we mean that the ending is not forced but rather eventuates as a reasonable outcome of the process. Both the therapist and client agree, and the end becomes mutually satisfying. This is not to say that all issues have been resolved or that there might not be some feelings of loss at the end of so intimate a relationship. What we mean is that both parties recognize that the purposes of the relationship have largely been met and that continuing the relationship might do more harm than good—creating dependency, for example, or an unnecessary financial burden. In such a complementary situation, the goals of termination will be most effectively accomplished.

Unplanned Termination

Endings are not always planned or even anticipated. Some happen quickly, and most unsatisfying of all is the situation in which there is no opportunity to bring closure to the therapeutic relationship.

Spontaneous Termination. Sometimes clients come to a session knowing that their work is finished. In the normal flow of the session, it may become clear that the client is ready to end, and the therapist may fully agree. In such a situation, the ending is mutual even though it has not been discussed prior to the ending session. This is a case, while not ideal, in which the goals of effective termination can be adequately accomplished. The counselor might have to simply throw open the client's folder and say, "Let's look at the goals we set in the beginning and review them together." The outcome can be satisfying, and even though accomplished on the "spur of the moment," it can be thorough enough and provide the opportunity for both a review of gains and a discussion of tasks yet left to be accomplished. Spontaneous endings might well signal a client's difficulty with "saying good-bye" in general. If this has not been a part of the therapy and if the opportunity presents itself, talking about this aspect of ending with the client might be worthwhile.

Arbitrary Termination. The least satisfying ending for a therapist is one in which the client simply stops coming to therapy without the opportunity for an ending session. Typically, there are clues to arbitrary endings that might include such things as missing sessions, not completing homework, or having trouble finding important issues to discuss in therapy or seeming less involved during sessions. When clients begin to show such signs, it may be possible to anticipate an arbitrary ending and instead make it a planned ending. It is important, of course, for therapists to understand that the client is the one who is in charge of termination and that although a mutually decided on ending may be more satisfying for the therapist, clients may end therapy any time they wish. It is possible, however, if the signs of restlessness can be recognized that the therapist request an ending session in which the goals of termination may be accomplished.

Another form of unplanned ending may not come from the client but from the therapist who may, for any number of reasons, find it necessary to end a therapy relationship before it is mutually satisfying to both parties. One of the authors, for example, recently moved from one community to another. As a part of the move, he had to end the counseling relationship with his clients. Some of them resulted in spontaneous endings, and some resulted in referrals. These situations may be unavoidable, and just as therapists sometimes move, so do clients.

Sometimes therapists might recognize some intrapersonal feelings that interfere with their effectiveness and realize the need to refer the client to another therapist as an ethical issue. In one example of this situation, one of the authors received a referral, and when he met with the new client, she expressed her frustration and irritation at being referred. She simply did not know why she had been referred. In fact, neither did the new therapist. He asked her permission to speak to the previous therapist to find out the reason for the referral. As it turned out, the previous therapist had gone through a divorce, and the client bore a striking resemblance to his former wife! He simply felt that he would not be able to get beyond her physical appearance. He consented to the current therapist's informing the client of his reasons and when that was done, the client was able to form a relationship with the new therapist and move on. In other situations, therapists may find that a client presents with a disorder that demands specialized knowledge. They may feel ethically bound to refer the client to a more competent practitioner. More often than not, clients accept these referrals as being in their best interests, especially when the situation is adequately explained.

In more unfortunate circumstances, death can come unexpectedly in anyone's life, and both clients and therapists have to cope if death takes a client or a counselor. A client might end his or her life by suicide, and this is a time when the therapist should seek the support and advice of other psychotherapists to deal with any feelings of guilt or mourning. Clients are in a more precarious place, and unless the therapist happened to work in a group setting, there might not be someone immediately available to meet with distraught clients.

The Meaning of Ending

Even in the best of circumstances, there can be issues in the termination of psychotherapy. Some are simply unavoidable and may even include the natural issues of ending any relationship. Others are peculiar to the therapeutic relationship. Psychotherapy is an intimate relationship. Both clients and psychotherapists can be taken off guard at how quickly an intimate and significant relationship can develop. While there is healing potential in such relationships, there can be danger as well. For the therapist, there is the danger of self-aggrandizement, misuse of power, manipulation, and exploitation (for example, financial, sexual, and so on).

For clients, there is the danger of dependency, hero worship, and a self-diminishing attitude in which they may believe that they are incapable of success in life without the therapist. Even when the dangers are avoided and the relationship is one of empowerment and mutual satisfaction, ending the relationship can bring feelings of loss and wishfulness for continued contact on a social or more informal level. We are not too far out on a limb to mention that we are a species that has made its way in the universe by togetherness. We are more comfortable in coming together than we are in separating. Saying good-bye is a task that many in our culture have reported as troublesome. Tears come easily to some, and even brief acquaintances may result in a tearful good-bye. While therapists recognize the importance of therapeutic distance, the end of a long and intimate relationship may still "tug at one's heartstrings."

For clients, who have not been through the training of managing detached concern (Welch, 1998), these separation issues can be more intense. They might have greater issues with feelings of abandonment and attachment than the therapist, and for them a good termination is one in which ample opportunity to discuss these feelings is provided.

Lame Duck Sessions

A final problem with which therapists must cope in termination is the tendency of clients to begin to withdraw emotional energy from the therapy once termination is mentioned as a possibility. Therapists may find themselves being "lame duck therapists" and unable to continue the effective work that was being done previously. Clients may begin to invest less and less energy in session as they anticipate their end in therapy. While we have made much of the point that psychotherapy always anticipates its ending, it is simultaneously true that the premature suggestion of ending can frighten clients and prevent effective work. It is a difficult task to decide accurately and collaboratively the appropriate time for ending without jeopardizing the therapy. Our suggestion is that termination should not be presented until the therapist is firmly convinced that the therapeutic issues have been addressed, and then approximately two weeks before the anticipated final session. An alternative to this procedure is the process in which clients are moved from weekly sessions, to biweekly, to monthly, to quarterly, and so forth until they feel fully comfortable in being on their own without the need for the support of therapy. While therapy should include planning for termination, its premature introduction can have a negative effect on therapy, and the introduction of the idea of ending should be approached cautiously.

Solidifying Gains

The termination session is a time in which clients can reflect on the changes they have made in therapy. It is a time to measure the space between the starting line and their present position. The therapist can be of help in being concrete and practical in the movement. It is a time when both the client and the therapist look back and make a judgment about the perceived changes. Again the client should lead, and the therapist should add what he or she believes the client has neglected. It may be useful for the therapist to bring in a written list of the formal goals established in the treatment plan. It might be helpful to have the client write out, along with the therapist, the goal, the progress made, and what is left to do with that goal.

Psychotherapy is not designed to do everything within the confines of the therapeutic session or for that matter within the confines of the therapeutic encounter. Obviously, much is done by the client outside the time spent in the therapy session. This reasoning extends to the time after psychotherapy has been completed. Welch (1998) discussed the need for clients to become "therapist to the self." In a discussion of work remaining, clients and counselors can talk about what the clients need to do to continue their progress as they continue their lives. This is a time for encouragement and support as the counselor helps clients begin the transition from having a supportive climate, that they can visit each week, to a sense that they are increasingly capable of coping on their own with the issues and problems of their lives. Again, it is important for clients to lead and for the counselor to add what seems necessary.

Referral

Referral presents a different set of issues with which the therapist must cope. In termination, it must be made clear that the possibility of returning is open for the client. If for some reason, this is not the case, then information should be provided in a concrete way so that clients can continue to receive the help they need. It may involve providing the client with the telephone number of a local mental health center and the names and telephone numbers of appropriate independent practitioners. In addition, it may include providing clients with ways in which organizations and support groups may be contacted to continue clients' progress.

As stated earlier, clients need to know that they can return if they feel the need. The therapist's job is to be encouraging without giving clients the impression that if they come back, they have somehow failed. It is, as is much in psychotherapy, a delicate time and task. Clients need to be encouraged to move out on their own and be reassured that the therapist is there to be of assistance if needed. One way to do this is to include a phrase that recognizes psychotherapy as one of the tools the clients now have as they cope with their life issues. A therapist might say, for example, "You know something now that you didn't know before and that is that when you are facing the stresses of your life that you have this place to come to if you want to." What is implied in this statement is that psychotherapy is just one more way in which to cope and not a sign of failure.

It may also be a time to refer clients into a different modality of psychotherapy, such as marriage and family or group therapy rather than individual sessions. It is a time to help clients become aware of community resources that might be appropriate and, if necessary, a time to refer a client to a therapist who specializes in the client's concern. Regarding referral, it is also a time to reassure clients that a referral is not needed and that the issues they came with and other issues that arose have been sufficiently dealt with—in the therapist's opinion—and that further psychotherapy does not appear to be necessary. This can be a powerful statement for clients.

Summary

The termination session is a time to spend looking back. The tasks of termination are straightforward and mirror the summary phase of an individual session. Just as in an individual session, there needs to be a summary, a solidifying of gains, a review of goals, a discussion of work remaining, and homework. Questions to ask are such things as "What were the presenting issues? What new issues emerged? What were the highlights, low points, struggles, and, perhaps, interpersonal issues?" It is a time to look back over the path that the client and counselor traveled together. This is both a cognitive (that is, intellectual/analytical) and emotional summary. It is important that the client take the lead in this summary. The therapist's role is to listen to the client's summary and then add anything that the client leaves out that seems important to the therapist.

Termination is not merely the end of psychotherapy, it is psychotherapy. It should not be treated as something that is separate from the process of therapy. Termination is ideally presented as one more therapeutic process in which therapists can be of service to the client. It is important to note that ending psychotherapy both efficiently and effectively is an ethical matter for psychotherapists and we are not in the business of unnecessarily extending the time a client spends with us. The goals of termination are to summarize the therapy in a cognitive, intellectual, and analytical way as well as to provide an emotional summary of the path taken in the therapy. It is important to review the gains made in therapy as well to review the presenting problem(s), formal goals, progress, and work yet left to be done. Finally, clients need to know that they can return to therapy if they want to without guilt and, that if the therapist thinks it necessary, a referral can be made to help the client continue the work initiated in the present therapy.

REFERENCES AND FOR FURTHER READING

Beitman, B. D. (1987). *The structure of individual psychotherapy.* New York: Guilford Press.

Bruckner-Gordon, F., Gangi, B. K., & Wallman, G. U. (1988). *Making therapy work.* New York: Harper & Row.

Castillo, R. J. (1997). *Culture and mental illness.* Brooks/Cole.

Combs, A. W. (1989). *A theory of therapy: Guidelines for counseling practice.* Newbury Park, CA: Sage.

Combs, A. W., & Gonzalez, D. M. (1994). *Helping relationships: Basic concepts for the helping professions* (4th ed.). Boston: Allyn & Bacon.

Connor-Greene, P. A. (1993, Fall). The therapeutic context: Preconditions for change in psychotherapy. *Psychotherapy, 30,* 375–382.

Cormier, L. S., & Hackney, H. (1993). *The professional counselor: A process guide to helping* (2nd ed.). Boston: Allyn & Bacon.

Curtis, R. C., & Stricker, G. (Eds.). *How people change: Inside and outside therapy.* New York: Plenum Press.

Davies, J. D. (1955). *Phrenology: Fad and science.* New Haven, CT: Yale University Press.

Egan, G. (1990). *The skilled helper* (4th ed.). Pacific Grove, CA: Brooks/Cole.

Hanna, F. J., & Ritchie, M. H. (1995, April). Seeking the active ingredients of psychotherapeutic change: Within and outside the context of therapy. *Professional Psychology—Research and Practice, 26,* 176–183.

Lauver, P., & Harvey, D. R. (1997). *The practical counselor: Elements of effective helping.* Pacific Grove, CA: Brooks/Cole.

Leahey, T. H., & Leahey, G. E. (1983). *Psychology's occult doubles: Psychology and the problem of pseudoscience.* Chicago: Nelson-Hall.

Martin, D. K. (1983). *Counseling and therapy skills.* Pacific Grove, CA: Brooks/Cole.

Maslow, A. H. (1970). *Motivation and personality.* New York: Harper and Row.

McConnaughy, E. A., DiClemente, C. C., Prochaska, J. O., & Velicer, W. F. (1989). Stages of change in psychotherapy: A follow-up report. *Psychotherapy, 26,* 494–503.

McConnaughy, E. A., Prochaska, J. O., & Velicer, W. F. (1983). Stages of change in psychotherapy: Measurement and sample profiles. *Psychotherapy: Theory, Research, and Practice, 20,* 368–375.

Maeder, T. (1989, January). Wounded healers. *Atlantic Monthly,* 37–47.

Mishara, A. L. (1995, Spring). Narrative and psychotherapy: The phenomenology of healing. *American Journal of Psychotherapy, 49,* 180–195.

Rogers, C. R. (1951). *Client-centered therapy.* Boston: Houghton Mifflin.

Rogers, C. R. (1962). Toward becoming a fully functioning person. In A. W. Combs (Ed.), *Perceiving, behaving, becoming: A new focus for education.* Alexandria, VA: Association for Supervision and Curriculum Development.

Safran, J. D. (Ed). (1991). *Emotion, psychotherapy, and change.* New York: Guilford Press.

Sommers-Flannagan, J., & Sommers-Flannagan, R. (1993). *Foundations of therapeutic interviewing.* Boston: Allyn & Bacon.

Steenbarger, B. N. (1992). Toward science-practice integration in brief counseling and therapy. *The Counseling Psychologist, 20,* 403–450.

Strong, S. R., & Claiborn, C. D. (1982). *Change through integration.* New York: Wiley.

Suler, J. R. (1991, March). The T'ai Chi images: A Taoist model of psychotherapeutic change. *Psychologia: An International Journal of Psychology in the Orient, 34,* 18–27.

Teyber, E. (1997). *Interpersonal process in psychotherapy: A relational approach.* (3rd ed.). Pacific Grove, CA: Brooks/Cole.

Tracey, T. J., & Ray, P. B. (1984). The stages of successful time-limited counseling: An interactional examination. *Journal of Counseling Psychology, 31,* 13–27.

Waters, D. B., & Lawrence, E. C. (1993). *Competence, courage, and change: An approach to family therapy.* New York: W. W. Norton.

Welch, I. D. (1998). *The path of psychotherapy: Matters of the heart.* Pacific Grove, CA: Brooks/Cole.

Welch, I. D., & Gonzalez, D. M. (1999). *The process of counseling and psychotherapy: Matters of skill.* Pacific Grove, CA: Brooks/Cole.

Zastrow, C. (1988, Spring). What really causes psychotherapy change? *Journal of Independent Social Work, 23,* 5–16.

CHAPTER

6 The Use of Techniques in Psychotherapy

DAVID M. GONZALEZ

I. DAVID WELCH

The word *technique* carries a variety of meanings in psychotherapy. In this chapter the word is used to refer to specific intervention strategies utilized during psychotherapy sessions for definite purposes. Examples of such techniques are visualization (Ayres & Hopf, 1987; Nelson, 1987; Turkington, 1987), and empty chair (Conoley, Conoley, McConnell, & Kimzey, 1983). This chapter provides a review of some of the potential benefits of using techniques for both the therapist and the client. Among the inherent dangers in advocating the use of techniques in psychotherapy is that more importance will be assigned to them than is appropriate. Our observations as clinical supervisors teach us that many therapists early in their careers move too quickly into problem solving without an adequate exploration and understanding of the client's issues. Armed with specific techniques, less experienced therapists may be too eager to "get on with it" without a clear understanding of the client's dilemmas (Williams, 1988). In this age of Empirically Validated Treatments (EVTs), there can be a danger of "manualized" psychotherapy—the application of "treatment" without understanding. There is a danger of dealing only with the client's surface presentation but not the underlying problems.

The Role of Techniques

Techniques by themselves do not necessarily lead to more effective coping skills. We agree with Highlen and Hill (1984) that the likelihood of successful therapy is found in more subtle predictors. The essence of therapy largely lies in the ability of the therapist to establish a therapeutic relationship with the client (Highlen & Hill, 1984; Kiesler & Watkins, 1989; Patterson, 1984). The most important dimension of that relationship is the therapist's capacity to understand the client and to communicate that understanding (Okun, 1987; Rogers, 1980). Without empathic understanding, any technique or attempt to problem-solve is merely a "shot in the dark." Occasionally, one will hit the target, but seldom will any prizes be won for marksmanship. The same is true in psychotherapy. One may prove to be of some help to another person through genuine concern and by accidental interventions without much preparation or training; however, one cannot reliably count on such accidents for consistent success. Thus, empathy forms the foundation for successful psychotherapeutic intervention.

The effective therapeutic relationship is characterized by empathy, but that is not the only important aspect (Carkhuff, 1987; Gazda, Asbury, Balzer, Childers, & Walters, 1984; Patterson, 1984). In such a relationship, the client ideally comes to trust the therapist with those parts of life that are frightening, embarrassing, and painful. Thus, the therapist's ability to suspend judgment is crucial in order for the early therapeutic relationship to develop into a strong therapeutic alliance or bond. As one of the author's professors used to say, "Anytime you can help a client *mention his or her unmentionables,* you have been helpful to the client" (Ossorio, 1999). "Unmentionable" material is not likely to be expressed unless the therapist is truly nonjudgmental.

One other aspect of the therapeutic relationship merits comment. Some therapists communicate a sense of faith in their clients' ability to contribute to their own realized dilemmas remarkably well. In a word, some therapists are especially respectful of their clients' capacity to explore, problem-solve, and cope. This is especially important, and a substantive body of literature demonstrates the significance of client collaboration and involvement in the therapeutic process (Gonzalez, 2000; Combs & Gonzalez, 1994; Welch, 1998). Weissmark and Giacomo (1998) noted in their review of research on effective psychotherapy that client involvement and participation have yielded the most consistent evidence in predicting positive therapeutic outcomes. Similarly, Orlinsky, Grawe, and Parks (1994) examined 54 findings related to client involvement and found that 65 percent of the 54 findings showed a significant positive association with outcome. Thus, therapists who work from a collaborative position rather than from an expert stance are more likely to have an effective therapeutic relationship.

These are the characteristics, along with others (for example, self-disclosure, confrontation, concreteness) used to describe the therapist–client relationship, that are predictive of successful therapy rather than techniques alone. A client's entry into therapy for the purpose of examining the fearful, embarrassing, and painful parts of life is the first prerequisite of successful therapy. The second prerequisite is a therapist who is able to understand and communicate understanding, suspend judgment, and convey a sense of personal respect for the client's strengths. These two qualities set the stage for the successful outcome of a therapeutic relationship (Garfield & Bergin, 1993; Gladding, 1988; Rogers, 1957). Techniques can enhance the effectiveness of the therapeutic relationship but using techniques alone is not predictive of successful therapeutic outcomes (Mahoney, 1986).

Recognizing the limitations of techniques does not imply that they are not important. Our experience, both as therapists and clinical supervisors of therapists early in their careers, is that techniques often provide useful structure for the therapist and valuable insights for the client. However, techniques present the therapist with both hazards and opportunities.

The hazards, which have been discussed above, are the assumption that the mastery of techniques makes one a master psychotherapist and the danger of premature, and therefore inaccurate, problem solving. The opportunities are discussed in the following section.

The Benefits of Techniques

Our experience has shown that techniques often provide a useful structure for the therapist and insight for the client. It seems clear that the appropriate use of techniques in psychotherapy provides benefits for both the therapist and the client.

Benefits for the Therapist

Energy. The introduction of a technique can make the session more active and alive. Techniques can add sparkle and vigor to sessions that seem dull, unhelpful, and boring.

Pace. Techniques can modulate the rate of a session. If the pace is too rapid, introducing a technique can slow it down so that information can be understood and even reflected upon. In this case, the therapist may employ purposeful interruption as a technique.

Obstacles. Techniques can "facilitate the process." Clients are sometimes so "well defended" that understanding and insight come with pain and grueling slowness. Techniques can be used to provide "end runs" around long-established "defenses" that are getting in the way of progress.

Content. Techniques can be used to expand the material of therapy. The techniques themselves may call to memory ideas, episodes, and events that were previously vague and undifferentiated.

Clarification. When the therapy is vague, when the issues elude, or when the etiology is just too slippery, techniques can serve to clarify the therapy, pin down the issues, and identify the origins of the pain in concrete and understandable ways. Introducing techniques specifically designed to address a particular knot can untie a therapy session and move it toward effectiveness.

Benefits for the Client

Energy. The use of techniques may enliven the session for the client just as it may for the therapist. The client may be invigorated, energized, and stimulated by techniques that introduce a different level of action into the process.

Novelty. Techniques inject a degree of novelty into therapy. The week-in-week-out strategy of therapy can bog down and give the appearance of a repetitive discussion of the same old issue session after session. Techniques can make the sessions new and make the client come to anticipate the session eagerly.

Participation. Techniques can help make the client an active participant in the therapy. They offer clients a variety of methods to better express themselves and to gain insights into their issues.

Integration. Techniques offer clients an opportunity to integrate what has been gained in therapy. They may provide the distance needed to see their lives in different perspectives. Insights that might escape clients in talking therapy might present themselves for inspection during the use of a technique.

Principles for Using Techniques

We have developed seven principles involving the use of techniques in psychotherapy. These principles serve to remind the psychotherapist of the place and usefulness of techniques. Each principle is presented as a declarative statement followed by a short discussion to clarify our meaning.

Principle 1. *Do not experiment with clients.* Without being maudlin and yet still making a point, we want to stress that people who enter therapy are too vulnerable to serve as subjects in a trial-and-error experiment. Therapists use a technique because they already know the technique is effective and useful in that particular situation. It is a tangible violation of clients to experiment in therapy with some strategy for which a general idea of the expected outcome is not already known. In a phrase, therapists do not "try something, just to see if it works." There must be some prior theoretical or experiential justification for the use of techniques in therapy.

Principle 2. *Do not rely on techniques.* Techniques are not the essence of therapy; they are supplements (perhaps even special enhancements) to the therapeutic relationship. The essence of therapy lies more in the relationship than in specific techniques. A danger for beginning therapists is to use strategic interventions too much in any given session. Just as passive listening can become boring and useless, too many techniques become gimmicky and trite. A "rule" we use is to use no more than three techniques in any single session.

Principle 3. *Do not overuse a technique.* Just as too many techniques in a single session can reduce effectiveness, so can using the same technique too frequently. It is important, of course, to cement the gains one has made in the therapy session, and the sensitive repetition of an effective technique can do that. However, if a single technique is used repetitively, then it may become routine and lose its ability to illuminate new information or insights. We suggest, allowing for professional judgment, that at least one session intervene before the use of a technique is repeated.

Principle 4. *Do not abandon technique.* Less experienced therapists often will attempt a technique, with encouragement and good results, and in later sessions will not grasp the opportunity to use it again when it is appropriate. In order to use techniques effectively, the therapist has to be sensitive to those points in therapy when a technique may be introduced with effectiveness. Also, remember not to abandon the technique too quickly during a particular session. A therapist may attempt a technique, fear that it is not working, and stop prematurely. It is important to stay with a technique. To some extent, this demands a belief, on the part of the therapist, that the technique will work and will provide useful information or insights for the therapy.

Principle 5. *Techniques rarely fail.* When supervising therapists in training, it is not uncommon to see a therapist who uses a technique in the therapy session only to report, "I tried what you said, and it did not work." What is missing in this situation is an understanding of the use of techniques. Whether or not a client is able to do what is asked in a technique is not the central issue when judging the success of the technique. In fact, no matter how the client responds, information is generated when a technique is introduced into the therapy session. If the client is able to respond in the predicted way, then the material produced is discussed. If the client does not respond in the predicted way and instead touches on some other aspect of his or her life, then that material may become the focus of therapy. If the client is unable to enter in the technique at all, then that is significant in and of itself and the inability to enter the technique may become the focus of therapy. In essence, no matter what occurs when a technique is introduced, the material produced is potentially useful to therapeutic progress.

Principle 6. *Use techniques with which you feel comfortable.* Not all techniques "fit" or are useful for all therapists. While we are familiar with many techniques, we do not use all of them in therapy sessions. Some techniques do not match the individual style or personality of particular therapists. Each therapist must struggle to find those techniques with which he or she is comfortable and use those.

Now let us discuss a bit of a paradox. Principle 1 advises that therapists not experiment with clients. That remains true. Nevertheless, one must experiment with techniques for one's own use. What is the answer to this seeming dilemma? Understanding the following attitude clears up the dilemma: When a therapist introduces a technique into therapy, the client is not being experimented on because the therapist already knows that this technique has proven to be effective with other clients in similar situations based on reports in the literature or the advice of a supervisor who has assured the therapist that the technique is appropriate. The therapist is testing whether or not he or she can use the technique effectively and comfortably. This is an important distinction.

Let us explore one more aspect of this problem. What is the role of creativity and spontaneity in therapy? How does one know that a creative intervention is not simply experimenting with a client? The answer to the first question is that creativity and spontaneity are important to effective therapeutic intervention. The answer to the second question involves the importance of being well versed in one's theoretical orientation. One way to discover which techniques are comfortable is to try them out for fit. Another approach is to test them intellectually against one's philosophy and theoretical orientation. Although many techniques can be justified by several theoretical orientations, some cannot. This test of fit is another consideration of degree of comfort. As far as creativity and spontaneity are concerned, an "on-the-spot" intervention still may not be considered trial and error because, theoretically, it should work. On the basis of one's theory, one may create spontaneous psychotherapeutic interventions.

Principle 7. *Use techniques with which the client feels comfortable.* When working with various clients, some techniques will prove to be more effective than others. Some may use audio cues. Others might be reluctant to enter into fantasy. Some might respond more readily to storytelling. Some might react negatively to behavioral rehearsal. Others might thoroughly object to an empty chair, while some seem to relish imagery.

> The principle of effectiveness is to honor the tendencies of the client. It is important to be sensitive to concerns such as learning style, gender, and culture.

Each of these may prove an impediment or a pathway to greater effectiveness with a client. To some extent, it is important to recognize that while "techniques rarely fail," some are more effective with particular clients.

Guidelines for the Selection of Techniques

In our experience, two guidelines for the selection of techniques have emerged. One deals with *when* to use a technique in therapy and the other deals with *what* techniques to use.

> Guideline 1. *Select a technique for a specific purpose.* A nontechnical way of phrasing this would be, "do not go on fishing expeditions to try to hook into something spicy and delicious." The technique should be selected because the therapist already knows the usefulness and predicted outcome in a particular situation. Although serendipitous results are possible, that is not the intention of the intervention.
>
> Guideline 2. *Select techniques that fit you as a therapist.* Therapists should only use techniques that fit their theoretical orientation, personal values, and personal style. One of the touchstones of effective therapy is that the client views the therapist as an authentic person. If the therapist uses techniques that make him or her uncomfortable, uneasy, or phony, then that discomfort is certain to be communicated to the client. Using the information presented in Principle 6, find those techniques that fit your theoretical orientation, personal values, and personal style. Those techniques stand a greater chance of successfully adding to the overall effectiveness of the therapy. Before using any techniques, we recommend that the therapist consider how he or she would feel if asked to engage in a particular technique. If such a thought creates a reluctance on the part of the therapist, then the technique is likely not a good fit. In other words, do not ask clients to do anything that you would not be willing to do. Along these lines, a number of years ago one of the authors was cofacilitating a group of adolescents. The coleader asked each member of the group to engage in the trust-building technique of falling backward and trusting the other members to catch them. After each member did so (some with a lot of trepidation that was eventually overcome), the group asked the coleader to do the same thing. She was unable to do so as she found the technique to be too frightening. She was unaware that the exercise would raise such fears in her. The group members were furious that they were asked to do something that the therapist would not or could not do. Thus, a mindful consideration of which techniques are chosen is recommended.

Suggested Techniques

While there are a number of sources of effective techniques (Dyer & Vriend, 1977; Rosenthal, 1998; Vriend, 1985; Welch, Zawistoski, & Smart, 1991), the techniques included here are ones that the authors use on a regular basis and have proven through our experience to be effective with clients.

Empty Chair

This technique employs a bit of imagination. Clients are asked to bring a person into the room with whom the client needs to speak—not in reality, but in their imagination. The process involves a number of steps:

1. Provide an empty chair. (The recommendation is that four chairs be used—two for the client and two for the therapist.)

2. Ask the client to identify the person in the empty chair, describe the person, and reach out with a hand to touch the empty chair. (This is to personalize the experience.)

3. Begin the exercise with a stem. The therapist might say (speaking as the client), "Dad, I need to talk to you about something important to me." Then, let the client do the speaking unless the client has trouble and needs to be "prompted." Then, as in the theater, give the client a line to speak: for example, "I'm having trouble getting started." This seems more effective than urging the client to speak, as in, "Say anything you want." Giving the client a line is more concrete and direct.

4. After the client has spoken to the empty chair for a few sentences, the counselor faces a decision. The decision is whether simply to allow the client to say whatever he or she wishes or to move toward some resolution. If a resolution appears necessary, or even close, then move the client into the other chair where the client will assume the role of the person to whom he or she has been speaking. When the client moves into the other chair, the therapist moves simultaneously into the second chair provided for the therapist. Graphically, the arrangement looks like this: _--_. The top dashes represent the role-playing chairs in which the client might move back and forth and the bottom two dashes represent the original counselor–client chairs in which the counselor moves back and forth. In this situation, the client may move back and forth between the chairs in a dialogue fashion.

5. When the episode is finished, which requires a judgment from the therapist, ask the client to move back into his or her original seat, say "good-bye" to the person to whom the client has been talking, move the empty chairs aside, and ask the client, "What did you learn in that exercise?" It is important at this point to ask what has been learned rather than what the client feels, since this step is to promote a cognitive processing of the experience.

6. The therapist might also have learned something in the dialogue, and it is acceptable to introduce that information at this step.

Application. The empty chair is an excellent technique for dealing with anger, unresolved issues, and death and dying, and as a behavioral rehearsal technique for some upcoming difficult situation in the client's life.

Sometimes clients may have difficulty expressing anger or frustration toward a loved one. They can experience a sense of guilt or betrayal if they express any negativity. In such cases, a prompt such as, "Let's take all of the loving feelings you have for this person and set them over here for now. After we are finished with this exercise, we will place them back with the person so they can remain intact and untarnished." Such an assist can free some clients to go ahead and express their pent-up feelings without worrying that somehow the relationship will be damaged.

Also, the empty chair technique can be used in cases in which clients may be feeling betrayed by their body as in the case of a serious, chronic, or terminal illness. By assuming the roles of each, some resolution of feelings may be achieved.

Role Playing

This technique asks the therapist to take the role of some person with whom the client has unresolved issues. The therapist may choose any sort of role (helpful, argumentative, insulting) as a way of understanding how the client responds in a particular situation or as a way of helping the client have an insight about the client's own behavior. It may be used as a method to teach the client other ways of responding. The therapist may act either the role of some other person in the client's life or the role of the client. The therapist acts the role faithfully until the exercise is finished, then a clear end to the exercise is marked as the therapist stops role playing. This clear stoppage is necessary to make clear to the client the distinction between the "role" and the therapist. When the exercise is finished, ask the cognitive, processing question, "What did you learn from that experience?"

Application. This technique is particularly useful for creating a dramatic understanding of how a client may be responding in actual fact as opposed to a verbal description of how the client says he or she is responding. A "job sample" is created in the therapy room that can be examined by both the client and therapist. It has the possibility of allowing a client to discover an insight into ineffective behavior and for teaching other ways of responding. It is also possible to use role playing as a behavior rehearsal technique.

Talking to Parts of the Self

This technique is a variation of role playing and the empty chair. The therapist asks the client to identify a part of the self (either in general or a specific part that has become the source of some problem, for example, "Can you get in touch with that part of yourself that is so condemning of you? Can you get in touch with that part of you that believes in you?"). The purpose is to place that part of the self in a chair for an interview so that it may be questioned for information about causes of behavior, motivations, dynamics, or underlying beliefs that are either hindering or helping the client. The steps in this exercise are straightforward:

1. Let's do something here. Close your eyes and get in touch with that part of you that __________. Let me know by a nod of the head or some gesture that you are in touch with that part.

2. Ask if it will talk to us. (If the client says no, ask the client to find another part that will talk for the original part.)

3. Then, have the client ask questions or dialogue with the part. The therapist may ask questions as well.

4. When the exercise is over, ask the client to slowly come back to the session and ask the cognitive, processing question, "What did you learn from that experience?"

Application. This technique is particularly good for exploring unknown influences in the client's life. It is a good exploratory technique that can help clarify for the therapist and client sources of influence in the client's life. Also, the client has the opportunity to more fully integrate all of his or her feelings, not just the ones that are acceptable to acknowledge.

This technique is intended for use with relatively intact personalities. If a client is prone to dissociative processes, the recommendation is to avoid this technique in order not to contribute to the lack of existing integration.

Ask the Expert

This technique is used in response to a direct question. The client might ask about what to do in a specific situation or why the client acts in some particular way. The process may involve a story to set up the exercise or it may be entered into directly. The story format involves setting up the situation as follows: "You need to know why you don't stand up to your father. What you need is an expert on family relations who can answer your question. Luckily, we have an expert right here in this office. I'll bring in the expert in just a minute. What exactly do you want to ask him or her?" Have the client formulate the question. Then, say to the client, "Come, sit in this chair" (the therapist's chair). Switch seats with the client. The therapist then asks the exact question formulated by the client. The therapist may role play if other questions occur as the client speaks in the role of the expert. (If the client says that he or she doesn't know, then the therapist should prompt the client by saying, "You must know. You are the expert. You have written a book on the subject!") When the exercise is finished, switch seats again and ask the client, "What did you hear the expert say?"

If the therapist sees no reason to create a story, then simply say, "Come sit here. You are the expert. Why doesn't a person stand up to a father?"

Application. This technique is useful in working with direct questions and for helping clients explore areas of confusion. It is also an empowering technique in which the client is allowed to discover his or her own solutions to personally felt issues. The therapist can demonstrate his or her genuine belief in the client's capacity for understanding and resolving his or her problems.

Mirroring the Body

Mirroring the body simply means that the therapist uses the gestures, posture, and physical attitude of the client as a way of demonstrating nonverbally that the therapist understands the client. It comes from the discovery that at high levels of empathy therapists tended to "mirror" the actions of the client. This was discovered, in part, from an analysis of videotapes that permitted slow-motion replay and delayed studies of therapist–client interaction. Mirroring the gesture or posture of a client may be done as a part of a verbal interaction (as the therapist speaks, he or she would make the gesture noticed in the client) or simply as a nonverbal behavior indicating that the therapist is with the client.

Application. The usefulness of this idea is, of course, limited. It is merely another way of demonstrating empathic understanding and allows a variation in sitting postures for the therapist in addition to the classic attending posture. A note of caution should be introduced here: It is not appropriate to "mirror" postures that are closed or defensive in nature.

Mirroring the Language/Metaphor of the Client

This technique is similar to mirroring the body except that it is used to match the language style and metaphor of the client. Some clients are visual ("I'm in a fog"; "I just can't see my way though this problem"); some clients are auditory ("I just said to myself, I'm going crazy"; "It just sounds bizarre"; "even when I say it out loud"); some clients are kinesthetic ("I just can't seem to get the jump on life." "Wham! Life just punched me in the nose"). The intent is to match the client so that a statement demonstrating understanding matches not only content but also the feelings of a client in a language style that is used naturally by the client ("I just seem to be in a fog" for example is not well-matched by a therapist phrase such as "I hear you saying . . ." since the former is visual and the latter is auditory. It would be mirroring the language to use a phrase such as, "You just can't seem to see your way clear.").

Application. This technique has somewhat more usefulness than mirroring the body since it, conceptually, offers more opportunity for genuinely demonstrating that what has been said has truly been understood by the therapist. The technique is largely based on the work of Grinder and Bandler (1976) that proposed the notion that different clients have different primary representational systems (visual, auditory, or kinesthetic). Using language that is representative of the primary system characteristic of a particular client may increase the effectiveness of the interactions between therapist and client.

Visualization

This technique asks the client to visualize metaphors used or implied in the therapeutic discussion. A client might say, "I'm blocked from reaching a solution." The therapist might say, "Close your eyes and visualize the block you see. Describe it for me." Or, the client might say, "I just feel like I am being attacked from all sides." The therapist would say, "Close your eyes and visualize what or who is attacking you." The therapist dialogues with the client during the visualization. The therapist has the freedom to suggest different aspects of the visualization and even to intervene to alter an ending or event in the visualization if it is therapeutically suggested.

Application. This is a helpful and widely useful technique. Visualization may be used in exploration, understanding, or in the action, problem-solving stage of therapy. Thus, it has a wide range of usefulness. It allows a client to use a metaphor brought up in therapy to actually explore, understand, or take action on a concrete issue in life. The important quality needed for the therapist is a creative imagination to quickly overcome any obstacles in the visualization presented by the client. The therapist can encourage the client to bring any necessary assistance in the form of people or objects to overcome any obstacle.

Fantasy

Fantasy differs from visualization in that it may involve a story begun by the therapist and ended by the client. It can begin with a metaphor suggested by the client, or it can come from some concrete event in the client's life that the therapist wishes to explore, understand, or problem-solve with the client through fantasy. The therapist starts by saying, "Close your eyes. I want you to imagine . . ." and then begins a short story that the client will finish. The therapist might even ask before beginning the fantasy, "What do you want to have happen in this situation?" For example, a client with a negative self-concept might profit from a fantasy in which the self is, in fantasy, nurtured and grown. The therapist might say,

> Close your eyes. I want you to imagine that you are a flower in a garden. In fact, at this point, see your self as a seed, newly planted in rich, loving soil. Imagine now the budding plant just emerging from the ground. The flower is small; tender at this point; perhaps, not very strong. Now see a warm, bright light shining on the flower. Imagine that rich, pure water is being poured around the earth in which the flower is growing. Even as you watch, you can see the flower respond to the light and the warmth and the water. The flower is growing stronger and stronger. Now, every day I want you to imagine the flower and the light and the water and the warmth. Watch as the flower grows stronger and stronger.

Another fantasy might involve a client who feels blocked from some goal or understanding. The therapist might say,

> Close your eyes. I want you to visualize the block. What does it look like? What is it made of? What do you need in order to knock it down or drill a hole in the wall? Now, drill a hole in the wall. Look on the other side, and tell me what you see. Now, when you are ready come back slowly to this room. Tell me "What did you learn from that experience?"

This last fantasy allows the therapist and client to metaphorically explore what the block might be hiding, thus presenting the possibility of deeper understanding.

Application. Fantasy is another technique that offers a wide range of uses. It is particularly useful in situations that have occurred in the past and seemingly have no solution in the present. It becomes metaphorically possible to solve some problems in fantasy that cannot be solved in reality. For example, it is especially good when the client feels powerless to do something about an event that occurred in the past and yet still troubles the client. It may have been something as serious as rape or physical abuse where the rapist or abuser cannot, in fact, be confronted. In fantasy, however, the outcome can be very different than previously. Give them in fantasy what you cannot give them in reality. The rapist in fantasy can be defeated, captured, frightened, beat up, if necessary, so that the client can reclaim the strength, dignity, and/or power over his or her own life. Problems can be solved in fantasy in hopes that there will be some carryover into actual life. There is no problem, issue, or dilemma that cannot be conquered in fantasy.

House of Control

The house of control is a specific guided fantasy to deal with a particular issue in the lives of clients. It is designed to help clients gain control over decisions that directly affect their lives. It is a fantasy in which the therapist must be creatively quick in order to overcome blocks, suggest alternatives, and be ever mindful that the purpose of this technique is to give power to the client. The name is derived from the notion that the center of control in every person must be housed, metaphorically, somewhere. The "house" metaphor is one of many that may emerge. The fantasy begins with the therapist saying, "Close your eyes. Find that place inside yourself where things are controlled. When you find it, give me a signal that you can describe it to me. Describe it to me." When the initial description is completed, the therapist has to do several things in the fantasy. "Now describe the inside to me." (In this description the therapist is listening for evidence of some device or mechanism by which messages are sent out to the self.) In the description of the exterior and interior of the "house," listen for the condition—the upkeep of the "house." If it is shabby, then in fantasy some repairs are going to have to be made so that the house of control is attractive on the outside and on the inside as well. Next, have the client explore the control room. Guide the client.

> Look inside the control room. Tell me what you see. Next, I want you to make sure that there is no other person in the control room with you. If there is, then do whatever you need to do so that that person or those persons leave. Now lock the door so that on one can get in. This is your control room, and no one has any right to be in there except you. Look around. Does the room need to be redecorated? Bring in rugs, or flowers or paintings so that this room is yours and yours alone. Now, look at the door. There is a picture on the wall beside the door. Underneath the picture there is a title: "Person in Charge." Whose picture is that? (If it is not a picture of the client, have the client remove the picture that is there and replace it with their own picture.) There may be various levers, dials, knobs, or other devices by which a message is sent out of the control center. I want you to look at those and see if they have labels. Read the labels to me. Now, do you want to send a message? (If the client sends a message, ensure that it is a positive message.) Now we are going to leave your house of control. Go outside and lock the door so that no other person can get in, and slowly return to this room in this place and time.

The therapist then asks, "What did you learn from that experience?"

Application. The house of control technique is designed for one purpose: to help clients, in fantasy, move toward control of their own lives. It is designed to empower clients with an attitude of control in which they see themselves as being able to make decisions, cope with stress, and deal with crises in life. They are the ones who make the decisions that rule their lives. This is the sole purpose of this fantasy exercise.

Whose Face Is That? Whose Voice Is That?

This is a quick intervention aimed at determining whether decisions in the client's life are being unduly influenced by some outside agent. It is triggered by negative statements the client makes about his or her life. For example, a client might say, "I'm just hopeless." The therapist can respond with, "Whose face do you see?" (If the client says, "I don't see anything," then repeat the phrase and say, "Whose voice is that?"). Since some clients are more visual or more auditory, be prepared to switch from one stimulus to the other. The typical responses will be parents, grandparents, the client, or the therapist. In each of these cases, it allows the client and the therapist to explore undue influence in the client's life.

Application. This technique is useful for discovering what person or persons in the client's life may be the source of negative feelings or who may be exerting influence which robs the client of a central role in self-determination.

Wise Old Man, Wise Old Woman

When clients seems genuinely confused about what direction to take, this exercise is helpful in allowing clients to give advice to themselves. After some appeal for advice or an expression of being stuck around some decision, the therapist might say, "Close your eyes. I want you to go inside yourself and search until you find the wisest part of yourself. When you find that part give me a signal. Describe what you see." What the therapist is looking for in this description is a wise old man or a wise old woman figure (a sage, saint, wizard, medicine woman, or the like). It should be an image that avoids youthfulness, a parent, or some representation of mere authority. "Ask that part for advice around the dilemma you are facing." Listen to the client talk to the wisest part of him- or herself. "Now, slowly return to this room in this time and place knowing that you can return to this wise part whenever you look for advice. What did you hear the wisest part of yourself say?"

It is important to listen closely to advice that comes from a part of the self that is spontaneously described as an old, old man or woman. It is important to downplay advice that comes from a part described as the self, as the client is, as a parent, or as some figure of authority such as a professor, minister, rabbi, or the like.

Application. This is an effective way to have clients give advice to themselves and to keep the therapist out of advice giving. It allows therapists to have a good idea of what level of advice the clients are able to give to themselves. It also permits therapists to appraise the advice in order to understand its usefulness in the lives of clients and to emphasize or downplay the advice heard.

You to I, But to And, and Can't to Won't/Don't Language

To some extent, the language used by people may be a part of the problems they are having. In a larger context, the thoughts we express to ourselves may profoundly influence the actions we take. This concept, of course, lies at the heart of many therapeutic interventions. This technique is less profound than that conception and yet akin to it. The language changes are meant to teach clients. First, changing "you" to "I" is meant to teach the concept of ownership of thoughts and emotions. Second, changing "but" to "and" is meant to teach the concept of noncontradictory language. Also, clients may make an important statement and then inject the word "but," which results in their not actually hearing their own important statement. For example, a client may say "I have some strong feelings about the situation *but* I am afraid to say them." The client may be stopped by saying "but" and not express the feelings that came before the "but." By using the word "and" clients are more likely to pay attention to their whole statement. Third, changing "can't" to "won't" or "don't" language is meant to teach the concept of empowerment and personal responsibility for decisions. The change is made in a gentle way and without confrontation. "I heard you say 'You can't trust yourself.' It sounds clear that you won't or don't trust yourself. Is that right? Yes? Could you just say it that way, 'I won't trust myself'?" In each case, the teaching would be the same—"but" to "and," and "can't" to "won't/don't." There is no need to explain. Model the sentence and check out how the client experiences the new statement.

Application. This clarification of language has only limited usefulness. It is a way of teaching clients to be clearer in their thinking and expression. That in itself, of course, is helpful.

Body Scan

This is an exploratory technique designed to identify the source of some emotional upset in a client. It is a form of bodywork. When the client is discussing some issue in his or her life but cannot seem to identify the emotion that accompanies the issue, this technique can be helpful. The technique involves a short description of what the client is to do and an identification of the emotion involved. The therapist identifies the issue with the client (for example, "I can't talk to my wife.") Then, the therapist might say, "I want you to do something. I'll describe it for you and then I want you to use your hand as a scanner for feeling in your body. You know how a computer might scan a photograph for a particular image or object. I want you to scan your body for feelings about this issue. Close your eyes and move your hand from the top of your head across your body down to your feet. When you feel something, a catch or any feeling, stop and then move on. Do you have any questions? Do it now." The therapist observes the scan and notes any stops. Ask the client to touch the places where the scan stopped. Label that part of the body.

There are common places clients touch, and each has a fairly literal interpretation of meaning:

Head = intellectual/cognitive (The client may feel stupid about the situation.)

Shoulders = heavy load (The client is carrying a burden.)

Mouth, throat = communication (The client may not feel comfortable talking about the issue.)

Throat = choking (The client may feel suffocated by the issue.)

Heart = love (The client may feel unloved.)

Chest = armor, box (The client may feel defensive or trapped; the client may feel something is hidden from him or her.)

Stomach = nurturance, guts (The client may feel unloved or may lack courage to face the issue.)

Genitals = sexual (The issue might be infidelity; the client is being "screwed.")

Back = pain (The issue or person is a pain.)

Feet = running (They want to get out of the situation.)

The secret of interpretation is to be as literal as you can be. Consider the first impression that comes to mind or a common cliché. It is important to have the client identify the part of the body touched and the symbolic meaning given to that part of the body. Then, the therapist can add anything additional.

Application. This technique is a quick way to identify the emotion attributed to an issue in the life of a client. While the description is long, the actual technique is short and is meant to quickly provide an insight for the client and therapist.

Homework

Not all the work clients do in therapy is, nor should it be, done in the session itself. Homework is a means of having clients do work outside the therapy session. The homework assignment should be concrete and ordinarily something that can be written down so that it may be demonstrated and discussed in the next session. For example, if the issue is one of grief, the therapist may say, "Next week, sometime during the week, I want you to write a letter to your dead husband explaining the trouble you are having now that you are being asked to go out to dinner with men and feel guilty about accepting." It is important, the authors believe, to assign homework that requires a written response. This seems more beneficial than homework that merely asks the client to "think about" some issue. The written component asks for a committed act. The client will bring the homework assignment into the next therapy session for discussion.

Application. Homework can be an effective method of trying out new skills, learning new things, and safely expressing thoughts and feelings that are too threatening to express directly. It may employ fantasy situations or real concrete situations in the person's life that need to be practiced and discussed later.

Put Yourself on the List

When a client has an overdeveloped sense of responsibility for others, this technique can be a way of providing some insight that the client can be responsible for himself or herself as well. The therapist merely asks the client to provide a list of all the people for whom the client is responsible. The therapist might say, "Tell me all the people for whom you are responsible." If the client does not list himself or herself, then the therapist would say, "Put yourself on the list. I'm not telling you that your name has to be number one, I am just saying that your name can be on the list of those people that you feel responsible to take care of." If the client does include his or her name on the list, then the therapist can say, "I see you are aware that one of the people you have to take care of is yourself."

Application. This technique is designed to help clients understand that they have some responsibility for taking care of themselves. It is especially useful when clients forget to list themselves.

Body Language/Work

Often clients make gestures or use the body in such a way that the gesture or posture provides clues into their underlying feelings. There are two essential ways in which the body may be used to better understand a client. First, it may be used as a clue to forming an empathy statement. For example, a client may rub a hand across the forehead. The therapist might say, "It is just such a feeling of relief" since the gesture gave a clue of relief. The second method is to directly use a gesture to help a client explore the meaning of the gesture to the client. The therapist might observe a client make a gesture with the arm out, palm up with a slight up and down motion. The therapist might say, "Look at your hand. What are you carrying?" in hopes that the attention brought to the gesture will allow the client to arrive at an insight.

Application. The use of body language, gestures, and posture in therapy can often be the source of the breakthrough in terms of insight for the client. It is often a powerful tool. The danger is that the therapist may read too much into the gesture or posture without being willing to acknowledge that sometimes the gesture does not carry symbolic meaning.

Self-Talk

This is a strategy that may be used with highly verbal and insightful clients. It simply asks the client to take a question they are puzzled about and talk about it without interruption for three to five minutes. The client is encouraged to ask the question over and over and answer it over and over. After the client stops, the therapist can ask, "What did you hear yourself say?"

Application. This technique challenges the client to speak rapidly about an issue of concern, answering it over and over in an attempt to overcome any resistance or reluctance the client may have to answer the question in some meaningful and important way that is difficult to say out loud for fear of judgment, embarrassment, or silliness. It is often the source of a breakthrough or insight for the client.

Lifeline

This is a method of collecting personal history that is more creative than a simple narrative or responses to a number of questions. It may be used as homework. The therapist says,

> I want you to draw a long line on this piece of paper. (Use the middle of the paper to allow for variations in how far from average an experience is judged to be. Use a+ on the top half of the page for positive experiences and a– on the bottom half of the page to designate negative experiences.) The right end of the line is the present. The other end is as far back as you wish to go. Place everything you think is important in your life and development on the line. Positive experiences go up above and negative experiences go down below. The line represents an average experience.

When the client is finished use the lifeline as a reference for material in therapy.

Application. This technique provides the therapist with a quick way of obtaining a developmental history that is meaningful to the client without a lengthy question and answer session. It is also useful with nonverbal clients as a way to generate material for discussion in therapy.

The Five Worst Things a Human Being Can Be

The therapist asks the client to list the five worst things a human being can be. Then, immediately after the client responds, the therapist asks, "Are you any of those things?"

The point here is that when clients are very condemning of themselves, this is a quick intervention to remind them that they are not the worst things in the world. It is a way of gaining some perspective for clients.

Application. This strategy is used for a quick intervention to address issues of self-concept and to disrupt the destructive process that highly self-condemning clients engage in. It is meant to provide clients with some perspective on themselves. Clients may have self-doubts and still recognize that they are not the worst imaginable human beings.

Paradoxical Intention

This technique, which should be used carefully so as not to violate the dimension of genuineness, essentially means that the opposite of what is intended is reflected. It may take the form of purposeful naiveté or over-reflecting/exaggerating the intention of the client. The therapist might say, "So, if I understand you correctly, your spouse is the crummiest human being alive and ought to be tortured to death." What usually happens is that the client is forced into a more moderate position than he or she originally stated. The therapist might say, "So the situation is hopeless," when the client is expressing difficulty. The outcome might be that the client would say, "Well, it is not hopeless. There is some hope."

Application. This technique may be used to "shock" a client into a different way of thinking and may be thought of as a form of confrontation. It is useful when rapport is highly established and a good deal of trust exists between the client and therapist.

Charting

This simple technique involves merely having the client write on a wall sheet (or a table sheet) a list of desires, needs, shortcomings, or any other range of topics that lend themselves to writing. The technique may also involve listing the issue on one side of the page and solutions or feelings on the other. It can be used to help clarify and separate a number of issues presented confusingly by a client. The purpose of the technique is to help both the client and the therapist clarify something vague or confusing in the client's thinking. The authors have found a strategy of making a number of columns that include:

1. The issue
2. The client's "feeling" associated with the issue
3. What is their wish(ed) for outcome?
4. What is stopping them from getting their wish?

5. What would they settle for if they could not get their wish?
6. Is it in their control or not (C/NC)?

Application. This technique actually provides two useful purposes in therapy. First, the primary use is to clarify the thinking of the client regarding some blockage or vaguely felt concern. Second, it introduces physical activity into the session since in using a wall sheet, the client and therapist are required to stand. This breaks the ritual of "sitting-talking-listening" that may become too passive.

Put It in the Box

This is a straightforward strategy to help a client deal with some troublesome behavior in therapy. For example, a client who laughs constantly may be asked to take the laugh and "put it in the box" for the therapy session. Or, a client who constantly replies, "I don't know" can be asked to take that phrase and "put it in the box" for the session.

Application. This technique permits a client to talk more seriously about presently felt concerns by symbolically deciding not to use a common defense. It permits more serious and meaningful talk about presently felt emotions and thoughts.

Card Sort of Emotions

In this technique, the therapist prepares approximately 100 3 × 5 index cards with one emotion on each card. The deck of cards should contain a mix of positive and negative emotions. Some attention should be paid to including emotions that the therapist suspects are felt, but not being expressed by the client. The client is asked to sort the cards according to those emotions that are felt by the client in the situation being discussed and those that are not (it is possible to have a third stack of "I'm not sure" cards). Once the cards are sorted, the stack of emotions that are descriptive of the client may be further sorted or ranked from most to least important.

Application. This technique is useful for clients who have difficulty identifying emotions characteristic of their situation or clients who have difficulty talking about their life situation. It is a stimulus activity that generates materials for the therapy session.

Hopes, Expectations, and Requirements

Typically, people have *hopes, expectations,* and *requirements* in their relationships (Ossorio, 1999). Complications arise when people confuse the three in their relationships and treat all three as requirements. Have the person write down their hopes, expectations, and requirements. In the process of clarification, the person may realize that he or she may have been treating hopes as requirements and thus having more conflict in relationships than is necessary. Clients can differentiate among hopes, expectations, and requirements by examining their feelings when any of these things are not met. The usual reaction to not having hopes met is *disappointment*. The usual reaction to not having expectations met is *surprise*.

Requirements are those things that are absolutely essential for clients to remain in relationships. In doing this exercise, clients will sometimes move items from the *requirements* column to the *hopes* or *expectations* column as their feelings become clearer.

Application. The most ready application of this technique is to assist couples dealing with dissatisfaction in their relationships. One or both persons in the relationship may be responding with great distress to problems in the relationship because they are treating their unmet needs as requirements, when, in fact, some may be hopes or expectations. By not treating so many things as requirements, the couple has a better chance of working out the problems in the relationship. The method can also be applied to an individual trying to sort out various aspects of living.

Grief and Bereavement Techniques

Some techniques have proved to be exceptionally effective with issues of death, dying, and bereavement. The techniques described below are those used most often by the authors.

Empty Chair

The empty chair technique, described earlier in this chapter, has demonstrated itself over the years as a particularly effective strategy for helping clients explore and cope with issues of grief.

Application. In fact, the empty chair is particularly useful for any sort of "unfinished business." It may be used to say good-bye, resolve some conflict, deal with guilt, or to advance the grief process.

Letter to the Deceased

Writing a letter to the deceased is another method of confronting "unfinished business." It is assigned as homework. The therapist simply says, "Before next week's session, I want you to write a letter to __________ about the feelings you are having. Bring it with you next week and we can talk about the letter then."

Application. Writing a letter is useful in advancing the grief process, asking for advice, confronting conflict, and as another way to say good-bye. Also, writing such a letter provides an avenue for the client to more fully express thoughts and feelings about the deceased.

Obituary

Similar to writing a letter, writing an obituary is a method of confronting grief. The therapist says, "Before next week's session, I want you to write an obituary for __________. Bring it with you to the session and we will talk about it then." (Obituary means a notice of a person's death with a short biographical account a person's life.)

Application. This technique is useful in the early part of the grief process or when clients are having trouble accepting the reality of the death. It is meant to advance the grief process. It allows the grieving person to relive some of the memories of the deceased by recounting a biographical account of the deceased's life.

Eulogy

Similar to writing a letter and an obituary, the client is asked to write a eulogy for the deceased. Be prepared to define what a eulogy is and to talk about the feelings it brings up for the client. This technique is also used early in the grief process. (Eulogy means a formal statement of praise for the deceased.)

Application. The purpose is to advance the grief process. It is a way for the grieving person to acknowledge the valuable contribution the deceased made to his or her life.

Poetry

The purpose of having the client write poetry about the loss is to help the client in the exploration of grief and to help the therapist understand the process the client is going through. It is an especially effective way of helping clients who are not highly verbal to bring important emotional material into the session. Stems for poetry writing might include the name of the deceased with each letter of the name beginning a line of the poem. Poems using the word "Death" have also proved to be effective in helping clients explore their feelings and the meanings associated with a death in their life.

Application. This technique is meant to advance the grief process and to bring more personally meaningful material into the sessions. It is useful for persons who are highly literate but not particularly verbal. Poetry may be used at any point in the grieving process.

Drawing/Painting

It is possible to use techniques such as drawing and painting with adults as well as children when dealing with death. You may have the client draw or paint scenes that are personally meaningful to stimulate memories and feelings for discussion in the session.

Application. This technique is useful for nonverbal clients and clients who have trouble expressing their emotions. It allows important material to be brought into the session and can be used to stimulate verbal interaction as well as previously unexpressed feelings.

Reality Testing

This strategy is meant to be somewhat confrontive in that it asks the client the same question several times. For example, "What did you do? What else? What else?" It is meant to challenge the irrational thoughts that somehow the client could have done something to have saved the life of their loved one or done something to have caused the death.

Application. This technique is helpful in dealing with guilt. A good deal of rapport between the client and therapist is usually needed for this to be an effective technique.

Memorabilia

Using memorabilia is a way of getting the client to talk about feelings of grief when the client is somewhat reluctant or confused about what to talk about in therapy. The therapist says, "Next week why not bring something that is important to you that reminds you of _______. It can be pictures or anything that holds special memory for you. We will talk about them when you bring them in."

Application. The usefulness of bringing memorabilia into the therapy session is that it promotes talk and the purpose is to advance the grief process. It is another technique that is especially good for low verbal clients and for children.

Trip to the Cemetery

At some point, in very difficult deaths especially, the therapist may learn that the client has not visited the cemetery. The therapist may either suggest to the client that going to the cemetery is an important thing to do or even suggest that the therapist accompany the client on the visit. Such an act is important in the grief process and can signal the beginning of a healthy grief process.

Application. This strategy is useful for the early stages of the grief process, and, in fact, for any stage of the grief process, where it is clear that the client is in denial and not dealing with the reality of the death.

Summary

This chapter provides a review of some of the potential benefits of using techniques for both the therapist and the client. Our experience, both as therapists and clinical supervisors of therapists early in their careers, is that techniques often provide useful structure for the therapist and valuable insights for the client. However, techniques present the therapist with both hazards and opportunities. These potential hazards are identified and discussed. While there are potential dangers, it seems clear that the appropriate use of techniques in psychotherapy provides benefits for both the therapist and the client.

The authors have provided a list and discussion of these benefits for the therapist and for the client. The chapter also provides both guidelines and principles for the use of techniques in therapy. Specific techniques are identified and described so that psychotherapists will be able to practice and integrate them into their therapy sessions. Techniques that have proven themselves to be especially helpful in exploring and coping with grief and bereavement are described and discussed.

REFERENCES AND FOR FURTHER READING

Ayres, J., & Hopf, T. S. (1987, July). Visualization, systematic desensitization, and rational emotive therapy: A comparative evaluation. *Communication Education, 36*(3), 236–240.

Bellack, A. S., & Hersen, M. (1985). *Dictionary of behavior therapy techniques*. New York: Pergamon Press.

Carkhuff, R. R. (1987). *The art of helping VI.* (6th ed.). Amherst, MA: Human Resource Development Press.

Combs, A. W., & Gonzalez, D. M. (1994). *Helping relationships: Basic concepts for the helping professions.* (4th ed.). Boston: Allyn & Bacon.

Conoley, C. W., Conoley, J. C., McConnell, J. A., & Kimzey, C. E. (1983, Spring). The effect of the ABCs of rational emotive therapy and the empty-chair technique of gestalt therapy on anger reduction. *Psychotherapy, 20*(1), 112–117.

Dyer, W. W., & Vriend, J. (1977). *Counseling techniques that work.* New York: Funk and Wagnalls.

Garfield, S. L., & Bergin, A. E. (Eds.). (1993). *Handbook of psychotherapy and behavior change.* (4th ed.). New York: Wiley.

Gazda, G. M., Asbury, F. S., Balzer, F. J., Childers, W. C., & Walters, R. P. (1984). *Human relations development.* Boston: Allyn & Bacon.

Gladding, S. T. (1988). *Counseling: A comprehensive profession.* Columbus, OH: Merrill.

Gonzalez, D. M. (2000). Client variables and psychotherapy outcome. In D. J. Cain & J. Seeman (Eds.). *Handbook of research and practice in humanistic psychotherapies.* Washington, DC: American Psychological Association.

Grinder, J., & Bandler, R. (1976). *The structure of magic II: A book about communication and change.* Palo Alto, CA: Science and Behavior Books.

Highlen, P. S., & Hill, C. E. (1984). Factors affecting client change in individual counseling: Current status and theoretical speculations. In S. D. Brown & R. W. Lent (Eds.). *The handbook of counseling psychology.* New York: Wiley.

Kanfer, F. H., & Goldstein, A. P. (1986). *Helping people change: A textbook of methods.* New York: Pergamon Press.

Karasu, T. B., & Bellack, L. (1980). *Specialized techniques in individual psychotherapy.* New York: Brunner/Mazel.

Kiesler, D. J., & Watkins, L. M. (1989, Summer). Interpersonal complementarity and the therapeutic alliance: A study of relationship in psychotherapy. *Psychotherapy, 26*(2), 183–194.

Mahoney, M. J. (1986, April). The tyranny of technique. *Counseling and Values, 30*(2), 169–174.

Nelson, R. C. (1987, October). Graphics in counseling. *Elementary School Guidance and Counseling, 22*(1), 17–29.

Okun, B. F. (1987). *Effective helping: Interviewing and counseling techniques* (3rd ed.). Pacific Grove, CA: Brooks/Cole.

Orlinsky, D. E., Grawe, K., & Parks, B. K. (1994). Process and outcome in psychotherapy: Noch einmal. In S. L. Garfield & A. E. Bergin (Eds.) *Handbook of psychotherapy and behavior change.* (pp. 270–376). New York: Wiley.

Ossorio, P. G. (1999). Personal communication.

Patterson, C. H. (1984, Winter). Empathy, warmth and genuineness in psychotherapy: A review of reviews. *Psychotherapy, 21*(4), 431–438.

Rando, T. A. (1984). *Grief, dying, and death.* Champaign, IL: Research Press.

Rogers, C. R. (1957). The necessary and sufficient conditions of therapeutic personality change. *Journal of Consulting Psychology, 21*(4), 95–103.

Rogers, C. R. (1980). *A way of being.* Boston: Houghton Mifflin.

Rosenthal, H. G. (Ed.). (1998). *Favorite counseling and therapy techniques: 51 therapists share their most creative strategies.* Muncie, IN: Accelerated Development.

Turkington, C. (1987, August). Help for the worried well. *Psychology Today, 21*(8), 44–48.

Vriend, J. (1985). *More counseling techniques that work.* Alexandria, VA: Association for Supervision and Development.

Weissmark, M. S., & Giacomo, D. A. (1998). *Doing psychotherapy effectively.* Chicago: The University of Chicago Press.

Welch, I. D. (1998). *The path of psychotherapy: Matters of the heart.* Pacific Grove, CA: Brooks/Cole.

Welch, I. D., & Gonzalez, D. M. (1999). *The Process of counseling and psychotherapy: Matters of skill.* Pacific Grove, CA: Brooks/Cole.

Welch, I. D., Zawistoski, R. F., & Smart, D. W. (1991). *Encountering death: Structured activities for death awareness.* Muncie, IN: Accelerated Development.

Williams, A. J. (1988). Action methods in supervision. *Clinical Supervisor, 6*(2), 13–27.

Worden, J. W. (1982). *Grief counseling and grief therapy.* New York: Springer.

CHAPTER

7 Motivational Interviewing

THERESA B. MOYERS

Motivated clients can accomplish amazing things. Therapeutic research indicates that they can change maladaptive and painful behaviors with remarkable success. It is clear that a determined client assisted by a competent therapist can expect to triumph over a number of distressing problems (Lambert, Shapiro, & Bergin, 1986; Chambless, 1998).

Yet, what can be done when clients are not motivated for change? What can the provider do when education, skills building, and encouragement have all failed to yield the desirable behavior change? Is it possible that some clients are hopelessly unmotivated to change?

Take a moment to consider what your response would be to the following clients. You might want to jot down a few of your thoughts about the clients themselves as well as what approach you might take with them.

> Mark B. is a 23-year-old diabetic client who takes insulin regularly but does not monitor his blood glucose levels to insure the correct dose. His lack of glucose control has resulted in complications from his diabetes including retinal degeneration and neuropathy. Mark's poor compliance means he is ineligible to receive an insulin pump, a device to reduce his need for frequent injections. His physician has tried everything she knows to encourage him to monitor more frequently, with no success.
>
> Jennie P. is 18 years old and expecting her first baby. Although she has cut her alcohol consumption since discovering her pregnancy, she continues to drink to intoxication every Friday with her friends. Jennie wants a healthy baby, and she is willing to make some changes in her alcohol use, but she does not believe it is necessary to quit drinking entirely just because she is pregnant. Her parents have referred her to a psychologist for help.

Clients of this kind are common in medical and psychological practice and account for a disproportionate amount of frustration on the part of providers. They are often labeled as being unmotivated or in denial. Providers may respond to these clients by redoubling their efforts to educate them about the risks of their behavior, they may give strongly worded warnings about the need for change, or they may give up altogether.

Motivational interviewing (Miller & Rollnick, 1991) is a therapeutic intervention that is used to help clients who are ambivalent about implementing behavior change, like Mark and Jennie. It begins with a different way of viewing the process of change.

Stages of Change Model

Prochaska and DiClemente (1986) have described a model for change, developed from their experience with clients who were attempting smoking cessation. They noted that clients appeared to move through a predictable series of steps when they were trying to stop smoking and that progression to each step seemed to depend on what happened in the previous one.

The stages of change model describes these four important steps or stages. In the initial stage (precontemplation), the client is unconcerned about making a change. Smokers in this stage of change, for example, are not considering making a change in their smoking in the foreseeable future. These clients may be unaware of the consequences of their behavior or may have decided that they are willing to accept them. Clients in this stage of change are often described by others as resistant or resigned (Prochaska, DiClemente, & Norcross, 1999).

Clients in the next stage of change (contemplation), by contrast, do feel some concern about their behavior and are considering a change. The contemplation stage of change is characterized by ambivalence. The client is simultaneously aware of both the benefits and the consequences of the behavior and is actively weighing them. Smokers in this stage of change report they are considering a change within the next six months but are not ready now. If the client's ambivalence is not resolved somehow, they may remain in contemplation indefinitely or slip into a precontemplative stage resignation. However, if the client transcends the rough waters of ambivalence, preparation for change will begin.

Next the client enters the action stage of change. Here the client's energy is genuinely focused on the attempt to change. Interventions from providers may, or may not, be necessary depending on the client's level of knowledge and skill.

Once the acute task of behavior change is accomplished, usually taking about six months, the client enters the maintenance stage of change. The client's task is to make long-term lifestyle changes to support the gains accomplished in the previous stage and to avoid relapse.

From the moment the client begins to prepare, the change process can be interrupted by relapse. Once a relapse occurs, the client may be transfixed by guilt or may struggle to cope with the disappointment of others. Permission-giving beliefs (Marlatt & Gordon, 1985) may prolong the relapse. Eventually the client may become contemplative or engage in action to terminate the unwanted behavior again, although it is unfortunately true that relapse can sometimes be permanent. Most people move through the change process more than once before they are successful in making a change. In fact, successful nonsmokers required an average of four serious attempts before quitting (Norcross, Ratzin, & Payne, 1989). For this reason, the stages of change model is represented by a wheel or circle, indicating that the client can repeat them or exit from the wheel of change (Prochaska, DiClemente, & Norcross, 1999).

One important contribution of the stages of change model is the notion that clients may require different strategies from providers depending on their stage of change. Clients in the action stage of change will be most likely to respond to specific strategies for accomplishing change, and they will probably respond well to a provider's encouragement and advice. Clients in the contemplation stage of change, by contrast, may become more resistant and therefore *less* likely to change if providers offer advice and encouragement. These clients need an intervention specifically useful for negotiating ambivalence, such as motivational interviewing.

Origins of Motivational Interviewing

Motivational interviewing (MI) is heavily indebted to the work of Carl Rogers (1957); many of the skills used are taken directly from client-centered therapy. For example, the emphasis on therapist empathy, reflective listening, eliciting core values, and responding to resistance in a nonconfrontational manner clearly derive from Rogers's work.

Motivational interviewing also incorporates elements of social psychology to understand why clients resist adaptive change. Reactance theory holds that a threat to a freedom evokes a motivation to restore that freedom (Brehm & Brehm, 1981). Threatened behaviors become, in effect, more valuable. Reactance can also be elicited when freedom is threatened by an internal event, such as a choice between two desirable alternatives. In this circumstance, there will be an "internal counteracting cost for exercising one freedom at the expense of another. The motivation to have the foregone alternative is increased and this alternative is seen as more desirable than it was" (p. 28). Reactance is likely to be increased in situations where clients view themselves as competent to exercise the freedom, such as Jennie's belief that she can regulate her alcohol use to avoid harming her infant. In social interactions, including therapy, reactance can be evoked when the therapist uses "commands, persuasion, attempts to bribe for compliance or threaten with punishment for noncompliance" or restricts the client's choice of treatment options, such as Mark's inability to receive an insulin pump (p. 31). When using MI, the therapist's task is to minimize reactance and increase the client's awareness of choice.

Motivational interviewing also borrows from the social psychological area of self-perception theory (Petty & Capioppo, 1981) in emphasizing the attributions the client makes about the reasons for the considered change. Clients are more likely to endorse ideas that they believe are their own, rather than those proposed by others. For this reason, MI places a high value on having the client, rather than the interviewer, verbalize the arguments for change.

From social-learning theory, MI incorporates an emphasis on the client's own expectancies about his or her self-efficacy or ability to change. Self-efficacy has consistently been shown to predict the ability to successfully change behaviors (Bandura, 1982). For this reason, enhancing a client's beliefs that he or she can, in fact, accomplish a difficult behavior change is a core feature of MI. Elements of cognitive-behavioral therapy found in MI include asking clients to explore incentives for maladaptive behaviors as well as examine specific situations that are most difficult (Beck & Weishaar, 1989).

Yet MI is not merely a compilation of parts of other approaches. It is directive, in that the therapist is explicitly working toward the goal of adaptive behavior change. Attempts are made to enlarge, rather than resolve, client discrepancy about needed changes. Resistance to change is viewed as a normal part of the change process and a vital source of energy for therapeutic work. Advice, teaching, and skills building are used cautiously. Motivational interviewing is unique in its emphasis on client motivation, with the assumption that behavior change is relatively straightforward (if not necessarily easy) when ambivalence and resistance diminish.

Assumptions of Motivational Interviewing

Central to the use of MI is the concept that the process of adaptive behavior change is often stymied by ambivalence or reluctance. The difficulty is not so much the implementation of the change but the appetite for it. Therefore, a MI approach focuses on the resolution of ambivalence and exploration of resistance about change, rather than on *changing*. Although the change process may be intricate and difficult, it is almost always eminently feasible once the client has made a firm commitment to it. Further therapeutic interventions may not be necessary. This is not to say that MI can replace a full spectrum of psychosocial interventions; some clients will certainly require help to implement change. But many will not, and this is clear from empirical studies that support MI as a successful stand-alone treatment (Project MATCH, 1997).

Another assumption of MI is that there are usually a variety of acceptable ways to achieve most behavior changes, and that clients are uniquely qualified to choose the optimal change strategy. For this reason, clients are viewed as the experts regarding their dilemmas, and the interviewer actively solicits advice about solutions from them. The interviewer explicitly declines the role of the expert, offering possible solutions carefully and inviting the client to disregard them if they are inappropriate. This approach may require a shift away from providers who have used a model that requires them to be experts and to provide advice and direction as part of their services. As noted, the expert model will work well for curious clients in the action stage of change, but may elicit resistance from contemplators.

There is also an assumption of optimism in MI. Pessimism is viewed as a disadvantage for the client, since provider's expectations are likely to influence outcome (Leake & King, 1977), and clients who are hopeful are more likely to change successfully (Frank, 1973). Interviewers accept responsibility for maintaining optimism and for remembering that change may happen at some point in the future, not necessarily when it is gratifying for the provider.

Because they are assumed to be counterproductive, power struggles are discouraged. The interviewer meets resistance with specific responses designed to diminish and redirect power struggles, much as an aikido master deflects the force of his opponent in a harmless manner. Resistance might be redefined as an example of client autonomy, individuality, or energy for success. Interviewers are facile at letting clients "win" or have the last word. Personal choice is emphasized, including the choice not to change.

Finally, motivation is not viewed as a fixed characteristic residing in clients. Rather, the influence of the therapist in eliciting and increasing motivation is emphasized. Motivation is considered a product of the interaction between the client and the interviewer. From this perspective, it makes little sense to describe clients as unmotivated; instead, the interviewer's behavior is used to increase whatever existing motivation is present. Motivational interviewing, like all therapeutic approaches, requires some degree of concern and cooperation from the client. It is ineffective in coercing change from unwilling participants.

The Spirit of Motivational Interviewing

In describing MI, Miller and Rollnick (1991) compared it to a song. That is, MI has both words and music as critical components of success. The techniques of MI, such as using double-sided reflections to deflect resistance and drawing the reasons for change from the client rather than supplying them, are essential. Yet they do not convey the spirit of MI, just as words cannot convey the music of a song. Ideally, those using MI will be familiar not only with the techniques but also with the larger spirit of MI. It is captured in the following guidelines:

1. Motivation to change is elicited from the client and not imposed from without.
2. It is the client's task, and not the counselor's, to articulate and resolve his or her ambivalence.
3. Direct persuasion is not an effective method for resolving ambivalence.
4. The counseling style is generally a quiet and eliciting one.
5. The counselor is directive in helping the client to examine and resolve ambivalence.
6. Readiness to change is not a client trait, but a fluctuating product of interpersonal interaction.
7. The therapeutic relationship is more like a partnership than an expert/recipient one.

The spirit of MI informs which techniques among many a therapist might choose in any particular interaction with a client (Rollnick & Miller, 1995).

Principles of Motivational Interviewing

So, what does MI actually look like? First, the interviewer conveys empathy. Empathy within an MI approach is defined as the ability to use reflective listening skills and to recognize opportunities to affirm the client's intents, goals, and values where possible. Having the same life experiences, agreeing with a client's point of view, or feeling sorry for the client are not considered necessary for therapist empathy. Rather, the interviewer's ability to accurately mirror the client's meaning is the important ingredient.

MARK: I know I should monitor four times a day, but I can't do that at work. I'm the breadwinner for my family, and I carry mail for a living. I'm always out walking. How can I stop and drag out all that stuff? I could do it at lunch, but that's just once a day anyway. My doctor wouldn't be happy with that.

INTERVIEWER: It's important to you to keep your job, and you don't see how you can monitor like your doctor wants you to and work at the same time.

MARK: I can never get it all done.

INTERVIEWER: You're always having to juggle, and they're both important to you.

Second, the interviewer attempts to elicit and amplify the discrepancy between the client's deepest goals and values and their current behavior. Consider Mark's desire for a long and healthy life. This is clearly in direct contrast to his lack of blood glucose monitoring. Similarly, Jennie's desire for a healthy baby is not consistent with her abuse of alcohol. From a motivational perspective, the discrepancy between core values and destructive behavior is the location of fruitful therapeutic work.

JENNIE: I'm going to those prenatal classes now to get the right diet so my baby will be healthy. I can't believe how much milk I have to drink.

INTERVIEWER: You want to do everything you can to help your baby's chances to be healthy.

JENNIE: That's the only thing that worries me about my happy hours. I'm not an alcoholic or anything, but I know it can hurt the baby when a woman is pregnant. They told me that in the prenatal class, too.

INTERVIEWER: So it's good to have the happy hour with your friends, but at the same time you worry what it might be doing to your baby.

JENNIE: I guess that's right, huh?

Third, the interviewer avoids direct confrontation of the client if possible. Although there are times when confrontation is unavoidable, the motivational interviewer does not use confrontation as a therapeutic technique. The benefits of confrontation are not worth the potential for eliciting resistance. Interviewers are explicitly permitted to sidestep areas that may lead to arguments with clients, such as accepting a specific diagnostic label or treatment goal.

MARK: I like my doctor, and I thought we were getting along great. But when I asked for the pump, she said I couldn't have it because I was "noncompliant." It makes it sound like I'm one of those idiots that doesn't even take insulin. I know I'm not perfect about my glucose control, but noncompliant? No way.

INTERVIEWER: You'd like to get some credit for all the hard work you put into staying healthy instead of the small part you don't do.

MARK: Exactly.

Fourth, the interviewer recognizes client resistance as a potential source of energy for therapeutic interventions rather than seeing it as a stumbling block or diversion. Indeed, the client's resistance to change is considered a normal part of the change process, consistent with the stages of change model. The interviewer implements specific strategies to cope with resistance, with the goal of using the energy the client has invested in it to provide momentum for exploration of underlying fears or resentments about change. Interviewers avoid becoming too enthusiastic in the face of the client's reluctance.

MARK: I know I'm supposed to tell people I have diabetes so they'll know what to do if my blood sugar bottoms out. But I never do it, because when they find out I have diabetes, they start looking at me differently; like I'm fragile or something. Some people ask me a bunch of questions because they know someone else who's diabetic or just because they're curious. I know it's nothing to be ashamed of, but I just don't want to be known for that.

INTERVIEWER: You don't want to be the poster boy for diabetes.

MARK: (*smiling*) Yeah, the next party I go to, I don't want them to introduce me as Mr. Diabetes.

INTERVIEWER: For you, it's better to keep this private, even if it isn't quite as safe.

MARK: For me, yes. Maybe I can tell some people, but not everyone.

Finally, the interviewer looks for opportunities to build confidence in clients and to encourage their belief that they are able to make a specific change. This may take the form of interviewers actively seeking evidence of client's past successes or emphasizing the important lessons learned in past relapses. Or, the interviewer may encourage the client to consider alternative methods for change or even different treatment goals.

JENNIE: Yeah, I cut down my drinking to take it easy on my baby, but I just can't let go of my happy hours. I've tried, but it's the only thing I've got left, so I couldn't do it.

INTERVIEWER: You cut down? How did you do that?

JENNIE: I just made up my mind to stop it and give my baby a chance. I used to drink every day, but I quit all that. Now I only have my happy hours.

INTERVIEWER: So, what did you do when you had an urge to drink?

JENNIE: Called up my mom, called up my girlfriends with kids, ate a lot of ice cream, and watched TV.

INTERVIEWER: You got encouragement and you found other indulgences, and that kept you away from drinking.

JENNIE: And I just kept daydreaming about my baby being born healthy.

INTERVIEWER: Thinking of your baby like that makes you strong.

JENNIE: I know that could keep me away from the happy hours, too.

INTERVIEWER: If you tried it.

JENNIE: I wouldn't try it; I'd do it.

Coping with Resistance. We have previously learned that ambivalence is viewed as a normal part of the change process when using MI. Given this perspective, there is some question about whether the word *resistance* is appropriate, carrying as it does the connotation of hindering or obstructing, rather than implying a natural consequence of change. Often, what is labeled *resistance* is nothing more than an expression of ambivalence. For this reason, Miller and Rollnick recently experimented with exchanging the term *resistance* for *countermotivational behaviors* (MINT, 1998). For some practitioners, however, this term seems anemic. For them, there is a clear difference between the hostility and resentfulness expressed by some clients (which most providers would choose to call resistance) and the more subtle insistence on autonomy expressed by other clients (which may be more indicative of true ambivalence). The point to be taken from this ongoing controversy is that resistance, like motivation, can be created by the provider. It can become a self-fulfilling prophecy, especially when the provider is predisposed to view it as an indication of poor outcome in the future.

TABLE 7.1 Principles of Motivational Interviewing

1. Express empathy
2. Develop discrepancy
3. Avoid argumentation
4. Roll with resistance
5. Support self-efficacy

Source: Miller & Rollnick, 1991.

So, how does the motivational interviewer respond to resistance? There are two approaches: reflective and strategic. The reflective responses emphasize using Rogerian mirroring as a way of defusing resistance.

JENNIE: I can't believe my obstetrician called me an alcoholic. What the hell does she know about my drinking, anyway?

INTERVIEWER: It doesn't make sense that someone would call you an alcoholic when you only drink once a week. (*simple reflection*)

JENNIE: I know I shouldn't drink at all during these nine months, but I've already given up everything else, and I have a right to enjoy something.

INTERVIEWER: If you were doing things strictly by the book, you'd give up drinking entirely; but, on the other hand, you feel you owe it to yourself to drink if it's just once a week. (*double-sided reflection*)

The interviewer may also use strategic responses to resistance; these are intended to turn the interview in another direction. This results in emphasizing the client's ultimate responsibility for change or may result in bypassing the resistance in favor of a more constructive topic.

MARK: If they don't give me the pump, why should I even try? If they want to keep something from me that will help me, then maybe I'll just quit monitoring completely.

INTERVIEWER: I can see you're really angry about them refusing the pump.

MARK: You're damn right.

INTERVIEWER: Tell me more about why you'd like to have it. (*shifting focus*)

JENNIE: My mom even threatened to turn me in to the law if I keep going to happy hour. What are they going to do about it? Throw me in jail just for a few beers?

INTERVIEWER: You're right about that. No one can force you to stop drinking. That kind of change could only come from you. (*emphasizing personal choice and control*)

Finally, the interviewer can respond by siding with the negative. This is not a true paradoxical response, in which the therapist would overtly prescribe the self-destructive behavior, but it is in the same ballpark. Here, the interviewer responds to an ambivalent client by explicitly arguing against change.

JENNIE: What would I do without friends if I skipped happy hour? It's the only time I get to really talk to them. If I missed Friday nights, I wouldn't have any friends at all. I'm already lonely enough since my boyfriend left.

INTERVIEWER: Maybe it's just too hard to give up time with your friends right now. (*siding with the negative*)

JENNIE: I would only do it if my baby's health depended on it.

The value of siding with the negative is that it pulls for the client to supply the *other* side of the statement. When a client is ambivalent, the discrepant statement is likely to follow

TABLE 7.2 Handling Resistance

Reflective	Strategic
Simple reflection	Shifting focus
Amplified reflection	Emphasizing personal choice
Double-sided reflection	Siding with the negative

immediately—this incongruity is the nature of ambivalence. From a motivational interviewing perspective, having clients present this argument for change is ideal since the clients are more likely to endorse that belief if they attribute it to themselves rather than the provider. Although it is a powerful intervention for coping with resistance, siding with the negative should be used cautiously. Like all resistance interventions, it can be damaging if the interviewer is sarcastic or deceitful.

Motivational Interviewing in Treatment Settings

Motivational interviewing has been used most extensively in substance abuse treatment settings, both as an add-on to enhance existing treatment (Heather, Rollnick, Bell, & Richmond, 1996; Handmaker & Miller, 1999) and as a stand-alone intervention (Bien, Miller, & Boroughs, 1993; Lawendowski, 1998). In a substance abuse setting, MI augments traditional interventions, such as outpatient counseling and peer support groups. In one model, used at the Substance Abuse Treatment Program at the Albuquerque VA Medical Center, clients who are ambivalent or resistant at intake can be enrolled for three sessions of motivational interviewing, called the Treatment Options Clinic. The goal is to resolve ambivalence about participation in substance abuse treatment and select which of the options offered by the program is best suited for the client. At the end of the sessions, the client may choose to discontinue altogether or to develop an initial treatment plan that he or she carries back to the traditional program. In this way, milieu disruptions and early dropouts caused by client ambivalence and resistance are decreased.

Motivational interviewing can be married with an assessment process to increase the effectiveness of initial contacts with patients. Feedback about substance use indicators gathered in the assessment process is provided in MI style, and change plans are discussed only if the client indicates readiness to do so (Miller, Zweban, DiClemente, & Rychtarik, 1992; Dimeff, Baer, Kivlahan, & Marlatt, 1999). Alternatively, MI can be used to *replace* the assessment process as the initial contact with patients in substance abuse treatment programs. Although some information is gathered by a brief self-report instrument before the client and interviewer meet, the focus of the initial session is on eliciting self-motivational statements from the client. The "million-dollar work-up" assessment, which leads to the treatment plan, is deferred until the client's engagement in treatment is secure.

Motivational interviewing can also be used in medical settings, for lifestyle problems that have medical consequences such as Mark's failure to monitor his blood glucose level (Rollnick, Heather, & Bell, 1992; Senft, Polen, Freeborn, & Hollis, 1997). Investigation continues regarding whether MI can be adapted to a briefer format to conform to time constraints of medical providers in primary care settings (Rollnick & Miller, 1995). Indeed, studies are currently in progress to investigate the use of MI for patients with hypertension, eating disorders, hyperlipidemia, diabetes, and schizophrenia (MINT, 1998).

There are now 11 randomly assigned, controlled studies investigating the use of MI. Eight show an advantage for patients receiving MI, usually in comparison to a control group receiving standard treatment or education (Noonan & Moyers, 1997). The largest controlled trial of MI was conducted in Project MATCH, an NIAAA funded study to discern a favorable strategy for matching substance abuse clients to differing treatments. In comparison to cognitive-behavioral and 12-step facilitated therapies, MI showed equal effectiveness with one-third the number of sessions (Project MATCH, 1997). In addition, clients with higher levels of hostility had a more favorable response to MI than the other two treatments, an interaction that remained even in the one year follow-up (Project MATCH, 1999).

Motivational interviewing clearly shows promise for clients who are unresponsive to advice to change, even when that change is obviously necessary. Nevertheless, MI is not a panacea; neither is it a substitute for a full spectrum of therapeutic care.

Conclusion

Let's return to our two clients from the beginning of the chapter. Mark and Jennie are in the contemplation stage of change; they are able to see both the costs and the benefits of their behavior and have concerns about it. While they are considering change, they can become resistant if that change is advised by others. They are both struggling with personal barriers to implementing change successfully, including isolation, social stigma, and time constraints. Based on what you have learned in this chapter, what would you do?

MARK: I might do it in the future, but not right now. I have a vacation coming up in a month, and I was considering going all out for that. If I could really see a difference when I monitored four times a day, maybe I'd be motivated to do it all the time, like they're always telling me to.

INTERVIEWER: Sounds like you're planning to give it a try when you have fewer work demands and then decide for yourself if it's worth it.

MARK: If my A1C's get better, my doctor might even decide I'm okay for the pump, but I'm still not going to ask her for it.

INTERVIEWER She'll have to remember to think about it herself, huh?

MARK: Well, if my sugars are really good, she can't help but notice.

INTERVIEWER: I think you're right. Is there anything that could get in the way of your plan to use your vacation to improve your health?

MARK: No, I know I need to do it. I'm getting ready. My wife might get nervous about it, because when I'm experimenting with my blood sugars, I get too low sometimes, and she worries I'll go into a coma. But she'd be happy if I were under better control, so I know she'll go with the flow if I explain it.

INTERVIEWER: Mark, this sounds great. I wonder if you'd feel free to come back and see me again if you get stuck with your plan or you'd like some extra help in the future with your monitoring?

MARK: Let me see how this works, and I'll get back to you if I need to. It might be awhile, because I'm not going to do it right away.

INTERVIEWER: My door is open.

MARK: How would I go about getting back in to see you?

Consistent with the philosophy of motivational interviewing, Mark's provider has not pushed him to make a change for which he is not ready. Nevertheless, the interviewer has set the stage for Mark to return in the future and has focused on building efficacy for the smaller approximation that Mark is willing to endorse. This focus on leaving the therapeutic relationship intact so that the client can return in the future is sometimes the most realistic goal for clients who are highly ambivalent.

JENNIE: I wonder if I could give up my happy hours, just for the rest of my nine months.

INTERVIEWER: You'd like to finish your pregnancy totally alcohol-free.

JENNIE: It would be hard on me, but good for my baby.

INTERVIEWER: I wonder if it would help to have some support for that. You mentioned that you used your mom and your friends for moral support when you quit drinking on other days.

JENNIE: I better, huh?

INTERVIEWER: It's totally up to you, Jennie. But if you're interested, we have a support group here of girls just like you who are trying not to drink and use drugs during their pregnancy.

JENNIE: They use drugs? At least I never did that.

INTERVIEWER: You've already done a lot to keep your baby safe. This is the last important bit left.

JENNIE: Yeah, I might as well finish it up right since I've done this much. I'll go to the group. But could I get counseling if my boyfriend comes back? We're gonna need it.

Jennie's interviewer can now move confidently forward to make a personalized change plan for abstinence during her pregnancy. There is nothing to keep her interviewer from working with Jennie to implement that change plan and explore any further areas of concern as they come up. If Jennie becomes ambivalent or resistant at any point in the therapeutic process, the provider can fall back on MI skills to respond. It is not unusual for ambivalence to recur, even if the client moves into the action stage of change.

INTERVIEWER: Sure, we can work on that. Let's write this down on paper so you can take a copy with you when you go home.

JENNIE: This is all right. I thought you were gonna yell at me when you found out I was drinking after I got pregnant.

INTERVIEWER: Well, what good would that do?

JENNIE: Not much, for sure.

REFERENCES

Bandura, A. (1982). Self-efficacy mechanism in human agency. *American Psychologist, 37,* 122–147.

Beck, A. T., & Weishaar, M. (1989). Cognitive therapy. In A. Freedman, K. M. Simon, L. E. Beutler, & H. Arkowitz (Eds.), *Comprehensive handbook of cognitive therapy.* New York: Plenum Press.

Bien, T. H., Miller, W. R., & Boroughs, J. M. (1993). Motivational interviewing with alcohol outpatients. *Behavioural and Cognitive Psychotherapy, 21,* 347–356.

Brehm, S. S., & Brehm, J. W. (1981). *Psychological reactance: A theory of freedom and control.* New York: Academic Press.

Chambless, D. (1998). Empirically validated treatments. In G. P. Koocher, J. C. Norcross, & S. S. Hill (Eds.), *Psychologist's desk reference* (pp. 209–219). New York: Oxford University Press.

Dimeff, L. A., Baer, J. S., Kivlahan, D. R., & Marlatt, G. A. (1999). *Brief alcohol screening and intervention for college students: A harm reduction approach.* New York: Guilford Press.

Frank, J. D. (1973). *Persuasion and healing* (2nd ed.). Baltimore: Johns Hopkins University Press.

Handmaker, N., & Miller, W. R. (1999). Findings of a pilot study of motivational interviewing with pregnant drinkers. *Journal of Studies on Alcohol, 60,* 285–287.

Heather, N., Rollnick, S., Bell, A., & Richmond, R. (1996). Effects of brief counseling among male heavy drinkers identified on general hospital wards. *Drug and Alcohol Review, 15,* 29–38.

Lambert, M. J., Shapiro, D. A., & Bergin, A. E. (1986). The effectiveness of psychotherapy. In S. L. Garfield & A. E. Bergin (Eds.), *Handbook of psychotherapy and behavior change* (3rd ed., pp. 157–212). New York: Wiley.

Lawendowski, L. (1998). A motivational intervention for adolescent smokers. *Preventive Medicine, 27,* A 39–46.

Leake, G. J., & King, A. S. (1977). Effect of counselor expectations on alcoholic recovery. *Alcohol Health and Research World, 11,* 16–32.

Marlatt, G. A., & Gordon, J. R. (1985). *Relapse prevention: Maintenance strategies in the treatment of addictive behaviors.* New York: Guilford.

Miller, W. R., & Rollnick, S. (1991). *Motivational interviewing: Preparing people to change addictive behavior.* New York: Guilford.

Miller, W. R., Zweban, A., DiClemente, C., & Rychtarik, R. G. (1992). Motivational enhancement therapy manual: A clinical research guide for therapists treating individuals with alcohol abuse and dependence (Volume 2, Project MATCH monograph series). Rockville, MD: National Institute on Alcohol Abuse and Alcoholism.

MINT: Motivational Interviewing Network of Trainers: Annual Meeting. Newport, RI. October 18–21, 1998.

Noonan, W. C., & Moyers, T. B. (1997). Motivational interviewing. *Journal of Substance Misuse, 2,* 8–16.

Norcross, J. C., Ratzin, A. C., & Payne, D. (1989). Ringing in the New Year: The change processes and reported outcomes of resolutions. *Addictive Behaviors, 14,* 205–212.

Petty, R. E., & Cacioppo, J. T. (1981). *Attitudes and persuasion: Classic and contemporary approaches* (pp. 165–173). Dubuque: Wm. C. Brown.

Prochaska, J. O., & DiClemente, C. C. (1986). Toward a comprehensive model of change. In W. R. Miller & N. Heather (Eds.), *Treating addictive behaviors: Processes of change* (pp. 3–27). New York: Plenum Press.

Prochaska, J. O., DiClemente, C. C., & Norcross, J. C. (1992). In search of how people change: Applications to addictive behaviors. *American Psychologist, 47,* 1102–1114.

Prochaska, J. O., DiClemente, C. C., & Norcross, J. C. (1999). Stages of change: Prescriptive guidelines for behavioral medicine and psychotherapy. In G. P. Koocher, J. C. Norcross, & S. S. Hill (Eds.), *Psychologist's desk reference* (pp. 230–236). New York: Oxford University Press.

Project MATCH Research Group. (1997). Matching alcohol treatments to client heterogeneity: Project MATCH post-treatment drinking outcomes. *Journal of Studies on Alcohol, 58,* 7–29.

Project MATCH Research Group. (1999). Project MATCH secondary a priori hypotheses. *Addiction, 92,* 1671–1698.

Rogers, C. (1957). The necessary and sufficient conditions for therapeutic personality change. *Journal of Consulting Psychology, 21,* 95–103.

Rollnick, S., Heather, N., & Bell, A. (1992). Negotiating behaviour change in medical settings: The development of brief motivational interviewing. *Journal of Mental Health, 1,* 25–37.

Rollnick, S., & Miller, W. R. (1995). What is motivational interviewing? *Behavioural and Cognitive Psychotherapy, 23,* 325–334.

Senft, R. A., Polen, M. R., Freeborn, D. K., & Hollis, J. F. (1997). Brief intervention in a primary care setting for hazardous drinkers. *American Journal of Preventive Medicine, 13,* 464–470.

FOR FURTHER READING

Motivational interviewing: Preparing people to change addictive behaviors by Miller and Rollnick is the seminal text for this topic (listed in references).

Motivational interviewing: Videotape series. Interviews with Miller and Rollnick as well as taped vignettes illustrating the points of MI using a variety of interviewers, clients, and treatment settings. Available from the University of New Mexico; 505-277-2805 for information and orders.

What is motivational interviewing? Rollnick and Miller (listed in references). A useful discussion about the spirit of MI.

Motivational enhancement therapy (MET) manual: A clinical research guide for therapists treating individuals with alcohol abuse and dependence. Miller et al. (listed in references). How-to manual for providing feedback about alcohol risk factors using MI strategies.

CHAPTER

8

Building Alternative Futures

The Solution-Focused Approach

BRIAN CADE

We believe that it is useful to think about solution-focused therapy as a rumor. It is a set of stories that circulate within and through therapist communities. The stories are versions of the solution-focused therapy rumor. Whilst the names of the major characters usually remain stable, the plots and contexts that organize the action may vary from one storytelling episode to the next.
—Miller & de Shazer, 1998, p. 364.

The Central Philosophy of Brief and Solution-Focused Therapy

1. *If it works, do more of it.*
2. *If it doesn't work, do something different.*
3. *If it ain't broke, don't fix it.*

This chapter will consider the approaches and techniques that have become subsumed under the general heading of "solution-focused" (Berg, 1994; Berg & Miller, 1992; de Shazer, 1985, 1988, 1991, 1994; de Shazer et al., 1986; DeJong & Berg, 1998; Furman & Ahola, 1992; Miller et al., 1996; Walter & Peller, 1992). I clearly take responsibility for the particular twists I will give to the "solution-focused rumor."

Some of the Historical Background

The origins of the approaches lie primarily in the brilliant and idiosyncratic work of Milton H. Erickson (Erickson & Rossi, 1979; Erickson et al., 1976; Haley, 1967, 1973; O'Hanlon, 1987; Rosen, 1982; Rossi, 1980) and in the work of the Brief Therapy Center, Palo Alto

(Fisch et al., 1982; Ray & de Shazer, 1999; Watzlawick, 1978; Watzlawick & Weakland, 1977; Watzlawick et al., 1974; Weakland et al., 1974; Weakland & Ray, 1995).

Milton Erickson worked from the assumption that people already have, from within their own personal experiences and histories, the resources and areas of competence they need in order to surmount their difficulties. He did not operate from a clearly articulated theory of personality or of dysfunction but seemed to work from an implicit theory of therapy, of what helped people to change. Neither did he operate from a deficit model. He believed that people made the best choices they see as being available for themselves at any given moment, and that the therapist should listen carefully to and respect all communications from the client. He saw it as the job of the therapist to meet the client in his or her own world rather than to try to work from or to impose elements of the therapist's world.

Equally as important as Erickson's legendary genius for constructing brilliant and unpredictable interventions was the profound level of respect he showed for his patients, for their beliefs, for their integrity, and for their capacity to change—however chronic or acute their problems. His influence on the development of the brief approaches was profound. In an interview, videotaped just a few months before his death, John Weakland, a founding member of the Brief Therapy Center, Palo Alto, was asked what he had learned from Erickson. He replied,

> A great deal. . . . I learned something about paying close attention to clients. I learned something about change being always possible even in what appear to be desperate and fixed and concrete situations; and I learned that it's the business of a therapist essentially to take charge and influence people to make changes in useful directions. . . . It was remarkable to us to see the things that Erickson could get people to do that were different from what they were accustomed to doing. (Chaney, 1995)

The Brief Therapy Center was set up in 1966 within the Mental Research Institute, Palo Alto, California, primarily at the initiative of Dick Fisch, and included John Weakland and Paul Watzlawick. This group had a profound effect on the subsequent interest in and rapid development of the brief approaches throughout the world. John Weakland, who with Jay Haley and Don Jackson, had earlier been part of the influential Gregory Bateson project, which studied the paradoxes of abstraction in communication and evolved the interactional view (Bateson, Jackson, Haley, & Weakland, 1956; Berger, 1978; Sluzki & Ransom, 1976; Watzlawick & Weakland, 1977), described the origins of the brief therapy project as follows,

> To my mind we only had two or three basic ideas, which led to everything else. One, of course, was that we would work as a group. One person would be the therapist; the others would observe, and then everything would be recorded and discussed.
>
> But the two main principles that I think were responsible for the directions we took within that framework were, one, that we would focus on the client's main presenting complaint and STICK TO IT; not try to look around it or behind it or beneath it but stick to what's the main presenting complaint. And the other thing was that, by that time, we realized that it was not so easy to get people to change. So . . . we would try anything that we could think of that was legal or ethical regardless of whether it was conventional, or a long, long way from conventional thinking. I think things just grew out of that." (Chaney, 1995)

It is difficult nowadays, with the use of teams, one-way mirrors, and video recorders being so commonplace, to appreciate how revolutionary, at that time, this procedural approach was. Particularly revolutionary was the decision to remain tightly focused on what the client defined as the problem, making no assumptions about the existence of "deeper," underlying issues or of the function of symptoms. The group proceeded to elaborate an approach to therapy that evolved out of the direct observation of the process of trying to help people change, and from the detailed analysis of tape-recordings of therapy sessions. No unprovable assumptions were evoked or used. The group took care not to stray too far from pragmatics, from what could be unequivocally observed and clearly described. This stood in considerable contrast to other models prevalent at the time in which the therapeutic approach arose out of the dictates of the tenets of sometimes quite complex theories. One of this group's most influential ideas was the notion that problems develop from and are maintained by the way that, under certain circumstances, particular, and often quite normal, life difficulties become perceived and subsequently tackled. Guided by reason, logic, tradition, or "common sense," various attempted solutions are applied (and can include a denial of the difficulty). These can either have little or no effect or, alternatively, can exacerbate the situation. A problem then becomes entrenched as *more of the same* solutions, or classes of solutions, become followed by *more of the same* problem, attracting *more of the same* attempted solutions, and so on. A vicious circle develops, and the continued application of "wrong" or inappropriate solutions that lock the difficulty into a self-reinforcing, self-maintaining pattern can be seen as becoming the problem. Therapy is focused on changing the "attempted solutions," on stopping or even reversing the usual approach, however logical or correct it appears to be. The assumption is that, once the feedback loops maintaining the problem are changed, a greater range of responses becomes available.

Among the increasing number of professionals who began to have contact with this project in the late sixties and early seventies were Steve de Shazer and Insoo Kim Berg, who were to become very influential in the development of the solution-focused approaches. de Shazer recently talked of the earlier influence on him of the work of Milton Erickson and of Jay Haley's groundbreaking book, *Strategies of Psychotherapy* (Haley, 1963):

> Until I read this book, as far as I can remember, I had never even heard the term "psychotherapy." Certainly this was the first book on the topic that I read. I enjoyed it perhaps more than any other "professional book" I'd read in philosophy, art history, architecture, or sociology. So, I went to the library and looked at its neighbors. I was shocked. I was unable to finish any of the others I tried to read: After *Strategies*—which made so much sense to me—everything else was (poorly written) nonsense until I found *Advanced Techniques of Hypnosis and Therapy*, which is a selection of Milton H. Erickson's papers. It is not going too far to say that these two books changed my life and shaped my future. Unlike so many other "professional books," the books by Erickson and Haley were well written. They were clear. (I then read everything else they had written and I followed their references to other authors and other articles and books.) Among other things these books implicitly and indirectly (at times) suggested many of the themes that would form my career, including the idea of "brief therapy." (de Shazer, 1999)

The Brief Family Therapy Center was set up in Milwaukee in 1978. As de Shazer commented,

> Insoo and I and a group of our colleagues—who had been working together (secretly) for many years—decided to set up an independent "MRI of the Midwest" where we could both

> study therapeutic effectiveness, train therapists to do things as efficiently as possible, and, of course, practice therapy. (de Shazer, 1999)

In addition to Steve de Shazer and Insoo Kim Berg, the original Milwaukee group included James Derks, Marvin Weiner, Elam Nunnally, Eve Lipchick, Alex Molnar, and Marilyn La Court. Over time, the membership of the team was continually to evolve. Among the later members who were also to make a significant contribution were Wallace Gingerich, Michele Weiner-Davis, John Walter, Kate Kowalski, Ron Kral, Gale Miller, Scott Miller, and Larry Hopwood. In those early days, the group was largely using a problem-focused model very similar to and influenced by that of the Palo Alto Brief Therapy Center. However, in the early 1980s, it became increasingly interested in what clients were already doing on their own to solve their problems and in clients' own ideas about what they wanted changed, how things could be different, and what it would take to bring about these changes. This focus on a description of solutions rather than on a clarification of problems and failed solutions led quickly to the realization that it was not necessary to know much or sometimes even anything about the problem or its origins, assuming they could ever reliably be established, to get the process of change started. The group began to see the client as the expert in their own lives.

Keys to Solution

In 1984, de Shazer and Molnar outlined a first-session task that was routinely being given to clients regardless of the nature of the presenting problem.

> "Between now and the next time we meet, we (I) want you to observe, so that you can tell us (me) next time, what happens in your (life, marriage, family, or relationship) that you want to continue to have happen." (de Shazer & Molnar, 1984, p. 298)

They discovered that, in a significant number of cases, concrete changes occurred between the giving of this task and the following session.

> With surprising frequency (50 of 56 in a follow-up survey), most clients notice things they want to have continue and many (45 of the 50) describe at least one of these as "new or different." Thus, things are on the way to solution; concrete, observable changes have happened. (de Shazer et al., 1986, p. 217)

Moshe Talmon described how, working in a medical health center, he would give a suggestion similar to de Shazer's first session task to patients during the initial phone contact while a first appointment was being set up (Talmon, 1990, p. 19). Weiner-Davis et al. found that, in a significant proportion of cases, significant changes frequently seemed to occur prior to the first appointment even where no such suggestion had been offered. They would ask the following question,

> "Many times people notice in between the time they make the appointment for therapy and the first session that things already seem different. What have you noticed about your situation?" (Weiner-Davies, de Shazer, & Gingerich, 1987, p. 306)

In *Keys to Solution in Brief Therapy* (de Shazer, 1985), de Shazer described the development of further "formula interventions" through which, it was argued, the process of building solutions could be started. He invoked the analogy of a skeleton key in that, with just one skeleton key, a whole range of different locks can be opened without the need to find the exact key that will fit the exact shape of each and every lock.

Molnar and de Shazer elaborated a list of these formula interventions,

> 1. Client is asked to do more of the behaviors which are satisfactory and different from the problem behavior.
> 2. Client is asked to: "pay attention to what you do when you overcome the temptation or urge to . . ." (perform the symptom or some behavior associated with the symptom).
> 3. Client is given a prediction assignment such as whether in the time between sessions there will be more instances of behavior that are an exception to the problem behavior.
> 4. Client is told: "Between now and the next time, I (we) would like you to do something different and then tell me (us) what happened."
> 5. Client is asked to do a structured task (such as keeping a log of certain incidents) which is related to those times when the problem behavior ceases or is not present.
> 6. Client is told: "The situation is very (complicated, volatile, etc.). Between now and the next time, attempt to identify why the situation is not worse." (Molnar & de Shazer, 1987, p. 355)

The common theme with each of these interventions is that they are concerned with and focus the client and the process of therapy on what has worked, is working, or is beginning to work, rather than with exploring or categorizing pathology. They operate from an assumption that change is inevitable and that people are already bringing it about or have all that is necessary to do so. The group continued to seek clearer and more precise descriptions of the essence of what it takes to be therapeutic. What works? On the way, they dropped those assumptions, ways of thinking or of intervening that they discovered to be unnecessary or unhelpful. Many of these latter included assumptions and approaches that are often seen as of central importance in many other approaches (e.g., clear problem definition, hypothesizing, and diagnosis). In 1988, with his next book, *Clues: Investigating Solutions in Brief Therapy,* de Shazer summarized the basic principles behind and techniques used in the solution-focused approach that have since then been its essential features (de Shazer, 1988). More recently, these characteristic features have been summarized as follows,

> 1. At some point in the first interview, the therapist will ask the "Miracle Question."
> 2. At least once during the first interview and at subsequent ones, the client will be asked to rate something on a scale of "0–10" or "1–10."
> 3. At some point during the interview, the therapist will take a break.
> 4. After this intermission, the therapist will give the client some compliments, which will sometimes (frequently) be followed by a suggestion or homework task (frequently called an experiment). (de Shazer & Berg, 1997, p. 123)

Language and Figure/Ground

Solution-focused therapy has developed within the tradition of the constructivist/constructionist thinking of the interactional view. In seeking to describe, understand, and explain human behavior, there is no one reality "out there" available for objective analysis. There are as many "realities" as there are observers or groups of observers. *The Tibetan Book of the Great Liberation* states, (Evans-Wentz, 1969)

> As a thing is viewed, so it appears.

Reality, in terms of the way it is experienced and reacted to, is constructed out of the way each individual perceives, divides up, makes sense of, allocates meaning to, *and talks about* his or her world. This is in turn embedded in and powerfully affected by the negotiations about reality that continually evolve in the interactions between people from the level of dyad, family, kinship, and friendship networks, through larger and larger communities of (and means of) connection, including local, national, and international social, political, and knowledge systems, up to, nowadays, the instant global reach of the media and the worldwide community(ies) of the Internet.

Language is clearly the primary medium through which such realities are negotiated and, in every area of discourse and at all levels of discourse, ways of using language develop that both reflect and transmit the needs and the essence of that particular area of discourse. Particular clusters of words and phrases and ways of using them, tend to be favored and take on meanings, or shades of meaning, relevant to the context. The philosopher Ludwig Wittgenstein evoked the term *language game* to highlight the way the meaning of words stands not in a fixed relation between each word and some aspect of reality that it denotes, but in a local convention of usage that varies from context to context and is dependent on the spirit within which it is being used. Different language games would be used in, for example, an attempt at seduction, negotiating a loan with a bank manager, union–employer bargaining, gossiping with a neighbor, discussing a scientific theory, and engaging in an act of communal worship. Each would clearly be conducted in a different manner, and the words used would be chosen and would take on conventions of meaning and association relevant to the activity and the traditions and customary expectations of those involved. We cannot move outside of language so, in the same way that a fish can be seen as being unaware that it is in water, we can remain unaware of the particular language game we are immersed in because it is so familiar to us. As an example of how a word can have a meaning within but be relatively meaningless outside of a language game,

> Take the word "good." What is common between a good joke, a good player, a good man, feeling good, good will, good breeding, good looking, and a good for nothing? There is no one common property which the word *good* refers to. We cannot analyze the word so that we reach some essence or element from which the concept is built up. . . . But there are resemblances between the various meanings of the term . . . The circumstances in which the words are used give the clue. Specificity does not belong to the *experience* but to the *language game* which enables us to talk about or express our desires, intentions, meanings, etc. Meaning depends on articulation rather than representation. What is specific is always a function of the language game and can only be articulated within it. (Heaton & Groves, 1994, pp. 127–129)

In any field toward which our attention is drawn, certain aspects of that field will stand out in a figure/ground relation to other aspects. Which aspects of the field become figure and which become ground will relate to our expectations of the situation and to our current and most pressing preoccupations and intentions. These will also both be affected by and affect the language games through which we customarily operate. Discussing figure/ground phenomena in a chapter on perception, Adcock commented that, "detail is observable in the portion regarded as figure whereas the background tends to be rather homogenous" (Adcock, 1964, p. 142).

> A friend of [mine], many years ago, bought a Victorian drawing which was a rather skillfully executed reversible figure/ground picture of the type frequently used in works on the psychology of perception. The picture could be seen either as a naked young woman or as a collection of gaunt human skulls. The friend had only seen the former figure and was unable to see the latter until some time after it was pointed out. He was looking absentmindedly at it several days later when suddenly he was able to see the skulls for the first time. Clearly, in such a drawing, the emergence of either subject depends on two totally different interpretations of which lines and which areas of shade constitute the figure against which all of the rest then goes to make up the ground. The two subjects cannot exist simultaneously for any one observer (although they can rapidly be alternated between, once you have developed the hang of it). (Cade & Hudson O'Hanlon, 1993, p. 27)

Troubled people tend to see and remember those aspects of their lives that confirm their problem-saturated sense of themselves or each other and which thus stand out as the figure against which everything else becomes the ground. Also, whether seen as residing in the individual, the family or in any other system, problems tend to be the focus of considerable preoccupation by the symptom bearer, his or her intimates, and often of other systems—legal, medical, school, psychotherapeutic, neighborhood, work, and so forth. These preoccupations will be embedded in family, community, or professional language games that consist of explanatory frameworks, affective responses, and behaviors for dealing with the problem and its various effects. This will mean that particular events, attributes, and so forth associated with problems will stand out as figure against which other possibilities will become ground. As the problem becomes embedded, it is as though a gestalt develops in which certain behaviors and beliefs, attitudes, and responses are continually being highlighted and repeated and thus reinforced within an interlocking web of language games.

There is an ever-burgeoning number of models of therapy (one recent estimate puts the number at over 250) with differing ways of explaining the development of problems, the relationship between problems and past, present, or future aspects of people's lives, or their inner and outer worlds, and with sometimes widely differing ideas as to what is the proper focus of attention for the therapist and the therapy. Each approach will have its own language game and, while there may well be "family resemblances" between the games, it cannot be assumed, from approach to approach, that terms used in common have the same meanings and carry the same implications. Many a primary worker with a case will be familiar with the feeling of total confusion and even of paralysis that can follow the experience of discussing the client(s) in a multiagency, multi disciplinary case conference.

Miller and de Shazer (1998) differentiated between the language games that are involved in creating stories about problems as opposed to those that are concerned with helping clients construct stories about solutions. The former tend to focus on deficits—what is wrong—to become part of a discourse that "constructs" and maintains a problem, and to be past focused. The latter tend to focus on client resources available for constructing solutions and on what is possible, to emphasize what can be defined as already working, and to be future focused. In many of the former, it is also assumed that there is a direct correspondence between things and events and the words that are used to describe them: He *is* depressed; she *has* a personality disorder; this cluster of symptoms *confirms* a diagnosis of schizophrenia; this family *is* dysfunctional. The latter would show no interest in such categorization and would see such labels as saying as much if not more about the categorizer than about the categorized.

Miller and de Shazer also differentiated between the language games used when therapy is seen as a job to be done, defined by what the client specifically seeks help with, to be evaluated in terms of whether it effectively does that job for the client, as opposed to those where therapy is linked to an overarching explanatory theory, an ideology, or a cause such that the client is encouraged to view themselves differently in relation to personal, political, social, or cultural patterns identified as important by the therapist. Solution-focused therapy—with its primary concern with the therapist attitudes and behaviors associated with most rapidly and effectively bringing about the sought for (by them) changes in clients' lives—clearly falls within the former group.

Who Wants What?

The customer is always right.

In the tradition of the work of the Brief Therapy Center, Palo Alto, close attention is paid to who wants help, with what, and for whom? Much of what is often seen as "resistance" in clients is the result of therapists failing to clarify whether somebody is a customer or not or, if they are, failing to clarify and respect exactly what it is that they are a customer for. Therapists thus try to "sell" something to a person who is *currently* not interested in buying anything, or they try to sell the client something other than what he or she came to buy. It is thus important to establish at the beginning whether it is the client's concerns or the concerns of some other person(s) that have led to the client's being there. If the client is there because of his or her own concerns, then the therapy can proceed with the job of establishing what those concerns are and what needs to happen for the session to be useful. Where the client has come because of the concerns of others, a respectful acknowledgment of this by the therapist can often lead to the beginning of a productive discussion (which might then lead to the development of an agenda for therapy or to a joint decision not to proceed).

THERAPIST: What brings you here?

CLIENT: My doctor thought it would be useful for me to come and talk about some things.

THERAPIST: Did you agree with him that it might be useful?

CLIENT: I don't know.

THERAPIST: What do you think your doctor hoped would happen by your coming here and talking?

CLIENT: He thinks I need grief counseling to help me get over the death of my mother.

THERAPIST: Do you agree with him?

CLIENT: I don't know. I don't like to talk about it. *(pause)* I don't know if I want to.

THERAPIST: When did she die?

CLIENT: About a year ago.

THERAPIST: What do you think makes him think that you need grief counseling?

CLIENT: Well, I've been depressed and not been sleeping too well, and I burst into tears at the slightest thing. I've not been able to work since I broke down earlier this year.

THERAPIST: And the doctor feels that this is related to the death of your mother?

CLIENT: I guess so.

THERAPIST: Do you agree?

CLIENT: I suppose it could be.

THERAPIST: Were you close to her?

CLIENT: Very. *(Client looks tearful.)*

THERAPIST: So, your doctor feels that talking about your mother's death might be helpful?

CLIENT: I guess so.

THERAPIST: What difference is he hoping that talking about it will make?

CLIENT: Well, ultimately, that I might get off of these antidepressants and even be able to go back to teaching. I used to be a primary school teacher.

THERAPIST: Do you want to go back to teaching?

CLIENT: Yes, I'd like to feel that I could.

THERAPIST: So what would need to start happening differently in your life so that you could say, maybe not today but in a couple of weeks or so, "I'm glad I took the doctor's advice and went to see that therapist?"

CLIENT: If I could just wake up one morning and find that I'm actually looking forward to the day.

THERAPIST: Suppose that happened. What would be the most likely small but significant thing you would start looking forward to?

CLIENT: Just something simple like going out for a walk and having a morning coffee in Eastwood. Perhaps meeting up with my friend. I've been putting off calling her for weeks, now.

THERAPIST: What else?

It is important that the therapist never be more enthusiastic than the client about the need for therapy or about a particular outcome for therapy. People will only change in ways that they themselves are a customer for. Often, clients can remain unenthusiastic about working on the goals of the people who have brought or sent them, but develop alternative goals of their *own* which they are prepared to work toward. For example, a young person sent by a teacher because of disruptive behavior in the classroom may show no interest in changing for the teacher but may well develop an interest in finding ways of getting the teacher off his or her back. An individual with anorexia is unlikely to want to put on the weight that the referrer wants her to, but may be prepared to work toward getting the energy for completing her university assignments. A problem drinker may have little motivation for working on his drinking habit but be quite concerned about losing his job, in relation to which he may draw his own conclusions about the need to cut back on his alcohol consumption.

At times, a therapist can become too clearly identified with the arguments in favor of a particular change, especially, for example, when operating on the behalf of an agency with statutory powers and responsibilities. Whether that urgency is explicitly or implicitly communicated, the therapist can become the main "customer" for how a client should be or for what a client should do. It then becomes as though the therapist has colonized the arguments in favor of that change, leaving available to the client only the counterarguments to the change together with the accompanying affect produced by those counterarguments. The perceived rights and wrongs of the therapist's view of how things *ought to be* are irrelevant if the pursuit of those ends has the effect of disempowering the client, increasing "resistance," or further entrenching attitudes.

The woman from the excerpt agreed to a second appointment and eventually came for a series of sessions with the goal of gradually increasing the number of things she was doing each day to which she would look forward on waking up. Apart from briefly acknowledging the important role her mother had played in her life and her profound sadness about her death, very little time was spent on issues to do with grief (which is not to say that the issue of grief was not important, nor that the woman did not have grief issues to work through; grief was just *not* what *she* wanted to work on in therapy).

Exceptions to the Problem

Is the glass half empty or is it half full?

Central to the solution-focused approach is the certainty that, in a person's, couple's, or family's life, there will always be exceptions to the behaviors, ideas, feelings, and interactions associated with what is seen as a problem. There will be times, even if they only occur occasionally, when a difficult adolescent *does* cooperate; when a depressed person feels *less* sad; when a shy person *is* able to feel more at ease in a social situation; when an obsessive person *is* able to relax; when a troubled couple *resolves* rather than escalates a conflict; when a bulimic *resists* the urge to binge and purge; when a child does *not* have a temper tantrum when asked to tidy up; when an overly responsible person *does* say no; when a problem drinker *does* contain drinking to within sensible limits; and so on. Yet, because clients have become immersed in the problem, they tend to see the problem as figure together with all the processes surrounding it, against which everything else becomes the ground. They tend to see what they expect to see and to miss, discount, or deny as significant that which does not fit in with their expectations. As de Shazer observed,

> Problems are seen to maintain themselves simply because they maintain themselves and because clients depict the problem as *always happening*. Therefore, times when the complaint is absent are dismissed as trivial by the client or even remain completely unseen, hidden from the client's view. Nothing is actually hidden, but although these exceptions are open to view, they are not seen by the client as differences that make a difference. (de Shazer, 1991, p. 58)

By questioning clients about these exceptions, clients can be invited to recognize and then to build on *what they have already done or are currently doing* that can be framed as successful or, at least, as heading in the general direction of dealing more effectively with the problem, even if it is only one small step in that direction. They are invited, as it were, to examine the ground and to find forgotten or unnoticed details there that can be highlighted and become a new figure.

For example, a harassed and demoralized parent was describing how her children would *always* ignore or defy her when she asked them to tidy away their toys and get ready for bed. The therapist responded with a hunch:

THERAPIST: But, sometimes they don't?

CLIENT: Yes, but not very often.

THERAPIST: What's different about you the times that they *have* done what you asked.

CLIENT: (*after a pause*) I guess it's when they realize that they have pushed me too far.

THERAPIST: How could they tell that?

CLIENT: (*another pause*) You know, it's funny. I think it's when I stop ranting and raving at them, and my voice goes very, very calm.

THERAPIST: What else is different?

CLIENT: I don't threaten or beg.

THERAPIST: What do you do, instead?

CLIENT: I tell them clearly and firmly what I want them to do.

THERAPIST: You mean it's when they realize they haven't gotten under your skin?

CLIENT: Yes, I think that's it. They know I really mean it. Once they get under my skin, they know they've got me on the run.

THERAPIST: What else is different about those days?

CLIENT: I think it's when I feel generally less harassed, when I feel I've got things done rather than spent the whole day worrying about getting things done. When I feel I've not been able to get on top of the housework, I tend to panic.

THERAPIST: So, what's different about those days when the kids do take note?

CLIENT: I get started early on and get things done. Then, I can have a break and relax a little before the kids come home from school. I think that helps me handle things better.

THERAPIST: So, on those days, it's clear to the kids that you mean business? They must be able to pick up the vibes? You presumably look somehow different on those days?

CLIENT: I guess so. Yes, I'm sure that's it. I think I just look calmer.

THERAPIST: What else?

CLIENT: I probably greet them more enthusiastically and smile more.

THERAPIST: And when is the last time you had a day like that, or at least part of a day like that?

CLIENT: In fact, now I think about it, it happened last Monday. I also took them to McDonalds.

The extent to which recognition of the existence of exceptions might start a different language game and become a springboard from which further changes can occur, clearly relates to the extent to which they are seen as meaningful to the client. As Cade and O'Hanlon commented,

> Clearly, it would be easy to highlight exceptions in such a way that the client or family feels patronized, or feels that the therapist really does not understand the seriousness of their problem, or the distress, guilt, anger, etc., that it has caused them. Thus it is important that the therapist avoids becoming overpreoccupied that a client or family *must* recognize the existence of a particular exception, or avoids entering into an argument with them about its significance. As John Weakland has said (personal communication), "Never argue with a client." It is often much better to maintain a puzzled skepticism rather than a crusading zeal. (Cade & Hudson O'Hanlon, 1993, p. 98)

When clients are talking about their problems in a negative, problem-focused way, the therapist can most usefully aid the process of deconstructing that language game by being not too quick to understand. According to de Shazer,

> perhaps the best that therapists can do is creatively misunderstand what clients say so that the more useful, more beneficial meanings of their words are the ones chosen. Thus, creative misunderstanding allows the therapist and the client to together construct a reality that is more satisfactory to the client. (de Shazer, 1991, p. 69)

> "I am *still* puzzled as to how you managed to avoid *totally* losing your temper. It can't have been easy. Many parents would have lost it within the first few seconds. Your daughter really does sound as if she could try the patience of a saint. So, how the hell did you resist wringing her neck last night?"

> "From what you have told me, I think anyone, including me, would have become depressed. How did you manage to keep yourself going? How did you manage to get on with what you had to do in spite of feeling that way?"

The asking of questions such as, "How did you do that?" can be very powerful. Not only do they implicitly highlight success, or degrees of success, but can also help elicit contingencies in people's lives that are, and can be highlighted as, associated with more successful functioning. For example,

THERAPIST: When was the last time you went a day or more without bingeing and purging?

CLIENT: It was quite some months ago.

THERAPIST: But you can remember that time?

CLIENT: Yes.

THERAPIST: How did you do it?

CLIENT: It was difficult. I managed to hold off for nearly a week. Mind you, I kept thinking about it all day long.

THERAPIST: Of course, but how did you manage it?

CLIENT: I was determined not to let it control me.

THERAPIST: How did you manage to do that, and for nearly a week?

CLIENT: Well, one thing I did was, after eating, I made myself go for really long walks with the dog.

THERAPIST: And that helped?

CLIENT: Yes, because, by the time I got back, I would feel less bloated.

THERAPIST: What else helped?

CLIENT: I wouldn't be sitting there with my parents watching and waiting; watching me out of the corners of their eyes, but pretending not to; and me getting more and more angry.

These questions are not part of a fact-finding mission, a hunt for the truth. They are an invitation to the client to enter a language game about themselves and their circumstances that allows for a different view of competence, of possibilities, of their potentials to develop solutions, of the inevitability of change. So the question "What else . . . ?" is used frequently either when looking at past or present exceptions or, as will be seen, when looking at how the future will be different.

It can also be affirming of people when the difficulties they have been struggling with are attested to by questions such as,

> "Given what you have told me about your situation, I am really surprised that things are not much worse. How have you kept going?"

As Miller has observed, "By asking how a client has been able to make some progress, or maintain or prevent their problems from becoming worse, the therapist and client are able to review situations that appeared to be failures as solutions that simply went unnoticed" (Miller, 1992, p. 7).

However, the usefulness of concentrating on exceptions—on solutions rather than on problems—and of using the miracle and scaling questions to be described next, still exists primarily in the experience of the client. It is always important to read the feedback. Some clients want to talk about their problems, to seek an understanding of why they have them, and to have an opportunity to "let off steam." Although the ultimate direction of therapy will be to look at what will be different in the future, it is no good if the therapist rushes ahead and leaves the client(s) behind feeling puzzled, unheard, and even angry. Clients know best what they find helpful.

The Miracle Question

A powerful way of helping people to focus on potential solutions rather than on problems and to set goals is the miracle question. It continues the process of developing a language game between therapist and client(s) from within which possibilities and probabilities of future success can be both anticipated and constructed. The client is implicitly invited to ignore the details of the problem—in fact, to bypass them completely—and go straight into the future to a time where the problem either no longer exists or is being handled more effectively and to describe that future in as specific a way as possible. The asking of the miracle question is usually prefaced with a comment such as, "I'm going to ask you a strange kind of question."

> Suppose that tonight after you go to sleep a miracle happens and the problems that brought you to therapy are solved immediately. But since you were sleeping at the time you cannot know that this miracle has happened. Once you wake up tomorrow morning, how will you discover that a miracle has happened? Without your telling them, how will other people know that a miracle has happened? (de Shazer, 1994, p. 95)

Clients are then encouraged to elaborate, in as detailed a way as they are able, what the observable differences will be.

WIFE: I'd be happy; feeling at ease at last. I'd be more pleasant to Bob, not jumping down his throat all the time.

THERAPIST: What will you do instead?

WIFE: Well, there would be more understanding between us. We'd listen to what each other was saying.

HUSBAND: Yes. At the moment, we don't really listen to each other. We just wait to get our own point in.

THERAPIST: So, you'd both be listening to each other more instead of behaving like politicians?

BOTH: Yes.

THERAPIST: How could you tell that the other is *really* listening?

WIFE: In the face, I think. We'd perhaps make more eye contact. (*pauses, then laughs*) We'd nod in the right places.

HUSBAND: Yes, we'd both respond to what the other was saying rather than just attacking or ignoring it.

THERAPIST: What else would be different about the way you talk together?

HUSBAND: Our voices would be different. We wouldn't be yelling so.

THERAPIST: How would your voices be, instead?

HUSBAND: Calmer. More tolerant. We might be putting our points firmly, but we wouldn't be hammering at each other.

THERAPIST: So, instead of hammering . . . ?

HUSBAND: We'd be talking calmly, respecting each other's right to a different opinion.

THERAPIST: Going back to the moment you first open your eyes tomorrow morning, what do you suppose would be the very first thing either of you would notice that would tell you things are different?

WIFE: He usually wakes up first so, before getting up to make a coffee, maybe he'd kiss my shoulder, like he used to.

THERAPIST: Suppose he did that tomorrow morning, what would you then do?

WIFE: I'd feel good.

THERAPIST: How could Bob tell?

WIFE: Well, if he could see my face he'd probably see a smile.

HUSBAND: And she wouldn't pull away from me.

WIFE: Well, you know why that is.

HUSBAND: (*to therapist*) She always assumes if I kiss her that I am after sex.

WIFE: Well, you usually are.

HUSBAND: Now, you know that's not true.

THERAPIST: So, Bob, how would you kiss her so that she would know it was different from an "I am interested in sex" kiss?

HUSBAND: I'd just kiss her gently on the shoulder then go off to make the coffee.

THERAPIST: Is that what you mean, Tania? Is that the kind of kiss you would respond to with a smile?

WIFE: Yes, if I knew it was that kind of kiss.

THERAPIST: Then what would happen?

WIFE: Well, if I knew it wasn't automatically going to lead to a grope and to "wishful thinking" time, I'd like to cuddle up to him for a while some mornings.

THERAPIST: How would that make a difference to you?

WIFE: Well, it would be a nice way to start the day. Maybe I wouldn't be so tense and irritable.

THERAPIST: What difference would the children notice?

WIFE: (*laughing*) I wouldn't be so tense and irritable.

THERAPIST: What would they see, instead, that would tell them that something had changed?

HUSBAND: If we were talking to each other instead of basically ignoring each other; if they saw us smiling and touching each other affectionately; if they saw us kiss when I left for work; they'd definitely see that something had changed.

THERAPIST: Is that right?

WIFE: Yes. Just us all having a pleasant breakfast together would be a nice change.

Often, the first answer to the miracle question is a somewhat general, global, even Utopian one.

"I (we) will be happy."
"I will be more confident."
"I will be tall and blonde."
"I will have my sight back again."

It is very difficult to do "happy" or "confident" (let alone suddenly become tall or regain sight). The level of description that is being sought is something specific that the client could do *even if he or she didn't feel like it*. For example, a young woman diagnosed as anorectic found it extremely difficult to answer the miracle question other than saying that she would know it had happened because she would wake up feeling happy. It took the whole session of patiently returning to the question for her finally to come up with two specific differences.

First, she would be able to look in the mirror on her way to the shower without being repulsed. The very fact that she looked in the mirror at all would prove that a miracle had happened because she could not normally stand to look at herself. Second, after her shower, she would go to her closet and choose something to wear because she liked it rather than automatically putting on her "anorectic uniform" of jeans and a bulky sweater.

She came to the next session wearing a short, sleeveless summer dress. It was not that the weather had suddenly become hot. It had been extremely hot and humid for many weeks. As O'Hanlon and Weiner-Davis said, "It appears that the mere act of constructing a vision of the solution acts as a catalyst for bringing it about." (O'Hanlon & Weiner-Davis, 1989, p. 106). Looking in a mirror or wearing a summer dress was something she could do, *even if she didn't feel like it*—feeling happy was not.

Sometimes a client can find it easier to describe what other people would notice than what they themselves would. For example,

CLIENT: I would be more confident.

THERAPIST: What would you do differently that would show that you were more confident?

CLIENT: I don't know. I just would feel more confident.

THERAPIST: Okay, so when you catch the train to work tomorrow morning, suppose there is someone who travels regularly on the same train who looks over at you and thinks, "That young woman looks far more confident today." What would they be noticing different about you?

CLIENT: That I would be holding my head up. I would be looking around and showing an interest in things.

THERAPIST: What else?

CLIENT: There would be a spring in my step. If it was someone who travels regularly on the same train, I might smile and nod a greeting to them.

THERAPIST: What else?

CLIENT: Instead of clutching my bag to my stomach, I might place it on the floor beside me.

Often, the client's initial response will be "I don't know." However, it is very rare to come across a client who cannot, with minimal prompting, begin building a picture of an alternative future.

Sometimes, clients do find it difficult to imagine that a miracle has happened. While it clearly is important not to push too hard for an answer, a gentle and respectful persistence over the course of an interview can help begin the process. For example, a woman who was struggling with two oppositional adolescents found she could not answer the miracle question. As she continued to describe the difficulties she had been experiencing, she told of a recent incident in which they had made her "lose the plot."

> **THERAPIST:** Suppose that miracle I talked about earlier had happened. How do you think you might have handled that situation differently?
>
> **CLIENT:** I guess I maybe would have walked out of the room and calmed myself down, first.
>
> **THERAPIST:** What else might have been different?
>
> **CLIENT:** I wouldn't have risen to the bait in the first place. They really know how to wind me up.
>
> **THERAPIST:** So, after this miracle, the kids will learn that you are not so easy to wind up?
>
> **CLIENT:** Yes.
>
> **THERAPIST:** What else would they learn?
>
> **CLIENT:** Maybe that I deserve some respect.
>
> **THERAPIST:** What will they see in you that will tell them that you deserve respect?

People typically find it easier to define how *other* people should be different (particularly the spouse with whom they are having difficulties, or a problem child). This tends to perpetuate more of the same "why can't you see what you are doing wrong" stance, which will often be insufficiently different from their usual interactions around the problem. It is better that they be encouraged to describe what differences others, such as their spouse, children, friends, work associates, or strangers, will notice about them.

> "Suppose your husband does begin to behave in a more considerate way, what differences will he see in the way you respond to him that will show him that you appreciate it?"
>
> "Suppose you two were to go to a restaurant tomorrow night and another couple was watching you having a meal together, and one of them said to the other, 'that couple looks as if they are getting on well,' what would they be seeing that would tell them that?"

Often clients describe differences in terms of an *absence* of either a behavior or an emotional state. It is useful to ask them what it is that they will be doing or feeling *instead.* Ultimately, it is much easier to engage in a clearly defined alternative behavior than it is just to resist doing something without having another activity to take its place.

> "So, when you are no longer sitting around crying and feeling sorry for yourself, what will you be doing instead?"

Descriptions of changes in feelings are also best translated into descriptions of the specific behaviors that would be clear evidence to others that their mood had changed.

"What specifically will your colleagues at work see different about you that would tell them that you were no longer depressed, without you telling them?"

Another way of focusing on the future is to ask a question such as, "Suppose you are coming back next week, and you are sitting there telling me that things have improved in small but significant ways, what is it that you will be telling me about?" or, when talking to a couple, "What will be the differences in you that your partner will be telling me about?"

When working with young children, it may be that the notion of a miracle is not one they will easily understand. It is always possible to use notions such as a magic wand, a good fairy, a guardian angel, a fairy godmother, a genie, Sabrina the teenage witch, and so on.

Scaling Questions

> As anyone who has played around with numbers knows, like words, numbers are magic. (de Shazer, 1994, p. 92)

Another important part of the solution-focused language game is the use of scaling questions, which can be used in a wide variety of ways. Scales of some sort or other have been used in many other approaches to therapy, usually as a way of measuring aspects of a client's behavior against some normative standard. In solution-focused therapy, scales are used to create (and reflect) an assumption of fluidity and change. They are a measure of a client's perception of themselves now compared to how they had been before and how they would wish to be. They have no external referents other than those that are meaningful to the client (even if they are not clearly able to articulate them). If it were hypothetically possible to have two people at exactly the same point vis-à-vis solving exactly the same problem, one of them might scale themselves at 4, the other at 7. Neither would be right or wrong. The usefulness of the scale is totally subjective and solely in terms of whether the number chosen helps clients have a sense that they are handling things better now than at some earlier point. It helps them develop a sense of moving forward, or the possibility of doing so, and a picture of what things will be like when that forward movement has been made. As Kowalski and Kral pointed out,

> the scale builds on an assumption of change in the desired direction. Since a scale is a progression, the number "7" assumes the numbers "10" as well as "5", "3", or "1." It assumes movement (change) in one direction or another, rather than stagnation. By virtue of this, an expectation of change is built into the process of asking scaling questions. . . . since the use of a scale enhances a suggestion of change in either the desired or dreaded direction, it also implies a degree of control on the part of the client for navigating the direction. . . . the business of goal setting is accomplished, since the poles and the area between the problem and the goal are made quantifiable and objectifiable. (Kowalski & Kral, 1989, p. 61)

By means of a scale, a precise figure can be elicited to represent a whole range of aspects of the client's experience, with components ranging from the specific to the global, even to the vague. A general sense of how the client is doing can be translated into a concrete number, which will have meaning for the client. Although it is possible to invite clients to spell out some specific things that are happening that tell them they have achieved a particular number, it is never possible to achieve a complete picture. There will always be more, and that creation of a sense that there will always be more is an important part of the solution-focused language game. The most frequently used scale in a first session is as follows:

> On a scale ranging from 0 to 10 where 0 represents when problems were at their worst (in subsequent sessions, it is more usual for 0 to represent the way things were when they first sought help) and 10 represents how things will be when these problems are resolved (or, if the miracle question has already been asked, 'when this miracle we've been talking about has happened'), where would you place yourself today?

Although there will be clients who will place themselves at 0, a surprising number will place themselves somewhere higher on the scale creating instantly a potential story of flexibility and a degree of success in dealing with the problem already, rather than a story of the problem as a monolithic fixed entity over which they have little or no control.

Whatever number clients come up with (3 is the number that seems most often to be chosen), two areas of expansion then become available. First, clients can be invited to describe how they have got themselves to 3. "How did you do that?" "What are you doing different that you were not doing when you were down at 0?" This will encourage them to concentrate further on exceptions. As highlighted earlier, it remains important that the therapist be cautious not to be more enthusiastic than the client, even potentially patronizing, about the importance of an exception. Second, clients can be invited to build a picture of future step-by-step change (as opposed to sudden miraculous change) through being asked what would need to be happening for them to feel they have moved from 3 up to 4. For example,

THERAPIST: On a scale ranging from 0 to 10 where 0 represents when things were at their very worst and 10 represents how things will be when your life is fully back on track again, where would you place yourself today?

CLIENT: (*after a pause*) About 3.

THERAPIST: How have you done that? How have you got yourself from 0 to 3?

CLIENT: I guess I decided I just couldn't go on that way any longer.

THERAPIST: So, what have you been doing different that has got you from 0 to 3.

CLIENT: Well, for a start, I contacted you.

THERAPIST: Okay. What else?

CLIENT: I've been making myself get up and take a shower first thing each morning. Also, on a couple of mornings, I went out for a walk. It was tough getting myself started. . . .

THERAPIST: I'm sure it was.

CLIENT: But I tend to feel better once I've done it.

THERAPIST: What else?

CLIENT: That's about it. (*short pause*) Oh, I did try to call a friend, yesterday. But she's away in Brisbane for a few days.

THERAPIST: So, you might try her again, later?

CLIENT: I guess so.

THERAPIST: Anything else that you're doing different that tells you you've moved from 0 to 3?

CLIENT: I can't think of anything else.

THERAPIST: Okay, suppose that we are now a week or two in the future and you are sitting there in that chair and telling me that you feel strongly that you've started edging toward or even that maybe you've reached 4. What will you be telling me about?

CLIENT: That I've called that friend and that we're meeting up for a coffee.

THERAPIST: Okay. What else?

CLIENT: That I am still getting up early and also still going out for walks. (*pause*) Maybe I'll have started looking in the paper for a job.

THERAPIST: Are you sure that looking for a job would be at 4? That sounds like quite a significant jump to me.

CLIENT: (*laughs*) I only said *looking* in the paper. I didn't say anything about actually going for one.

THERAPIST: You're right. I was jumping the gun. So where would you have to be on the scale to be actually going for a job?

CLIENT: 6 or 7, I guess.

THERAPIST: So, what else would you be doing that would tell you you were at 4?

CLIENT: I wouldn't be sitting around feeling sorry for myself all day.

THERAPIST: What would you be doing, instead?

CLIENT: Maybe I'd start painting again.

THERAPIST: Painting?

CLIENT: Yes. I used to paint with watercolors. You know, flowers, landscapes, and things. I used to enjoy that.

Scales can be used to consider a whole range of aspects of a client's life or of the therapy. In fact, there are few experiences that cannot, in some way, be looked at through the lens of a scaling question.

> scaling questions can be used to assess self-esteem, pre-session change, self-confidence, investment in change, willingness to work hard to bring about desired changes, prioritizing of problems to be solved, perception of hopefulness, and evaluation of progress, and so on—things usually considered too abstract to quantitate (Berg, 1994, p. 102).

The following are some examples of scales that can be used:

> (To a couple) "If 0 represents 'I couldn't really give a damn' and 10 represents 'I'm really motivated to work on our relationship,' where would you place yourself today between 0 and 10?" (or "where do you think your partner would place him- or herself?")

> What will have happened over the next week or so for each of you to feel you have moved up a point or two?"
>
> "If 10 represents 'this relationship has the potential to be a really good marriage' and 0 represents 'this relationship has no future at all,' where would you put yourselves today between 0 and 10?"
>
> "If 0 means you believe you are basically going to be like this for the rest of your life and 10 that you are very confident that you'll have this problem beat at some point in the future, where would you place yourself on that scale today? What would it take for you to move up half a point or even one point on the scale?"
>
> "If 10 represents having as much confidence as anyone could expect to have, and 0 is the opposite, absolutely no confidence at all, where would you put yourself today?"
>
> "If 0 represents how you were when I first met you and 10 represents when that miracle we talked about has happened, where are you today between 0 and 10?"
>
> "If 10 represents that you'll do more or less anything to get over this and 0 represents that you're only prepared to wait it out and hope it will all go away, where are you between 0 and 10 today?"

It is important when inquiring about movements up the scale that the therapist choose realistic gradations erring on the side of the conservative rather than the over-optimistic. If a client is experiencing a high degree of optimism, it is better that he or she has to persuade the therapist about that. If the therapist seems to be pushing too quickly for change such that the client feels pressured, he or she is more likely to adopt a "yes, but" position.

Looking at a client's progress through the medium of a scale can often give him or her a different perspective on how things are going. A young man apologetically admitted that he felt he'd only reached 3 on the scale. He was surprised and encouraged when it was pointed out to him that he was "almost a third of the way there." A young woman who was still expressing many negatives about her progress, in spite of the many "exceptions" the therapist had been able to elicit (which were clearly, at that stage, more meaningful to him than to her), became more optimistic about her situation when, after scaling her overall progress as 5, she realized she was "halfway there."

Scaling questions can be used with young children as well as with adults. Words are, of course, not the only medium to be used. The therapist can draw pictures, or ask the child to draw them. There are many creative ways young children can be helped to depict where they feel they are. A young girl who had been sexually abused was invited to draw a picture of herself that showed the way she saw herself now and then a picture of how she would look when she really liked herself. She first drew an ugly, distorted figure in brown and black, covered with spots and with a miserable mouth. Her second picture was of a pretty girl wearing brightly colored clothes and smiling a big smile. She drew flowers around the feet and a sun in the sky. It was then possible both to talk about and to draw the small changes that would tell her and her friends that she was moving from the one picture to the other.

> As I struggled to find a way of expressing a scale that would be meaningful for her to help her *envisage* and measure her progress from being the girl in the first drawing to the girl in the second, Melinda came up with a wonderful insight which also provided us with an evoca-

tive scale. She said that getting better was a bit like being in a game of snakes-and-ladders. As you moved forward you sometimes went up a ladder and felt that you were beginning to get there. Then, every now and then you would slip down a snake. Some days you would feel that you had gone up one of the big ladders and things were really good. "Then you slide down that bloody big snake and feel you've gone right back to the beginning again." She put a hand over her mouth realizing she had cussed. I told her that it was alright; that I used to be a truck driver and was not easily shocked. She went on to say, "But you mustn't let yourself get too upset because, if you keep on going and don't let sliding down the snakes upset you too much, everyone gets to the finish in the end."

From that time on, each session I would draw a snakes-and-ladders board and Melinda would indicate what her position was on the board that represented how good she felt about herself on that particular day. She agreed with me that the difference between snakes-and-ladders and real life was that, in real life, you could often make your own mind up about how you wanted to act and react, although sometimes it was difficult not to "slide on down that snake." I suggested, both at school and at home, that she keep a watch out for any time that she could easily have slipped down a snake but didn't and did something else instead. (Cade, 1998, p. 8)

The Intermission

Solution-focused therapists typically take a break before ending each session, whether or not there is a team behind a one-way mirror with whom to consult. De Shazer described the beginnings of this tradition,

> One day in 1977, we watched while the therapist and client were trying to define and describe the problem, i.e., the client's complaint and the associated, failed attempts to resolve that complaint much in the same way that MRI would do it. The client and therapist were focused on this frame: She was depressed and, therefore, she was fat. Naturally she believed she needed to stop being depressed before she could lose weight. Behind the mirror, the group was thinking the opposite: She's fat and therefore she's depressed. Using that punctuation, interventions could be aimed at her ways of accidentally maintaining and increasing her weight. We phoned in a couple of suggestions based on this view but the therapist did not find our help helpful. This frustrated both the therapist and the group. Finally, the therapist excused himself for a couple of minutes to talk to the team. He was going to straighten us out. I don't remember the outcome of that discussion, but we soon started to routinely take a break in the session during which the team and therapist would meet, a procedural intervention that we continue to this day. It was not long before we started to take a break "to think about things" even when working alone. (de Shazer, 1999)

Before leaving the room, however, it is important that the therapist ask whether there is anything that so far has not come up in the session that the client feels is important for the therapist to know about at this point. Sometimes a client will then bring up an issue that is important and which may require further clarification before the break is taken. At times, a client will bring up an issue that may not seem particularly relevant to the therapist. However, it remains important to ask the question. If this is not done and the client believes there is something important the therapist should know, or should have asked about, then whatever the therapist says to end the session will become diluted or lost behind the client's sense that the therapist lacks (or has shown insufficient interest in) this important knowledge.

A break allows the therapist to collect his or her thoughts, compose a concluding statement, construct an appropriate homework assignment, and, of central importance, make sure that all of the former relate to the client's primary expressed concern. An interview can range over a wide number of issues, many of which may be of intense interest and concern to the client but are *not* the central concern that brought the client to therapy. It can be easy for the therapist to frame the concluding comments and the task around one of these issues (particularly if it is an issue about which the therapist holds strong views) rather than around the specific concern that brought the client there. This can lead then to "resistance" on the part of the client.

A break also gives the client time to think about the session and heightens his or her sense of anticipation about what the therapist's (and, where relevant, the team's) opinion and suggestion is going to be. Also, clients often come to therapy expecting to be probed and exposed in areas of their greatest doubts or emotional sensitivity and/or to be "told the error of their ways." The break brings the realization that this is not about to happen.

For example, a woman remained both verbally and nonverbally totally unresponsive throughout the whole of a first session. She had had two previous experiences of more traditional therapies during which, according to her husband, she had also been totally "uncooperative." The therapist was careful not to try to persuade her to respond, though she would ask the woman occasional questions. However, she was careful, when receiving no response to a question, not to turn to the husband for the answer, but would ask him a totally different question, thus avoiding the trap of seeming to enter a "co-therapy" relationship with him. When the therapist returned from her break, the woman instantly and spontaneously began to respond, firstly with silent nods of agreement at the validating feedback, then verbally, and finally laughing and joking. It is interesting to speculate on the importance of the break to let this woman know that the pressure to respond she had doubtless been anticipating from the therapist was actually not going to occur.

Summary, Compliments, and Tasks

A solution-focused therapy session always ends with a final intervention, which includes a summary, compliments, and, following on logically from those, a task, often described as an experiment.

The final summary first of all indicates to clients that they have been listened to and understood. People tend to hear best when they feel that they themselves have been heard. The summary, therefore, clearly must address their primary concerns. It should acknowledge the difficulties they have been struggling with and the positive attempts they have made to deal with the situation. It can be helpful and affirming, where possible, to reproduce or paraphrase a client's own language, including the idiosyncratic ways they use particular words or phrases. Consistent with the development of a solution-focused language game, this summary should concentrate on complimenting positive aspects of a client's achievements, intentions, and desires. It must obviously be sincere and avoid being either glib or patronizing. Client goals should be identified and validated as important and worthy of the hard work that might be necessary to achieve them. As Berg and Miller pointed out,

> The team at the Brief Therapy Center has been using and studying compliments for close to 20 years, and we continue to be amazed at their therapeutic power and usefulness as an intervention tool. The compliment is used with all cases . . . regardless of the type of client–therapist relationship, and throughout the treatment process. Except on rare occasions when the client is squeamish about receiving compliments, and in extremely rare situations where the therapist is unable to find anything positive at all, we find that using compliments enhances the cooperation with the client. . . . The use of compliments is one of many tools a therapist has at his disposal that takes advantage of socially accepted norms of discourse. We discovered through our cross-cultural and international presentations that all cultures use compliments as a means to cementing social relationships at all levels. However, the cultural norm dictates the manner in which compliments are presented. (Berg & Miller, 1992, pp. 101–102)

The task that is then suggested should follow logically and naturally from themes highlighted in the summary: "Because it is so clear to us that . . ." or "because it is obviously important to you that. . . ." A critical reason for giving an assignment to be carried out between sessions is that it emphasizes therapy to be primarily about helping the client do things differently out there *in the real world* rather than some process that takes place in the therapy room. Also, an important thing about giving a task that encourages people to engage in different behaviors is that—as has been shown when people engage in particular behaviors associated with, or promoted by, particular beliefs or attitudes (the new language game)—commitment to those beliefs or attitudes becomes confirmed or strengthened more quickly and profoundly than from just talking about them (Kiesler, 1971). Clearly any task that is suggested must be seen to be relevant to the concerns that brought the clients there and must be seen to make sense.

The most frequently suggested task is one that requires clients to observe between this session and the next whatever it is that they do that moves them one step up a scale (whichever scale seems most relevant, given their primary concerns). They are not asked to try to make the changes, just to notice when they do. This is part of a language game in which change in the desired direction is assumed to be inevitable—the task just draws the clients attention to this. A figure/ground reversal is thus made such that clients are more likely to notice naturally occurring exceptions that otherwise would probably remain hidden.

Illustrations

The following example is an intervention given to a young woman who, following a breakdown during her final year at high school, had been embroiled in the psychiatric system for three years. This also included three periods of in-patient treatment. Over this time, she saw herself as having been passed from one worker to the next with nobody seeming to care or wanting to listen to her side of the story. Earlier in this first session, she had put herself at 2 on a scale in which 0 represented when things were at their worst and 10 represented when her miracle had happened. Her reason for coming into therapy again was her wish to "get her act together" and to move back into some kind of basic education.

THERAPIST: First, let me say that I think it was courageous of you to come here today. After all you have been through, to take the risk of coming to see yet *another* therapist took guts, and also tells me that you are very serious about wanting to get your life sorted out. And, the way that you *really* checked me out at the beginning of the session!!! You seem to know pretty clearly what you are looking for, and it's also clear that, in future, you are determined to make your *own* mind up about who you will see and who you won't see, and when. Have I got that right?

CLIENT: That's it. I've really decided I'm not going to be pushed around anymore.

THERAPIST: From what you tell me, you have clearly had a difficult life with lots of losses and a whole heap of terrible disappointments. However, you are still wanting to get your act together and to go back to studying. You still want to catch up with the education that you lost out on back then. That's impressive! After years of feeling pushed from pillar to post and being given drug after drug by people who you feel did not listen to what you *really* wanted, you still have this level of determination. That *is* impressive.

You obviously are aware that getting your HSC (Higher School Certificate) will take a lot of hard work, but you clearly think it is worth the effort. I agree that the effort, however hard it may be, could set you up for a better future. But you are also aware of your tendency to be discouraged easily if things do not go exactly as you wish. This important insight could hold you in good stead when the going gets tough. As you said earlier, that's when the tough get going.

Because you are clearly *so* determined, and because you seem to recognize the importance of not biting off more than you can chew—otherwise you can easily become discouraged—I have a suggestion for you to try by way of a sort of experiment. Then, if you would like to, we can set up another appointment. Is that okay?

CLIENT: Yes, I'd like to come back.

THERAPIST: I would, first of all, suggest you be careful of shooting for 10 straight away. Shooting for 10 tends to mean you only end up seeing how far short you fall. Do you know what I mean?

(The young woman nods.)

THERAPIST: Between now and the next time we meet, I would like you to make a mental note of what you do that begins to move you from 2 up to 3 on that scale we looked at. I'm not asking you to write it down but, of course, you can if you would find it easier. I am particularly interested in small steps. I am sure you know the story of the tortoise and the hare.

(The young woman nods.)

THERAPIST: It's always the tortoise that gets there first by taking small, steady steps. So, notice anything you do, any way that you respond differently, that tells you that you have begun to move up from 2 to 3. If on any day you go higher than 3, enjoy that day as a bonus but be careful not to judge the next day by that higher number. Okay?

CLIENT: Okay.

THERAPIST: Do you have any questions you want to ask about this?

CLIENT: No, I don't think so.

THERAPIST: Let's set up another appointment. What do you think would be a good gap between now and the next session so that it is not too close but also not too far away?

CLIENT: A couple of weeks?

THERAPIST: Okay.

Although the timing of subsequent appointments often has to fit into real limitations imposed by worker or agency schedules, where possible, clients should be asked both whether they want another appointment and, if so, when. It should not necessarily be assumed that a second session is either wanted or needed. Therapists tend to see therapy as, by definition, involving a series of sessions; clients do not necessarily do so. Working in a medical center, Moshe Talmon looked at why so many of his clients did not return for second interviews. As he observed,

> In spite of my fears about what I would hear, the results of my follow-ups seemed almost too good to be true: 78 percent of the 200 patients I called said that they got what they wanted out of the single session and felt better or much better about the problem that had led them to seek therapy. (Talmon, 1990, p. 9)

He also examined the practice of colleagues employed in the center, including psychiatrists, psychologists, and social workers, to find that clients not returning for a second session was far from uncommon. He also found that "the therapeutic orientation of the therapists had no impact on the percentage of SSTs in their total practice" (p. 7). In a subsequent, more formal research project, 88 percent reported "much improvement" or "improvement," 79 percent found the one session to have been sufficient, and 65 percent had experienced changes in areas other than those for which they had initially sought therapy.

A wide range of different tasks can be suggested limited primarily by the particular style and creativity of the therapist and (where in use) the team. People new to the approach often become fascinated by some of the tasks they see in demonstration interviews or that they read about, and often become preoccupied with coming up with similar ideas. It is important to keep in mind that the most important part of any intervention is the first part where the therapist summarizes and compliments the client and agrees with his or her goals. If that first part is not adequately addressed, then the best task in the world is likely to be ineffective, whereas a well thought out, confirmatory summary may well make a significant contribution to a client making changes even though no task is suggested. After all, much of the outcome research has suggested that a client's positive feelings about the encounter with the therapist—and the experience of feeling heard and understood—are major predictors of a positive outcome to the therapy, while specific techniques make a much more modest contribution (Miller, Duncan, & Hubble, 1997).

A useful class of tasks are those in which the client is asked—at particular times between one session and the next—to pretend that a desired change has occurred and to observe what difference it makes to both the client's behaviors and to the ways that significant others respond. For example, a woman struggling with a difficult six-year-old, had identified a heavy legacy of guilt from the past as underpinning much of what she described as her inadequacy as a mother. It was suggested that on dates with even numbers she should pretend to herself that she had had a "guiltectomy" and see how it affected the way that she handled her daughter and the way that her daughter responded to her. On the dates with odd numbers, she was to go about things just as she normally did.

De Shazer described such a task given to a troubled couple, both with long psychiatric histories:

> We have some ideas, an experiment we'd like you two to do between now and next time we meet.
>
> Each of you pick two days over the next week, secretly, and on those days, we want you to pretend that that miracle we talked about has already happened. OK?
>
> And observe how the other person reacts to what you do. Then, see if you can figure out which two days she picks, you see if you can figure out which two days he picks. Don't say anything about it. Do it secretly, just observe. Observe how he reacts, observe how she reacts. You might even pick the same day by accident; that's OK. You might learn something extra that way. But it has to be by accident. It's got to be a secret; don't discuss it. (de Shazer, 1991, p. 144)

An interesting variation on this is to suggest that the client toss a coin each day. When it comes up heads, for example, the client is to carry out the suggested experiment and when it comes up tails, the client is to behave as normal. It is interesting how often people change their behaviors on the days when they do not have to change. For example, a young woman was making herself ill by obsessively overstudying for her final exams. She literally had to be carried out from a trial examination, violently sick with anxiety and exhausted. Although she knew she had already done enough preparation to pass with high grades, she was finding it impossible to relax. It was suggested that, each day, she toss a coin. If it came up heads, she was not to do any work at all on that day, however hard that might be. She was to go to the beach or do something similar and to be sure to take no textbooks with her. If it came up tails, she could study as hard as she wanted. It is interesting that she found it difficult but possible not to work when the coin came up heads, but easy to work in moderation when it came up tails.

Berg and Miller described the use of a prediction task in situations where the client feels there is no pattern to, and that they have no control over, the occurrence of problems.

> Between now and the next time we meet I suggest the following: Each night before going to bed, you make a prediction about what kind of drinking you will do the next day and keep a record of it. Next day you go about your day as usual but at the end of the day compare your activities with your previous day's prediction to see whether or not your prediction came true. Also, jot down on a piece of paper what differences you noticed about your life. Then make another prediction for the following day. We would like you to repeat this for a week and come back with the results. (Berg & Miller, 1992, p. 126)

In situations of extreme client pessimism, it is possible to summarize how extremely difficult things have been, and to declare that, given what has happened, it is surprising that things are not much worse. Ask clients to pay particular attention to what they do between now and the next session to keep things at the level they now are (or at whatever point on a scale they have put themselves) and to prevent things becoming worse. As scales are purely subjective entities, where clients place themselves at 0, it is possible to ask about how they have prevented themselves from going sub-zero.

As already indicated, people will usually only follow suggestions if they are ready for change and if the behaviors they are being asked to try are consistent with their ideas about how they want to be, rather than how the therapist or some other person wants them to be. However, sometimes clients will accept an odd, even a bizarre, suggestion, even one they do not fully understand the reason for. This usually tends to happen only when they feel profoundly understood, respected, and positively engaged with the therapist.

For example, an 18-year-old, bulimic young woman was somewhat demoralized after what she described as the lack of success of a previous therapy. She talked about her symptoms with a very serious demeanor. She had been advised that her condition would require prolonged and intensive therapy. Having made a positive initial connection with her, the therapist asked her suddenly whether she had tried any creative experiments with different foods to see if they made different patterns in her vomit. She burst out laughing and said she hadn't. The therapist went on to ask her if she had tested the Scottish comedian Billy Connelly's hypothesis that whenever you vomit there is always some diced carrot in it even if you haven't eaten carrots for months; that they must lurk around waiting for you to be sick. She again burst out laughing. At the end of the session, she was asked if she had a good sense of humor. She said she did, and the therapist confirmed that it was certainly his impression that was the case. She was then asked whether she would be prepared to try an experiment that had a touch of absurdity to it. She said she did not mind being absurd. "Or looking absurd?" She was happy to go ahead. It was suggested that, for the next week, whenever the urge to binge overcame her, she was not to waste time fruitlessly fighting it, then failing, but to go ahead. In fact, she was advised not to try to go a whole week without bingeing at this early stage. However, before bingeing, she should go to her bedroom and put on her oldest clothes, but put them all on back to front. She clearly should not do this with her shoes because this would mean she would have to dislocate her feet. It was suggested she also buy a cream cake each day and, after eating all that she felt she could eat, she was to finish off with it. Then, before vomiting, she was to go back to her bedroom and change into her smartest outfit and then go ahead with getting rid of the food. She left the session still laughing and clearly much more optimistic about her ability to deal with her problem.

> A 13-year-old girl was continually being checked up on by her elderly parents. She was seen as untrustworthy, aggressive, lazy, uncooperative and unhelpful. Though the girl showed no motivation to be involved in therapy, she began to express interest when asked by the therapist whether she would be prepared to trick her parents. To this she readily agreed. She was asked to do a number of things over the next couple of weeks that she knew would definitely please her parents. However, she was to do them in such a way that they did not know what it was that she had done. Neither was she to let on, even if asked. She was to deny that she had done anything, even if they were to guess correctly.
>
> The parents, meanwhile, were to make every possible attempt to find out what it was she had done and to keep a written list. They could discuss it together but were not allowed to ask her.
>
> At the next session, the girl was seen separately. She admitted that she had not really made any efforts to do anything but admitted that things had been much better between her

> and her parents. When the parents were seen, they brought with them a long list of all the things that they had detected that they thought she had done in order to please them.
>
> It seems that, whether the girl undertook her part of the suggestion or not, her normal behaviour patterns contained sufficient nonconfrontative, cooperative acts, which perhaps were normally not noticed, to satisfy the parents that things were changing. From the daughter's point of view, the parents' constant vigilance, against which she was normally rebelling, had taken on a new meaning and become an attempt to discover evidence of good rather than bad behaviour. (Cade & Hudson O'Hanlon, 1993, p. 129)

Although the girl in this example had been asked to do something her parents wanted (usually unwise with adolescents), the intervention did not actually require her to comply. More important was the invitation to the parents to look for evidence of cooperation instead of constantly looking for evidence of transgressions. We tend to see what we expect to see. When we treat a person as though they have certain attitudes or traits, they are more likely to exhibit them. A reversal of the usual figure/ground led to the parents seeing cooperative behaviors that were already happening. The change in her parents' attitude probably also led to the girl being spontaneously more cooperative without her necessarily having to have any conscious intention to change.

Subsequent Sessions and Endings

It is usual to commence the second (and subsequent) sessions with some variation or other of the question, "What's been better since we last met?" The responses to this opening will range from those who are able to elaborate a range of changes to those who indicate that either nothing is better or that things are worse. However, with a little persistence on the part of the therapist, it is very rare for people not to be able to point to times when *something* in the situation was better, even if only a little and briefly.

THERAPIST: What's been better since last time?

WIFE: Nothing. We have had a terrible week.

HUSBAND: And we've just had a God Almighty row in the car on the way over here.

THERAPIST: Okay. Let's come back to that. Taking the last week as a whole, even if only a little bit, what has been better?

WIFE: *(after a pause)* We did go for a coffee after we left here last time, and we talked quite a lot more about things. In fact, for us, we had quite a civilized conversation.

THERAPIST: In what way?

HUSBAND: We listened to each other. We actually had a pleasant couple of hours.

WIFE: Then we went home and the wheels fell off, again.

THERAPIST: What else was different about the time over the coffee?

HUSBAND: We were both feeling more relaxed.

THERAPIST: How did that show itself?

HUSBAND: Well, we were smiling at times rather than frowning.

WIFE: (*grinning*) We had our knives back in their sheaths rather than plunged into each other's backs.

THERAPIST: What else has been better?

WIFE: We went to the cinema the other night. The film was awful, but we had quite a good time, now I think back to it, didn't we?

THERAPIST: In what way?

WIFE: We had a meal before the film, which was quite nice. And we had sex that night; the first time for some weeks.

Such conversations are not to deny that things are still very difficult, but to help people identify the small building blocks that, if there is potential in their situation, will go toward constructing a different future. Also, a recent setback, such as the "God Almighty row on the way over here" that this couple reported, can often color the way that the rest of the week is seen. It is interesting how, even when clients say that there has been no change or that things have become worse, these are still only partial descriptions of their situation—only part of their problem-saturated language game. Once an exception has been identified, however small, clients will often, over the course of the session, go on to describe others that they had initially forgotten or just not noticed. As they move into the new language game, these small events take on greater levels of significance. Sometimes changes of considerable importance can become hidden under the general picture that things are the same or worse. For example, it was three-quarters of the way through a second session, during which he had been describing his situation as no better, that a man "let slip" that he had been offered a job (he had spent many months looking for one). In the case of the couple who were invited secretly to pretend a miracle had occurred, from the de Shazer example described in the last section, it was some way into the second session that the wife let slip that she had successfully completed her first day as a substitute teacher. The husband, having earlier described himself as floundering throughout the whole of that same day, went on gradually to elaborate a busy day in which a list of small but important chores had been completed.

When changes or exceptions are identified, it is important to amplify and reinforce them. The two questions, "How did you do that?" and "What else?" remain of central importance.

> Eliciting and amplifying the small but significant changes the client has made can be achieved by asking detailed questions regarding the events the client describes. This detailed questioning can easily last up to twenty minutes during the follow-up interview. Asking about the chain of events, sequences, and who else noticed the changes also amplifies the positive changes: When did this happen? What did you do? Who else noticed? What did they do when they saw you doing that? What tells you that they noticed the changes in you? What was going on at that place that helped you do things that way? What else did you do? . . . What gave you the idea to do it that way? . . . Is that new for you? How did that help you? How did that help your family? What did your husband do when he noticed you doing it that way? How did that help him? (Berg & Miller, 1992, p. 132)

It is obviously important when asking such questions to avoid being patronizing and also to avoid being more enthusiastic about the changes or their implications than the client. A position of respectful curiosity rather than persuasion appears to help clients more effectively enter the new language game and draw positive conclusions themselves. The importance of continuing to ask "What else?" is that, as mentioned, many of the behaviors that are involved in the building of a different future and that can be incorporated into a new language game tend to be the small and apparently trivial minutiae of day-to-day life and thus easily overlooked or dismissed as of no significance.

Scaling questions also help focus on change. A frequently asked question in second and later sessions is "If 0 represents how things were when you first came to see me and 10 represents when things are all sorted out, where would you put yourself today?" Again, as elaborated earlier in the section on scaling, questions can focus on the details of how they achieved whatever steps they identify and then what needs to happen for them to move up one more step on the scale.

When clients continue to say that things are either no better or that things are worse, it is important that the therapist points out that he or she now understands more clearly how difficult and/or complex the situation is. Thus validated, it is surprising how often clients will begin to talk about small changes that have occurred. Sometimes, the feeling that things are no better or even worse may be because the client was looking or hoping for a substantial or even a complete solution and therefore is either not able or not prepared to see small changes as of relevance. It is also important that the therapist be sure that he or she had not veered away in the previous session from the agenda that the client had originally come with. If this were to have been the case, then getting back on track quickly is likely to start things moving along.

Interventions at the end of second and subsequent sessions take essentially the same shape as those previously described. It remains important to summarize, to compliment, and to suggest a relevant task, maintaining what has been achieved and building on what has changed.

> I am really struck by the determination you have shown and the changes that you have begun to make. In spite of the difficulties that you are still encountering, you nevertheless have moved from 3 up to 5 on the scale by relaxing more with the children, by cleaning up the house, by making contact with a friend to go out for lunch. This is impressive. Many people know what they have to do but continue to talk themselves out of it. You clearly have not done that this week. You also know that life rarely runs smoothly and that you are going to have setbacks and it is clear that you are ready to tackle them. It is also clear that you feel the future benefits of being more available to your children is worth the hard work. Because this is so clear, what I suggest you do between now and when we next meet is to watch very carefully what you do to keep yourself at 5 or even to begin to creep toward 6, but especially to watch how, if things get tough and you go back down the scale, how you get yourself back up to 5 again.

In this approach to therapy, the end comes as quickly as possible and is defined not so much by the ultimate goals being attained (although that can happen) but by the clients' feeling that they are now sufficiently on track not to need the therapist's inputs anymore. Clearly, the end is defined by what the client thinks not what the therapist thinks. Often clients will indicate that they do not need another session, that they feel things are now moving along in the right direction. Alternatively, the therapist may see that things have begun to move and can end a session saying something like,

> It seems you have begun to make some significant steps forward. We can do one of several things at this point. We can make another appointment if you think that will be helpful, or we can make a time for a couple of months or so away, or we can say, "let's see how it goes," and you give me a call if you would like to meet again.

Applications and Outcome Studies

Over the last decade or so, the solution-focused approach has grown rapidly throughout the world and is used in a wide range of settings. From early on, it began to be used in residential settings and in schools. It is used in mental health settings, public social services agencies, hospitals, the probation service, in prisons, and in child welfare. It is used with groups, as an approach to supervision and in institutional or business consultations. It has been used with child and adolescent problems; domestic violence; survivors of sexual abuse; drug and alcohol problems; mental illness; people who have physical handicaps; marital problems; multi-problem, multi-agency families; the problems of aging; eating disorders; adoptive families; and in family medicine. This is, of course, by no means an exhaustive list. For a continually updated list of publications (now over 1,000 items), readers are referred to Patrick Triggiano's comprehensive compilation, *The Solution Papers Revisited: A Compilation of the Beginning, Integration, And Ever Expanding Guide to Solution-Focused Publications.* This is available on the Internet at <www.talkingcure.com/solutionfocused.htm>.

Over the years that it has been developing the approach, the Brief Family Therapy Center has systematically followed up its clients by contacting them at between 6 to 18 months and asking whether they felt they had achieved their treatment goals or, at least, made significant progress toward them. Results have consistently shown between 70 and 80 percent answering in the affirmative (de Shazer et al., 1986; Kiser, 1988; De Jong & Hopwood, 1996). However, such subjective and uncontrolled studies, while providing useful early indicators, do not have the necessary rigor to allow more conclusive statements about the effectiveness of the approach.

Increasing numbers of outcome studies are now being published, many of them using a similar design to those above and reporting varied levels of effectiveness. However, in a recent conference paper given in April, 1999, Wallace Gingerich, an early member of the Milwaukee group, and Sheri Eisengart reported on a more recent substantial rise in controlled studies. They identified 15 such studies, 7 of which assert that,

> SFBT (solution-focused brief therapy) equaled or surpassed the outcomes of standard treatment. SFBT sometimes produced better outcomes, and sometimes produced comparable outcomes in less time. Only one study (Littrell et al., 1995) failed to report any positive outcomes for SFBT. . . . The fifteen studies included a wide range of modalities, ranging from the individual and family therapy, to group, consultative, supervisory and network interventions. Five of the six studies that employed individual or family therapy of two or more sessions

> duration, the modality most consistent with the original form of SFBT, had positive outcomes. However, studies that used indirect interventions such as consultation or supervision had a comparable success rate. Most of the studies used real-world clinical populations, and client problems ranged all the way from common mental health problems, to school functioning, self-sufficiency, delinquent behaviour, and work hardening. This represented an unexpectedly wide range of application of SFBT.
>
> We also find it interesting that in all but one of the studies (Lambert et al., 1998) the SFBT intervention appeared to be implemented by relatively inexperienced therapists, in many cases just newly trained. In psychotherapy research generally, experienced therapists tend to get better results than inexperienced therapists. (Gingerich & Eisengart, 1999)

However, Gingerich and Eisengart referred to the lack of proceduralization, the lack of evidence of treatment integrity, and the fact that over half of investigators were advocates of SFBT as important reasons for caution. They commented that, while "providing promising evidence . . . None of the studies meet accepted standards for empirically validated treatments."

Nevertheless, as Gingerich and Eisengart pointed out,

> That 15 studies have appeared in so short a time is rather remarkable for an intervention approach that has been in existence for less that 20 years. It is all the more remarkable when one considers that SFBT evolved out of a clinical context, not a quantitative research context, and that all of the published studies were carried out by investigators outside the original Milwaukee group. (Gingerich & Eisengart, 1999)

OUTCOME RESEARCH PAPERS SELECTED BY GINGERICH AND EISENGART

Cockburn, J. T., Thomas, F. N., & Cockburn, O. J. (1997). Solution-focused therapy and psychosocial adjustment to orthopedic rehabilitation in a work hardening program. *Journal of Occupational Rehabilitation, 7*(2), 97–106.

Eakes, G., Walsh, S., Markowksi, M., Cain, H., & Swanson, M. (1997). Family centered brief solution-focused therapy with chronic schizophrenia: A pilot study. *Journal of Family Therapy, 19*(2), 145–158.

Franklin, C., Corcoran, J., Nowicki, J., & Streeter, C. (1997). Using client self-anchored scales to measure outcomes in solution-focused therapy. *Journal of Systemic Therapies, 16*(3), 246–265.

Geil, M. (1998). *Solution focused consultation: An alternative consultation model to manage student behavior and improve classroom environment.* Unpublished doctoral dissertation, University of Northern Colorado, Greeley, CO.

LaFountain, R. M., & Garner, N. E. (1996). Solution-focused counseling groups: The results are in. *Journal for Specialists in Group Work, 21*(2), 128–143.

Lambert, M. J., Okiishi, J. C., Finch, A. E., & Johnson, L. D. (1998). Outcome assessment: From conceptualization to implementation. *Professional Psychology: Research and Practice, 29*(1), 63–70.

Lindforss, L., & Magnusson, D. (1997). Solution-focused therapy in prison. *Contemporary Family Therapy, 19*(1), 89–103.

Littrell, J. M., Malia, J. A., & Vanderwood, M. (1995). Single-session brief counseling in a high school. *Journal of Counseling and Development, 73*(4), 451–458.

Polk, G. W. (1996). Treatment of problem drinking behavior using solution-focused therapy: A single subject design. *Crisis Intervention, 3*(1), 13–24.

Sundman, P. (1997). Solution-focused ideas in social work. *Journal of Family Therapy, 19*(2), 159–172.

Sundstrom, S. M. (1993). *Single-session psychotherapy for depression: Is it better to focus on problems or solutions?* Unpublished doctoral dissertation, Iowa State University, Ames, IA.

Triantafillou, N. (1997). A solution-focused approach to mental health supervision. *Journal of Systemic Therapies,* 16(4), 305–328.

Zimmerman, T. S., Jacobsen, R. B., MacIntyre, M., & Watson, C. (1996). Solution-focused parenting groups: An empirical study. *Journal of Systemic Therapies, 15*(4), 12–25.

Zimmerman, T. S., Prest, L. A., & Wetzel, B. E. (1997). Solution-focused couples therapy groups: An empirical study. *Journal of Family Therapy,* 19(2), 125–144.

REFERENCES

Adcock, C. J. (1964). *Fundamentals of psychology.* Harmondsworth, Middlesex: Penguin Books Ltd.

Bateson, G., Jackson, D. D., Haley, J., & Weakland, J. H. (1956). Toward a theory of schizophrenia. *Behavioral Science, 1*(4), 251–264.

Berg, I. K. (1994). *Family based services: A solution-focused approach.* New York: W. W. Norton.

Berg, I. K., & Miller, S. D. (1992). *Working with the problem drinker: A solution-focused approach.* New York: W. W. Norton.

Berger, M. M. (Ed.). (1978). *Beyond the double bind.* New York: Brunner/Mazel.

Cade, B. (1998). A game of snakes-and-ladders. In F. N. Thomas & T. S. Nelson (Eds.), *Tales from family therapy: Life-changing clinical experiences.* New York: Haworth.

Cade, B., & Hudson O'Hanlon, W. (1993). *A brief guide to brief therapy.* New York: W. W. Norton.

Chaney, S. (1995). Personal communication.

DeJong, P., & Berg, I. K. (1998). *Interviewing for solutions.* Pacific Grove, CA: Brooks/Cole.

DeJong, P., & Hopwood, L. E. (1996). Outcome research on treatment conducted at the brief family therapy center, 1992–1993. In S. D. Miller, M. A. Hubble, & B. L. Duncan (Eds.), *Handbook of solution-focused brief therapy* (pp. 272–298). San Francisco: Jossey-Bass.

de Shazer, S. (1985). *Keys to solution in brief therapy.* New York: W. W. Norton.

de Shazer, S. (1988). *Clues: Investigating solutions in brief therapy.* New York: W. W. Norton.

de Shazer, S. (1991). *Putting difference to work.* New York: W. W. Norton.

de Shazer, S. (1994). *Words were originally magic.* New York: W. W. Norton.

de Shazer, S. (1999). *Beginnings.* BFTC Website (www.brief_therapy.org).

de Shazer, S., & Berg, I. K. (1997). 'What works?' Remarks on research aspects of solution-focused brief therapy. *Journal of Family Therapy, 19*(2), 121–124.

de Shazer, S., Berg, I. K., Lipchik, E., Nunnally, E., Molnar, A., Gingerich, W., & Weiner-Davis, M. (1986). Brief therapy: Focused solution development. *Family Process, 25*(2), 207–222.

de Shazer, S., & Molnar, A. (1984). Four useful interventions in brief family therapy. *Journal of Marital & Family Therapy, 10*(3), 297–304.

Erickson, M. H., & Rossi, E. L. (1979). *Hypnotherapy: An exploratory casebook.* New York: Irvington.

Erickson, M. H., Rossi, E. L., & Rossi, S. I. (1976). *Hypnotic realities: The induction of clinical hypnosis and forms of indirect suggestion.* New York: Irvington.

Evans-Wentz, W. Y. (Ed.). (1969). *The Tibetan book of the great liberation.* Oxford: Oxford University Press.

Fisch, R., Weakland, J. H., & Segal, L. (1982). *The tactics of change: Doing therapy briefly.* San Francisco: Jossey-Bass.

Furman, B., & Ahola, T. (1992). *Solution talk: Hosting therapeutic conversations.* New York: W. W. Norton.

Gingerich, W. J. & Eisenhart, S. (1999, April). *Solution-focused brief therapy: A review of the outcome literature.* Unpublished paper given to the International Family Therapy Association, Akron, Ohio.

Haley, J. (1963). *Strategies of psychotherapy.* New York: Grune & Stratton.

Haley, J. (Ed.). (1967). *Advanced techniques of hypnosis and therapy: Selected papers of Milton H. Erickson.* New York: Grune & Stratton.

Haley, J. (1973). *Uncommon therapy: The psychiatric techniques of Milton H Erickson.* New York: W. W. Norton.

Heaton, J., & Groves, J. (1994). *Wittgenstein for beginners.* Cambridge: Icon Books.

Kiesler, C. A. (1971). *The psychology of commitment: Experiments linking behaviour to belief.* New York: Academic Press.

Kiser, D. J. (1988). *A follow-up study conducted at the Brief Family Therapy Center of Milwaukee, Wisconsin.* Unpublished manuscript. Milwaukee, WI: Brief Family Therapy Center.

Kowalski, K., & Kral, R. (1989). The geometry of solution: Using the scaling technique. *Family Therapy Case Studies, 4*(1), 59–66.

Miller, G., & de Shazer, S. (1998). Have you heard the latest about . . . ? Solution-focused therapy as a rumor. *Family Process, 37*(3), 363–377.

Miller, S. D. (1992). The symptoms of solution. *Journal of Strategic and Systemic Therapies, 11*(1), 1–11.

Miller, S. D., Duncan, B. L., & Hubble, M. A. (1997). *Escape from Babel: Toward a unifying language for psychotherapy practice.* New York: W. W. Norton.

Miller, S. D., Hubble, M. A., & Duncan, B. L. (Ed.). (1996). *Handbook of solution-focused brief therapy.* San Francisco: Jossey-Bass.

Molnar, A., & de Shazer, S. (1987). Solution-focused therapy: Toward the identification of therapeutic tasks. *Journal of Marital and Family Therapy, 13,* 349–358.

O'Hanlon, W. H. (1987). *Taproots: Underlying principles of Milton H Erickson's therapy and hypnosis.* New York: W. W. Norton.

O'Hanlon, W. H., & Weiner-Davis, M. (1989). *In search of solutions: A new direction in psychotherapy.* New York: W. W. Norton.

Ray, W. A., & de Shazer, S. (Ed.). (1999). *Evolving brief therapies: In honour of John H. Weakland.* Galena, IL: Geist & Russell.

Rosen, S. (1982). *My voice will go with you: The teaching tales of Milton H. Erickson, M. D.* New York: W. W. Norton.

Rossi, E. L. (Ed.). (1980). *The collected papers of Milton Erickson.* New York: Irvington.

Sluzki, C. E., & Ransom, D. C. (Eds.). (1976). *Double bind: The foundation of the communicational approach to the family.* New York: Grune & Stratton.

Talmon, M. (1990). *Single-session therapy.* San Francisco: Jossey-Bass.

Walter, J. L., & Peller, J. E. (1992). *Becoming solution-focused in brief therapy.* New York: Brunner/Mazel.

Watzlawick, P. (1978). *The language of change: Elements of therapeutic communication.* New York: Basic Books.

Watzlawick, P., & Weakland, J. H. (Eds.). (1977). *The interactional view.* New York: W. W. Norton.

Watzlawick, P., Weakland, J. H., & Fisch, R. (1974). *Change: Principles of problem formation and problem resolution.* New York: W. W. Norton.

Weakland, J. H., Fisch, R., Watzlawick, P., & Bodin, A. (1974). Brief therapy: Focused problem resolution. *Family Process, 13*(2), 141–168.

Weakland, J. H., & Ray, W. A. (Eds.). (1995). *Propogations: Thirty years of influence from the Mental Research Institute.* New York: Haworth.

Weiner-Davies, M., de Shazer, S., & Gingerich, W. J. (1987). Building on pretreatment change to construct the therapeutic solution: An exploratory study. *Journal of Marital and Family Therapy, 13,* 359–363.

FOR FURTHER READING

Berg and Miller's *Working with the Problem Drinker: A Solution-Focused Approach* is an excellent description of the use of the model that has applicability far outside its focus. De Shazer's succession of books, *Keys to Solution in Brief Therapy, Clues: Investigating Solutions in Brief Therapy, Putting Difference to Work,* and *Words Were Originally Magic,* give a brilliant and highly readable insight into the development of the model over time, are full of practical ideas and examples, and are highly recommended. Walter and Peller's *Becoming Solution-Focused in Brief Therapy* is a clear and comprehensive guide to developing the approach. Miller, Hubble and Duncan's *Handbook of Solution-Focused Brief Therapy* is full of suggestions and brings together from a range of settings 28 experts who present research information, case examples, and a host of practical techniques. The following web sites are also of particular relevance and will give links to other sites:

Brief Family Therapy Center, Milwaukee:
<www.brief-therapy.org>

The Institute for the Study of Therapeutic Change:
<www.talkingcure.com>

The European Brief Therapy Association:
<www.ebta.nu>

CHAPTER

9 Psychological Assessment

ROBERT WALRATH

Psychological assessment has traditionally been viewed as a skill that differentiates psychologists from other mental health professionals. Historically, assessment has been seen as a mainstay of clinical practice, although conventional wisdom suggests psychologists are doing less testing due to managed care limitations. Despite this perception, Phelps, Eisman, and Kohut (1998), in a survey of licensed psychologists, found that psychological assessment "continues to be a prominent activity of practice" (p. 36). However, Piotrowski, Belter, and Keller (1998) found that a number of psychologists have changed their use of tests and the number of different tests used over the past five years due to managed care pressures. Ball, Archer, and Imhof (1994) found a "limited set of 20–40 psychological tests" reported to be most popular among psychologists surveyed in their study, with five or six common to both adult and adolescent test batteries. Acklin (1996) has also reported that psychologists are doing less "traditional" psychological assessment due to managed care practices that "have been uniquely restrictive in psychological testing" (p. 195).

Two factors within the managed care environment seem to have led to less assessment: (1) The reduction in total reimbursement given to all mental health services. (2) The tendency toward general non-approval of assessment services per se. These practices appear to have redefined psychological assessment, especially in relation to psychotherapy. Assessment has been increasingly viewed as superfluous, with clinicians seeking to fight "bigger battles" with managed care companies over authorizations for ongoing treatment rather than for assessment. From a managed care perspective, formal and extensive psychological assessment for treatment or other purposes is considered a luxury for clinicians and a waste of resources by insurers, who claim that its "utility and incremental validity for health service delivery is questionable" (Finn & Tonsager, 1997, p. 374).

The exception to this trend away from formal assessment has been the more "specialized" applications of psychological assessment, namely school psychology, forensics, and neuropsychology. Unfortunately, only the latter is commonly reimbursed by third party payers, and then (typically) grudgingly.

For psychotherapists, most conventional assessment or evaluation occurs during the intake process. This regularly involves an initial interview, perhaps the completion of intake forms or symptom checklists, and, rarely, more formal diagnostic psychological testing. With the profound influence of managed care on the provision of psychotherapy services, the more characteristic demand for assessment outside of the initial evaluation is to help justify continued treatment or a certain treatment approach, to show progress or "outcome" of treatment interventions, and for treatment planning.

More and more insurers are demanding that clinicians demonstrate the benefit of treatments through cost-effective and repeatable measures that show progress toward measurable psychotherapy goals. Despite advocacy by managed care organizations of the flawed premise that outcome research may serve to identify more effective treatments (Seligman & Levant, 1998), and their unwillingness to fund such research through appropriate reimbursement, there will likely be more and more instruments developed for this express purpose. The clinical utility of many existing instruments has not been demonstrated, but some useful tests for measuring outcomes will be described below.

Overall, clinicians who practice in the realm of psychotherapy and counseling may increasingly need to utilize formal and, more importantly, informal types of psychological assessment, not only to aid in understanding patients for briefer interventions, but to provide outcome assessment information to third party payers in a cost-effective manner.

The following sections discuss the most widely used psychological assessment instruments and their applications in psychotherapy. There are many more clinically sound and widely used tests and techniques, which cannot be covered here, and other uses outside of psychotherapeutic applications for the tests that are described. In general, tests and techniques have been included due both to their wide acceptance in the field and to their ease of use as adjuncts to treatment.

Clinical Interviewing

Assessment for the purposes of psychotherapy is "probably the most complex, subtle, and highly skilled procedure in the whole field" of psychology (Malon, 1979, p. 210). Prior to managed care, clinicians most often used assessment as an adjunct to treatment in two main areas: differential diagnosis and treatment planning. For example, Olin and Keatinge (1998) describe the most common reasons for psychological evaluation or assessment: "diagnosis, treatment planning, identifying functional status (assessment of the client's cognitive and emotional abilities), self-control (concerns of suicidality, dangerousness, or substance abuse), and history" (p. 3–4).

The diagnostic interview has typically been the basic method used by most clinicians to gain information from clients for these purposes. Smelson, Kordon, and Rudolph (1997) report that 95 percent of clinical psychologists use the interview to assess their patients. The usefulness of the interview is also apparent as a means of establishing rapport, as a prelude to more formal procedures for patients of all ages, and with almost all referral questions. There are probably as many variations on the diagnostic interview as there are clinicians, depending on training and experience. Interviewing to determine diagnosis, for example, as opposed to developing a clinical formulation expressly for treatment purposes, may vary in style based on the clinician's theoretical orientation. Smelson et al. (1997) and others (Rudolph et al., 1998; Prieto, 1997) have raised concerns about the lack of formal training and supervision in graduate schools for psychological assessment and clinical interviewing in general, citing lack of consistency in methods and supervision and a need for more structured protocols.

Clinical interviewing is both an art and a science. The art is to encourage patients to talk frankly in less than optimum situations, while the science is to know what to ask to get the most complete clinical information. As there are an infinite number of ways to interview clients, clinicians (especially in the early stages of their professional practice) would do well to "standardize" their interview methods with clients. Having a standard interview format or method assures that, within the complexity of the interpersonal relationship of therapist and client, important areas of functioning are not neglected or skipped. Many new (and seasoned) clinicians have ended an initial interview with a very solid understanding of a patient's depressive symptoms and no clue as to, say, their medical or substance abuse histories, either of which may bear directly on etiology and treatment.

Developing a personal interview "outline" and creating a form that the therapist can refer to and fill out during an initial interview can help to insure that all areas of importance are at least touched upon. The danger, however, is that the clinician may become too dependent on this format and rigidly attempt to go through a "checklist" of questions, sometimes without regard for the patient's desire to talk in more detail on certain subject areas—or, in many cases, to talk around sensitive subjects. This approach typically damages rapport and creates the impression that the therapist is not listening to the patient, or that the questions are more important than the answers. The net result may be either that the patient feels disconnected and does not return for a second session, or that the clinician misses important information that may not come up again for a number of sessions. As an aside, while there are actually few "missed opportunities" in psychotherapy, it is important to be as thorough as possible initially. The most central or important issues for treatment are bound to come up again in ongoing interviews, but it is crucial to develop as complete a picture of presenting problems and concerns as early in treatment as possible, especially given the managed care dictate for brief interventions.

Overall, interview guidelines help the clinician remain cognizant of areas that need to be addressed (though not in rigid order). Probably the most important skill is the ability to listen, and the most successful interviewer will likely find him- or herself moving around on an interview "form," letting the patient's responses and needs balance the interviewer's need for information. As a starting point, an annotated outline of suggested content areas for the initial or diagnostic interview is offered in Appendix 9.A.

A second important benefit of having a somewhat standardized interview approach is that it allows the new clinician to begin building a personal "database" of responses within the clinician's ongoing experience to help interpret and categorize patient responses most effectively. For example, the child therapist who always asks "three wishes" of every youngster at intake will soon have a very important frame of reference for the multitude of responses this question brings by age and developmental level. Similarly, responses to standard questions on a mental status exam with adults (such as naming the last five U.S. presidents or defining a specific proverb) can help the clinician to understand patients and their cognitive abilities in the general context of their peers.

Many beginning clinicians are more comfortable with the idea of interviewing a patient than with that of performing psychotherapy, which seems a daunting task. It often helps to realize that the patient is generally much more anxious than the therapist. For beginning psychotherapists, a helpful concept may be to consider the psychotherapy session a form of evaluation interview that is ongoing and broken into segments. Each psychotherapy session can thus be viewed as an opportunity to assess change from previous meetings, to progress toward goals, and to evaluate new circumstances or stressors impacting treatment. This approach helps supply a sense of structure and purpose to each meeting that can facilitate clinical work for the "uncertain" psychotherapist.

The Mental Status Exam

The mental status examination (MSE) is probably the most formal and consistent type of clinical or diagnostic interview, with a number of methods in use. Appendix 9.B provides an annotated sample mental status examination method that can be used in conjunction with the outline for the diagnostic interview. Trzepacz and Baker (1993) have provided comprehensive definitions, explanations, and guidelines for the adult mental status examination from a medical and psychiatric perspective, most of which are also applicable for general assessment purposes. Franzen and Berg (1998) have provided a similar resource for children, concentrating on information that can be gathered directly from both parents and children. There are also specialized and more structured versions of the mental status exam, the most popular being the Mini-Mental Status Exam (Folestein, Folestein, & McHugh, 1975), with increased acceptance and use thanks to the availability of reliability, validity, and normative data for formal scoring of this test (Spreen & Strauss, 1998).

Since the mental status exam is widely used across a number of disciplines, the clinician should be careful, as with other forms of the diagnostic interview, to become familiar with a set of skills and techniques that can be mastered and applied with ease and proficiency. It should also be noted that the mental status exam is generally considered a starting point rather than an end to the evaluation process. Typically, the MSE is used to screen for indications of gross cognitive or emotional concerns that should be evaluated more fully. Very poor performance is frequently more informative than moderate impairments or lack of significant findings due to general validity problems with such brief exams (Hawkins & Cooper, 1996). As an extension of an intake or general diagnostic interview, the MSE helps the clinician focus and systemize observations and interactions to elicit different kinds of information than are generally provided by a more history-based interview. A helpful distinction is to think of the MSE as a more performance-based than content-based component of the assessment, in contrast to the history segment. However, many aspects of a patient's mental status will be apparent during the diagnostic or intake interview. Often, the mental status exam will suggest more complete evaluation of cognitive or memory functions; a psychiatric exam, due to the presence of thought process or content disturbances; or a more formal psychological assessment, due to disturbances of mood, affect, or thinking that are diagnostically and functionally ambiguous.

Objective Psychological Testing

Objective psychological tests are criterion-referenced, norm-based, standardized assessment tools that are widely used in many clinical and research settings. Criterion-referenced tests are developed using an empirical approach, with test items selected based on their ability to discriminate between "clinical" or diagnostic groups and normal groups (Aiken, 1996). The best-known and most widely used objective personality test is the Minnesota Multiphasic Personality Inventory, second edition (MMPI-2; Hathaway et al., 1989), the adolescent version (MMPI-A) being broadly accepted as well (Butcher & Williams, 1992). Also widely used are the Millon scales, including the Millon Clinical Multiaxial Inventory, third edition (MCMI-III; Millon, Millon, & Davis, 1994); the Millon Adolescent Clinical Inventory

(MACI; Millon, Millon, & Davis, 1993); and the Millon Adolescent Personality Inventory (MAPI; Millon, Green, & Meagher, 1982). The Personality Inventory for Children (PIC; Wirt et al., 1984) is probably the most widely used objective personality measure for children and is completed by parents. A self-report version for adolescents, the Personality Inventory for Youth (PIY; Lachar & Gruber, 1994) is also available. All of these inventories provide validity and clinical scales that provide an overall view of personality or psychological functioning across a number of areas, making them global indicators of an individual's personality or presentation of symptoms and symptom patterns. These self-report, paper-and-pencil inventories are increasingly favored as computer scoring (and, in many cases, computerized administration) help minimize staff and clinical time, leading to more cost-effective utilization.

An in-depth discussion of the psychometric properties of and test interpretation strategies for these tests is beyond the scope of this chapter. A thorough review is available in Aiken (1996) or Lanyon and Goodstein (1997). There is a substantial body of research regarding the uses of these tests with specific populations and in specific settings. Clinicians must always be cognizant of the accepted clinical- and research-based applications of these tests, being careful not to step outside of accepted practice guidelines in most situations.

Much has been written regarding the utility of objective personality tests in psychotherapy for selecting patients (Hilsenroth et al., 1995), predicting outcome (Chisholm, Crowther, & Ben-Porath, 1997), providing feedback and direction during psychotherapy (Clair & Pendergast, 1994; Finn, 1996), and in more formal treatment planning activities (Butcher, 1990; Ben-Porath, 1997). The utility of these tests for psychotherapists lies in two major areas: first, the ability to use test results to "zero in" and help focus initial treatment efforts with potentially resistant, psychologically unsophisticated or guarded, or greatly distressed patients; and second, to help the therapist work through treatment impasses.

To avoid managed care restrictions on psychological testing, this type of assessment can often be accomplished by having the patient complete the test in the waiting room or a spare office either following or preceding a therapy session, avoiding the need for direct clinician involvement. Computer-assisted scoring helps minimize professional time and client expense, and can provide narrative interpretative statements, scaled score comparisons, and lists of critical items to facilitate the interpretation of results to the patient. Interpretation of objective personality tests is typically based on a "cookbook" approach of looking at combinations of high and low clinical scales, together with patterns on validity scales and a review of critical items. Graham (1998) and Olin and Keatinge (1998) provide brief, excellent summaries of MMPI-2 interpretation by scale elevation and "code type," or by combination of highest two or three clinical scale scores.

Most patients expect and will appreciate an indication of test results and major findings. Newman and Greenway (1997) found that discussion of test results from the MMPI-2 with university students resulted in an immediate increase in self-esteem and a decrease in symptomatic distress at the time of a two-week followup. Similarly, Finn (1996) describes positive benefits to patients from a systematic discussion of psychological test results. Butcher (1990) describes a series of steps to provide effective feedback with the MMPI-2, with care taken to describe the rationale for testing, what the MMPI-2 is used for and what the scales measure, and how the client's scores deviate from the test norms.

In all provisions of feedback, care must be taken to explain the functioning of the specific test used while not compromising test security. Also, as many patients experience a degree of anxiety while awaiting test results (much like the anxiety experiencing in awaiting medical test results), the clinician should consider the need for a timely and reassuring approach to the evaluation session. Scheduling a review of results for the beginning of the therapy session following the taking of the test is recommended. This allows a timely review of results in the context of the therapeutic work and provides ample time for discussion and questions. Avoiding jargon and providing a global interpretation of both difficulties and strengths indicated by the test results are probably helpful to the patient.

One specific interpretation strategy is to review the patient's responses to the "critical items" of a test. Critical items are specific test items that, when answered in a noteworthy manner, suggest areas of general clinical or diagnostic significance. A review of critical items can help clarify diagnostic questions, point to areas of particular gravity or clinical concern for further discussion within the therapy interview, and identify problems not readily verbalized by the patient. For example, responses to critical items may point to significant delusional or paranoid thought content, admit to issues of sexual abuse or molestation, or admit to patterns of alcohol or drug use that may not be readily acknowledged in a face-to-face initial interview. Review with the patient of responses that admit to suicidal or homicidal thoughts, prior suicide attempts, or other dangerous behaviors or ideations may provide a less threatening or intrusive method of broaching these sensitive subjects.

Many objective tests that measure specific rather than global aspects of personality, or assess specific symptoms or disorders, are available for both children and adults. The Beck Depression Inventory–II (Beck, Steer, & Brown, 1996) is one of the most frequently used tests among practicing clinicians, providing a relatively "narrowband" measure of psychopathology in older adolescents and in adults (Piotrowski, 1996). Similarly, the Beck Anxiety Inventory (Beck et al., 1988) measures anxiety symptoms in adults, although some criticisms have suggested that it primarily measures symptoms of panic attack rather than general anxiety (Cox et al., 1996). Child and adolescent versions of these more narrow self-report measures are also widely used, with the Children's Depression Inventory (Kovacs, 1992), Reynolds Child Depression Scale (Reynolds, 1989), and the Multidimensional Anxiety Scale for Children (March, 1997) being representative of the more popular instruments available. These tests provide a brief, easily-obtained view of a narrow slice of potential psychopathology and have some utility in measuring changes in symptom presentation over time and in relation to treatment efforts. These tests are, however, limited in some ways regarding generalizing results among populations, and caution should be exercised in diagnostic uses to utilize supporting information from other tests or clinical sources (Fristad, Emery, & Beck, 1997).

Projective Testing

Projective testing allows for a more "indirect" measure and access to a patient's unconscious emotional state than objective testing due to the unstructured and ambiguous nature of the test materials. The assumption with all projective techniques is that the nature of the task allows the individual to "project" or insert structure and content into the task that is dependent on internal processes of personality. Projective techniques in general are controversial, despite their widespread use, with typical criticisms being that these techniques have less demonstrable reliability and validity than the objective personality tests described in the previous section, a general lack of objective scoring procedures, and too much sensitivity to variable conditions when administered.

Rorschach Test

The most widely used projective technique, and the second most widely used assessment procedure after the MMPI-2, is the Rorschach Psychodiagnostic Test. In this task, subjects are asked to describe their impression of ten achromatic and chromatic inkblots, with the resulting protocol scored according to "determinants" or card characteristics used by the subject to formulate a response. The examiner elicits determinants during an "inquiry" (series of questions about the specific responses) after the initial presentation of the cards. Determinants can include form, color, shading, texture, movement, and content. Different scoring systems list a variety of similar determinants for use in developing formal scores for interpretation.

The Rorschach has been controversial throughout its 60-plus years of use. Due to its complexity, it is considered more of a technique than a formal test by some (e.g., Exner, 1997). Aronow, Reznikoff, and Moreland (1995) suggest that the Rorschach should be considered a "test" when interpreted under a nomothetic perspective (i.e., according to general laws of interpretation) and a "technique" when interpreted in an idiographic approach (i.e., seeking to understand the unique qualities of the individual). Despite the acceptance of five major Rorschach scoring systems in the United States (Ganellen, 1996), it was not until the development of the Comprehensive System (CS) for scoring by Exner (1986) that the Rorschach was considered to have psychometrically sound and empirical scoring criteria. The CS, despite creating a resurgence of interest in the Rorschach (Aiken, 1996), has been criticized as too complicated and time-consuming to lend itself to anything less than formal use, thus not allowing for the more traditional "projective" uses of the test (Willock, 1992). Critics also charge that the CS has failed in its attempts to establish reliability and validity according to accepted standards of test development.

There is a large body of research utilizing the Rorschach to help in differential diagnosis (Archer & Krishnamurthy, 1997; Khadavi, Wetzler, & Wison, 1997), in treatment planning (Finn, 1996; Frank, 1995), to determine treatment outcome (Weiner & Exner, 1991; Greenberg, Pearlman, & Schwartz, 1997), and to help predict certain behaviors such as suicide (Conti et al., 1996).

A less well described but equally important use of the Rorschach is the informal interpretation of the manifest content of responses in order to help understand the individual patient's unique view of the world. This approach corresponds to the more traditional, projective use of the Rorschach, and is described by Aronow et al. (1995) as the "content-idiographic" approach. This approach may prove most useful in providing direction in psychotherapy and helping in what Aronow et al. (1995) describe as "clarifying and removing logjams in therapy."

Consider the following Rorschach responses of Laurel, a 16-year-old female with a history of serious depression and school-related difficulties. Initial responses are listed verbatim with responses to the inquiry following in parentheses.

Card I
Someone is falling and reaching out to somebody. (*Inquiry:* It's the little hands . . . falling . . . just the way it looks, somebody in that position looks like falling . . . this looks like the side view of a person.)

Card II
Someone sad who is crying. (*Inquiry:* It looks like a sad person . . . puddles of tears.)

Card III
I don't know . . . looks like two people fighting over one thing. (*Inquiry:* Two things look like people . . . both have hands on one thing . . . fighting on it and yelling at each other . . . this here is just background stuff . . . focus on black more.)

Card IV
A giant with big feet, about to hurt somebody. (*Inquiry:* It's the shape . . . this looks like a little person underneath him . . . looks like about to hurt him.)

Card V
A person, standing in a crowd. (*Inquiry:* Just looks like a huge crowd of people . . . one little white dot looks like a person looking up in the crowd . . . feeling crushed in, wants to get out but no one will move . . . want to crush him and make sure he's sad.)

Card VI
Looks like a bird flying up from a big, large puddle. (*Inquiry:* A puddle, bird, wings . . . just flying up out of a puddle, doesn't want to get wet.)

Card VII
Two people fighting, not speaking to each other, and they are sad. (*Inquiry:* Two shapes of person, sour faces, not saying anything . . . mad at each other, sitting and waiting for one to speak.)

Card VIII
Looks like a house with a lot of people in it and bears are attacking the house. (*Inquiry:* People inside, looking outside at the bears . . . bears on the side attacking on two legs, arms are on the house.)

Card XI
A girl hiding from people and she's crying . . . hiding behind stuff so no one will see her and she can cry. (*Inquiry:* It's all the stuff she's hiding behind . . . girl is in here, hiding so no one can see her . . . she looks sad where she is.)

Card X
A girl, everybody she loves attacks her, and they didn't want her around anymore, they try to force her to leave . . . gather around her to bother her so she leaves . . . eventually she leaves. (*Inquiry:* Girl here, everybody in family trying to hurt her, yell at her,

hurt her feelings . . . this is her leaving, doesn't want to be sad anymore but will be because she doesn't want to leave her family.)

Utilizing a "content-idiographic" approach to analyze these responses provides a great deal of rich clinical material for exploration in psychotherapy without the time-consuming formal scoring of the CS. This is not to diminish the value of formal scoring of Rorschach responses. Te'eni (1998) has suggested that the nomothetic-idiographic distinction should be encouraged to help define the different purposes and uses of the Rorschach test. Realities of practice in the managed care environment suggest that a more formal, nomothetic treatment of test responses may not be cost-effective, while a more informal, idiographic approach may help uncover patient issues more efficiently, enabling briefer psychotherapy interventions. It is important to recognize that the Rorschach test is probably the most complex in terms of scoring and interpretation of any described in this chapter. As such, the reader should not take this brief treatment as a substitute for the vast literature that is available and should be studied for a complete understanding of this instrument.

Thematic Apperception Test

Another widely used projective test is the Thematic Apperception Test (TAT) (Murray, 1943). The TAT consists of 31 possible cards from which 5–10 can be selected for a brief administration which can be written or oral and completed in small groups or with individuals (Aiken, 1996). Many cards deal with interpersonal situations, making the TAT extremely useful for eliciting themes regarding relationship issues, interpersonal conflicts, and family difficulties. A version for young children, the Children's Apperception Test (CAT), is also available, with alternate forms of stimulus cards featuring animal characters or children's scenes to help elicit more developmentally relevant themes (Bellak, 1993). Patients are typically asked to tell a "dramatic" story about the scene depicted on the card, including what the characters are thinking, feeling, and doing; what may have led up to the scene; and what might happen next. An inquiry after the initial administration of cards has been recommended (Bellak, 1993), and some clinicians ask specific questions about the "moral" of the story or other matters. Liberal questioning with children and adolescents often elicits more complete and useful stories. TAT responses have been used to identify victims of sexual abuse (Pistole & Ornduff, 1994), to make a differential diagnosis (Pillai, 1982), and to identify personality traits, relationship variables, and treatment outcome (McGrew & Teglasi, 1990; Osborn, 1996; Alvarado, 1994). Although no widely accepted formal system exists for scoring, interpretation is based on the premise that the individual will project their own inner states (needs) and environmental or external pressures (press) on the main character and the character's environment in each story (Lanyon & Goodstein, 1997). Individual cards are considered to have a particular "pull" for certain themes based on their content combined with the subject's personality and emotional state. When responses deviate significantly from the more common themes, it can be assumed that there is more of a "projection" of inner states or conflicts for that subject.

To illustrate the possible range of responses to one TAT card by a number of patients with different presenting problems and needs, four responses to Card I (which depicts a young boy staring at a violin) are given below. Questions from the examiner are in parentheses;

patient demographics and diagnostic impressions based on all assessment results are listed at the end of each story.

Samuel
Looking at violin, doesn't want to play it . . . maybe his mom is making him play. He's going to hide it or say that he lost it or break it, whatever. (What happens next?) I don't know, he probably grows up not knowing how to play the violin. (Is that the end?) Yes. (What's the moral of the story?) If you don't want to do something, then don't do it. (18-year-old male, seen in an inpatient unit following two serious suicide attempts, diagnosed with Major Depression and antisocial personality traits.)

Laurel
He's in violin, music class playing the violin. Parents want him to do good, he doesn't want to do violin, wants to do drums. He thinks the violin is boring, wants to be a rock star. (What happens next?) So he tries to tell his parents he wants to play drums, they yell at him, say he can't play the drums because the violin is much better. He cries and runs to his room. (How does the story end?) He never got to play drums; his parents didn't understand why he wanted to play. (16-year-old female whose Rorschach responses are listed above, diagnosed with Major Depression.)

William
This kid likes the way the violin looks, likes his music teacher, likes the way people tell him about the bow of the violin, how it's made from hair of the horse tail . . . thing is he hates Mozart, hates the way the violin sounds when he has it in his clutches, and he wants to smash it. (What does he do?) Sits there like a sullen little baby; he hasn't developed the skills of an adult to know how it pays to put effort into it. But he hates Mozart, wants to play Beatles or a guitar. His mother makes him take violin lessons. (How does it end?) At about 4:30, when his mom picks him up. He goes on and on until something drastic happens like his mom picks him up and he can go out and play under the sun. (20-year-old male, seen on an inpatient unit, diagnosed with a Brief Psychotic Disorder.)

Jennifer
He probably paid a lot of money to get the violin and then it broke and nobody cared so he has to figure out in his own way to repair it and learn how to play. He's really sad about it. (What does he do?) He probably forgets about it in a couple of months, doing other things. (Then what happens?) He probably tries to save money, but helps his friends out with money, uses more money, and doesn't repair it for a long time. (How does it end?) Probably nothing, he just grows up, finds it one day, remembers how he felt then. (15-year-old female, in foster care due to neglect, diagnosed with Dysthymic Disorder.)

An analysis of the above stories provides a unique glimpse of each subject's personality and needs as revealed by her or his response to a stimulus card that has "pull" to elicit themes of parental relationships, ability to deal with frustration, and problem solving. Clearly, the variation of responses is based on each person's perception as defined by their internal emotional status and experiences. This is the clear value of projective testing: providing a view of the typically unconscious psychological processes that define the individual's reaction to the people and events in their life.

Projective Drawing

Along with the Rorschach and the TAT, there are other, more informal projective techniques with widespread acceptance. Projective drawing tasks, namely the Human Figure Drawing Test (Koppitz, 1984), the House-Tree-Person Test, and the Kinetic Family Drawing Test are the three projective techniques most commonly used with children and adolescents (Halpern & McKay, 1998). Subjects are asked to complete various drawings of people, family members interacting, and houses and trees, with interpretation centering around unusual treatments of individuals and characteristics of individuals, and through comparisons of differences across drawings based on their content. Family drawings are interpreted by the nature of the interactions (or lack thereof) depicted by the subject. All drawings are considered to have some significance for personality style based on the individual's approach to the task, qualitative aspects of the drawing (such as placement on the page or line quality), and content. With children and adolescents, results are often interpreted along developmental and cognitive lines, with emotional indicators considered secondarily. Emotional indicators have been used to help evaluate self-esteem, interpersonal relationships, and family attachments. Projective drawings have been used in a similar fashion with adults. Mitchell, Trent, and McArthur (1993) suggested that human figure drawings are useful indicators of internal and external pressures as well as general conflicts and concerns. Despite reliability and validity problems that stem from a lack of useful research (Vass, 1998) projective drawings are routinely and widely used with all ages. Groth-Marnat (1984) reviewed the development of projective drawing techniques and provided extensive guidelines on interpretation for adults, and DiLeo (1983) provided guidelines for children using a large number of actual children's drawings as case examples.

The best use of projective drawings may be to help the psychotherapist understand individual patient characteristics and bring them to the patient's awareness within the therapy hour, and to help understand and diagnose specific patient characteristics. For example, Figure 9.1 depicts the family drawing of a 15-year-old male anorexic with significant depressive affect. His unusual depiction of self and family without faces, his distance from female family members (who are behind a vivid barrier), and his depiction of himself holding a pool cue in a defensive/aggressive fashion paints a literal picture of the likely dysfunctional nature of his family life. Simply asking the patient to describe his family interactions or impressions of family life would probably not provide the depth of information this simple picture provides. Figure 9.2 illustrates the self-portrait of a 34-year-old female experiencing a significant major depressive episode. Describing the sense of hopelessness and desolation this picture suggests may help the patient approach these issues in treatment more effectively. Also, comparing drawings such as this to reports of family life or self-description obtained from parents, family, or the patient at intake may provide a means of assessing the validity of some self-report information.

FIGURE 9.1 Family Drawing by 15-Year-Old Male Anorexic with Significant Depressive Affect

FIGURE 9.2 Self-Portrait by 34-Year-Old Female Experiencing Major Depressive Episode

Sentence Completion

Sentence completion tasks are also widely used in projective testing. In these tasks, the subject is presented with a list of sentence stems and asked to complete them with their own ideas and feelings. There is agreement that sentence completion is more a "semi-projective" task as there is more structure and opportunity to discern the purpose of the test or question and therefore censor responses (Aiken, 1996). However, the results from sentence completion tasks are widely regarded as reliable and valid with many populations (Ames & Riggio, 1995). While there are a few formal administration and scoring systems available, such as Rotter's Incomplete Sentences Blank (1992), interpretation strictly by content allows for the formulation of any number of sentence stems on any number of topics. The utility of this task for the psychotherapist is similar to a review of critical items from the objective personality inventories. Using responses as a basis for discussion in the therapy session, the therapist may be able to broach more sensitive subjects, validate findings from other measures, and help to create a hierarchy or prioritized list, with the patient, of concerns and problems that need to be addressed over the course of treatment.

A sample of sentence completion items from Laurel, the 16-year-old girl whose projective test responses appear throughout this section, are listed below:

I feel . . . so annoyed with life.
I can't . . . stop crying when I am upset.
I sometimes . . . wish I was someone else.
I wish . . . I could leave and be happy.
I secretly . . . want to live somewhere out of my mom's house.
I am most ashamed of . . . everything about me.
My weakest point is . . . when I'm crying (that's a lot).
If I only . . . had a better body and was pretty someone would like me.
To me freedom means . . . I have no freedom.

Comparing Laurel's responses here to her Rorschach and TAT responses helps provide a solid understanding of the depression, low self-esteem, and family problems this hopeless youngster experiences.

Behavior Rating Scales and Symptom Checklists

Behavior rating scales have a long history of use with children and adolescents as a means of gathering objective data about emotional and behavioral symptoms from parents and teachers and through self-report. Checklists have been categorized as either "broadband" (sampling general categories of behavior) or "narrowband" (assessing more specific behavioral domains such as anxiety, attention, or social skills). Many broadband checklists describe one or two "factors" (such as internalizing or externalizing) to categorize clusters of behavior and have scales that may relate to narrowband sets of symptoms or behaviors such as depression, aggression, or hyperactivity. Popular broadband behavior rating scales include the Behavior Assessment System for Children (BASC; Reynolds & Kamphaus, 1992) and Achenbach's Child Behavior Checklist (CBCL; 1991). The most popular narrowband behavior checklists are the Conners Rating Scales–Revised (Conners, Sitarenios, Parker, & Epstein, 1998), which are used primarily to help diagnose attention problems and hyperactivity in children and adolescents.

Behavior checklists are useful both as an initial assessment tool and as a means of monitoring behavioral changes throughout psychotherapy or a program of focused behavioral interventions. Most scales include a parent, teacher, and self-report version, allowing for comparisons to check reliability and validity of ratings, and changes over time. There is some support for the use of behavior checklists as a measure of psychological or behavioral treatment outcome (LeBuffe & Pfeiffer, 1996) and of response to medication for some specific behaviors such as hyperactivity (Pelham et al., 1996).

For psychotherapists, behavior checklists may be a useful and cost-effective way to gain initial impressions of behaviors and problems. Rating forms can be mailed to parents and teachers prior to an initial meeting, and the widespread availability of computer scoring for many scales reduces clinical staff time for scoring and administration. As a screening device, a combination of broadband and narrowband measures may help identify areas of functioning requiring more detailed assessment, or may help in the development of treatment plans.

Behavior checklists are limited in that they only provide a "slice of time" measurement of a rater's subjective view of an individual, with no information generally available regarding antecedents or consequences of the behaviors being rated. Also, ratings are susceptible to the biases and opinions of the rater, which may skew results. As a consequence, comparing multiple raters and validating findings through interviews, observations, or other formal measures is consistently recommended.

Symptom checklists are similar to behavioral ratings scales, although they are typically self-report questionnaires rather than ratings completed by observers or family members. The Brief Symptom Inventory (BSI; Derogatis, 1993) is a typical symptom checklist completed at or prior to intake to assess subjective levels of distress and expression of symptoms in specific areas of functioning such as interpersonal sensitivity, depression, anxiety, hostility, psychoticism, and others. Multiple administrations may be used to track changes in levels of subjective distress, and results can be graphed to show changes over time relative to treatment efforts. The brief administration time and ease of scoring of the BSI has led to its use in the measurement of treatment progress and outcome (through comparison of pretreatment and post-treatment results).

Cognitive Testing

Although the majority of psychologists who engage in psychological assessment perform intellectual evaluations (Watkins et al., 1995), the usefulness of this type of testing for psychotherapy is quite limited. Although it may be helpful in assessing intellectual or cognitive abilities to help determine a patient's capacity for insight or ability to participate in and benefit from cognitive behavioral interventions, this does not typically require or justify a formal intellectual evaluation using instruments such as the Wechsler scales. For most patients, a brief mental status exam provides sufficient information about orientation, attention, memory, and cognition to make judgements regarding treatment-related issues. In some instances, brief cognitive measures such as the Kaufman Brief Intelligence Test (Kaufman & Kaufman, 1990) or the Slosson Intelligence Test–Revised (Nicholson & Hibpshman, 1991) may be utilized when a very basic measure of intellect is required. However, the validity of these instruments is limited, and correlation with more comprehensive intellectual measures such as the Wechsler scales is variable (Kamphaus, 1993). Also, as there is little research linking these briefer intellectual measures to contemporary theories of intellectual ability (McGrew & Flanagan, 1998), their use is generally discouraged.

When cognitive testing results are available, they may help provide some confirmation of levels of impairment or diagnosis. For example, Boone (1992) found that psychiatric patients had less intra-subtest scatter on WAIS-R subtests than normals matched from the standardization sample. Similarly, Piedmont, Sokolove, and Fleming (1990) found that WAIS-R results were useful in discriminating personality disorders. Teeter and Korducki (1998), in their summary of the uses of the WISC-III in assessing emotionally disturbed children, suggest an inverse relationship between IQ and emotional disorders, although there is significant variability across studies within the existing literature. Teeter and Korducki report numerous studies suggesting that emotionally disturbed children tend to have higher Performance IQ scores compared to Verbal IQ scores on the Wechsler scales, and that depressed verbal abilities have been associated with conduct-disordered youth.

Should the clinician administer intellectual measures during an evaluation, a review of test behaviors and actual responses can be useful in understanding personality variables that relate to problem solving, motivation, and cognition, which in turn may be useful in understanding an individual's approach to psychotherapy. Also, specific responses to some of the more unstructured verbal tasks, such as Comprehension, Vocabulary, or Similarities on the Wechsler scales, can provide more "projective" types of information as the patient provides answers to questions that require verbal concept formation which may be dependent on moods, conflicts, or stressors.

Integrating Test Results

Finn and Tonsager (1997) have differentiated the use of psychological assessment into two complementary views or paradigms. First is the "information-gathering paradigm," in which the goal of assessment is to gather data to use in treatment planning and decision-making about patients. This is in contrast to the "therapeutic model of assessment" paradigm, where the goal of evaluation or testing is to produce positive change in clients. When using psychological assessment as an aid to psychotherapy, this distinction may be helpful in orienting the clinician to choice and use of assessment technique. Certainly, the use of full battery assessments—typically involving at least an interview and a series of objective and projective personality measures—is required for clinical decision-making regarding competency, placement in a treatment program or facility, custody of children, or any equally grave matter. For the purposes of psychotherapy, where the primary goal is not so much information-gathering as therapeutic assessment, as described by Finn and Tonsager (1997), the use of less rigorous testing is justified and should be encouraged as a more cost-effective way to improve psychotherapy outcomes.

Ben-Shakhar et al. (1998) suggest that psychodiagnostic test results may reflect the expectations of the tester. In therapeutic assessment, this is a pitfall that may be avoided by a review of test results with the patient, providing an opportunity for discussion and use of the patient's reactions to confirm or disconfirm hypotheses.

One way to avoid examiner bias is to score and interpret each test in a battery separately, and then list hypotheses or major findings for each test. Such a comparison of results helps reveal trends in the results that may be combined to develop a working hypothesis. If we are to review the projective test results presented in this chapter for Laurel, for example, themes of depression, low self-esteem, and family problems are prominent. If objective testing using instruments such as the Millon Adolescent Clinical Inventory or the Deck Depression Scale–II is administered and reveals subscale elevations on similar symptom patterns, then the diagnostic hypothesis of depression and treatment directions to intervene with individual and family therapy would likely be confirmed and fine-tuned.

It should be noted that using the convergence of test results to formulate treatment hypotheses in this manner runs some risk of over-generalization, especially if limited test data is available from a brief or less-formal evaluation. Integrating test results effectively requires some knowledge of the strengths and weaknesses of the different test instruments and how they are best utilized. Some common uses of objective and projective tests discussed in this chapter are summarized in Table 9.1.

As implied earlier, use of these tests to help understand psychotherapeutic impasses or in treatment planning will likely require less comparative integration of results by the examiner and more "interaction of results" with the patient and his or her progress in therapy. In this sense, the more important integration is not among different test results but among treatment efforts.

Most psychological assessments will result in the creation of a written report to document and communicate findings. The exception to this may be when the clinician uses tests

TABLE 9.1 Usefulness of Common Psychological Tests

Measure	Ease of Use/ Scoring	Norm-Based Interpretation	Axis I Diagnosis	Axis II Diagnosis	Assessing Reality Testing	Defense Mechanisms	Interpersonal Relationships
Rorschach	difficult	limited to CS	good	good	very good	good	fair
TAT	easier	poor	good	good	good	excellent	excellent
Incomplete Sentences	easiest	poor	fair	fair	good	good	very good
Drawings	easiest	poor	poor	poor	good	poor	good
MMPI-2/ MMPI-A	easier	excellent	very good	good	good	poor	fair
MCMI-3	easier	very good	good	excellent	good	poor	fair
MACI/MAPI	easier	very good	good	very good	good	poor	fair
Behavior Checklists	easiest	good	fair	fair	poor	poor	fair
Beck Scales	easier	good	very good	poor	poor	poor	poor
Child Depression/ Anxiety Scales	easier	fair	fair	poor	poor	poor	poor

more informally to understand a client, develop treatment plans or approaches, and shares this information with the client only. Clinicians who accept a referral for testing must generate a report to describe their findings in relation to the referral question, which itself may not always be clear. There are as many methods and styles of report writing as there are clinicians, and an infinite number of referral questions. Appendix 9.C lists the necessary sections of a test report with some brief guidelines and comments about content and style. Authors of test reports should always keep in mind that many reports travel far beyond their initial audiences, and once a report is released, the evaluator has virtually no control over who might read the report in the future. Reports should therefore be written with the expectation that they will be read by a wide audience, the members of which will have varying degrees of sophistication regarding the tests used and interpretation of the results gathered. With this in mind, completeness in reporting the results from specific procedures used in the evaluation is of greatest importance in report writing. Furthermore, the writer must make sure that the referral question is answered as completely and clearly as possible, with minimal use of psychological jargon.

Unfortunately, many referral sources can be extremely vague about the questions they would like answered by an assessment, and it is strongly encouraged that the referral question be clarified as much as possible. Typical and traditional referrals from physicians, therapists, and courts may include testing for differential diagnosis; to assess treatment suitability and aid in treatment planning; or to assess competence in some area of functioning.

As with other aspects of testing, however, managed care pressures have altered referrals for psychological assessment. Bindler and Shapiro (1995) suggest that brief or informal psychological testing should be used more in brief psychotherapy to answer referral questions such as helping to delineate a patient's cognitive style, to assess symptoms and complaints, and to monitor treatment, while advocating greater acceptance of this type of testing by managed care. Similarly, Groth-Marnat (1999) suggests that psychological testing is actually cost-effective in managed care if used to reduce risk of adverse outcomes such as suicide or violence, to diagnose more "expensive" conditions in order to target effective therapies, and to measure patient variables that can relate directly to treatment planning and outcome. Cates (1999) suggests that the validity of a test battery can only be determined by how well it answers the referral question, with the psychologist who administers the battery using his or her own judgment in this area.

The role of psychological assessment in clinical and counseling psychology is changing. Increasingly, referrals are made for psychological assessment due to treatment impasses or the need for second opinions to either justify a level of treatment (e.g., more restrictive treatment for a suicidal patient) or to insure that correct diagnosis and treatment have been considered to avoid potential litigation (Groth-Marnat, 1999).

Ethics and New Directions for Psychological Assessment

Basic ethical considerations in the use of psychological testing have traditionally centered on qualifications for use, appropriate training for interpretation, and adequate knowledge of tests and measurement theory in order to make appropriate clinical judgments on test use with specific populations and in specific clinical situations. Users of psychological tests should be familiar with the general ethical principles that govern uses of psychological tests (American Psychological Association, 1992), as well as specific guidelines on computer-based tests and interpretation published by the American Psychological Association (1986) and general standards for test development (American Psychological Association, 1985). While the emphasis in this chapter has been on the informal uses and interpretation of many psychological tests, this by no means is meant to encourage the casual use of testing without proper training in administration, scoring, and interpretation. Ben-Porath (1997) and others have made a strong case that a more formal and statistically-based method of interpretation for most tests is preferable. Informal use of any test is neither ethical nor realistic without formal training.

Multicultural issues in psychological assessment are an ongoing concern that has been gaining much-needed attention recently. Ridley, Li, and Hill (1998) argue that "assessment always occurs in a cultural context" (p. 829), and voice concern that managed care pressures, lack of clinician sensitivity to cultural issues, and inappropriate application of standardized tests can lead to "incomplete assessments" and flawed clinical decisions. Similarly, Constantine (1998) discusses the "ethics of conducting appropriate multicultural assessment in spite of potential managed care threats" (p. 926). Some researchers have voiced concern that test validity is threatened by using cultural adaptations of tests that simply translate test items to another language (Cates, 1999), while some studies have suggested that there are limited differences in measures of psychopathology across ethnic groups using tests such as the MMPI-2 (e.g., Hall, Bansal, & Lopez, 1999).

Discussions in the literature have distinguished the "emic" approach to assessment (Ridley, Li, & Hill, 1998), which advocates the use of culturally specific measures to evaluate culture-specific psychological issues, from the "etic" approach (Hall et al., 1999), which suggests that psychological constructs exist across all cultures and can therefore be measured without using culture-specific measures. Most clinicians advocate for the "emic" approach in assessment as well as in treatment (Arbona, 1998) to insure that cultural issues are considered across a continuum of services. Ridley et al. (1998) list 16 suggestions for practitioners to help incorporate a multicultural approach to assessment, and warn that "incomplete assessments can render unsound assessment decisions" (p. 866). Clearly, all clinicians who engage in psychological assessment must be aware of cultural diversity in their patient populations and act both ethically and responsibly to address these issues in practice.

Recent advances in technology have also impacted the ethics of psychological assessment. While computers have been used for some time to score and provide interpretive hypotheses for many tests, the last few years have seen a drastic increase in interest in computer-administered psychological assessment. McMinn, Ellens, and Soref (1999) have investigated the use of computer scoring and interpretation for many psychological tests together with clinician's perceptions of whether or not such uses are ethical. They differentiate between "support" functions of computer-aided scoring and interpretation (as adjuncts to typical assessment procedures) and "replacement" functions (replacement of some aspects of the typical testing procedure). Based on their findings, there is general agreement that computer-based test interpretation should not be used as a primary source of information and that such use is unethical (McMinn, Ellens, & Soref, 1999). There is less agreement on the ethics of "cut and paste" word processing of actual computer-scored reports, but it is generally agreed that computer scoring for many tests in not only ethical but more accurate (McMinn et al., 1999).

A growing interest has focused on computerized administration of tests and clinical interviews. Computer-based interviews such as the Present State Examination (Dignon, 1996) have been administered together with a clinician interview to evaluate validity and reliability in hopes of developing more cost-effective procedures for gathering important patient information. Although reliability and validity of computerized interviews has been low (Brugha et al., 1996), computer-administered ratings scales have shown promise (Kobak et al., 1996). Some test subjects have actually expressed a preference for a computer rather than a clinician when interviewed (Dignon, 1996). Campbell et al. (1999) report that test-retest reliabilities for computer-administered personality inventories, symptom checklists, and behavior ratings scales are acceptable and have reliability coefficients comparable to (if not exceeding) those of most other tests, even when computer and paper-and-pencil administrations were mixed. This suggests that there is great potential for more "automated" assessment.

As there is increasing interest in Internet and computer-based psychotherapy (Wright & Wright, 1997), the logical extension is to expect the increased use of computerized assessment tools to aid diagnosis, treatment planning, and outcome measurement of long distance "computer patients." There are more and more concerns for the ethical use of computers and the Internet in this manner (Sturges, 1998; Bloom, 1998) and increasing need for research in all aspects of computer use in psychological research and practice (Childress & Asamen, 1998).

Psychological assessment techniques will continue to be an important part of psychological practice. While the worth of these activities is slighted by the powers that currently manage health care, the real worth of any psychological test is the unique ability it affords us to understand and help our clients. There is no greater value for any technique we use.

REFERENCES

Achenbach, T. (1991). *Manual for the Child Behavior Checklist/4-18 and 1991 Profile.* Burlington, VT: University of Vermont Department of Child Psychiatry.

Acklin, M. (1996). Personality assessment and managed care. *Journal of Personality Assessment, 66,* 194–201.

Aiken, L. R. (1996) *Psychological assessment: Methods and practices* (2nd ed.). Toronto: Hogrefe & Huber.

Alvarado, N. (1994). Empirical validity of the Thematic Apperception Test. *Journal of Personality Assessment, 63,* 59–79.

American Educational Research Association, American Psychological Association, & National Council on Measurement in Education. (1985). *Standards for educational and psychological testing.* Washington, DC: American Psychological Association.

American Psychological Association (1992). Ethical principles of psychologists and code of conduct. *American Psychologist, 47,* 1597–1611.

American Psychological Association, Committee on Professional Standards and Committee on Psychological Tests and Assessment. (1986). *Guidelines for computer based tests and interpretations.* Washington, DC: American Psychological Association.

Ames, P. C., & Riggio, R. E. (1995). Use of the Rotter Incomplete Sentences Blank with adolescent populations: Implications for determining maladjustment. *Journal of Personality Assessment, 64,* 159–167.

Arbona, C. (1998). Psychological assessment: Multicultural or universal. *Counseling Psychologist, 26,* 911–926.

Archer, R., & Krishnamurthy, R. (1997). MMPI-A and Rorschach indices related to depression and conduct disorder: An evaluation of the incremental validity hypotheses. *Journal of Personality Assessment, 69,* 517–533.

Aronow, E., Reznikoff, M., & Moreland, K. (1995). The Rorschach: Projective technique or psychometric test. *Journal of Personality Assessment, 64,* 213–228.

Ball, J. D., Archer, R., & Imhof, E. (1994). Time requirements of psychological testing: A survey of practitioners. *Journal of Personality Assessment, 63,* 239–249.

Beck, A. T., Epstein, N., Brown, G., & Steer, R. A. (1988). An inventory for measuring clinical anxiety: Psychometric properties. *Journal of Consulting and Clinical Psychology, 56,* 893–897.

Beck, A. T., Steer, R. A., & Brown, G. K. (1996). *Beck Depression Inventory manual* (2nd ed.). San Antonio, TX: Psychological Corporation.

Bellak, L. (1993). *The TAT, CAT, and SAT in clinical use* (5th ed.). Boston: Allyn & Bacon.

Ben-Porath, Y. (1997). Use of personality assessment instruments in empirically guided treatment planning. *Psychological Assessment, 9,* 361–367.

Ben-Shakhar, G., Bar-Hillel, M., Bilu, Y., & Shefler, G. (1998). Seek and ye shall find: Test results are what you hypothesize they are. *Journal of Clinical Decision Making, 11,* 235–249.

Bindler, P., & Shapiro, R. (1995). Psychological testing in brief psychotherapy: How testing, appropriately applied, can enhance managed care's "therapy of choice." *Behavioral Health Management, 15,* 18–23.

Bloom, J. (1998). The ethical practice of WebCounseling. *British Journal of Guidance & Counseling, 26,* 53–59.

Boone, D. (1992). WAIS-R scatter with psychiatric inpatients: I. Intrasubtest scatter. *Psychological Reports, 71,* 483–487.

Brugha, T., Kaul, A., Dignon, A., Teather, D., et al. (1996). Present state examination by microcomputer: Objectives and experience of preliminary steps. *International Journal of Methods in Psychiatric Research, 6,* 143–151.

Butcher, J. N. (1990). *The MMPI-2 in treatment planning.* New York: Oxford.

Butcher, J. N., & Williams, C. L. (1992). *MMPI-A user's guide for the Minnesota report: Adolescent interpretative system.* Minneapolis: University of Minnesota Press.

Campbell, K., Rohlman, D., Storzbach, D., Binder, L., Anger, W. K., Kovera, C., Davis, K., & Grossman, S. (1999). Test-retest reliability of psychological and neurobehavioral tests self-administered by computer. *Assessment, 6,* 21–32.

Cates, J. A. (1999). The art of assessment in psychology: Ethics, expertise, and validity. *Journal of Clinical Psychology, 55,* 631–641.

Childress, C., & Asamen, J. (1998). The emerging relationship of psychology and the Internet: Proposed guidelines for conducting Internet intervention research. *Ethics & Behavior, 8,* 19–35.

Chisholm, S., Crowther, J., & Ben-Porath, Y. (1997). Selected MMPI-2 scales' ability to predict premature termination and outcome from psychotherapy. *Journal of Personality Assessment, 69,* 127–144.

Clair, D., & Pendergast, D. (1994). Brief psychotherapy and psychological assessments: Entering a relationship, establishing a focus, and providing feedback. *Professional Psychology: Research & Practice, 25,* 46–49.

Conners, C. K., Sitarenios, G., Parker, J., & Epstein, J. (1998). The revised Conner's Parent Rating Scale (CPRS-R): Factor structure, reliability, and criterion validity. *Journal of Abnormal Child Psychology, 26,* 257–268.

Constantine, M. G. (1998). Developing competence in multicultural assessment: Implications for counseling psychology training and practice. *Counseling Psychologist, 26,* 922–929.

Conti, L., Giannoni, A., Falco, P., & Tognazzo, D. (1996). Death between reality and imagination: Rorschach's test in suicide attempters. *Giornale Italiano di Suicidologia, 6,* 83–91.

Cox, B., Cohen, E., Direnfield, D., & Swinson, R. (1996). Does the Beck Anxiety Inventory measure anything beyond panic attack symptoms? *Behaviour Research & Therapy, 34,* 949–954.

Derogatis, L. R. (1993). *Brief Symptom Inventory: Administration, scoring and procedures manual–II.* Minneapolis: National Computer Systems.

Dignon, A. (1996). Acceptability of a computer-administered psychiatric interview. *Computers in Human Behavior, 12,* 177–191.

DiLeo, J. H. (1983). *Interpreting children's drawings.* New York: Brunner/Mazel.

Exner, J. (1986). *The Rorschach: A comprehensive system. Volume I: Basic foundations* (2nd ed.). New York: John Wiley.

Exner, J. (1997). The future of Rorschach in personality assessment. *Journal of Personality Assessment, 68,* 37–46.

Finn, S. (1996). Assessment feedback integrating MMPI-2 and Rorschach findings. *Journal of Personality Assessment, 67,* 543–557.

Finn, S., & Tonsager, M. (1997). Information-gathering and therapeutic models of assessment: Complementary paradigms. *Psychological Assessment, 9,* 374–385.

Folestein, M. F., Folestein, S. E., & McHugh, P. R. (1975). A practical method for grading the cognitive status of patients for the clinician. *Journal of Psychiatric Research, 12,* 189–198.

Frank, G. (1995). Use of the Rorschach in planning psychotherapy. *Psychological Reports, 77,* 607–610.

Franzen, M., & Berg, R. (1998). *Screening children for brain impairment.* New York: Springer.

Fristad, M. A., Emery, B. L., & Beck, S. J. (1997). Use and abuse of the Children's Depression Inventory. *Journal of Consulting & Clinical Psychology, 65,* 699–702.

Ganellen, R. (1996). Comparing the diagnostic efficiency on the MMPI-2, MCMI-II, and Rorschach: A review. *Journal of Personality Assessment, 67,* 219–243.

Graham, J. R. (1998). Characteristics of high and low scores on the MMPI-2 clinical scales. In G. Koocher, J. Norcross, & S. Hill (Eds.), *Psychologists desk reference.* New York: Oxford.

Greenberg, R., Pearlman, C., & Schwartz, W. (1997). Using the Rorschach to define differences in schizophrenics and the implications for treatment. *Journal of the American Academy of Psychoanalysis, 25,* 399–408.

Groth-Marnat, G. (1984). *Handbook of psychological assessment.* New York: Van Nostrand Reinhold.

Groth-Marnat, G. (1999). Financial efficacy of clinical assessment: Rational guidelines and issues for future research. *Journal of Clinical Psychology, 55,* 813–824.

Hall, G., Bansal, A., & Lopez, I. (1999). Ethnicity and psychopathology: A meta-analytic review of 31 years of comparative MMPI/MMPI-2 research. *Psychological Assessment, 11,* 186–197.

Halperin, J., & McKay, K. (1998). Psychological testing for child and adolescent psychiatrists: A review of the past 10 years. *Journal of the American Academy of Child and Adolescent Psychiatry, 37,* 575–584.

Hathaway, S. R., McKinley, J. C., with Butcher, J. N., Dahlstrom, W. G., Graham, J. R., Tellegen, A., & Kaemmer, B. (1989). *Minnesota Multiphasic Personality Inventory 2: Manual for administration and scoring.* Minneapolis: University of Minnesota Press.

Hawkins, K., & Cooper, M. (1996). Limitations of cognitive status exams: A case based discussion. *Psychiatry: Interpersonal & Biological Processes, 59,* 382–388.

Hilsenroth, M., Handler, M, Toman, K, & Padawer, J. (1995). Rorschach and MMPI-2 indices of early psychotherapy termination. *Journal of Consulting and Clinical Psychology, 63,* 956–965.

Kamphaus, R. (1993). *Clinical assessment of children's intelligence.* Boston: Allyn & Bacon.

Kaufman, A. S., & Kaufman, N. L. (1990). *Kaufman Brief Intelligence Test.* Circle Pines, MN: American Guidance Service.

Khadavi, A., Wetzler, S., & Wilson, A. (1997). Manic indices on the Rorschach. *Journal of Personality Assessment, 69,* 365–375.

Kobak, K., Greist, H., Jefferson, J., & Katzelnick, D. (1996). Computer administered clinical rating scales: A review. *Psychopharmacology, 127,* 291–301.

Koppitz, E. M. (1984). *Psychological evaluation of Human Figure Drawings by middle school pupils.* Orlando, FL: Grune & Stratton.

Kovacs, M. (1992). *Children's Depression Inventory manual.* North Tonawanda, NY: Multi-Health Systems.

Lachar, D., & Gruber, C. P. (1994). *Personality Inventory for Youth: Manual.* Los Angeles: Western Psychological Services.

Lanyon, R. I., & Goodstein, L. D. (1997). *Personality assessment* (3rd ed.). New York: John Wiley.

LeBuffe, P., & Pfeiffer, S. (1996). Measuring outcomes in residential treatment with the Devereux Scales of Mental Disorders. *Residential Treatment for Children & Youth, 13,* 83–91.

Malon, D. H. (1979). *Individual psychotherapy and the science of psychodynamics.* London: Buttersworth.

March, J. (1997). *Multidimensional Anxiety Scale for Children.* North Tonawanda, NY: Multi-Health Systems.

McGrew, K., & Flanagan, D. (1998). *The intelligence test desk reference (ITDR).* Boston: Allyn & Bacon.

McGrew, M., & Teglasi, H. (1990). Formal characteristics of Thematic Apperception Test stories as indices of emotional disturbance in children. *Journal of Personality Assessment, 54,* 639–655.

McMinn, M., Ellens, B., & Soref, E. (1999). Ethical perspectives and practice behaviors involving computer-based test interpretation. *Assessment, 6,* 71–77.

Millon, T., Green, C. J., & Meagher, R. B. (1982). *Millon Adolescent Personality Inventory manual.* Minneapolis: National Computer Systems.

Millon, T., Millon, C., & Davis, R. (1993). *Millon Adolescent Clinical Inventory manual.* Minneapolis: National Computer Systems.

Millon, T., Millon, C., & Davis, R. (1994). *Manual for the MCMI-III.* Minneapolis: NCS Assessments.

Mitchell, J., Trent, R., & McArthur, M. (1993). *Human Figure Drawing Test.* Los Angeles: Western Psychological Services.

Murray, H. A. (1943). *Thematic Apperception Test.* Cambridge, MA: Harvard University Press.

Newman, M., & Greenway, P. (1997). Therapeutic effects of providing MMPI-2 feedback to clients at a university counseling service: A collaborative approach. *Psychological Assessment, 9,* 122–131.

Nicholson, C. L., & Hibpshman, T. L. (1991). *Slosson Intelligence Test-Revised.* Los Angeles: Western Psychological Services.

Olin, J. T., & Keatinge, C. (1998). *Rapid psychological assessment.* New York: John Wiley.

Osborn, C. (1996). The feasibility of the Thematic Apperception Test for adolescent clients. *Measurement & Evaluation in Counseling and Development, 29,* 48–55.

Pelham, W., Swanson, J., Furman, M., & Schwindt, H. (1996). Pemoline effects on children with ADHD: A time-response by dose-response analysis on classroom measures. *Annual Progress in Child Psychiatry & Child Development, 1996,* 473–493.

Phelps, R., Eisman, E., & Kohut, J. (1998). Psychological practice and managed care: Results of the CAPP practitioner survey. *Professional Psychology: Research & Practice, 29,* 31–36.

Piedmont, R., Sokolove, R., & Fleming, M. (1990). Discriminating personality disorders using the WAIS-R: A comparison of three approaches. *Journal of Personality Assessment, 54,* 363–378.

Pillai, A. (1982). Paranoid schizophrenics and the Thematic Apperception Test. *Psychological Studies, 27,* 56–60.

Piotrowski, C. (1996). Use of the Beck Depression Inventory in clinical practice. *Psychological Reports, 79,* 873–874.

Piotrowski, C., Belter, R., & Keller, J. (1998). The impact of managed care on the practice of psychological testing: Preliminary findings. *Journal of Personality Assessment, 70,* 441–447.

Pistole, D., & Ornduff, S. (1994). TAT assessment of sexually abused girls. *Journal of Personality Assessment, 63,* 211–222.

Prieto, L. (1997). The supervision of psychological assessment: Toward parsimony and empirical evidence for developmental supervision theory. *Professional Psychology: Research & Practice, 28,* 593–594.

Reynolds, C., & Kamphaus, R. (1992). *Behavior Assessment System for Children manual.* Circle Pines, MN: American Guidance Services.

Reynolds, W. (1989). *Reynolds Child Depression Scale professional manual.* Odessa, FL: Psychological Assessment Resources.

Ridley, C., Li, L., & Hill, C. (1998). Multicultural assessment: Reexamination, reconceptualization, and practical application. *Counseling Psychologist, 26,* 827–910.

Rotter, J., Lah, M., & Rafferty, J. (1992). *Rotter Incomplete Sentences Blank: Manual.* San Antonio, TX: Psychological Corporation.

Rudolph, B., Craig, R., Leifer, M., & Rubin, N. (1998). Evaluating competency in the diagnostic interview among graduate students: Development of generic scales. *Professional Psychology: Research & Practice, 29,* 488–491.

Seligman, M., & Levant, R. (1998). Managed care policies rely on inadequate science. *Professional Psychology: Research & Practice, 29,* 211–212.

Smelson, D., Kordon, M., & Rudolph, B. (1997). Evaluating the diagnostic interview: Obstacles and future directions. *Journal of Clinical Psychology, 53,* 497–505.

Spreen, O., & Strauss, E. (1998). *A compendium of neuropsychological tests: Administration, norms and commentary* (2nd ed.). New York: Oxford.

Sturges, J. (1998). Practical use of technology in professional practice. *Professional Psychology: Research & Practice, 29,* 183–188.

Te'eni, D. (1998). Nomothetics and idiographics as antonyms: Two mutually exclusive purposes for using the Rorschach. *Journal of Personality Assessment, 70,* 232–247.

Teeter, P., & Korducki, R. (1998). Assessment of emotionally disturbed children with the WISC-III. In A. Prifitera & D. Saflofske, *WISC-III Clinical Use and Interpretation: Scientist-practitioner perspectives.* Boston: Academic Press.

Trzepacz, P., & Baker, R. (1993). *The psychiatric mental status exam.* New York: Oxford.

Vass, Z. (1998). The inner formal structure of the H-T-P drawings: An exploratory study. *Journal of Clinical Psychology, 54,* 611–619.

Watkins, C. E., Campbell, V. L., Nieberding, R., & Hallmark, R. (1995). Contemporary practice of psychological assessment by clinical psychologists. *Professional Psychology: Research & Practice, 26*(1), 54–60.

Weiner, I., & Exner, J. (1991). Rorschach changes in long-term and short-term psychotherapy. *Journal of Personality Assessment, 56,* 453–465.

Willock, B. (1992). Projection, transitional phenomena, and the Rorschach. *Journal of Personality Assessment, 49,* 346–355.

Wirt, R. D., Lachar, D., Klinedinst, J. K., & Seat, P. D. (1984). *Multidimensional description of child personality: A manual for the Personality Inventory for Children, Revised 1984.* Los Angeles: Western Psychological Services.

Wright, J. H., & Wright, A. S. (1997). Computer-assisted psychotherapy. *Journal of Psychotherapy Practice & Research, 6,* 315–329.

FOR FURTHER READING

Franzen, M., & Berg, R. (1998). *Screening children for brain impairment.* New York: Springer.

Provides a good overview of mental status exams with children, as well as testing with children in general.

Koocher, G., Norcross, J., & Hill, S. (Eds.) (1998). *Psychologists desk reference.* New York: Oxford.

A comprehensive but brief description of test usage, ethics, and scoring guidelines for many objective and projective tests. Also covers a number of other issues of interest to practicing clinicians.

Morrison, J. (1995). *The first interview: Revised for DSM IV.* New York: Guilford.

Guidelines on how to conduct an effective first interview, how to deal with unusual or sensitive problems or topics, and symptom presentation according to DSM IV diagnostic criteria.

Olin, J. T., & Keatinge, C. (1998). *Rapid psychological assessment.* New York: John Wiley.

An excellent reference for usage and scoring of many commonly used psychological tests. Designed to help the reader find information quickly and easily.

Trzepacz, P., & Baker, R. (1993). *The psychiatric mental status exam.* New York: Oxford.

Although written primarily for physicians with much medical information, provides an exhaustive reference to sections of the metal status exam and guidelines for assessment.

Zimmerman, M. (1994). *Interview guide for evaluating DSM IV psychiatric disorders and the mental status examination.* East Greenwich, RI: Psych Products Press.

Provides coverage of all areas of a mental status exam, with actual questions to be used in decision tree format for conducting the interview.

APPENDIX 9.A
Annotated Diagnostic Interview Format

The following is provided as a guideline. Not all interviewers will follow the order presented here, but these content areas are inclusive of the important areas to be covered in an initial diagnostic contact with a patient. The information described here may need to be elicited in more than one session, depending more on the amount and complexity of the information rather than on the skill of the interviewer. Child interviews may differ somewhat from what is presented here, mainly because parents or guardians will likely be the primary informants in many areas, and direct questioning of the child may involve more rapport-building statements than information-eliciting questions.

Content areas of the interview as well as the clinical record of the interview are noted.

I. Informed Consent
Regardless of whether you are doing a one-time diagnostic interview, a formal evaluation, or intake for ongoing psychotherapy, it is crucial that the patient know the purpose of the interview, who you are as the interviewer, and how the information gathered will be recorded and used. The client's understanding of and assent to proposed uses of evaluation information should be clearly noted in the record.

II. Presenting Problem/Chief Complaint
A brief description of the reason the patient is seeking treatment or evaluation should be obtained. Eliciting and noting a description of the problem in the patient's own words is helpful. A patient who describes feeling "anxious" may in fact be describing something totally different than a clinical concept of anxiety, however. Precipitants, ongoing stressors, onset, and reasons for seeking treatment (whose idea it is, for example) should be addressed at this time. Consequences of behaviors or problems, circumstances where difficulty occurs, and level of subjective distress should be assessed. Specific current treatments such as medications and referrals or recommendations for treatment (such as from primary care physicians) should be discussed. Be sure to ask about potential or complicating medical factors or symptoms. This is also a good time to attempt to elicit a client's expectations for treatment, goals, and general attitudes about treatment.

III. Psychosocial History
Family, medical, and emotional history should be obtained, as well as academic and work histories, developmental history (especially for children), and substance use history. If not already mentioned in the prior section, current living situation and life events should be discussed here. History of marital and social relationships is important, as is history of legal problems, military service, and leisure activities. Sensitive subjects, such as sexual history, job or social failures, and substance use, may be difficult to broach, and subtlety and good timing may be needed to help the patient feel open in these discussions.

Family history should include current and extended family constellation, family medical and psychiatric history, and the nature of contact between family members. Medical history should be comprehensive and include any major illnesses and injuries, surgeries, and history of both prescription medication and "over-the-counter" medicines. Academic and work history should include general discussions of activities during school-age years as well as highest degree obtained. Reasons for events such as leaving school before completion should be discussed. History of learning disabilities or difficulties with learning, special education services, or educational coding should be discussed for both patient and family histories. Work history should include all experiences—successful employment as well as problems. Efforts should be made to ascertain if the individual is underemployed due to academic failures, emotional difficulties, or motivational factors.

IV. Treatment History

Prior experiences in both inpatient and outpatient settings should be explored. This is also a time to briefly discuss transfers of records, contacts with previous therapists, and signing of appropriate releases. Precipitants and lengths of past treatments, past uses of medication (including over-the-counter uses and possible side effects), and reasons for terminating past treatment are all important, even if they appear to have little bearing on the present treatment episode. Always ask about the reactions of significant others to past treatment episodes, as many patients drop out of treatment due to negative comments or reactions from family and friends.

V. Critical Topics

Critical topics such as suicidal or homicidal thinking, substance use, or victimization may be evaluated at any time during an interview, but are discussed separately here to underscore the importance of discussing these in an initial evaluation. Morrison (1995) provided concrete examples of questions and approaches for what he considers these "sensitive subjects." Many novice interviewers are apologetic to the patient for having to raise difficult issues such as these. It is helpful to keep this reaction from the patient as it may diminish the patient's perception of the interviewer's competence and inhibit the elicitation of information. The patient may be reluctant to "burden" or risk disapproval from the therapist who presents as uncomfortable with this or any other type of information.

Assessment of suicidal or homicidal thoughts or actions should be addressed in every initial or diagnostic contact. The question "Have you had recent or past thoughts of harming yourself or others?" may be sufficient to raise the issue, and, if the response is consistent with the patient's presentation in other aspects of the interview, remove it from the interviewer's concern. Obviously, positive responses should be explored in detail, which is typically easier once the subject has been raised and the patient's responses have been accepted by the therapist.

Substance use issues are similarly important to discuss, as many psychiatric disorders and relationship difficulties that patients present with have some symptomatic substance abuse aspect. To avoid activating denial mechanisms, which are often a part of substance use, avoid asking first if drinking or drug use is problematic. Asking about family history and social activities may provide clues to potentially problematic substance use and ease into a more direct discussion. While gaining a sense of the pattern of usage is important, it may be most useful and somewhat easier with some patients to elicit adverse effects, problematic effects, or relationship difficulties related to drug or alcohol use.

Victimization issues, which can be emotional, physical, or sexual, sometimes cause more anxiety for the interviewer than for the patient. Again, history-taking may provide information that facilitates a transition to this subject, but often the interviewer will need to ask some simple, inoffensive, and open-ended questions. The interviewer should be prepared, if any abuse is disclosed during the interview, to discuss their ethical and legal obligation to report abuse to state agencies, or any other legally-mandated procedures in their locality. In many states, mandated reporting has been expanded from minor children to adults.

VI. Ending the Interview

Second only to opening the interview, closing the session deserves special consideration. Many patients will ask for some summation of the interviewer's impressions or findings, usually couched in questions such as: "Well, how crazy am I?" or "Is there any hope for me?" Providing a summary of impressions, directions to take in the next interview, suggestions for starting a basic treatment plan, or simple reassurance that the first meeting is always difficult and that further contacts will tend to be less anxiety provoking—all are excellent ways to provide a sense of closure and direction toward future contacts.

APPENDIX **9.B**

Annotated Mental Status Exam Format

The mental status exam (MSE) should proceed from simpler to more complex tasks. The patient who is unable to perform simple tasks of attention and concentration, for example, will probably not need formal assessment of short-term memory skills, as attention is considered a necessary component to register information for use in short-term memory. This approach saves clinical time for more fruitful investigation, and avoids putting the patient through unnecessary and potentially frustrating exercises. Many concerns of the MSE will be assessed throughout the course of a history-taking interview, as well as in the formal exam for mental status. General areas to assess in the MSE are as follows:

Appearance and Demeanor

Does the patient appear his or her stated age? Is dress appropriate for the situation? Are there important physical characteristics (e.g., scars, tattoos, bandages) or mannerisms (i.e., poor eye contact, grimaces, evidence of hallucinations)? Is the patient cooperative, angry, or hostile? Does demeanor and attitude change over the course of the interview? If so, is this change specific to a topic or area of investigation? Are there apparent (observable) motor difficulties such as tremors, tics, staggering, or slurred speech?

Orientation/Attention/Cognition

Is the patient properly oriented to person, time, and place? If not, are there specifics to be noted and further evaluated? For example, a patient disoriented to person may also present some delusional material around this disorientation. A patient mildly disoriented to date or time while in the first few days of an acute psychiatric hospitalization is less seriously impaired than the patient who reports the date to be months or years different from the present.

Attention to directions to complete tasks within the interview, as well as to tasks themselves, is necessary for many components of the MSE and should be assessed early in the interview through requests to do simple, multistep tasks. Simple attention can also be assessed through a digits-forwards-and-backwards task, while more focused attention (concentration) is typically assessed with a serial seven task (successively subtracting 7 from 100), although the patient must have the capacity and training to perform simple arithmetic to do this successfully.

Abstract thinking is an important cognitive function that allows the patient to conceptualize and generalize information. Proverb interpretation, perception of similarities and differences between common objects, and conceptualization of object categories are common tasks to assess abstraction ability versus concreteness of thought.

Speech and Language

Speech and language ability, both receptive and expressive, is typically assessed throughout the interview and should involve written language and reading as well as spoken language. Comprehension of language involves responding to verbal commands, reading a command from a piece of paper and completing it, writing a dictated sentence, and making appropriate responses to conversational questions throughout the interview. These abilities are considered *receptive* speech skills. Writing a sentence of the patient's choice, reading aloud, and the speaking of thoughts and answers to questions are examples of *expressive* language abilities.

Both expressive and receptive language skills are assessed in terms of comprehension and fluency, with expressive speech evaluated in terms of pragmatics (subtle or more abstract meaning related to communication), prosody (intonation), semantics (content), and use of grammar. In some patients, it may be necessary to differentiate functional language problems from speech abnormalities related to psychiatric difficulties. Trzepacz and Baker (1993) provide comprehensive guidelines to assess speech and language problems and make this distinction.

Memory

Immediate recall, that is, the naming of two or three objects shown to the patient or repeating two or three words, should be assessed first to establish that attention is sufficient to proceed with the assessment of short-term memory. Trzepacz and Baker (1993) describe this immediate recall task as "registration."

Short-term memory of both visual and verbal material should be assessed. Verbal material can include short paragraphs or lists of unrelated words that are read by the examiner and then recalled by the patient. Word lists are typically presented over a series of learning trials prior to a free, or uncued, recall. Visual material typically involves designs that are presented, removed, and then drawn by the patient. Working memory, that is, the ability to hold information in short-term memory while in pursuit of a specific outcome, can be assessed through more complex, two- or three-step math problems, digits backwards, or a similar task that involves active use of information not typically accessed from long-term memory.

Assessment of long-term memory requires an understanding of the differences between declarative memory (of factual information) and procedural memory (behaviorally based memory for specific actions or skills). Declarative memory involves both semantic memory (specific knowledge of the environment and general information) and episodic memory (of personal experiences and events). Questioning about well-known historical facts or events can assess semantic memory, but the examiner must have access to personal information to validate and assess the accuracy of answers involving episodic memory.

Mood and Affect

Mood is the patient's self-report of their internal emotional state, and *affect* is the outward display of emotion or feeling. As mood is considered more stable, affect is often assessed in terms of potential changes over time (lability) and by the strength or intensity of the emotion. Is affect congruent with mood? Is it appropriate in terms of consistency with the situation and the content of verbalizations? Are there behavioral or nonverbal clues as to intensity or appropriateness? Is there a range of affect over the course of the evaluation and if so, how quickly and easily does it change?

Thought Content and Process

Assessment of thought content may occur throughout an interview. The distinction to be drawn is between more normal concerns or preoccupations and pathological or abnormal thoughts such as delusions, obsessions, or suicidal or homicidal thinking. A productive method is to take a less-structured approach to the initial portion of the interview, allowing for the spontaneous expression of unusual thoughts, which can then be questioned more closely.

Difficulties in the patient's process or organization of thinking are readily apparent for the most part. Common thought process difficulties include loose associations, tangential thinking, or circumstantiality. Typically, patterns of speech can be considered in terms of flow and general "connectedness" to assess potential thought process difficulties.

Perceptual abnormalities such as hallucinations or depersonalization are often difficult to evaluate, as they can be subtle and hard to observe directly. They can often be inferred from some unusual behavior such as appearing to attend to something not in the room, and that behavior can then be questioned more closely.

Judgment and Insight

Judgment involves the forming of decisions, conclusions, or opinions about events or situations that are appropriate and based on realistic interpretations of facts known to the patient. *Insight* is that awareness of self and problems which allows a patient to make sound and realistic observations about the effects of their behavior on others, the potential consequences of their actions, and to make realistic judgments about such issues as need for treatment. Insight and judgment are interrelated; insight is considered a precursor to sound judgment.

Assessment of both insight and judgment is usually accomplished by careful questioning of the patient's understanding of their illness and related symptoms, their views on the need for treatment, and the effects their behavior or symptoms have had in various areas of their life such as home or work, or in specific roles such as spouse, parent, or employee.

APPENDIX 9.C

Sections of the Test Report

Identifying Information
Name
Date of birth
Date seen and report date

The above information should be listed as a minimum. This section may also include a brief statement of identifying characteristics, special or notable events surrounding the assessment, or any other information deemed crucial to understanding the report. The examiner and her role with the patient may also be described here.

Referral
By whom
What is the question? BE SPECIFIC!!

This section may include a description of where the patient was seen relative to the referral, how the information will be used to answer the referral question, or any other information that helps understand why this patient was referred.

Procedures
All tests and procedures used
Observations
Record review
Formal or standardized tests
Anecdotal information

It is important to list every method used to obtain information about the patient, as the validity of your report depends on these sources. There should be total agreement between any list of sources here and all references to specific tests in the body of the report; a test report that lists procedures with no mention of results, or that provides results from a test not listed, is suspect.

History and Observations
General and test-specific observations

At times, there is so much history available on a patient that to try to describe everything known would be both confusing and too lengthy. History pertinent to the referral question or having direct bearing on circumstances of testing, interpretation of results, or recommendations should be described as concisely as possible. Similarly, observations of any behaviors, attitudes, response styles, or mannerisms that may affect test responses or findings should be discussed.

Results
General
By areas assessed
Test by test

There are a number of different formats for presenting and discussing results. Generally, test scores should be reported with some brief explanation of what the scores mean and how they are derived.

Some clinicians prefer a test-by-test presentation of findings, building to a conclusion that integrates the commonalities or agreements across tests. Another approach is to present general results based on specific areas of functioning (cognitive versus personality functions, for example). Statements regarding the validity of results may be emphasized here as well. Attention should be paid to the referral question, with results described as they relate specifically. Findings that are unrelated to the referral question or unusual or unexpected should not be ignored, but reported in the context of your understanding of the patient as a whole.

Summary/Conclusions

Unfortunately, this is the section of the test report that many people read first, or even exclusively. The results described in the previous section should be distilled down to their most important details and described in terms of the "answer" to the referral question. Recommendations can be described here in terms of need for further assessments, treatment issues or plans (if part of the referral question), or any unexpected or unusual findings. The writer should resist the temptation in this section to go beyond the referral question to theorizing about behavior or results and describing recommendations, unless they relate directly to unexpected findings.

Signature

Your signature and credentials verify that a person with a specific level of training and expertise completed the testing. Without a signature, the best report will be worthless in some situations.

CHAPTER

10 Foundations of Pharmacopsychology

Toward an Integration of Psychopharmacology and Psychosocial Therapy for Mental Health Practitioners

CLIFFORD N. LAZARUS

Introduction

Spurred on by the prevailing biopsychosocial zeitgeist and the dramatic reforms of "managed" health care, more and more psychologists are seeking out and undergoing intensive training in psychopharmacology. Psychologists are increasingly involved in the psychopharmacotherapeutic management of their patients by way of collaborative practice with primary care physicians, psychiatrists, and other medical specialists. Hence, a solid grounding in psychopharmacology is essential for many currently practicing clinical psychologists (and certainly most future ones) to enable them to meaningfully participate in the full spectrum of their patients' mental health care.

Beyond purely collaborative practice, many psychologists are interested in obtaining autonomous prescribing privileges in the hope that, one day soon, they may provide comprehensive, seamlessly integrated, biopsychosocial interventions including the safe and effective prescribing of psychotropic medications. Thus, the discipline of "pharmacopsychology" has recently evolved as an inevitable feature of the mental health field, yet one that awaits legislative change before it can truly enter the mainstream of psychological practice.

Legislative changes aside, the evolution of pharmacopsychology and the emergence of prescribing psychologists seems a natural development in the field of psychology. Psychology originated as a philosophical discipline many centuries ago. Within the past century it has become an experimental science. At about the same time, the foundations of clinical psychology as a therapeutic process were being laid. In the latter half of the twentieth century, with the advent of behavior therapy, the discipline of clinical psychology became a science of psychological therapy (e.g., A. Lazarus, 1958) by marrying experimental methods with the art of psychotherapy. Subsequently, given the growing evidence that human psychology is significantly influenced (if not determined outright) by biological processes, a degree of "medicalization" has become necessary to evolve a comprehensive model and method of contemporary psychological practice.

It will come as no surprise that the idea of prescribing psychologists is fraught with controversy and is a subject greatly debated among health care professionals. Even practicing psychologists are heavily divided on the issue. However, despite the issue's enormous importance, an analysis of the pros and cons of pharmacopsychology is not the focus of this chapter. This chapter will emphasize the process of collaborative practice, since this is a reality that many non-medical mental health care providers already face. In essence, this chapter will aim to weave the "bio" into the biopsychosocial tapestry of mental health therapy so that, even without autonomous prescribing privileges, present-day non-medical clinicians can be better equipped to participate in the medical management of their patients' mental health care.

It will be necessary to cover much interrelated material, since psychologists who wish to practice collaboratively with medical providers need to be fully conversant with a variety of subjects. Furthermore, sometimes the most important intervention a therapist can perform is to persuade a patient to agree to a trial of a psychotropic medication, and usually, the more he or she knows about psychopharmacology the better they are able to do so.

This chapter is divided into seven parts. The first will review the origins of psychopharmacology (i.e., the practice of prescribing drugs to reduce or alleviate psychological disturbance). The second will introduce the structure and function of the human brain, since a solid grounding in neuroscience is essential to understanding the processes through which psychotropic drugs work. The third will summarize some fundamental aspects of general pharmacology. The fourth will survey the major classes of psychotropic medications. In the fifth part, the importance of differential diagnosis will be discussed (i.e., discrimination of true psychological disturbances from medical conditions that can masquerade as psychological disorders). The sixth will survey several advanced topics such as therapeutic blood monitoring and augmentation strategies. Finally, the biological emphasis of the preceding parts will be linked with the processes of psychosocial therapy.

The Evolution of Psychopharmacology

The fact that certain substances can affect perception, thought, sensation, emotion, and behavior has long been known. Indeed, alcohol, opiates, and tobacco (to name only a few) have been used recreationally and ceremonially for centuries. The medicinal use of such substances is equally ancient. It was only in the middle of the twentieth century, however, that pharmaceutical compounds were scientifically demonstrated to be useful in treating psychological disorders. Interestingly, the discovery of psychotropics was far from deliberate; the first few generations of psychotropics were discovered entirely serendipitously. For example, lithium, one of the oldest and best established mood-stabilizing agents (Hyman, Arana, & Rosenbaum, 1995) was found to be efficacious in treating manic patients when J. Cade noted its calming effect on animals in the late 1940s. In an intuitive yet reasonable leap, he administered it to ten manic patients and noted dramatic improvement in their symptoms.

In the early 1950s a compound originally labeled #4560 RP was developed as a potential antihistamine. Soon thereafter it was used as a preanesthetic to calm patients prior to surgery. Within two years it was found to be effective in the treatment of psychotic patients, and by 1954 the drug chlorpromazine was approved for use and was marketed in the United States under the brand name Thorazine. Similarly, the first antidepressant, iproniazid, a monoamine oxidase (MAO) inhibitor, was developed in the early 1950s to treat tuberculosis. Though iproniazid proved a dismal failure in treating TB, it was noted that depressed TB patients became significantly less depressed when taking it. The first tricyclic antidepressant, imipramine (Tofranil), was originally intended as an antipsychotic agent but was fortuitously found to have potent antidepressant properties. Thus the first few psychotropic (literally, "mind-turning") medications entered the pharmacologic arsenal almost by accident, allowing physicians to bring new weapons to bear in the fight against psychopathology.

Today, owing to tremendous advances in neuroscience and molecular biology, drugs are being rationally designed, sometimes one atom at a time, to have precise therapeutic effects. Nevertheless, despite the astonishing progress in rational drug development, serendipity will probably continue to play an important role as specific medications are discovered to have important "off-label" uses. For example, although originally labeled as antidepressants, Anafranil (clomipramine) and Prozac (fluoxetine) were observed to be effective in reducing the symptoms of obsessive-compulsive disorder (OCD). For years they were used "off label" to treat OCD sufferers until the FDA approved their use in OCD as well as depression. Now they can be prescribed "on-label" for both conditions, a fact that has more implications for third party payers, however, than for prescribers and patients.

Similarly, in the past few years several antiepileptic agents (e.g., Neurontin, Lamictal, and Topamax) have demonstrated efficacy in treating bipolar illnesses and are being used "off-label" with increasing frequency in bipolar patients. Indeed, even that arch-nemesis of good health, nicotine, is being investigated as a therapeutic for Parkinson's and Alzheimer's disease. Thus, despite the advancements that have brought us closer and closer to the design of pharmacologic "magic bullets," fortuitous discoveries continue to contribute to our therapeutic armamentarium.

The Human Brain

The practice of psychopharmacology and pharmacopsychology requires a thorough understanding of neuroscience since psychotropic drugs produce their effects by affecting neurochemistry. The term "psychotropic" literally means "mind-turning"; psychotropic agents aim to turn the mind from disorder to order, from imbalance to balance. Thus, to participate responsibly in the prescribing of psychotropics (whether autonomously or collaboratively) a good working knowledge of the brain is necessary. Obviously, a comprehensive review of neuroanatomy and neurophysiology would fill several books, so the following discussion is intended to provide only a glimpse into the wondrous territory of the brain. Indeed, even for readers who already possess a solid base of biological learning, this chapter can only commence what must be a career-long journey toward an increasingly broad and detailed understanding of neuroscience.

The human brain is without doubt the most complex organ, and perhaps the most complex single structure, on the planet. It is a three-pound, gelatinous blob of tissue carried in a bony, spherical container on our shoulders, yet it produces all human experience. When astronomers talk about outer space they speak in numbers so vast they boggle the imagination: 15 billion light-years of space-time folded around billions of galaxies containing trillions of stars, planets, and other celestial bodies. Similarly, when neuroscientists describe our brains—the tissue that gives rise to our universe of inner space—they speak of equally mind-numbing numbers: 15 billion transmitting neurons encased in more than a hundred billion supporting cells and creating trillions of interconnections. To put these numbers in perspective, consider that if you counted at the rate of one per second around the clock, 24 hours a day, seven days a week, it would take you more than 11.5 days to count to one million. To count up to one billion would take more than 31.5 years, and to reach one trillion would take 31,688 years!

To reduce this amazingly complicated organ to more manageable terms we will begin with a single brain cell. Then we will build up and out until we have integrated both the microscopic and macroscopic features of the brain into a coherent whole. Before venturing deeper into the territory of the central nervous system, however, it is helpful to define a few of the basic terms that form the foundation of neuroscience. These terms may seem esoteric at first, but by the time you have completed this section they should be well-understood and easily placed within the context of psychopharmacology. For a more detailed discussion see Lazarus, 1998.

Action potential: A self-propagating electrochemical impulse; the temporary loss or reversal of membrane polarization of a segment of the axon initiates the same sequence of events in the immediately adjacent portion of the axon, and so on in chain reaction, ultimately resulting in neurotransmitter release from the nerve terminal.

Axon and axon terminal: Axons are the transmitting neurofilaments of neurons. Electrochemical impulses called action potentials travel down the axon, resulting in the release of neurotransmitters from the terminal area, where they are stored in discrete packages called vesicles. The axon terminals are small knob-like swellings sometimes referred to as "boutons" from the French for "button." The terminal is synonymous with the presynaptic membrane.

Dendrites: The receptive neurofilaments of neurons, containing receptors where neurotransmitters bind. Also referred to as the postsynaptic membrane.

EPSP: Excitatory postsynaptic potential. A depolarizing stimulus that increases the likelihood that the receiving neuron will "fire" or initiate an action potential.

IPSP: Inhibitory postsynaptic potential. A stimulus that decreases the likelihood that the receiving neuron will fire, usually by hyperpolarizing it.

Neurofilaments: Fine threadlike structures (dendrites and axons) that are unique features of neurons which enable them to send and receive electrochemical signals.

Neuroglia: Literally, "nerve glue." Neural cells that support transmitting neurons both physically and nutritionally. There are two main types: (1) astrocytes, which are relatively large, star-shaped cells that connect neurons with the brain's blood supply and anchor them in place; and (2) oligodendroglia, which function principally to encase axons in insulating myelin sheaths which increase the rate at which they conduct impulses.

Neuron: A nerve cell that receives, integrates, and transmits electrochemical signals; the functional unit of the nervous system.

Neurotransmitter: A chemical messenger that carries information from one neuron to another at the synapse. (Auto-transmission can also occur. This is when a single neuron synapses with itself.) There are three general categories of neurotransmitter: (1) monoamines such as serotonin, norepinephrine, dopamine, and acetylcholine (the term *amine* simply refers to any organic molecule containing a nitrogen atom derived from ammonia, NH_3); (2) amino acids like γ-aminobutyric acid (GABA) and glutamate; and (3) neuropeptides or small proteins like beta-endorphin.

Polarization: The state of having opposite charges; the difference in electrochemical charge that develops between the outside and inside of the neural membrane such that the interior is negatively charged relative to the exterior. For all intents and purposes, polarization is synonymous with a neuron's resting membrane potential.

Receptors: Specialized molecular binding sites where neurotransmitters dock, thereby producing physiologic effects. Most receptors are large proteins that span the neural membrane thus having portions on the exterior of the cell where the neurotransmitters bind and portions in the cell's interior that subsequently initiate biochemical reactions within the neuron.

Soma: The cell body of the neuron, containing the nucleus and many other cytoplasmic organelles ("little organs" of the cell); also the point of origin of the neurofilaments, dendrites, and axon.

Synapse: The junction between two neurons' transmitting and receiving membranes. Usually a physical gap across which neurotransmitters diffuse when released.

TOE: Threshold of excitation. A critical degree of excitation or depolarization at which the neuron initiates an action potential or fires in an all-or-nothing fashion.

Neural Transmission: The Language of Chemical Communication

Neurons, also referred to as nerve cells, are the functional units of the nervous system. Essentially, neurons receive, integrate, and transmit electrochemical impulses via neurotransmitter-dependent, ionic and/or enzymatic interactions across cellular membranes (Carpenter, 1996; Hyman & Nestler, 1993). While at first this definition seems dauntingly complex, the elegance of neural structure and function will soon become clear.

Neurons have the complement of organelles typical of nucleated animal cells (i.e., cells having a nucleus, or eukaryotes), but have in addition unique features that make them especially well adapted to their roles as signal senders and receivers. Among these unique characteristics are the neurofilaments (fine threadlike structures), which include dendrites and axons (see Figure 10.1).

Although it is a slight oversimplification, dendrites can be thought of as the neuron's receptive membrane—the site where most incoming messages are received. Dendrites can originate at many points on the soma of a neuron. The axon, the neuron's transmitting component, is the structure that sends signals. While both dendrites and axons may branch out into numerous offshoots, usually the axon originates from a single site called the axon hillock where it leaves the cell body. Neurons synthesize neurotransmitters in their cell bodies, package them in membranous sacks called vesicles (which protect the neurotransmitter from en-

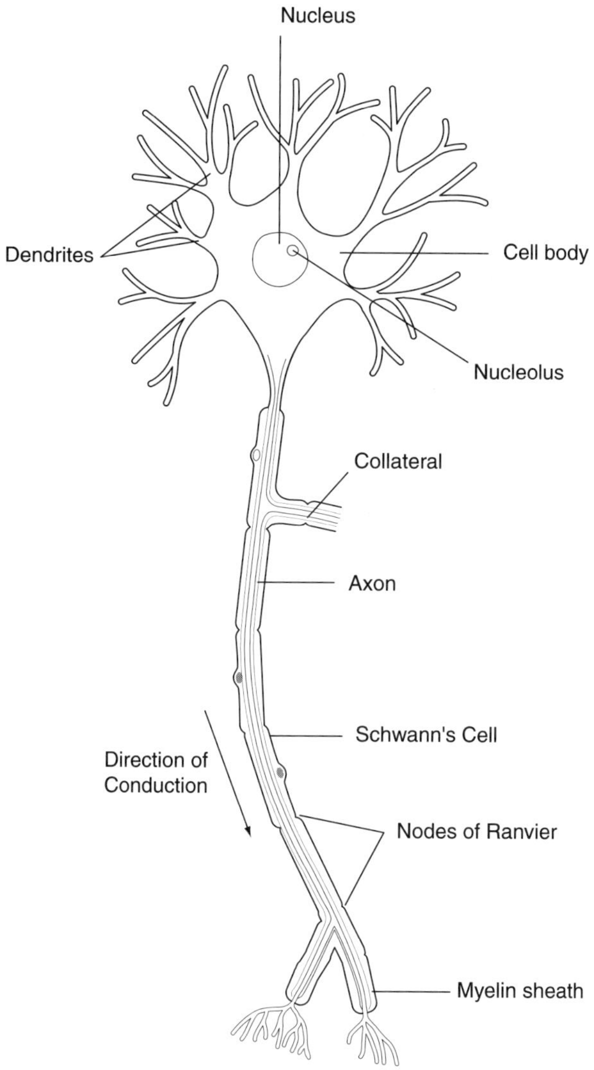

FIGURE 10.1 A Typical Neuron: Cell Body, Dendrites, and Axon with Myelin Sheath and Unsheathed Nodes

zymatic degradation), and store them in their axon terminals, where they await release upon the arrival of an action potential, as described below and illustrated in Figure 10.2.

When a neuron is at rest (i.e., not "firing" or sending an impulse) a very narrow layer of the axon's interior is negatively charged. Conversely, a very narrow layer of the fluid surrounding the axon is positively charged. This separation of charge, which ensures that the interior of the neuron is usually negatively charged relative to its exterior, is termed *polarization*. Polarization is due to a property of the cellular membrane called selective permeability, which

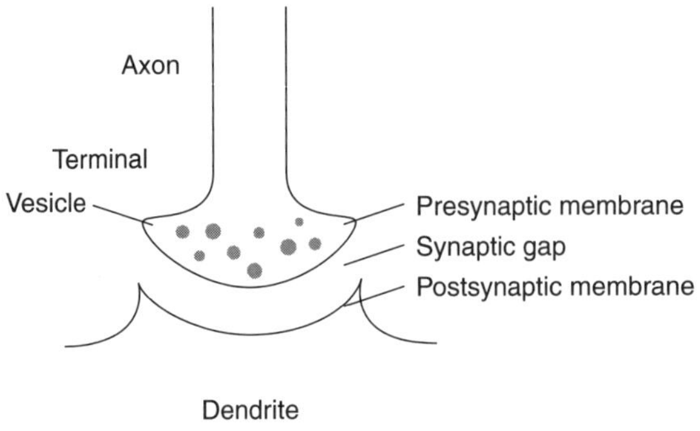

FIGURE 10.2 Close-up of a synapse, indicating axonal terminus with vesiculated neurotransmitter, gap junction, and postsynaptic dendritic membrane.

means that the membrane allows some molecules to cross into or out of the cell, but not others. Another important device that helps to polarize the neuron is an active (energy-requiring), membrane-bound, molecular pump that extrudes sodium ions and retrieves potassium ions. Since the pump has three binding sites for sodium atoms, but only two for potassium atoms, for every three sodium ions pumped out of the cell only two potassium ions are taken in. Because the resting neural membrane is normally impermeable to sodium, a concentration gradient develops so that the quantity of sodium ions outside the neuron is much greater than the quantity of sodium within it. Since substances tend to seek equilibrium by moving down concentration gradients (i.e., molecules will randomly move by diffusion from areas of high concentration to areas of lower concentration) a significant tension builds, tending to force sodium into the cell. Similarly, inside the cell's axon a concentration gradient develops that favors the movement of potassium ions out of the neuron.

The net result is that the immediate interior of the neuron is negatively charged relative to the immediate exterior. This charge difference of about 70 millivolts is called the neuron's *resting membrane potential* and can be thought of as analogous to a cocked crossbow (see Figure 10.3 for an illustration of this concept).

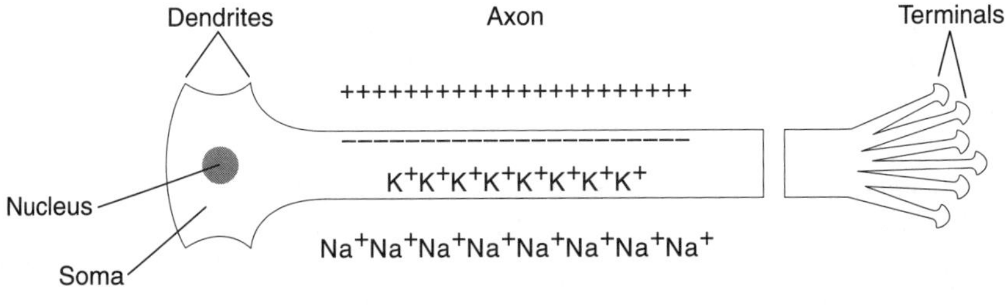

FIGURE 10.3 Schematic of a neuron's resting membrane potential illustrating the distribution of sodium and potassium ions and resultant charge differential.

If, by analogy, anything occurs to pull the trigger, the crossbow will fire by suddenly releasing its stored energy. Similarly, since the sodium and potassium ions are seeking to equalize their distribution across the axon's membrane (they are "cocked"), if anything occurs to increase the permeability of the membrane to them, an immediate rush of sodium into and potassium out of the cell will result. This flip-flop of ions—sodium in, potassium out—causes a change in the neuron's polarity so that its interior becomes momentarily positive relative to its exterior. When this happens, as shown in Figure 10.4, the neuron is said to have depolarized.

Certain neurotransmitter–receptor interactions increase membrane permeability to sodium ions, which decreases the degree of polarization (i.e., partial depolarization) because the interior membrane margin becomes less negatively charged due to the influx of positively charged sodium ions. This is referred to as an EPSP, or excitatory postsynaptic potential, and tends to push the neuron toward firing. Other neurotransmitter–receptor interactions produce an increase in the degree of polarization (i.e., hyperpolarization), either by increasing membrane permeability to negative ions like chloride, thus adding additional negative molecules to the already negative intracellular environment, or by further decreasing permeability to positive ions (so that even more accumulate outside the membrane). Such an event is called an IPSP, or inhibitory postsynaptic potential, which tends to inhibit the neuron from firing.

At any moment a neuron can be receiving dozens, perhaps even hundreds or thousands, of signals from many other neurons. Some might be EPSPs while others might be IPSPs. When the amount of excitation from EPSPs crosses a threshold—the threshold of excitation or TOE—the neuron fires (Carlson, 1994). What happens is basically a domino effect that proceeds as follows. When the TOE is reached, sodium ion channels open, thus increasing the membrane's permeability to sodium, which allows it to rush down its concentration gradient into the cell. This causes the membrane to become more permeable to potassium which, almost simultaneously with the sodium influx, rushes down its concentration gradient out of the cell. As this is happening the membrane's sodium ion channels close, restoring its resistance to sodium. Next, the membrane rapidly becomes resistant to potassium ions again. At this point, the sodium–potassium pump removes sodium ions and retrieves potassium ions, thus restoring the membrane's resting potential. This complete sequence of events is termed the *action potential* and is initiated at the axon hillock, the conical area of origin of the axon from the nerve cell body.

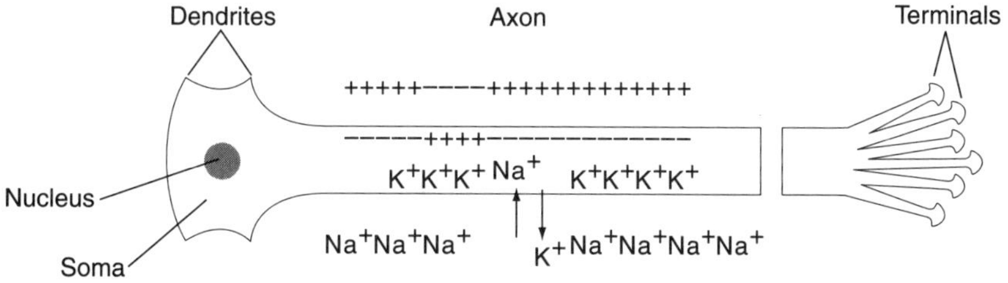

FIGURE 10.4 Axonal Depolarization with Charge Reversal Due to Sodium Influx and Potassium Efflux

The occurrence of an action potential at any point along the axon triggers a similar succession of changes in the immediately adjacent portion of the axon. As the sequence is replicated there, a similar series of events arises in the next axonal segment and so on down the line. In this manner, the action potential self-propagates like a wave along the entire length of the axon (Swonger & Constantine, 1983). Most neurons, furthermore, have myelin sheaths covering most of their axons like insulation around an electric cord. Unlike an electric cord's continuous cover, the myelin sheaths surrounding axons have discrete segments called nodes where the axon's membrane is unsheathed. This allows the action potential to jump from node to node, rather than traversing the entire length of the axon, thus increasing the speed of nerve signals. According to Sherwood (1993), some large myelinated nerve fibers, such as those supplying skeletal muscles, conduct impulses as fast as 120 meters per second (360 miles per hour), compared with speeds of only a few millimeters per second (2 or so miles per hour) in small, unmyelinated fibers like those supplying the digestive tract.

When the action potential reaches the terminal portions of the axon, a cascade of events takes place that results in the release of neurotransmitters into the synaptic space, a process called *exocytosis*. Once released, the neurotransmitters diffuse across the synapse where some of them bind to specific molecular receptors on the postsynaptic membrane. Depending on the type of neurotransmitter and the nature of the receptor, the neurotransmitter–receptor interaction will produce either an EPSP or an IPSP. When the sum of the EPSPs exceeds the TOE, the postsynaptic neuron will fire. This entire process, illustrated in Figure 10.5, is referred to as *neural transmission*.

In addition to regulating ion channels in the cellular membrane, many neurotransmitter–receptor interactions activate second-messenger systems. While a detailed discussion of second-messenger systems is beyond the scope of this chapter, suffice it to say that second-messenger systems involve complex cascades of biological reactions that take place in the cell's interior. In such cases, the neurotransmitter is the "first messenger" that, upon binding to its receptor, activates or inhibits other chemicals inside the cell that then also function as chemical messengers. These second messengers in turn initiate a variety of physiologic

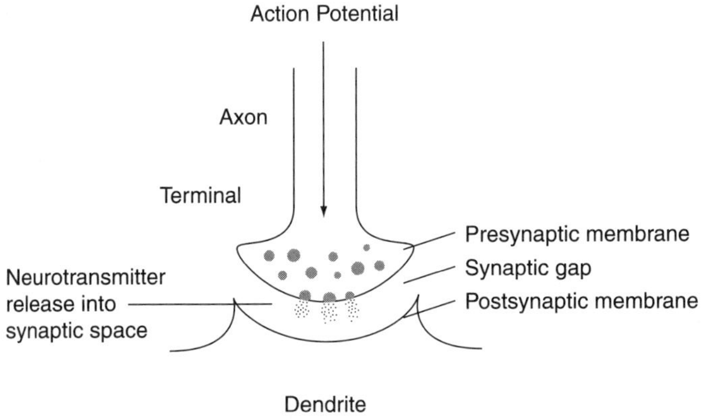

FIGURE 10.5 Close-Up of Synapse with Arrival of Action Potential and Release of Neurotransmitter into Synaptic Gap

events, usually involving activation of specific enzymes, that produce additional (third) chemical messengers and biochemical reactions that can ultimately influence the genetic functions of the cell (e.g., Craig & Stitzel, 1994; Hyman & Nestler, 1993). Indeed, it is through these second-messenger mediated intracellular phenomena that most psychotropic medications are believed to exert their therapeutic effects.

Neurotransmitters

As described above, neurons are specialized cells uniquely adapted to receiving, integrating, and transmitting electrochemical impulses by way of neurotransmitter molecules. Currently three major types of neurotransmitters are known, classified according to their chemical composition or molecular structure: monoamines, amino acids, and neuropeptides. While a detailed summary of all of the known transmitter molecules is beyond the scope of this chapter, I shall highlight some of the important aspects of each type.

Often students of neurophysiology are eager to know if a given neurotransmitter is excitatory or inhibitory. The answer to this commonly posed question is "it depends." That is, while some transmitters are typically described as inhibitory (e.g., GABA) and others as excitatory (e.g., norepinephrine), whether or not a given neurotransmitter produces an IPSP or an EPSP depends on the receptor it binds to. Most transmitters bind to several subtypes of receptors, not just one. For example, there are at least seven varieties of serotonin receptors, five kinds of dopamine receptors, and several receptors for norepinephrine (Hyman & Nestler, 1993). At some receptors norepinephrine is excitatory (e.g., at most of its targets in the sympathetic nervous system) while at others it is inhibitory (e.g., at alpha-2 receptors in the locus ceruleus, a brain stem structure implicated in acute anxiety and panic). Thus, there are probably no absolutely excitatory or invariably inhibitory neurotransmitters. Postsynaptic potentials always depend on the specific transmitter–receptor interaction. Furthermore, many neurotransmitters are found all through the body, not only in the central nervous system (CNS), and play many different roles at these peripheral locations. Serotonin is widely distributed throughout the gut and on the surface of red blood cells. Epinephrine and norepinephrine are hormones released from the adrenal gland, and acetylcholine is the transmitter present at all neuromuscular junctions (i.e., the points where nerves connect with muscles), to name only a few examples.

The best-known small molecule neurotransmitters are the monoamines, which consist of a variety of chemicals, including serotonin, norepinephrine, epinephrine, dopamine, acetylcholine, and histamine. Serotonin has many important functions in the CNS and is thought by some to be the "workhorse" of neurotransmitters. It is involved in sleep, arousal, motivation, appetite, and sex. Norepinephrine plays a "Paul Revere" role in the brain, in that it sounds the alarms that mobilize our fight-or-flight stress response. Both serotonin and norepinephrine appear to be involved in depressive illnesses. Norepinephrine's chemical cousin, epinephrine, is not well-understood as a neurotransmitter, but appears to be involved in regulating some autonomic (life support) processes. Dopamine is critically important in mediating extrapyramidal motor control (see below), and when deficient results in symptoms of Parkinson's disease. It is also involved in regulating the release of some important pituitary hormones, and seems inextricably woven into the processes that underlie psychotic disorders like schizophrenia. Acetylcholine's role in the CNS seems related to learning and memory. Alzheimer's disease, a progressive neurodegenerative illness whose hallmark is memory loss, appears to involve the degeneration of the brain's major acetylcholine-producing structure, the hippocampus. Although histamine is now known to be a neurotransmitter as well as ubiquitous outside of the CNS, its function in the brain is not well understood.

The amino acid neurotransmitters that have been best elucidated are the predominantly inhibitory transmitters GABA (γ-aminobutyric acid) and glycine; also glutamate and aspartate, which both appear to be predominantly excitatory. In addition to monoamines and amino acids, the brain contains an unknown number of peptide (small protein) neurotransmitters called *neuropeptides.* Two of the best-studied neuropeptides are β-endorphin, which is a naturally occurring opiate-like molecule, and substance P, which appears to be important in conveying pain sensations and is now under investigation for its suspected role in depression. Many of the peptide transmitters are believed to act as neuromodulators or neuroregulators by modulating or regulating the binding of other transmitters, such as the monoamines and amino acids, at their receptors. They are also thought to exert longer-lasting postsynaptic influences than monoamine and amino acid transmitters (Carlson, 1994).

By far the best-studied neurotransmitters are the monoamine transmitters, especially acetylcholine and norepinephrine, since they occur in high concentrations in the peripheral nervous system and are, therefore, more accessible and more segregated than centrally located transmitters. Ironically, despite being so well-studied relative to other neurotransmitters, the monoamines collectively account for only 5 to 10 percent of the synapses in the human brain, whereas the amino acid transmitters account for up to 60 percent of CNS synapses (Kaplan & Sadock, 1991).

While only a handful of neurotransmitters have been confidently classified to date, it is believed that as many as several hundred neurotransmitters are yet to be identified. To make matters still more complex, it is now known that most neurons have co-localized neurotransmitters (Hyman & Nestler, 1993); that is, a single neuron may produce and release more than one neurotransmitter. This recent discovery flies in the face of the long-held Dales hypothesis, which states, "one neuron, one neurotransmitter." Indeed, it appears to be the norm that a given neuron can release as many as three different neurotransmitters simultaneously, usually one of each of the three major types—a monoamine, an amino acid, and a neuropeptide.

To complicate things even further, there are numerous permutations of synaptic connections (Hyman & Nestler, 1993). Most synapses are axodendritic (i.e., the axon of one neuron synapses with the dendrite of another). But there are also axosomatic (axon to cell body) and axoaxonic (axon to axon) synapses. In addition, dendrites may also synapse with each other in dendrodendritic connections. And to introduce yet another layer of complexity, not all neurons communicate at chemical synapses. Some neurons interconnect at electrical synapses and actually pass ions back and forth directly into each other's cytoplasm (Kandel, Schwartz, & Jessell, 1991).

Neurons in and of themselves are not especially smart. As we have described, they can do very few things, such as fire or not fire, and communicate with a relatively limited vocabulary of only a few types of chemicals. But put one hundred billion of them together in a small area, and let each "speak" with thousands of others in very specific and precise ways, and a literal brainstorm of activity will take place, resulting in the infinite diversity of human conscious experience—experience that depends on an extremely delicate biochemical balance. Even a slight change in the concentration or activity of a single neurotransmitter can cause a physiologic chain reaction, resulting in profound and far-reaching psychological repercussions. Having outlined the fundamentals of neurophysiology and neural transmission, we will now discuss the structure and function of the adult brain.

Structure and Function of the Adult Human Brain

On a macroscopic level, our brains are actually three brains in one—an amazingly complex origami of tissue folded into a single organ. At the base of our brain, just above the spinal cord, is the brain stem, which regulates the basic mechanisms of life support; nonconscious or autonomic processes like breathing, digestion, and circulation. This is the part of our nervous system inherit from the earliest true-brained creatures. Resting on top of and wrapped around our brain stem is the limbic system, which derives its name from the Latin word *limbus* meaning a border or edge. The limbic system is a group of interrelated structures that appears to mediate many biological drives and emotional states. This is the legacy of the reptiles—the so-called "reptilian brain" that made vertebrate survival on land possible. But by far the most recent part of the brain is its cerebral cortex, literally its crowning glory. The intricately convoluted outer layer of the brain, a mere ¼ inch thick, gives rise to all the conscious, sensory, and perceptual phenomena we think of as human experience. It is our cortex that allows us to perceive the world through our senses; to see, smell, hear, taste, and touch. And perhaps most importantly, the cortex serves as our thinking cap. It allows us to plan, to learn, to speak, and to behave in a manner that is uniquely human.

Since a comprehensive atlas of structural and functional neuroanatomy would more than fill more than this entire book, we will instead provide an overview of some of the brain's most obvious features. To reiterate an important point, our brains are really three brains in one: a primitive brain stem responsible for basic life support and some aspects of motor integration; a reptilian brain or limbic system responsible for much of our motivation, emotional experience, and biological drives; and the cerebrum, the seat of consciousness, intellectual abilities, and voluntary behavior. Refer to Figure 10.6 for an illustration of this structural arrangement and some important neuroanatomical landmarks.

The brain stem is the portion of the CNS at the very top of the spinal cord, at the base of the brain. It consists of two major parts, the medulla oblongata (often just called the medulla) and the pons, plus an adjacent structure called the cerebellum. The medulla lies closest to the spinal cord and contains centers for the regulation of heartbeat, breathing, blood pressure, and muscle tone. It also houses important reflex centers for vomiting, coughing, sneezing, swallowing, and hiccuping. In addition, the medulla gives rise to the reticular (net-like) formation, one of the oldest structures in the brain—a direct descendant of the primitive nerve nets that still function as nervous systems in such primitive creatures as the hydra. The reticular formation receives sensory information from various pathways and relays it to the spinal cord, limbic system, and cortex. It plays important roles in sleep, arousal, selective attention, and many of the reflexes mentioned above.

The pons is a rather large bulge in the brain stem lying right above the medulla and directly in front of the cerebellum. Like the medulla it contains a portion of the reticular formation, and is similarly important in sleep and arousal. Behind the pons sits the cerebellum ("little brain") which, as its name implies, resembles a miniature cerebrum. It is covered by a cerebellar cortex and has a cluster of deep cerebellar nuclei that project to its cortex just

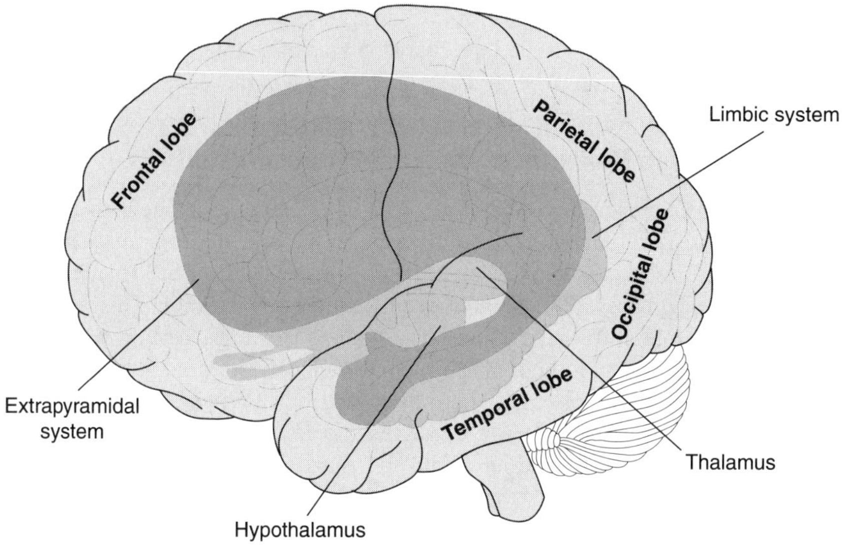

FIGURE 10.6 Cross Section of a Human Brain Illustrating Brain Stem, Limbic/Subcortical Structures, and Cerebral Cortex

as the cerebrum has a set of internal nuclei that project to its. (In neuroanatomy, nuclei—plural for nucleus—are essentially homogeneous groups of nerve cells in the brain or spinal cord that can be clearly demarcated from neighboring cell groups.) The cerebellum enables us to stand, walk, and perform highly coordinated movements. It receives information from the cortex about vision, hearing, equilibrium, and individual muscle actions, which it integrates to exert a coordinating effect on movements. Damage to the cerebellum results in abnormal motion patterns such as jerky and poorly coordinated movements. New evidence based on neuroimaging data (positron emission tomography and functional magnetic resonance imaging or MRI) suggests that the cerebellum has some cognitive functions as well (e.g., Raichle, 1998).

The limbic system is a set of interconnected structures lying deep within the brain. It appears that the limbic system originally formed most of the cortical surface of the CNS, but over time was eclipsed by the neocortex (literally, "new cortex"), which swelled into the modern cerebral hemispheres, completely engulfing the older limbic structures, which now appear as a curved border ("limbus" is a circular edge or border) deep in the brain's interior. The functions of the limbic system are many and complex. Much of the limbic system appears to be dedicated to governing emotion and motivation. It contains nuclei that are important in regulating the body's inner environment (e.g., temperature) and biologic drives like hunger, thirst, and sex. In addition, some of the limbic system is integrally involved with learning and memory.

The largest portion of the human brain is the cerebrum, which is responsible for conscious experience and voluntary behavior. The cerebrum is divided into halves by a deep longitudinal groove, producing right and left cerebral hemispheres which are connected by a massive bridge of nerve fibers called the *corpus callosum* (see Figure 10.7).

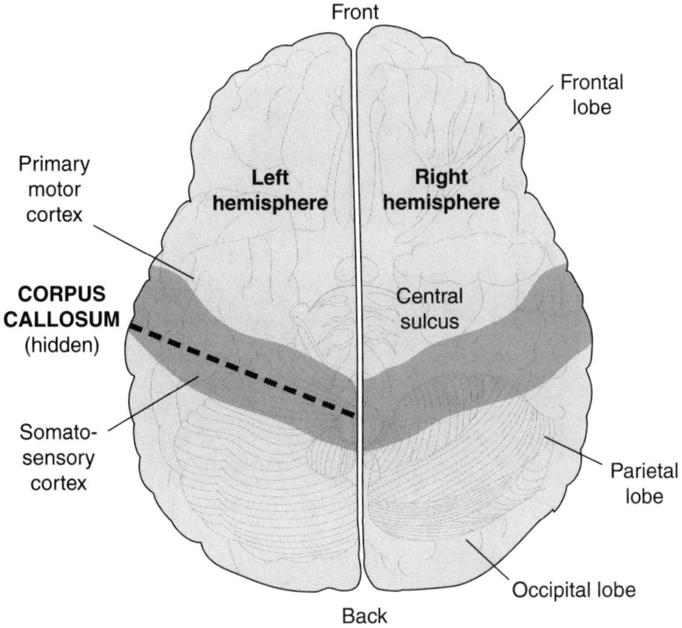

FIGURE 10.7 Top View of the Brain Illustrating Longitudinal Division into the Right and Left Hemispheres and Indicating the Corpus Callosum

The cerebral hemispheres are dramatically convoluted, which greatly increases their surface area relative to an equally-sized smooth brain. These convolutions consist of large grooves called *fissures,* smaller grooves called *sulci* (plural of *sulcus*), and *gyri* (plural of *gyrus*), the conspicuous bulges between adjacent grooves. In general terms, the entire cerebrum can be mapped according to its three major functions. First, there are association areas which are believed to produce and control intellectual, creative and artistic, learning, and memory processes. Second, there are sensory areas which receive afferent (i.e., directed toward the CNS) nerve impulses from the sense organs to produce sensory experience. Third, the motor areas of the cerebrum initiate voluntary movements by way of efferent (outgoing) nerve impulses that send signals from the CNS to effectors such as muscles.

As shown in Figure 10.8, each cerebral hemisphere is further divided into four lobes, the frontals, parietals, temporals, and occipitals, which govern specific aspects of cognitive, sensory, and motor functions. The frontal lobes are responsible for much of the higher intellectual processes including planning, concentrating, language, complex problem solving, and judgment. In addition, the posterior region of the frontal lobe is the primary motor cortex that allows us to move our skeletal muscles voluntarily. Some people have suggested a dichotomy vis-à-vis the different functions of the right and left frontal lobes: the left lobe thinks in words and mediates rational, logical, and analytical operations; the right lobe thinks spatially and governs processes like creativity, intuition, and artistry. While some data support this division-of-labor model of the brain (e.g., Gazzaniga & LeDoux, 1978), it is generally agreed that the

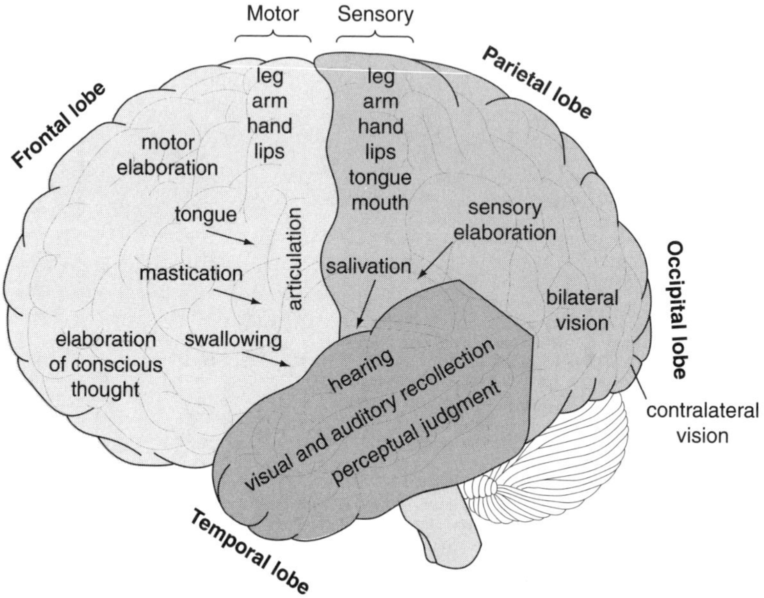

FIGURE 10.8 Side View of a Cerebral Hemisphere Indicating Its Four Lobes

two hemispheres share information via the corpus callosum, and thus think holistically. One truly dichotomous aspect of the brain, however, is that as far as motor and sensory functions are concerned, the left hemisphere controls most of the right side of the body and the right hemisphere controls most of the left side of the body (see discussion of decussation below).

The parietal lobes, which sit between the frontal and occipital lobes at the top of the brain, contain the somatosensory cortexes that allow us to perceive sensations from our bodies and skin like touch, temperature, pressure, and pain. They also have association areas that function in the understanding of speech, interpretation of sensations, and use of words to express thoughts and feelings. Below the parietal lobes and partially under and behind the frontal lobes are the temporal lobes, which have sensory areas responsible for hearing and smell. Their association areas, like the parietals, aid in the interpretation of sensory experiences, especially complex sensory patterns such as those involved in music and visual memory. The occipitals are the rearmost lobes of the cerebrum and contain the primary visual cortexes. This is where the neurophysiological phenomena that give rise to the conscious experience of vision take place. The association areas of the occipital lobes function in visual interpretation and combine visual images with other sensory experiences.

Another crucial function of the brain is the initiation, coordination, and integration of voluntary movement. This aspect of behavior is carried out by the brain's motor systems, some of which we have already touched on, but which warrant additional discussion since some psychotropics can have dramatic impact on motor functioning. Voluntary movement is the end-product of a complex sequence of neuronal and muscular events involving the three major components of the motor system: the corticospinal tracts, the basal ganglia, and the cerebellum. The corticospinal nerve fibers originate at cell bodies in the motor cortex of the frontal lobe and pass through structures deep in the brain stem before continuing along the spinal cord (hence the name "corticospinal") to their targets at neuromuscular junctions.

Corticospinal nerve tracts decussate (i.e., cross over like the arms of an X, X being the Roman symbol for the number 10, "decussis" in Latin) where they pass through conspicuous, pyramid-shaped structures in the medulla called the *medullary pyramids*. For this reason the corticospinal tracts are often referred to as the *pyramidal tracts* or the *pyramidal motor system*. Lesions of these fibers result in weakness or total paralysis of voluntary movement. Decussation of nerve fibers explains how many sensory and motor functions are controlled by opposite sides of the brain. Sensory and motor fibers originating in the left cerebral hemisphere cross over to innervate corresponding tissues on the right side of the body and vice versa. Thus, damage to left cerebral sensory-motor tissue results in deficits on the right side of the body and right hemisphere damage results in left-side deficits.

Another important motor system is the basal ganglia, a group of interrelated structures lying deep in the forebrain. Unlike the corticospinal or pyramidal tracts, motor output from the basal ganglia does not pass through the medullary pyramids and hence is called the *extrapyramidal system*. Lesions of this system cause involuntary movements such as those seen in patients with Parkinson's disease. Indeed, as we will discuss in more detail later, some psychotropic medications, mainly the typical antipsychotic agents, produce Parkinsonian side effects and other so-called extrapyramidal symptoms (EPS), by interfering with dopamine transmission at the basal ganglia.

The last of the major motor systems is the cerebellum, which we have already discussed. Disorders of the cerebellum are associated with abnormalities in the rate, range, and force of movement. In a healthy individual the three motor systems work in concert to produce, integrate, refine, coordinate, and execute all voluntary motor behavior.

Having laid down the conceptual foundation of neuroscience, we will now consider basic pharmacology. We can then synthesize the two into a coherent discussion of psychopharmacology, and segue into the fundamentals of pharmacopsychology.

Basic Pharmacology

One of the most fundamental concepts in pharmacology is that of molecule–receptor interactions. Recall from the discussion above on neural transmission that receptors are specialized molecular binding sites where substances such as neurotransmitters dock, thereby producing physiologic effects. Most receptors are large proteins that span the cellular membrane, having portions on the exterior of the cell where molecules bind, and portions in the cell's interior that subsequently initiate intracellular biochemical reactions. This concept applies not only to the action of naturally occurring or endogenous substances such as neurotransmitters and hormones, but also to exogenous substances like drugs. Indeed, many drugs mimic the effects of hormones and neurotransmitters because they bind with the same receptors as these endogenous substances do. Hence, most drugs do not do anything radically new to the body. Rather they mimic or influence naturally occurring processes. Of course, with the advent of gene therapies, new mechanisms of drug action will no doubt involve physiologically unprecedented phenomena; for the present, however, and certainly with most currently available psychotropics, the traditional mechanisms of drug action are sufficient to explain how drugs work, or at least how they initiate physiologic and cellular events that lead to a therapeutic response. A summary of most of the postulated mechanisms of drug action follows.

Drugs can:

- mimic a neurotransmitter or hormone. If the drug produces an effect to the same extent as the naturally occurring molecule it is called a *full agonist.* If it produces the same general response but to a lesser effect than the endogenous substance, it is a *partial agonist.* If a drug augments or facilitates an endogenous compound's effects without actually binding to the natural substance's receptor it is referred to as an *indirect agonist.*
- prevent endogenous compounds from binding to their receptors by occupying the receptor without producing a physiologic response. Such drugs are referred to as *antagonists.* As is the case with agonists, if a drug diminishes or prevents an endogenous compound's effects without actually binding to the natural substance's receptor it is referred to as an *indirect antagonist.*
- bind to a receptor and provoke an action opposite to that of the endogenous substance. Such drugs are called *inverse agonists.* Just as there are full and partial agonists, there are full and partial inverse agonists.
- inhibit or activate enzymes. Since enzymes are crucial in orchestrating a myriad of biological processes, this mechanism has many implications. For example, a drug can inhibit an enzyme that is an essential link in the chain of events necessary to synthesize some product, thereby preventing that product from being produced. Or, a drug can paralyze an enzyme that is necessary to deactivate a biologically active substance, thereby increasing or prolonging its activity.
- block transporters or reuptake pumps that usually operate to recycle neurotransmitters.
- cause more or less neurotransmitters to be released from axon terminals, for example by causing more vesicles to release their contents upon depolarization or by causing the vesicles themselves to become leaky, thus depleting their contents.
- influence the degree that ion channels open or close in the cell membranes.

While this is by no means an exhaustive summary, it is a reasonable sample of the most common mechanisms through which drugs produce their effects. What is more, a single drug can act through more than one mechanism at a time. That is, some drugs have multiple drug actions that produce not just the desired therapeutic effect but side effects as well. For example, the tricyclic antidepressant amitriptyline (Elavil) acts as an indirect agonist for the neurotransmitters norepinephrine and (to a lesser extent) serotonin by blocking their neuronal reuptake pumps. At the same time, it acts as an acetylcholine antagonist by occupying the acetylcholine receptor, thus blocking the action of acetylcholine at its binding site and causing such anticholinergic side effects as dry mouth and constipation. Amitriptyline inhibits sodium ion channels, which results in slowed depolarization, especially in the cardiac muscle, causing this medicine to be prescribed with great caution to patients with compromised cardiac function. We will explore mechanisms of drug action further in the sections of this chapter that deal with pharmacodynamics and psychopharmacology. But before turning to the topic of pharmacodynamics, which involves studying the actions of drugs in the body, we will first discuss the subject of pharmacokinetics, which deals with what the body does to drugs.

Pharmacokinetics

Pharmacokinetics is the mathematical description of the rate and extent of absorption, distribution, metabolization, and elimination of drugs in the body (Gwilt, 1994). Rather than describing these phenomena in mathematical terms, we will discuss them from a conceptual viewpoint. In simplest terms, pharmacokinetics is what the body does to a drug once it is administered—namely absorb, distribute, metabolize, and finally eliminate it. Hence, the four phases of pharmacokinetics are usually referred to as absorption, distribution, metabolization, and elimination, and are denoted by the acronym ADME. (Sometimes the term *biotransformation* is used synonymously with metabolization, rendering the alternative acronym ADBE. Some people refer to the final phase as *excretion* rather than *elimination,* but, of course, this doesn't change the acronym.)

Absorption

Absorption involves the passage of the drug from its site of administration into the blood. Obviously, for a drug to have any effect it must be absorbed into the system. Usually, drugs are taken orally (i.e., "po," from the Latin *per os,* "by or through the mouth") and most absorption, therefore, takes place in the gastrointestinal tract, chiefly in the duodenum and first few feet of the small intestine, the proximal jejunum. While there are several other routes of administration, the vast majority of psychotropics are taken by mouth and unless specifically stated otherwise, all examples in this chapter assume the oral route of administration. Nevertheless, for the sake of thoroughness, we will mention in passing the other ways through which drugs can enter the body. Drugs can be administered through the skin by topical preparations or transdermal patches; subcutaneously (under the skin), intramuscularly, or intravenously via injection; rectally or vaginally with suppositories; in the eye or ear with drops; and even through inhalation, as with gases. Generally, the terms *take, apply, insert,* and *place* refer to the oral, topical, rectal/vaginal, and eye/ear routes, respectively. One additional route that warrants mention is the sublingual, which involves placing the drug under the tongue. This circumvents the gastrointestinal tract by allowing the drug to be absorbed directly into venous circulation through the capillary bed at the base of the tongue, which, as we will discuss later, can have great significance.

As mentioned above, most drugs are taken by mouth, which means that they are absorbed in the stomach and small intestine. Indeed, in much the same way that nutrients are absorbed, drugs enter circulation by absorption into the venous blood supply of the digestive tract. This means that the drug must pass through several biological barriers before it can enter circulation, including the membranes of the cells lining the stomach and intestines and the walls of the blood vessels into which the drug need enter. Broadly speaking, there are two mechanisms by which molecules can cross cell membranes: passive processes in which the driving force is a concentration gradient, and active transport, which requires the expenditure of cellular energy and can drive molecules against concentration gradients.

The most common passive means by which a drug can cross a cellular membrane include diffusion (random movement of molecules from an area of high concentration to one of low concentration), filtration (movement of molecules through pores in the membrane), and facilitated diffusion (when a substance temporarily binds to a specific carrier molecule that ferries it across the membrane). Active transport is the energy-dependent movement of molecules across membranes, usually against their concentration gradient. In active transport, as with facilitated diffusion, the substance to be transported reversibly binds to a carrier molecule (usually a protein) that conveys it across the membrane. In general, drugs will not be actively transported unless they very closely resemble the endogenous substances (such as glucose and amino acids) that are the normal passengers for the carrier system involved. Most drugs are absorbed from the intestinal tract through passive processes, particularly diffusion (Gram, 1994).

There are many factors that can influence the degree to which a drug is absorbed, most of which can be grouped into two categories: physiochemical (i.e., relating to the physical and chemical) properties of the drug, and patient variables. Physiochemical properties include such factors as the drug's dissolvability, its solubility in fat (lipophilicity) versus its solubility in water (hydrophilicity), whether it is an acid or a base, and its molecular size, to name only a few. Patient variables include whether the drug is taken with food or on an empty stomach, as well as a variety of other factors including the patient's age, weight, gender, and general health.

Distribution

Distribution involves those processes by which the drug, once absorbed, is delivered to the tissues and eventually to its sites of action. The system responsible for this phase of pharmacokinetics is the circulatory system, which delivers a prodigious assortment of materials to the furthest outposts of the body. Once absorbed into the blood supply of the digestive tract, a drug is considered to be in general or systemic circulation. Before it can be delivered to its site of action, usually the CNS in the case of psychotropics, it must journey through a series of blood vessels. Substances that are absorbed into the blood supply from the digestive system enter into small veins called *venules* which, along with tiny arteries call *arterioles,* make up the capillary beds. In addition to absorbing nutrients and drugs, capillary beds deliver fresh, oxygenated blood to organs and remove their waste products. Venous blood from the digestive tract eventually makes its way to the heart, where it is pumped to the lungs for oxygenation (and to remove gaseous waste, mostly carbon dioxide), then returned to the heart, from which it enters systemic circulation. As a general rule, veins convey deoxygenated blood *to* the heart, arteries transport oxygenated blood *from* the heart. (An exception to this is in adult cardiopulmonary circulation, where arteries carry deoxygenated blood from the heart to the lungs and veins return it, once oxygenated, to the heart for pumping to the rest of the body.)

As a drug proceeds to its ultimate destination, it must cross many barriers before reaching its site of action. Much as it had to pass through various biological membranes to enter the bloodstream, it must cross various membranes to reach its site of action. One important obstacle that most centrally acting drugs must surmount is the blood–brain barrier (BBB) which insulates and protects the CNS from toxins by allowing only certain molecules to enter the brain. Most psychotropics are fat-soluble compounds, and since the BBB preferentially allows fat-soluble substances to pass, as a general rule psychotropics have little difficulty entering the CNS. Similar to the blood–brain barrier is the blood–testis barrier, which also confers a degree of protection by allowing passage of only certain molecules. Indeed, the relative impenetrability of the blood–testis barrier is why it is so difficult to deliver chemotherapeutic compounds to testicular neoplasms.

Generally, distribution of a medication throughout the body is a two-phase process. Initially, most of the drug is delivered to the organs that have the richest supply of blood, such as the liver, heart, lungs, kidneys, and brain. Subsequently, the drug moves into tissues that have less extensive perfusion, such as muscles, fat, and bone. These latter areas are referred to as *reservoirs* or *compartments,* because drugs can accumulate in them. Usually an equilibrium is reached, and the flow of drug between compartments becomes relatively stable. With most drugs, equilibrium is reached fairly rapidly (within several minutes), at which time the process of distribution is said to be complete (Preston et al., 1997) and the drug is believed to be uniformly distributed throughout the body. That is, the concentration of the drug in the blood is assumed to be the same as the concentration in organs and tissues. A mathematically derived value called the *apparent volume of distribution* (V_d) provides a rough estimate of the overall distribution of a drug in the body.

Although many drugs reach equilibrium relatively quickly, some psychotropics do not distribute uniformly throughout the body, because of their affinity for muscle and fat cells. After chronic administration, significant concentrations of drug can accumulate in these reservoirs, which has obvious implications when the drug is discontinued, since it can leach out of these compartments and thus prolong the life of the drug in the system. While this can be problematic in some cases, this phenomenon also has important therapeutic utility in that some drugs can be delivered to these reservoirs deliberately to allow for sustained therapeutic action. For example, some antipsychotic agents (e.g., Prolixin) can be administered by injection once every several weeks, which greatly improves patient compliance due to ease of dosing and consistent drug effects.

Another important mechanism through which drugs can be compartmentalized in the body involves the binding of drugs to plasma proteins. Blood plasma is the fluid (noncellular) portion of circulating blood and contains a great many dissolved substances such as electrolytes, sugars, hormones, and proteins. One of the most common proteins in blood plasma is albumin. Although some drugs are simply dissolved in the blood fluid, most are associated with plasma proteins, like albumin, to which they bind reversibly. Recall that the receptors to which neurotransmitters bind are large proteins into which the neurotransmitter fits like a key into a lock. Also, recall that many drugs act by binding to these same receptors. Plasma proteins are very similar in structure to receptors. Hence it is not surprising that many drugs bind to the plasma proteins in much the same way that they couple with receptors. The extent of this binding will significantly influence the drug's distribution, concentration at effectors (i.e., sites of action), and rate of metabolization and elimination, because only the unbound drug can diffuse through membranes. Thus, only the unbound fraction of the drug is biologically active. Furthermore, extensive protein binding results in the blood's serving as a circulating drug reservoir. As free or unbound drug is eliminated from the body, more drug dissociates from the plasma proteins, replacing the unbound drug that has been lost. Therefore, extensive protein binding can prolong drug availability and duration of action.

Another important phenomenon is displacement of drug from plasma proteins. The binding of drugs to plasma proteins is usually nonspecific, meaning that many different drugs can interact with the same binding site. A drug with a higher affinity for the protein's binding site may displace a drug with a weaker affinity from it. Since only the unbound portion of a drug is biologically active, this can have profound pharmacologic and clinical implications. For example, if drug B displaces a significant amount of drug A from its protein binding sites, there will be more free drug A available to cross cell membranes, which will result in a greater concentration at its site of action and an intensified pharmacologic effect.

Metabolization

Before blood from the gastrointestinal system reaches the heart and enters systemic circulation, it first passes through the liver, the major organ of metabolization or biotransformation. By gross simplification, the liver can be likened to a biochemical processing plant that modifies substances passing through it. Indeed, the liver contains an enormous amount and variety of enzymes that act as molecular processors, ultimately changing or transforming the biological substances that encounter them. This is why the term *biotransformation* is synonymous with *metabolization*—because through the metabolic action of its enzymes, the liver biologically transforms molecules from their original form, the parent compound, to new products called *metabolites.*

The major drug-metabolizing enzymes of the liver are often called the *cytochrome P450 system* and include more than 30 related enzymes. These enzymes, which evolved over one billion years ago during the era of plant–animal differentiation (Preskorn, 1996), have the ability to metabolize foreign biological substances ("xenobiotics"). These enzymes allowed the animals that possessed them to metabolize plant toxins before they could enter the animal's systemic circulation, thus protecting them from harm. Obviously, such a system would confer tremendous survival advantages and be passed on to future generations and new species. Since many drugs originally come from plant products, and resemble plant toxins, they are readily metabolized by this same system of enzymes. In addition to providing protection from toxicity, these enzymes serve to transform substances into forms that can be readily eliminated from the body. Indeed, these enzymes determine, in part, what compounds can become drugs, because if a mechanism does not exist to eliminate a substance from the body it cannot be (safely) used as a drug.

The activities of the cytochrome P450 enzymes are subject to change. Basically, their numbers and activity can be increased (enzyme induction) or decreased (enzyme inhibition) through the actions of drugs and their metabolites. Although the analogy is not precise, these phenomena can be thought of as similar to the agonist and antagonist effects that drugs produce at receptors, which in many cases resemble the enzymes structurally. For example, the antiepileptic and mood-stabilizing agent carbamazepine (Tegratol) induces certain enzymes which can cause a reduction in another drug's bioavailability, if that drug happens to be metabolized by the enzymes that Tegratol induces. Alternatively, the SSRI fluvoxemine (Luvox) is a potent inhibitor of the enzyme that metabolizes the antianxiety agent alprazolam (Xanax). Therefore, if Luvox and Xanax are co-administered, the effects of the Xanax can be significantly amplified because of Luvox's inhibitory effect on the enzyme that Xanax depends on for its biotransformation and eventual elimination from the body. Other factors, such as smoking and liver disease, can induce or inhibit many of the cytochrome P450 enzymes and thus influence the metabolization of many drugs.

Another important aspect of metabolization is the "first-pass" effect, which simply refers to the fact that drugs absorbed into the bloodstream from the digestive tract first pass through the liver before entering systemic circulation. On this pass through the liver, drugs can undergo extensive metabolization by the cytochrome P450 system and other enzymes present in the liver. On one hand, this phenomenon can significantly reduce the concentration of many drugs, resulting in a diminished therapeutic effect. On the other, some drugs (called *prodrugs*) must be metabolized before they become biologically active. For example, the benzodiazepine clorazepate (Tranxene) is an inactive prodrug which becomes the active compound desmethyldiazepam once it has been metabolized by liver enzymes. Parenteral drug administration (i.e., administration other than through the digestive tract, such as by injection, topical, rectal, vaginal, or sublingual routes) circumvents the first-pass effect.

It is important to note that some metabolites are more pharmacologically active than the parent drug. For example, Prozac (fluoxetine) is metabolized into norfluoxetine, which is believed to be more potent than Prozac at inhibiting the serotonin reuptake pump (Preskorn, 1996). In addition, some metabolites are more potent enzyme inhibitors than their parent drugs and/or have much longer half-lives (the amount of time it takes to eliminate one-half of the substance from the body) or biological activity.

Elimination

To completely terminate the pharmacological effects of a drug, it must be eliminated from the body. Indeed, in addition to detoxifying substances, the process of metabolization also prepares them for removal from the body by transforming them into metabolites, which are more readily excreted than the original compound. *Excretion* is the process whereby substances are translocated from the internal environment to the outside of the body. Several systems participate in drug elimination, such as the lungs (through exhalation), the gastrointestinal tract (through defecation), and the skin (through perspiration). As important as these routes of elimination are, the most import organ of drug elimination is the kidney, which excretes drug metabolites through urine. The kidney filters almost 2,000 liters of blood a day (about 475 gallons) to produce a mere liter of urine. Nevertheless, this amount of urine is sufficient to eliminate the vast majority of drugs and metabolic waste products from the body. It is important to consider that the physiochemical properties of a drug which govern its absorption also apply to drug excretion. While it is beyond the scope of this chapter to discuss the details, the urinary elimination of drugs can be influenced by modifying the acidity or alkalinity of the urine. Increasing the acidity of urine hastens the elimination of basic substances while increasing its alkalinity speeds up excretion of acidic compounds.

Any drug that influences one or more phases of pharmacokinetics can result in a pharmacokinetically mediated drug–drug interaction that may intensify or diminish therapeutic effects. For example, antacids are known to interfere with benzodiazepine absorption, thus diminishing their therapeutic onset. Displacement from plasma proteins of one drug by another can significantly increase the bioavailability of the displaced drug, resulting in a greater therapeutic effect (or even toxicity) than would be predicted based on the original dose of the displaced drug. This would be an example of a pharmacokinetic drug–drug interaction involving the distribution phase. We have already provided an example of a pharmacokinetic interaction involving metabolization: Luvox inhibits one of the enzymes Xanax depends on for its biotransformation, thus intensifying or prolonging its effects. Moreover, the fact that certain drugs can change the acidity of urine can influence the rate of elimination of other drugs from the body.

Having provided a general overview of some of the most fundamental pharmacokinetic processes—what the body does to the drug—we will now turn to what the drug does to the body, what is often called *pharmacodynamics*.

Pharmacodynamics

Following absorption and distribution to its sites of action, a drug will produce physiological effects that ultimately result in a therapeutic response. With psychotropic medications, the major organ effected is the brain. In most cases, psychotropics produce their therapeutic effects by binding to specific receptors or enzymes. In many cases, psychotropics mimic the effects of neurotransmitters or, by passively occupying receptors, prevent neurotransmitters from binding at those sites. Ultimately, psychotropics produce therapeutic effects by changing neural activity, as a consequence of affecting the traffic patterns of neurotransmitters or, in some cases, intracellular, second-messenger systems.

In general terms, drugs produce both acute effects and long-term compensatory changes in the flow of neurotransmitters and cellular activity. Acute effects are the rapid changes in neurotransmitter concentrations that follow within minutes or hours of a drug's administration. Long-term compensatory effects are adaptations that neurons undergo after chronic administration of a drug. Usually these adaptations involve modifying populations of receptors, a genetically mediated process that requires the cell to synthesize and insert into its membrane new receptor molecules. These adaptations, which compensate for the change in neurotransmitter traffic, are often referred to as *receptor down-regulation* or *up-regulation,* depending on whether the end result is that the cell has fewer receptors (down-regulation) or more (up-regulation). These phenomena, also called *neural plasticity,* take up to several weeks to occur. This time frame is highly correlated with the therapeutic onset of many psychotropics, leading to the compelling hypothesis that the therapeutic effects of these drugs result from these compensatory adaptations. Similarly, the reversal of these adaptations upon discontinuation of the drug can take several weeks to occur, explaining why relapse is often delayed much as response lags initiation of the drug. Some psychotropics, however, such as the benzodiazepines, act therapeutically by producing short-term effects. Hence, these drugs work relatively quickly and only while present at the receptors where they exert their influence.

Phramacodynamic processes involve drug effects at receptors. Just as there are many pharmacokinetically mediated drug–drug interactions, there are also many important pharmacodynamically mediated drug–drug interactions. In essence, any drug that influences another drug at its receptors or sites of action will produce pharmacodynamic interaction that will either potentiate or attenuate pharmacologic effects. For example, tricyclic antidepressants have effects at several types of receptors. Hence they often potentiate antihistamines (via effects at histamine receptors), several antihypertensives (via effects at the α_1-adrenergic receptor), anticholinergic agents (via blockade of muscarinic cholinergic receptors), and certain antiarrhythmics (via direct membrane-stabilizing properties).

Some additional terms and concepts that are essential knowledge for any student or practitioner of pharmacology include *efficacy, potency, toxicity,* and *therapeutic index. Efficacy* refers to the capacity of a drug to produce a desired result or effect and can be thought of as synonymous with effectiveness. If drug A (e.g., morphine) is capable of relieving more pain than drug B (e.g., ibuprofen), drug A is said to have greater analgesic efficacy than drug B. Hence, even at enormous doses ibuprofen cannot match morphine's analgesic effectiveness. *Potency* concerns the dosage of a drug needed to produce a therapeutic effect. If less of drug A is needed to produce a given response than of drug B, drug A is more potent than drug B. For example, since 200 mg of ibuprofen is able to produce the same amount of pain relief as 500 mg of acetaminophen, ibuprofen is more potent than acetaminophen. Interestingly, a drug that is more potent than another is not necessarily more efficacious. For example, both alprazolam (Xanax) and diazepam (Valium) are equally efficacious in reducing anxiety, but alprazolam is about ten times as potent as diazepam. Thus 1 mg of alprazolam has about the same efficacy as 10 mg of diazepam.

Toxicity refers to a substance's potential for producing injury or death. Toxicity and lethality are directly and positively correlated; the more toxic a substance, the greater its lethality. A critical parameter that directs safe and effective drug use is the *therapeutic index,* which is a quantitative comparison of a drug's effective concentration (efficacy) and its toxic concentration (toxicity). The closer together these two measurements are, the narrower the index, and therefore the less safe the drug. In psychopharmacology, lithium and tricyclic compounds have small therapeutic indices (and are therefore more dangerous) than benzodiazepines and selective serotonin reuptake inhibitors (SSRIs), which have large therapeutic indices.

Basic Psychopharmacology

This section surveys the major classes of psychotropics. Because most psychotropics belong to a specific class or family of compounds, all members of which share many common features, classes of drugs rather than individual medications will be discussed. Unique or novel agents will be discussed separately. It must be underscored at the outset that we really do not have a complete or even adequate understanding of how psychotropics work. What we do know with a high degree of confidence is that psychotropic medications are significantly more effective than placebos in relieving many symptoms of psychopathology. We also know that most psychotropics have identifiable immediate interactions with one or more neurotransmitter receptors, enzymes, or intracellular second-messenger systems.

Antidepressants

Monoamine Oxidase Inhibitors. Monoamine oxidase inhibitors (MAOIs) are among the oldest antidepressants in the psychopharmacopia. Monoamine oxidases are a family of enzymes primarily responsible for the catabolism (breakdown) of the monoamine neurotransmitters and structurally related molecules, including the biologically active amines such as the amino acid tyramine. (A monoamine is a biomolecule that contains a single amine group. An amine is a molecular component derived from ammonia, NH_3, and thus contains a nitrogen atom with hydrogen or other atoms attached to it.) MAOIs permanently paralyze the enzyme(s) that break down, and thus deactivate, several monoamine neurotransmitters, including norepinephrine, serotonin, and dopamine. When the monoamine oxidases are taken out of commission, amounts of monoamine neurotransmitters increase, which boosts their levels at synapses.

The traditional MAOIs are very effective antidepressants and antipanic agents. Nevertheless, because of their potential to produce a wide range of troublesome and even potentially lethal side effects (i.e., treatment-emergent adverse events or TEAEs), they are best used only in cases of refractory illness. The TEAEs most commonly reported by patients on MAOIs are dizziness, headache, sleep disturbance, agitation, gastrointestinal disturbance, postural or orthostatic hypotension (a sudden drop in blood pressure upon standing), weight change, and sexual dysfunction. Of far more concern, however, is their potential to cause sudden and dramatic elevations in blood pressure, and even fatal cerebral hemorrhage if combined with tyramine-containing foods or certain drugs such as the pain-killer Demerol (meperidine) or sympathomimetic agents (substances that mimic the effects of the predominant sympathetic nervous system transmitters epinephrine/adrenaline and norepinephrine/noradrenaline) like those found in many over-the-counter decongestants. These potentially fatal reactions, referred to as hypertensive or hyperadrenergic crises, necessitate that patients using MAOIs follow a specific diet to ensure that they avoid tyramine-containing foods such as cheese. They are also cautioned to avoid other drugs that may contain sympathomimetics.

Another catastrophic reaction, serotonin syndrome, can occur if MAOIs are combined with SSRIs. Since MAO acts as an important mechanism by which serotonin is deactivated, if serotonin agonists are taken while the enzyme is inhibited, an extreme elevation in serotonin levels can result—leading to a possibly fatal dysregulation of serotonin activity in the brain stem. For this reason, special care must be taken when switching a patient from MOAIs to SSRIs and vice versa. In switching from a MAOI to a SSRI a two-week washout is recommended because it takes that long for the body to replenish its normal MAO levels. A two-week washout is also sufficient when switching from most SSRIs to a MAOI. The one exception is when switching from fluoxetine (Prozac), which requires at least a four-week washout because fluoxetine has very active metabolites with long elimination half-lives.

An interesting phenomenon sometimes seen with MAOIs is the cycling of depressed patients into mania. While all antidepressants can do this, the likelihood is greatest with the MAOIs. Hence, clinicians must be alert to the warning signs that a patient might be becoming manic during the early stages of therapy with a MAOI. Given their concerning résumé of side effects and bad reactions, it is no surprise that the traditional MAOIs are mostly used as last-resort medications. The good news is that a new class of MAOIs is just entering the portfolio of psychotropics. These agents are reversible inhibitors of one specific type of MAO (MAO A) and are called RIMAs (reversible inhibitors of MAO A). Unlike their predecessors RIMAs do not require dietary restrictions, yet have the same therapeutic effects as the irreversible MAOIs. Currently, the traditional MAOIs available are phenelzine (Nardil) and tranylcypromine (Parnate). The best-studied RIMA is meclobemide (Aurorix).

Tricyclic/Heterocyclic Agents. The tricyclic antidepressants (TCAs) were so named because their molecular structure has three ring-shaped elements called *cyclic groups* in organic chemistry. Long after their antidepressant efficacy was observed it was discovered that TCAs block the reuptake pumps for both norepinephrine and serotonin (and for dopamine, to a much lesser extent). This is believed to mediate their therapeutic effects. They also have strong affinity for other binding sites, such as the histamine, acetylcholine, and α_1-norepinephrine receptors, which is thought to account for their side effects.

The TEAEs most commonly associated with TCA are anticholingeric side effects such as dry mouth, blurred vision, constipation, and urinary retention. They also produce dizziness, sedation, postural hypotension, and weight gain. The most serious adverse effect associated with TCAs, however, is the blocking of the electrical conduction fibers in the heart. Indeed, for this reason, the TCAs are among the most lethal drugs in the pharmacoepia.

By current standards the term *tricyclic antidepressant* is archaic because many newer agents in this class have one, two, or four rings in their structures, which is why the term *heterocyclic* is sometimes used. Moreover, they are not merely antidepressants since some of them have important antipanic effects, and others have powerful anti-obsessive–compulsive effects. Some of the more commonly prescribed TCAs are imipramine (Tofranil), desipramine (Norpramine), nortriptyline (Pamelor), and the very effective anti-OCD agent clomipramine (Anafranil).

Selective Serotonin Reuptake Inhibitors (SSRIs). Since the U.S. introduction of fluoxetine (Prozac) in 1988, the SSRIs have essentially elbowed the older antidepressants aside and now account for the vast majority of prescriptions written for depressive and OCD-spectrum disorders. In addition to their well-established therapeutic efficacy, the SSRIs are extremely safe drugs, all having very broad therapeutic indices. In addition, they all appear to have broad-spectrum effects and are, therefore, effective in treating a range of conditions other than depression. For example, OCD, panic, general anxiety disorder (GAD), bulimia, many phobias, and some impulse control disorders often respond well to SSRIs. As their name suggests, the SSRIs are named on the basis of their primary pharmacologic effect, which is to selectively block only the reuptake pump (transporter) that shuttles serotonin back into neurons. Unlike TCAs, SSRIs have no appreciable effects on the norepinephrine transporter, nor do they strongly interact with other receptors. Thus they are *selective* serotonin reuptake inhibitors.

Most people tolerate SSRIs quite well; however, they are very likely to produce sexual side effects such as delayed ejaculation and anorgasmia. Other common side effects include mild headaches, nausea, diarrhea, nervousness, insomnia, dry mouth, and fatigue. Unlike the sexual side effects, which usually persist, most of these other TEAEs often remit within the first few weeks of therapy. In the United States, the currently available SSRIs are fluoxetine (Prozac), sertraline (Zoloft), paroxetine (Paxil), fluvoxamine (Luvox), and the recently approved citalopram (Celexa).

Bupropion (Wellbutrin). Bupropion (Wellbutrin) is a prototypical antidepressant of the dopamine and norepinephrine reuptake blocker group (Stahl, 1996). While bupropion has only weak effects at these neurotransmitter transporters, it has an active metabolite that is much more powerful and is also concentrated in the brain. In some ways, therefore, bupropion is more of a prodrug than a drug. Bupropion is a very stimulating antidepressant that has several advantages over other antidepressants including SSRIs. It is essentially devoid of sexual side effects, is extremely unlikely to cause weight gain or fatigue, and is very cardiac-safe.

What is more, there is increasing evidence that it is effective in treating attention deficit/hyperactivity disorder (ADHD) (mostly inattentive type) and has recently received an indication for aiding in smoking cessation under the trade name Zyban.

Bupropion is generally very well tolerated, but can cause some transient side effects such as nervousness, agitation, and insomnia. The only significant drawback with bupropion is that it is slightly more likely to induce seizures than other antidepressants. Nevertheless, if patients who are at risk for seizures are screened out (e.g., patients with a history of prior seizures, eating disorders, significant head trauma, etc.), bupropion can be very safely prescribed. Recently, a sustained-release formulation of bupropion was approved that should further reduce seizure risk. Some psychopharmacologists (e.g., Goldberg, 1996) are so impressed by bupropion that they insulate patients against seizures with concurrent anticonvulsants and then titrate patients to as much as 600 mg daily, or 25 percent more than the FDA-approved upper limit of 450 mg per day.

Venlafaxine (Effexor). Venlafaxine (Effexor) is a prototype serotonin–norepinephrine reuptake inhibitor agent or SNRI. Thus, venlafaxine shares the serotonin and norepinephrine reuptake inhibitory effects of the classical TCAs, but without any significant effects at cholinergic, hisaminergic, or α_1-adrenergic receptors. Although well-documented as an effective antidepressant, it is not clear if venlafaxine has any advantages over SSRIs vis-à-vis efficacy or tolerability. Some anecdotal reports suggest that venlafaxine has a more rapid therapeutic onset than other antidepressants, but this might be due to its activating properties, which can cause an initial boost in energy (as a side effect) that can be mistaken for actual clinical improvement, especially in anergic patients.

As suggested above, the TEAEs associated with venlafaxine resemble the SSRIs although it is less likely to produce fatigue or sexual side effects. It is more likely, however, to cause diaphoresis (sweating) and is occasionally associated with elevations in diastolic blood pressure and blood lipids. In addition, although it now comes in an extended-release form, it still requires at least bid (twice-a-day) dosing. For these reasons, venlafaxine is considered by most prescribers to be a second-line treatment.

Nefazodone (Serzone). Like the SSRIs, nefazodone (Serzone) inhibits serotonin reuptake, but unlike the SSRIs it also blocks a specific type of postsynaptic serotonin receptor (the serotonin type 2 receptor). Thus, nefazodone is a mixed agonist/antagonist (serotonin transporter inhibition = agonism; postsynaptic serotonin type 2 receptor blockade = antagonism). The makers of nefazodone, Bristol-Myers Squibb, are trying to gain market share by emphasizing that nefazodone has fewer sexual side effects than the SSRIs and also reduces anxiety more rapidly than they do. Clinical trial data do suggest that initial anxiety is less of a problem with this agent than with the SSRIs and that sexual side effects are also less frequent. Clinical experience, however, suggests that nefazodone is not as efficacious as the SSRIs in most cases of depression. Indeed, like its predecessor, the pharmacologically similar compound trazodone (Desyrel), many prescribers are using nefazodone as a potentiator and/or soporific (i.e., co-prescribing it with a SSRI or bupropion to amplify efficacy and/or to promote sleep when insomnia is present) rather than as a solo therapeutic agent.

Mirtazapine (Remeron). Mirtazapine (Remeron) is the first antidepressant that works primarily through antagonizing central presynaptic α_2-adrenergic receptors which is believed to enhance noradrenergic and serotonergic activity. In addition, mirtazapine is a potent blocker of postsynaptic serotonin type 2 and type 3 receptors, as well as histamine receptors. This latter effect (i.e., histaminergic antagonism) is believed to account for mirtazapine's most common side effect, somnolence. Other common TEAEs reported in clinical trials include dizziness, increased appetite, weight gain, and elevated blood lipids. Clinical data suggest that although an effective antidepressant, given its unfavorable side effect profile mirtazapine, like nefazodone, is best used in cases of agitated depression or as a potentiator/soporific and not as a first-line antidepressant.

Anxiolytics and Sedatives/Hypnotics

In much the same way that the SSRIs and new-generation antidepressants eclipsed the older TCAs and MAOIs in the 1990s, 30 years previously a similar pharmacologic shift took place when the benzodiazepines were introduced. Prior to the benzodiazepines, barbiturates were the state-of-the-art-and-science for pharmacologic treatment of anxiety. Benzodiazepines (BZs) are anxiolyic (literally, "anxiety-dissolving") agents that in addition to relieving psychic anxiety also have sedative, muscle-relaxing, and anticonvulsant properties. Compared to barbiturates, BZs have a greater dose margin between anxiolysis and sedation; less tendency to produce tolerance and dependence; less abuse potential; and, most importantly, very large therapeutic indices. Indeed, the lethality of barbiturates is well documented whereas death from BZ overdosage is essentially unheard-of, unless other substances are co-ingested.

The efficacy of the dozen or so BZs available in the United States is basically the same. The choice in selecting one over the others rests mostly on their pharmacokinetic properties, which do differ significantly. Most of these factors involve speed of onset after oral dose, distribution, metabolization, and elimination parameters. Another consideration in clinical decision making is potency, since only the high-potency agents have efficacy in treating panic (e.g., alprazolam [Xanax] and clonazepam [Klonopin]).

The prevalence of anxiety, coupled with the effectiveness and safety of BZs, has lead to their extensive use. Despite concerns about addiction and abuse, which have caused a steady decline in prescriptions for BZs over the past 20 years, they are still widely prescribed. It is true that clinically significant dependence can occur even at therapeutic doses in the course of long-term use (more than 6 months), and that dependence is more likely to result from use of high-potency, short-acting agents (e.g., alprazolam [Xanax]). Nevertheless, it appears that the risks of dependence, even during long-term use, have—given proper therapeutic management—been exaggerated (Hyman, Arana, & Rosenbaum, 1995). Paradoxically, it is probable that excessive fear of addicting patients to BZs may be responsible for withholding extremely effective therapy from many anxious patients.

Pharmacologically, BZs' action is due to their affinity for a specific binding site on a very large protein that functions to draw negatively charged chloride ions into neurons, thus hyperpolarizing them and inhibiting their firing. Also on this large chloride channel, called the gamma-aminobutyric acid–benzodiazepine chloride channel receptor complex (or GABA-BZ receptor complex for short), are binding sites for the inhibitory neurotransmitter GABA (gamma-aminobutyric acid). In essence, BZs boost the effects of GABA by binding to the receptor complex. This results in GABA exerting a more powerful effect when it occupies its binding site, causing the chloride channel to open more, than it does when GABA binds in the absence of BZ molecules. Therefore, BZs allow GABA to hyperdilate the chloride channel, which allows extra chloride to enter the neuron, resulting in a hyperpolarized cell that is pushed away from its threshold of excitation. Commonly prescribed BZs include diazepam (Valium), alprazolam (Xanax), lorazepam (Ativan), clonazepam (Klonopin), temazepam (Restoril), and chlordiazepoxide (Librium), to name only a few.

A new class of nonbenzodiazepine anxiolytic has recently entered the psychopharmacopia, a group of compounds called asapirones. In the United States, the only one of these drugs to be approved for the treatment of anxiety is buspirone (BuSpar). Buspirone is neither chemically nor pharmacologically related to the benzodiazepines, barbiturates, or other sedative/anxiolytic drugs. Its major advantages over BZs are that it is nonsedating, does not impair motor function, and has shown no potential for dependence or abuse. Its biggest disadvantages are that it takes several weeks to produce anxiolysis, and can paradoxically intensify anxiety during the early stages of treatment. While clinical trials have demonstrated buspirone's efficacy in treating anxiety, it has proved rather disappointing in general clinical use. This finding may be due in part to inappropriate expectations and use on the part of prescribers and patients who are accustomed to the rapid effects of BZs. In terms of its putative mechanism of action, buspirone is believed to exert its anxiolytic effects by acting as a partial agonist at serotonin type 1A receptors. Precisely how this produces anxiolysis remains to be determined, but it is clear from the well-established efficacy of SSRIs in treating anxiety disorders that serotonin plays an important role in the pathophysiology of anxiety.

Mood Stabilizers and Antimanic Agents

In the treatment of bipolar disorders the question of when to consider drug therapy is not the main issue; rather, it is which medication to use with a particular patient, since pharmacological management of bipolar illness is almost always necessary. The primary agents to consider include lithium and the anticonvulsants carbamazepine (Tegratol) and valproic acid (Depakote). In addition to being mood stabilizers, these drugs are also referred to as *antimanic* agents, but this is a bit of a misnomer since they also work to treat depression symptoms.

Until recently, the most frequently prescribed drug for bipolar illness was lithium, which has been partly eclipsed by some of the anticonvulsant agents, as will be discussed. Unlike most psychotropics, lithium does not produce its actions within synapses. Rather, it works beyond the receptor intracellularly, acting to influence the phosphatidyl inosital second-messenger system. Since it is an ion, not a multiatomic molecule, another unusual feature of lithium is that it is not at all protein-bound.

Unfortunately, lithium has many side effects and a very narrow therapeutic index (meaning its therapeutic dose is uncomfortably close to its toxic dose), seriously limiting its utility in clinical practice. Moreover, due to its significant toxicity, consistent blood levels must be obtained to ensure that patients are being maintained within the therapeutic window. Examples of TEAEs common with lithium therapy include nausea, vomiting, and diarrhea. These gastrointestinal side effects are usually transient and resolve with continued therapy. If they emerge later in treatment, it is usually a sign of toxicity. Other side effects include increased thirst (polydipsia), increased urination (polyuria), tremor, lethargy, weakness, and cognitive dulling. Another important TEAE seen with lithium is hypothyroidism, which in most cases can be managed by the addition of thyroid hormones. In addition, lithium has been known to alter cardiac physiology, produce dermatologic reactions such as acne and psoriasis, increase white blood cell count, and cause weight gain.

Despite its concerning side effect profile, lithium remains one of the most frequently prescribed drugs in the treatment of bipolar disorders. Nevertheless, several other drugs are being used with increasing frequency. Based on a theory that mania may "kindle" further manic episodes, just as a seizure will increase the incidence of future seizures, trials of certain anticonvulsants have been conducted. It was discovered that two agents—valproic acid (Depakote) and carbamazepine (Tegratol)—were effective in controlling manic depression, especially for patients who either could not tolerate or were nonresponsive to lithium (such as rapid cyclers or patients with Bipolar II Disorder). In many cases, however, these anticonvulsants are used in conjunction with lithium. Although their mechanism of action is unclear, there is some evidence that they work by modulating the GABA system (e.g., Stahl, 1996). Other anticonvulsant agents are gaining increasing popularity in treating bipolar disorders. While controlled studies proving their efficacy are lacking, some of the more promising agents are lamotrigine (Lamictal), gabapentin (Neurontin), and topiramate (Topamax). As we will discuss later, many of the mood stabilizers, especially lithium, are used to augment the efficacy of other psychotropics and thus have clinical utility that extends beyond the treatment of bipolar illness.

Typical and Atypical Antipsychotic Agents

The advent of antipsychotic drugs in the 1950s ushered in a new era in the treatment of severe mental illness. The traditional agents used in treating psychotic disorders are a group of compounds belonging to the neuroleptic class, all of which block dopamine receptors, mostly type 2 receptors. The term *neuroleptic* means "causing a neurological disorder"; these agents often produce profound motor side effects that resemble neurological disorders such as Parkinson's disease. These motor side effects are referred to as *extrapyramidal symptoms* (EPS) because they result from the blockade of specific dopamine receptors in the basal ganglia motor system (the extrapyramidal tracts) rather than in the corticospinal system (the pyramidal tracts). While most EPS can be tolerated or managed with adjunctive agents (e.g., anticholinergics, β-blockers, or benzodiazepines), long-term use of typical antipsychotics can result in tardive dyskinesia (literally, "late onset, bad or difficult movement"). Tardive dyskinesia (TD) is a syndrome of long-standing or permanent abnormal involuntary movements usually involving the face, mouth, and tongue (buccolingualmasticatory movements). Interestingly, some data suggest that concurrent treatment with anticonvulsants may prevent the development of neuroleptic-induced TD or suppress its expression (e.g., Swanson et al., 1996).

In addition to their propensity for producing EPS and TD, typical antipsychotic drugs cause a host of other troublesome side effects. These include dry mouth, blurred vision, constipation, delayed urination, postural hypotension, sedation, restlessness, weight gain, and elevated prolactin levels. What is more, they have been associated with two potentially fatal side effects: neuroleptic malignant syndrome (NMS) and agranulocytosis. NMS is a rare, idiosyncratic reaction characterized by fever, confusion, rigidity, and autonomic instability, which if not recognized and treated immediately can lead to coma and death. Once a patient suffers from NMS, he or she should never be rechallenged with any antipsychotic agent unless compelling reasons exist to do so. Agranulocytosis is a potentially life-threatening hematologic side effect seen extremely rarely with typical neuroleptics. It is characterized by a severe decrease in white blood cell count, and therefore renders victims susceptible to fatal infection. Hence, clinicians need to alert patients to be on the look out for signs of significant infection, such as sore throat accompanied by lesions in the mouth. When agranulocytosis is associated with a specific antipsychotic drug in a particular patient, that drug must never be given to that patient again. One final point about typical antipsychotic agents is that they have minimal efficacy on the negative symptoms of schizophrenia. Thus, ironically, despite the fact that they have broad therapeutic indices and are much less lethal than TCAs and lithium, optimizing their use is difficult.

It is believed that the therapeutic actions of typical antipsychotic drugs are exerted via blockade of dopamine receptors in the mesolimbic and mesocortical dopamine pathways. Their untoward motor effects are thought to be due to dopamine blockade in the nigrostriatal pathway (Stahl, 1996). In theory, a drug that acts preferentially at the mesolimbic and mesocortical pathways, while sparing dopamine blockade at nigrostriatal projections, should have good efficacy without producing EPS. Indeed, it seems the new atypical antipsychotic agents do just that. In contrast to the typical neuroleptics, the atypical antipsychotics are strong serotonin-receptor blockers and relatively weaker dopamine antagonists. Furthermore, they seem to be associated with much lower incidences of EPS and TD.

The first, and perhaps still the most efficacious, of these drugs to gain use in the United States is clozapine (Clozaril). Unlike the typical antipsychotics, atypical neuroleptics like clozapine not only reduce the positive symptoms of schizophrenia, but have good efficacy with negative symptoms and refractory patients as well. Although clozapine represents a leap forward in the treatment of psychotic illnesses, it produces many TEAEs, such as sedation, hypersalivation, dizziness, postural hypotension, and lowers the seizure threshold. The most serious side effect, however, is agranulocytosis, which can occur in 1–3 percent of patients (Hyman, Arana, & Rosenbaum, 1995). Given this incidence, patients on clozapine must have regular blood tests to ensure that their white blood cell count remains within normal limits.

During the past few years, several new atypical antipsychotic agents have entered the market. Like clozapine, they seem to have efficacy in both positive and negative symptoms, but do not require blood monitoring due to their lack of association with hematological side effects. These newer agents are risperidone (Risperdal), olanzapine (Zyprexa), and quetiapine (Seroquel).

Psychostimulant Medications

Many substances can produce CNS stimulation (e.g., caffeine), but the ones used in psychopharmacology are the sympathomimetic amines (i.e., amines containing molecules that mimic the effects of the predominant sympathetic nervous system transmitters epinephrine/adrenaline and norepinephrine/noradrenaline). The prototype psychostimulant is amphetamine. The clinical utility of the psychostimulants has been limited by their ability to cause tolerance, dependence, and by their abuse potential. Indeed, in 1970 the FDA reclassified them as Schedule II, the most restrictive classification for drugs that are medically useful. They are currently approved only for the treatment of ADHD and narcolepsy. Nevertheless, they are often used off-label for other conditions such as severe, refractory depression. Interestingly, before MAOIs and TCAs supplanted them, psychostimulants were used regularly in the treatment of depression.

Amphetamine and similar agents are indirect agonists of several monoamine neurotransmitters, and act by amplifying the release of norepinephrine, dopamine, and serotonin from presynaptic nerve terminals (as opposed to having direct agonist effects on the postsynaptic receptors themselves). In addition, amphetamine inhibits norepinephrine and dopamine reuptake, thus prolonging their synaptic effects. Enhanced monoamine release in the reticular activating system is thought to account for the increased alertness these agents produce. Their effects at hypothalamic nuclei explain their anorectic properties, and facilitation of dopaminergic activity in mesolimbic pathways and the striatum is believed to produce their characteristic euphoric and increased-locomotor effects. The most frequently used psychostimulants are dextroamphetamine (Dexedrine), methylphenidate (Ritalin), and, although it is not widely used anymore, Pemoline (Cylert). One additional psychostimulant that warrants mention is Adderall, actually a combination amphetamine product composed of dextroamphetamine saccharate, amphetamine aspartate, amphetamine sulfate, and dextroamphetamine sulfate. Interestingly, Adderall was once indicated for the treatment of obesity under the brand name Obetrol but was withdrawn from the U.S. market in 1973. Since its re-release in 1994, it is rapidly becoming a favorite among prescribers who use it to treat ADHD due to its long-acting effects, which minimize the rebound irritability seen with shorter-acting compounds such as the regular formulation of Ritalin.

Cognitive Enhancers

One final class of psychotropic that deserves mention is the cognitive enhancer group. These compounds are used in the treatment of dementia, especially Alzheimer's disease, which is at least in part due to degeneration of the hippocampal nuclei. The hippocampus is known to contain a large number of acetylcholine-producing neurons. Moreover, hippocampal lesions produce memory impairment. Therefore, it is rational to assume that if a drug can replenish acetylcholine in a dementia patient, memory and cognitive function should improve. Indeed, this does seem to be so. While in most cases they do not produce dramatic improvement, two cognitive enhancers have recently entered the pharmacopia: tacrine (Cognex) and donepezil (Aricept). Both of these compounds are classified as acetylcholine esterase inhibitors (AchIs). Acetylcholine esterase is analogous to monoamine oxidase, in that it catabolizes acetylcholine much as MAO breaks down monoamines. By inhibiting the enzyme that deactivates acetylcholine, the AchIs increase the amount of acetylcholine in the CNS, thereby enhancing cognitive function.

Differential Diagnosis of Medical Conditions and Psychopathologies

Earlier in this chapter, we referred to the human brain as the most complex single entity in existence (at least on our planet, as far as we know). Perhaps the only thing even more elaborate than the brain itself is the human organism in toto. Indeed, the brain exists in the ecosystem of the body and participates in a multitude of reciprocal relationships with all other organ systems. Just as the brain controls and influences the other tissues of the body, the other organs of the body can influence and affect the brain. Since the brain is the seat of conscious experience and gives rise to thoughts, feelings, and actions, anything that affects the brain can have a profound effect on psychological functioning. Thus, it will come as no surprise to learn that there are a great number of medical illnesses and conditions that can masquerade as psychological disturbances. Clearly, before one can treat a problem it must first be confidently identified, since the foundation of effective therapy is accurate diagnosis. Therefore, all competent clinicians must be good diagnosticians who are well versed in the science and art of differential diagnosis (i.e., differentiation among a range of possible conditions and their systematic exclusion, one at a time, until the most probable diagnosis has been rendered). Again, since many diseases and conditions can present as apparent psychological disorders, it is imperative that nonpsychiatric medical illnesses be ruled out before one proceeds with psychopharmacologic treatment.

Good and Nelson (1991) have suggested the useful mnemonic MED'CL to help categorize many of the medical conditions that present as or with psychological symptoms. *M* for Metal poisoning; *E* for Endocrine system malfunction; *D* for Drug reactions such as side effects and toxicity; *C* for Cancers and malignancies that produce psychological symptoms; and *L* for Lots of others, since a hodgepodge of other important medical disorders mimic psychopathologies.

Some of the more common metal poisonings include lead (most common in children who live in older homes with lead-based paint), mercury (in people who work in vacuum-pump and thermometer manufacturing), aluminum (present in many antacids), manganese (used in the battery-manufacturing industry), arsenic (found in some pesticides), and bromides (found in some old-time medicinal preparations). All of these metals can affect the CNS by binding to crucial metabolic enzymes, thus leading to a host of physical, psychological, and neurological symptoms. Often a simple blood test can diagnose metal intoxication. In some cases, as with lead and mercury, treatment involves chelation therapy. This is when substances called *chelating agents* (pronounced KEY-*late-ing*), like ethylene diamine tetracetic acid (EDTA) and dimercaprol, are administered. In the body, chelators pull the metal out of circulation, or away from enzymes, by binding to it, resulting in a metal–chelate complex that can be eliminated in the urine.

There are a variety of endocrinopathies (pathologies of the endocrine system) that masquerade as psychopathologies, especially thyroid and adrenal disorders. The thyroid gland, located in the front of the neck, is responsible for regulating general metabolism, which it does through its principal hormone thyroxine. If the thyroid produces too little thyroxine, hypothyroidism results and can present as almost identical to depressive illness. In other cases, excessive production of thyroxine (hyperthyroidism) can mimic symptoms of anxiety disorders. Similarly, hypo- or hyper-function of the adrenal glands (the pyramid-shaped glands that sit atop the kidneys) can lead to a host of psychological symptoms. The outer layer of the adrenals (called the *adrenal cortex*) produces a variety of steroid hormones, which participate in many physiologic processes. One of them, cortisol, acts on carbohydrate metabolism and influences the nutrition and growth of various tissues. When the adrenals produce too much cortisol a condition called Cushing's disease may result, which can produce psychological symptoms akin to mania and depression. The opposite condition, adrenocortical hypofunction, can result in a condition called Addison's disease, which can also mimic depression. Thyroid and adrenal function can be easily assessed by standard medical evaluations including blood tests that measure the amount of circulating hormones and of hormone-releasing or -stimulating factors.

One additional endocrinopathy that warrants mention is a condition called *pheochromocytoma*. As mentioned, the adrenal cortex produces and releases steroid hormones like cortisol. The inner portion of the adrenal gland is referred to as the *adrenal medulla* and produces and releases the catecholamines epinephrine and norepinephrine—the same chemicals that function as neurotransmitters in the brain—which are important hormones in the periphery. When a tumor in the adrenal medulla causes great bursts of epinephrine and norepinephrine to enter the bloodstream, it can feel like a panic attack to the patient. Besides mimicking panic symptoms, pheochromocytoma cause discrete episodes of hypertension, which can aid in its diagnosis. In addition to blood pressure monitoring, a 24-hour urine collection test can determine the presence or absence of abnormal catecholamine metabolite levels, providing a useful "compass" for the diagnostician.

Certain medications, including prescription, over-the-counter (OTC), and "recreational" drugs, are notorious for causing psychological disturbances. Some of the most common offenders are the older antihypertensives (e.g., reserpine and propranolol), which are known to cause depression. The misuse of amphetamines can lead to psychotic reactions and so can illicit drugs like phencyclidine (PCP). Interestingly, many people think that just because a drug is available OTC it is safe to use. The truth is that many OTC preparations can be extremely dangerous. For example, OTC diet pills can lead to severe insomnia, nervousness, and even dangerous elevations in blood pressure. Even seemingly innocuous substances like antacids can lead to severe metabolic imbalances if used too frequently. As for recreational drug use, alcohol is a huge contributor to the incidence of depression, and caffeine use is linked to chronic anxiety and acute panic attacks. The list goes on almost endlessly. Just about any drug, or other substance for that matter, if used improperly, can lead to toxicity and dramatically affect psychological functioning.

Malignancies can also cause changes in mental status, personality, and psychological functioning. Pancreatic cancers frequently cause severe depression, which can be the presenting complaint. Lung tumors can have a dramatic impact on the CNS and lead to psychological symptoms like dementia. And as mentioned, pheochromocytomas can produce a clinical picture similar to that seen with panic disorder.

A large assortment of other medical conditions can produce or present as psychological problems. These include metabolic disorders like Wilson's disease (a disorder of copper metabolism) and acute intermittent porphyria (which afflicted King George III), to name only two. There are also hereditary illnesses (e.g., Huntington's disease), vitamin deficiencies, electrolyte imbalances, and hard-to-detect seizure phenomena that can all challenge the most skillful diagnostician.

The upshot is simple. Many people seeking professional attention for a psychological complaint should have a thorough medical evaluation before being treated with either psychosocial or psychotropic interventions. Of course, this doesn't mean that every patient with mild complaints of everyday living or of relationship problems should be given a complete medical workup before starting psychotherapy. It does mean, however, that psychologists need to be aware of the myriad organic causes of psychopathologies. Only then can they intelligently refer to other clinicians for further tests or treatment and co-manage their patient's pharmacotherapy.

Advanced Topics in Psychopharmacology

Therapeutic Drug Monitoring

Although the TCAs have fallen out of favor, they do offer one important advantage over the SSRIs and other newer antidepressants: namely, many of them have empirically established therapeutic windows. That is, there is a range within which they work optimally, and measuring precisely where within this range a given patient's serum concentration is can be readily done by standard laboratory assessment. (Serum is the fluid portion of the blood, obtained by removal of cells and clotting factors.) The importance of such monitoring is based on the TCAs' narrow therapeutic indices. While annoying anticholinergic and antihistaminergic side effects begin to occur at subtherapeutic concentrations, potentially lethal cardiac and CNS effects develop at the upper end of the therapeutic range. Since a 10- to 30-fold difference in the rates of metabolization and elimination exists among individuals taking TCAs, it is estimated that approximately 5 percent of patients taking standard doses will have serum concentration in the life-threatening range (Azzaro & Ward, 1994). Therefore, to avoid serious toxicity, monitor compliance, and optimize therapeutic response, therapeutic drug monitoring of TCAs should be standard clinical practice.

Unlike with TCAs, therapeutic drug monitoring (TDM) with SSRIs will probably never be a standard-of-care issue since avoiding serious toxicity is the main purpose of TDM and SSRIs have very little toxic potential. In addition, most studies to date have failed to show a strong correlation between SSRI serum concentration and therapeutic response (Preskorn, 1996). Nevertheless, therapeutic drug monitoring with SSRIs can have important clinical utility. For example, TDM can provide valuable information about whether a patient is failing to respond to a standard dose of a SSRI because he or she is not responsive to its mechanism of action or is rather an aggressive metabolizer of the drug. Also, during the early stages of treatment, SSRIs can produce side effects that mimic depression symptoms. If TDM indicates a blood level higher than predicted based on oral dose, the dose can be titrated downward without compromising efficacy. Alternatively, if TDM reveals a low serum concentration, upward titration can be performed without too much risk of exacerbating the patient's symptoms.

With respect to the antipsychotic drugs, at present only haloperidol (Haldol) seems to have a blood level that is correlated with therapeutic effects (i.e., levels greater than 5–10 ng/ml). Generally, however, serum levels for antipsychotic drugs are more misleading than they are clinically useful because the therapeutic range reported for each drug has yet to be shown to correlate with symptom improvement (Hyman, Arana, & Rosenbaum, 1995). Therefore, clinical observation and documentation of patient status over time remains the cornerstone of assessing antipsychotic drug efficacy.

With lithium, TDM is the mainstay of safe and effective therapy because oral dosage is not an adequate guideline. Since the half-life of lithium is 24 hours, and the time to steady state serum concentration for all drugs is 4–5 half-lives, levels should be drawn no sooner than five days after a change in dose or the initiation of therapy unless toxicity is expected. It should be noted that regimens in which the entire dose is taken at bedtime generally produce trough (morning) levels 10–20 percent higher than regimens with divided dosing. For acute mania, a therapeutic response is usually achieved at serum levels of 1.0–1.2 mmol/L (sometimes reported as mEq/L), which typically requires a daily oral dose of 1200–2400 mg.

For prophylaxis, serum levels of 0.8–1.0 mmol/L have been shown to be more effective than lower levels. This usually can be achieved with a daily oral dose of 600–1800 mg. If side effects are severe enough to compromise compliance, the lowest effective serum level should be determined empirically. If a patient cannot tolerate lithium at a therapeutic level, carbamazepine or valproic acid should be considered as alternatives.

Strategies for Treating Refractory Depression

A significant number of patients respond only partially or not at all to an initial antidepressant trial. *Refractory,* or *treatment-resistant, depression* refers to a depressive episode that has failed to respond to two or more adequate trials of antidepressant medication, and may describe as much as 20 percent of depressed patients (Preston, O'Neal, & Talaga, 1997). In such cases, the first thing to do is to ensure that the diagnosis is correct (e.g., rule out PTSD and psychosis) and that there is no unsuspected comorbid condition such as hypothyroidism or chemical dependence that could be undermining treatment response. If all of these considerations are ruled out, there are three general strategies that can be systematically employed: optimization, augmentation, and substitution. Of course, when all else fails, electro-convulsive therapy (ECT) should be considered.

Optimization involves ensuring adequate drug dose and adequate length of treatment for the individual, which may be higher than the usual doses. This often means a patient must be challenged with the upper end of the dose range for at least six weeks (e.g., 80 mg of fluoxetine, 200–300 mg of desipramine). Often, failure to respond is due to inadequate compliance. Therefore, patient education is also a vital element of the optimization strategy.

Augmentation refers to the addition of another medication to the established antidepressant regimen. In essence, augmentation strategies take advantage of pharmacodynamic, and to a lesser extent pharmacokinetic, drug–drug interactions to boost therapeutic efficacy. The usual agents added are lithium (at subtherapeutic doses, e.g., 300–600 mg/day), thyroid hormones (T3 and T4), low-dose psychostimulants such as methylphenidate, or another antidepressant such as bupropion. In this way, a therapeutic synergism is hoped for, wherein 1 + 1 = 3. That is, the response elicited by the combined drugs is greater than the combined responses of the individual drugs.

Substitution involves changing the primary drug to another medication usually in a different class. For example, if a patient fails to improve after an adequate trial of a SRRI (a serotonergic drug) changing to a TCA (a noradrenergic drug) might produce a better response. If, however, the first drug fails because of side effects, switching to another drug in the initial class may be productive if it is better tolerated. For example, some patients have great difficulty tolerating fluoxetine, but have no trouble tolerating sertraline or paroxetine.

Weaving the Bio into the Psychosocial Tapestry

Comprehensive Assessment and History

To repeat: on occasion, the single most important intervention a psychologist can perform is getting a patient to agree to try psychotropics. Often, the more a clinician knows about psychopharmacology the more able she or he is in achieving this goal. Clearly, before recommending a trial of medication, clinicians must be confident that the patient is suffering from a condition that has been empirically shown to respond well to drug therapy (i.e., an Axis I condition). Therefore, proper diagnosis and thorough biopsychosocial assessment is crucial for treatment success. Comprehensive assessment will, of course, inquire into the mental health histories of the patient's biological family, which can provide important information vis-à-vis genetic diatheses. In addition, it can alert clinicians as to what medications might have efficacy, since knowing that a patient's first-degree relative responded well to a specific drug can serve as a useful clinical compass. Obviously, if a patient has a history of a favorable response to a particular drug, that drug should be tried first for the current illness.

Perhaps one the most comprehensive assessment tools available in adult outpatient settings is the Multimodal Life History Inventory (Lazarus & Lazarus, 1991). This patient-self-report questionnaire assesses the complete spectrum of biopsychosocial functioning across seven dimensions (i.e., behavior, affect, sensation, imagery, cognition, interpersonal relationships, and biological/medical factors) and can serve as a valuable framework for symptom identification, treatment planning, and medication selection. For a thorough discussion of how multimodal therapy is the most elegant and comprehensive model of biopsychosocial assessment and psychotherapy, see A. Lazarus, 1997.

Informed Consent

In previous eras, clinicians were viewed as beneficent healers who, it was assumed, knew what was best for a patient and had no obligation to explain decisions or ask permission to perform actions. Hence, in the traditional model of the doctor–patient relationship, the doctor treated the patient as a caring parent would treat a child, and the patient had no fundamental right to informed consent, truth-telling, or confidentiality. Today, based on the writings of Immanuel Kant, the doctor–patient relationship is conceptualized as (more) egalitarian. Patients are treated as responsible, rational, and self-governing, with rights of self-determination that must be respected even when they make decisions that work against them (e.g., the right to refuse treatment). At the very heart of this autonomy-based model of patient care is the process of informed consent.

Regrettably, much of psychopharmacology, and especially of clinical research, involves consent forms that would baffle the editor of a scientific journal. Most informed consent forms are designed by hospital or drug company lawyers and are court-tested, boilerplate documents intended to protect prescribers from litigation, rather than to inform patients about treatments. Yet, ironically, even the most carefully constructed consent form has little chance of standing up in court, since almost any attorney three days out of law school can shred even the most meticulously crafted document. In addition, all a patient has to say is "I didn't understand a word of it, but the doctor told me I had to sign it." Furthermore, there is an intrinsic paradox of consent forms—if complete enough to be comprehensive they are incomprehensible, and if short enough to be comprehensible they are invariably incomplete.

Many clinicians, mainly prescribers, tend to think of informed consent as a single event that has the sole purpose of informing the patient about the risks of a particular treatment. It is best to conceptualize informed consent neither as a single event nor only in terms of information. It is not a form or a signature on a form. Informed consent (IC) is a moral and ethical dimension of the therapeutic relationship that starts with the first moment of eye contact and evolves throughout the entire duration of treatment. Conceptualized in this way, IC is an ongoing and evolving process of discussion and information exchange that forms the very foundation of the therapeutic alliance. Indeed, as Lazarus and Fay (1984) have underscored, regardless of the intervention, it is the fertile soil of the therapeutic relationship itself that enables the specific methods to take root. In addition to being an excellent method from the standpoint of information exchange, this way of construing IC also serves as a powerful risk-management tool because the degree of relatedness engendered by this kind of process tends to forestall litigation (Gutheil, 1994); patients who see themselves as part of a solid therapeutic alliance almost never sue their doctors. (It is a great pity that most risk management seminars teach clinicians to see their patients as potential litigants. This impels them to adopt rigid boundaries that adversarialize the relationship and ironically render them *more* susceptible to litigation. See A. Lazarus, 1994, for a controversial discussion of boundaries in psychotherapy.)

In the evolving IC process there are three technical aspects that must be considered: *information, voluntarity,* and *competency* (Arnott, 1998). *Information* is the "informed" aspect of IC and must be presented in clear and understandable language. Therefore, instead of shoving a bolus of drug facts down the patient's throat, the doctor must collaborate with the patient in exploring the available information about the drug or treatment being considered. *Voluntarity* refers to the "consent" dimension of IC and implies that the patient can say "no" as easily as "yes," thus indicating the absence of coercion and that the therapeutic decision is consensual. Hence, IC can be withdrawn. The final aspect of IC is *competency,* the capacity to take in, process, and weigh information and then make a rational decision based on the facts supplied. Again, it is a mistake to think that a document is a good IC mechanism; at best it is a formality, literally. A patient cannot have a relationship with a document and it is the relationship that is the very heart of the IC process. Nevertheless, there are some settings in which one must use the forms; but one uses the forms as an adjunct to the IC process described here, not in lieu of it.

Regarding the information to be discussed during the IC process, three important options must be considered vis-à-vis benefits and risks: the proposed treatment, alternative treatments, and no treatment. Most clinicians do well in discussing the proposed treatment, but often fail to give enough attention to the other two branches in the decision tree. For example, a depressed patient is likely to hear a lot from a prescriber about SSRIs (the proposed treatment), but not as much about bupropion or cognitive–behavioral therapy (alternative treatments) or the no-treatment option. In discussing the benefits and risks of drug therapies (or any treatment), the clinician should address preferentially side effects that are serious, common, and specifically relevant to a particular patient. Examples of serious side effects include arrhythmias (TCAs), serotonin syndrome (SSRIs), seizures (bupropion), and TD (typical antipsychotics). Common side effects include dry mouth (TCAs), headache (SSRIs), agitation (bupropion), and akathisia (typical antipsychotics). Relevant adverse events might be constipation in geriatric patients (TCAs), anorgasmia in a newlywed with an active libido (SSRIs), tremor in a calligrapher (bupropion), and blurred vision in an avid reader (typical antipsychotics).

Record Keeping as Informed Consent and Risk Management

Oddly enough, given the limitations of "boilerplate" IC forms, a much better way of documenting the IC process is a simple progress note in the patient's file. Naturally, a thorough biopsychosocial history and assessment must be the foundation of this record. Since most psychotropics belong to a class or family of compounds, all sharing many features, it is relatively easy to develop a standard discussion of the effects, benefits, and risks for most of the drugs commonly used. For example, TCAs, SSRIs, typical neuroleptics, and benzodiazepines can all be discussed in general terms. Unique or novel agents, of course, need to be discussed as such. Following comprehensive evaluation, record that the discussion of the benefits and risks of the recommended treatment (class of drug or specific compound) took place. Underscore any precautions that were noted, such as the MAOI diet, use of dangerous equipment, care in getting up, adequate hydration and sodium intake, and avoidance of alcohol and certain OTC drugs. Then, assiduously document, verbatim, pertinent questions the patient asked and your answers to them. This is very important, because if a patient has the presence of mind to ask relevant questions, he or she is clearly demonstrating competency during this vital part of the IC process.

Again, not only is this a better IC process than any document can perform, but it also serves as a very powerful risk management tool. Imagine that ten years after your last contact with a patient, you are on the witness stand being cross-examined by an attorney who is trying to convince a jury that your patient was sitting there like a potato while you nonchalantly sprinkled informed consent on him or her like pepper. The attorney asks, "What did you tell my client about that toxic swill you foisted on him, doctor?" And you look the attorney right in the eye and say with tremendous confidence and great aplomb, "I don't remember. It was ten years ago and memory is unreliable. But, I see by my notes that the patient and I had the standard discussion about the medication I recommended—the same discussion I have had with every patient before and every patient since—which goes as follows . . ." You continue, "I also see that I specifically cautioned him not to use his power tools until we were sure he was tolerating the medicine well." Then you add, "I also see in my notes that the patient asked me about drinking beer while using the drug and I advised him not to since it could intensify some of the side effects, such as fatigue, as well as worsen his depression." This is rock-solid evidence. If your clinical record documents that you did something it is up to the plaintiff to prove that you didn't. (Of course, for a record to stand up in court, it must be part of an authentic patient file, not some fresh-looking pages shuffled in with old, yellowed papers.)

Maximizing Compliance and Safety

One of the strangest paradoxes in the mental health field is that the providers who have the most liability for their patients' safety (i.e., prescribers) usually spend the least amount of time with their patients. Indeed, the most common complaint among patients is that doctors do not spend enough time with them. The second most common complaint, no doubt a corollary of complaint number one, is that doctors do not provide enough specific information. As discussed above, the best methods of informed consent and risk management depend on the therapeutic relationship itself (e.g., Lazarus & Fay, 1984; Gutheil & Gabbard, 1998). Similarly, the best strategies for optimizing compliance and patient safety also rely heavily on a solid therapeutic alliance that, obviously, cannot be achieved by spending 10 or 15 minutes with someone once a month or less. Since establishing rapport and alliance building are the pillars on which psychosocial therapy rests, most psychologists and nonmedical mental health care providers are already well-versed in these processes.

Beyond basic rapport, an "open door policy" is one excellent method for furthering these aims. That is, patients should be encouraged to call anytime if they have any concerns, worries, or fears. (Of course, patients with severe somatization disorders and/or significant Axis II pathology such as Borderline Personality Disorder need to have firmer therapeutic boundaries. Nevertheless, they, too, should be made to feel welcome in sharing rational concerns as often as necessary.) Interestingly, inviting patients to call anytime for any (rational) reason usually results in their calling seldom.

Another fundamental strategy for ensuring compliance and safety is to avoid surprises. Therefore, in keeping with the practice of good informed consent, patients should be informed of common or dramatic medication side effects. Patients can tolerate tremendous distress if they are told what to expect. Even severe dystonias and oculogyric crises (side effects of typical antipsychotic agents) can be withstood with sufficient warning. To concretize this suggestion, consider the two following scenarios. Scenario one: a patient experiencing dystonias without adequate warning. "Oh my god! What is this medicine doing to my body? Why are my muscles so stiff and cramping like this?" Scenario two: a patient experiencing dystonias after being told to expect them, "Oh, there's that muscle stiffness the doctor told me I might experience. She told me it might happen and not to let it worry me too much." The take-home message here is to *prevent surprise.* A prescriber need not provide a patient with an exhaustive compendium of every possible side effect associated with a drug; however, a "heads up" warning on the most frequent or disconcerting treatment-emergent adverse events cannot only improve compliance, but also strengthen the doctor–patient alliance.

In keeping with the no-surprises theme, it is important to alert patients to the fact that progress in therapy is not usually linear, but rather resembles a "saw tooth," in that a graph of progress over time would look something like a chart of the Dow Jones Average. Hence patients must be cautioned to expect "two steps forward, one step back," and to not let their hope for a good recovery get chewed up in the saw teeth of their progress.

Finally, patients must be educated about what to expect from drug therapy. While a few patients have a profound, primary endogenous illness that requires medication and little else in the way of psychosocial therapy, most patients will require the synergism of a comprehensive biopsychosocial treatment. This will not only maximize their therapeutic gains, but will also armor them against relapse if the balance of their therapy is a psychoeducative, cognitive–behavioral approach that emphasizes skills acquisition rather than insight (e.g., Lazarus & Lazarus, 1997). Therefore, to use a football analogy, drug therapy might take a patient to midfield, or even to within field goal range, but to get into the end zone, she or he will have to do something about their problems as well as take something for them.

As for getting a person to agree to a trial of medication, especially one who is drug-averse, it is vital that every effort be made to destigmatize the illness and provide a concrete rationale for medical therapy. Again, by virtue of the emphasis that most nonmedical clinicians place on relationship building, this is relatively easy if the process is part of an alliance-based discussion and the clinician exudes confidence and knowledge about psychopharmacologic treatments. Ironically, many patients who refuse to comply with a trial of psychotropics prescribed by a psychiatrist will adhere to an identical regimen if their therapist convincingly recommends it.

Perhaps the best way to destigmatize clinical conditions requiring drug treatment is to emphasize that they are *illnesses,* not weaknesses, character flaws, or personality defects. There are several useful points to emphasize in this regard. First, refuting the false dichotomy of mind/psychology versus body/physiology is helpful. Most patients like to hear that the mind and the body are different sides of the same coin. Hence the brain, our organ of consciousness, is from one point of view an enormously important gland that functions reciprocally with the other organs in the body's ecosystem. Thus, the separation between physical and mental illness is fundamentally nonsensical; illness is illness is illness.

Second, drawing a parallel between certain endocrine disorders that usually require medical correction is helpful in this regard. For example, pointing out that diabetes mellitus and hypothyroidism are but two of many glandular–hormonal imbalances that can have dramatic impact on mood and cognitive functioning serves to lower the threshold of acceptance for the idea that most clinically significant psychopathologies are brain disorders or neurochemical imbalances that might similarly benefit from medical treatment. Of course, this does not mean medical therapy is always necessary. For instance, some cases of type II diabetes and essential hypertension respond well to "behavioral medicine" (i.e., salubrious life-style changes such as exercise, weight loss, sensible nutrition, and relaxation training). Likewise, many brain disorders such as OCD, phobias, panic disorder, and unipolar depression respond well to nonmedical, cognitive–behavioral treatment as well (e.g., Baxter, 1991; Baxter et al., 1992). Nevertheless, despite the fact that drug treatment may not be absolutely necessary, "jump starting" recovery and symptom reduction with an appropriate chemical "catalyst" is often desirable. In this way, progress can be optimized and in the long run, reliance on medication can be minimized.

Third, underscoring that diagnostic labels like "depression" and "anxiety" are vague and medically imprecise is very helpful (e.g., C. Lazarus, 1991). That is, discussing the pathophysiology of brain disorders in more medically sophisticated language often reassures patients that they are indeed suffering from a treatable illness. For example, in cases of major depression, point out that a crucial neural structure called the hypothalamus regulates sleep, appetite, energy, pleasure, and libido, the core functions affected by depressive illness. Then emphasize that due to genetic factors or chronic or acute stress the hypothalamus is vulnerable to becoming underactive (like the thyroid or pancreas) and often needs chemical replenishment to restore balance and achieve symptom remission. Thus, while more of a heuristic than a confirmed medical definition, depression can be referred to as "hypothalamic hypofunction."

Of course, the artistry of this process involves providing the necessary information in a manner a medically unsophisticated consumer can understand and relate to. Hence, the use of metaphors can be additionally useful. One such metaphor is to liken the cognitive, emotional, and perceptual distortion of affective illness to a kind of "cataract" clouding the psychological lens. As laser surgery can burn away the opacity of an optical cataract, thus restoring clear vision, psychotropics can burn away the fog obscuring the phenomenological lens, thus restoring psychological clarity and focus. Another metaphor is to compare normal psychological functioning with a finely tuned orchestra. In an orchestra, if a single instrument is just slightly out of tune, it can diminish the acoustic harmony of the entire arrangement. Similarly, the brain requires a finely tuned and precisely balanced chemical ensemble to produce psychologically harmonious experience. If a single chemical is just slightly out of balance, it can result in significant psychological disharmony.

The art and science of pharmacopsychology and collaborative, prescriptive mental health care is an enormous undertaking. It is, however, the immediate and inevitable direction toward which the field of psychology is moving. While offering no more than a peek through the keyhole, we hope this chapter has helped build a foundation for understanding this crucial development in the mental health field.

REFERENCES

Arnott, S. (1998). Medicolegal issues in clinical practice. *Hospital Medicine, 59*(2), 149–153.

Baxter, L. R. (1991). PET studies of cerebral dysfunction in major depression and obsessive–compulsive disorder: The emerging prefrontal cortex consensus. *Annals of Clinical Psychiatry, 3,* 103–109.

Baxter, L. R., Schwartz, J. M., Bergman, K. S., Szuba, M. P., Guze, B. H., Marriotta, J. C., Alazvaki, A., Selin, C. E., Feung, H. K., Munford, P., & Phelps, M. E. (1992). Caudate glucose metabolic rate changes with both drug and behavior therapy for obsessive-compulsive disorder. *Archives of General Psychiatry, 49,* 681–689.

Carlson, N. R. (1994). *Physiology of behavior* (5th ed.). Boston: Allyn & Bacon.

Carpenter, R. H. S. (1996). *Neurophysiology* (3rd ed.). New York: Oxford University Press.

Craig, C. R., & Stitzel, R. E. (1994). *Modern pharmacology* (4th ed.). Boston: Little Brown.

Gazzangia, M. S., & LeDoux, J. E. (1978). *The integrated mind.* New York: Plenum Press.

Goldberg, I. K. (1999). Optimizing therapy with bupropion. Personal communication, October 30, 1999.

Good, W. V., & Nelson, S. E. (1991). *Psychiatry made ridiculously simple.* Miami, FL: MedMaster.

Gram, T. E. (1994). Drug absorption and distribution. In C. R. Craig and R. E. Stitzel (Eds.), *Modern pharmacology* (4th ed.), (pp. 19–32). Boston: Little Brown.

Gutheil, T. G. (1994). Risk management at the margins: Less-familiar topics in psychiatric malpractice. *Harvard Review of Psychiatry, 2*(4), 214–221.

Gutheil, T. G., & Gabbard, G. O. (1998). Misuses and misunderstanding of boundary theory in clinical and regulatory settings. *American Journal of Psychiatry, 155*(3), 409–414.

Gwilt, P. R. (1994). Pharmacokinetics. In C. R. Craig and R. E. Stitzel (Eds.), *Modern pharmacology* (4th ed.), (pp. 55–64). Boston: Little Brown.

Hyman, S. E., & Nestler, E. J. (1993). *The molecular foundations of psychiatry.* Washington, DC: American Psychiatric Press.

Hyman, S. E., Arana, G. W, & Rosenbaum, J. F. (1995). *Handbook of psychiatric drug therapy* (2nd ed.). Boston: Little Brown.

Kandel, E. R., Schwartz, J. H., & Jessell, T. M. (1991). *Principles of neural science* (3rd ed.). Norwalk, CT: Appleton & Lange.

Kaplan, H. I., & Sadock, B. J. (1991). *Synopsis of psychiatry: Behavioral sciences clinical psychiatry* (6th ed.). Baltimore, MD: Williams & Wilkins.

Lazarus, A. A. (1958). New methods in psychotherapy: A case study. *South African Medical Journal, 32,* 660–664.

Lazarus, A. A. (1994). How certain boundaries and ethics diminish therapeutic effectiveness. *Ethics and Behavior, 4,* 255–261.

Lazarus, A. A. (1997). *Brief but comprehensive psychotherapy: The multimodal way.* New York: Springer.

Lazarus, A. A., & Fay, A. (1984). Behavior therapy. In T. B. Karasu (Ed.), *The psychiatric therapies* (pp. 485–538). Washington, DC: American Psychiatric Association.

Lazarus, A. A., & Lazarus, C. N. (1991). *Multimodal Life History Inventory.* Champaign, IL: Research Press.

Lazarus, A. A., & Lazarus, C. N. (1997). *The 60-second shrink: 101 strategies for staying sane in a crazy world.* San Luis Obispo, CA: Impact.

Lazarus, C. N. (1991). Conventional diagnostic nomenclature versus multimodal assessment. *Psychological Reports, 68,* 1363–1367.

Lazarus, C. N. (1998). Biological foundations of clinical psychology. In S. Cullari (Ed.), *Foundations of clinical psychology* (pp. 274–304). Boston: Allyn & Bacon.

Preskorn, S. H. (1996). *Clinical pharmacology of selective serotonin reuptake inhibitors.* Caddo, OK: Professional Communications.

Preston, J., O'Neal, J. H., & Talaga, M. (1997). *Handbook of clinical psychopharmacology for therapists* (2nd ed.). Oakland, CA: New Harbinger.

Raichle, M. E. (1998). *Searching for images of the mind.* Princeton University Public Lecture Series, December 2, 1998.

Sherwood, L. (1993). *Human physiology: From cells to systems* (2nd ed.). St. Paul, MN: West.

Stahl, S. M. (1996). *Essential psychopharmacology: Neuroscientific basis and practical applications.* New York: Cambridge University Press.

Swanson, J. M., Christian, D. L., Wigal, T., Clevenger, W., Cavato, K. F., Ackerland, V., Dean, D. B., Carreon, D., Potkin, S., & Crinella, F. M. (1996). Tardive dyskinesia in a developmentally disabled population: Manifestations during the initial stage of a minimal effective dose program. *Experimental and Clinical Psychopharmacology, 4*(2), 218–223.

Swonger, A. K., & Constantine, L. L. (1983). *Drugs and therapy: A handbook of psychotropic drugs* (2nd ed.). Boston: Little Brown.

FOR FURTHER READING

All books suggested below are cited in the chapter and reference section.

Hyman, S. E., & Nestler, E. J. (1993). *The molecular foundations of psychiatry.* Washington, DC: American Psychiatric Press.

Hyman and Nestler's small text on neuroscience and psychiatry is a powerhouse. While many of its concepts are for advanced students and academically oriented clinicians, it is written so that advanced concepts, which are defined by vertical rules in the left margin, can be skipped without loss of the overall message.

Lazarus, A. A. (1997). *Brief but comprehensive psychotherapy: The multimodal way.* New York: Springer.

One of the most important books on biopsychosocial therapy ever written. A must for any mental health practitioner interested in maximizing his or her clinical effectiveness.

Preston, J., O'Neal, J. H., & Talaga, M. (1997). *Handbook of clinical psychopharmacology for therapists* (2nd ed.). Oakland, CA: New Harbinger.

One of the most clearly written and "reader-friendly," yet comprehensive, books on the subject of psychiatric diagnosis and psychotropic drug therapy.

Stahl, S. M. (1996). *Essential psychopharmacology: Neuroscientific basis and practical applications.* New York: Cambridge University Press.

This book explains the neurobiological concepts underlying the drug treatment of psychiatric disorders and is an essential text for students, scientists, psychiatrists, psychologists, and other mental health professionals.

CHAPTER

11 Working with People with Serious Mental Illness

DALE L. JOHNSON

The term *serious mental illness* (SMI) is broad and has general rather than specific meaning. If it is to include people who have such disorders as schizophrenia, schizoaffective disorder, bipolar disorder, and major depression, it could refer both to some long-time disabled residents of state and VA hospitals and to Nobel Prize winners such as Nash and Hemingway. Using diagnostic status alone, the range of functioning denoted by SMI is enormous, and thus not very helpful. In an attempt to narrow the definition, the following has been developed for the Healthy People 2010 Objectives: "Serious mental illness (SMI): A diagnosable mental disorder found in persons aged 18 or over of such severity and duration as to result in functional impairment that substantially interferes with or limits major life activities" (U.S. Department of Health and Human Services, 2000). *Functional impairment* is defined as "difficulties that substantially interfere with or limit role functioning in one or more major life activities, including basic daily living skills (e.g., eating, bathing, dressing); instrumental living skills (e.g., maintaining a household, managing money, getting around the community, taking prescribed medication); and functioning in social, family, and vocational/educational contexts. Adults who would have met functional impairment criteria during the referenced year without the benefit of treatment or other support services are considered to have serious mental illnesses" (*Federal Register,* 1993). People with schizophrenia, schizoaffective disorder, bipolar disorder, and major depression frequently meet these criteria. People with such disorders as anxiety and obsessive–compulsive disorders are less often so disabled.

Terminology has been controversial in this field. The term *chronic* has been rejected as too negative. *Serious mental illness* is accepted by many people and is used here. Others prefer *severe and persistent mental disorders*. The term *patient* is used here for people in a hospital, and *client* for people actively receiving services in the community. *Consumer* is used for people who have a history of SMI but who may or may not be in regular contact with service providers. Other terms are in use in other countries, but everyone finds terminology controversial. For this chapter, an attempt has been made to identify and use terms that seem to be acceptable to most people without regard to their relationships with the mental health community.

Epidemiology

The lifetime prevalence of schizophrenia is estimated to be approximately 1 percent of the population (Tsuang & Farone, 1997). This prevalence is believed to be the same worldwide and applies equally to women and men. The incidence of schizophrenia is approximately 22 cases per 100,000 individuals (Tsuang & Farone, 1997); however, incidence estimates have varied greatly owing to differences in diagnostic and recording practices. Although schizophrenia may occur in childhood and middle age, the modal onset of first psychotic symptoms is age 19 for men and 22 for women (Tsuang & Farone, 1997).

Bipolar disorder occurs in about 1.6 percent of the population using lifetime prevalence figures (Kessler et al., 1994). The disorder affects the genders equally. Onset is typically in adolescence with depressive symptoms.

Major depression has a lifetime prevalence of 17.1 percent of the population, the prevalence being 21.3 percent for women and 12.7 percent for men. Onset may occur in childhood or at any time during the life span.

Social Costs

In the United States, the annual cost of dealing with schizophrenia has been estimated at $65 billion (Wyatt et al., 1995) and the annual cost of bipolar disorder at $45 billion (Wyatt & Henter, 1995). The economic burden of depression has been estimated at $43.7 billion. Direct treatment costs of major depression have been estimated at $19 billion and indirect costs, such as loss of wages and productivity, at $10 billion (Rice & Miller, 1993).

The costs in terms of human suffering are more difficult to estimate. For example, the mortality rate is higher for persons with schizophrenia due to suicide and death through natural causes (Brown, 1997). Persons with affective disorders have much higher suicide rates than the general population; indeed, most suicides are committed by depressed people (Goodwin & Jamison, 1990).

Patients/clients/consumers are, of course, the persons whose lives are most adversely affected by mental illnesses, but their families also experience increased subjective and objective burden (Johnson, 1990).

People with serious mental illness make up approximately one-third of the 600,000 homeless persons in the United States on a given day (Federal Task Force on Homelessness and Severe Mental Illness, 1992). Seven percent of the 426,479 people in jails in 1991 had a serious mental illness, and it is estimated that 10–15 percent of the 1990 prison population of 771,243 have DSM-III-R diagnoses involving thought disorder or mood disorder (Torrey, 1995). Rates of homelessness and criminal incarceration are indicators of social distress, with the burden falling not only on the people with serious mental illness but also on members of society in general. Some observers have reported increasing rates of homelessness and use of jails and prisons as a function of the decline in availability and quality of community mental health services that has occurred with the advent of managed care in the United States and its limits on treatment options.

Etiology

Psychosocial Causes. Although psychosocial factors such as child abuse are clearly involved in the development of depressive disorders, they have not been implicated in the essential development of schizophrenia or bipolar disorder.

Genetic Causes. There is evidence for a genetic etiology for all three of the major SMIs. Evidence is strongest for bipolar disorder and weakest for major depression (NIMH Workgroup on Genetics, 1998). All are believed to have polygenic modes of inheritance with multiple genes in interaction.

Neurodevelopmental Causes. It is likely that the cause of schizophrenia is genetic and involves some type of damage to the developing brain during mid-pregnancy (Weinberger, 1987). Viruses associated with maternal pregnancy have also been implicated (O'Reilly, 1994).

Unipolar depression has been found to be related to maternal influenza during the second trimester of pregnancy (Machon, Mednick, & Huttunen, 1997).

These SMIs are believed to have neurodevelopmental essential causes, but their expression is highly complex and may involve psychosocial stressors (Johnson, 1997).

Course

The course of schizophrenia has been described many times. Warner (1985) listed 68 studies in his review. Schizophrenia is an episodic disorder with relatively symptom-free periods marked by psychotic episodes. In general, people with schizophrenia tend to improve over time. In a 32-year followup of Vermont State Hospital patients released to the community, Harding et al. (1987) found that 72 percent showed slight or no symptoms. The quiet rural setting and relative absence of drugs may have contributed to this high recovery rate. Warner's review found that "complete recovery occurs in roughly 20–25 percent of schizophrenics and social recovery in 40–45 percent" (p. 79).

Depressive symptoms tend to diminish with time, but the rate of recurrence is high. In the Zurich followup study (Angst, Kupfer, & Rosenbaum, 1996) 50 percent of patients with major depression relapsed within five years. The researchers found depression had an unfavorable outcome in terms of treatment in 75–80 percent of cases over 20 years.

Bipolar disorder is also a recurrent illness. Gitlin and associates (1995) followed 82 patients for five years after hospital treatment. Medication treatment was optimal and most patients were compliant. Nevertheless, they found that 73 percent relapsed into mania or depression. Angst, Kupfer, and Rosenbaum (1996) found that for bipolar patients the relapse rate was 50 percent in only two years.

The SMIs are thus indeed serious and generally in need of continued treatment over a long period of time.

Comorbidity or Dual Diagnosis

When the term *comorbidity* is applied to the SMIs, the reference is most often to substance abuse as the comorbid condition. This is the case for alcohol in 3.8 percent of individuals with schizophrenia and 13.4 percent of individuals with affective disorder. Rates for drug comorbidity are higher: 6.8 percent and 26.4 percent, respectively (Regier et al., 1990). Kessler and associates (Kessler et al., 1997) found much higher comorbidity rates for lifetime depression and alcohol dependence. Men had a 24.3 percent rate and women, a 48.5 percent rate.

Comorbidity with many other disorders may also exist. It is not uncommon for people with schizophrenia to have depression, anxiety, posttraumatic stress disorder (PTSD), or obsessive–compulsive disorder, or for major depression to be associated with anxiety. In each case, the comorbid condition requires treatment attention.

Intervention Settings

People with SMI may be treated in a wide range of settings. These include independent practices, group practices, community mental health centers, hospitals, jails, and prisons. Although some of the special techniques to be discussed below can be implemented by individual psychologists, most require the efforts of a group of mental health workers. A key role for psychologists is to manage such teams of workers. By virtue of their training, psychologists are prepared to carry out key leadership functions such as supervision, training, evaluation (individual and agency), and planning, including grant-proposal writing.

Competencies for Work with People with SMI

Although the basic skills of clinical and counseling psychology are required for treating people with SMI, they are not sufficient. Too often psychologists underestimate the severity of SMI or its persistence. Other special problems are described below. The special competencies that are needed have been described in detail in Johnson, 1990b. Some states, such as New York, have developed less extensive descriptions of desirable competencies (Surles, 1994).

Considerations for Intervention

People with SMI, by definition, have multiple and severe problems. The presence of these problems means that certain special treatment considerations are required. This does not mean that individuals in this group are especially difficult to work with; this is not necessarily the case. Perhaps because of their experience with disability, many are highly cooperative, even enthusiastic about treatment and rehabilitation.

Special issues in treatment and rehabilitation include the following.

Stress Management. All of the SMIs show a high susceptibility to stress (Hooley, Orley, & Teasdale, 1986; Zubin & Spring, 1977; Ellicott et al., 1990), and working with patients to manage stress has priority. It is not enough to help people to reduce stress in their lives, although that is a beginning; it is also important that they learn to manage stress as it occurs and to anticipate and avoid stressful situations. An emphasis on stress reduction by itself may lead to impoverished, stagnated lives.

Impaired Insight. Insight is often impaired with SMIs, in the sense that the person does not realize that he or she has a mental illness, that treatment is necessary, and that his or her ideas and beliefs are at odds with those of most people in the community. Lack of insight is most profound during acute psychotic episodes, but may persist well after major symptoms have resolved (David, 1990). This is especially true in schizophrenia.

One of the serious consequences of this lack of insight is noncompliance with recommended treatments. Insight problems, along with dislike of medication side-effects, are the main causes of noncompliance, and therefore, a major impediment to treatment. This facet of SMI must be recognized and dealt with.

Insight improves with symptom improvement, but this process can be accelerated with patient psychoeducation. Eckman and associates have shown that with an intensive training program, medication compliance improves as does acceptance of the illness (Eckman et al., 1992). Their work was with people who have schizophrenia, but their methods would presumably work as well with other forms of SMI.

Cognitive Deficit. A major problem for some people with SMI is a persistent cognitive deficit. Not all have this, but for those that do the deficit is an obstacle to participation in rehabilitation programs and to obtaining and retaining employment. Deficit is recognized through interviews and neuropsychological assessment where deficiencies are found in attention, memory, and executive functioning.

Although cognitive deficit appears most often in schizophrenia (Bilder, 1997; Gold & Harvey, 1993), it is also apparent in the other SMIs and is one of the reasons so many people with bipolar disorder or major depression are unable to work at expected levels even when they are apparently symptom-free (Gitlin et al., 1995).

Impaired Social Skills. Manfred Bleuler once said that whatever the essential cause of schizophrenia was found to be, it was nevertheless clear that social relatedness is profoundly disturbed. In depression, social skills are impaired by the tendency to be negative about so many things (Coyne, 1976). In bipolar disorder social relations are smashed during the manic phase, often with consequences that last long after the manic episode.

Social skills problems make relationships with the therapist difficult, but also point out why psychosocial interventions are so important.

Trust. People with paranoia by definition do not trust others. This lack of trust is problematic for many people who have schizophrenia, not just in times of acute disturbance, but lastingly. Similar problems appear for the other SMIs. Early proponents of psychotherapy for this group, such as Sullivan (1960), noted this problem and were concerned with developing ways of managing it.

Empowerment. It is now widely recognized that treatment and rehabilitation depend more on doing *with* than doing *for* or *to* the other person. People who have SMI work with professionals to further their rehabilitation. This point should be considered in every interaction with people with SMI (and with other clients as well) (Corrigan & Garman, 1997).

Assessment

It is the psychologist's responsibility to provide a detailed and accurate assessment of the patient's condition. This assessment comprises examination both of problem areas, including presence and severity of symptoms, and of personal strengths that can be brought to bear as the person develops a therapeutic alliance with the therapist.

A diagnosis must be determined, but this is primarily for research or reimbursement purposes; treatment direction depends on a more specific assessment of the patient's strengths and weaknesses. For example, bipolar disorder is divided into Bipolar I and Bipolar II in the DSM-IV manual (American Psychiatric Association, 1994), but practical management considerations require that it be known whether the patient is a rapid cycler or not, and if the person has a mood-incongruent or mood-congruent form of the disorder (Miklowitz, 1992). These distinctions become clear only with a thorough, structured interview of the patient and, if possible, a significant other.

In the assessment of SMI, some psychologists have moved away from the use of projective techniques to structured interviews, questionnaires, observational procedures, and neuropsychological testing. Thus, instead of inferring depression from Rorschach responses, a structured interview such as the Structured Clinical Diagnostic Interview (SCDI) and a self-report measure such as the Beck Depression Inventory–II (BDI–II) or Hamilton Depression Inventory is used. For the assessment of positive symptoms, specific measures of hallucinatory and delusional experiences are used.

Core Treatments and Forms of Rehabilitation

Psychopharmacy

Psychotropic medications have an important role in the treatment of serious mental illnesses; many would say the role is central. Medications are regarded as a first-line form of treatment and with the reduction in services forced by managed care, many community mental health centers have become little more than medication clinics. This has minimized the place of psychologists in such centers, but well-informed administrators realize that (1) medication alone usually is not sufficient for treatment or rehabilitation and (2) effective medication use is dependent on ongoing assessment and intensive medication-compliance training. Psychologists have key roles in implementing each of these functions. In this chapter, it is assumed that psychologists will work with physicians who have prescription privileges. This relationship is described by Smyer et al., 1993.

Examples of the major medications used in the treatment of SMI are shown in Table 11.1. The chemical name is given first with the brand name below. The term *older* is used for typical antipsychotics and tricylclic or heterocyclic antidepressives. *Newer* refers to atypical antipsychotics and selective serotonin reuptake inhibitor (SSRI) antidepressants. For bipolar disorder, the *newer* medications are anticonvulsants.

Antipsychotics. These drugs are used in the treatment of schizophrenia and other disorders in which psychosis is present. Thus, they are also used in the treatment of bipolar disorder, major depression, and autism. Chlorpromazine was first used in 1956. It was followed by a large number of other similar-acting drugs, all of which had their main effects on the dopamine receptor system. Not until 1990 were chemically different drugs approved for use by the FDA. The first of these, clozapine, was actually synthesized in 1965, but owing to agranulocytosis-associated deaths of some patients in drug trials in Finland, the drug was withdrawn and not approved until arrangements were made for regular blood tests for early detection of blood disorders. The success of clozapine encouraged the development of other medications and other atypicals soon followed. These are all approximately equal to the typical antipsychotics in effectiveness, but have fewer side effects. Only clozapine is especially effective with patients whose symptoms are not relieved by typical antipsychotics (Tamminga, 1997).

TABLE 11.1 Examples of Medications Used to Treat the Serious Mental Illnesses

	Antipsychotics	Antidepressives	Mood Stabilizers
Older	chlorpromazine Thorazine	imipramine Trofranil	lithium Lithobid
	fluphenazine Prolixin	amitriprpyline Elavil	
	thioridzine Mellaril	bupropion Wellbutrin	
	haloperidol Haldol	doxepin Adapin	
Newer	clozapine Clozeril	fluoxetine Prozac	valproate Depakote
	risperidone Risperdal	paroxetine Paxil	carbmazepine Tegretol
	olanzapine Ziprexia	sertraline Zoloft	
	quetiapine Seroquel	venlafaxine Effexor	
	ziprasidone Zeldox	citalopram Celexia	

Among the newer antipsychotics, there are some important differences in side effect profiles. Although most have fewer unpleasant side effects than typical antipsychotics, several still have side effects that promote nonadherence. Weight gain is one of these. It is less likely, however, with ziprasidone (Tandon, Harrigan, & Zorn, 1997).

Antidepressives. There are many medications available for the treatment of affective disorders. These are discussed in Chapter 10.

Psychosocial Methods

The major forms of psychosocial intervention that psychologists should know about and be prepared to implement when working with people who have SMI are listed in Table 11.2 and discussed below. For most, efficacy has been determined with randomized controlled clinical trials. The American Psychological Association Division 12 (Clinical) Task Force on Promotion and Dissemination of Psychological Procedures developed standards for empirically validated therapies; see Chambless et al. (1998) for details.

American Psychological Association (APA) reviews of published research on psychological treatments for adults revealed several in the field of SMI (DeRubeis & Crits-Christoph, 1998; Baucom et al., 1998), and these are mentioned in following sections. Other guidelines to treatment of people with SMI were also consulted for reviews of efficacy of

TABLE 11.2 Important Psychosocial Methods

Psychotherapy		Drop-In Centers	*
Cognitive–Behavioral	***	Case Management	
Interpersonal	***	Broker Model	*
Group Psychotherapy	**	Assertive Community Training	***
Patient Education	**	Fairweather Lodges	**
Family Interventions		Social Learning Program	**
Family Consultation	*	Cognitive Rehabilitation	***
Family Education	*	Vocational/Educational Rehabilitation	
Family Psychoeducation	***	Supported	***
Social Skills Training	***	Transitional	**
Psychosocial Clubhouses	**	Job Club	**

*** Effectiveness demonstrated in multiple controlled trials. ** Effectiveness demonstrated in at least one controlled trial. * Effectiveness not known.

treatments. For schizophrenia these guidelines were those of Frances, Docherty, and Kahn (1996), American Psychiatric Association (1997), and Lehman et al., 1995); for bipolar disorder, American Psychiatric Association (1994); and for depression, American Psychiatric Association (1993) and Depression Guideline Panel (1993). In addition, Mojtabai, Nicholson, and Carpenter (1998) conducted a meta-analysis of a wide range of psychosocial treatments and found that most, but not all, were effective in attaining a variety of treatment goals.

Table 11.2 shows the status of each of the treatments mentioned by APA Task Force criteria, as judged by the Task Force, or as I have judged them using Task Force criteria.

In the great majority of cases, clients in psychosocial interventions also take medication.

Psychotherapy

Until the 1950s the main treatments for the serious mental illnesses were shock therapies (insulin and electroshock), lobotomies, and physical soothing techniques such as the cold-wet sheet pack and hydrotherapy (Valenstein, 1986). When psychotherapy was offered as a humane alternative, it was greeted with relief and enthusiasm. Early reports suggested great success; however, these were based on uncontrolled or methodologically flawed research. There have been two controlled, random-assignment, large-scale studies of psychodynamic therapy with schizophrenia, the first with relatively inexperienced therapists and the second with highly experienced therapists. The results were not favorable (May et al., 1976; Gunderson et al., 1984).

These results do not mean that psychotherapy per se is not effective in treating schizophrenia. Five more recent randomized controlled studies have demonstrated the effectiveness of cognitive-behavioral psychotherapy or of a related kind of therapy, personal therapy. Three of these (Drury et al., 1996; Kuipers et al., 1997; Tarrier et al., 1998) focused on positive symptom relief. Of these, Drury's group worked with acutely disturbed cases and the other two worked with clients in the community. All significantly reduced the salience of such positive symptoms as delusions and hallucinations. Buchkremer and associates (1997) added family psychoeducation to cognitive therapy and found the combination more effective than cognitive therapy alone in reducing relapse rates, and better than standard treatment. In all of these studies, emphasis was placed on reviewing delusions and learning how to check ideas for veracity, on problem solving, and on coping skills training.

Personal therapy, as described by Hogarty and associates (1997), is more complex and requires a longer period of time. It is staged to take place over three years beginning just after hospital discharge. Although problem-solving and coping skills are included, emphasis is on becoming aware of and learning to manage affective states. Successful managing of stress is a major goal of the therapy. The evaluation of personal therapy by Hogarty and associates was extensive, and it appears that this may be the most potent of this group of psychotherapies. It is also more demanding of time and requires more special training.

The evaluations of these new therapies are sufficiently positive to recommend their wide application. Cognitive-behavior therapy is taught in most graduate programs today, and the special application of these methods can perhaps be learned through the manuals that are available for the Drury cognitive therapy (Chadwick, Birchwood, & Trower, 1996) and for the Kuipers cognitive-behavioral therapy (Fowler, Garety, & Kuipers, 1995).

Active, cognitively oriented therapies also are the choice for the treatment of depression. Antonuccio, Danton, and DeNelsky (1995) reviewed the literature comparing psychotherapy with pharmacotherapy for depression. They concluded that cognitive–behavioral therapy is at least as effective, short-term and long-term, as antidepressant medication and is more acceptable to clients. Interpersonal therapy is also effective, but psychodynamic therapies have not demonstrated effectiveness.

In a six-year followup, cognitive behavioral therapy (CBT) was found to be effective in reducing relapse for up to four years, but effects then faded. CBT did reduce total number of relapses during the six-year period (Fava et al., 1998). Borderline personality disorder has also been treated with CBT (Linehan, 1993a, 1993b).

Effective cognitive–behavioral therapies may have the following characteristics:

> a) A well-elaborated rationale and theory guiding the treatment, b) training in skills the patient can learn, c) an emphasis on the independent practice of the skills outside of the therapy session, d) a time-limited treatment with specific goals, e) encouragement for patients to attribute changes to their own efforts and skills rather than to the skillfulness of the therapist, and f) a maintenance plan for follow-up assessment and follow-up intervention (Antonucci, Danton, & DeNelsky, 1995, p. 576).

The efficacy of psychotherapy with bipolar disorder is not known. There is evidence from a number of methodologically weak studies that group therapy, cognitive therapy, behavioral family management therapy, family therapy, family psychoeducation, and interpersonal/social rhythm therapy improve medication compliance and reduce hospitalizations (Parikh et al., 1997). The complexity of the issues involved in the use of CBT with bipolar disorder has been discussed by Basco and Rush (1996).

Group Psychotherapy

Group psychotherapy has long held an important place in the treatment of people with SMI, being one of the standard forms of treatment in hospitals and outpatient settings. Nevertheless, evidence for effectiveness with people with SMI is scant. For acutely disturbed patients, Schooler and Keith (1993) have warned of dangers: "[W]e find little theoretical rationale for exposing an acutely psychotic and disorganized patient to the multitude of stimuli, potentially intrusive, over-involved, and critical, that can be part of group therapy on an inpatient unit" (p. 17).

In a number of treatment evaluation studies, group therapy has been the control group and has not fared well (e.g., Hayes, Halford, & Varghese, 1995). It appears that more skills-directed, training-oriented interventions do better.

Group therapy may differ from *therapy in groups*. Rehm's (1984) cognitive–behavioral program for depression is conducted in groups, but never referred to as group therapy. Group cohesion is a key part of the social learning program (Paul & Lentz, 1977) and the Fairweather Lodge program (Fairweather et al., 1969), but neither approach is considered group therapy.

Meeting with patients or clients in groups to identify and solve ongoing, day-to-day problems may be the best use of the group. Patients learn they are not alone in having problems, that others have confronted some of the same problems, and that others have solved successfully some of these problems.

Patient Education

The complexities of treatment of SMI plus the cognitive effects of the illnesses themselves make it essential that patients be educated in their illnesses and the management thereof. When this is done in thorough and extensive training programs, patients know more about their illnesses and are more likely to participate actively in their own treatment (Eckman et al., 1990, 1992). Other programs have extended the range of topics to include legal matters, stress management, and so forth (Ascher-Svanum & Krause, 1991; Barter, Queirolo, & Ekstrom, 1984; Goldman & Quinn, 1988).

Family Interventions

For a great many people with SMI, the family is their most important social group. In the past, the family was viewed as a negative factor, an entity that was part of the cause of the disorder, and a continuing obstacle to rehabilitation (Johnson, 1990a). This negative view of the family has changed to one in which the family is seen as a source of support and an aid to positive change. The family also constitutes a key part of the environment of the person with SMI; if this environment exerts positive influences, the person does better. This new view has led to the development of several ways of working with families.

Family Consultation. One form of help is family consultation. This form of assistance to families has been proposed by Bernheim (1989) and Wynne and associates (Weber, McDaniel, & Wynne, 1987; Wynne, McDaniel, & Weber, 1987). Family consultants offer expert information and advice to families who retain responsibility for setting their own goals and ways of attaining these goals. Consultants may help families make decisions that the families themselves find difficult. They are faced with difficult questions. For example: "Should our ill relative live with us or in some other place?" Or: "Our relative is taking medication for his disorder, but should he be doing something more?" Families need help with such questions.

Although there has been no evaluation research on family consultation, families appear to benefit from contacts on an ongoing basis and they report liking this form of help. Consultation during crises appears especially valuable. This method is especially valuable for psychologists in independent practice.

Family Education

The relatives of people with SMI experience a great deal of stress, especially when symptoms are acute. They are troubled by both positive and negative symptoms; they must make decisions that offend their sense of family unity, as when they must decide whether to seek hospital commitment; they are often frightened by threatening behaviors; and they find their own routines disrupted to an extreme degree. In addition, they often feel they are alone in coping with these problems and stigmatized by the nature of the illness. They need help, and a major part of that help is information.

The formats of family education sessions vary, as do their contents, but that described by Anderson, Reiss, and Hogarty (1982) is typical. The essential elements are that the family (1) learn about the National Alliance for the Mentally Ill (NAMI) and/or the National Depression and Manic Depression Association (NDMDA), and be introduced to one or more members of local chapters at the session; (2) understand the essential neurobiological cause of serious mental illnesses; (3) appreciate the role of stress and its management; and (4) be given ample opportunity to ask questions and to interact with each other.

Anderson, Reiss, and Hogarty (1986) used a full-day session. Others have included the same contents, but have made use of a series of evening sessions.

The NAMI can be reached at www.NAMI.org or by telephone at 703-524-7600. The NDMDA can be reached at www.ndmda.org or by telephone at 800-826-3632.

In my own work with families, I have adapted the Anderson, Reiss, and Hogarty Survival Skills Workshop to place more emphasis on NAMI and to include bipolar disorder and major depression along with schizophrenia. The medications section is presented by a psychiatrist invited for that purpose and briefed with an outline of recommended topics and procedures. We have found it is better to have relatives and patients in separate sessions. Both groups are able to be more open about their concerns in separate sessions.

Several studies have shown that family education increases knowledge about serious mental illnesses and that family attitudes change toward greater acceptance of the mental illness. These are important results, and mental health professionals should work to attain them. However, there is little evidence that family education alone results in positive changes for the patient or that it eases family burden (Johnson, 1994b).

Family Psychoeducation

Family psychoeducation is a form of family work developed out of research on relapse in schizophrenia. Leff and Vaughn (1985) found that certain features of family interaction, including criticism, hostility, and over-involvement (expressed emotion), were associated with higher rates of relapse. Their research has been replicated many times all over the world and has been extended to nonfamily living situations, such as board and care homes. It is quite clear that interpersonal stress is related to increased relapse, not only in people with schizophrenia, but also in people with bipolar disorder, depression, and other psychiatric disorders.

In an attempt to counter these forms of stress, Leff and Vaughn (1981), in London, developed ways of working with families that emphasized training in coping skills, problem solving, and managing stress. Families met in the sessions with the ill relative. This early family psychoeducation work was extended by Falloon et al. (1987), in Los Angeles, by Hogarty (Hogarty et al., 1991) in Pittsburgh, by Tarrier (Tarrier et al., 1989) in Manchester, and by McFarlane (McFarlane et al., 1995) in New York, with random controlled group studies. (For manuals, see Mueser, 1998.)

All demonstrated strong effects on relapse. With all research patients on medication, control group subjects tended to relapse at a rate of about 40–50 percent after nine months, while those in family psychoeducation relapsed at a rate of about 10–15 percent (Lam, 1991). The effects remained, although somewhat weakened after two years, and Tarrier has found them to still be present after eight years. This work has been replicated in China, Norway, Germany, Italy, and many other parts of the world.

Family psychoeducation now ranks with medication as one of the most effective ways of reducing symptom levels and improving quality of life of people with SMI. It should be on the priority list for psychologists working with people with SMI.

Social Skills Training

The problems of negotiating social interactions compound the difficulties of many people with SMI. It has seemed obvious for many years that social skills training (SST) should be a part of treatment (e.g., Johnson et al., 1965). Social skills training includes providing information about skills such as getting dates or obtaining directions when in an unfamiliar location; modeling relevant behaviors; rehearsing skills in role playing; corrective feedback to shape targeted behaviors; and rewards for positive performance. SST methods have improved and been found to be quite efficacious. SST generalizes and has effects over a range of behaviors (Penn & Mueser, 1996). Training effects appear to vary as a function of patient characteristics; that is, patients with negative symptoms do less well than those with a preponderance of positive symptoms (Kopelowicz et al., 1997).

It also appears that SST is a useful adjunct to other treatments. For example, Hogarty and associates found SST and family psychoeducation together were more effective than either alone (Hogarty et al., 1991).

Case Management

People with SMI often do not make an effort to utilize services or do not show up for appointments. In recognition of these facts, case management systems have been developed to reach out to people where they live.

Furthermore, the mental health system in most states is highly fragmented, with services located in many places and with only tenuous connection. Clients are expected to find their way through this maze. One solution is to make use of case managers. In this arrangement, a client is assigned to a case manager who helps the client in a variety of ways, depending on the client's needs and the case manager's work load. One of the case manager's roles is to go *to* people. Patients often lack transportation, as people with SMI frequently do not drive; if transportation is available its use may be too complex for people who have cognitive deficits.

Two types of case management have been identified. In the first, the case manager serves as broker to locate services and help the client make contact. Evaluations of the effectiveness of the broker model have had mixed results, perhaps because case managers are often poorly trained, services are not available, and case loads are too high (Holloway et al., 1995; Mueser et al., 1998).

The second model is clinical case management, in which the case manager is concerned with helping the client in a variety of ways, including providing counseling and training. There are several forms of clinical case management (Holloway et al., 1995; Mueser et al., 1998). The most widely used form is Assertive Community Treatment (ACT) or also called Programs in Assertive Community Training (PACT), developed by Stein and Test (1980). This model was created in Wisconsin to reduce relapse rates and foster social skills. In this model, a team of mental health professionals works with a group of people with SMI. Team members go to the client's home and teach home management skills, if they are lacking. They go with the client to the supermarket to teach shopping skills. They explain in detail the need for and action of prescribed medication. In short, they become a major part of the life of the person in the community. Working as a team, it is possible for these mental health professionals to assist each other as needed and to call on the wide range of skills present in the team. ACT was found to be highly successful in attaining its goals and was quickly replicated in Australia by Hoult et al. (1983) who also found the program efficacious. Since then the model has been evaluated many times and with diverse groups of people with SMI. Results for fully formed programs have been consistently positive (Bond et al., 1988; Burns & Santos, 1995; Olfson, 1990). It is very important to note that ACT does have essential elements, and if some of these are missing, outcomes are less favorable (McGrew et al., 1994).

The empirical base for the ACT program is strong, making this a priority model to consider in providing services. However, it is not a complete model. It is limited in providing rehabilitation and offers only limited opportunities for socialization and development of social skills.

Psychosocial Clubhouses

The first psychosocial clubhouse was Fountain House, established in New York City in 1948. Clubhouses are first of all places where members can meet as peers. Empowerment is a major goal of clubhouses. Secondly, they are social centers where people with SMI can meet other people and have a pleasant time. Thirdly, clubhouses are settings for vocational rehabilitation. Depending on local conditions, experiences, and preferences, various types of vocational rehabilitation are offered. These include transitional employment, sheltered employment, and supported employment.

There has been relatively little research on the effectiveness of the clubhouses. In one of the few studies, Beard, Malamud, and Rossman (1978) reported lower rehospitalization rates over a five-year period for Fountain House members than for randomly assigned controls.

Drop-In Centers (DIC)

People with SMI often have small social networks and, while desiring social interaction opportunities, lack the skills and motivations necessary to meet people and maintain relationships with others. Drop-in centers (DICs) were developed to meet this need. These are nearly always socialization settings first of all; only rarely are rehabilitation efforts added. Their main problem seems one of having enough people drop in on a regular basis to justify their existence. This is a problem even when the DIC is located at a transportation hub and provides attractive social opportunities. The negative symptoms of SMI are the obstacle.

Johnson (1994b) reviewed the small body of research on DICs and found they had little impact on symptoms, relapse rates, or employment rates. Drop-out rates are high. Nevertheless, in some settings they may provide social interaction experiences that have value. In addition, those DICs run by mental health consumers provide a good rehabilitative work experience for the employees.

Fairweather Lodges

Fairweather's program (also called "achievement lodges") began at the Palo Alto Veterans Administration Hospital as a way to motivate patients to leave the hospital (Fairweather et al., 1969). It was effective in doing so, but researchers noted that the relapse rate was high. They modified the program to maximize the length of stay in the community.

This program is an elegant adaptation of social psychological research findings. Small-group research was used to develop cohesive working groups of patients. Trained initially in the hospital to work together in solving problems and in coping with adversity, patients moved into the community, where they lived together and operated competitive businesses. Many of the lodges operated janitorial services. In Houston, at one time, one lodge had a contract to maintain the Coca-Cola warehouse and another maintained buildings in the medical center.

By working as a team, lodge members are able to compensate for work deficiencies in the performance of individual members. One person may not be able to negotiate contracts or deal with managers, but can operate a floor buffer.

The effectiveness of the lodge program was evaluated with a matched-group design. Using time in the community as an outcome measure, Fairweather found the lodge program participants did significantly better than the controls at 6–40 months. In addition, lodge members were much more often employed at each followup time point.

The lodge program was at one time very popular, with more than 200 lodges in operation around the nation. Today it seems to be neglected, which is unfortunate, as it is still a highly appropriate program for many people, especially those who do not have good prospects for surviving and working in the community without strong support.

Social Learning Program (SLP)

The development of token economies for the treatment of long-term institutionalized patients was a methodological breakthrough (Allyon & Azrin, 1968), and such procedures were widely adopted. The token economy is essentially a motivational system and, used alone, has limitations as a training system. In a token economy certain behaviors are targeted for change; if the person changes in the desired way, he or she obtains tokens that may be used to purchase desirable objects or events (e.g., permission to go to the hospital canteen for coffee, or an extended pass). If the person violates rules, tokens are taken away. For example, if a person speaks aggressively, tokens will be removed.

Paul and Lentz (1977) improved treatment further by developing a highly integrated system of treatment. Specific excessive behaviors such as hitting or spitting are identified and targeted for modification. Behavioral deficits such as personal grooming also receive specific attention. Identification of problem behaviors is accomplished with an objective, highly reliable observational procedure, the Time-Sample Behavioral Checklist (Paul, 1987).

A thorough evaluation of the program was conducted and the SLP was found to be superior to a conventional treatment control and a milieu therapy control. Patients had been hospitalized an average of 16 years at the beginning of the study. At the 5-year followup, 97.5 percent of the SLP patients were functioning in the community, compared with 71 percent of the milieu group and only 44.8 percent of the conventional treatment group. The SLP was very successful in eliminating dangerous aggressive behavior. Medication use declined as treatment progressed.

The SLP is the only effective treatment for people who have psychotic disorders and who do not respond well to medications (Glynn & Mueser, 1986).

Cognitive Rehabilitation

There have been several attempts to remediate the cognitive deficit so often found in schizophrenia. In general, the focus of these efforts has been on executive functioning, attention, and memory. Some of this work has been reviewed by Green (1993). It appears that remediation is possible, but to date, the gains have been small. It is likely that more intensive training is necessary over much longer periods of time to attain meaningful goals (Wexler et al., 1997). One exciting new development is the Cognitive Enhancement Therapy developed by Hogarty and Flesher (1999). People with schizophrenia who have been stabilized on medication participate in an intensive all-day, every-day rehabilitation program. Specific cognitive deficits, such as those of attention or complex planning, are identified and the person receives remedial training with the aid of computer programs. These programs are gamelike and were developed initially for the rehabilitation of people with traumatic head injuries. In addition, small group discussions are held to work on how to get to the gist of a problem. Hogarty had observed that this was an especially great problem for people with schizophrenia. Training includes reading editorials from *USA Today* and, in the group, identifying the main point of the editorials. Early results indicate that cognitive deficits are essentially eliminated and people become symptom-free. Patients also *like* the program and continue to make gains on their own after the formal program is ended.

There do not seem to be reports of similar work with the other SMIs, even though the cognitive deficit research suggests it may be warranted (Purcell et al., 1997).

Vocational/Educational Rehabilitation

Several forms of vocational/educational rehabilitation are used and research results have been reported (Lehman et al., 1995). At present, the oldest of these, sheltered employment, seems not to be in favor, but it should not be minimized. For some quite-disabled people, working under noncompetitive conditions and receiving low wages provides an opportunity to add structure to their lives and to have some sense of accomplishment.

Transitional Employment. Transitional employment has a key role in many psychosocial clubhouses and has been a part of the Fountain House virtually since its inception. In transitional employment, the person receiving rehabilitative services is part of a group of people receiving similar services. The host agency arranges for employment and guarantees that the job will be carried out. For example, if the job is one of stuffing envelopes for a mail-out company, the agency assures the company that the letters will be mailed, if not by people in rehabilitation, then by staff. People receive competitive wages, and it is assumed that they will work into regular employment.

Supported Employment/Education (SE). Supported employment appears to be the most popular form of employment today. It is a method for moving people from stigmatized situations into normal adult roles in the community. It assumes that people with psychiatric disabilities can work in competitive situations, full-time or part-time, if given adequate support.

SE begins with a comprehensive interview about work abilities, experiences, preferences, and limitations. A job coach is assigned to the person to help in selecting a job, applying, and following through after the person has found work. Support after entering the work force is an essential part of the model.

The effectiveness of SE has been reviewed by Bond et al. (1997). In six experimental studies, the mean percentage of clients employed in SE was 58 percent, compared with 21 percent for control clients.

Similar procedures are used for educational involvement. SMI commonly afflicts young people who are in the midst of their educational experience. They are eager to return to school, but too often have unrealistic views of what they can do. They enroll in a difficult school and take an impossible course load. SE helps to develop acceptable and attainable goals and to lay out a plan for attaining them.

Job Club. The job club was developed by Azrin and Besalel (1979) as a tightly integrated form of group support for people searching for and attempting to retain jobs. For an SMI group, the job finding rate was 90 percent compared with 33 percent for controls (Azrin & Philip, 1980). Other evaluations found lower rates of job finding, but significant differences between the job club and controls are typical (Bond, 1992). Retention of the job remains a problem.

Work Cooperatives. These are widely used in Northern Italy as part of the radical deinstitutionalization plan put into effect two decades ago (Savio & Righetti, 1993). In Trieste, for example, nearly all community mental health center (CMHS) clients are members of the work cooperative. This is run jointly by clients and staff. One CMHS operates 13 businesses, including a tourist hotel, a sailboat for tourists, a janitorial service, and a handbag design studio, factory, and sales shop. Members of the co-op share earnings. Cooperatives have been used rarely in the United States, perhaps for political reasons.

Other Forms of Intervention

Therapeutic Contracting. This is a system for engaging the person with SMI as a colleague in developing and carrying out a treatment program (Heinssen, Levendusky, & Hunter, 1995). The psychologist serves as a expert guide. The system "is based on principles of behavior change that stimulate [the] client's perceptions of self-control, personal effectiveness, and self-worth through milieu-based and individual goals-setting interventions" (p. 523).

Multimodal Community Treatment. This is a service-delivery system rather than a treatment as such, but psychologists working with people who have SMI should be aware of this system (Bedell, Hunter, & Corrigan, 1997). The method makes use of a wide range of behavioral assessments that are carried out at baseline and on a continuing basis thereafter. Members of the clinic team are assigned responsibilities for working with the client on targeted problems or symptoms and making periodic reports to the team about progress. The team works with the client in finding ways to continue to make progress. It should be noted that at a time when many people have called for regular outcomes-assessment, this system is one of the few that provides such data on a routine basis.

Symptom Management. Hallucinations and delusions that continue even with medication adherence may be managed with behavioral and cognitive–behavioral methods. As noted, the methods developed by Drury, Kuipers, and Tarrier were all successful in reducing the severity of these positive symptoms. Weiss and Weiss (1998) reviewed other methods. In addition, Jenner, van de Willege, and Wiersma (1998), using an uncontrolled, naturalistic outcome study, found cognitive therapy highly effective in treating auditory hallucinations. It is clear at this time that most patients can be helped with one or more of this set of methods.

Diversity Issues

The treatment and rehabilitation methods described have been used with women and men, and apparently with virtually all ethnic groups in the United States. All groups of people are susceptible to SMI, and all seem to respond to the methods described here. Furthermore, most if not all of these methods have been successfully adopted for use in other countries. Many new methods, such as CBT for the symptoms of schizophrenia, were developed in England, Germany, and Holland and are only now being used in the United States. It should be noted that none of the methods can be applied in a mechanical way; all must be modified to meet the individual needs, abilities, and limitations of the people for whom they are intended. Programs or types of treatment provide structures and general plans for action that make it possible for therapy to occur. Therapy also depends on the relationship of the patient, client, or consumer with the therapist.

From Symptom Control to Recovery

Mental health professionals recognize the need for a full range of psychosocial services in addition to medication and, in some instances, instead of medication. Nevertheless, few people with SMI today receive the full range of recommended services (Lehman et al., 1998).

The availability of medication has made the reduction of relapse rates possible. Clearly we have knowledge from research that would further reduce relapse and improve quality of life, but this knowledge is not being implemented widely.

In addition, with major symptoms under control for most clients, and with the rise of the mental health consumer movement whereby many people who have been seriously disturbed are now coming forward to tell their stories and to show that recovery is possible, a new goal is established, which is an improved quality of life and normalization.

Course of SMI and Implications for Treatment

All people with SMI cannot and should not receive the same package of treatments. Perhaps the most important aspect of treatment planning is to individualize. Nevertheless, it is possible to think of five aspects to the course of most disorders needing treatment: (1) pre-psychosis prevention, (2) first-episode treatment, (3) standard, long-term treatment, (4) treatment of the most disabled, and (5) rehabilitation or recovery.

Pre-Psychosis Treatment. Researchers have long doubted that the state of scientific knowledge is sufficient to prevent any of the SMIs (Goldstein, 1981). Now, even with limited knowledge of the etiologies of these disorders, preventive efforts have been undertaken. Falloon (1992) published a provocative report on prevention of schizophrenia making use of the early identification of prodromal signs in adolescence. This identification is done by primary care physicians who have been specially trained for this purpose. The prodromal signs are: "Marked peculiar behavior; inappropriate or loss of affect; vague, rambling speech; marked poverty of speech or thought; ideas of reference; depersonalisation or derealisation; perceptual disturbances" (Falloon, 1992, p. 6). Treatment consists of moderate, short-term use of anti-psychotic medication and family psychoeducation. Continuing mental health monitoring is also included. Evaluation of the prevention effort did not include a randomized control design, but the incidence of diagnosable schizophrenia that was present at four-year followup was compared with the incidence of schizophrenia found in an earlier study of the community. The incidence rate was 0.75 per 100,000 compared with an expected rate of 7.4 per 100,000. This remarkable reduction in incidence has prompted others to attempt prevention (e.g., Yung et al., 1996), but results from controlled trials have not been reported as yet.

The prevention of depression has much promise, as discussed by Munoz (1993). While there seem to have been no attempts to prevent the onset of bipolar disorder, a good approach might resemble that taken by Falloon to schizophrenia. In a survey of National Depressive and Manic-Depressive Association members, it was found that 59 percent of respondents had first symptoms during childhood or adolescence and that there were long delays between the beginning of prodromal signs and treatment for bipolar disorder (Lish et al., 1994). This period of delay is a ripe time for preventive intervention.

First-Episode Treatment. With all SMIs it is important to make an accurate diagnosis and identification of the full range of problem behaviors (symptoms) as soon as possible. Ideally, a person suffering a psychotic episode for the first time would be rushed to a specialty hospital. This is done in parts of The Netherlands (de Haan, Linszen, & Gorsira, 1998), where experts on psychosis thoroughly examine the patient and initiate treatment consisting of a wide range of intervention modalities. Treatment is individualized, but in general includes the following: medication, compliance training, family psychoeducation, cognitive–behavioral therapy, case management, social skills training, and vocational rehabilitation. This program resulted in a 14 percent relapse rate after one year compared with the expected rate of 40 percent.

Standard, Long-Term Treatment. The full range of interventions already mentioned can be considered here. People in this group relapse fairly often and may be in and out of care; therefore, it is especially important to use active forms of contact, such as ACT.

Severely-Disabled SMI. People in this group have severe and persistent symptoms that resist medical treatment. Many are institutionalized because they are assaultive, uncommunicative, and unable to provide even basic care for themselves. The Social Learning Program (Paul & Lentz, 1977) was developed to meet the needs of this group and seems to be the only programmatic treatment that is effective with this population.

Rehabilitation. At the fifth level of treatment are people whose symptoms have been quite successfully treated, but who still have cognitive deficits or other problems that prevent them from being fully integrated into the community. For this group, rehabilitation in its various forms is essential. Several forms of vocational rehabilitation have been mentioned. Cognitive rehabilitation may be especially important. This stage of the treatment/rehabilitation continuum has received least research.

Conclusions

People with SMI have multiple disabilities and treatment is a challenge: a challenge that brings many rewards, because it is possible to intervene with methods that not only reduce symptom severity, but also lead to improved quality of life for most people. The problem today is not a lack of effective methods; it is that there are so many social and economic obstacles to the application of these methods.

REFERENCES

Alford B. A., & Correia, C. J. (1994). Cognitive therapy of schizophrenia: Theory and empirical base. *Behavior Therapy, 25,* 17–33.

Allyon, T., & Azrin, N. H. (1968). *The token economy.* New York: Appleton-Century-Crofts.

American Psychiatric Association. (1993). Practice guidelines for major depressive disorders in adults. *American Journal of Psychiatry, 150* (Suppl. April), 1–26.

American Psychiatric Association. (1994a). Practice guidelines for the treatment of patients with bipolar disorder. *American Journal of Psychiatry, 151* (Suppl. December), 1–36.

American Psychiatric Association. (1994b). *DSM-IV: Diagnostic and statistical manual for mental disorders* (4th ed.). Washington, DC: American Psychiatric Press.

American Psychiatric Association. (1997). Practice guidelines for the treatment of patients with schizophrenia. *American Journal of Psychiatry, 154* (Suppl. April), 1–63.

Anderson, C. M., Reiss, D. J., & Hogarty, G. E. (1986). *Schizophrenia in the family: A practitioner's guide to psychoeducation and management.* New York: Guilford.

Angst, J., Kupfer, D. J., & Rosenbaum, J. F. (1996). Recovery from depression: Risk or reality? *Acta Psychiatrica Scandinavica, 93,* 413–419.

Antonucci, D. O., Danton, W. G., & DeNelsky, G. Y. (1995). Psychotherapy versus medication for depression: Challenging the conventional wisdom with data. *Professional Psychology: Research and Practice, 26,* 574–585.

Ascher-Svanum, H., & Krause, A. A. (1991). *Psychoeducational groups for patients with schizophrenia: A guide for practitioners.* Gaithersburg, MD: Aspen.

Azrin, N. H., & Besalel, V. B. (1979). *Job club counselor's manual: A behavioral approach to vocational counseling.* Baltimore, MD: University Park Press.

Azrin, N. H., & Philip, R. A. (1980). The job club method for the job handicapped: A comparative outcome study. *Rehabilitation Counseling Bulletin, 23,* 144–155.

Barter, J. T., Queirolo, J. F., & Ekstrom, S. P. (1984). A psychoeducational approach to educating chronic mental patients for community living. *Hospital & Community Psychiatry, 35,* 793–797.

Basco, M. R., & Rush, A. J. (1996). *Cognitive–behavioral therapy for bipolar disorder.* New York: Guilford.

Baucom, D. H., Shoham, V., Mueser, K. T., Daiuto, A. D., & Stickle, T. R. (1998). Empirically supported couple and family interventions for marital distress and adult mental health problems. *Journal of Consulting and Clinical Psychology, 66,* 53–88.

Beard, J. H., Malamud, T. J., & Rossman, E. (1978). Psychiatric rehabilitation and long-term rehospitalization rates: The findings of two research studies. *Schizophrenia Bulletin, 4,* 622–635.

Bedell, J. R., Hunter, R. H., & Corrigan, P. W. (1997). Current approaches to assessment and treatment of persons with serious mental illness. *Professional Psychology: Research and Practice, 28,* 217–228.

Bilder, R. M. (1997). Neurocognitive impairment in schizophrenia and how it affects treatment options. *Canadian Journal of Psychiatry, 42,* 255–264.

Bond, G. R. (1992). Vocational rehabilitation. In R. P. Liberman (Ed.), *Handbook of psychiatric rehabilitation* (pp. 244–275). Boston: Allyn & Bacon.

Bond, G. R., Drake, R. E., Mueser, K. T., & Becker, D. R. (1997). An update on supported employment for people with severe mental illness. *Psychiatric Services, 48,* 335–346.

Bond, G. R., Miller, L. D., Krumweid, R. D., & Ward, R. S. (1988). Assertive case management in three CMHCs: A controlled study. *Hospital and Community Psychiatry, 39,* 411–418.

Bouchard, S., Vallieres, A., Roy, M. A., & Maziade, M. (1996). Cognitive restructuring in the treatment of psychotic symptoms in schizophrenia: A critical analysis. *Behavior Therapy, 27,* 257–277.

Brenner, H. D., Boker, W., Hodel, B., & Wyss, H. (1989). Cognitive treatment of basic pervasive dysfunctions in schizophrenia. In S. C. Schulz & C. A. Tamminga (Eds.), *Schizophrenia: Scientific progress* (pp. 358–367). New York: Oxford University Press.

Brown, S. (1997). Excess mortality of schizophrenia. *British Journal of Psychiatry, 171,* 502–508.

Buchkremer, G., Klingberg, S. Holle, R., Schulze, M. H., & Hornung, W. P. (1997). Psychoeducational psychotherapy for schizophrenic patients and their key relatives or care-givers: Results of a 2-year follow-up. *Acta Psychiatrica Scandinavica, 96,* 483–491.

Burns, B. J., & Santos, A. B. (1995). Assertive community treatment: An update on randomized trials. *Psychiatric Services, 46,* 669–675.

Chadwick, P., Birchwood, M., & Trower, P. (1996). *Cognitive therapy for hallucinations, delusions and paranoia.* Chichester: Wiley.

Chambless, D. L., Baker, M. J., Baucom, D. H., Beutler, L. E., Calhoun, K. S., Crits-Cristoph, P., Daiuto, A., DeRubies, R., Detweller, J., Haaga, D. A., Johnson, S. B., McCurry, S., Mueser, K. T., Pope, K. S., Sanderson, W. C., Shoham, V., Stickle, T., Williams, D. A., & Woody, S. R. (1998). Update on empirically validited therapies. II. *The Clinical Psychologist, 51,* 3–21.

Corrigan, P. W., & Garman, A. N. (1997). Considerations for research on consumer empowerment and psychosocial interventions. *Psychiatric Services, 48,* 347–352.

Coyne, J. C. (1976). Toward an interactional description of depression. *Psychiatry, 39,* 28–40.

David, A. S. (1990). Insight and psychosis. *British Journal of Psychiatry, 156,* 798–808.

de Haan, L., Linszen, D. H., & Gorsira, R. (1998). Early intervention, social functioning and psychotic relapse of patients with recent-onset schizophrenic disorders. *International Clinical Psychopharmacology,* 13(Suppl. 1) S63–S66.

Depression Guideline Panel. (1993). *Depression in primary care: Volume 2. Treatment of major depression. Clinical Practice Guideline Number 5.* Rockville, MD: U.S. Department of Health and Human Services, Public Health Service, Agency for Health Care Policy and Research. AHCPR Publication No. 93-0550.

DeRubeis, R. J., & Crits-Christoph, P. (1998). Empirically supported individual and group psychological treatments for adult mental disorders. *Journal of Consulting and Clinical Psychology, 66,* 17–52.

Drury, V., Birchwood, M., Cochrane, R., & MacMillan, F. (1996). Cognitive therapy and recovery from acute psychosis: A controlled trial. I. Impact on psychotic symptoms. *British Journal of Psychiatry, 169,* 593–607.

Eckman, T. A., Liberman, R. P., Phipps, C. C., & Blair, K. E. (1990). Teaching medication management skills to schizophrenic patients. *Journal of Clinical Psychopharmacology, 10,* 33–38.

Eckman, T. A., Wirshing, W. C., Marder, S. R., Liberman, R. P., Johnston-Cronk, K., Zimmerman, K., & Mintz, J. (1992). Technique for training schizophrenic patients in illness self-management: A controlled trial. *American Journal of Psychiatry, 149,* 1449–1555.

Ellicott, A., Hammen, C., Gitlin, M., Brown, G., & Jamison, K. (1990). Life events and the course of bipolar disorder. *American Journal of Psychiatry, 147,* 1194–1198.

Ernst, E., Rand, J. I., & Stevinson, C. (1998). Complementary therapies for depression: An overview. *American Journal of Psychiatry, 155,* 1026–1032.

Fairweather, G. W., Sanders, D. H., Maynard, H., & Cressler, D. L. (1969). *Community life for the mentally ill: An alternative to institutional care.* Chicago: Aldine.

Falloon, I. R. H. (1992). Early intervention for first episodes of schizophrenia: A preliminary exploration. *Psychiatry, 55,* 4–15.

Falloon, I. R. H., McGill, C. W., Boyd, J. L., & Pederson, J. (1987). Family management in the prevention of morbidity of schizophrenia: Social outcome of a two-year longitudinal study. *Psychological Medicine, 17,* 59–66.

Fava, G. A., Rafanelli, C., Grandi, S., Canestrari, R., & Morphy, M. A. (1998). Six-year outcome for cognitive behavioral treatment of residual symptoms in major depression. *American Journal of Psychiatry, 155,* 1443–1445.

Federal Register, 1993, 58, No. 90, 29425.

Federal Task Force on Homelessness and Severe Mental Illness. (1992). *Outcasts on main street.* Washington, DC: Interagency Council on Homelessness.

Fowler, D., Garety, P. A., & Kuipers, L. (1995). *Cognitive behaviour therapy for psychosis: Theory and practice.* Chichester: Wiley.

Frances, A., Docherty, J. P., & Kahn, D. A. (1996). The expert consensus guideline series: Treatment of schizophrenia. *Journal of Clinical Psychiatry, 77* (Suppl. 12B), 58.

George, M., Wasserman, E., Callahan, A., Ketter, T., Post, R., Hallett, M., & Williams, W. (1996). Daily repetitive transcranial magnetic stimulation (rTMS) improves mood in depression. Neuroreport, Oct. 2.

Gitlin, M. J., Swendsen, J., Heller, T. L., & Hammen, C. (1995). Relapse and impairment in bipolar disorder. *American Journal of Psychiatry, 152,* 1635–1640.

Glynn, S., & Mueser, K. T. (1986). Social learning for chronic mental inpatients. *Schizophrenia Bulletin, 12,* 648–668.

Gold, J. M., & Harvey, P. D. (1993). Cognitive deficits in schizophrenia. *Psychiatric Clinics of North America, 16,* 295–311.

Goldman, C. R., & Quinn, F. L. (1988). Effects of a patient education program in the treatment of schizophrenia. *Hospital and Community Psychiatry, 39,* 283–286.

Goldstein, M. J. (1981). *Preventive intervention in schizophrenia: Are we ready?* Rockville, MD: U.S. Department of Health and Human Services, #81-1111.

Goodwin, F. K., & Jamison, K. R. (1990). *Manic-depressive illness.* New York: Oxford University Press.

Gould, R. A., & Clum, G. A. (1993). A meta-analysis of self-help treatment approaches. *Clinical Psychology Review, 13* , 169–186.

Green, M. F. (1993). Cognitive remediation in schizophrenia: Is it time yet? *American Journal of Psychiatry, 150,* 178–187.

Gunderson, J. G., Frank, A. F., Katz, H. M., Vannicelli, M. L., Frosch, J. P., & Knapp, P. H. (1984). Effects of psychotherapy in schizophrenia: II. Comparative outcome of two forms of treatment. *Schizophrenia Bulletin, 10,* 564–598.

Harding, C. M., Brooks, G. W., Ashikaga, T., Strauss, J. S., & Breier, A. (1987). The Vermont longitudinal study of persons with severe mental illness, I: Methodology, study sample, and overall status 32 years later. *American Journal of Psychiatry, 144,* 718–726.

Hayes, R. L., Halford, W. K., & Varghese, F. T. (1995). Social skills training with chronic schizophrenic patients: Effects on negative symptoms and community functioning. *Behavior Therapy, 26,* 433–449.

Heinssen, R. K., Levendusky, P. G., & Hunter, R. H. (1995). Client as colleague: Therapeutic contracting with the seriously mentally ill. *American Psychologist, 50,* 522–532.

Hogarty, G. E., Anderson, C. M., Reiss, D. J., Kornblith, S. J., Greenwald, D. P., Ulrich, R. F., & Carter, M. (1991). Family psychoeducation, social skills training, and maintenance of chemotherapy in the aftercare treatment of schizophrenia. *Archives of General Psychiatry, 48,* 340–347.

Hogarty, G. E., & Flesher, S. (1999). Practice principles of Cognitive Enhancement Therapy for schizophrenia. *Schizophrenia Bulletin,* 25(4), 693–708.

Hogarty, G. E., Greenwald, D., Ulrich, R. F., Kornblith, S. J., DiBarry, A. L., Cooley, S., Carter, M., & Flesher, S. (1997). Three-year trials of personal therapy among schizophrenic patients living with or independent of family, II: Effects on adjustment of patients. *American Journal of Psychiatry, 154,* 1514–1524.

Hogarty, G. E., Kornblith, S. J., Greenwald, D., DiBarry, A. L., Cooley, S., Ulrich, R. F., Carter, M., &

Flesher, S. (1997). Three-year trials of personal therapy among schizophrenic patients living with or independent of family, I: Description of study and effects on relapse rates. *American Journal of Psychiatry, 154,* 1504–1513.

Holloway, F., Oliver, N., Collins, E., & Carson, J. (1995). Case management: A critical review of the outcome literature. *European Psychiatry, 10,* 113–128.

Hooley, J. M., Orley, J., & Teasdale, J. D. (1986). Levels of expressed emotion and relapse in depressed patients. *British Journal of Psychiatry, 148,* 642–647.

Hoult, J., Reynolds, I., Charbonneau-Powis, M., Weeks, P., & Bragg, J. (1983). Psychiatric hospital versus community treatment: The results of a randomised trial. *Australian and New Zealand Journal of Psychiatry, 17,* 160–167.

Jenner, J. A., van de Willege, G., & Wiersma, D. (1998). Effectiveness of cognitive therapy with coping training for persistent hallucinations: A retrospective study of attenders of a psychiatric out-patient department. *Acta Psychiatrica Scandinavica, 98,* 384–389.

Jeste, D. V., Gladsjo, J. A., Lindamer, L. A., & Lacro, J. P. (1996). Medical comorbidity in schizophrenia. *Schizophrenia Bulletin, 22,* 413–430.

Johnson, D. L. (1990a). The family's experience of living with mental illness. In H. Lefley & D. L. Johnson (Eds.), *Families as allies in treatment of the mentally ill* (pp. 31–63). Washington, DC: American Psychiatric Association Press.

Johnson, D. L. (Ed.). (1990b). *Service needs of the seriously mentally ill: Training implications for psychology.* Washington, DC: American Psychological Association Press.

Johnson, D. L. (1994a). Current issues in family research: Can the burden of mental illness be relieved? In H. Lefley & M. Wasow (Eds.), *Helping families cope with serious mental illness* (pp. 309–328). New York: Breach & Gordon.

Johnson, D. L. (1994b). Drop-in centers are a great idea, but do they work? *Innovations & Research, 3,* 43–44.

Johnson, D. L. (1997). Overview of serious mental illness. *Clinical Psychology Review, 17,* 247–257.

Johnson, D. L., Hanson, P. G., Rothaus, P., Morton, R. B., Lyle, F. A., & Moyer, R. (1965). A follow-up evaluation of human relations training for psychiatric patients. In W. Bennis & E. Schein (Eds.), *Personal and organizational change through group methods* (pp. 188–196). New York: Wiley.

Kessler, R. C., Crum, R. M., Warner, L. A., Nelson, C. B., Schulenberg, J., & Anthony, J. C. (1997). Lifetime co-occurrence of DSM-II-R alcohol abuse and dependence with other psychiatric disorders in the National Comorbidity Study. *Archives of General Psychiatry, 54,* 313–321.

Kessler, R. C., McGonagle, K. A., Zhao, S., Nelson, C. B., Hughes, M., Eshleman, S., Wittchen, H. U., & Kendler, K. S. (1994). Lifetime and 12-month prevalence of DSM-III-R psychiatric disorders in the United States. *Archives of General Psychiatry, 51,* 8–19.

Kirsch, I., & Saperstein, G. (1998). Listening to Prozac but hearing placebo: a meta-analysis of antidepressant medication. *Prevention and Treatment, 1,* 1–17.

Kopelowicz, A., Liberman, R. P., Mintz, J., & Zarate, R. (1997). Comparison of efficacy of social skills training for deficit and nondeficity negative symptoms in schizophrenia. *American Journal of Psychiatry, 154,* 424–425.

Kuipers, E., Garety, P., Fowler, D., Dunn, G., Bebbington, P., Freeman, D., & Hadley, C. (1997). London–East Anglia randomised controlled trial of cognitive–behavioural therapy for psychosis. *British Journal of Psychiatry, 171,* 319–327.

Lam, D. (1991). Psychosocial family intervention in schizophrenia: A review of empirical studies. *Psychological Medicine, 21,* 423–441.

Leff, J., & Vaughn, C. (1981). The role of maintenance therapy and relatives' expressed emotion in relapse of schizophrenia: A two-year follow-up. *British Journal of Psychiatry, 139,* 102–104.

Leff, J., & Vaughn, C. (1985). *Expressed emotion in families: Its significance for mental illness.* New York: Guilford.

Lehman, A. F., Steinwachs, D. M., & the Survey Co-Investigators of the PORT Project. (1998). Patterns of usual care for schizophrenia: Initial results from the Schizophrenic Patient Outcomes Research Team (PORT) client survey. *Schizophrenia Bulletin, 24,* 11–20.

Lehman, A. F., Thompson, J. W., Dixon, L. B., & Scott, J. E. (1995). Schizophrenia treatment outcomes research. *Schizophrenia Bulletin, 21,* 561–566 (see related articles in same issue).

Linehan, M. M. (1993a). *Cognitive behavioral therapy of borderline personality disorder.* New York: Guilford.

Linehan, M. M. (1993b). *Skills training manual for treating borderline personality disorder.* New York: Guilford.

Lish, J. D., Dime-Meenan, S., Whybrow, P. C., Price, R. A., & Hirschfeld, R. M. (1994). The National Depression and Manic-Depression Association survey of bipolar members. *Journal of Affective Disorders, 31,* 281–294.

Machon, R. A., Mednick, S. A., & Huttunen, M. O. (1997). Adult major affective disorder after prenatal exposure to an influenza epidemic. *Archives of General Psychiatry, 54,* 322–328.

May, P. R. A., Tuma, H. H., Yale, C., Potepan, R., & Dixon, W. J. (1976). Schizophrenia: A follow-up study of results of treatment. *Archives of General Psychiatry, 33,* 481–486.

McFarlane, W. R., Lukens, E., Link, B., Dushay, R., Deakins, S. A., Newmark, M., Dunne, E. J., Horen, B., & Toran, J. (1995). Multiple-family groups and psychoeducation in the treatment of schizophrenia. *Archives of General Psychiatry, 52,* 679–687.

McGrew, J. H., Bond, G. R., Dietzen, L., & Salyers, M. (1994). Measuring the fidelity of the implementation of a mental health program model. *Journal of Consulting and Clinical Psychology, 62,* 670–678.

Miklowitz, D. J. (1992). Longitudinal outcome and medication noncompliance among manic patients with and without mood-incongruent psychotic features. *Journal of Nervous and Mental Disease, 180,* 703–711.

Mojtabai, R., Nicholson, R. A., & Carpenter, B. N. (1998). Role of psychosocial treatments in management of schizophrenia: A meta-analytic review of controlled outcome studies. *Schizophrenia Bulletin, 24,* 569–587.

Mueser, K. T. (1998). Helping families manage severe mental health. *Psychiatric Rehabilitation Skills, 1,* 21–42.

Mueser, K. T., Bond, G. R., Drake, R. E., & Resnick, S. G. (1998). Models of community care for severe mental illness: A review of research on case management. *Schizophrenia Bulletin, 24,* 37–74.

Munoz, R. F. (1993). The prevention of depression: Current research and practice. *Applied and Preventive Psychology, 2,* 21–34.

NIMH Workgroup on Genetics. (1998). *Genetics and mental disorders: Report of the National Institute of Mental Health's Genetics Workgroup.* Rockville, MD: National Institute of Mental Health.

Olfson, M. (1990). Assertive community treatment: An evaluation of the experimental evidence. *Hospital and Community Psychiatry, 41,* 634–641.

O'Reilly, R. L. (1994). Viruses and schizophrenia. *Australian and New Zealand Journal of Psychiatry, 28,* 222–228.

Parikh, S. V., Kusumaker, V., Haslam, D., Matte, R., Sharma, V., & Yatham, L. N. (1997). Psychosocial interventions as an adjunct to pharmacotherapy in bipolar disorder. *Canadian Journal of Psychiatry, 42* (Suppl. 2), 74S–78S.

Paul, G. L. (1987). *The Time-Sample Behavioral Checklist.* Champaign, IL: Research Press.

Paul, G. L., & Lentz, R. J. (1977). *Psychosocial treatment of chronic mental patients.* Cambridge, MA: Harvard University Press.

Penn, D. L., & Mueser, K. T. (1996). Research update on the psychosocial treatment of schizophrenia. *American Journal of Psychiatry, 153,* 607–617.

Perris, C., & Skagerlind, L. (1994). Cognitive therapy with schizophrenic patients. *Acta Psychiatrica Scandinavica, 89* (Suppl. 382), 65–70.

Purcell, R., Maruff, P., Kyrios, M., & Pantelis, C. (1997). Neuropsychological function in young patients with unipolar major depression. *Psychological Medicine, 27,* 1277–1285.

Regier, D. A., Farmer, M. E., Rae, D. S., Locke, B. Z., Keith, S. J., Judd, L. L., & Goodwin, F. K. (1990). Comorbidity of mental disorders with alcohol and other drug abuse. *Journal of the American Medical Association, 264,* 2511–2518.

Rehm, L. (1984). Self-management therapy for depression. *Advances in Behavior Therapy and Research, 6,* 83–98.

Rice, D. P., & Miller, L. (1993). The economic burden of affective disorders. In Teh-Weh Hu & A. Rupp (Eds.), *Advances in health economics and health services research: Research in the economics of mental health* (pp. 37–53). Greenwich, CT: JAI Press.

Savio, M., & Righetti, A. (1993). Cooperatives as a social enterprise in Italy: A place for social integration and rehabilitation. *Acta Psychiatrica Scandinavica, 88,* 238–242.

Schooler, N. R., & Keith, S. J. (1993). The clinical research base for the treatment of schizophrenia. In U.S. Department of Health and Human Services. *Health care reform for Americans with severe mental illnesses: Report of the National Advisory Mental Health Council* (pp 2–30). Washington, DC: Superintendent of Documents, U.S. Government Printing Office.

Smyer, M. A., Balster, R. L., Egli, D., Johnson, D. L., Kilbey, M. M., Leith, N. J., & Puente, A. E. (1993). Summary of the Report of the Ad Hoc Task Force on Psychopharmacology of the American Psychological Association. *Professional Psychology: Research and Practice, 24,* 394–403.

Stein, L. I., & Test, M. A. (1980). Alternative to mental hospital treatment: I. Conceptual model, treatment program, and clinical evaluation. *Archives of General Psychiatry, 37,* 382–397.

Sullivan, H. S. (1960). *Schizophrenia as a human process.* New York: Norton.

Surles, R. C. (1994). *Potential clinical roles for psychologists in the public mental health system.* Unpublished paper.

Tamminga, C. A. (1997). The promise of new drugs for schizophrenia treatment. *Canadian Journal of Psychiatry, 42,* 265–273.

Tandon, R., Harrigan, E., & Zorn, S. H. (1997). Ziprasidone: A novel antipsychotic with unique pharmacology and therapeutic potential. *Journal of Serotonin Research, 4,* 159–177.

Tarrier, N., Barrowclough, C., Vaughn, C., Bamrah, J. S., Porceddu, K., Watts, S., & Freeman, H. (1989). Community management of schizophrenia: A two year follow up of a behavioural intervention with families. *British Journal of Psychiatry, 154*, 625–628.

Tarrier, N., Yusupoff, L., Kinney, C., McCarthy, E., Gledhill, A., Haddock, G., & Morris, J. (1998). Randomised controlled trial of intensive cognitive behaviour therapy for patients with chronic schizophrenia. *British Medical Journal, 317*, 303–307.

Torrey, E. F. (1995). Jails and prisons—America's new mental hospitals. *American Journal of Public Health, 85*, 1611–1613.

Tsuang, M. T., & Farone, S. V. (1997). *Schizophrenia: The facts* (2nd ed.). New York: Oxford University Press.

U.S. Department of Health and Human Services. (2000). *Healthy People 2010*. Washington, DC: Author.

Valenstein, E. (1986). *Great and desperate cures*. New York: Basic Books.

Warner, R. (1985). *Recovery from schizophrenia: Psychiatry and political economy*. London: Routledge and Kegan Paul.

Weber, T. T., McDaniel, S. H., & Wynne, L. C. (1987). Helping more by helping less: Family therapy and systems consultation. *Psychotherapy, 24*, 615–620.

Weinberger, D. R. (1987). Implications of normal brain development for the pathogenesis of schizophrenia. *Archives of General Psychiatry, 44*, 660–669.

Weiss, K., & Weiss, K. (1998). Treatment of auditory hallucinations: What to do when pharmacology is inadequate. *Psychiatric Rehabilitation Skills, 2*, 188–205.

Wexler, B. E., Hawkins, K. A., Rounsaville, B., Anderson, M., Sernyak, M. J., & Green, M. F. (1997). Normal neurocognitive performance after extended practice in patients with schizophrenia. *Schizophrenia Research, 29*, 173–180.

Wyatt, R. J., & Henter, I. (1995). An economic evaluation of manic-depressive illness—1991. *Social Psychiatry and Psychiatric Epidemiology, 30*, 213–219.

Wyatt, R. J., Henter, I., Leary, M. C., & Taylor, E. (1995). An economic evaluation of schizophrenia—1991. *Social Psychiatry and Psychiatric Epidemiology, 30*, 196–205.

Wynne, L. C., McDaniel, S. H., Weber, T. T. (1987). Professional politics and the concepts of family therapy, family configuration, and systems consultation. *Family Process, 26*, 153–166.

Yung, A. R., McGorry, P. D., McFarlane, C. A., Jackson, H. J., Patton, G. C., & Rakkar, A. (1996). Monitoring and care of young people at incipient risk of psychosis. *Schizophrenia Bulletin, 22*, 283–303.

Zubin, J., & Spring, B. (1977). Vulnerability—a new view of schizophrenia. *Journal of Abnormal Psychology, 86*, 103–126.

FOR FURTHER READING

Bernheim, K. F., & Lehman, A. F. (1985). *Working with families of the mentally ill*. New York: W. W. Norton.

Anyone who works with families with psychiatric disorders—and this should include families themselves—should begin with this sensible, informative book.

Mueser, K. T., & Glynn, S. M. (1999). *Behavioral family therapy for psychiatric disorders* (2nd ed.). Oakland, CA: New Harbinger.

This is about more than family therapy; it is an excellent overview of many therapies and how and why they work.

Tsuang, M. T., & Farone, S. V. (1997). *Schizophrenia: The facts* (2nd ed.). New York: Oxford University Press.

This is an excellent, accurate introduction to the study of schizophrenia.

CHAPTER

12 The Predoctoral Internship

JAMES P. GUINEE

All students enrolled in doctoral training programs approved by the Committee on Accreditation of the American Psychological Association (APA) must complete an *internship* as part of their requirements. The internship in professional psychology is a predoctoral experience that occurs after a student has completed formal course work, appropriate practica and clinical training experiences, and other relevant academic hurdles (e.g., comprehensive exams). Notwithstanding completion of the doctoral dissertation, the internship often looms large as the "last leg" of a student's formal training.

The duration of the internship is typically an entire calendar year (e.g., September 1 of the current year to August 31 of the following year) of full-time employment, although some internship sites offer half-time positions over a two-year period. According to the Association of Psychology Postdoctoral and Internship Centers (APPIC), the organization that regulates most predoctoral internships, an internship must (1) occur in an agency that employs at least two full-time doctoral-level, licensed psychologists; (2) involve a minimum of 1,500 hours, to be completed between nine and twenty-four months after inception; (3) involve direct client contact at least 25 percent of the time; and (4) involve at least two hours per week of direct supervision and at least two hours per week of other didactic training (e.g., seminars, case conferences).

Thus, while the intern is a full-time employee at his or her internship setting, the internship is also a training program, typically comprised of supervised activities (e.g., group counseling, supervising practicum students) in which the trainee is given opportunities to advance to the level of an *independently functioning professional.* "Independently functioning" means that the graduate will still need consultation with other professionals and continuing education for maintaining licensure, but no longer must be supervised by another professional. Therefore, internship is truly an exciting time—a time when a graduate stands on the cusp of leaving the classroom and beginning a career.

A Brief History of the Internship

The character of the internship experience has evolved over the history of the profession and has been significantly affected, directly and indirectly, by a number of major professional conferences and activities that have occurred during the last 50 years. Six major activities during this 50-year period will be reviewed.

1949: The Boulder Conference

Fifty years ago, the first national conference on the graduate education of professional psychologists was held in Boulder, Colorado. It was at this conference that the now-famous and controversial *scientist-practitioner* training model was developed. Strickland (1998) noted that the importance of the Boulder Conference in shaping professional psychology cannot be overemphasized. The decision that professional psychologists should be trained as scientists *and* practitioners was a bold move, and assured that professional psychology would fall squarely in the sciences, marked by an empirical base and generating knowledge via the scientific method. One contemporary consequence of the scientist-practitioner model is the length of doctoral programs. While students often feel they are quite ready to go on to an internship and finish their graduate studies, internships are often delayed by a lack of progress in completing the research requirements set forth by their academic departments.

Phares (1984) noted that the scientist-practitioner model asserts that professional psychologists should pursue their training in university departments; they should be trained as psychologists first and clinicians second; they should be required to serve a clinical internship; they should attain competence in diagnosis, psychotherapy, and research; and finally that the culmination of their training should be the Ph.D. Thus, while internship training was not a focus of the Boulder Conference, nevertheless its primordial seeds were planted there.

1950s: Accreditation of APA Programs

The 1950s witnessed remarkable growth in the psychological profession. The membership of the APA rose from 7,250 in 1950 to 16,644 in 1959—a phenomenal increase (Phares, 1984). It was during this period, as a measure of quality control, that the APA accredited academic programs in clinical and counseling psychology programs; in 1956, through its Office of Accreditation, it began accrediting clinical and counseling internships.

The designation *APA-accredited* essentially means that an academic or internship program meets acceptable professional training standards. The APA continues to maintain a committee on accreditation, and routinely (i.e., every 3–5 years) reviews academic and internship programs to ensure that they are providing training that meets specified guidelines. (The list of approved schools and internships are published each year in the December issue of the *American Psychologist*.) With respect to internships, students can apply to non-accredited internship programs, but this decision should be made only after careful investigation of the program and the potential consequences of graduating from a non-accredited internship program. For example, the Department of Veterans Affairs will no longer hire psychologists who have not completed internships at programs approved by the APA (Department of Veterans Affairs, 1995). Even today, there is still little doubt that graduating from an APA-accredited psychology program with an APA-accredited internship is the best insurance for all types of future credentialing (Stedman, 1997).

1968: Association of Psychology Internship Centers

In 1968 the Association of Psychology Internship Centers (APIC, now the Association of Psychology Postdoctoral and Internship Centers) was established to respond to a growing number of internship issues and problems. Some considered the psychology internship selection process to be chaotic, stressful, and unregulated (Stedman, 1989). Therefore, in 1972 APIC established a uniform selection process that remained largely unchanged until recently. While internship programs were generally free to design their own application and interview procedures, the selection process became governed by a set of guidelines (Hall et al., 1997) that strictly defined how internship sites and applicants were to communicate during the process, as well as how offers of positions were to be tendered by programs and accepted or rejected by applicants.

These guidelines were developed with the goal of providing an orderly national internship selection process while reducing the probability that applicants would experience undue pressures or unfair tactics (e.g., pressuring candidates to reveal their rankings) on the part of internship programs. All internship offers and acceptances were restricted to a predefined notification period, which was gradually shortened over the years from five days to four hours. This notification period was called *Uniform Notification Day* (UND), or Selection Day, and occurred annually on the second Monday in February.

1973: The Vail Conference

In the early 1970s a growing concern within the profession for quality control in graduate education was met by the development of more definitive standards by professional organizations, such as the American Psychological Association (APA), the Association of Psychology Internship Centers (APIC), and the American Association of State Psychology Boards (AASPB). Many internship programs were not accredited by APA, and much of the training was inconsistent across sites (Holloway & Roehlke, 1987).

Vail Conference delegates reviewed issues in the training of professional psychologists such as professionalization, social responsibility, and evaluation of training services that significantly influence internship training. Most significant was the declaration that the internship should be a substantial part of graduate education in professional psychology; therefore, APA accreditation standards were revised to require that a predoctoral internship become part of the doctoral degree in counseling, clinical, and school psychology. Thus, students may be surprised to note that the automatic inclusion of internships in a psychologist's training has a relatively short history!

1987: The Gainesville Conference

In 1987, the first (and to date only) conference focusing solely on predoctoral internship training was held in Gainesville, Florida. It sought to address such issues as the purpose of internship training, the timing of internship training in graduate education, and the entrance criteria for internship training (Belar et al., 1989). One of the most significant changes pertained to how the delegates conceptualized internship training. Until this conference, the model of a one-year internship had been considered the "capstone" of graduate education (Holloway & Roehlke, 1987).

The conference delegates agreed that the predoctoral internship should become a two-year training process; however, given the logistical problems of implementing an actual two-year position (e.g., there was already a national shortage in one-year positions), it was maintained that in order for trainees to become independently functioning professionals, their one-year internship should be supplemented with an additional year of supervised postdoctoral work.

The two-year internship model is consistent with licensure requirements in most states. Further, this supervised experience is often incorporated into the graduate's first year in her or his position (e.g., a new hire is often supervised by a licensed psychologist on staff). However, despite delegates maintaining that entry-level psychologists should be supervised their first year out of school, they also maintained that graduates should become immediately eligible for employment and licensure upon the completion of their internship.

Another significant issue delegates debated pertained to the doctoral dissertation, typically the last rite of passage before permanent employment. Delegates maintained that the internship should occur *after* the completion of the dissertation (prior to this it was not uncommon for a student to return to graduate school after completing the internship); however, they stopped short of implementing this as a strict policy. Nonetheless, since the Gainesville conference, academic programs have consistently instituted these minimum requirements before students can apply and be accepted into an internship program: (a) completion of all formal course work, (b) passing of comprehensive or qualifying exams, and (c) acceptance of the dissertation proposal.

Before a student begins the process of applying for internship, he or she should seriously consider the ramifications of going on internship with little progress made on the dissertation. Despite the hardships of staying at school yet another year, applicants might be better served over the long term by completing as many dissertation subgoals as possible. (As a professor once remarked, "Make sure you at least collect your data!") The internship year is fast and furious, and leaves little time for hunting and begging for subjects. Most interns do not do their internship in the same area as their academic program, therefore the trainee loses daily contact with the faculty, as well as with familiar resources (e.g., library). The inability to make adequate progress on one's dissertation during the internship year can have significant repercussions—delayed licensure, lower salary offers, or being precluded from certain jobs due to not being license eligible (i.e., one does not have a license but has met all of the requirements to apply for one). Further, even though a trainee may have procured gainful employment, the initial adjustment to a new job (and new setting) will likely postpone completion of graduate school for a substantial period of time.

1998–1999: APPIC Computerized Matching Program

Over the years, the APPIC selection process came under serious criticism, and many advocated significant change. Flaws in the process included undue stress and anxiety on the part of the applicants, pressures on applicants to prematurely disclose their ranking of sites, frequent violations of APPIC guidelines, and difficulties in enforcing the guidelines (Keilin, 1998).

In 1998, APPIC voted to adopt a computerized matching program, to be implemented beginning with the 1998–1999 selection process. This program matches internships and applicants on the basis of their expressed rank-ordered preferences and replaces the events that previously occurred on Uniform Notification Day. The computerized matching program will be discussed further later in this chapter.

Structure of the Internship

Now that a brief history of professional activities relevant to internship training has been reviewed, students are likely to formulate concrete questions about specific aspects of internship training. How many positions are available? What types of internship sites do students train in? How do students obtain more information about the application process and specific information about internship sites?

Number of Internship Positions

According to recent studies (Pederson, 1995; Stedman, 1997), each year approximately 2,500 to 3,000 graduate students in psychology apply for an internship position. There are roughly 550 different internship programs that participate in the APPIC; this translates into approximately 2,500 full-time internship positions. Further, while the number of students in psychology programs has increased during the past decade, the number of internship positions has, unfortunately, remained relatively stable.

Most internship sites are participating members of the APPIC. As stated, the primary focus of APPIC is to help assure high-quality training and recruitment practices at professional psychology internship sites throughout the United States (and Canada). This helps students ensure that these programs have maintained consistent recruitment, selection, and training standards and practices in accordance with APPIC ethical guidelines.

Students can also choose to apply to non-APPIC internship sites, but typically less is known about these programs (e.g., it is not known how many positions are currently available at non-APPIC programs). Students considering a non-APPIC site should obtain the materials for licensure from the state psychology licensing board (or boards) in the state (or states) where the student intends to practice, and verify that the site meets all of the requirements of the licensing board. Once the details are finalized, they should be spelled out in a contract that is signed by the applicant, the university training director, and the on-site training supervisor. Following these steps will help ensure that the site abides by the contract and provides interns with the experience they need (Mellott, Arden, & Cho, 1997). To locate possible sites, it may be helpful to consult the *Directory of Graduate and Undergraduate Internships: Training of a Mental Health, Rehabilitative, or Educative Nature in Human Services Agencies and Institutions.*

For all APPIC internships, APPIC puts out an annual directory that contains specific information regarding each participating internship program. At a minimum, internship sites provide such information as location, address and phone number, contact person (typically the training director), number of vacancies, APA-accreditation status (full, provisional, probationary, none), types of services offered, benefits, and salary. All academic departments that participate in APPIC should have a current copy of the *APPIC Directory* (1999–2000). For more information on how to obtain a copy of the *APPIC Directory,* students can access the APPIC web site (http://www.appic.org/) or write to: APPIC—Association of Psychology Postdoctoral and Internship Centers, 733 15th Street NW Suite 719, Washington, DC 20005.

Types of Settings and Services

Clinical and counseling psychology trainees are currently trained in over 500 settings, which include every type of setting in which psychologists practice. From most to least common, these training sites include university counseling centers, Veterans Administration (VA) medical centers, medical schools, community mental health centers, state institutions, child care facilities, private general hospitals, private practice consortia, private psychiatric facilities, military hospitals, and a variety of other facilities. Further, while some types of settings—such as medical schools—accept predominantly clinical students, and while individual programs may state a preference for one specialization over another, it is more typical that students from both counseling and clinical psychology are given equal consideration for available positions.

Although there can be vast differences in internship programs in terms of setting, clientele, size of training program, and professional responsibilities, accredited program guidelines do assure some degree of standardization in the organization of the internship training program. The typical internship program is embedded in the larger organization of the service agency in which it is housed (e.g., a counseling center internship in a university setting). Therefore, the internship program is in a multidisciplinary setting—one where the trainee has the opportunity to interact and learn from different professionals (e.g., a hospital setting with psychologists, psychiatrists, social workers and nurses), and perform different services and activities. This should enhance the likelihood that the primary mission of the internship program is that of *training,* not service. Interns have their entire professional career to see thousands of clients; therefore, internship is the final and possibly most important mechanism for dedicated learning, and the intern's responsibilities should not be equivalent to that of professional staff members.

Some activities, such as individual, group, and couples counseling, are featured in nearly every internship site, while others such as family counseling, vocational counseling, supervising graduate students, and research, vary from site to site in terms of emphasis. One of the most exciting aspects of internship is that interns have the opportunity to deepen their knowledge and enhance their skills in a variety of activities. Students should consider the importance of such activities to their professional development, as well as to licensure and employment considerations, and examine which programs offer (and to what extent) forensic psychology, psychological testing, neuropsychology, outreach and programming, consultation, gerontology, hypnosis, and so forth.

The Internship Training Director

The initial contact person for an internship site is typically a staff psychologist whose primary job function is that of training director. Training directors are responsible for disseminating accurate information about the internship to APPIC; developing printed materials and brochures about the training program; maintaining affiliation with appropriate organizations (e.g., Association of Counseling Center Training Agents); and corresponding with, scheduling interviews with, and making offers to intern applicants. They are also the link between the internship program and the APA accrediting body, the student's academic program, the administrative head of the agency, and the rest of the training staff.

The director of training sets the overall climate, attitudes, and standards for that particular internship program—he or she plays a crucial role in developing a training environment that facilitates the intern's professional and personal development. Intern applicants should carefully consider how the training director presents herself or himself during the application and selection process. Some training directors are extremely accessible, others remote. Some internship directors are largely involved in the interview process, others partial off interviews to the rest of the staff. The training director is essentially the intern's "boss"—they make supervision assignments, conduct evaluation meetings, and can be instrumental in the intern's job search process during the latter part of internship. Finally, the training director is ultimately responsible for ensuring that application and selection process is conducted in an equitable and ethical manner. Therefore, the applicant's assessment of the training director is often instrumental in choosing between internship sites.

A Developmental Model of Internship

The predoctoral internship has been described as distinctly different from academic preparation or professional employment, a bridge between graduate education and professional employment. Moreover, although the internship may only consist of one out of four to seven years of training, it is a unique and immensely important endeavor. Some authors (e.g., Guinee, 1998; Kaslow & Rice, 1985; Lamb et al., 1982) even believe that the internship year is so unique from the rest of graduate school that a predictable set of issues and conflicts develop during it.

Further, these writers believe that viewing internship from a developmental perspective (i.e., how does the intern change over the course of the year?) can help interns and training staff to better understand the different professional and personal issues that arise during internship. One such developmental model has been proposed by Guinee (1998), in which he argues that the psychosocial development theory of Erik Erikson (1975) can serve as a useful metaphor for conceptualizing the challenges of internship. The internship year is viewed as having a "life of its own," and by Erikson's lifespan theory is seen as a series of challenges, or "crises," from beginning to end.

Training staff that have worked with interns are more likely to resonate with the ideas presented below; students, on the other hand, may not fully grasp some of the concepts presented until they are going through, or possibly have completed, their internship experience. Nevertheless, developmental issues should be immediately recognizable to any student, and minimally the themes presented next should provide students with insight into the issues they will likely encounter throughout the internship year.

Trust versus Mistrust

Erikson's first psychosocial stage, "trust versus mistrust," pertains to how parents care for an infant; a healthy resolution occurs when parents (and other care givers) help the infant develop a realistic sense of trust and distrust in the world. Trust may emerge as an issue for interns even before the internship has begun. Clearly, intern applicants must gather enough information to make informed decisions about which programs best match their preferences. Thus, it is imperative that an intern applicant be able to trust that the information they glean from brochures, individual staff members, and other sources is accurate.

No training staff will be guilty of egregiously misrepresenting information about their internship program, but there are internship programs that may bend the truth in order to compete for quality students. For example, Constantine and Keilin (1996) found that 40 percent of the intern applicants that they surveyed perceived that violations of the APPIC guidelines had occurred during the selection process. Further, training staff members may be innocent of commission but guilty of omission. It is clearly difficult for intern applicants to know what information they might need that has *not* been transmitted. Students may wish to consult with faculty, supervisors, and especially current interns about essential information needed to make decisions. Current interns, uninvolved in the decision-making process, are often a great way of getting the "straight scoop" (Gloria & Robinson, 1994). Further, new professionals can be helpful resources as well, in discussing what they wish they would have known about internship sites (e.g., evaluation process).

Autonomy versus Doubt

Erikson's second crisis is typified by a struggle for self-confidence. Successful resolution involves appropriate guilt for mistakes, but there is also a strong and persistent belief in one's competence. During the initial weeks of internship, interns often feel confused, even overwhelmed, due to the ominous number of new responsibilities, both central (e.g., clinical responsibilities) and peripheral (e.g., compliance with office policies and procedures). Most interns have never seen so many clients before, and in all likelihood they have little experience in some of the clinical activities (e.g., crisis intervention) required of them.

Intern applicants should carefully examine the consistency and structure of supervised activities in the internship program. For example, the internship program should have some kind of orientation program—very often a useful time for allowing new interns to become familiar with their responsibilities, their fellow interns, the staff, and the agency (Shemberg & Leventhal, 1981). Orientation can provide new interns with opportunities to formally meet with each of the training staff members who coordinate a particular aspect of the training program (e.g., case management, outreach programming, supervision of practicum students), and learn the specific expectations each training staff member has for the interns.

Confusion is not only a product of professional change but also personal stress. The typical interns will complete their internship in a different town than that of their academic department. Interns should consider visiting their new home several times prior to a permanent move, in order to procure living arrangements, find their way around town, and inquire among staff members and others about personal resources (e.g., health care, insurance). New interns should also make their move at least a few weeks prior to the start of internship, to give themselves adequate time to settle into their new communities before they endure the stress of a new job.

Initiative versus Guilt

In this stage, ego skills acquired during the second stage result in the ability to plan and pursue goals more effectively. A person's healthy resolution of this stage will result in an appropriate sense of when he or she can pursue goals by themselves, take risks and try new experiences, and know when it is appropriate to wait until further instruction. In describing the internship experience, Solway (1985) suggested that internship is indeed a time for taking risks and confronting weaknesses. The intern is faced with many new challenges—adjusting to a new setting (both personally and professionally), working with new types of clients (with respect to presenting problem and/or demographics), and experimenting with new types of interventions.

It is conceivable that during the initial months interns will struggle with defining their own goals and with taking risks while working under the shelter of necessary and sufficient supervision. At times interns may experiment with client interventions but then tacitly, or explicitly, ask their supervisors "Was that okay?" A difficult but important task in supervision is helping interns delineate between when to venture forth and when to check first with their supervisors (e.g., trying a new clinical intervention). Thus, it is clearly integral to the intern's development that the training staff reinforce appropriate risk-taking. This may be mediated by a supervisor's ability to make the transition from seeing the intern as a dependent trainee to a competent, independently functioning professional.

Industry versus Inferiority

Erikson contends that during the industry and inferiority crisis the child's world widens and the influences become increasingly broad. The chief new influence and battleground is the school, where the child's intellectual and interpersonal abilities are tested, and a sense of identity outside the home is acquired. A healthy resolution is a realistic appraisal of one's talents and abilities as well as of one's shortcomings and weaknesses.

Many interns have had a well-established position in their graduate school programs, and were respected by the faculty and admired by the other students in the program. However, once interns come to their internship program, they may have to prove themselves all over again, to the training staff or supervisors as well as fellow interns, and in a short period of time. Interns may compete with each other to be viewed by the training director (and the entire staff) as the "best intern."

As previously stated, the internship typically represents the last formal training experience, thus it is imperative that the training staff provide the intern with specific, concrete, and accurate feedback, and this should be provided as early in the internship as possible. Hahn and Molnar (1991) noted that a particular "thorny" aspect of internships is intern evaluation. Intern applicants should carefully inquire as to the modes, criteria, and timing frequency of intern evaluations.

One significant aspect of intern evaluation is intern impairment, defined as any physical, emotional, or educational condition that significantly interferes with the quality of the intern's professional performance (Rangel & Boxley, 1985). Note that an impaired intern is not just a trainee who has trouble developing a certain skill, but one who, through personal or professional reasons becomes significantly deficient in a particular area (e.g., intern is unsuccessful with running a group, public speaking, being on time for clients). On occasion, interns may suffer a personal crisis (e.g., divorce, death of a loved one) that might temporarily impede ability to perform their duties. Therefore, it is essential that the training program have a mechanism for helping the trainee through this time of duress.

Identity Development versus Role Confusion

Erikson's "identity crisis" is typified by the increasing need to find one's role in life as a productive, responsible adult, with a set of core beliefs and values. The positive side of the struggle is a sense of identity—a sense of continuity and consistency of self over time. The negative side is a sense of confusion about one's identity or role—a lack of certainty about who one is, or about the part one is playing in society, or more universally, in the grand scheme of life.

Much as an adolescent may face turmoil in being less than an adult and more than a child, an intern may continually feel a conflict between defining herself or himself as a student and as a professional. Interns are no longer students, but they are not yet professionals; therefore they experience a special kind of status with their agency, a status that may be unclear (Lamb et al., 1982). Staff members sometimes unknowingly add to this problem by using such terms as "the interns" or "the junior staff," perpetuating interns' role-ambiguity as well as reinforcing the notion that interns are not unique individuals. It may be several months before each intern is able to truly display their unique talents and differences.

Skovholt and Ronnestad (1992) argued that training staff must continually help interns examine their uniqueness as professionals (e.g., each intern can be challenged to understand how their cultural background may influence their professional identity), and to use their internship experience to develop their professional identities. Further, they state that training programs should emphasize professional development in all aspects (e.g., individual and group supervision, staff meetings, seminars) of the training program. Finally, Ducheny et al. (1997) suggested that training staff should encourage interns to enhance their identity development by networking with professionals in the community, particularly those who have similar academic experiences, training, and interests.

Intimacy versus Isolation

According to Erikson, after the identity crisis is fairly well resolved an individual can more adequately develop fully intimate relationships, and resolve the extent to which "intimacy versus isolation" will occupy their lives. Once interns typically begin to settle into different roles within the training site, they move from a preoccupation with themselves, and become more aware of the differences among each other without the intense competitive feelings experienced earlier during the year. Personal friendships may develop between particular interns and staff members, as well as the interns themselves; on the other hand, interns may also choose to partially (or fully) isolate themselves professionally (i.e., work independently) or personally from others.

One aspect of affiliation is that interns will inevitably question the types of clients they wish to work with, as well as the types of settings where they will seek permanent employment with upon completion of internship. Interns may make decisions during the year about clients and settings based on their own awareness of interests, needs, and perhaps even personality (Holland, 1985). Interns may also struggle with professional affiliations, making decisions on joining national organizations (e.g., American Psychological Association, American Psychological Society, American Counseling Association, American Mental Health Counselors Association, American College Personnel Association), regional or state divisions of those organizations, and even specialty groups (e.g., those focusing on marriage and family therapy, hypnosis). Dividing their loyalties may at times be overwhelming, and training staff can facilitate interns' opportunities to experience and explore different groups and settings in order to answer those questions.

Generativity versus Stagnation

The generativity crisis is typified by an individual's desire to produce something that will outlive him- or herself, usually through parenthood or occupational achievements. The struggle is between a sense of generativity, or leaving one's mark in some way, and the sense of stagnation, or self-absorption. A healthy resolution, then, is one that results in the individual feeling that they are being productive in such a way that their life will leave an indelible mark. At some point, each intern will become (perhaps painfully) aware of termination—that one day the internship will end. Erikson might argue that with this realization it is natural for each intern to aspire to "make one's mark."

Interestingly, there is little in the internship literature that focuses on this stage of development. Interns certainly want to do well, and once they develop more and more confidence in their work may begin to wonder if their presence has made a difference. Interns may begin to make recommendations to the staff about specifics of the training program; they may even challenge certain policies and procedures. This can be difficult for training staff, and they may (at least initially) resist making any permanent modifications to the internship program.

Integrity versus Despair

The last of Erikson's eight psychosocial crises is brought on by a growing awareness of the finitude of life and of one's closeness to death. The crucial task during this stage is to evaluate one's life and accomplishments and to affirm that one's life has been a meaningful adventure in history; this would be the sense of *integrity.* Its opposite is despair and disgust—the feeling that one's life was wasted.

Initial awareness of termination probably begins about midway through the internship. Specific events such as completing the dissertation, applying for jobs, and planning to relocate may reinforce the fact that the internship will come to an end. Interns may plunge into these activities and deny that termination is approaching. However, interns clearly begin to experience one loss after another—saying goodbye to each other, their supervisors, the staff in general, and perhaps even people from their neighborhood or community. Interns will terminate clients and may also have to help their supervisee terminate their clients as well.

Most graduating interns pursue professional employment, while a minority will return to their graduate departments to complete the dissertation, pursue a postdoctoral fellowship, or even travel before exploring the job market. Training staff will hopefully reinforce whatever appropriate post-internship plans interns make. Clearly, as interns look back on the year, they desire to feel that they have made the most of their training experiences, and while facing regrets and mistakes, will hopefully leave the internship believing they have successfully completed this stage of their graduate training—perhaps the last.

Internship Application Issues

The process of finding an internship can be very anxiety-producing (Gloria & Robinson, 1994); in recent years, that anxiety has been compounded by the increased number of unplaced applicants due to academic programs accepting higher numbers of applicants while internship spots have decreased. Therefore, due to the limited availability of internship positions, applicants must work hard at finding a site that will best meet their needs. Similarly, most internship agencies put significant effort into obtaining highly qualified graduate students to train in their facilities.

In the last ten years, the majority of published articles on internship training have focused on the application process, both from the perspective of the applicants as well as internship training directors (Stedman et al., 1995). This is clearly indicative of how time-consuming and stressful the entire process can be. What follows is a compilation of different application strategies based on studies examining the application and selection process from both the applicants' and the agencies' perspectives.

The Applicant's Perspective

In a recent article, Mellott, Arden, and Cho (1997) discussed how applicants can prepare for internship application early on in their graduate work by establishing a mentor, preparing an application portfolio, and collecting information on internship sites. This is an important issue; often, students will wait until the last minute (several months prior to applications being due) to initiate the process. It is not necessary that students know where they will apply, but to simply begin to plan for applying for internships in the future, and to know that the more planning they do early on, the less work they will have to do in those last several months.

It can be argued that there is a six-step process in choosing and selecting one's internship of choice. (Whether the site makes an offer to the student is another matter.) In addition to the aforementioned three steps—(1) developing a mentoring relationship, (2) preparing an application portfolio, and (3) collecting information about internship sites—students will also eventually (4) prepare and submit applications, (5) prepare and conduct interviews, and finally (6) rank their final selections.

Developing Mentoring Relationships. The role of a mentor is unquestionably integral to the success of many students in graduate school. The internship selection process, as well as graduate school in general, is a time-consuming and stressful endeavor. It is imperative for many students that early on they seek to affiliate themselves with faculty members who share their interests, who are dedicated to working with students, and are perhaps someone they generally enjoy being around. Students can also be mentored by older students in the program (e.g., current interns)—these students can be very instrumental in helping a student find internship sites that match their career objectives, as well as provide sound advice on applying and interviewing strategies. A mentor may even provide helpful feedback in the event they feel the student is not adequately prepared, professionally or personally, to apply for internship.

Preparing an Application Portfolio. Development of an application portfolio should also start early in a graduate student's academic career. Students should keep detailed records of all clinical experience gained through different training modules (e.g., practicum) and maintain a file (and make copies) of all supervised activities. Students should minimally keep an accurate count of the number of hours devoted to client contact (e.g., individual counseling, intake interviews), individual and group supervision hours, types of clients, tests administered, and hours on-site. Internship sites may also request copies of write-ups and psychological assessments (after the student has removed identifying information from the reports). The maintenance of accurate and up-to-date information about the student's clinical experiences will save the student from having to retrieve (or, worse, remember) information.

Collecting Information about Internship Sites. The summer prior to applying for internship is generally a good time to request materials (e.g., brochures, applications) from internship sites. The summer is also a good time to gather information before paring down one's preferences. The best place to start searching is through the *APPIC Directory* for a listing of internships; students should carefully review the information regarding each program, and then write to each agency for more information. It is important to remember that writing to an agency does not obligate a student to anything—it is simply gathering data. Students should request materials from *any* site that appeals to their interest—it is easiest to start with a large pool of sites (i.e., 30–50) and then sort through the materials, weeding out programs until one has reached a reasonable number of sites.

Most experts suggest applying to no more than 15–20 sites. However, in a recent study, Lopez, Oehlert, and Moberly (1996) found that internship sites, on average, receive 155 inquiries regarding their training programs (range 40–550); 45 percent of those inquiring (M = 70, range 17–298) actually return a completed application, and on average, training sites sift through 70 applications to fill five available slots. Therefore, students may need to strongly consider a large pool of sites simply to remain competitive.

On the other hand, there are also reasons for students to refrain from applying to a large number of sites. One reason is that applying to internship sites can be costly. Many internship sites request transcripts, students will want to make long-distance calls to individual sites to gather more information, and some interviews may require (or the student desire) travel to the internship site (which entails costs for gas, lodging, and food). It is also important that a student spend considerable time examining the contents of the internship program and put together a solid application. This is time-consuming, and it is better that the student spend considerable time on highly desired sites, as opposed to a little bit of time on numerous ones.

Preparing and Submitting Applications. Once students have narrowed down their list of potential sites to a reasonable number, they should then construct a checklist of requirements for each agency and write down the due date for each agency's applications. Students should ensure that transcripts are ordered well in advance of application deadlines, and that letters of recommendation are also sent out as early as possible. Some internship programs are so inundated with applications that a training director may eliminate an application simply due to a missing item.

With respect to completing applications, it is imperative that students spend considerable time on completing these, and to work on them early in the semester (applications are often due in late November to early January, at a time when students are busy with projects, papers, and exams). The typical internship application requests such information as a student's professional goals, theoretical orientation, specific goals for internship, and reasons for choosing the site (Mitchell, 1996).

Preparing and Conducting Interviews. After the applications have been completed and mailed, students should continue perusing internship brochures in order to prepare for upcoming interviews. Applying to an internship site does not guarantee a student an interview, although internship sites typically attempt to interview as many applicants as possible. When an internship site calls to schedule an interview, it is important that the student write down the name of the internship site (the student does not want to confuse internship sites!), the names of the individuals conducting the interview, and the date, time, and length of the interview. Students should keep in mind that they have the right to coordinate the time of the interview with the agency. For example, it is not unheard-of for an internship site to call a student early in the morning and desire to conduct the interview right then! Further, with respect to time, applicants should ascertain the time zone of each internship site (e.g., "It is 3:00 where you are, 2:00 here—that means that my 11:30 a.m. interview will take place at 10:30 a.m., right?").

Students should also inquire as to the format of the interview: How long will the interview take? Will the applicant have time to ask questions? Will the applicant be required to prepare anything in advance? Lopez et al. (1996) found that on average, nine staff persons per internship are involved in the interview process; programs are just as likely to schedule applicants with one-on-one interviews with staff members or to conduct team interviews. Further, the typical person-to-person interview process lasts about two hours, while the typical phone interview ranges from 30–45 minutes.

In order to prepare for the interview, applicants should consider what questions they may be asked, as well as what questions they want to ask the professional staff and current interns. A careful perusal of internship brochures and materials is likely to elicit additional questions that are specific to that site. Faculty and current interns can also be good sources for developing questions. In general, the most common questions applicants are asked include: "Why are you interested in this internship?" "What advantages and disadvantages do you see to doing your internship with us?" "What are your goals for internship?" "What is unique about you?" "What are your plans for after internship?" "What clients do you enjoy working with the most? Least?" "What kind of supervisory relationship do you like?" "What diverse populations have you worked with?"

Ranking the Internships. After the interview process has been completed, each applicant is faced with the difficult task of rank-ordering internship sites. Stedman et al. (1995) suggested that most applicants heavily emphasize an affective ("gut feeling") sense of "fit" with the program. However, students should also take into account objective criteria, such as the accreditation status of the program, the match between the student's interests and the training program's experiences, the specific training opportunities, and the desire to work in that setting. Additional factors include geographics, ease of application, cost of living, stipend, proximity to significant other or family, and the work hours (e.g., how many evening hours are required?).

Stewart and Stewart (1996a) noted the importance of considering professional and personal variables that may affect the selection and completion of internship. The more sites the applicant applies to, the more information the applicant must process, the less time they will likely have to process that information, and the more difficult the task of comparing individual sites will be. Therefore, Stewart and Stewart offered a strategy (modified by the author) for applicants to use in making their decisions about internships.

The first step begins with the applicant's selection of professional, personal, and practical criteria that will be used in comparing sites to one another. Common professional criteria include the amount and quality of supervision, ability to work with desired clientele, reputation and prestige of site, salary, job opportunities after internship, opportunities to work on the dissertation, availability and amount of didactic experiences, ability to choose rotations, and opportunities for test administration and interpretation. Personal and practical variables include location, proximity to partner and family members, work opportunities for partner, cost of living at internship site, benefits (e.g., health and dental insurance, sick and vacation leave), simplicity and ease of preparing application, and costs of moving and settling.

Students may or may not wish to rank the importance of selection variables. In other words, students can simply weigh each variable equally, or they may wish to assign different weights to the different variables (e.g., giving supervision more weight than location). To weight criteria, students can simply number them; for example, if there are ten variables, then the most important variable is assigned a weight of ten points, the next most important variable is assigned nine points, and so on. Clearly, the more variables the applicant chooses, the more time-consuming and difficult the task of rank ordering the variables; therefore, variables of minor importance can be eliminated from the list.

The third step then involves listing all of the internship sites. This entails constructing a grid, so that the names of the internship sites are written along the rows of the grid, and the selection criteria are written along the columns of the grid. Although all sites may be compared, it is probably most beneficial to compare only sites that the applicant is actively considering. Sites that are marginal or that have all but been eliminated should probably be omitted from the exercise.

While Stewart and Stewart (1996a) recommended a somewhat laborious method of pairwise comparisons for all selection criteria, it is probably just as informative, and much simpler, to use a rating scale of 1 ("low") to 10 ("high") for all criteria. Thus, for each variable (e.g., freedom to choose rotations), applicants can rate each internship site using the simple rating scale (e.g., Site A gets 5 points, Site B gets 7 points, etc.). Once the grid has been completed, then each internship site's total can be produced, and applicants can examine and compare totals for internship sites. While applicants shouldn't necessarily base their ranking for internships on the grid, nonetheless it should be helpful in arriving at the student's top two or three choices.

The ranking of internship sites can take a while and should not be done prematurely. Even after applicants have ranked sites, they should continue to solicit information about different sites as much as possible. Applicants may not initially see much difference between choice #3 and choice #4, for example; worse, some applicants may presume that they will be placed with their first choice and see little reason to research other sites. However, given the increasing competition for sites, the "hidden" selection criteria that sites may use (e.g., applicants can be skipped over for lower-ranked candidates based on demographic needs of the center), and that part of the decision making is based on agency needs as well as the computer matching program, it is imperative that every "preference" be carefully examined.

The Training Director's Perspective

In addition to looking at the process of choosing which internship sites to apply to, as well as how to rank order them, it is useful for students to know what training directors are actually looking for. Without sufficient knowledge of what internship sites tend to look for in their applicants, the internship application and selection process could very well become a very time-consuming, wasteful endeavor. What follows is not only information regarding selection criteria from the training director's perspective, but also information based on empirical evidence (surveys of training directors).

Lopez et al. (1996) surveyed a representative sample of 115 training directors from APA-accredited internship programs. The results suggest that candidates who are not selected or who are not competitive for internship spots frequently evidence (based on their application materials) deficits in clinical experience, experience with special populations, poor writing skills, or poor specialty skills (e.g., testing). Further, training directors typically rank the candidate's amount and variety of clinical experience, strength of interview, letters of recommendation, graduate course work, and special training experiences as most important, and graduate grade point average, academic prestige of applicant's program, and approval of doctoral dissertation proposal as least important. In general, training directors state that the most important factor in selecting applicants is typically the particular set of opportunities (e.g., supervising practicum students) that the agency offers and how much interest (and experience) the applicant demonstrates regarding those opportunities.

Gloria et al. (1997) surveyed 342 training directors from the *APPIC Directory (1993–1994)*. They found that most internship sites rate the applicant's personal interview, supervised therapy experience, and letters of recommendation as most important. In contrast to earlier findings, results of this study indicate that personal interviews have increasingly become more and more integral to the selection and application process. As sites continue to seek the most competitive and desirable candidates possible, the personal interview provides the opportunity to more thoroughly question or get to know the candidate, or to hear how the candidate conceptualizes and provides treatment for different clients and issues.

In that same study, training directors were also asked which academic courses are most important in evaluating internship applicants. Respondents rated the five most important academic courses as Psychopathology, Personality Assessment, Individual Intellectual Assessment, Personality Theory, and Group Therapy. Moreover, training directors felt that Multicultural Counseling will increase in importance, but at the time of the survey, many programs did not offer a course in multicultural counseling. Many programs simply offer it as an elective.

In addition to the specific courses and experiences provided, internship training directors were asked to identify two courses or professional practice experiences that they believed "set a top candidate apart from other applicants." Responses included (a) clinical experience with specific clients (e.g., ethnic minorities, children, severely disturbed); (b) knowledge of specific therapies (e.g., family, group); (c) supervisory experience; (d) assessment experiences (e.g., projective and objective tests); (e) scholarship (e.g., publications and/or affiliation with professional organizations); (f) specific courses (e.g., psychopharmacology, multicultural counseling); and (g) experiences in specific agencies.

As stated, it is never too early for graduate students to begin the process of preparing for internship. Students in their first year clearly may have only begun to consider the types of settings they are interested in with respect to internship and post-graduate employment. Nonetheless, a sound knowledge of the coursework and experiences that internships tend to emphasize can be acquired regardless of future considerations.

Additional Issues in Selecting Internship Sites

Given the abundance of information that has been presented regarding the application and selection process, it is hoped that students can take advantage of this data in successfully applying for internships. In addition to how students can better prepare themselves to be competitive candidates, other factors should be considered when exploring and applying to internship sites.

APPIC Ethical Guidelines

Over the years, internship applicants have consistently reported that they encounter a great deal of stress in finding a training site (Allen & Dressel, 1992). Further, despite recent attempts by APPIC to clarify the selection process (e.g., computer matching, early notification), many students, faculty, and training directors believe that it is fraught with ethical problems and in need of revision. Constantine and Keilin (1996) surveyed students, faculty, and training directors alike in an attempt to investigate prevalence and types of ethical violations during the application and selection process.

Applicants were specifically asked whether or not they had experienced a violation of APPIC guidelines over the course of the 1994–95 selection process. Surprisingly, 40 percent of applicants reported that they had indeed perceived *at least* one violation by at least one particular internship site. When asked to describe these violations, the three most frequent violations were (1) applicants being pressured by at least one agency to disclose their site rankings ("Where do you have us ranked?"), (2) internship sites hinting about making an offer to applicants before selection day ("I think we have a spot for you"), and (3) applicants not being notified about their status by sites on selection day.

With respect to the pressure to disclose site rankings, an important side note is that it used to be appropriate practice for applicants to disclose which internship site was their number one choice. This practice was considered acceptable as long as the agency did not solicit rank-ordered information from applicants. However, in recent years, APPIC has instituted a policy that explicitly discourages applicants from revealing their rankings to any sites, including their first choice.

The Constantine and Keilin (1996) study also revealed that applicants rated the three most perceived violations (i.e., they are not true violations of APPIC guidelines) were (1) applicants were asked personal questions (e.g., race, marital status, age), (2) internship sites asked applicants about other sites to which they had applied, and (3) training directors called applicants on the weekend before selection day. Further, Constantine and Keilin found that most applicants did not report a violation or perceived violation to anyone, and while a small percentage of applicants did notify other individuals (e.g., faculty members) about violations, none of the respondents reported the violation to APPIC. Constantine and Keilin suggested that students should carefully review the ethical guidelines set forth by APPIC regarding the application and selection process, and that internship sites that commit violations will continue to do so until students are willing to speak up. Further, if an internship site does not conform to the selection rules, what kind of setting will it be for the student to work in?

Internship Evaluation

In addition to the importance of internship sites "playing by the rules," it is also important that students carefully examine the evaluation procedures of particular internship sites. Hahn and Molnar (1991) found that there is great variability between internship sites when it comes to how often and in what manner interns are evaluated. Further, they noted that even though many sites provide the student's academic department with written feedback, that feedback is typically global and uninformative. Students need to know the mode, manner, and frequency with which they will be evaluated. Students also need to know the mechanism for responding when they receive a negative evaluation.

Another aspect of internship evaluation is that there exists the possibility that an intern can be terminated. While internship sites do not regularly dismiss interns, nevertheless it does happen (Hahn & Molnar, 1991). It is absolutely imperative that the student determine if a particular internship site has a mechanism for (1) early identification of problems, (2) assisting interns with the remediation of those problems, (3) giving interns an opportunity to challenge a negative evaluation, and most importantly, (4) providing interns with the opportunity to challenge a dismissal.

According to the internship literature, internship training staff need to understand that interns are going to have problems with certain aspects of their performance. Interns are in training, and capable of making mistakes. However, there needs to be a distinction between an intern having some difficulty with a certain aspect of training and the notion of intern impairment. Tedesco (1982) defined intern impairment as an interference in professional functioning as a result of one or more of the following: inability and/or unwillingness to acquire and integrate professional standards into one's repertoire of professional behavior; inability to acquire professional skills in order to reach an acceptable level of competency; inability to control personal stress or other emotional reactions. Further, criteria which link this definition of impairment to particular professional behaviors should be incorporated into all competency-based evaluations during the internship.

While no intern wants to be thought of as "impaired," it is in everyone's best interests that, should an intern clearly have significant difficulties with their professional functioning, these difficulties be appropriately and accurately identified and remediated. Further, the American Psychological Association (1992) has instituted ethical guidelines designed to (1) observe ethical and legal protection of clients' and trainees' rights; (2) meet the training and professional needs of trainees in ways consistent with the clients' welfare and programmatic requirements; and (3) establish policies, procedures, and standards for implementing programs.

Therefore, it is in the intern's best interests to know that an internship site will adequately and appropriately respond should the internship year be less than successful. Many things can happen in a year—an intern could experience the death of a family member, a divorce, or even succumb to the enormous pressures and stress of completing the internship, dissertation, and job search process in a short amount of time. Interns should want to be in a setting where the staff will seek to protect some or all clients from the intern's difficulties, but that the intern's needs should be attended to as well. The intern might simply have some clients reassigned, take a week off, or even receive additional supervision.

Personal Considerations

In addition to the weighty issues of ethics and evaluation, students will also need to examine personal factors in contemplating the decision to apply for internship. While personal factors are not often examined in the internship literature, nonetheless they are extremely important. Each student will very likely weigh their unique personal interests, emotional needs, responsibilities, limitations, and role obligations when applying and choosing internship sites (Stewart & Stewart, 1996b). The most common personal factors are location, finances, and family obligations.

Location. While internship training staff do not want interns to prize the location of the site over more central variables (e.g., types of clients), nonetheless intern applicants do use location to narrow their choices. *Location* refers to the geographic place in which you desire to work as an intern. It can also mean that you need to stay in a certain town or city, within an hour commute, within a weekend commute, or in a certain geographic locale. For example, when surveying sites it may be important for students to consider the feasibility of traveling back and forth from the site to the location of significant others or family.

Another variable is the extent to which the student will need to remain in contact with their academic program during the internship year. If the student is attempting to complete the dissertation, several trips back to their home campus may be needed in order to finish certain aspects of that work (e.g., the defense). The choice of an internship location may also be affected by where the intern wants to live and develop professionally after the internship.

Stewart and Stewart (1996b) note that location considerations often interact with financial ones, such as the cost of interviewing and interning, cost of relocating to a new site, cost of living there, and opportunities for employment of partners. Some applicants may spend as much as $1,000 on applications and interviews. Therefore, it is imperative that students at the beginning of the application process carefully examine their financial needs and resources, to examine their available resources (e.g., income, savings, family) in conjunction with the potential costs that will arise. Further, Stewart and Stewart suggested students should consider financial considerations that may influence their choice of internship sites, including travel, relocation, tuition, and insurance.

Travel. Internship sites do not typically require that applicants conduct their interviews on site. Yet, with the increasing competition for internship sites, it is often in the best interests of the applicant to interview on site. This can be costly. Air travel can be expensive, especially if you are invited for a site interview but cannot purchase an airline ticket with advance purchase discounts. On the other hand, if an applicant chooses to drive, they still need to pay for gas and wear and tear on the vehicle. Further, staying overnight will require paying for a hotel, food, and possibly other expenses.

Students should also assess the cost of living at a prospective internship site. Two internship sites can offer the same stipend, yet the cost of living may be different in those communities. Stewart and Stewart (1996b) offered such recommendations as contacting local chambers of commerce, visitor centers, and real estate agencies to ascertain living expenses. Students should also consider the cost of the physical move from their present home to the internship site, which may require at least one trip prior to moving to procure living arrangements, visit local schools, and become familiar with the area.

Tuition. Since the internship is part of a student's academic course work, he or she will likely be required to register for classes during the internship year, minimally for internship credit, and possibly for dissertation credit. This is often an unexpected expense for students, and depending on the tuition at their home institution, as well as residency status, can be very costly. In some cases, students may be able to apply to their university for a special fee waiver or deferment for internship tuition costs, or the student may have earned enough graduate credit to enroll for zero hours (which should lower the tuition rate).

Insurance. Finally, the issue of insurance may be important to some students, particularly those students with spouses or children. When a student relocates to a different state, he or she may experience a significant increase in car insurance rates, or the insurance carrier may not even offer insurance in that particular state. Students will also need to examine the availability of health and dental insurance, for themselves, and possibly their spouses or children. For example, counseling center internship sites typically offer health and dental insurance as part of their benefits package; on the other hand, most Veterans Administration medical centers offer higher salaries but do not include these benefits directly. Students should contact their insurance companies and internship sites to determine the best course of action for them and their families.

The issue of insurance is also relevant on a professional level. Intern applicants should make inquiries into the agency's malpractice insurance policy, to ensure that they are covered under the umbrella of that agency's insurance. It is common practice in training agencies that interns are indeed automatically covered under the agency's insurance policy, and therefore privately purchasing malpractice insurance during internship is typically unnecessary. Nonetheless, intern applicants should verify that this is the case.

Future Changes in Internship Training

Things change, and changes will likely affect the nature and focus of internship training in the coming years. Further, since events and issues outside of the profession can often influence the field in ways that are difficult to predict, it follows that it is difficult to predict what changes will occur in internship settings. Nevertheless, what follows is an examination of factors that are most likely to influence internship training in the next decade.

APPIC Computerized Matching Program

It is likely that no other factor will impact the internship application and selection process as much as the APPIC computerized matching program. According to Keilin (1998), the decision to adopt a computer-based matching program is based on nearly 30 years of discussion, debate, and controversy within the profession on how to improve upon the existing application and selection process. With the adoption of this program, the membership of APPIC hope to (1) provide a more fair and efficient selection process, (2) reduce participants' stress and anxiety, (3) provide better results for applicants and programs, and (4) eliminate many of the incentives that previously existed for participants to violate the APPIC guidelines.

The New System. Keilin (1998) noted that the idea of a computerized program has existed for many years. However, previous efforts to implement such a system were unsuccessful, for reasons such as technological problems, procedural difficulties, and the administrative time burden placed on APPIC. In 1996 APPIC moved to hire an outside vendor to handle the technical aspects of a matching program, and in 1998, the membership of APPIC adopted the proposal for immediate utilization in the 1998–1999 selection process.

It is important that students understand that the computerized program has completely changed how students are selected for internship, and may very well render much of the literature on the application and selection process obsolete. The APPIC matching program replaces the four-hour period known as Uniform Notification Day (UND). In the past, unless an internship site had notified the applicant more than a week prior to UND (typically held the second Monday in February), the applicant was to consider himself or herself a viable candidate for that site. Therefore, applicants typically spent the last week prior to UND ranking their choices. On Monday, at 9:00 a.m. central daylight time, applicants would stay home and wait for the phone to ring, hoping that at least one call would bring an offer from an internship site. While applicants were ethically obligated to "hold" no more than one offer at a time, gridlocks typically developed from applicants concurrently holding multiple offers. Further, many applicants reported feeling undue pressure to immediately accept an internship's offer, even though there was no obligation to accept such an offer until the end of the day. With the new program, students are instructed that on a predetermined day they can learn what site they have been chosen for; further, all students who participate must understand that the decision via the computer model is *binding* and therefore cannot be altered by either the student or the site.

Reducing Applicant Stress. It is hoped that the computerized program will do more than just abolish UND. The matching program is an attempt to create an equitable and orderly mechanism for matching internship programs and applicants, based on the preferences of both. Because all offers by programs, acceptances, and rejections by applicants occur simultaneously, decisions by programs and applicants can be based entirely on their "true" preferences without concern for the procedural difficulties of the previous system (e.g., holding offers). Moreover, the APPIC matching program does not dictate any changes to the existing application and selection procedures; instead, applicants and programs submit ranked lists of their preferences to National Matching Services, Inc. (the vendor). The company then uses its proprietary software to match applicants and distributes the *binding* results to participants on a predetermined date.

Keilin (1998) noted whereas under the old system applicants did not often wait on UND for their best offers, or that sites made offers to lower-ranked candidates who they believed were likely to accept those offers, a potential advantage of the computerized program is that participants can now be assured of receiving the best possible match. Further, by reducing the incentive for a training program to coerce a student into premature acceptance, as well as leaving indecisive applicants to stress over decisions on UND, it is hoped that the new program will significantly reduce the amount of anxiety that applicants have experienced (and complained about) in recent years.

New Opportunities for Couples. Finally, Kielin also noted an advantage that was nonexistent with the old system: couples will be able to coordinate their internship decisions. The new program allows couples to submit a single rank-ordered list consisting of paired internship sites. In essence, a couple's first choice might be that one partner chooses a particular site contingent on the other partner getting an offer from another site (probably in close proximity to the first site). Thus, any two applicants may choose to officially be designated as a "couple" and submit a single, paired rank-ordered list of any length.

While there appear to be many advantages to the new system, only time and experience will prove to be a true indication of how much computerized matching improves upon the previous system. Certainly the program cannot guarantee that applicants and training staff will change any past inappropriate behavior. In the coming decade, much research will likely be conducted on the application and selection process under the new system, and students are admonished to share their successes and their struggles with all appropriate personnel.

Preliminary Results. According to statistics from the APPIC match interim report (1999) for the most recent computerized matching, 2413 applicants were successfully matched to internship positions. Nearly half (46 percent) of all matched applicants received their top-ranked choice of internship site, two-thirds (66 percent) received one of their top two choices, and nearly four in five (78 percent) received one of their top three choices. The match interim report emphasizes that comparing this data to previous years is difficult because of the limited prior data available.

Nonetheless, the preliminary results from the matching program suggest that it is comparatively equivalent, if not superior, to the Uniform Notification Day system. Based on a survey of applicants and training directors from this most recent match (APPIC, 1999), respondents' answers to such items as overall satisfaction with the internship selection process, stress as a result of the application and selection process, and perceived ethical violations from internship agencies and applicants all indicate that the new system is indeed a marked improvement.

The Problem of Unplaced Intern Applicants

As stated previously, students are increasingly finding difficulty in finding internship placements, especially due to the increasing number of students being admitted to psychology programs. A very critical variable is the economics of managed care, which affect internship availability. Managed care and hospitals may seek to eliminate internship positions or eliminate training staff in those internship sites. At this point, it is difficult to predict how managed care will affect internship availability in the next decade, but early indications suggest that the problem will get worse before it gets better (Gloria et al., 1997).

In November of 1998, APA co-sponsored with APPIC a national conference on the supply and demand of professional psychologists. While internship supply and demand was only a part of the conference agenda, the perceived internship shortage for predoctoral clinical, counseling, and school psychology students was extensively discussed. It is unlikely that the number of internship positions will appreciably increase within the next five to ten years. Counseling and clinical psychology programs will need to reduce the size of incoming classes in order to reduce the "glut" of applicants. Further, as long as the internship process remains highly competitive, students will need to heed many of the aforementioned suggestions in order to remain as attractive as possible in terms of their candidacy. Less experienced, less competitive students may need to delay their decision to go on internship.

Finally, in the past few years, the APPIC Doctoral Clearinghouse has received approximately 300 requests annually from students who remained unplaced after UND, and this number is likely to increase (Mellott et al., 1997). The Clearinghouse is an internship placement program that has been offered through APPIC since 1976. Its primary purpose is to assist internship programs that have unfilled positions, as well as intern applicants who are not selected by an internship site, so that these programs and applicants can locate each other. For students, this is an important service—those who are unfortunately not offered an internship site get a second chance at placement. In recent years, more students have used the Clearinghouse. Because of increased competition for sites, even more may do so. Applicants are advised to check with the director of their academic program to ensure that their program is a member or subscriber of this service.

Postdoctoral Internships

Another issue pertaining to the supply and demand of professional psychologists becomes the issue of obtaining an internship beyond the predoctoral experience. It is conceivable in the future that more graduates may need to consider a postdoctoral internship in order to remain competitive and marketable. Postdoctoral internships are typically one- or two-year positions where one is supervised and trained in a particular agency (somewhat similar to the predoctoral experience). The practice of obtaining postdoctoral experience is already commonplace in certain specialty fields (e.g., neuropsychology), and APPIC has a number of sites that students can apply to for this type of advanced training.

A strong advantage of postdoctoral positions is that they offer an organized, strategic training experience; thus, a postdoctoral experience can make one quite competitive when it comes to seeking permanent employment. However, while postdoctoral training can provide graduates with additional experience and training in an area of specialization, most postdoctoral interns are paid significantly less than full-time professional staff members. Therefore, it means that the graduate commits to another year of being in training while making a meager salary. Further, with the exception of postdoctoral neuropsychology sites, other types of postdoctoral internships are difficult to find and are not always regulated.

It is also conceivable that the predoctoral internship will *become* postdoctoral. In 1998 the Council of University Directors of Clinical Psychology (CUDCP) voted to move the timing of the clinical internship to the postdoctoral period. According to Thorn (1998), the vote was viewed by many of its members as a call for relevant training and organizational bodies to examine the issue of internship timing, and not as a move to immediately change the current system. Further, although organizations outside of CUDCP (including APPIC) reaffirmed the predoctoral internship timing after learning of the CUDCP's vote, nonetheless the vote has initiated much dialogue within different training bodies. Moreover, in direct response to CUDCP, the APA Board of Educational Affairs has appointed a committee to study the impact of moving the internship from pre- to postdoctoral, and to summarize the implications for such a move on the quality of training, financial and administrative support, accreditation, and licensure.

Being License-Eligible upon Completion of Internship

With respect to licensure, the postdoctoral internship experience may ultimately help resolve a thorny problem regarding new graduates—being unlicensed while looking for professional positions that typically require licensure. An agency that advertises a job opening may require that the individual who is hired for that position be licensed in that state (or immediately able to transfer their license from another state). Given that many state licensing boards require an *additional* year of supervision beyond the internship experience, this can preclude the newly graduated intern from being hired. Yet, clearly the graduate cannot get supervision if they are not hired by an agency!

Most states offer newly graduated interns some type of temporary licensure, or bona fide applicant status. Essentially, this temporary licensure allows the professional to practice psychology during the first year after internship (under supervision), and therefore one can be hired at an agency as a "licensed" psychologist before actually completing the requirements for being licensed in that particular state.

It is difficult to speculate about the future of temporary licensure, and each state is autonomous enough on its regulations that states may vary widely on the existence, status, and conditions of temporary licensure. In recent years, some states have revoked the temporary license, or made changes to the conditions under which one can be temporarily licensed. Therefore, interns are encouraged to contact the licensing boards of the states in which they are seeking employment, and to ascertain their eligibility for temporary licensure. Certainly the job search process is stressful enough while one is completing an internship; nonetheless, it is important that interns be familiar with state licensing regulations so that they do not needlessly apply for positions from which an inability to be immediately licensed after internship precludes them.

Standardization of APPIC Predoctoral Internship Applications

In the past, each internship agency has developed its own application form. This practice has resulted in numerous complaints by students that filling out applications is cumbersome, tedious, and a poor use of time. In recent years, with the increased competition for internships, the number of complaints regarding applications has increased (Holaday & McPhearson, 1996). Anxious applicants can literally spend hours on each application, writing and rewriting and tailoring their specific answers to that particular agency. Further, questions on application forms are often vaguely worded and excessively detailed (Gloria & Robinson, 1994).

Holaday and McPhearson, who conducted a study on the written application forms of internship sites, noted several benefits of a standardized form sent via computer, including (1) saving internships time and money because they would not have to design or duplicate their own form; (2) saving staff time and energy because analyzing information received and stored on a computer is more efficient and more accurate; and (3) information stored on a computer takes up less space. However, they also noted some disadvantages, most notably that students may decide to apply to more sites than they have in the past due to the ease of copying the same application over and over.

In 1997–1998, APPIC implemented a standardized application form that internship sites may or may not choose to use. Will sites eventually be required to adopt this standardized form? Given the trend toward increasing use of technology, as well as APPIC's efforts to ensure that the application process is conducted as smoothly as possible, it is very likely that this will occur. Students are encouraged to contact APPIC regarding their interest in this issue.

Conclusion

The predoctoral internship can be an extremely rewarding experience, both personally and professionally, and with preparation and training experiences, students can increase the likelihood that they will find sites that satisfy their personal and professional needs. It is hoped that after reading this chapter, students will view the internship as a wonderful opportunity, as something that should not be feared but eagerly anticipated.

Much information has been presented regarding internship training—that presented on the application process alone may result in some readers feeling anxious. Nevertheless, it is imperative that students use this information to improve their chances at procuring a quality internship. The internship is far too important to be relegated to the status of "getting to it later."

REFERENCES

Allen, C., & Dressel, J. (1992). 1991 intern selection practices survey. *APPIC Newsletter, 17*(1), 26–29.

American Psychological Association. (1992). Ethical principles of psychologists and code of conduct. *American Psychologist, 47,* 1597–1611.

Association of Psychology Postdoctoral and Internship Centers. (1999). *APPIC Match interim report from the APPIC Board of Directors.* Web site: www.appic.org/m10statistics.html. Washington, DC: Author.

Association of Psychology Postdoctoral and Internship Centers. (1999–2000). *APPIC Directory (28th ed.).* Washington, DC: Author.

Belar, C. D., Bielauskas, L. A., Larsen, K. G., Mensh, I. N., Poey, K., & Roehlke, H. J. (1989). The national conference on internship training in psychology. *American Psychologist, 44,* 60–65.

Constantine, M. G., & Keilin, W. G. (1996). Association of Psychology Postdoctoral and Internship Centers' guidelines and the internship selection process: A survey of applicants and academic and internship training directors. *Professional Psychology: Research and Practice, 27,* 308–314.

Department of Veterans Affairs. (1995). *Psychologist (clinical and counseling) GRANDSON-180-11/12/13* (Announcement No. VA-0180). Richmond, VA: Author.

Ducheny, K., Alletzhauser, H. L., Crandell, D., & Schneider, T. R. (1997). Graduate student professional development. *Professional Psychology: Research and Practice, 28,* 87–91.

Erikson, E. H. (1975). *Life history and the historical moment.* New York: W. W. Norton.

Gloria, A. M., Castillo, L. G., Choi-Pearson, C. P., & Rangel, D. K. (1997). Competitive internship candidates: A national survey of internship training directors. *The Counseling Psychologist, 25,* 453–472.

Gloria, A. M., & Robinson, S. E. (1994). The internship application process: A survey of program training directors and intern candidates. *The Counseling Psychologist, 22,* 474–488.

Guinee, J. P. (1998). Erikson's life span theory: A metaphor for conceptualizing the internship year. *Professional Psychology: Research and Practice, 29,* 615–620.

Hahn, W. K., & Molnar, S. (1991). Intern evaluation in university counseling centers: Process, problems, and recommendations. *The Counseling Psychologist, 19,* 414–430.

Hall, R. G., Cantrell, P. J., Boggs, K. R., & Hercey, C. M. (Eds.). (1997). *APPIC directory: Internship and postdoctoral programs in professional psychology* (26th ed.). Washington, DC: Association of Psychology Postdoctoral and Internship Centers.

Holaday, M., & McPhearson, R. (1996). Standardization of APPIC predoctoral psychology internship application forms. *Professional Psychology: Research and Practice, 27,* 508–513.

Holland, J. L. (1985). *Making vocational choices: A theory of vocational personalities and work environments* (2nd ed.). Englewood Cliffs, NJ: Prentice-Hall.

Holloway, E. L., & Roehlke, H. J. (1987). Internship: The applied training of a counseling psychologist. *The Counseling Psychologist, 15,* 205–260.

Kaslow, N. J., & Rice, D. G. (1985). Developmental stresses of psychology internship training: What training staff can do to help. *Professional Psychology: Research and Practice, 16,* 253–261.

Keilin, W. G. (1998). Internship selection 30 years later: An overview of the APPIC matching program. *Professional Psychology: Research and Practice, 29,* 599–603.

Lamb, D. H., Baker, J. M., & Jennings, M. L. (1982). *Passages of an Internship in Professional Psychology, 13,* 661–669.

Lopez, S. J., Oehlert, M. E., & Moberly, R. L. (1996). Selection criteria for American Psychological Association-accredited internship programs: A survey of training directors. *Professional Psychology: Research and Practice, 27,* 518–520.

Mellott, R. N., Arden, I. A., & Cho, M. E. (1997). Preparing for internship: Tips for the prospective applicant. *Professional Psychology: Research and Practice, 28,* 190–196.

Mitchell, S. L. (1996). Getting a foot in the door: The written internship application. *Professional Psychology: Research and Practice, 27,* 90–92.

Pederson, S. L. (1995). *Internship supply and demand: A preliminary report.* Unpublished report for the Association of Psychology Postdoctoral and Internship Centers and the Council of Chairs of Training Councils.

Phares, E. J. (1984). *Clinical psychology: Concepts, methods, and professions* (2nd ed.). Homewood, IL: Dorsey Press.

Rangel, D., & Boxley, R. (1985). Clinical impairment in American Psychological Association approved internship programs. *APPIC Newsletter, 19,* 18–21.

Shemberg, K. M., & Leventhal, D. B. (1981). Attitudes of internship directors toward preinternship training and clinical training models. *Professional Psychology, 12,* 253–260.

Skovholt, T. M., & Ronnestad, M. H. (1992). Perspectives on professional development. In *The evolving professional self: Stages and themes in therapist and counselor development* (pp. 1–21). New York: Wiley.

Solway, K. (1985). Transition from graduate school to internship: A potential crisis. *Professional Psychology: Research and Practice, 16,* 50–54.

Stedman, J. M. (1989). The history of the APIC selection process. *APIC Newsletter, 14,* 35–43.

Stedman, J. M. (1997). What we know about predoctoral internship training: A review. *Professional Psychology: Research and Practice, 28,* 475–485.

Stedman, J. M., Neff, J. A., Donahoe, C. P., Kopel, K., & Hays, J. R. (1995). Applicant characterization of the most desirable internship training program. *Professional Psychology: Research and Practice, 26,* 396–400.

Stewart, A. E., & Stewart, E. A. (1996a). A decision-making technique for choosing a psychology internship. *Professional Psychology: Research and Practice, 27,* 521–526.

Stewart, A. E., & Stewart, E. A. (1996b). Personal and practical considerations in selecting a psychology internship. *Professional Psychology: Research and Practice, 27,* 295–303.

Strickland, B. R. (1998). History and introduction to clinical psychology. In S. Cullari (Ed.), *Foundations of clinical psychology.* Boston: Allyn & Bacon.

Tedesco, J. (1982). Premature termination of interns. *Professional Psychology, 13,* 695–698.

Thorn, B. (1998). Clinical psychology directors focus on supply and demand. *APA Monitor, 29,* 58–60.

Williams, G. (1992). APPIC predoctoral clearinghouse—1992. *APPIC Newsletter, 17*(2), 24–25.

FOR FURTHER READING

Association of Psychology Postdoctoral and Internship Centers. (1999). *APPIC Directory* (28th ed.). Washington, DC: Author.

Contains a list of all APPIC sites and relevant information regarding each site.

Hahn, W. K., & Molnar, S. (1991). Intern evaluation in university counseling centers: Process, problems, and recommendations. *The Counseling Psychologist, 19,* 414–430.

Gives a framework for developing an intern rating system, considering both what areas of intern training to evaluate and how to select appropriate content items.

Holloway, E. L., & Roehlke, H. J. (1987). Internship: The applied training of a counseling psychologist. *The Counseling Psychologist, 15,* 205–260.

Provides a brief history and definition of the internship, the organization and management of internship programs, the major types of internship settings, the influence and impact of pressures from within and outside the profession on internship training, and questions and concerns relevant to the internship of the future.

Keilin, W. G. (1998). Internship selection 30 years later: An overview of the APPIC matching program. *Professional Psychology: Research and Practice, 29,* 599–603.

Summarizes some of the problems and issues inherent in the previous selection process and provides an overview of the new program.

Levinger, C., & Schefres, I. (1996). *Everything you need to get a psychology internship.* Los Angeles: Internship Publishers.

The title is a good description of this book.

Lipovsky, J. A. (1988). Internship year in clinical psychology training as a professional adolescence. *Professional Psychology: Research and Practice, 19,* 606–608.

Through presentation of personal experiences and observations of a clinical psychology intern, elements of the internship year are compared with the identity process of adolescence.

Megargee, E. J. (1992). *A guide to obtaining a psychology internship* (2nd ed.). Muncie, IN: Accelerated Development.

Provides students with helpful insights into the application and selection process of internships.

Mitchell, S. L. (1996). Getting a foot in the door: The written internship application. *Professional Psychology: Research and Practice, 27,* 90–92.

Offers guidelines for developing a written application that accurately and thoughtfully conveys who the applicant is in a manner that is more likely to capture the attention of prospective internship sites.

Ross, R. R., & Altmaier, E. M. (1990). Job analysis of psychology internships in counseling center settings. *Journal of Counseling Psychology, 37,* 459–464.

The critical incident technique was applied in order to determine dimensions of performance among psychology interns.

CHAPTER

13 Outcome Evaluation in Psychological Practice

DAVID C. SPEER

We have witnessed dramatic changes in psychological practice in just the past two decades. Managed mental health care is firmly entrenched and practitioners not on approved provider lists are finding survival difficult. Annual incomes are decreasing. Practitioners are confronted on a daily basis with ethical dilemmas of attempting to help clients within the constraints of third party reimbursement practice guidelines. The mental health professions are scurrying to compile lists of empirically documented effective treatments for specified psychological conditions and psychiatric disorders (e.g., Nathan & Gorman, 1998). The financial and treatment merits of "carve-in's" and "carve-out's" are being debated. Although the intrinsic interaction of mind and body has been long acknowledged (Goleman & Gurin, 1993), and in spite of ample evidence of the medical cost-offset effect and significant reductions in medical utilization following brief behavioral health interventions (Cummings, 1997b), the integration of behavioral health services and medical practice is a relative rarity (Cummings, 1997a).

In addition to these intense economic forces, pressures for accountability in terms of documented benefits or service outcomes are building. Third party payers, managed care entities, employers, and the public are increasingly asking, "What are we getting for our money?" The mental or behavioral health industry has had a checkered history with respect to benefit accountability; Eysenck's 1952 review of the available research on the effectiveness of psychotherapy suggested that the passage of time was as effective as therapy in ameliorating "neurotic" symptoms (Eysenck, 1952). The resulting furor precipitated an avalanche of laboratory research which, by the mid-1980s, had documented the efficacy of standardized, time-limited psychosocial interventions (e.g., Lambert, 1991; Lambert & Bergin, 1994). Unfortunately, because of chauvinism both in academia and among providers, this work was largely ignored by practicing psychologists. A more serious consequence of this breakdown in communication was that almost no efforts were made to evaluate the effectiveness of mental health services in the field; there were no efforts to replicate in the community the methods and results provided by clinical researchers in university settings. Technically, this is referred to as the lack of *external validity* of laboratory-tested interventions (Speer, 1998). It was not until the early 1990s that concern developed about the absence of outcome information from community-based mental health services. As a result, we are "behind the curve" in developing, piloting, and implementing valid and unbiased measures of how consumers' problems respond to our services. A lot has been said about the need for outcome evaluation, but little has been done (Speer & Newman, 1996).

Further complicating relations with the public has been the very poor job of the mental health industry in informing or educating lay people about the counseling or treatment process. Psychoanalysis is admittedly obscure for many professionals. Unfortunately, the majority of mental health interventions, too, are trade-secret "black boxes" from the public's standpoint. Thus, trust of behavioral health providers becomes an issue, particularly when accountability is under discussion. The public accepts pills to deal with problems; counseling and psychotherapy are something else (for an exception to this, however, see Mental Health: Does Therapy Help?, 1995). Lost in the turmoil of recent years is Lipsey and Wilson's demonstration (1993) that psychological and behavioral interventions are as effective for mental health problems as most medical interventions are for medical illnesses, and more effective than many medical procedures for medical conditions.

Practical Outcome Evaluation

One manifestation of the mutually distrustful relationship between psychologists in academia and practicing psychologists during the 1960s and 1970s was their differences about appropriate evaluation methodology in service delivery settings. The prevailing view, represented by Campbell (e.g., Campbell & Stanley, 1963), was that the only appropriate approach was the experimental model with random assignment, extensive assessment with well-validated instruments, and carefully selected homogeneous participants/subjects. Practitioners in the field, clinics, and other settings rebelled at the ethical dilemmas of random assignment, depriving clients of treatment, and the generally disruptive intrusion of laboratory methods into the helping environment. When field practitioners attempted to implement less rigorous but more feasible methods to study service delivery, they were criticized for being "unscientific" and it was intimated that data generated by quasi-experimental approaches were not of value. Eventually practitioners allowed themselves to be intimidated by this criticism, and efforts to evaluate services in the field ceased.

In the early 1980s Lee Cronbach and his colleagues confronted and addressed the "clay feet" of the high-science and experimental approaches to evaluation of community services (Cronbach et al., 1980). These authors pointed out that total or absolute control of all potentially confounding factors is impossible even under highly controlled laboratory conditions. Further, efforts to control or rule out other explanations of treatment or service effects (thus maximizing internal validity) created such artificial service conditions that they had little likelihood of being used in the field, community clinics, and so forth. Thus, the external validity of interventions tested and validated in the laboratory could only very rarely be examined in field settings. Weisz and his colleagues and Seligman have eloquently described the many dramatic differences between field clinical practice and laboratory investigation of structured psychosocial interventions (Weisz, Weiss, & Donenberg, 1992; Seligman, 1995). Cronbach and his group pointed out the ipsative relationships between internal validity and external validity (generalizing methods and findings to other situations). They also pointed out that findings from highly controlled experimental studies usually had little meaning to and utility for policy and program decision-makers. These researchers recommended sacrificing some scientific "certainty" for the greater relevance and usefulness of less rigorous program evaluation; imperfect information is better than no information. Recently, Goldfried and Wolfe (1996) expressed the view that efficacy studies and clinical trials are the wrong methods for investigating the effectiveness of services, as services are usually provided in community settings.

For Cronbach and his colleagues, the purpose of program evaluation is not to produce new knowledge, prove cause and effect, or communicate with the scientific community. It is to provide comprehensible information, relevant to current public and social issues, that will be pertinent to and inform or enlighten discussions of public policy or program decision matters (Cronbach et al., 1980). Some rigor and certainty are to be sacrificed for relevance and utility. Reduced rigor can be compensated for by replication in other field settings, and creative combinations of less elegant quasi-experimental methods (e.g., Campbell & Stanley, 1963). Cronbach and colleagues (1980) and Campbell and Stanley (1963) argued that alternative explanations of the observed change involving extraneous factors must be "plausible" and cogent, not just theoretically possible. Recently, Sperry et al. (1996), too, challenged the role of experimental methods or randomized clinical trials in practical outcome evaluation. These authors recommended a "quasi-naturalistic" approach that systematically uses exploratory methodology. Methods that enhance generalizability of findings and replication are to be encouraged.

Having challenged the primacy of a rigid scientific approach in program outcome evaluation, we need to pause and consider some other aspects of scientific reasoning and methods. Scientific investigation and program evaluation overlap and have some important things in common. This overlap is depicted in Figure 13.1.

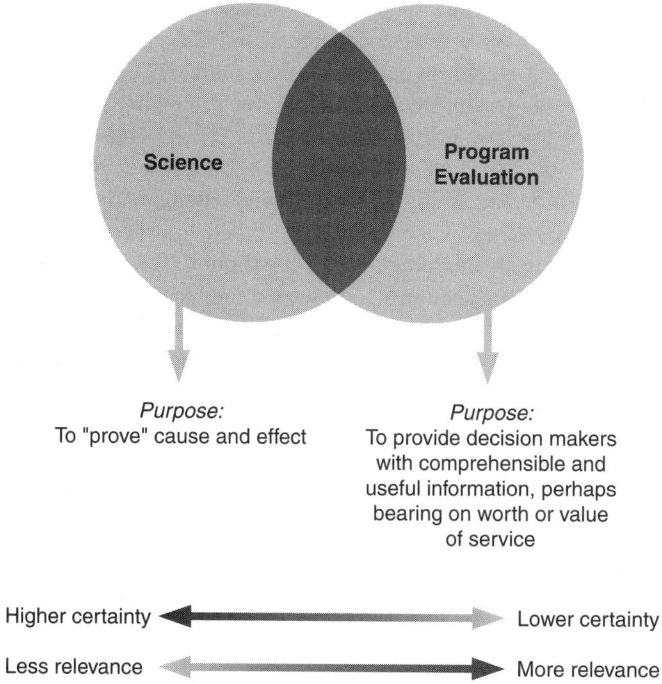

FIGURE 13.1 The Relationship between Program Evaluation and Science

Slavish devotion to the randomized experimental model has been questioned. However, we do need to be concerned about matters that affect drawing defensible conclusions. Cronbach, while proposing that we accept the tradeoff of some certainty for greater feasibility, also urges that we use the most rigorous methods possible in any given situation. We cannot be cavalier about measurements' reliability and validity, bias-producing methods and procedures, or comparison conditions. An example of a biasing procedure is having therapists ask consumers about consumer satisfaction with the therapist's services; the pressure to compliment the nude emperor on his fine attire is obvious. Similarly, using therapist ratings of consumer depression to evaluate the effectiveness of the therapist's services, rather than direct consumer report, is arguable (i.e., the effects of vested interests must be considered).

Practical Outcome Evaluation Designs

When discussing outcome evaluation, we are usually implicitly talking about consumer change. The study of change involves *comparisons:* comparison of one group of consumers with another (perhaps from a different time period), comparison of consumer scores with normative data, comparison of consumer termination or followup scores with admission scores, or comparison of consumer data with data from some other group of people. Evaluation *designs* are, simply, (1) specification of the clients or consumers of primary interest; (2) specification of what data, and from whom, will constitute the comparison reference point for interpretation of the primary data; and (3) the timing of the assessments involved. Design also includes procedural rules specifying how these things will occur.

In acute care settings we are usually concerned with documenting or demonstrating that positive change or improvement has occurred; a minimum of two assessments is required. On the other hand, programs serving people with chronic problems such as severe and persistent mental illness may be primarily concerned with helping consumers maintain their functional status, and to not deteriorate to the point of needing placement in restrictive treatment settings. Evidence is accumulating, in fact, that individuals with severe and persistent mental illness who receive intensive case management rarely improve symptomatically or in functioning, in spite of being able to remain in the community (Speer & Stiles, 1997).

In outcome evaluation in community settings, we need to be cautious about use of the terms "sample" or "sampling." In field settings, true random sampling is rarely possible. Instead, we usually are working with *cohorts* of clients or consumers. That is, we specify time periods during which new clients, or clients with some specific characteristics, are to be included in the evaluation. For example, consumers admitted for service or treatment during consecutive three-month intervals might be specified as the "study" and comparison cohorts. Although we cannot use random selection to ensure that the selected consumers are representative of all consumers in whom we are interested, through comparison of the demographic and clinical characteristics of our evaluation cohorts with those of consumers in general, we can investigate similarity and make judgments about the likely representativeness of our study groups. Most treatment settings will have information about the ages, gender, ethnicity, education, income, diagnoses, and so forth of their clientele.

Let us now consider some evaluation designs that are often used in community mental health treatment settings or would be feasible in most of them (Speer & Newman, 1996).

Most of these designs are quasi-experimental (Campbell & Stanley, 1963). The original symbols used by Campbell and Stanley will be used to describe these designs: O = observation or assessment, X = treatment or intervention, R = random assignment, and ------ = non-random selection, or non-equivalent groups. Because most readers will have had this material during their training, the designs will not be discussed at length. The strengths and weaknesses of these designs are summarized in Table 13.1.

Single Cohort Pre-post-test Design

O X O

This is the very familiar single group method in which specified consumers are assessed at the beginning of service and again on some later occasion, such as toward the end of service or at followup. Although feasible in most settings, given an appropriately unobtrusive measure, and capable of demonstrating that consumers are different later (or not), Campbell and Stanley (1963) considered this a "pre-experimental design" (not even qualifying

TABLE 13.1 Characteristics of Evaluation Comparison Strategies

Strategy	Purpose	Strengths	Weaknesses
1. single cohort pre-post-test	describe change	acceptable to most providers	weak evidence that treatment caused change
2. nonequivalent comparison groups			
a. normative groups	compare pre- and/or post-treatment status to status of a nonconsumer group	provides a static but meaningful nonconsumer reference point to aid in evaluating change data	groups are likely to differ in many ways except for a few demographic characteristics (e.g., age)
b. different setting groups	compare change in one group with change in another group	provides a comparison group external to study group to aide interpreting data	groups may differ in ways that affect outcomes; organization and population characteristics that affect outcomes may differ
c. same service setting groups	same as 2.a	consumer and organizational variables of the groups likely to be similar	groups may differ in ways that affect outcomes
3. experimental or randomized control groups	prove that innovative service caused consumer change	eliminates many other explanations of the observed change	is often unacceptable to providers; requires administrative logistic action

as "quasi-experimental"). This design is descriptive at best. Examples of its use are Galligan's evaluation of a specialized residential unit and day treatment program for 36 intellectually challenged adults who also had psychiatric disorders (1990). At one-year followup, the residents had made substantial gains in independence, but 60 percent were still having significant weekly behavior problems. Johnson et al. (1992) used the design to evaluate a four-day, close-to-the-battle-zone crisis treatment program for 22 combat veterans with combat fatigue. Anxiety, depression, and hostility decreased significantly, and 21 returned to duty.

The single cohort pre-post-test design is of modest rigor and should probably be considered the weakest of the field-setting outcome evaluation designs. It can provide descriptive base-rate information about rates of improvement, no change, and deterioration, however.

Nonequivalent Normative Comparison Group Design

O X O
- - - - - - - - -
O

Although this design has been around for some time, it has been seriously overlooked and neglected. In this approach, the general public norms for a particular assessment instrument are used as the comparison group to assist in interpreting pre- and/or post intervention data from the cohort of interest (Kazdin, 1994; Kendall & Grove, 1988). The obvious disadvantage is that the normative group may have little in common with the service cohort demographically, as regards timing of the assessments, geographically, and so forth. The major advantage is that it is possible to determine where the cohort falls at admission in relation to the mean, and in relation to points one or two standard deviations from the normative mean. Thus the cohort can be described in terms of its relative deviation from people in general. Another serious weakness is that the design is locked to a specific measure with norms; not all popular evaluation instruments have norms (e.g., Hamilton Rating Scale for Depression, Hamilton, 1960).

Speer (1994) provided an example of this design in a descriptive study of 92 older adults seen in a mental health outpatient clinic. Dupuy's 18-item General Well-Being Scale (mean = 80, standard deviation = 18), was administered at admission and at discharge (1977). The findings of the study are presented graphically in Figure 13.2. The cohort's mean was significantly below the normative mean at admission (nearly two standard deviations), and though improved statistically significantly at discharge was still significantly below the normative mean. Comparisons such as this are important, particularly for the humility of the evaluator. We will return to the interpretation of these findings later.

Nonequivalent Different-Setting Comparison Group Design

O X O
- - - - - - - - - - - - - - - - -
← O → ← O →

Here, the comparison group is from a different place and setting, and usually from a different time period. The group is chosen because hopefully it has something in common, usu-

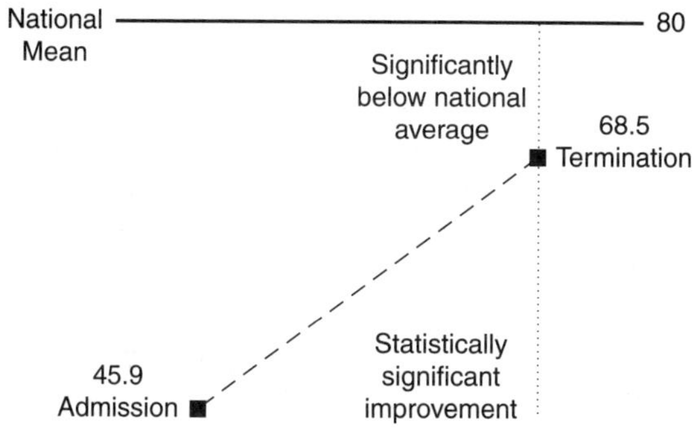

FIGURE 13.2 Well-Being among Older Outpatients (N = 92; General well-being range, 0–110)

ally demographically or clinically, with the cohort of interest. The same or highly similar outcome measures are used. The weakness is that the two groups may differ markedly on any number of variables, including historical events such as an intervening economic recession, for example. The diagram suggests that the time interval between assessments may also vary considerably. An example is Shern and his colleagues' five-year evaluation of an enhanced and subsequently defunded case management program for chronically mentally ill adults in one area of Colorado (1994). The comparison group was consumers from a similar case management program in a nearby geographic area for which enhancements were not planned and for which defunding did not occur. The enhancements did increase services and reduced unmet needs, while defunding reversed these relative to the comparison group.

Nonequivalent Same-Setting Comparison Group Design

O X O
O   O

This design is a significant step toward a tighter and more rigorous approach to outcome evaluation. Here, both groups are constituted in the same service setting and from the same service population. The ideal circumstances occur when a new service component or a change in some service element is being planned. Even though the culture of the treatment setting may not be able to accept experimental random assignment, a sophisticated and fairly robust design can be crafted if sufficient time is permitted. The most common situation is that a program change is planned for some time in the future. The desire to evaluate its effectiveness leads to a decision to use current services, in combination with pre-post assessment, prior to implementation of the change as the comparison condition. The strengths of this design are that staff, administration, funding streams, socio-economic status (SES), and clinical characteristics of the treatment population, geography, and so forth are all held constant and cannot be easily used to explain away the demonstrated treatment effects of the new process. Usually, the current-treatment cohort and the cohort receiving the new or changed service are contiguous in time so that there is relatively little opportunity for extraneous events to differentially affect the two groups.

An example is the evaluation of a new intensive community service program for state hospital discharges reported by Bigelow et al. (1991). Seventeen clients discharged from the hospital during the two months prior to beginning the new community program were specified as the comparison cohort and were assessed two to three months after discharge, as were the 25 clients discharged after the beginning of the new program. Although there was a mixture of positive differences and lack of differences between the two groups, the new program clients had a significantly lower rate of hospital re-use and distress scores, and significantly higher well-being and interpersonal relationship scores than the prior-program consumers.

Another situation that lends itself to creation of a same-setting comparison group is when the intervention under investigation can accomodate fewer consumers than the total number of people needing and requesting the service. An example is the evaluation of a structured six-week substance abuse program in a jail by Peters et al. (1993). Many more inmates requested the program than could be accommodated by the available staff and space. Because those who could not be admitted had requested the service, they were similar to the treated group on motivation to participate. These inmates who requested service but who could not be accepted into the program provided an excellent nonrandom comparison group.

The Experimental or Randomized-Comparison Group Design

R O X O
O X O

Here, a single cohort of particular interest and relevance for a specific new intervention or new modification of an existing service is specified. After estimating the number of participants needed in each of two groups to ensure acceptable power (with the help of a consultant, or as described in Cohen, 1992), members of the cohort are randomly assigned to the experimental service group or to the routine currently available service (the comparison condition). The larger cohort from which the randomized groups are constituted could simply be all new consumers admitted following a certain date, and then randomly assigned until the necessary number in each group is attained.

Note that there has been no reference to a "no treatment" control group. There has now been sufficient laboratory efficacy research demonstrating that psychosocial interventions consistently provide effects markedly greater than the simple passage of time; thus, efforts to surpass "no treatment" control conditions are no longer needed. This should provide reassurance to service providers and administrators. The comparison group of greatest interest and relevance is now what is referred to as "treatment as usual" (TAU; e.g., Addis, 1997). The new gold standard to which innovative treatments and innovative services are to be compared and evaluated are those services and treatments which are generally accepted as (or are proven to be) the "best" or most effective available ("best practices").

An important implication of this evolutionary methodological development is that "no treatment" or "inadequate treatment" can no longer be used as excuses for avoiding use of randomizing experimental designs in service delivery settings. That is, the door is opened for greater use of this robust design in outcome evaluation research involving new or innovative intervention technology in clinical field settings. The caveat or downside is that the process must still be sold to and accepted by the consumers (assuming acceptance by providers, management, and appropriate institutional review entities charged with the protection of human "subjects"). In the above scenario, members of the larger, newly admitted consumer cohort would have to be informed of the nature of the research and would have to be willing to indicate in writing their willingness to accept random assignment to either the experimental or usual treatments or interventions prior to being included in the study. This does involve some "hassle" and development of new administrative procedures that will not be happily accepted by harried administrative and provider staff in managed care environments. However, progressive profit and not-for-profit provider organizations will recognize the public relations and marketing potential of being perceived by the public as being in the vanguard of organizations exploring and testing new service and treatment technology, as being on the "cutting edge," so to speak.

As indicated, TAU as a randomized comparison condition is still in the process of gradual acceptance in service delivery settings. (Old attitudes die hard.) Some examples follow. Clarkin et al. (1991) studied the effectiveness of a new program of six psychoeducational sessions for family members of consumers currently receiving treatment in a psychiatric inpatient unit. The comparison condition was inpatient treatment as usual for the consumer (previously, family members had received no particular services). Family members who agreed to participate in the study were then randomly assigned to the psychoeducational program or to treatment as usual. At followup six months after the consumer was discharged, consumer functioning and symptoms and family attitudes toward treatment among the psychoeducational families were significantly better than among those who had received TAU.

Henggeler, Melton, and Smith (1992) conducted an experimental evaluation of an intensive in vivo family treatment and support services program for juvenile offenders. The comparison condition was the usual youth services provided for youthful offenders. Qualifying families were randomly assigned to either family treatment or usual services. Youth in the experimental program, as a group, had fewer arrests and days of incarceration, and higher family cohesion scores, than did the usual-services youth. Morse et al. (1992) reported an experimental evaluation of an assertive outreach and intensive case management program for homeless mentally ill persons, in which 100 consumers were randomly assigned to intensive case management, a daytime drop-in center, or routine outpatient services at a mental health center. The case management consumers had significantly fewer homeless days than consumers in the other two services, but did not differ from other consumers on income, symptoms, self-esteem, or alienation.

In summary, I have discussed four pre- and quasi-experimental designs that are feasible and provide useful information in most service delivery settings. I have also discussed the randomized experimental design, the feasibility of which is gradually increasing with the emergence of TAU as a highly desirable comparison condition. These five designs represent a continuum of methodological rigor that is diagrammed in Figure 13.3. As we move down the scale from program evaluation to basic research, control of extraneous variables and internal validity increases (in some cases, however, not by much) and degree of uncertainty decreases. To the extent that the experimental design can be implemented in service settings, the problems with the external validity of laboratory efficacy studies will be greatly ameliorated.

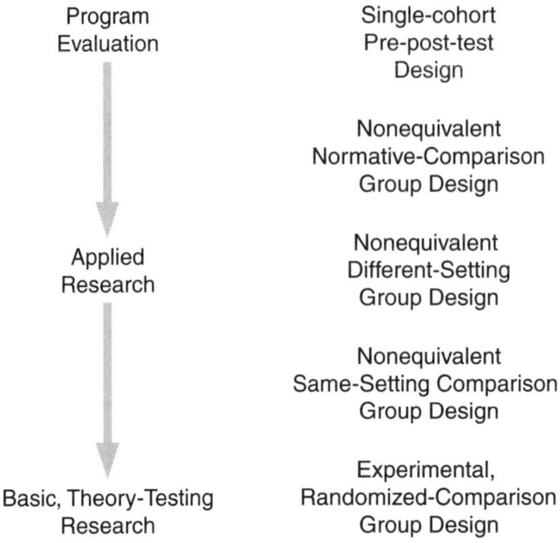

FIGURE 13.3 A Continuum of Evaluation Designs

Classifying Consumers as Improved, Not Changed, or Worse

The study of human change over time has probably been one of the most methodologically enigmatic domains in psychology, and this has been particularly true in psychological practice areas such as mental health services. The major culprit has been the purported *regression to the mean* phenomenon. For decades, there was consensus that regression artificially inflated judgments about improvement because of error of measurement. However, there has also been a universal lack of consensus about what to *do* about regression to the mean. There has been much discussion and many recommended statistical methods for adjusting or correcting for regression to the mean. We will return to this matter shortly.

As indicated earlier, another problem has been the difficulty that we have had in communicating change data or information to lay policy and decision makers. Attempting to attach meaning to group averages for laypeople has always been difficult. Efforts such as Smith, Glass, and Miller's statement (1980) that the average person who receives psychotherapy is better off at the end of therapy than 80 percent of people with similar problems who do not receive therapy, though accurate, is confusing to non-statistically trained people. We need to find ways of better communicating outcome information to the public and non-scientist decision-makers (Speer, 1994; 1998).

The Reliable Change Index (RC) has been proposed by Jacobson and his colleagues as a statistical method for classifying individual clients as improved, unchanged, or worse using *d* score methodology; that is, the difference between an admission and a discharge score on some instrument for which a reliability coefficient is available (e.g., Jacobson & Truax, 1991). RC was initially introduced in the early 1980s; since then, it has been criticized by a number of investigators, including myself, as being vulnerable to confounding by regression to the mean. A number of statistical adjustments have also been suggested to compensate for regression (e.g., Hsu, 1995; Speer, 1992).

Also in the early 1980s, independent of Jacobson's work, education research methodologists (led by David Rogosa) were doing early work on growth-curve approaches to the study of change (e.g., Rogosa, Brandt, & Zimowski, 1982; Rogosa & Willett, 1985). In a startling chapter in a book on methodology and aging research in 1988, Rogosa declared that the idea that regression to the mean is ubiquitous a "myth." Depending on a variety of factors, second scores may be no different than the first score, and sometimes farther from the mean than the initial score. Rogosa, and Willette (1994), also asserted that the *d* or difference score is a reliable and "fair" estimate of change (not necessarily the best estimate, but at least unbiased). Rogosa went on to declare (1988) that the belief that residual change methodology can be used to fix *d* scores is also a myth. A variety of residual change approaches have been suggested as corrections for RC. Unfortunately, because these developments were occurring in the fields of educational and human development research, clinical researchers were unaware of them until relatively recently. Taken together, however, these arguments challenged the veracity of many of the criticisms of RC and of many of the suggestions for "fixing" RC. To Rogosa and his colleagues, many of the proposed corrections created more logical and statistical problems than existed in straightforward use of uncorrected or unadjusted *d*.

It is my belief that, for the immediate future, Jacobson's RC, based on unadjusted *d* scores, is the most justifiable statistical approach for use with two-wave data in classifying consumers as improved or worse for purposes of communicating client outcomes to the public and non-scientist decision-makers (Speer, 1998; Speer, in press).

The application of RC to pre-post intervention measurement scores is straightforward. Keep in mind that the data are examined for each consumer individually; decisions are made about whether each individual client has improved, is unchanged, or has become worse from a statistical reliability standpoint. In addition to the pre-post scores for each individual, the only required statistics are the standard deviation of all admission scores (s_A) and a reliability estimate (r). Either internal consistency (Cronbach's alpha) or test–retest reliability coefficients may be used. The only caveat regarding reliability is to keep in mind that instruments with low reliability coefficients will produce lower improvement rates than instruments with greater reliability (Speer, 1992).

Using the above statistics, the first step is to compute the standard error (SE) according to the following formula:

$$(1)\quad SE = s_A(1 - r)^{1/2}$$

Thus, the reliability coefficient is subtracted from one, the square root of this result is obtained, and this number is multiplied by the standard deviation of the admission scores. This is the standard error. The next step is to compute the standard error of the differences (SED) according to this formula:

$$(2)\quad SED = (2[SE]^2)^{1/2}$$

The SE from step one is squared, the result is multiplied by two, and the square root of the resulting number is determined. RC is then computed (theoretically) for each individual consumer by this formula:

$$(3)\ RC = (X_L - x_A)/SED,$$

where x_L is the consumer's termination (last) score and x_A is the consumer's admission or initial score. The difference between the two scores is then divided by the standard error of the differences. If RC is greater than 1.96 the client has improved reliably at $p = .05$, and if RC is less than –1.96 the client has reliably deteriorated. RCs inbetween indicate that the client has not undergone statistically significant change. In practice, the RC for each individual client will not need to be computed. As one works through the clients' scores, the RC for each difference score can be recorded and referred to the next time this difference arises; division by SED is constant and does not have to be repeated after it has been done once. As one proceeds, a table of difference scores and RCs is generated. If the same instrument is used in future analyses, the same table can be kept and reused, after computing the admission standard deviation and determining that the two admission standard deviations are not significantly different.

After all consumer RCs have been determined and classified as improved, unchanged, or worse, they are simply added up and divided by the total number of clients to determine the percentage improved, unchanged, and worse. The evaluative study of older adult mental health outpatients introduced above provides an example of the use of improvement and deterioration rates. Recall that the cohort of 92 improved significantly from admission to termination, but on average was still significantly below the national adult norm on general well-being at termination (see Figure 13.2; Speer, 1994). This study also exemplifies difficulties in interpreting group means. Although using a slightly different variation of RC, the change of each individual client was tested for statistical significance and the change data were aggregated. Fifty-one percent of the consumers were classified as improved, 44 percent as unchanged, and 5 percent as worse. Thus, part of the reason that the group's termination mean was still reliably below the national mean was that nearly half the cohort reported no significant change or became worse.

So, what basis is there for thinking that these rates are valid indices of program effectiveness? First, the improvement and deterioration rates are consistent with those of a small group of other studies of adult outpatients reported by Jacobson and his colleagues (e.g., Jacobson et al., 1984; Jacobson, Wilson, & Tupper, 1988). These studies generally found improvement rates in the 50–60 percent range and deterioration rates in the 5–10 percent range. Second, these rates are consistent with my clinical experience in CMHC outpatients services. Most outpatients tend to drop out of therapy unilaterally, and generally after four or fewer sessions (Phillips, 1991). Many clients that we describe as clinically improved in actuality have changed little behaviorally, and many experience only a sense of emotional relief. Change rates of these magnitudes are credible to me. Third, further investigation of the change rates by diagnosis makes clinical sense. For example, 73 percent of clients with major depression were improved, as were 71 percent of those receiving a diagnosis of adjustment disorder; no client in either group deteriorated. However, only 53 percent of clients with dysthymia were improved and 9 percent were worse (Speer, 1994). This example suggests the potential communication value of change-rate information.

Another aspect of change is consumer movement, or lack thereof, from dysfunctionality to functionality (or abnormality to normality). Jacobson and Truax (1991), among others, suggested that for instruments with norms, a point two standard deviations away from the normative mean be used as the cutoff point defining dysfunctionality. This has been a consensually accepted statistical definition of abnormality in clinical psychology for some time. For example, it was recommended by the original authors of the Minnesota Multiphasic Personality Inventory (MMPI) as an aid in interpretation of test results using the original form of the test. Jacobson and Truax suggest that stringent criteria for mental health service effectiveness are statistically significant change *and* movement from the abnormal to the normal range after treatment. They reported exemplifying data from 30 couples who received marital therapy and who scored in the dysfunctional range on the Dyadic Adjustment Scale prior to treatment. After treatment, 37 percent neither improved significantly nor moved into the normal range; 30 percent had improved significantly, but their final score was still in the abnormal range; 33 percent improved reliably and moved into the normal range (Jacobson & Truax, 1991). Parenthetically, these results also demonstrate the fairly common finding that requiring positive change *and* "normality" can give service programs the appearance of quite modest effectiveness.

Measurement Issues

Although one would think that selecting outcome measures would be a fairly straightforward task, having mainly to do with why clients are seeking services in the first place, this is not the case. Admittedly, psychology has produced vast numbers of respectable and validated tests and measures of various constructs. However, the vast majority were created for reasons other than program outcome evaluation. For example, many instruments were developed primarily for research purposes with strong emphasis given to reliability. This emphasis can lead to lengthy instruments that are simply not feasible in the hurry and scurry of field-based service delivery (e.g., the 500-plus items of the MMPI).

A word about consumer satisfaction: In spite of the popularity of the concept among managers, the research evidence bearing on the relationship between client satisfaction and client outcomes suggests that the two constructs are unrelated (Lambert, Salzer, & Bickman, 1998). That is, many studies report non-significant, zero-order correlations. Significant positive relationships are occasionally reported. Seventy-five to eighty percent of mental health clients report satisfaction with services, how they are treated, promptness of services, courtesy, and so forth. I believe, however, that consumer satisfaction should *not* be considered an outcome measure at this time. Future research may suggest differently, but for the time being, consumer satisfaction is best considered a quality-of-care or marketing variable.

Quality of life has also received a lot of recent attention in the evaluation literature, particularly in investigations of services for persistently and severely mentally ill persons and of services for older people. The most popular quality-of-life measures, e.g., the Quality of Life Index for Mental Health (Becker, Diamond, & Sainfort, 1993), and the Lehman Quality of Life Interview (Lehman, Kernan, & Postrado, no date), are multidimensional instruments that assess consumers in a variety of domains. For example, it is common to ask consumers about their satisfaction with their housing, their health, the adequacy of their income, their mood, social network, and so forth. Collectively, clients' characteristics and reports over these domains are considered an assessment of their quality of life. Thus, although a popular concept, quality of life ordinarily does not have a single referent, and is not a unidimensional construct. Although quality of life has summary interpretive value, more information is produced by focusing on the multiple dimensions that constitute the particular instrument.

A recent review of published mental health outcome evaluation studies by Speer and Newman (1996) revealed that when multiple measures are used consumers may improve in some domains (such as distress), and not change or get worse in other areas (such as functioning or role performance). The moral here is, whenever time and resources permit, multiple measures assessing different aspects of consumers, emotions, conditions, adjustment, and/or behavior should be used. Single measures do not adequately sample the complexity of the human condition. An example is the Clarke et al. (1992) study of intensive family and school "wrap-around" treatment services for severely maladjusted children and youth. The results were that the youth improved significantly at home but not at school. Failure to assess adjustment in either setting would have led to highly misleading conclusions.

A theoretical matter with potentially important practical implications is the distinction between "states" and "traits." This distinction should be attended to in the selection of outcome measures. Many of the variables assessed in outcome studies are "state" variables which can be expected to change over time, such as distress, stress, and some kinds of anxiety and depression. *Traits*, on the other hand, are more stable. Thus, one should be cautious in use of "personality" tests as outcome measures because of their frequent focus on assessment of traits. For example, the Hypochondriasis, Hysteria, Psychopathic Deviant, and Hypomanic scales of the MMPI seem to measure trait or characterological features upon which change may take a long time to occur in treatment. Injudicious choice of outcome measures may have dire consequences for the appearance of a treatment program's effectiveness. A useful strategy is to begin the planning of an outcome evaluation by examining the mission and goals of the service organization.

An important, complex, and somewhat fuzzy issue involves the *who* that is the source of the data. In a classic paper, Strupp and Hadley (1977; also see Strupp, 1996) proposed that different stakeholders will have different perspectives on the effectiveness of mental health services, and that each may be inherently valid. They suggested, for example, that clients are the best judges of their own pain or distress. Significant others, such as family members, neighbors, and coworkers, may be in less-biased positions to assess consumers' daily functioning and role performance than the consumers themselves. This point of view is consistent with the enigmatic finding in measurement validity research that correlations with different criteria are often of modest magnitude, in the .30–.60 range, indicating only a modest amount of common variance. Such low-to-modest validity coefficients undoubtedly also reflect the fact that different people will be seeing clients in situations which may elicit different behaviors (e.g., home versus work). Outpatient therapists typically see consumers in very limited and atypical settings, and for small amounts of time.

Given this state of affairs, how do we proceed? First, it is important to acknowledge that some people will have views that are inherently more valid than other people's, e.g., the consumer versus his neighbor regarding the consumer's distress. An expanded Struppian matrix representing different observer perspectives and different domains of consumer conditions and behavior is presented in Table 13.2. I believe that these different perspectives also vary in

TABLE 13.2 A Measurement Variable by Date Source Framework

Source	Distress	Symptoms, Disorders, Diagnosis	Functioning, Role Performance
Client	A	B	c
Significant Others	d	e	F
Public Gatekeepers	g	h	I
Independent Observers	j	K	l
Therapists/Providers	m	N	o

their inherent validity depending on the domain under consideration. In Table 13.2, the relatively more-valid perspectives for the different domains are represented by capital letters in bold print. Clients will be intrinsically better judges of their own distress and those symptoms reflecting pain such as depression or anxiety. Family members, neighbors, and employers will probably be good judges of consumers' hygiene, social skills, conformity, reliability, role performances, and so forth. Public gatekeepers such as law enforcement or public records workers can also be good reporters of behaviors such as drunken driving arrests or disorderly conduct; bank employees will know about checks written on insufficient funds. Independent observers are people employed to observe and record behavior for research purposes. They are usually used to administer standardized procedures such as structured clinical interviews for research diagnostic purposes. Therapists or clinicians may also be knowledgeable about consumers' symptoms and psychiatric conditions. Some caution must be exercised in using clinicians as sources of data, however; we will return to this matter below.

Measures

A comprehensive survey of all measures potentially relevant to the outcome evaluation of psychological practice is obviously beyond the scope of this chapter. Most readers will be familiar with the Mental Measurement Yearbook series (e.g., Conoley & Impara, 1995). Other sources of possible outcome instruments are *The 1996 Behavioral Outcomes & Guidelines Sourcebook* (1995), *2000 Behavioral Outcomes & Guidelines Sourcebook* (Coughlin, 1999), and *Outcomes Assessment in Clinical Practice* (Sederer & Dickey, 1996). The Veteran Affairs has put out publications which survey and review measures. Two that are worth considering are *Outcomes Assessment Tools* (Jacobs, Nelson, & Berrio, 1997) and *Toward Enhanced Outcomes Measurement: An Outcomes Measurement Reference Book* (Buffum & Dean, 1996). For those working in healthcare or primary care settings, *Understanding Health Care Outcomes Research* (Kane, 1997) is worth perusing.

Some instruments worth considering are as follows: An excellent but little-used broad spectrum measure of clients' distress is Dupuy's General Well-Being (GWB) scale (1977). This is an 18-item, self-administered questionnaire that takes less than five minutes to complete. It has the further advantage of having normative data available from a randomly selected national sample of nearly 7,000 adults. It has demonstrated reliability and validity. In spite of being a composite of depressive affect, anxiety, stress, physical well-being, and sense of emotional control, it has excellent internal reliability (suggesting again that different aspects of maladjustment tend to co-vary). Because of its excellent range, 0–110, there is plenty of room for clients to demonstrate improvement as well as deterioration. The GWB can be thought of as a broad index of satisfaction with self or quality of life. This was the instrument used in Speer's evaluation of outpatient mental health services for older adults reported earlier (1994).

Another broad-spectrum measure of distress that is rising in popularity in mental health services research is the heterogeneous five-item Mental Health Scale of the SF-36 instrument (Ware et al., 1993; Ware & Sherbourne, 1992). The scale is a self-administered report measure for which age- and gender-stratified norms are available.

Another excellent nonsymptom measure of malaise is Cohen and Williamson's Perceived Stress Scale (PSS; 1988). An important feature of this instrument is that it is available in four-, ten-, and fourteen-item forms, all of which have norms from a randomly selected national sample of over 2,000 adults. The norms are reported by age, gender, income level, education, and ethnic group. Extensive validity data are available. The scales reflect the stress-coping framework of Lazarus and Folkman (1984). An evaluation example of the use of the PSS was a two-year longitudinal study of a supported housing program for older people with severe and persistent mental illness (O'Sullivan & Speer, 1995). One of the significant findings of the study was that in spite of generally successfully avoiding rehospitalization, these older patients experienced significant stress and marked fluctuations in stress over time.

The most widely used self-administered self-reports of psychological symptoms, both in practice and in research, are the Hopkins Symptom Checklist-90–Revised (Smith, 1996) and its companion short-form, the Brief Symptom Inventory (Smith, 1996). Both instruments consist of the same nine-symptom and three global- or summary-score scales. There are 90 items on the former, which take about 30 minutes to complete, and 53 items on the latter, which take about 15 minutes to complete. The scales of both instruments have good internal and test–retest reliability, both have been extensively researched, and there are norms based on over 900 nonpatients available for both instruments. The main drawback is that these measures are copyrighted, manuals and forms must be purchased, and large-scale use can become costly. These instruments have been used in outcome evaluation studies by Henggler, Melton, and Smith (1992) to study the effectiveness of experimental family therapy for juvenile offenders and their families; by Lehman et al. (1994) to evaluate case management for adults with chronic mental illness; and by Speer and Swindle (1982) in a study of community mental health center adult outpatients services.

Two widely used and well researched self-report measures of depression are the 20-item Center for Epidemiologic Studies–Depression Scale (Radloff, 1977) and the 30-item Geriatric Depression Scale (Sheikh & Yesavage, 1986). Neither scale has available norms, although both have recommended cutoff scores suggesting severe clinical depression. Several recent studies have reported that these scales can be administered using an interview format, or over the telephone, with validity and reliability that are equivalent to self-administration (Speer, 1998).

An instrument that was developed specifically for mental health outcome evaluation, and designed to capture the perspective of significant others, is the Personal Adjustment and Role Skill Scales (Coughlin, 1999; Ellsworth, 1975). Why this instrument has received as little attention as it has is not clear. One possible reason is that obtaining information from significant others is complicated, not least because the client's permission is needed. The instrument consists of nine scales, each consisting of three or four items. All of the scales have excellent internal consistency and reliability, and the instrument differentiates clients and nonclients. Although there are scales that seek the significant other's perceptions of the consumer's depression, confusion, substance abuse, and anxiety, the scales particularly pertinent to functioning and role performance are household maintenance activities, employment and income, relationships with children, close interpersonal relationships, and outside social activities. Because the scales are brief, they lend themselves to by-mail administration and inclusion with other brief measures. The issue of norms is complicated. Nonpatient norms are not available. However, the author developed "change norms" that describe the average amount of change demonstrated by adult consumers over a three-month period. These change scores are cumbersome to interpret to policy and funding personnel. The Personal Adjustment and Role Skill Scales do have considerable "face" validity and are useful for assessing pre- and post-treatment change. The close-interpersonal-relationship scale and the relations-with-children scale are among the few outcome-evaluation-friendly measures that attempt to assess relationships with others. These scales were also used in O'Sullivan and Speer's two-year longitudinal evaluation of a supported housing program for older adults with severe and persistent mental illness (1995). Although their average stress levels did not change over time, involvement in social activities outside their homes did increase over the two-year period.

An instrument developed to assist in assessment of older adults, the Instrumental Activities of Daily Living (Lawton & Brody, 1969), may be considered in evaluation studies of consumers with significant impairments. This is an eight-item scale evaluating a person's ability to perform everyday activities such as shopping, using a telephone, handling finances, and taking medications. The instrument was designed to be used by others who know the consumer's functioning on a day-to-day basis, and has good inter-rater agreement and reliability. Although there are no general public norms, the items are face valid and are useful in assessing daily functioning over time. Speer (1993) used this instrument in a study of the functioning and adjustment of Parkinson's disease patients and caregivers over a 12-month period.

Measures in the "Public Gatekeepers" category are usually unstandardized events or behaviors that come to the attention of a variety of people in a community. Some of these people may be public employees such as law enforcement or public records managers, while others may have knowledge because of their place in the community. These might include child protection workers and public health nurses. Types of public or community phenomena that have been used in outcome evaluations include hospitalizations, arrests, incarceration, employment status, income level, type and quality of housing, and quality of self-care and hygiene. Hospitalization has frequently been used as an outcome variable in evaluations of community support services for severely and persistently mentally ill adults (e.g., Bigelow et al., 1991; Brown et al., 1991; Hiday & Scheid-Cook, 1989).

Arrests and incarceration are frequently used as outcome variables in programs serving consumers with severe alcohol or drug problems. Another group of pertinent consumers are those with violence-control difficulties such as spouse and child abusers. These measures were used by Marques et al.'s evaluation (1994) of intensive inpatient cognitive behavioral treatment of adult sex offenders, and in Peters et al.'s evaluation (1993) of an in-jail cognitive-behavioral and relapse-prevention substance abuse treatment program. A problem with these kinds of measures is the relatively low rate of crimes that result in arrest and conviction (perhaps 10–20 percent).

Employment, as an indicator of ability to care for and support oneself, is often used to study the effectiveness of support services for severely and persistently mentally ill persons. Employment was used as an outcome variable in Caton et al.'s study (1990) of on-site mental health day treatment for mentally ill men in a homeless shelter; in Cook, Graham, and Razzano's evaluation (1993) of residential, rehabilitation, and intensive case-management services for deaf and mentally ill adults; and Leda and Rosenheck's study (1992) of intensive medical, psychiatric, rehabilitation, and substance-abuse treatment in a domiciliary program for homeless mentally ill veterans.

Housing and quality of home have been used as dependent variables by themselves or as components of quality of life in outcome evaluation studies. The first question is whether the consumer has a home or is homeless; the next, whether the home is some form of supervised or sheltered residence. Physical quality of housing can be judged by peeling paint, broken windows, adequacy of plumbing and heating, and so forth. Such variables have been used by Morse et al. (1992) to evaluate the effectiveness of assertive outreach and intensive case management relative to a daytime drop-in center and routine outpatient treatment for homeless consumers with mental illness; by Bigelow et al. (1991) to evaluate intensive community services for former state hospital residents; and by Bybee, Mowbray, and Cohen's study (1995) of outreach, linkage, advocacy, and case-management services for homeless adults with mental illness.

A final functioning and role-performance group of measures are those involving self-care or self-maintenance. Dimensions here include personal hygiene, cleanliness, care of clothing, cooking, and nutrition, and occasionally include such capacities as making and keeping medical appointments and being responsible for taking medications. The two ultimate goals here are health maintenance and appearance in the service of social relationships. Gatekeepers who are often aware of and capable of assessing these variables include visiting nurses, anyone making home visits, intensive case managers, and health-care workers. The Bigelow et al. study (1991) and the Hiday and Scheid-Cook study (1989) cited above are examples of evaluations using these kinds of variables as outcome measures.

Although the writer is concerned about the possible biasing effects of vested interests when provider rating scales are used as outcome measures, two widely used instruments need mentioning. (We will return to biases below.) One of the most widely used traditional clinician interview-based symptom measures is the Hamilton Rating Scale for Depression (HRSD; Hamilton, 1960). The scale assesses such symptom components as feelings of guilt, suicidal ideation, insomnia, gastrointestinal symptoms, and weight loss. Part of the popularity of this 24-item scale in treatment and drug studies is that the various rating points for each item are relatively well defined in behavioral terms. Although the HRSD has standing in psychiatric research, it does presuppose some clinical experience and sophistication, and, to my knowledge, does not have nonpatient norms available.

The other widely used provider rating scale instrument is the Brief Psychiatric Rating Scale (BPRS; Overall & Gorham, 1962). The BPRS consists of 18 seven-point rating scales with the rating points ranging from "not present" to "extremely severe." Sample scales are emotional withdrawal, conceptual disorganization, grandiosity, hallucinatory behavior, and blunted affect. Again, public norms do not appear to be available, but the BPRS can be used in pre-treatment–post-treatment assessment situations to examine change in dimensions of psychopathology.

Potential Sources of Confounding of Conclusions

If one exchanges some methodological rigor for feasibility and relevance in outcome evaluation, one's conclusions are more vulnerable to various biases than those drawn in more rigorous scientific studies. One of the potentially most-troublesome sources of bias and distortion is *provider "vested interest" in provider rating measures*. This is a variation of the conflict-of-interest situation in which the sources of the information have a stake or interest in the conclusions drawn from the information (i.e., the results have consequences for the sources of the data). Even the *appearance* (or suspicion) of conflict of interest may be as damaging to the credibility of the conclusions as the potential bias introduced by the sources of the data.

This potentially biased method is particularly problematic at the time of this writing because a number of states are implementing performance or outcome evaluation systems based in large part on provider rating data. The complexity and seductiveness of provider ratings are related to the fact that provider ratings *obviate a different potential source of bias*—that introduced by data loss and consumer attrition from the study cohort. When a sizeable proportion of consumers in the evaluation study refuse to participate or cannot be located, the remaining members of the group tend to be unrepresentative of consumers designated to be in the original cohort and in the program in general. Because providers are theoretically under administrative control, provider ratings should theoretically be obtainable for 100 percent of the cohort members. This approach also simplifies the logistical hassles of administering questionnaires, conducting interviews, and so forth.

The downside of using provider ratings as outcome or response to treatment measures is the possible suspicion among public funding sources, third-party payers, and public decision-makers that providers will be tempted to "gild the lily" when an evaluation of their own service program is involved. One need not assume that providers are dishonest, or will falsify data, for this to be a reasonable concern. Providers are first of all human beings, and most human beings like to think of themselves and be perceived by others as doing a good job. In a real sense, providers are being asked, perhaps unreasonably, to evaluate their own work (although the evaluation effort is usually not described in these terms). It is a natural and normal human tendency, when in doubt or when the consumer's adjustment is unclear, to give the consumer and thereby *the provider* the benefit of the doubt. That is, when a significant period of time has elapsed or when the provider does not have information about a particular aspect of the client's adjustment, the provider may be inclined to rate the consumer as better adjusted than someone else with more direct or more current information might do. It is worth noting that when the stakes or consequences for the provider or his or her employer increase, the implicit and unintentional pressure on providers to "gild the lily" may also increase (e.g., when the agency's level of funding during the following year is determined in part by outcome performance during the previous year). There are other complication as well (Speer, 1998).

Fortunately (or unfortunately, as the case may be), there is some empirical evidence suggesting that there may be substance to the concern about the effects of provider-vested interest on provider ratings. In a review of the sensitivity to change of different kinds of measurement techniques in psychotherapy research, Lambert and Hill (1994) concluded that therapist-based data suggest greater change, or improvement, than do data from consumer self-reports, significant others, and institutional records. Data reported by Nicholson (1989) exemplify the dilemma. In a followup evaluation of the outpatient treatment of 241 adolescents, she compared the ratings provided by parents with those provided by therapists. The parents of 21 percent of the teenage clients indicated that the referral problem was "completely better," whereas the therapists of 42 percent of the young people rated the referral problems as "completely resolved"; the "completely resolved" rate of the therapists was *twice* the "completely better" rate of the parents. One of the earliest studies of this phenomenon was conducted by Lambert et al. (1986) using meta-analytic methods. They found that consumer ratings of their own depression on two self-report scales—the Zung and Beck depression scales—indicated significantly less change than did the ratings by providers using the Hamilton Rating Scale for Depression.

It should be noted that the vested-interest bias concern is most salient in the outpatient treatment domain, where provider contacts with consumers are almost exclusively office-based and occur once a week or less. There is some evidence that this bias may not be as serious an issue in situations where providers have greater contact with consumers in their homes and in the community, such as in intensive case-management programs. In a comparison of the ratings on several dimensions of community functioning, Massey and Wu (1994) found that case managers agreed with family members, and that both rated consumers *less* favorably than did the consumers themselves in several areas.

Another potentially serious source of distortion of findings is *data loss or consumer attrition*. At issue is the representativeness of those clients from whom outcome data are obtained. The intent in doing an outcome evaluation study is obviously to generalize consumers as a whole on the basis of data from a group of consumers; there is a significant and increasing body of evidence, however, that indicates that persons who drop out or refuse to participate in research and evaluation studies tend to have more and more serious problems, greater health problems, and fewer resources of almost all kinds than people who participate completely in such studies (e.g., Epstein et al., 1994; Norton et al., 1994). When dropout or refusal rates exceed 20–25 percent of the intended group, the group from whom data are obtained will tend to have demographic, social, and psychological characteristics which make them better able to use and benefit from counseling and psychotherapy than non-participants. The risk is that the data may provide a misleading picture of greater improvement or impact than would be obtained from a more representative cohort. Representativeness can be estimated by comparing the demographic and admission characteristics of participants and nonparticipants. Consumers tend to be more cooperative in providing outcome data while they are still involved in service programs. As much as possible, it is advantageous to try to obtain a final assessment prior to clients leaving the program. By-mail return rates, in studies which attempt to solicit outcome data from consumers by mail, are notoriously low, often on the order of 40–50 percent. This is another reason for attempting to obtain the assessment data while consumers are still "on the premises."

In the harsh world of service delivery, there are often situations in which time and resources do not permit obtaining outcome data from large numbers of consumers. This is the domain of adequate group sizes and power. With the emphasis that has been placed on power in recent years, the reader is undoubtedly aware of the issues. However, evaluation studies continue to appear in the literature with inadequate sample and cohort sizes (Speer & Newman, 1996). Therefore, the risks of drawing erroneous conclusions will be briefly discussed. If the evaluator is prescient and knows that statistically significant differences will be found, there is no problem.

Problem situations occur when statistical testing indicates "no significant differences," that is, that the Null Hypothesis is tenable. There are two such situations. First, when cohorts are small and the power or sensitivity to differences is low, we risk concluding that "no difference exists" when differences between the service in which we are interested and the comparison group really do exist (Type II Error). Thus, the service of interest may have great potential for significant improvement over existing services but we will not know it because the groups are too small. Rattenbury and Stones (1989) made this mistake in a nursing home study of the effectiveness of Reminiscence Group Therapy because there were only eight participants in each of the three groups they were comparing; they failed to find important differences.

The second (and particularly dangerous) situation, when cohorts that are too small are involved and no differences are found, tempts the evaluator to conclude that the innovative service is "no worse" than the alternative or usual service. Lack of statistical sensitivity cuts both ways. Reality may be that the innovative service is in fact harmful or less effective than the alternative, but because of the small groups we do not detect the difference. Just as some consumers become worse while receiving services, so are some innovative programs less effective than usual services (e.g., the 1992 study by Soloman et al. of a residential alternative to usual military treatment of combat veterans with post-traumatic stress disorder).

Two examples of outcome evaluation studies follow in which the evaluators risked drawing the erroneous conclusion that one service is "as good as" or, conversely, no worse than another. Hoffman, DiRito, and McGill (1993) studied the effectiveness of a psychoeducational track for thought-disordered consumers in a program for comorbid mentally ill and substance-abusing adults. They found no differences on a number of variables and concluded that the cognitively impaired consumers did as well with the psychoeducational program as did the other consumers who received the standard treatment. However, there were only 12 consumers in one group and 18 in the other, too few for a fair test. Hiday and Scheid-Cook (1989) compared three groups of persistently and severely mentally ill adults: those involuntarily committed to outpatient treatment, those committed to a hospital, and those released from commitment. Six months later there were no differences among the groups on the vast majority of outcome measures studied. However, there were only 38, 11, and 50 consumers in the three groups, about half the number needed for a fair test—estimated as follows.

The ideal situation, if time and resources permit, is either to do a formal power analysis of needed group size on the front end, that is, during design of the outcome study, or to seek the guidance of a knowledgeable statistical consultant. If resources do not permit these methods, some rough guidelines are available for judging the number of consumers needed per group for reasonably fair statistical tests. Cohen (1992) suggested that for moderate-sized group differences, to achieve reasonable statistical sensitivity (power = .80 and p = .05 or less), 65 consumers per group are needed for comparing two groups. For comparing three groups, 50 consumers per group will result in an appropriately sensitive and fair test, and so on. If only one group of consumers is being studied over time (i.e., repeatedly assessed on several occasions),

Kraemer and Thiemann's methodology (1987) suggests that a group of 36 will produce adequate test sensitivity for a medium-sized service effect. (Recall the efficiency in number of participants if participants "serve as their own control" in repeated measures analyses.)

Where does this leave the small-scale service program that may be intensively treating only a few consumers over an extended period of time? It is important to remember that statistical tests are only tools to help the evaluator make reasonable judgments and draw justifiable conclusions. With small numbers, statistical tests may be tools inadequate to the task. One approach is to simply compute and report percentages of consumers in various categories of outcomes. For example, Lerner et al., in a study of opioid-dependent adults, 17 in short-term and 17 in long-term psychotherapy (1992), did not statistically test their data. Instead, they simply reported the percentages of each group who were abstinent during treatment, dropped out of therapy, and reentered treatment. Some differences, such as the 63 percent in short-term therapy versus the 22 percent in long-term who reentered therapy, have considerable face validity. Similarly, Asay and Dimperio (1991) simply reported the percentages of parents of former child psychiatry inpatients who described the young person as "much" or "greatly" improved at one year followup (68 percent). Bath, Richey, and Haapala (1992) simply reported the percentage of children at risk for removal from their own homes who were still in their own homes one year after admission to an intensive community family-oriented treatment program (83 percent).

Other alternatives involve simply plotting data means over time on graphs for visual inspection and interpretation (e.g., O'Sullivan & Speer, 1995). If justifiable criteria for "improvement" or significant change can be agreed upon, data can be reported in terms of percentages of improved, unchanged, and deteriorated (see the Reliable Change Index earlier in the chapter, Speer, 1994, and Speer et al., 1996). Without the guidance of statistical tests, however, greater professional judgment and responsibility are required of the evaluator in interpreting the data and drawing conclusions. A moderately conservative, or humble, approach is recommended.

A final issue to keep in mind in selecting outcomes measures for an outcome evaluation study is the apparent phenomenon, particularly in outpatient services, that *emotions change more rapidly than do behaviors* (e.g., Ellsworth, 1975; Howard et al., 1993). That is, the empathy, reassurance, and focused attention of a compassionate clinician appears to have significant ameliorating effects on consumer distress in only a few sessions. Behavioral changes take longer. Thus, it is wise whenever possible to include measures that reflect both emotional relief *and* changes in behavior patterns such as communication, coping responses to stress, conflict resolution, and so forth. If evaluative judgments are based solely on changes in emotions, the program will appear erroneously efficient (i.e., rapid impact); if based solely on behavioral change, the program may appear to have only very slow effects.

Other Issues

There is a serious need in the mental health field for much more longitudinal clinical and treatment followup research. It is well-documented that psychological interventions are efficacious and effective when evaluated at the end of treatment and for short intervals thereafter, e.g., three months. However, we know very little about the longer-term effects or the durability of the effects of our interventions (Speer, 1998). There are practical reasons for this. As indicated above, the longer the interval between termination and the request for evaluation information, the higher the attrition and the higher the risk for a biased followup cohort. This is not an insoluble problem and Ribisl and his colleagues (1996) have offered a number of recommendations for obtaining high completion rates in longitudinal and followup research. The complication is that more cost and effort are involved in obtaining followup data than obtaining data at termination or during treatment. Nonetheless, readers are encouraged to consider and whenever possible pursue longer-term followup data. A strategy to consider is use of brief telephone calls using a standard set of questions and perhaps even brief symptom or stress scales with norms such as from the BSI or the Perceived Stress Scale (mentioned previously). Several studies have found that questionnaires originally designed to be self-administered can be administered by interview and by telephone with no decrement in reliability and validity (Burke et al., 1995; Morishita et al., 1995; Parmelee & Katz, 1990).

If an organization is involved when an outcome evaluation project is being considered, the first issue to be resolved is whether or not the project has strong support and commitment from top management and, perhaps, the governing board. If endorsement of the project receives only lip-service support from executive-level management, all staff will soon realize it. Data collection and aggregation will sink on the priority list of organizational activities. Data loss and attrition will accumulate with the result that interpretation of the results of analysis will be difficult or impossible. With lip-service support comes the likelihood that the report and findings will receive only cursory consideration before being filed; such a study is unlikely to have noticeable effects on services or the organization.

Another issue that must be resolved before implementation of an outcome evaluation project is whether or not the organization—management and provider staff alike—is professionally mature enough to handle, internally and publically, findings indicating that significant proportions of consumers either do not change or in fact become worse while receiving services. As indicated earlier, with projects in which indices of change such as Jacobson's Reliable Change Index are used, it is not unusual to find that 40 percent or more of consumers do not change and that 5–10 percent appear to deteriorate (e.g., Jacobson et al., 1984; Jacobson, Wilson, & Tupper, 1988; Speer & Greenbaum, 1995). Experienced clinical providers know that not all their clients improve substantially and that some do, in fact, become worse while being treated. These experiences have generally not been discussed or considered from a programmatic standpoint. It also appears that the more stringent the criteria for classifying consumers as improved, the lower the proportion found to be improved and the less effective the appearance of the program or service (e.g., Elkin, 1994; O'Sullivan & Speer, 1995; Speer & Newman, 1996). "Sunshine" laws and regulations require that such findings be made available for public inspection in publicly funded service programs. Management personnel had best be prepared to discuss and explain such results. It is helpful, in this respect, to keep in mind that mental health services are, statistically, as effective as, and in some instances more effective than, medical treatments for medical conditions (Lipsey & Wilson, 1993).

Finally, a matter of significance is the ultimate utilization of the outcome evaluation findings. The history of program evaluation is littered with ignored, unread, and "filed" evaluation reports. Recently Sperry et al. (1996) pointed out that there are at least two important uses of outcome findings. The first is the auditing or accounting function of tabulating relative "success and failures" by program for policy makers, funding sources, governing bodies, and upper management. The second, and probably more important, function of outcome data is incorporation of outcome assessment into quality monitoring, assurance, and improvement processes. This might best be accomplished by providing individual providers, team managers, and the quality assurance committee with the outcome-monitoring data by individual consumers. This will provide clinical staff with feedback about their consumers and allow everyone to be aware of consumers who appear not to be progressing or who seem to be getting worse. Discussions of such consumers can lead to decisions to change treatment approaches, different service strategies, and perhaps a change of specific providers. The accumulation of insights gained through such monitoring and clinical management discussions can also potentially lead to programmatic and treatment management changes that enhance the overall quality and effectiveness of services. Such feedback can also make outcome evaluation procedures more real and useful to line staff providers, thus increasing their interest and cooperation.

In conclusion, the field of psychological practice is currently a turbulent mix of cost and utilization reduction pressures, aggressive management, questions about service effectiveness, proprietary and public interests, potential opportunities, and professional and public outcries about the apparent erosion of quality care and seeming lack of concern about the care consumers receive. There is much agitation, distrust, apprehension, and resentment in the various constituent sectors of the industry. Increasingly noisy concerns about the quality, effectiveness, and quantity of services, and potential backlash against the current narrow focus of mental health management and funders on cost containment may well provide opportunities for improved services and care in the future. The vehicles for transforming these concerns and opportunities into improvements will be outcome assessment; identification of groups of consumers who do not respond to current interventions or who have high relapse rates, and seeking answers to why they do not respond; service modification; and increasing use of outcome management and continuous quality improvement mechanisms. When the wave of concern about quality of care and effectiveness peaks, we must be positioned to vigorously address more sophisticated outcome and effectiveness issues. These are tense and stressful but exciting times that provide much opportunity for development of new ways of providing improved care for troubled people.

REFERENCES

Addis, M. E. (1997). Evaluating the treatment manual as a means of disseminating empirically validated psychotherapies. *Clinical Psychology: Science and Practice, 4*, 1–11.

Asay, T. P., & Dimperio, T. L. (1991). Outcome of children treated in psychiatric hospitals. In S. M. Mirin, J. T. Gossett, & M. C. Grob (Eds.), *Psychiatric treatment: Advances in outcome research* (pp. 21–30). Washington, DC: American Psychiatric Press.

Bath, H. I., Richey, C. A., & Haapala, D. A. (1992). Child age and outcome correlates in intensive family preservation services. *Children and Youth Services Review, 14*, 389–406.

Becker, M., Diamond, R, & Sainfort, F. (1993). A new patient focused index for measuring quality of life in persons with severe and persistent mental illness. *Quality of Life Research, 2*, 239–251.

Bigelow, D. A., McFarland, B. H., Gareau, M. J., & Young, D. J. (1991). Implementation and effectiveness of a bed reduction project. *Community Mental Health Journal*, 27, 125–133.

Brown, M. A., Ridgway, P., Anthony, W. A., & Rogers, E. S. (1991). Comparison of outcomes for clients seeking and assigned to supported housing. *Hospital and Community Psychiatry, 42*, 1150–1153.

Buffum, M., & Dean, H. (Eds.). (1996). *Toward enhanced outcome measurement: An outcomes measurement reference book.* Department of Veterans Affairs, Research Constituency Center, Nursing Service.

Burke, W. J., Roccaforte, W. H., Wengel, S. P., Conley, D. M., & Potter, J. F. (1995). The reliability and validity of the Geriatric Depression Rating Scale administered by telephone. *Journal of the American Geriatrics Society, 43*, 674–679.

Bybee, D., Mowbray, C. T., & Cohen, E. H. (1995). Evaluation of a homeless mentally ill outreach program: Differential short-term effects. *Evaluation and Program Planning, 18*,13–24.

Campbell, D. T., & Stanley, J. C. (1963). *Experimental and quasi-experimental designs for research.* Chicago: Rand McNally.

Caton, C. L. M., Wyatt, R. J., Grunberg, J., & Felix, A. (1990). An evaluation of a mental health program for homeless men. *Evaluation and Program Planning, 18*, 13–24.

Clarke, R. T., Schaefer, M., Burchard, J. D., & Welkowitz, J. W. (1992). Wrapping community-based mental health services around children with a severe behavioral disorder: An evaluation of Project Wraparound. *Journal of Child and Family Studies, 1*, 242–261.

Clarkin, J. F., Glick, I. D., Haas, G., & Spencer, J. H. (1991). The effects of inpatient family intervention on treatment outcome. In S. M. Mirin, J. T. Gossett, & M. C. Grob (Eds.), *Psychiatric treatment: Advances in outcome research* (pp. 47–58). Washington, DC: American Psychiatric Press.

Cohen, J. (1992). A power primer. *Psychological Bulletin, 112*, 155–159.

Cohen, S., & Williamson, G. (1988). Perceived stress in a probability sample of the United States. In S. Spacapan & S. Oskamp (Eds.), *The social psychology of health: Claremont Symposium on Applied Psychology* (pp. 31–68). Newbury Park, CA: Sage.

Conoley, J. C., & Impara, J. C. (1995). *The twelfth mental measurement yearbook.* Lincoln, NE: The University of Nebraska–Lincoln.

Cook, J. A., Graham, K. K., & Razzano, L. (1993). Psychosocial rehabilitation of deaf persons with severe mental illness: A multivariate model of residential outcomes. *Rehabilitation Psychology, 38*, 261–274.

Coughlin, K. M. (1999). *2000 behavioral outcomes & guidelines sourcebook.* New York: Faulkner & Gray.

Cronbach, L. J., Ambron, S. R., Dornbush, S. M., Hess, R. D., Hornik, R. C., Phillips, D. C., Walker, D. E., & Weiner, S. S. (1980). *Toward reform of program evaluation.* San Francisco: Jossey-Bass.

Cummings, N. A. (1997a). Pioneering integrated systems: Lessons learned, forgotten, and relearned. In N. A. Cummings, J. L. Cummings, & J. N. Johnson (Eds.), *Behavioral health in primary care: A guide for clinical integration* (pp. 23–36). Madison, CT: Psychosocial Press.

Cummings, N. A. (1997b). Behavioral health in primary care: dollars and sense. In N. A. Cummings, J. L. Cummings, & J. N. Johnson (Eds.), *Behavioral health in primary care: A guide for clinical integration* (pp. 3–22). Madison, CT: Psychosocial Press.

Dupuy, H. J. (1977). *A concurrent validational study of the NCHS General Well-Being Schedule* (DHEW Publication No. HRA 78-1347). Hyattsville, MD: National Center for Health Statistics, U.S. Department of Health, Education, and Welfare.

Elkin, I. (1994). The NIMH treatment of depression collaborative research program: Where we began and where we are. In A. E. Bergin & S. L. Garfield (Eds.), *Handbook of psychotherapy and behavior change* (pp. 114–139). New York: John Wiley & Sons.

Ellsworth, R. B. (1975). Consumer feedback in measuring the effectiveness of mental health programs. In M. Guttentag & E. L. Struennig (Eds.), *Handbook of evaluation research* (Vol. 2, pp. 239–274). Beverly Hills: Sage.

Epstein, E. E., McCrady, B. S., Miller, K. J., & Steinberg, M. (1994). Attrition from conjoint alcoholism treatment: Do dropouts differ from completers? *Journal of Substance Abuse, 6*, 249–265.

Eysenck, H. J. (1952). The effects of psychotherapy: An evaluation. *Journal of Consulting and Clinical Psychology, 16*, 319–324.

Faulkner & Gray's Healthcare Information Center. (1995). *The 1996 behavioral outcomes & guidelines sourcebook.* New York: Faulkner & Gray, Inc.

Galligan, B. (1990). Serving people who are dually diagnosed: A program evaluation. *Mental Retardation, 28*, 353–358.

Goldfried, M. R., & Wolfe, B. E. (1996). Psychotherapy practice and research: Repairing a strained alliance. *American Psychologist, 51*, 1007–1016.

Goleman, D., & Gurin, J. (1993). *Mind-body medicine.* New York: Consumer Reports Books.

Hamilton, M. A. (1960). A rating scale for depression. *Journal of Neurological and Neurosurgical Psychiatry, 25*, 56–62.

Henggeler, S. W., Melton, G. B., & Smith, L. A. (1992). Family preservation using multisystemic therapy: An effective alternative to incarcerating serious juvenile offenders. *Journal of Consulting and Clinical Psychology, 60,* 953–961.

Hiday, V. A., & Scheid-Cook, T. L. (1989). A follow-up of chronic patients committed to outpatient treatment. *Hospital and Community Psychiatry, 40,* 52–59.

Hoffman, G. W., DiRito, D. C., & McGill, E. C. (1993). Three-month follow-up of 28 dual diagnosis inpatients. *American Journal of Drug and Alcohol Abuse, 19,* 79–88.

Howard, K. I., Lueger, R. J., Maling, M. S., & Martinovich, Z. (1993). A phase model of psychotherapy outcome: Causal mediation of change. *Journal of Consulting and Clinical Psychology, 61,* 678–685.

Hsu, L. M. (1995). Regression toward the mean associated with measurement error and the identification of improvement and deterioration in psychotherapy. *Journal of Consulting and Clinical Psychology, 63,* 141–144.

Jacobs, M. D., Nelson, A., & Berrio, M. W. (Eds.). (1997). *Outcome assessment tools.* Veterans Health Administration, Nursing Research Constituency Center.

Jacobson, N. S., Follette, W. C., Revenstorf, D., Baucom, D. H., Hohlweg, K., & Margolin, D. (1984). Variability in outcome and clinical significance of behavioral marital therapy: A reanalysis of outcome data. *Journal of Consulting and Clinical Psychology, 53,* 497–504.

Jacobson, N. S., & Truax, P. (1991). Clinical significance: A statistical approach to defining meaningful change in psychotherapy research. *Journal of Consulting and Clinical Psychology, 59,* 12–19.

Jacobson, N. S., Wilson, L., & Tupper, C. (1988). The clinical significance of treatment gains resulting from exposure-based interventions for agoraphobia: A reanalysis of outcome data. *Behavior Therapy, 19,* 539–552.

Johnson, L. B., Cline, D. W., Marcum, J. M., & Intress, J. L. (1992). Effectiveness of a stress recovery unit during the Persian Gulf war. *Hospital and Community Psychiatry, 43,* 829–831.

Kane, R. L. (Ed.). (1997). *Understanding health care outcomes research.* Gaithersburg, MD: Aspen.

Kazdin, A. E. (1994). Methodology, design, and evaluation in psychotherapy research. In A. E. Bergin & S. L. Garfield (Eds.), *Handbook of psychotherapy and behavior change* (4th ed., pp. 19–71). New York: Wiley.

Kendall, P. C., & Grove, W. M. (1988). Normative comparisons in therapy outcome. *Behavioral Assessment, 10,* 147–158.

Kraemer, H. C., & Thiemann, S. (1987). *How many subjects?* Newbury Park, CA: Sage.

Lambert, M. J. (1991). Introduction to psychotherapy research. In L. E. Beutler & M. Crago (Eds.), *Psychotherapy research: An international review of programmatic studies* (pp. 1–12). Washington, DC: American Psychological Association.

Lambert, M. J., & Bergin, A. E. (1994). The effectiveness of psychotherapy. In A. E. Bergon & S. L. Garfield (Eds.), *Handbook of psychotherapy and behavior change* (4th ed., pp. 143–189). New York: Wiley.

Lambert, M. J., Hatch, D. R., Kingston, M. D., & Edwards, B. C. (1986). Zung, Beck, and Hamilton rating scales as measures of treatment outcome: A meta-analytic comparison. *Journal of Consulting and Clinical Psychology, 54,* 54–59.

Lambert, M. J., & Hill, C. E. (1994). Assessing psychotherapy outcomes and process. In A. E. Bergin & S. L. Garfield (Eds.), *Handbook of psychotherapy and behavior change* (pp. 72–113). New York: John Wiley.

Lambert, W., Salzer, M. S., & Bickman, L. (1998). Clinical outcome, consumer satisfaction, and ad hoc ratings of improvement in children's mental health. *Journal of Consulting and Clinical Psychology, 66,* 270–279.

Lawton, M. P., & Brody, E. M. (1969). Assessment of older people: Self-maintaining and instrumental activities of daily living. *Gerontologist, 9,* 179–186.

Lazarus, R. S., & Folkman, S. (1984). *Stress, appraisal, and coping.* New York: Sage.

Leda, C., & Rosenheck, R. (1992). Mental health status and community adjustment after treatment in a residential treatment program for homeless veterans. *American Journal of Psychiatry, 149,* 1219–1224.

Lehman, A., Kernan, E., & Postrado, L. (no date). *Toolkit for evaluating quality of life for persons with severe mental illness.* Baltimore: Center for Mental Health Services Research, University of Maryland School of Medicine.

Lehman, A. E., Postrado, L. T., Roth, D., McNary, S. W., & Goldman, H. H. (1994). Continuity of care and client outcomes in the Robert Wood Johnson Foundation program on chronic mental illness. *Milbank Quarterly, 72,* 105–122.

Lerner, A., Sigal, M., Bacalu, A., & Gelkopf, M. (1992). Short term versus long term psychotherapy in opioid dependence: A pilot study. *International Journal of Psychiatry and Related Sciences, 29,* 114–119.

Lipsey, M. W., & Wilson, D. B. (1993). The efficacy of psychological, educational, and behavioral treatment: Confirmation from meta-analysis. *American Psychologist, 48,* 1181–1209.

Marques, J. K., Day, D. M., Nelson, C., & West, M. A. (1994). Effects of cognitive-behavioral treatment on sex offender recidivism: Preliminary results of a longitudinal study. *Criminal Justice and Behavior, 21,* 28–54.

Massey, O. T., & Wu, L. (1994). Three critical views of functioning: Comparisons of assessments made by individuals with mental illness, their case managers, and family members. *Evaluation and Program Planning, 17*, 1–7.

Mental health: Does therapy help? (1995). *Consumer Reports, 60*, (11), 734–739.

Morishita, L., Boult, C., Ebbitt, B., Rambel, M., Fallstrom, K., & Gooden, T. (1995). Concurrent validity of administering the Geriatric Depression Scale and the Physical Functioning dimension of the SIP by telephone. *Journal of the American Geriatrics Society, 43*, 680–683.

Morse, G. A., Calsyn, R. J., Allen, G., Tempelhoff, B., & Smith, R. (1992). Experimental comparison of the effects of three treatment programs for homeless mentally ill people. *Hospital and Community Psychiatry, 43*, 1005–1010.

Nathan, P. E., & Gorman, J. M. (Eds.). (1998). *A guide to treatments that work.* New York: Oxford University Press.

Nicholson, S. (1989). Outcome evaluation of therapeutic effectiveness. *The Australian and New Zealand Journal of Family Therapy, 10*, 77–83.

Norton, M. C., Breitner, J. C. S., Welsh, K. A., & Wyse, B. W. (1994). Characteristics of nonresponders in a community survey of the elderly. *Journal of the American Geriatrics Society, 42*, 1252–1256.

O'Sullivan, M., & Speer, D. (1995). *The supported housing program, Broward County elderly services, Ft. Lauderdale, FL: Evaluation final report.* Tampa, FL: de la Parte Florida Mental Health Institute.

Overall, J. E., & Gorham, D. R. (1962). The Brief Psychiatric Rating Scale. *Psychological Reports, 10*, 799–812.

Parmelee, P. A., & Katz, I. R. (1990). Geriatric Depression Scale. *Journal of the American Geriatrics Society, 38*, 1379.

Peters, R. A., Kearns, W. D., Murrin, M. R., Dolent, A. S., & May, R. L. (1993). Examining the effectiveness of in-jail substance abuse treatment. *Journal of Offender Rehabilitation, 19*, 1–39.

Phillips, E. L. (1991). George Washington University's international data on psychotherapy delivery systems: Modeling new approaches to the study of therapy. In L. E. Beutler & M. Crago (Eds.), *Psychotherapy research: An international review of programmatic studies* (pp. 263–273). Washington, DC: American Psychological Association.

Radloff, L. S. (1977). The CES-D Scale: A self-report depression scale for research in the general population. *Applied Psychological Measurement, 1*, 385–401.

Rattenbury, C., & Stones, M. J. (1989). A controlled evaluation of reminiscence and current topics discussion groups in nursing homes. *The Gerontologist, 29*, 768–771.

Ribisl, K. M., Walton, M. A., Mowbray, C. T., Luke, D. A., Davidson, W. S., & Bootsmiller, B. J. (1996). Minimizing participant attrition in panel studies through the use of effective retention and tracking strategies: Review and recommendations. *Evaluation and Program Planning, 19*, 1–25.

Rogosa, D. (1988). Myths about longitudinal research. In K. W. Schaie & S. C. Rawlings (Eds.), *Methodological issues in aging research* (pp. 171–209). New York: Springer.

Rogosa, D., Brandt, D., & Zimowski, M. (1982). A growth curve approach to the measurement of change. *Psychological Bulletin, 92*, 726–748.

Rogosa, D. R., & Willett, J. B. (1985). Understanding correlates of change by modeling individual differences in growth. *Psychometrika, 50*, 203–228.

Sederer, L. I., & Dickey, B. (1996). *Outcomes assessment in clinical practice.* Baltimore: Williams & Wilkins.

Seligman, M. F. (1995). The effectiveness of psychotherapy: The *Consumers Report* study. *American Psychologist, 50*, 965–974.

Sheikh, J. I., & Yesavage, J. A. (1986). Geriatric Depression Scale (GDS): Recent evidence and development of a shorter form. In T. L. Brink (Ed.), *Clinical gerontology: A guide to assessment and intervention* (pp. 165–174). New York: Haworth.

Shern, D. L., Wilson, N. Z., Coen, A. S., Patrick, D. C., Foster, M., Bartsch, D. A., & Demmler, J. (1994). Client outcomes II. Longitudinal client outcome data from the Colorado treatment outcome study. *Milbank Quarterly, 72*, 123–148.

Smith, M. L., Glass, G. V., & Miller, T. I. (1980). *The benefits of psychotherapy.* Baltimore: Johns Hopkins University Press.

Smith, V. L. (1996). Symptom Checklist–90—Revisited (SCL-90-R) and the Brief Symptom Inventory (BSI). In L. I. Sederer & B. Dickey (Eds.), *Outcomes assessment in clinical practice* (pp. 89–91). Baltimore: Williams & Wilkins.

Solomon, Z., Shalev, A., Spiro, S. E., Dolev, A., Bleich, A., Waysman, M., & Cooper, S. (1992). Negative psychometric outcomes: Self-report measures and a follow-up telephone survey. *Journal of Traumatic Stress, 5*, 225–246.

Speer, D.C. (In press). What is the role of two-wave designs in clinical research? Comment on Hageman and Arrindell. *Behaviour Research and Therapy.*

Speer, D. C. (1992). Clinically significant change: Jacobson and Traux (1991) revisited. *Journal of Consulting and Clinical Psychology, 60*, 402–408.

Speer, D. C. (1993). Predicting Parkinson's Disease patient and caregiver adjustment: Preliminary findings. *Behavior, Health and Aging, 3*, 139–146.

Speer, D. C. (1994). Can treatment research inform decision makers? Nonexperimental methods issues and examples among older outpatients. *Journal of Consulting and Clinical Psychology, 62,* 560–568.

Speer, D. C. (1998). *Mental health outcome evaluation.* San Diego: Academic Press.

Speer, D. C., & Greenbaum, P. E. (1995). Five methods for computing significant individual client change and improvement rates: Support for an individual growth curve approach. *Journal of Consulting and Clinical Psychology, 63,* 1044–1048.

Speer, D. C., & Newman, F. L. (1996). Mental health services outcome evaluation. *Clinical Psychology: Science and Practice, 3,* 105–129.

Speer, D. C., O'Sullivan, M. J., & Lester, W. A. (1996). Impact of mental health services in nursing homes: The clinicians' perspective. *Journal of Clinical Geropsychology, 2,* 83–92.

Speer, D. C., & Stiles, P. G. (1997). Severely and persistently mentally ill older adults and case management. *Continuum, 4,* 13–25.

Speer, D. C., & Swindle, R. (1982). The "monitoring model" and the mortality X treatment interaction threat to validity in mental health outcome evaluation. *American Journal of Community Psychology, 10,* 541–552.

Sperry, L., Brill, P. L., Howard, K. I., & Grissom, G. R. (1966). *Treatment outcomes in psychotherapy and psychiatric interventions.* New York: Brunner/Mazel.

Strupp, H. H. (1996). The tripartite model and the *Consumer Reports* study. *American Psychologist, 51,* 1017–1024.

Strupp, H. H., & Hadley, S. M. (1977). A tripartite model of mental health and therapeutic outcomes. *American Psychologist, 32,* 187–196.

Ware, J. E., & Sherbourne, C. D. (1992). The MOS 36-item short-form health survey (SF-36). *Medical Care, 30,* 473–481.

Ware, J. E., Snow, K. K., Kosinski, M., & Gandek, B. (1993). *SF-36 health survey manual and interpretation guide.* Boston: New England Medical Center, the Health Institute.

Weisz, J. R., Weiss, B., & Donenberg, G. R. (1992). The lab versus the clinic: Effects of child and adolescent psychotherapy. *American Psychologist, 47,* 1578–1585.

Willett, J. B. (1994). Measuring change more effectively by modeling individual growth over time. In T. Husen & T. N. Postlewaite (Eds.), *The international encyclopedia of education* (2nd ed., pp. 1–9). Oxford, UK: Pergamon Press.

FOR FURTHER READING

Cronbach, L. J., Ambron, S. R., Dornbusch, S. M., Hess, R. D., Hornik, R. C., Phillips, D. C., Walker, D. F., & Weiner, S. S. (1980). *Toward reform of program evaluation.* San Francisco: Jossey-Bass.

This is the classic first treatise in which a nationally renowned psychological methodologist called into question the universal applicability of the scientific model and experimental design. Cronbach et al. argue that the classical approach in applied service delivery community settings is usually inappropriate and often counterproductive. The pros, cons, and mystique of the scientific model are thoroughly discussed.

Campbell, D. T., & Stanley, J. C. (1963). *Experimental and quasi-experimental designs for research.* Chicago: Rand McNally.

Although there are many other excellent (and more recent) texts on social science research design, this classic contains some extremely creative quasi-experimental designs that are not discussed in academic texts on methods and designs. Although Campbell publicly defended the experimental approach in the Campbell-Cronbach debates, some of these quasi-experimental designs show that he was very knowledgeable about the pragmatic issues of research and evaluation in the "real world."

Strupp, H. H., & Hadley, S. M. (1977). A tripartite model of mental health and therapeutic outcomes. *American Psychologist, 32,* 187–196. Also: Strupp, H. H. (1996). The tripartite model and the *Consumer Reports* study. *American Psychologist, 51,* 1017–1024.

Strupp's 1977 paper introduced the concept that different perspectives on behavior change may be equally valid. Provided a social psychological framework and explanation for some of the .30–.60 range validity correlation coefficients between certain clinical validity criteria.

Ribisl, K. M., Walton, M. A., Mowbray, C. T., Luke, D. A., Davidson, W. S., & Bootsmiller, B. J. (1996). Minimizing participant attrition in panel studies through the use of effective retention and tracking strategies: Review and recommendations. *Evaluation and Program Planning, 19,* 1–25.

Excellent practical discussion of issues and solutions to problems of losing contact with longer-term follow-up evaluation participants.

CHAPTER

14 How to Open and Operate an Office in an Era of Managed Care

ALAN R. GRAHAM

In the current era of managed care, traditional models of practice may not be as viable as they may have been in the past. Much has been written about emerging patterns of practice. Division 42 (Independent Practice) of the American Psychological Association (APA) has recently established an Emerging Patterns of Practice Committee in order to help currently practicing psychologists explore new ways to provide psychological services in the market. This chapter describes some of these options.

Therapists interested in establishing an office must be aware that they are going into business. Therapists typically get no training in business and have little knowledge and understanding of what it takes to run a successful business. To this end, the Practice Directorate of the APA has published a series of books on practice entitled the *APA Practitioner's Toolbox Series*. This chapter aims to further fill this gap by highlighting those issues that must be considered when opening an office. Office systems and clinical systems will be described and references given for more detailed information.

With managed care largely controlling the stream of patients into therapists' practices, there is a growing awareness among therapists that they need to learn more about the marketplace in order to tailor their skills to what people want. Therapists often have negative feelings about marketing, yet marketing is simply the communication of information about one's skills to potential clients or patients. A marketing plan is a systematic process by which a therapist determines the specific behavioral health needs of a population and develops a plan to meet those needs. After reading this chapter, it is hoped that you will feel more comfortable with marketing principles and be able to implement, even enjoy, the process.

Two Remarks. First: The terms *patients* and *clients* will be used interchangeably. Second: this chapter is by no means a complete guide. The bibliography provides more specific information and sample practice forms.

Personal Assessment

Professional Goals

Where do you see yourself in your career? Do you see yourself in a small office like Judd Hirsch in *Ordinary People*? Do you want to work in hospital or organizational settings? Are you entrepreneurial and interested in building a business? Do you want flexible time to pursue writing, public speaking, or research? Do you want to work full-time or part-time in your practice? Do you want to work alone or with others? What kinds of populations do you want to serve? These are some of the questions you must ask yourself before opening a practice. Below are some strategies for developing your vision and the differing practice models that are available.

Edward Lundeen and Laura Geiger (1999) suggested strategies for developing a vision and attitude for succeeding in a private practice. The first is to stay focused on what you want—and on what people want. There is always a market for good therapists. Second, Lundeen and Geiger advised patience. Do not panic. Stay the course. Third, always focus on giving excellent service in your work and everything you offer. Always give your best effort. Customer service is highly prized in the market, and those who provide it will be successful. Lastly, Lundeen and Geiger implore you to fight against managed care whenever you can. They believe that managed care has harmed our profession and our patients. They recommend that you keep informed about health care alternatives and "keep ahead of the curve" in providing services that people want.

While Lundeen and Geiger see managed care as something to fight, some therapists have been successful in developing a managed care practice. Managed care covers a significant portion of the U.S. populace, and there are opportunities in this market. Just be aware of what you are getting when you sign managed care contracts. Ask an attorney to review the contract so you understand all its provisions. Managed care contract provisions often cover credentialing requirements, billing procedures and policies, hold-harmless clauses, contract termination clauses, and the like.

I have built a successful practice by courting managed care and becoming one of its premier providers. ACP Consultants has three offices about 25 miles away from each other. ACP stands for Associated Clinical Psychologists, the original name of the business. Two years ago, when I decided to branch out into personal, professional, and executive coaching, and consulting, I changed the name of the practice to ACP *Consultants*. People in business often feel more comfortable working with a coach or a consultant than a psychologist. Additionally, I employ social workers and licensed professional counselors in the practice, so the old name could be considered misleading. Two of ACP's three offices are full-service offices with office support staff and multiple therapy rooms. The third office is a satellite office where a room is sublet from another provider. My group practice currently gets about 60 new patients per month for the eight full-time-equivalent (FTE) therapists in my group. This keeps everybody quite busy.

Under managed care, we have had to take up to 50 percent discounts from our regular fee and wait for payment, often for periods of up to six months or longer. These slow payments have caused frequent cash flow problems—bills to be paid and no money in the bank to pay them. As a result, I decided to change our focus to more fee-for-service business. This decision was based on an external assessment of the current marketplace. A more thorough review of marketplace strategies will be presented later in this chapter.

Models of Practice

Therapists can participate in a number of different practice organizations from the relatively simple solo practice to a highly complex group practice. The solo practice is by far the simplest practice model. Expenses are low, with overhead requirements of only one office and simple business systems. The solo practitioner need only hire administrative staff as needed to manage the business end of the practice. Advantages include greater autonomy than in other models and fewer administrative burdens. Disadvantages include being limited as to the managed care organizations that will do business with a solo practitioner (not *necessarily* a disadvantage!), having to develop complex systems to handle any managed care business in the practice, and the loneliness and isolation that can accompany solo practice. Many therapists only work at their practice on a part-time basis to augment their full-time incomes. They may work only a couple of evenings a week, seeing eight to ten clients or fewer a week. These therapists can often find office space by renting on an hourly or daily basis from other therapists.

One way to combat the isolation of a solo practice is to join peer supervision or consultation groups. This provides an opportunity to talk about cases and grow professionally. (If the therapist chooses to join a group like this, she or he must be sure to inform clients that their cases may be reviewed with other clinicians.) These informal alliances are often expanded to provide additional benefits to their members. The group may choose to pool its resources into a purchasing co-op and buy office supplies at a discount. They may share office space, support staff, and referrals, thereby increasing each other's practices. There are disadvantages as well. The therapists have no formal business relationship and so cannot benefit from shared contracting. Most managed care organizations want to bill services to a single tax identification number, and so will not recognize these informal alliances. There may also be a liability risk. Since the members of the group may share office space and support staff, they may appear to be the same company to the client. If a legal action is taken against one of the members of the informal alliance, all other members could be sued as well. To deal with this issue, it is strongly recommended that you include a clear statement in your intake materials, and post it prominently in your office, to the effect that you are not affiliated with any other therapist or organizations within your office suite.

It may be most beneficial for you either to join an already existing group practice—developing a formal alliance with one—or to start your own group practice. A group practice is a legally formal organization in which practitioners agree to share offices, records, and administrative staff and to share financial risk. In such an arrangement, you invest time and money (if you are an owner or have shares of the group practice) and are part of the group; the world views your practice as a single legal entity. Mental health delivery systems are moving toward contracting with larger and larger entities, so a group practice that can provide "one-stop shopping" under one tax identification number is going to be looked on favorably. A group practice can also provide economies of scale, as only one administrative system needs to be in place for many clinicians. Referrals can be shared among group members, and if the group is multidisciplinary, the referred patient can be treated within the practice.

There are many different types of group practice arrangements: groups without walls, single-specialty groups, multi-specialty groups, multidisciplinary groups, independent practice associations, health maintenance organizations (HMOs), preferred provider organizations (PPOs), provider–hospital organizations (PHOs), management services organizations (MSOs), behavioral health organizations, and numerous other combinations. A more detailed description of these types of groups can be found in Yenney (1994). Appendix 14.B offers a glossary of common managed care terms.

Group without Walls. In a group without walls, therapists remain in their own offices but create a legal entity that oversees the group. The group members (or representatives of the group members) make all management decisions that are necessary to maintain the functioning of the group. Decisions are made regarding purchasing, contracting, personnel, clinical management, and so forth. The major drawback of a group without walls is that the practitioner gives up some level of autonomy, as many of the decisions that would be made by the solo practitioner now are made by the group. Therapists need to merge their goals with that of the group, which may be difficult for some clinicians.

Single-Speciality Group. A single-specialty group is one where practitioners of the same specialty come together to form a group. For example, the group may consist of only neuropsychologists. Developing common goals may be easier for this group, as all members' training has been similar. The biggest difficulty may be getting differing personalities to mesh together. The primary disadvantage to this type of group is that the marketplace may not be interested in contracting with a group that is too narrowly focused. Managed care organizations (MCOs) are often looking for groups with a broader skill set. However, for some specialized settings a single-specialty group may be ideal.

Multi-Specialty Group. A multi-specialty group provides a broader scope than a single-specialty group. Its primary advantage over the single-specialty group is that it provides third-party payers such as MCOs, employee assistance programs (EAPs), and other contracting entities with the "one-stop shop" that they seek. Another advantage is the ability to cross-refer within the group. A child therapist can refer a parent for individual therapy to a colleague in the group who specializes in adults; the referral (and its revenue) does not have to be sent outside of the group. The disadvantages of a multi-specialty group are that different specialists may have differing goals. Making individual goals compatible with group goals can be a formidable task. Once that hurdle is overcome, different specialists attract differing types of business, which requires more complex billing and administrative systems.

Multidisciplinary Group. The multidisciplinary group is one level of complexity higher that the multi-specialty group. Not only do group members have differing specialties, but they are of different professions with various goals, ethical and professional standards, and legal regulations. Further, there are often legal barriers to creating such a group. In many states, different professionals are unable to go into business with each other. An attorney is needed to determine how the group can avoid running afoul of state or federal laws. While this is the most difficult of practices to organize and maintain, it is the most desired organization for third-party payers. Their desire to contract with as few administrative organizations as possible is best served by a group of this sort. Another advantage of this type of group is the broader array of professionals available to provide service within the group; patients are less likely to be referred outside the group, with less revenue being drained from the organization.

Independent Practice Organization and Provider-Hospital Organization. An independent practice association (IPA) is an organization designed to contract with large-volume payers. The provider–hospital organization (PHO) is a variation of an IPA. In an IPA, physicians and other health care professionals join together. In a PHO, the provider group partners with a hospital to create a contracting entity that provides even broader services than an IPA and is thus even more attractive to third-party payers. The IPA then contracts with practitioners, either in groups or solo practices, to provide the services. The IPA usually negotiates a capitated rate as reimbursement for service provision and then pays its providers on a reduced fee-for-service basis. A capitated rate is a dollar amount calculated on the basis of the number of covered lives (or members in the payer's health plan) per month for which the IPA is required to provide service. For example, if the payer covered 10,000 people in its health plan ("covered lives") and paid the IPA \$3.50 per month for the provision of mental health services for each covered life, the IPA would receive \$35,000 per month to treat all the mental health needs of those 10,000 people. The advantage here is that the IPA has a clear notion as to how much money it will have with which to pay expenses. The disadvantage is that poor planning, with too many people accessing their benefits and using high-cost services, could bankrupt an IPA very quickly. And at that point, 10,000 people may have no coverage.

Capitation, critics charge, offers a perverting incentive to providers; clearly, the less service provided, the more money the IPA can keep. That is why IPAs generally pay the actual providers-of-service on a fee-for-service basis, so the disincentive to treat is not on the provider. A portion of the fee may also be withheld in a risk pool to be distributed at the end of a specified length of time if utilization of services was within expectation. However, IPA utilization reviewers, quality improvement managers, executives, and shareholders all put pressure on the providers to be more "efficient" and treat the patients as quickly and as "cost-effectively" as possible.

Health Maintenance Organization and Preferred Provider Organization. The health maintenance organization (HMO) and preferred provider organization (PPO) are provider organizations that contract with high volume payers. HMOs differ from PPOs in that the patient has a limited choice of providers and must generally go through the primary care physician (PCP), who acts as a gatekeeper. The PCP is encouraged—often given incentives—to treat the patient and not refer to specialists. In the HMO, all providers and patients agree to have their cases reviewed by a representative of the HMO.

With PPOs, providers are placed on a panel of participating providers. Generally, the patient may choose from any participating provider without going through a gatekeeper. The provider receives a reduced fee-for-service but usually does not have the treatment "case managed" by a utilization reviewer. There often is an "out-of-network" benefit in a PPO that allows the patient to be seen by a provider that is not a participating provider. In this case, the patient receives a reduced benefit. For example, when seeing an in-network provider, the patient may pay 20 percent of a discounted fee. When seeing an out-of-network provider, the patient may pay 50 percent of the provider's full fee. There is another product currently being offered by MCOs: the point-of-service plan (POS). This is an HMO with PPO-type out-of-network benefits.

Management Services Organization. A management services organization (MSO) exists to provide management services to practices with which it has contracts. It is often jointly owned by the practices that use its services. Since it is a legal entity, it has assets and liabilities and can contract with third-party payers and feed referrals to the member practices. The MSO provides administrative and management functions for each practice, and each practice pays the MSO a fee for these services.

Behavioral Health Organization. The behavioral health organization is a specialty managed-care organization. There are currently four or five national companies that cover most of the mental health needs of the U.S. population. Current statistics suggest that over 75 percent of the U.S. public is covered by some form of behavioral health, managed-care organization. Magellan Behavioral Health is the largest such organization, having merged Greenspring, Merit Behavioral Care, and Human Affairs International. The next largest companies are Value/Options, United Behavioral Health, Managed Health Network, and CIGNA Behavioral Health. Therapists can become providers for these organizations and receive reduced fee-for-service with case management oversight. The current trend with these organizations is further reduction in reimbursement rates to providers. Many providers have been dropping their membership in these provider panels in recent months as reimbursement rates have declined and more people choose health plan options that offer out-of-network benefits.

Owner or Employee? A mental health professional has an opportunity to be an owner, shareholder, or employee of any of the above group practice options. In some organizations, the practitioner may be engaged more in administrative duties than clinical duties; this needs to be considered when choosing a practice model.

Personal Goals

How much time do you want to spend on marketing a practice? How much clinical work do you really want to do? How much time do you want to spend with your family and other interests? How much vacation time do you need? What level of control do you require in your work life? Do you feel comfortable working for somebody else, or do you need to be master of your own ship? Do you like working alone, or do you need people with whom you can collaborate and consult about cases? Do you need a job that allows you flexibility in hours? These are all questions that you need to consider before opening a practice. If you are unhappy in your work, you will not have the enthusiasm and commitment needed to be successful.

Financial Goals

You need to determine how much money you want to make. Consider setting up a personal financial plan that includes current personal expenses and anticipated personal expenses five years from now. How will you be able to meet these expenses? It is often said that it takes two to five years to build a full-time practice. If that is your goal, how will you sustain yourself in the meantime? Many people start with a part-time practice and work full-time. As they build a practice, they cut back on their full-time job, if they can, or find a part-time job. At some point, they "make the leap" to full-time practice.

What kind of clients will you need to see in order to make the amount of money that you project? Do you want to have a solo practice and refer cases out if you have an overflow, or do you want to hire associates to take the cases you cannot see? Will you need to see managed care patients? Will you have to contract with group practices to fill up your open hours? These questions overlap with your treatment philosophy and personal and professional goals, but all need to be considered.

Developing a Business Plan

When first considering setting up your own practice, it is important to develop a business plan. This is meant to be a road map identifying your practice's long-term destination and what is required to get there. A business plan typically includes a financial plan, a long-term strategic plan, an operations plan, a human resources plan, an information-management plan, and a statement of goals for the coming year. A good business plan anticipates problems and has contingencies in place for those problems. It is a guide for your practice and should be brief, between three and five pages.

Kalman Heller (1997), in *Strategic Marketing,* recommended the following structure for your written business plan:

- *Mission statement:* Defines your practice.
- *Internal assessment:* A current picture of your practice including its strengths and weaknesses. Incorporates your office staffing, operations, and information management.
- *External assessment:* Includes a current picture of your competition, the business climate, and needs of the marketplace.
- *Strategic vision:* Your three-to-five year projection of your practice, and key changes required to achieve your vision.
- *Specific goals and tactics:* Includes plans for your coming year, including measurable goals, dates for achieving those goals, and tactics to be used.
- *Financials:* Includes projections for income and expenses for the coming year and what your financial requirements will be needed to achieve these goals.

Mission Statement

A good mission statement indicates clearly why your practice is being formed. It specifies what services and activities will be provided, who will be served, where your practice will be providing these services, and what makes it unique. Dana Ackley, in *Breaking Free of Managed Care* (1997), offers a method for defining your business. He suggests making four lists. The first will be the results of your market study—in other words, what issues appear to be of urgent concern for people within the community you plan to serve. The second describes the kinds of services you are interested in providing. List what excites you, not necessarily what your training has been. You may choose to seek training in one of these areas if you are interested in providing the service. Third, list the services for which you are trained. The fourth list is of services you choose not to offer. Often you may be offered work that you do not want to take; you may have no interest, training, or expertise in the work being offered. It is important to keep yourself focused on the services that you want to provide rather than venturing off into areas that will distract you from the work you want to do. Once these four lists are reviewed, it is possible to write a clear mission statement that communicates what you are about. This statement need not be more than three sentences long.

The following is the mission statement I developed for my group practice:

> The mission of ACP Consultants is to provide comprehensive, high-quality psychological and related services utilizing a consultative team approach. Within the Chicago area, persons of all age ranges and organizations can be served. Emphasis is on proper assessment, consultations with other professionals, and the development of clear goals, objectives, and interventions, and on finding solutions that promote positive growth.

The above statement lets the reader know that the practice is located in the Chicago area and aims to be a *comprehensive* organization. ACP Consultants is owned and operated by a psychologist and most of the members of the group are psychologists, but it also employs licensed clinical social workers and licensed clinical professional counselors. Services are not limited to psychotherapy and assessments, as services also are offered to organizations. One can see that the practice philosophy is solution focused and collaborative. This is also the mission statement of an organization that is in transition, as it is general in nature. The more focused your mission is, the easier it is to develop a plan to pursue that mission. ACP Consultants is moving out of the managed care business and is exploring other areas. The mission statement reflects this exploration.

Internal Assessment

Business Operations

Office Space. Choosing office space sets the tone for your practice. Many therapists work out of their home or in small offices in an effort to appear relaxed and inviting; the image projected is one of informality and privacy. While such a relaxed atmosphere may reduce stress for some clients, be comfortable, and offer flexibility, it may adversely effect business operations. In these settings, business policies are often individualized for each client. Policies may become erratic and inconsistent, negatively impacting on fee collection and ultimately on the financial viability of the practice. Some clients may view the small office as meager and unprofessional.

Yenney (1994) made a number of suggestions about choosing office space. First, select office space that represents the image you want to project. Review your long-range plans for your practice and try to find a setting that will help you reach your goals. If you are starting out, renting a smaller office in a professional building or subletting an office from a colleague may be advisable. If you only plan to maintain a small, part-time practice, a home-like atmosphere may be the image you want to project.

A second consideration is location. Choose a location that will be accessible to the people that you want to see. Are you close to public transportation? Is the parking lot well lit at night? Will clients feel safe coming to your office? Knowing the type of clients you want to see will help in this selection. If you are looking for a predominantly self-pay practice, you may need to locate in a fairly affluent neighborhood. If you plan on providing services to chronically ill patients, you may want to locate near a medical center. You also will want to pay attention to whether the space you are considering is handicapped-accessible. Knowing when you plan to offer appointments (weekends, evenings, daytime, and so forth) may help you choose a location that will make it convenient for your potential clients to schedule their sessions.

Determine whether you want to have more than one location. By subletting a satellite office from a colleague, you can broaden the geographical scope of your practice without significantly increasing your office overhead. Some therapists swap offices on different days. Managed care organizations (MCOs) make their referrals based on zip codes and often have access requirements built into their contracts. They may have to offer patients access to a practitioner within a certain radius of their home or place of employment (often in five-, ten-, and 25-mile increments). Having office addresses sufficiently spread out may increase the number of referrals you receive from the MCOs with whom you have contracted.

Make sure that your reception area is warm, approachable, and pleasant. Attend to lighting, seating, and decor. If you plan on having plants in your offices, consider the message they send. If your plants are dying from neglect, what does that say to the client about how you will attend to *them*? Alternately, if you have artificial plants, will your client think that you tend to take the easy way out? Reading materials are often found in reception areas. Are they out of date? Are they communicating the proper messages to the clients as they wait to see you? Some type of sound masking machine is also advisable to aid in the maintenance of privacy; music or white noise machines are often used. Ensure privacy and confidentiality in your offices. Some therapists provide a private exit for patients so they do not have to pass through the reception area. Position your office staff so that people in the reception area cannot hear telephone conversations.

Once you have chosen a potential office space, ask a friend or relative to help you assess your office. Does it present the ambience you want to convey? What changes do you need to make in order to make the space fit your needs?

Business Office. Once you have found your space and furnished the therapy offices and reception area, attention needs to be paid to the business office. Most practitioners' offices need business equipment of some sort. While it is possible to contract the management of your practice to an outside source, there are some pieces of equipment that, in the current environment, are required to maintain an office. A computer is a critical necessity for word-processing of reports, letters, and other correspondence. Billing is best handled with billing software that tracks charges, payments, and accounts receivable and maintains a patient database. Accounting software is needed to track expenses and income. All of these processes are more efficient when computerized. The Internet and e-mail can help the clinician keep in contact with colleagues and stay current on recent research, as well as help with marketing. E-mail is currently not a secure enough medium to send sensitive clinical material, but encryption processes are continually improving and may soon provide a sufficiently secure environment for transmittal of clinical material.

A fax machine and a copier are necessary for providing timely quality service. In most clinical cases, other providers are involved in the client's life; they are often in need of your information and need to send information to you. A fax machine allows for timely exchange of data. Confidentiality may be an issue here. Some organizations will not communicate via fax or e-mail for privacy reasons. A fax, for example, can be inadvertently sent to an incorrect recipient. Whenever a fax is sent, be sure to include a confidentiality statement on the cover page.

As copies of materials are often requested by colleagues, clients, and others, having a copier in the office saves time. When choosing a copier, it is important to determine the level of need and to purchase or lease a copier that suits them.

The purchase of a phone system can be a major investment. A solo practitioner may only need one phone for voice but may need another line for data (fax or modem). A group practice may need several phone lines to accommodate all therapists' needs.

Insurance. It goes without saying that professional liability insurance is a prerequisite to practice. There are, however, other insurances that you will need. Business liability insurance, general liability insurance, umbrella insurance, and insurance for your equipment and furnishings all need to be obtained. What if you cannot work for a time due to an unexpected illness or accident? You may want to purchase disability insurance. If you are hiring employees you need workers' compensation and unemployment insurance. Contact an insurance broker to review your insurance needs.

Initial Contact. Most practice consultants caution therapists to pay careful attention to how the initial contact with a client is handled. It is during this initial contact that you have the first opportunity to sell yourself and your practice. When a person first calls to arrange an appointment, they are looking for a compassionate individual to help them. If they do not feel satisfied by this first contact, they will most likely seek another therapist.

How quickly do you respond when the phone rings? Managed care organizations measure the number of seconds it takes them to answer a call, and track the number of call abandonments (callers who hang up before the phone is answered). Many of their contracts with HMOs and other companies they serve require them to track this data. This is an access-to-care issue and MCOs know the importance of responding quickly. MCOs are often perceived as large, bureaucratic organizations that are difficult to approach; by responding rapidly with a caring, live voice, MCOs can counter that perception. If an MCO values rapid response as a means of satisfying a client, a solo practitioner also needs to respond quickly.

Most people would prefer to speak to a live voice than a machine, but it is not always possible to do this. Whether you have a solo practice and do not have a receptionist, or have a group practice, you will probably want to have an answering machine or voice-mail system with a pager or answering service backup. Such a system allows the caller to leave complete and detailed messages if there is no live voice to answer the phone. The greeting on your system should be as brief as possible and gently presented. It should include a welcome message to identify your practice and state what the client should do in an emergency or how you can be reached if the situation is urgent. Our group practice uses a voice-mail branching system that lets the caller leave a message directly and confidentially for the therapist they are contacting. Our greeting is offered as an example.

> Thank you for calling ACP Consultants. If you know the extension you wish to reach, you may press it at any time. You will have 60 seconds to leave your message. A dialing directory will follow this message. Only if this is an emergency, dial "zero" and the answering service will assist you. If you are a new client calling for a first appointment or have a question about billing, please press "one." If you would like leave a message for Dr. Graham, please press "two" (etc).

Choosing an answering service can be difficult. Certainly, you want one that has experience answering for physicians or other therapists. One answering service used to respond to our emergency message by an automated voice that told the caller "an operator will be right with you." The caller was then treated to music until the call was answered, sometimes waiting two to three minutes. This is not an optimal situation, particularly if the client is suicidal. I found that by calling the voice mail and dialing the emergency number regularly, I could monitor the answering service and initiate corrective action.

Another system that a number of therapists have been happy with is a pager system that sends an automatic page to the therapist if someone leaves a message. This system assures that calls are answered quickly—but can be very disruptive to the therapist. No system is perfect and you may need to experiment with different systems until you find the one that best works for you.

Scheduling. Purchase an appointment book or software. Determine the hours that you will be seeing clients and the blocks of time required for each service. Some therapists see a client longer at a first session in order to complete a full diagnostic assessment. Other clinicians will use a shorter first session just to determine if the therapist and client can work together; psychological testing can take a longer block of time.

While individual therapists in a group practice may use differing scheduling tools and see clients at varying hours and for varying lengths of time, the receptionist will need some standardized form for recording everyone's schedule. It has been our experience that without some standardization, appointments get lost or incorrectly scheduled, placing our practice before the client in a bad light. Some group practices use a central person to do all the scheduling, particularly for new clients. It is our policy to have therapists make their own appointments and report back to the receptionist or intake person. We feel that treatment begins with the first call, and that by having the therapist make a personal connection with the client as soon as possible, the number of first-session cancellations and no-shows is reduced.

Managing a schedule is a simple task for some therapists and a very difficult one for others. Remember to keep the client's satisfaction a prominent consideration during your initial contacts. If you continually run late or double-schedule, clients will become annoyed and may drop out of treatment or seek another therapist. By maintaining a timely and organized schedule you provide a reliable and comforting environment for the client in which they feel valued by a competent, caring professional. Another tip for managing a schedule, particularly when first opening a practice: Leave space in your schedule to accommodate new clients as quickly as possible. As new clients do not have a relationship with you or your practice, a long wait may lead them to become impatient and seek treatment elsewhere. Time slots that are not filled can be devoted to marketing activities aimed at bringing new clients through the door. Make sure that your clients are clearly informed about your cancellation and no-show policy. Typically, therapists require at least 24 hours for a cancellation or the client will be charged. After all, a therapist only has his or her time to sell, and if a client does not show or cancels late, the therapist loses the revenue that would be generated by that hour.

Finally, be aware of the population you serve. If you are seeing children, expect to have late-afternoon, evening, and possibly Saturday appointments available. Some therapists schedule very early appointments, i.e., 7 a.m., in order to accommodate employed workers. The more you can tailor your schedule to the schedule of the population you serve, the more convenient you will be perceived as being and the greater the likelihood of receiving more referrals.

Billing and Insurance. You must develop a billing system that maintains cash flow. Dealing with financial issues is often uncomfortable for therapists, but if it is ignored or neglected you may find yourself doing more unintended pro bono work than you had anticipated. When a client comes to see you for the first visit, set out the expectations for payment. What services do you bill for and how much do you charge? Do you charge for telephone calls, report-writing, other paperwork? Creating and providing to your clients a fee schedule and payment policy at the first session increases the likelihood that you will be paid. By having the client sign a payment or treatment contract at the initial visit, you have a document that will be invaluable if you must turn over the account to a collection agency or initiate legal proceedings.

You must decide what forms of payment you will accept. The use of credit cards is increasing. The APA offers a credit-card program for psychologists. There are other credit-card programs available from banks, each charging about 2–4 percent of the transaction amount as their fee. An advantage to using credit cards is that you get paid in a more timely manner while the credit card company assumes the collection risk. As a therapist, you need to monitor your client's use of credit; if you have a client who runs up credit card balances, and this is part of the client's purpose in seeking treatment, it might make good clinical sense to develop an alternative payment plan at the initial visit.

The guiding principle regarding insurance is that insurance is a contract between the patient and the insurance company to aid the patient in paying claims. You, as the therapist, are not part of that contract; your contract is with the patient. As a result, you need to make an agreement with the patient as to how you will handle insurance claims. Managed care organizations often require the practitioner to file the claims, with the patient making a copayment at every session. If you have many such patients, you will need to complete the HCFA 1500 form (the industry standard for insurance claims) on a timely basis. Our practice prints out insurance claim forms on a monthly basis.

You may choose to have a managed care–free practice but accept insurance. In this case, you may ask patients to pay in full at the time of service and provide the patient with a bill that they can submit to insurance for reimbursement. If you allow the patient to make partial payment with you collecting the remaining balance from the insurance company, you need to have the patient sign an assignment-of-benefits form which authorizes the insurance company to make payments directly to you. Without such a signature, the insurance company will send payment to the patient and you will have to collect the entire debt from the patient.

There are some clients who cannot pay in full at every session. You may want to work out a payment plan with these clients. Keep in mind that when you do this, you will need to send out bills on a regular and timely basis. This increases your overhead costs and decreases the cash flow into your business. Some practices, however, do this on a regular basis and thus have a steady flow of income coming into the practice.

What do you do when a client gets behind in their payments? In our practice, the office staff notifies the therapist if the client is still in treatment. The issue becomes an integral part of the treatment process. If the patient builds up a large balance with no plan for payment, a dual relationship is created between the therapist and the client. The client also becomes a debtor. This may lead the therapist to have to drop the debtor as a client (after dealing with the ethical issues surrounding client abandonment). The therapist and the client may rework the repayment schedule as a way of rectifying the situation. In either case, the practice manager is involved to assure that the financial arrangements make sense from a business perspective.

There are occasions when a client gets behind in their payments after treatment is completed. In these cases, having a practice policy can increase collection rates. In our practice, we have a series of letters that are mailed to the client. In the first letter, they are reminded of the unpaid debt and asked for payment. The second letter is a bit more forceful, asking the client to either repay the debt in full at once or indicate a new payment schedule with which they would feel comfortable; they are told that if they do not respond to the letter, their account will be turned over to a collection agency in 30 days. Collection agencies typically charge 20–40 percent of the money they collect. Be sure to choose a collection agency that is experienced in working with mental health professionals. These agencies are more likely to be sensitive to the needs of mental health patients, paying attention to confidentiality and privacy needs.

Professional Consultants. A businessperson always needs a good accountant and attorney. Our training usually does not include business and accounting, nor are we trained as lawyers. The counseling profession has many legal requirements that we must take into account and when we have a question we need to have someone we can rely upon to provide an answer. Any financial decisions should be reviewed with an accountant to assure that nothing has been overlooked and that your business will not have significant tax exposure. If your practice is organized in such a way that taxes are not routinely taken out of your check, then you must make quarterly tax payments. Consultation with an accountant will help you to anticipate such payments. You only need to be audited once by the IRS to know that an accountant is a necessity.

Many therapists purchase clinical consultation. A solo practitioner may find that practice is too isolating and scheduling a weekly or twice monthly clinical consultation with a senior clinician is both an exercise in risk management and an opportunity to learn and grow as a therapist. Some therapists join consultation groups in which a number of clinicians meet on a regular basis to review cases or to learn new skills.

Information Management

Clinical Record. The clinical record of a patient's treatment traditionally was only for the benefit of the therapist: to keep track of the patient's progress, to aid in the treatment of other patients, and to document treatment in the event that questions arose. With the advent of managed care and accompanying requirements for oversight of treatment, clinical records are subject to more stringent rules and guidelines. In order to satisfy the requirements of the NCQA (National Council of Quality Assurance, an organization created by managed care companies to oversee quality within these managed care entities) and of other accrediting organizations who might want to review your charts, it is essential to create a client record that will include the information needed to pass their reviews.

The clinical record should be organized in a standardized manner for all your clients. Further description of clinical documentation in an outpatient practice can be found in

Graham (1996), and Appendix 14.A contains a number of client forms that can be adapted for use. The following is a suggested setup for a clinical record. In a manila folder (you may color code these folders to designate different populations, programs, or any other relevant schema), utilize the left side for:

1. Intake information sheet
2. Patient information sheet
3. Insurance information sheet
4. Legal documents (i.e., signed consent for release of information forms)
5. Treatment contract
6. Verification of contacts with relevant parties (physicians, schools, third-party payers, etc.)

The right side may include:

1. Treatment plan
2. Progress notes
3. Test reports, letters and any other clinical information generated within your practice
4. Clinical information gathered from other sources (i.e., medication records, consultations)
5. Communications provided by the patient (i.e., letters, e-mail, lists)
6. Consultation notes if patient was referred for additional care
7. Treatment updates
8. Termination summary

What follows is a description of the forms needed to enable the therapist to successfully pass a records review by a managed care organization or other accrediting body.

Intake Information Sheet. When a patient or client calls the practice for the first time, certain data must be collected and information transmitted to the caller. An intake sheet commonly includes the name of the caller, the name of the patient, the caller's relationship to the patient, phone numbers (home, work, car, pager, and so forth), referral source and their phone number, insurance information, employer, the patient's copayments, and a brief description of the reason for the call. This information can be collected by either the clinician or an intake worker. The caller is given fee information, instructions for getting preauthorization for services (if necessary), and is either offered an appointment (if the clinician is the intake worker) or told that a clinician will call back and set an appointment time with the caller. In a group practice where appointments are made by the intake worker, an appointment can be made on the initial call. In my group practice, we have the clinician call back and make the appointment, as this starts the therapeutic alliance and makes the patient more likely to attend the first appointment. There is a space on the bottom of the form for the time and date of the first appointment.

Patient Information Sheet. The patient's name, address, phone number, social security number, etc., are marked on this form. Additional information such as whether the patient has a spouse, children, brothers, and sisters may also be relevant. Also included on this form is the name, address, and phone number of the financially responsible party. A separate form records insurance information. It is best to make a copy of the patient's insurance card and have the insurer provide the addresses and phone numbers necessary to submit the claim. Even if you do not submit claims, having this information may be useful if the claim is paid incorrectly or the patient asks you to help with the filing.

Insurance Information Sheet. In the era of managed care, when providers are required to file insurance forms, insurance information provided by the patient is essential. To repeat, it is advisable to make a copy of the patient's insurance card. This often has most of the important information on it. It is also a good idea to have the patient write the information on the form as well. Included on the form is the name and address of the patient, the insured's employer, the employer's address, the phone number and address of the insurance company's claims-processing center, the phone number of the managed care company (if necessary), and a legal statement allowing the practice to communicate any information needed to process the claim to the insurance company. This statement must be signed by the patient. In some states, if the patient is an adolescent, a parent must sign as well.

Consent Forms for Disclosure of Records. Each state has its own requirements as to what a properly executed release-of-information form must include. Be sure to check your state's laws. Typically, a consent form includes the patient's name and identifying information; the identity of the person or persons whom the information is to be released to or received from; the nature of the information to be released; the possible consequences of not releasing the information; a time frame for which the release is valid; the patient's dated signature; and the signature of a witness. In our state (Illinois), you must have a separate consent form for each person or institution from which information is requested or to which it is to be released. Consent forms should be completed for anyone whom the therapist will contact (e.g., schools, physicians, other therapists, insurance companies, managed care companies, clergy, attorneys). Complete as many consent forms as needed at the initial session, particularly for release to the referral source, primary care physician, and managed care organization (if any).

Treatment Contract. A treatment contract is a necessary part of a clinical record as a means of risk management. In the age of informed consent, a clinician must inform the patient of payment policies and procedures, treatment procedures, possible risks involved, collection procedures, patient rights and responsibilities, etc. This can be handled in many different ways. Using a mutual expectations letter and a consent-for-treatment contract is one way to handle this issue.

In the mutual expectations letter, the clinician informs the patient of the necessary information in a factual and professional but friendly style. This includes an introduction to the practice which explains the patient's and clinician's need to be clear about their expectations of each other. It also describes the services offered by the practice. Next, a more complete explanation of the treatment process is provided, including what to expect in the first interview. The practice's expectations of the patient may include waiting room etiquette, appointment and cancellation policies, fees, handling of insurance, financial expectations and policies, confidentiality, referrals, and termination. In our practice we have added a section describing what the patient should know about managed care and its implications for treatment and privacy. What the patient can expect from the clinician and practice, and her or his rights and responsibilities, is last. Right to information, confidentiality, access to clinicians, complaint and grievance procedures, and courtesy are included here.

Once the patient has reviewed the mutual expectations document, they are given the consent-for-treatment contract, a form devised with the help of an attorney to meet state and federal laws regarding mental health. In this contract, the patient agrees to everything in the mutual-expectations letter. Essentially, this contract states that the practice agrees to provide services to the patient and the patient agrees to pay for these services. The responsibilities and rights of the patient and practice are briefly reviewed and the patient signs the document, witnessed by the clinician or other nonrelative of the patient. Fee, payment, and collection policies are spelled out for the patient. The patient indicates by signing this contract that they assume financial responsibility for any charges incurred during the course of treatment. An important clause in this document is the statement that the patient agrees to pay for any costs that are incurred in the collection of fees. In the event that the courts have to be used to collect past due accounts, this contract significantly increases the chances that you will get paid.

Generally, the person who signs the treatment contract is the responsible party. Parents in a divorce situation will often claim that they are not the responsible party and that they have a court decree that states their ex-spouse is the responsible party. If the ex-spouse is willing to sign the treatment contract, then this is not a problem. If not, then the person signing the treatment contract must be told that they are the responsible party, and that any disputes about payment are between the signee and their ex-spouse.

These two documents could be incorporated into one but it has been my experience that patients often do not read our mutual expectations letter completely at the first session, but are more likely to read a brief, one-page contract that they must sign.

Verification of Contacts with Relevant Parties. Many separate acts of communication are involved in working with clients. Information often needs to be exchanged with attorneys, physicians, third-party payers, schools, probation officers, etc. Maintaining a log in the client's chart helps the clinician keep track of what information has been sent to and received from which source. If a treatment plan is developed that indicates the need for case coordination, maintaining a communications log provides documentation of what information has been exchanged. This also helps with risk management.

Treatment Plan. The treatment plan is a document that provides a guide for the treatment process. It contains the problems presented, the goals of treatment, the interventions planned, target dates for completion, and motivation for treatment. Many treatment plans also include the initial assessment completed by the clinician. The initial assessment consists of identifying data, the presenting problem or chief complaint, a history of the current problem, other relevant history (developmental, family, educational, marital, work, military, social, etc.), a substance-abuse evaluation, previous psychiatric history (including family history), medical history (e.g., current medications, known drug allergies), mental status exam, and diagnosis (usually a DSM-IV diagnosis on all five axes). These items are required by the NCQA and are examined by such site visitors as accrediting organizations and managed care companies. Jongsma (1996) offers many ways to document problems that are the focus of treatment, goals directed at the problems presented, and interventions used to produce measurable and attainable outcomes.

Risk Assessment Form. Completing a formalized risk assessment is helpful as it alerts the clinician to clinical risk factors. Many managed care companies complete formal risk assessments on all their patients. Suicidal or homicidal thinking, evidence of need for hospitalization, legal problems, severity of symptoms, etc., are all possible risk factors when treating a patient and are thus covered in such a form.

Progress Notes. Progress notes relate specifically to the treatment plan and serve to document progress toward goals. In the past, all a progress note required was a date, the name of the patient, a narrative of what occurred in the therapy session, and a signature. In the current accountability climate, the progress note should also include identifying data such as the session number; length and type of session (individual, marital, family, or group); current diagnosis; problems and goals addressed in the session; interventions used and their effect; ongoing determination of risk assessment; and an updated plan for further treatment.

Treatment Updates. Managed care companies require regular updates regarding the treatment of the people they cover if they are to continue authorizing more treatment. By maintaining her or his own procedure for treatment reviews, a clinician builds outcome data that may convince an MCO that the clinician does not have to be monitored so closely. The four criteria often reviewed by MCOs are (1) Are the symptoms presented still severe enough to warrant treatment? (2) Is the patient or family compliant with treatment recommendations? (3) Is progress being made where it can be reasonably expected? (4) If there is little or no progress, is treatment serving to stabilize the patient and thus avoid more intensive levels of care?

In my group practice, we complete a treatment update one session prior to the end of a treatment authorization by an MCO. For example, if MCO X authorized eight sessions, we would complete our treatment update at session seven. If no MCO is involved, treatment update forms are completed after the tenth session. Our treatment update form contains all the same information in a progress note but includes a more elaborated plan and a check-off system for replying to the above four criteria. The clinician and clinical director of the practice sign off on the update.

Closing Summaries. The closing summary indicates that treatment has been completed. Prognoses are estimated, reasons for case closure are indicated and recommendations for further treatment included if the patient were to return. By maintaining this information, outcomes data can be collected and quality improvement issues addressed.

Other Clinical Information. Psychological test reports, letters, other clinical information generated within your practice, clinical information gathered from other sources (e.g., medication records, consultations), communications provided by the patient (e.g., letters, e-mail, lists), and consultation notes (if the patient was referred for additional care) all belong in the clinical record. They help provide a thorough running record of your treatment of the patient, benefiting not only the patient but you. Complete data contributes to your learning process and is an effective risk-management tool.

Financial Records. Maintaining accurate financial records is a critical business consideration. These records need to be kept separate from clinical records for reasons of confidentiality and convenience. These records are used primarily by the person in your practice that is responsible for billing procedures and insurance claim filing. The following forms make up a complete financial record package for each patient: the patient information form, the insurance information form with an assignment of benefits, the superbill, and the HCFA 1500. The patient and insurance information forms have been described above.

The *superbill* is completed after every patient contact. It documents the nature of the service rendered and the charge for that service. It is called a *superbill* because it contains all the information necessary for a patient to attach it to a claim form and submit for reimbursement. This information includes the patient's name; a DSM-IV or ICD-10 diagnosis; a CPT (current procedure terminology) code; the service provided; the fee charged; the date when and location where the service was provided; the therapist's name, address, phone number, signature, and license number; and any other relevant license numbers (e.g., federal tax identification number, Medicare number). The superbill can also serve as documentation for your internal accounting procedure. By completing a superbill for every billable patient contact, you can keep track of your practice's revenue.

The *HCFA 1500 form* is the industry standard for insurance claims. Most insurance companies and Medicare require that insurance claims be submitted on this form. While the superbill can replace the HCFA 1500 form for single charges, multiple charges can be included on the latter. A HCFA 1500 form is generally submitted on a monthly basis in our practice, although there is no required frequency for submission. Many insurance companies require, however, that charges must be submitted within a certain time frame, often within 45 days of the date of service. If a charge is submitted after this date, it may be rejected. HCFA 1500 forms can be obtained from authorized publishers. The American Medical Association is an authorized publisher, although there are less expensive alternatives.

Risk Management

The American Professional Agency, Inc. provides professional liability insurance for mental health professionals. It publishes a newsletter called *Insight: Safeguarding Psychologists Against Liability Risk.* In the second edition for 1998, general documentation guidelines are listed as a risk management tool:

1. Document every patient contact.
2. Don't needlessly record embarrassing or potentially damaging information about the patient.
3. Don't discuss your countertransference experiences.
4. Document your contacts with suicidal patients, paying particular attention to precautionary steps taken.
5. Remember that personal notes (or process notes) can be subpoenaed in a trial.
6. Don't audiotape or videotape patient sessions if you don't have to.
7. Make sure that computer-maintained records are backed up.
8. When patients discontinue treatment prematurely, make sure you document your recommendation against termination.

These recommendations are summarized from an interview *Insight* conducted with psychologist and attorney Bryant L. Welch, J. D., Ph.D (Welch, 1998). He emphasized that psychologists must maintain a balance between accurate clinical record-keeping, client confidentiality, and liability exposures.

Quality Improvement Plan

The scope and purpose of a quality improvement plan is to continuously review and improve all services provided by the practice. All activities within the organization are subject to the quality improvement process. Example areas for review are: clinical chart documentation, intake and referral, case management (including utilization review and clinical risk management), billing and accounting, and personnel.

Developing and documenting practice guidelines and clinical protocols helps to assure that quality is maintained throughout your practice. By standardizing clinical records, this increases your confidence that when a third party asks for clinical information, you will have useful data to provide. Standardized data also allow you to judge the efficacy of treatment.

Data collection is much easier should you choose to develop clinical research protocols. Standardized procedures should be developed for intake, documentation and maintenance of clinical and financial records, clinical management of cases, confidentiality, emergencies, management of disabled patients, and fees and payments. In a solo practice, these procedures may be housed in your head. By putting them down on paper, you are engaging in an important risk-management exercise. If your treatment is challenged, you have documentation to back up your actions.

Documenting procedures and policies helps therapists new to a group learn how things are done. It also benefits personnel management. If a therapist has a dispute with the owner or owners of the practice, the policy and procedure manual can provide not only a policy for resolving the dispute but the specific documentation to support or deny the allegation. As such, personnel policies are appropriate for inclusion in a policy and procedure manual. Issues such as hiring; ongoing review of staff credentials; benefits of being a therapist in the practice (e.g., use of support staff and services such as voice mail, pagers, business cards); therapist voluntary termination and involuntary termination; and therapist compensation policies can all be covered in the manual. It is critical that an attorney participate in the creation of these policies to reduce legal exposure. For further information regarding the creation of a policy and procedure manual for an outpatient psychotherapy practice, see Graham (1996).

In order for a quality improvement program to work, it needs regular review. The frequency of these reviews is usually dictated by the size and age of the organization. It makes sense for a new organization to document its systems as they are being created; such an organization will want to look at its policies and procedures frequently in order to find appropriate systems as soon as possible. Once systems are in place, they may need only to be reviewed on a quarterly, semi-annual, or annual basis. In a larger organization, reviews may be necessary on a monthly, twice-monthly, or even weekly basis. The NCQA requires that an active quality improvement program be in place in order for the organization to receive NCQA accreditation.

Outcomes Research

Outcomes research can document the efficacy of treatment. Such data can be used when pursuing contracts with third party payers and can be reported in marketing materials. Information such as average number of sessions per outpatient case, total cost per episode of care, number of cases referred for higher levels of care, and client satisfaction can be presented to third party payers to persuade them to contract with your practice. Matching this data with diagnoses and global assessments of functioning (GAF) may help you assess the effectiveness of treatment in your practice.

When assessing clinical outcome, the three most important criteria to measure are reduction of symptomatology, increase in functionality, and client satisfaction. Assessment tools are on the market that attempt to measure these variables. Such information can be used to help define which treatments are more effective, whether referrals to specialists aid in treatment, and so forth. More information about outcomes evaluation can be found in Chapter 13.

External Assessment

Market Research

Awareness of the marketplace helps in formulating strategies for getting referrals. Each area has unique marketplace trends, and these should be researched. National trends will also influence your practice. These are current national trends in mental health care delivery in the United States:

1. The large, behavioral health managed care organizations have been merging and consolidating. The top companies are controlling an increasing share of the market. For example, Magellan Behavioral Health—a merger of Greenspring, Merit Behavioral Care, and Human Affairs International—now covers more than 60 million lives in the United States. ValueOptions covers 27 million lives and United Behavioral Health covers 14 million lives. Together, the top 12 companies cover 144 million lives.
2. Managed care companies have squeezed all the excess out of mental health care and are now looking at new ways to cut costs. Some of their strategies are to pare down networks and cut reimbursement rates (*Psychotherapy Finances,* 1999).
3. Managed care companies are vigorously pursuing NCQA accreditation. In order to receive it, they must demonstrate an active quality improvement program and an active preventive health program.
4. The number of people choosing HMOs has been declining recently, for the first time since their creation. While the large companies continue to hold on to their patients, patients are increasingly choosing health plans that allow for more choice. Point-of-service plans and preferred-provider organizations allow their members to use out-of-network benefits to see the provider of their choice.
5. Legislative initiatives are increasingly designed to regulate the MCOs. Patients' rights laws have passed in many states and are being considered at the federal level.
6. The federal Mental Health Parity Act of 1996 requires that the annual and lifetime maximum dollar amounts of coverage for general medical health must be the same as for

mental health. While this may not have a significant impact at present, the issue of parity has its "foot in the door," suggesting that further legislation is on the way.

7. Corporate America still distrusts mental health practitioners. A study by the SAMHSA (Substance Abuse and Mental Health Services Administration), a part of the Department of Health and Human Services (DHHS), found that corporate leaders feel that the only way parity can work is if the benefits are managed (Office of Managed Care, CMHS, SAMSHA, 1998). They are still spooked by the psychiatric hospital scandals of the late 1980s (see http://www.samhsa.gov).

8. Mental health spending has been dropping. In the late 1980s, mental health spending consumed 8–10 percent of the health care dollar. In 1998, mental health spending had been cut to 3–5 percent of the health care dollar (Shalala, 1999).

9. Psychologists and other mental health practitioners are diversifying their practices. New areas of practice include coaching, preventive health initiatives, seminars for business and other groups, divorce mediation, expert testimony in child custody cases, and so forth.

10. Mental health professionals are becoming more technologically savvy and integrating computers and the Internet into their practices.

Further, you will need to know your competition and the demographics of the area in which you plan to open your office. Who are the current mental health practitioners operating in your area, and where are they getting their business? Open the Yellow Pages and look under psychologists, social workers, psychiatrists, marriage and family counselors, and counselors. How many listings are there? Do you recognize any of them? What do you know about them? Participation in your local professional organization will also help identify who is currently in business in your area.

Census figures, available in the public library, can inform you of the age distribution, socioeconomic status, education level, and so on of the population in the area in which you plan to open your office. This information will help you tailor your programs to the population you serve. Would it make sense to open an office that specializes in child therapy if there are mostly retirees in your area?

Developing a Marketing Strategy

Heller (1997) described eight practice strategies for achieving your mission. By being clear on your mission and choice of strategies toward that mission, you increase the likelihood of success.

Specialization. Developing a specialization to serve a specific market niche is a strategy highlighted by *Psychotherapy Finances,* a monthly newsletter published by Ridgewood Financial Institute. *Psychotherapy Finances* advertises itself as "the leading practice resource for behavioral health providers." Nearly every month, it includes an article on *niche* marketing. Filling a market niche fulfills the needs of a well-defined target group such as people with a specific disorder, people of a particular age range, or people who share a common life situation. Some niches are disease management and working with infertile couples, compulsive gamblers, or hearing-impaired children. Selection of your target group is central to this strategy. You must carefully assess the need for a given service in the community and the potential for income and growth.

The community needs to view your service as better than any other service offered in the community; this requires promotion of your service. Giving presentations or writing a newsletter or a column for the local newspaper are ways to get your message across.

Heller (1997) suggested that specialization is a good strategy for solo practitioners. He states that the rule of thumb is that the smaller you are, the more you need to specialize. Being small means you do not need a lot of referrals to keep busy and that promotion is more efficient. Once you have established yourself as an expert, you can charge premium fees. One fear is that you will only see one type of patient; however, experience has shown that over time, people will refer other types of problems to you as well.

Quality Leader: The "Expert." This strategy usually requires that the practitioner has special credentials that sets them up as an expert in the field. As such, they become the person that everyone wants to see. Public relations is an important component to this strategy. Experts usually appear on talk shows, write columns in newspapers, and give workshops. They can charge premium prices because they are perceived as experts. The most difficult task in this strategy is to achieve expert status. It often takes time to build one's reputation in the minds of the public.

Low Price Leader. In this strategy, you position yourself as having a high-volume, low-cost approach to service. The key is to generate business from contracts with organizations that can feed you a high volume of referrals. Managed care companies are attracted to practices that pursue this strategy. The tradeoff is that you need low-cost staff to see these patients and systems to monitor quality. Start-up costs for such a venture can be high, as volume-handling systems must be put in place. This strategy may be attractive to someone who is entrepreneurial—willing to take significant risk.

Eclectic Strategy. This strategy is a middle-ground position in which you try to provide good quality services at a reasonable cost. By offering a range of services, you try to meet the needs of a wide range of patients. Heller suggested that this is a risky approach in the current market because there is little differentiation from other practices. As a result, there is no compelling reason to go to *you,* and your practice may see a slow decline in referrals.

Technology Leader. The computer and the Internet have created many opportunities, but mental health practitioners are still trying to figure out how to use the current technology to generate revenue. While computers have entered into most practitioners' offices to help with billing, accounting, treatment planning, and clinical records, the use of such technology appears to be in its infancy. E-mail expands the number of communication avenues available to patients and professionals. Creating a Web site as a means to advertise your services, develop referral services, or create chat rooms is one way to connect to an ever-expanding market. The greatest lure of the Internet is that it is interactive, thus you can develop relationships with people around the world or set up (or participate in) virtual communities. These may center around a specific niche that can enhance your professional growth or help build your business.

Integration Strategies. These strategies are more feasible for the larger group practice models. *Vertically integrated* systems provide services at every level of care; for example, a physician–hospital organization (PHO) can provide services to a patient with mental health and substance-abuse problems who first needs hospitalization, then a partial hospitalization program, then an intensive outpatient program, and finally traditional outpatient therapy. This patient can be followed by a psychiatrist, a therapist, and a substance-abuse counselor, all services provided by the PHO. This type of organization is attractive to MCOs, which strive to limit the number of organizations with whom they contract. A *horizontal integration* strategy may involve a number of outpatient practices joined together to form a medical service organization (MSO) to consolidate administrative and management functions within a specified geographic area.

Managed Care Strategy. The goal of this strategy is to get on as many managed care panels as possible. It can be quite difficult to get on MCO panels, as most MCOs are striving to reduce the size of their panels. The best way to be considered is to have a specialty that is under-represented on the panel or to be in a geographic area, particularly in a rural setting, where there are few providers. One drawback of this strategy is that you are in business at the whim of large organizations that may change their reimbursement rates or policies and procedures at any time. This strategy also requires you to develop standardized clinical, quality improvement, and financial systems to manage your business.

Alternate Income Strategy. There are other arenas where a therapist's skills have application. Using an alternative income strategy, you may explore services that do not include direct patient treatment. Heller (1997) suggested a number of opportunities available to therapists, in six categories: legal, corporate, schools, psychoeducation, government, and training/supervision. All of the professional psychological organizations are promoting these options as an alternative to direct patient contact.

Building a Network

In order to develop a successful practice, a practitioner needs to build a strong referral network that will provide patients and consultations. One of the most effective ways to build a referral network is through word-of-mouth marketing. This entails talking to people, developing relationships with them, and educating them about what you do. There are "leads" groups that exist in the business community; these meet regularly, often weekly, for members to provide business leads to other members. Business Networks International (BNI) operates leads groups through out the world. Each group consists of local business owners who educate other members about their work and distribute referrals to each other. Only one representative from each profession or industry may be in a local group. BNI headquarters provides guidance for the local groups and educates members about the power of word-of-mouth marketing. You can find BNI on the World Wide Web at <www.bni.com>.

Other ways to develop relationships are to attend community group meetings or professional association meetings, get on hospital staffs, take prospective referral sources to lunch, write a column for a local newspaper, and distribute a newsletter. Newsletters educate your audience and address problems they may encounter which would lead them to make a referral to you.

Specific Techniques and Tactics

Deciding how large you want your practice to become and how you will attract new clients can be part of your practice plan. By making your goals as concrete, achievable, and measurable as possible, you can devise specific interventions to meet each goal. The American Psychological Association Practice Directorate, along with Coopers & Lybrand, L.L.P., have developed the *Practitioner's Toolbox Series* (1996), in particular the volume entitled *Marketing Your Practice,* to aid in your goal-setting and intervention planning. *Marketing Your Practice* is a guidebook for developing a marketing program for your practice. Communicating your message to potential referrals and referral sources occurs through personal and nonpersonal communication. A marketing checklist is provided by *Psychotherapy Finances* (1999). Examples of personal communication channels include promotional tools (e.g., sending letters to referral sources, exhibiting at health fairs and trade shows, and providing demonstrations of your work); public relations (e.g., speeches, seminars, charitable donations, sponsorships, publications, health and wellness events, articles in magazines and newspapers); and personal contact (e.g., word of mouth, educational presentations). Advertising tools such as newspaper ads, brochures, educational booklets, leaflets, directories, symbols, and logos are examples of nonpersonal communication. Utilizing these tools can help bring new referrals into your practice as you develop a reputation in your community.

Financials

Start-Up Costs

When considering opening your own office, you need to develop a budget for expenses and income. Initial costs can be substantial. Consider the costs of renting office space; if you rent space for yourself, you may be faced with security deposits and decorating costs. Purchasing furniture, computer systems, office equipment (e.g., fax, copier, telephone systems), and office supplies all contribute to your initial cash needs. Promotional activities are necessary during the start-up phase of a practice, entailing costs for business cards, brochures, Web sites, and Yellow Pages ads. Engaging an accountant and an attorney in the initial stages is also critical, and paying them to develop billing and accounting systems and contracts and policies must be added to the mix. Considering all these costs, you may decide to ease into practice slowly, using strategies already described in this chapter. If you are ready to take the risk, you will need to find capital.

Sources of Capital

The first place to look for capital is in your own savings and investment accounts. How much of your own money are you willing to invest in your business? Are you willing to look to your relatives to help you out? If you still cannot gather the necessary funds to start your practice, you will need to look for other sources of capital. Contacting a banker is a good place to start. If you own a home, you may be able to obtain a home equity line of credit that can help fund your practice. Using credit cards may be too expensive as a primary funding source. After reviewing possible funding sources, you may decide that sharing the risk with a colleague and going into partnership may be your best choice.

Financial Management

Developing a sound financial management system for handling income and expenses is fundamental to good business. Poor planning in this area can lead to cash shortages or trouble with the IRS. The advice of an accountant whom you know and trust is essential in setting up your financial system. Yenney (1994) suggested that your accounting system provide: (1) a daily listing of all clients and charges for services to them; (2) a daily listing of all receipts (cash, checks, and credit card charges); (3) a daily update of accounts receivable including aging (aging of accounts receivable tells you how long the bill has been outstanding, and it is usually reported in 30-, 60-, 90-, 120-, and over 120-day increments); (4) all bank deposits and transactions; (5) a daily balance; (6) an individual record of each client's charges and payments; (7) a listing of all expenses aggregated into appropriate categories. All this information is used to provide monthly income and expense statements. With this system, you can set up realistic budgets and engage in appropriate financial planning.

Billing and accounting software programs are available. "Shrink" is a billing program marketed by Multi-Health Systems, Inc. (North Tonawanda, NY). "Therapist's Helper" is another billing program. There are many others. The *APA Monitor,* the monthly newsletter of the APA, is filled with advertisements for billing programs. Accounting software is also available. "QuickBooks" by Intuit is a simple accounting program designed for small businesses. Your accountant will probably have a favorite accounting software program; I recommend that you take your accountant's recommendation, to assure compatibility.

When budgeting, all your practice income may be considered professional income. You may, however, want to break your income down into categories that help you track where your money is coming from. For example, in our practice we break income down by office location and type of service. It is thus possible to determine, at a glance, how much psychological testing is being done, how much inpatient work is being delivered, and which offices are generating the most income. Expenses are divided into categories as well. Office expenses including rent, telephone, supplies, office wages, and utilities are lumped together for each office. One office is our "main" office and the others are considered satellites; there are some expenses for our main office not duplicated for our satellites. Insurance is in one category, as are transportation, professional development, clinical salaries, and discounts. A good financial management system will give you a snapshot at any time of where you are financially.

Yenney (1994) suggested that you complete a financial checkup to see if you are operating effectively. She listed five steps. The first is to calculate the total charges for each of the past three years, compare them with your total receipts for each period, and determine your collection ratio. This will help you see whether your collections are adequate and can help you decide what to do to increase your collections. Secondly, review your accounts receivable. Use a monthly average of the amount of money outstanding or use actual data if you have it. By these means you can figure out ways to increase your income. Third, review all your expenses. Try to keep your overhead within 25 percent to 35 percent of your revenue.

The fourth step is to review your adjustment rate. This is determined by looking at all the discounts and writeoffs you have given. In a managed care environment, this number may be quite large and may even threaten the viability of your practice. You may need to reduce the adjustments you make in your fees. Finally, compute your net income before taxes. Do you see a positive or negative trend? As a result of this checkup, you may make changes to your financial plan.

Conclusion

This chapter has been designed to bring to your attention issues that you will face when you open a practice. When you open an office, you are starting a business, and so you must think as a businessperson. A good businessperson develops a business plan; the rudiments of a good business plan have been included here. It is not possible to be exhaustive in the space available, but an attempt has been made to lead you to resources that can aid in the business planning process.

Operating a private practice can be a rewarding experience professionally, personally, and financially if you take the time to think through what you want to do and develop a sound plan for accomplishing it.

REFERENCES

Ackley, D. (1997). *Breaking free of managed care.* New York: Guilford Press.

American Professional Agency (1998). Walking the documentation tightrope. *Insight* (2nd Edition). Amityville, NY: Author.

American Psychological Association, & Coopers & Lybrand, L.L.P. (1996). *Marketing your practice.* APA Practitioner's Toolbox Series. Washington, DC: American Psychological Association.

Graham, A. R. (1996). Developing a clinical policy and procedure manual for an outpatient practice. In C. E. Stout, G. A. Theis, & J. M. Oher (Eds.), *The complete guide to managed behavioral healthcare* (pp. I.A.3–I.A.8). New York: John Wiley & Sons.

Graham, A. R. (1996). Clinical documentation in an outpatient setting. In C. E. Stout, G. A. Theis, & J. M. Oher (Eds.), *The complete guide to managed behavioral healthcare* (pp. I.B.1–I.B.13). New York: John Wiley & Sons.

Heller, K. M. (1997). *Strategic marketing.* Sarasota, FL: Professional Resource Press.

Jongsma, Jr., A. E., Peterson, L. M., & McInnis, W. P. (1996). *The child and adolescent psychotherapy treatment planner.* New York: John Wiley & Sons.

Lundeen, E., & Geiger, L. (1999). Thoughts on succeeding in private practice. *The Independent Practitioner, 19,* 18–20.

Managed care: Heavy-duty rate cuts finally hit the East Coast. (1999). *Psychotherapy Finances, 24,* 1–2.

Marketing: Here's a set of checklists to aid your marketing efforts. (1999). *Psychotherapy Finances, 25,* 3–4.

Marketing: Two solid marketing strategies any therapist can try. (1999). *Psychotherapy Finances, 24,* 3–4.

Office of Managed Care, CMHS, SAMHSA. (1998). Insurance benefits: The costs and effects of parity for mental health and substance abuse insurance benefits (DHHS Publication No. SMA 98-3205). Washington, DC: Government Printing Office.

Shalala, D. E. (1999). Mental Health: A report of the Surgeon General. Washington, DC: Government Printing Office (available online at http://www.surgeongeneral.gov).

Welch, B. (1998). Safeguarding psychologists against liability risk. *Insight, 2,* 1–2.

Yenney, S. (1994). *Business strategies for a caring profession: A practitioner's handbook.* Washington, DC: American Psychological Association.

FOR FURTHER READING

Ackley, D. (1997). *Breaking free of managed care.* New York: Guilford Press.

Dr. Dana Ackley, a psychologist in Virginia, writes about how to provide psychological services to business as part of a strategy for building a fee-for-service practice.

Beckwith, H. (1997). *Selling the invisible: A field guide to modern marketing.* New York: Warner.

This easy-to-read book is helpful in developing your marketing strategies. Beckwith distinguishes between selling a product and selling a service.

Graham, A. R. (1996). Clinical documentation in an outpatient setting. In C. E. Stout, G. A. Theis, & J. M. Oher (Eds.), *The complete guide to managed behavioral healthcare* (pp. I.B.1–I.B.13). New York: John Wiley & Sons.

A further description of the forms used in a client chart and samples of those forms can be found here.

Heller, K. M. (1997). *Strategic marketing.* Sarasota, FL: Professional Resource Press.

Kalman Heller is a psychologist who manages and owns a group practice in the Boston area. His book can serve as an effective guidebook.

Insight.

Available from the Editor, 82 Hopmeadow St., Simbury, CT. 06070-7683. Each edition covers different professional topics for therapists.

Kolt, L. (1999). How to build a thriving fee-for-service practice: Integrating the healing side with the business side of psychotherapy. New York: Academic Press.

New on the market. Ms. Kolt is also a psychologist who has made practice work.

Psychotherapy Finances. Ridgewood Financial Institute, Inc. Juno Beach, FL.

A monthly newsletter with invaluable information about the psychotherapy marketplace, with practical ideas on practice building.

Yenney, S. (1994). *Business strategies for a caring profession: A practitioner's handbook.* Washington, DC: American Psychological Association.

The American Psychological Association's attempt to address business strategies in opening and building a practice; excellent.

APPENDIX 14.A
Sample Patient Forms

1. Patient Referral Form
2. Insurance Form
3. Consent for Release of Information Form
4. Treatment Contract
5. Superbill
6. Child Information Form
7. Adult Information Form

PATIENT REFERRAL DATA

REFERRAL FOR: ______________________________ OFFICE: DP CL NB

DATE: ___/___/___ TIME: ___:___ RELATIONSHIP TO PATIENT: ____________

NAME: ____

PT NAME: ______________________________ D.O.B. ___/___/___ AGE: ____

PHONE H: ____/____-______ PHONE W: ____/____-______

REFERRAL SOURCE: ____________________________ PHONE: ____/____-______

INSURED'S SOCIAL SECURITY NUMBER _____-_____-_____

REASON FOR REFERRAL

PLEASE ADVISE PATIENT TO NOTIFY CASE MANAGER THAT APPT IS SCHEDULED

INSURANCE COMPANY: ______________________________

COPAYMENT: $_____._____ EMPLOYER: ______________________________

QUOTE ALL FEES TO THE PATIENT, IF THEY DON'T HAVE MANAGED CARE.

DIAGNOSTIC INTERVIEW PRIOR TO TESTING $XXX.XX

INTERMEDIATE DIAGNOSTIC INTERVIEW $_____._____

EXPLAIN THAT THE THERAPIST WILL DETERMINE WHICH FEE WILL BE CHARGED FOR THE FIRST VISIT BASED ON THE TIME SPENT

(PATIENT AGREES TO PAY AT FIRST VISIT: FULL ½ $___________)

INDIVIDUAL THERAPY ____________________ FAMILY THERAPY ____________________

GROUP THERAPY ____________________ PSYCHOLOGICAL TESTING—PER TEST

FIRST APPOINTMENT OFFERED: DATE: ___/___/___ TIME: ___:___

APPOINTMENT SCHEDULED: DATE: ___/___/___ TIME: ___:___

WITH: ____ (THERAPIST)

ACP Consultants

2604 EAST DEMPSTER, SUITE 407 DES PLAINES, IL 60016

847/ 824-1235

FEIN: 36-3419655 STATE LIC #: 060-004314

INSURANCE INFORMATION FORM

Please fill in the portion below OR attach a copy of your insurance card. We will copy your card in the box below. Please be sure to SIGN BELOW.

PATIENT NAME ____________________

INSURANCE COMPANY ____________________

INSURANCE ADDRESS ____________________

INSURANCE COMPANY PHONE # ____/____-______

GROUP # ____________________ POLICY # ____________________

INSURED'S SOCIAL SECURITY # _____-_____-_____

NAME OF INSURED ____________________

EMPLOYER OF INSURED ____________________

EMPLOYER'S ADDRESS ____________________

ATTACH INSURANCE CARD HERE

DOES YOUR INSURANCE REQUIRE AUTHORIZATION FOR THIS VISIT?

Y or N (circle one)

IF YES, WHAT IS THE AUTHORIZATION NUMBER?

____

I/WE AUTHORIZE THE RELEASE OF ANY INFORMATION NECESSARY TO PROCESS THIS CLAIM. I/WE ALSO AUTHORIZE THE PAYMENT OF BENEFITS DIRECTLY TO THE ABOVE NAMED SUPPLIER WHO ACCEPTS ASSIGNMENT. IT IS UNDERSTOOD THAT THE UNDERSIGNED HAS THE RESPONSIBILITY FOR PAYMENT OF SERVICES. ASSIGNMENT OF BENEFITS DOES NOT RELEASE THE UNDERSIGNED FROM RESPONSIBILITY FOR PAYMENT.

SIGNED ____________________ DATE: ___/___/___

(INSURED PERSON AND/OR PATIENT)

ADDRESS ____________________

TELEPHONE ____/____-______

SIGNED ____________________ DATE: ___/___/___

(PATIENT—IF AGE 12 OR OLDER)

CONSENT FOR RELEASE OF INFORMATION FORM

NAME OF PATIENT: ____

DATE OF BIRTH: ___/___/___ AGE: ____

ADDRESS: ____

I/WE HEREBY AUTHORIZE: **ACP Consultants**

TO RELEASE TO/REQUEST FROM:

ADDRESS:

PHONE:

THE FOLLOWING INFORMATION FOR THE PURPOSES OF TREATMENT PLANNING

__________ HEALTH/MEDICAL RECORDS

__________ EDUCATIONAL RECORDS

__________ CONSULTATION WITH CLERGY

__________ SOCIAL HISTORY

__________ PSYCHIATRIC EVALUATIONS

__________ NEUROPSYCHOLOGICAL EVALUATIONS

__________ PSYCHOLOGICAL ASSESSMENTS AND DIAGNOSIS

__________ PRIOR TREATMENT RECORDS AND REPORTS

__________ OTHER (PLEASE SPECIFY)

I/WE UNDERSTAND THAT I/WE HAVE THE RIGHT TO INSPECT AND COPY THE INFORMATION TO BE DISCLOSED. I/WE UNDERSTAND THAT I/WE MAY REFUSE TO CONSENT TO DISCLOSURE PRIOR TO THE INFORMATION BEING SENT. I/WE UNDERSTAND THAT INFORMATION MAY BE TRANSMITTED VIA TELEPHONE, MAIL OR FACSIMILE.

I/WE HAVE READ THE ABOVE AND HAVE HAD THE OPPORTUNITY TO ASK QUESTIONS CONCERNING THIS CONSENT, **INCLUDING THE CONSEQUENCES, IF ANY,** OF REFUSAL TO CONSENT. THIS CONSENT IS VALID FOR SIX MONTHS FROM THE DATE IT IS SIGNED.

______________________________ DATE ___/___/___

PATIENT SIGNATURE
AGE 12 AND OLDER MUST SIGN

______________________________ ______________________________

PARENT/GUARDIAN WITNESS

THIS RELEASE EXPIRES SIX MONTHS FROM DATE SIGNED

TREATMENT CONTRACT

PATIENT NAME: ____

You have requested professional services from a member of our clinical staff and have received a copy of the Mutual Expectations Letter. This letter sets forth the agreement concerning our understanding of such services. This agreement shall become effective upon our receipt of a counter-signed copy of this letter.

1. You understand that these services involve evaluation and therapy, and that whatever services are provided will be by mutual agreement between you and the therapist.
2. If you participate in whatever services are recommended by your therapist, you agree to pay for these professional services according to the fee schedule you have received.
3. We will charge you on the basis of time expended, and we reserve the right to terminate the doctor–patient relationship for non-payment. Any payments received from third parties will be credited to your account; however, you are primarily responsible for the payment of the monthly statements.
4. You will be charged the full fee for late cancellations and missed appointments. The fee for our written reports will be $XX per 15 minutes. A $XX service charge will be applied for checks returned from your bank for any reason. If two or more checks are returned, we will no longer accept checks and you will be asked to pay cash.
5. Please be reminded that the Patient Accounts Manager will arrange a fee payment schedule, upon your request if the need for such arrangements can be established.
6. We reserve the right to designate the performance of professional services to our associate(s) if it becomes necessary in order to provide appropriate care.
7. In the event that it becomes necessary to utilize the courts to collect any unpaid balance, you agree to pay reasonable attorneys' fees and any and all court costs which may be incurred by us in connection therewith.

Please counter-sign this agreement and return it to us so that we will have a mutual memorandum of our understanding.

Very truly yours,
ASSOCIATED CLINICAL PSYCHOLOGISTS, LTD

FEE SCHEDULE AND MUTUAL EXPECTATIONS GIVEN, UNDERSTOOD AND APPROVED:

____ DATE ___/___/___

WITNESSED ______________________________________

ACP CONSULTANTS
2604 E. Dempster Street, Suite 407
Des Plaines, Illinois 60016
847/824–1235

FEDERAL ID # OFFICE: DP ______ CL ______ NB______

STATE LICENSE #

BC/BS PROVIDER #

MEDICARE #

DATE OF SERVICE: ___/___/___

REFERRING M.D.: ____________________

PROFESSIONAL SERVICES RENDERED TO: ____________________

PATIENT #: ____________________

ICD-9-CM DIAGNOSIS: AXIS I: ____________________ AXIS II: ____________________

CPT CODE	SERVICE		FEE
90801	DIAGNOSTIC INTERVIEW	50 MINUTES	______
90801-22	DIAGNOSTIC INTERVIEW	TIME: ______	______
90808	PSYCHOTHERAPY	TIME: ______	______
90806	PSYCHOTHERAPY	45–50 MIN.	______
90804	PSYCHOTHERAPY	25 MINUTES	______
90847	FAMILY THERAPY	45–50 MIN.	______
90847-22	FAMILY THERAPY	TIME: ______	______
90853	GROUP PSYCHOTHERAPY		______
00000	____________________		______

COPAY: ____________________

PAID: $ ____________________ CASH

CHECK #: ______________ TOTAL ______________

____________________ YOUR NEXT APPOINTMENT

DATE: ____________________

____________________ TIME: ____________________

LICENSED CLINICAL PSYCHOLOGIST

PAYMENT IS REQUESTED AT TIME OF SERVICE

ACP Consultants
Child Information Form

Date: ____________________

Patient's Name: ____

Patient's Address: ____

Patient's City: ____________________ State: ____________ Zip: __________

Home Phone #: ____________________ Date of Birth: ___/___/___ Age: ________

Name of School: ____________________ Grade: ______ Male: _____ Female: _____

Referred By: ________________________________ Phone #: ______________

Name Of Physician: ____________________ Physician Phone #: ______________

Medication Allergies: ____

Emergency Contact: ____

Relationship: ____________________________ Contact Phone: ______________

Brothers and Sisters:

Name: ______________________ Age: ________ School Name: ______________

Name: ______________________ Age: ________ School Name: ______________

Name: ______________________ Age: ________ School Name: ______________

Person Responsible for Account: (person who signed the treatment contract)

Name: ____

Billing Address: ____

Billing City: ________________________________ State: ________ Zip: ________

Billing Phone: ______________ Employer: ______________________________

Work Address: ____

Work City: ________________________________ State: ________ Zip: ________

Work Phone #: __________________ Driver's License #: ______________________

Next-of-Kin Information

Mother's Name: ______________________ Occupation: ______________________

Home Phone: __________________ Work Phone: ______________ Age: ________

Address (if different than patient): ________________________________

City: ______________ State: ________ Zip: ________ SS#: ______________

Father's Name: ______________________ Occupation: ______________________

Home Phone: __________________ Work Phone: ______________ Age: ________

Address (if different than patient): ________________________________

City: ______________ State: ________ Zip: ________ SS#: ______________

ACP Consultants
Adult Information Form

Date: ____________________

Patient's Name: ____________________

Patient's Address: ____________________

Patient's City: ____________________ State: __________ Zip: __________

Home Phone #: ____________________ Date of Birth: ___/___/___ Age: ________

SS#: _____-_____-_____ Driver's License #: _____-_____-_____ Male: ____ Female: ____

Referred By: ____________________ Phone #: ____________________

Name Of Physician: ____________________ Physician Phone #: ____________________

Medication Allergies: ____________________

Patient's Employer: ____________________ Phone #: ____________________

Work Address: ____________________

Work City: ____________________ State: ________ Zip: ________

Occupation: ____________________ Education: ____________________

Emergency Contact: ____________________ Relationship: ____________________

Contact Phone: ____________________ Marital Status: ____________________

Name of Spouse: ____________________

Spouse Employed by: ____________________ Occupation: ____________________

Spouse's Work Address: ____________________

Spouse's Work City: ____________________ State: ________ Zip: ________

Spouse's Work Phone #: ____________________

Children:

Name: ____________________ Age: ________ School Name: ____________________

Name: ____________________ Age: ________ School Name: ____________________

Name: ____________________ Age: ________ School Name: ____________________

Name: ____________________ Age: ________ School Name: ____________________

APPENDIX 14.B

Glossary Of Managed Care Terms

alternate delivery systems Health services provided in other than an inpatient, acute-care hospital, such as partial hospitalization programs, intensive outpatient programs.

Administrative Services Only (ASO) A relationship in which an insurance company or other management organization performs administrative services only, such as billing, practice management, marketing, etc., and does not assume any risk on behalf of a self-funded plan or group of providers.

capitation A method for payment to providers in which the provider is paid per procedure. Capitation involves a set amount paid per month to the provider per covered member (per member per month, PMPM). The provider is then responsible for providing all contracted services (such as behavioral health) required by members of the specified group during that month for a set fee, regardless of the amount of charges incurred.

carve-outs A strategy in which a payer such as an employer in a self-funded plan, insurance company, or HMO separates ("carves out") a portion of a benefit (such as behavioral health) and hires a managed behavioral health program to provide these benefits.

case rate Flat fee paid for a client's episode of care. For this fee the provider covers all of the services the client requires for treatment of their condition. Case rates may be negotiated for specific services only, such as outpatient services.

closed panel A provider network in which only a specific limited number of providers will be reimbursed for provision of services to the health plan's members.

concurrent review A review during the course of a patient's treatment to determine if continued treatment is medically necessary.

direct contracting Providing health services to members of a health plan by a group of providers contracting directly with an employer.

discounted fee-for-service An agreed-upon rate for service between the provider and payer that is usually less than the provider's full fee. This may be a fixed amount per service, or a percentage discount. Providers generally accept such contracts because they represent a means to increase their volume or reduce their chances of losing volume.

Exclusive Provider Organization (EPO) A type of provider organization similar to an HMO. These organizations are exclusive because the member must remain within the network to receive benefits.

Employee Retirement Income Security Act of 1974 (ERISA) This act, also called the Pension Reform Act, regulates the majority of private pension and welfare group benefit plans in the United States. ERISA also exempts most large self-funded benefit plans, which include health plans, from state regulation.

fee-for-service A method of billing by health providers whereby the patient is billed a fee for each service performed. Reimbursement comes from the patient or from a third party payer such as an insurer.

fee schedule A listing of fees for specified medical or health procedures, which usually represents the maximum amounts a plan will pay for specified procedures.

gatekeeper An individual or organization who controls the access to healthcare services for members of a health plan.

HCFA 1500 The standard form for submitting physician service claims to third party (insurance) companies, created by the Health Care Finance Administration.

Health Maintenance Organization (HMO) An HMO is a health plan organization that provides health care to its members for a preset amount of money on a PMPM (per member per month) basis. Most HMOs utilize PCPs (primary care physicians) as gatekeepers, and members are usually limited to a closed panel of providers. Some providers to the HMO share financial risk with the HMO.

Integrated Delivery System (IDS) A legal entity that is able to negotiate with the marketplace. All health care services are provided under the same legal umbrella. In its most integrated form, even the insurance or financing function is included.

indemnity health insurance A traditional health insurance plan with little or no benefit management, a fee-for-service reimbursement model, and few restrictions on provider selection.

Independent Physician Association or Independent Practice Association (IPA) Organizations that contract with groups of providers for the provision of health care services. Each provider agrees to see patients/clients from health plans who contract with the IPA. Such IPAs often contract with many HMOs and health plans.

Managed Behavioral Health Organization (MBHO) An organization that assumes the responsibility for managing the behavioral health benefit for an employer or payer organization under a "carve-out" arrangement. Management of benefit may range from management services to the actual provision of the services through MBHO's own organization or provider network. Reimbursement may be on a fee-for-service, shared-risk, or full-risk basis. Also called a Managed Care Organization or MCO, though this is a specialty MCO.

Managed Health Care or Managed Care Organization (MCO) Administrative systems created to control the cost of health care. Financial incentives, utilization review, and management controls are mechanisms used to provide cost-effective treatment.

medically necessary This is the standard that most MBHOs use to determine whether they will authorize payment for services. Medical necessity is diagnostically and functionally defined. For services provided for a clinical psychiatric condition to be considered medically necessary, there must be evidence of a psychiatric illness based on symptoms, a level of clinical instability, and a degree of functional impairment such that the patient's ability to self-care, perform activities of daily living, and maintain interpersonal relationships and vocation or educational activities are compromised. Medically necessary services must be provided at the most appropriate level of service that can reasonably considered safe for the patient.

Management Services Organization (MSO) An organization designed to provide business-related services such as marketing, contract negotiation, and data collection to a group of providers like an IPA or PHO.

member Any person eligible, as either a subscriber or a dependent, in an employee benefit plan.

network model A health plan that contracts with multiple provider groups or other independent providers to deliver health care to members.

Primary Care Physician (PCP) A Primary Care Physician is a family practitioner, general internist, pediatrician, or sometimes ob/gyn who supervises, coordinates, and provides medical care to members of a plan. Some PCPs may initiate all referrals for specialty care.

Physician–Hospital Organization or Provider–Hospital Organization (PHO) An arrangement among physicians, providers and hospital(s) wherein a single organization, the PHO, agrees to contract to provide services to insurers' members.

Preferred Provider Organization (PPO) Physicians, dentists, hospitals and other practitioners contract with a payer to provide members with services at discounted fee-for-service rates. The member may see a provider outside of the network but pays a higher fee or copayment.

Point-of-Service (POS) Plan In a POS benefit plan the member can choose to use a non-participating provider at a reduced coverage level and with more out-of-pocket cost although the plan encourages the use of network providers.

pre-certification Authorization required by some payers prior to provision of services in order for health benefit payments to be paid.

self-funded health plans An employer or group of employers provides for the reimbursement of medical expenses incurred by its employees and dependents. In such instances, the employer assumes all the financial risk.

self-insurance Group insurance with benefits financed entirely by the policyholder, usually large employers, rather than purchasing coverage from commercial carriers. Self-insured and self-funded plans are exempt from state insurance laws under ERISA.

sub-capitation When an organization being paid under a capitated system contracts with other providers and shares a portion of the original capitated premium.

Third-Party Administrator (TPA) A professional firm usually contracted by self-insured plans to provide such administrative services as paying claims, collecting premiums, and carrying out other administrative support services for employee benefit plans.

treatment episode Period from the start of treatment in a specific modality, such as outpatient services, to the end of such treatment.

CHAPTER

15 Consultation in Mental Health Settings

A Culturally Sensitive, Eclectic Approach

DUANE BROWN

Consultation is often used colloquially as a euphemism for advice giving. However, consultation in the mental heath professions is a far more complex process than the mere dispensation of information, although advice giving is often part of the consultation process. Consultation is at times confused with *supervision,* perhaps because some authoritative publications lump supervision and consultation together as strategies that can be used by mental health professionals to enhance their skills (e.g., Poindexter, Valentine, & Conway, 1999). However, equating consultation and supervision is an inaccurate representation of both processes. Unlike consultation, supervision involves a superordinate–subordinate relationship between two persons, the supervisor and the supervisee. Supervision and consultation do have a common goal, the improvement of the functioning of supervisees and consultees, but they cannot be viewed as interchangeable.

Further, some people use *consultation* and *teaching* interchangeably. Consultants may indeed teach, but to be effective the relationship that develops during the consultation process must be far different from the relationships between most teachers and their pupils. Additionally, teachers set the agenda for their classes. The educational agenda in consultation grows out of the interaction between the consultant, consultee, and a client.

Conversely, psychotherapy and consultation are rarely confused even though they share some common elements. Perhaps the most important of these commonalities is that both psychotherapy and consultation are aimed at delivering mental health services to clients. Consultation is not simply advice giving, supervision, teaching, or therapy, but does share common processes and goals with all of these processes. What then *is* consultation, and what are the factors that have shaped consultation as it is currently practiced?

Many factors have shaped consultation as it is currently practiced in mental health settings. However, Gerald Caplan's pioneering work (1970), which began in Israel after World War II, stands out as the contribution that has had the greatest impact. Mental health practitioners were overwhelmed by the wave of refugees that flowed into Israel at the end of the war. Caplan hit on the idea of using consultation as a tool to extend his services and those of other mental health professionals so that the needs of the refugees could be met. Consequently, he consulted with professionals such as nurses and teachers, who had little training in the delivery of mental health services, to enable them to provide these services to children and adults. After Caplan completed his work in Israel, he continued to develop the idea that mental health professionals can serve clients indirectly through consultation. In 1970 he set forth his ideas about his psychoanalytically based approach to consultation in his classic book, *The Theory and Practice of Mental Health Consultation.* Caplan indicated that mental health consultation is an indirect, triadic process engaged in by a consultant who has specialized training in the delivery of mental heath services, and by consultees who are professional caregivers, for the purpose of improving the mental health of a third person, the client. Further, Caplan specified that in order for mental health consultation to be successful the consultant must come from outside the consultee's organization and the relationship between the consultant and consultee must be coordinate, that is, a relationship between equals. Caplan also stipulated that mental health consultation is divided into four subcategories, each with its own specific focus.

The four subcategories of mental health consultation identified by Caplan are client-centered case consultation, consultee-centered case consultation, program-centered administrative consultation, and consultee-centered administrative consultation.

In client-centered case consultation the focus is on the delivery of mental health services to a specific client or group of similar clients. For example, a mental health professional with a specialty in substance abuse might consult with teachers in an alternative school to increase their sensitivity to the issues involved in withdrawal from drugs and to prepare them to assist students to develop the skills they need to avoid relapse.

Consultee-centered case consultation focuses on helping consultees remediate deficiencies that contribute to their inability to assist clients. Caplan indicated that the deficiencies typically experienced by consultees are categorized as lack of knowledge, lack of skill, lack of confidence, and lack of objectivity. Lack of objectivity often results when the relationship between professionals and clients changes from professional to personal. For example, nurses who become friends with their patients may lack objectivity. Lack of objectivity may also result from simple identification with the client, according to Caplan. Professionals who once experienced an intense rivalry with an older sibling may not be objective when their clients are experiencing the same dilemma. Transference, the third reason for lack of objectivity, occurs when a consultee repeatedly ascribes certain patterns of behavior or attitudes to a particular type of client because of his or her own unresolved conflicts. Also, lack of objectivity may result if the consultee has a characterological disorder. Caplan (1970) believed that this is the most serious condition that results in lack of objectivity because there is a portion of the consultee's personality that interferes with his or her ability to function with some clients. Theme interference is the most frequent cause of lack of objectivity according to Caplan. Theme interference manifests in faulty decision making regarding certain clients. For example, a professional may conclude that a certain group of clients is untreatable, in the face of evidence to the contrary. However, a consultee's faulty decision making must be ascertained on the basis of how clients are treated, rather than on her or his verbal behavior. That is, the consultee may be less enthusiastic about the treatment of certain clients and may engage in half-hearted efforts on their behalf. The consultee is unconsciously predicting that no matter what he or she does, the client will not do well.

Program-centered administrative consultation focuses on the improvement of an existing program or the design of a new one. As was the case in client-centered case consultation, here the consultant is viewed as an expert who can "diagnose" the problem and assist the program administrator to make changes in the existing program or design an effective new program.

The purpose of consultee-centered administrative consultation is to improve the functioning of the administrator. Caplan recommended that the consultant engaged in this type of consultation should be employed on a long-term basis and should have relatively unrestricted access to the organization.

Although Caplan's ideas about consultation (Caplan, 1970; Caplan & Caplan, 1993) have been influential, many consultants in mental health settings have adopted other approaches because of disagreements with Caplan's underlying theory and assumptions. For example, Gallessich (1982) took exception to Caplan's belief that theme interference is the major factor that interferes with consultee–client interactions. Bergan (1977) set forth an entire theory of consultation based largely on operant learning theory, which was later restated (Bergan & Kratochwill, 1990) to include somewhat more emphasis on cognitions, has little, if any, similarity to Caplan's ideas. Brown, Pryzwansky, and Schulte (2001) also disagreed with several of Caplan's ideas, including his assumption that consultants must come from outside consultees' organizations and that consultation can occur only with professional consultees. In fact, many consultants in mental health organizations consult with paraprofessionals, parents, and other nonprofessionals. Brown, Pryzwansky, and Schulte (1998) agreed with Caplan's assumption that the consultee–consultant relationship should be collegial, and recommended that consultants who are engaged in consultee–centered, client-centered cases, or consultee-centered administrative consultation, incorporate Caplan's taxonomy of consultee problems—lack of knowledge, lack of skill, lack of self-confidence, and lack of objectivity—into their diagnostic system. However, the eclectic model they presented took a different view of the bases for lack of objectivity than Caplan's (1970). Factors such as transference and theme interference undoubtedly play a role in consultee–client relationships although there are other ways to conceptualize them. However, biases and prejudices regarding gender, race, and ethnicity that are routinely inculcated into people in our society are more likely to be contributors to lack of objectivity than the sources identified by Caplan (Brown et al., 2001).

The remainder of this chapter will be devoted to discussing an approach to consultation that has direct application in mental health settings. It, like most approaches to consultation, has some discernible links to Caplan's ideas about mental health consultation. However, the approach set forth here borrows from systems theory, social learning theory, values theory, and multicultural psychology for its framework, as well as Caplan's theory. In the next section each of these areas will be discussed briefly. Because of space limitations, the focus of the discussion that follows will be largely on what Caplan termed client-centered and consultee-centered case consultation, one major difference being that the approach outlined in this chapter is culturally sensitive. Also, Caplan's assumption that there is a dichotomy between client-centered and consultee-centered case consultation is viewed as faulty. Most consultation engaged in by mental health professionals has the twin foci of improving the treatment received by clients and improving the ability of consultees to deliver mental health services in the future; thus they are engaged in consultee-centered and client-centered case consultation simultaneously. Further, it is viewed as inappropriate and unethical to engage in activities that improve a consultee's functioning in areas other than those directly related to work with the consultee. Consultation is a triadic process entered into by the consultant, consultee, and ultimately the client, with the primary purpose of improving the mental health of the client and with the secondary intention that the consultee will be better able to deliver mental health services to the client and to similar clients in the future. Consultation should not begin until the consultant and consultee have explicitly contracted to proceed toward these goals. Any deviation from these twin foci, such as providing counseling or psychotherapy to the consultee, requires either that the contract be renegotiated and/or that consultation be terminated to avoid the resulting dual relationship.

The Model

As noted above, the eclectic model of consultation presented here has a number of precursors, including Caplan's work. In this section these precursors will be discussed in more detail.

Caplan's assumption that the consulting relationship must be coordinate has been adopted for the model presented here with one difference. A coordinate relationship is a relationship between equals. Consultees typically engage consultants because they are perceived to have knowledge or skills that are needed in the treatment of clients. Consultants almost always have expert power. However, the ultimate power in the consulting relationship rests with the consultee because they can accept or reject the recommendations made by the consultant. In the model presented here, in accordance with Caplan, the consultee is fully responsible for delivering the intervention. The consultant's role is to help the consultee assess the clients' problem, assess their own knowledge and ability to deal with the problem, help the consultee to identify objectivity issues that are interfering with their treatment of their client, remediate deficiencies, identify treatment approaches, teach or arrange to have taught the knowledge and skills needed to deal with the client, monitor the intervention process, and assist consultees in evaluating the outcomes of their interventions.

This model is unlike the expert model of consultation often practiced in the medical profession, in which one physician refers a patient for treatment to a specialist who not only diagnoses the patient's problem but administers the treatment. The problem with the medical expert model is that the consultee (the referring physician) gains little in the way of additional expertise in the treatment of his or her patient's problem. Further, in situations in which the consultant is from outside the consultee's organization, the consultant must rely extensively on the consultee for much of the information needed in the consultation. The consultant is not *precluded* from gathering information about the school, hospital, mental health center, or drug and alcohol treatment facility in this model, but the reality of many consulting situations is that this is not possible. Therefore, a consulting relationship must be established that is based on mutual respect and trust so that authentic communication will result.

The exception to Caplan's assumption about the collegial nature of the consulting relationship occurs in cross-cultural consultation. Consultees from some cultures hold a collective-lineal social relationship value and *insist* on placing mental health professionals in a superordinate position (Sue & Sue, 1999). In these cases consultants must accept the status accorded them or run the risk of alienating their consultees. This issue of the role of cultural values in consultation will be taken up in more detail later.

The model presented here is consistent with Brown et al.'s assumption (2001) that the problems experienced by consultees can be classified into lack of knowledge, lack of skill, lack of self-confidence, and lack of objectivity. As noted earlier, it is assumed that one major source of lack of objectivity is bias or prejudice and, as Caplan stated (1970), a consultee's psychological problems may also result in lack of objectivity.

An open system, according to systems theory, is an organization or group established for the purpose of producing some product. It is differentiated from its environments by certain boundaries that have various degrees of permeability. For example, a private hospital has a carefully defined set of boundaries and the people who influence the functioning of the hospital are easily identified. People who come into the hospital do so through prescribed channels, and their behavior is carefully regulated. In some instances insiders and outsiders are identified through the use of uniforms or other forms of identification. On the other hand, the boundaries of schools are highly permeable. Many members of the community have access to decision-makers and ready access to faculty members and administrators, and the overall functioning of a school is often disrupted by governmental interventions.

Systems have norms, values, reward strategies, and patterns of communication. People in systems are interdependent and have a tendency to differentiate their roles. For example, organizations typically have six subsystems: managerial, goals, values, structure, psychosocial, and technology. The purpose of each of these subsystems is as follows:

- Managerial—provides leadership to the system, sets policies, and makes decisions. Typically there is a formal and an informal dimension to the managerial subsystem.
- Goals—relates to the "products" produced by the system. Families usually expect to produce certain types of children and schools hope to graduate students with a certain level of knowledge. A hospital that decides to add a drug and alcohol treatment center has altered its goals subsystem. The products produced by mental health organizations are typically related to clients.
- Values—associated with the manner in which the system meets the needs of people in the system. Some systems are more oriented toward producing products while others are devoted to meeting the needs of the people in the system.
- Structure—pertains to the control of behavior within the system and includes policies, rules, and reward strategies.
- Psychosocial—comprises the beliefs and perceptions of people in the system about the systems and their behavior in it. The beliefs and emotions of the people in the system interact to form the culture of the system.
- Technology—involves the use of technological devices such as computers to increase the effectiveness and efficiency of the system.

Just as systems have boundaries, roles within systems have boundaries with varying degrees of permeability. For example, in some families the roles of parents and children are rigidly defined and members of the familial system are forbidden to assume duties outside their own roles. In other families role boundaries are more flexible, and in dysfunctional families few boundaries exist.

Consultants need to be aware of the systems to which consultees belong, the rules and communication patterns within those systems, and the norms that have been established for their consultees. For example, many mental health agencies have adopted a norm of treating clients using individual therapeutic strategies in spite of evidence that group approaches are as effective as individual therapy and more efficient. Consultants who ignore this norm in their attempts to improve the efficiency and effectiveness of their consultees will undoubtedly encounter resistance. Consultants may also discover that formal communication mechanisms and the information relayed through them is at least partially ignored in favor of the information that is relayed through informal channels in the organization.

Clients also belong to systems, including families, classrooms, treatment units, friendship groups, and so forth. Therefore, a necessary part of any consultation process is to make consultees aware of the systems variables that influence their clients' functioning. Teachers often come to mental health consultants such as social workers, school counselors, and school psychologists with concerns about one or more children in their classrooms. Observation may reveal that the teacher ignores some of the less able students, responds differently to students of color, waits longer for boys to respond to questions than she or he waits for girls to respond to questions, and so forth. Students are aware of the unwritten rules and the messages being communicated, and respond accordingly. Their teacher may have received exceptional evaluations and will resist efforts to change for fear these evaluations will suffer. Consultants must be aware that changing one aspect of a system, such as the way one mental health practitioner deals with clients, will have consequences—often unfortunate, unintended consequences—in other parts of the system, because of the interdependence of the people in the system.

Consultants may find it useful to take the stance that it is difficult to establish blame (causality). For example, consultees such as therapists, teachers, or parents may blame themselves or others for the problems experienced by their clients, students, and children respectively. To minimize guilt and defensiveness, consultants may wish to reassure their consultees that the problems manifested by their clients, students, or children are rarely the result of a single act or set of actions. However, consultants are in the business of bringing about change by altering the knowledge, attitudes, and behaviors of consultees, that is, of influencing causal relationships.

Every consultant must have a well-developed sense of how behavior develops and is changed. Caplan (1970) anchored his theory of mental health consultation in psychoanalytic theory. The model discussed in this chapter has eclectic roots, two of which are variations of learning theory: Bandura's social learning theory (1971, 1986) and Feather's expectancy–valence framework (1988). Another precursor to the model discussed in this chapter is the research of Rokeach (1973) on the role of values in human behavior. Both Bandura and Feather subscribed to the idea that human behavior is acquired through various types of learning including classical conditioning, operant conditioning, and observational learning, with the latter category of learning being the most important. They also posited that human beings engage in self-regulatory thought and that there are three factors that influence such thinking: self-efficacy, expected outcomes, and goals. Bandura (1986) emphasized the importance of self-efficacy in his theory while Feather (1988) placed greater emphasis on expected outcomes. *Self-efficacy* is defined as an individual's belief that he or she can perform specified tasks within certain contexts. The adolescent who indicates that she is "good student" is making a statement based on her belief that she can perform a set of complex tasks in a variety of learning environments. The self-efficacy beliefs of most therapists ebb and flow during their own educational process as they gain more knowledge, skills, and experience, but even experienced therapists encounter cases that they believe are beyond their skill level. They have low self-efficacy.

Outcome expectations are forecasts of what will occur if certain courses of action are undertaken and are obviously tied to self-efficacy. If an individual believes that he or she can perform a task (self-efficacy is high) and that the performance of the task will result in a desired outcome (positive outcome expectations), they are likely to engage in that behavior.

The third dimension of self-regulatory cognitions is *goals*. The position here is that goals are linked to values, which introduces a construct not considered by Bandura (1986) or Feather (1988). However, the idea that values are central to human behavior is in accord with the pioneering work of Rokeach (1973). *Values* are central beliefs that are the basis of goal-setting once they are crystallized and prioritized. They are experienced as oughts and shoulds and are the basis for self-evaluation as well as evaluation by others (Rokeach, 1973). Individuals who do not engage in behavior that is consistent with their values will have negative emotional responses. Moreover, people who do not act in accord with the values held by an individual are likely to be viewed critically by that person. The classic example of this latter phenomenon is ethnocentrism.

During their training most mental health professionals have been involved in experiences that make them aware of their values and how they can influence their behavior. However, few of the people with whom mental health professionals consult have had similar experiences. Consultants can help consultees crystallize and prioritize their values through simple contemplation (What do you believe? What is important to you?). Values are also crystallized and prioritized when conflict occurs in an individual's life (Rokeach, 1973). Many mental health professionals working in low-paid jobs in public agencies have experienced a conflict between their desire to help people as the primary focus of their life and the desire to make more money. The perceived worth of engaging in an activity or set of activities (outcome expectations) is determined by its relationship to one's values and the goals growing out of those values, and some of the people who experienced discomfort with their jobs because of their salaries resolved the situation by taking other jobs. Some of the values that influence the goal-oriented behavior of consultants, consultees, and clients are listed below:

- Financial prosperity—it is important to accumulate money/property
- Achievement—it is important to challenge yourself and work hard
- Creativity—it is important to create new things or ideas
- Belonging—it is important to be accepted by others
- Concern for others—the well-being of others is important
- Concern for the environment—it is important to protect and preserve the environment
- Health and activity—it is important to be healthy and physically active
- Humility—it is important to be modest about one's accomplishments
- Independence—it is important to make one's own importance and do things your own way
- Loyalty to family or group—it is important to follow the traditions and expectations of your family or group
- Privacy—it is important to have time alone
- Responsibility—it is important to be dependable and trustworthy

- Scientific understanding—it is important to use scientific principles to solve problems
- Spirituality—It is important to have spiritual beliefs and to believe that you are a part of something greater than yourself. (Crace & Brown, 1996)[1]

It is expected that the values listed above routinely influence the work of consultees. For example, consultees who value Health and Physical Activity are likely to emphasize diet and exercise, consultees who value Scientific Understanding may encourage clients to make decisions based on facts, and so forth. Consultee's values only become a problem when they interfere with their work with clients. This occurs when the consultee pushes an agenda such as challenging one's self to achieve at a higher level (Achievement) when the client does not share that value. Consultees who value Independence, a value frequently held by white European Americans, are likely to be in conflict with clients who value Loyalty to Family or Group. Similarly, consultees who value Concern for Others may be in conflict with clients who eschew interpersonal involvement in their pursuit of wealth (Financial Prosperity), and so forth.

Once goals are established, individuals engage in activities to increase the skills needed to reach their goals, that is, to increase their self-efficacy. A consultee's self-efficacy can be increased through the successful performance of a task; observing a model who is similar to the consultee perform the skill to be leaned; encouragement; and, in those cases where anxiety is a barrier to performance, by reducing anxiety (Bandura, 1986). If an individual determines that they cannot develop the skills needed to reach their goals because the tasks involved are too difficult or because of contextual variables such as lack of access to training, goals will be adjusted in concert with their values.

In the forgoing discussion the issue of ethnocentrism was mentioned. Ethnocentrism is the perception by one cultural group that it is superior to other cultural groups who hold different beliefs and practice different customs. Sue and Sue (1990) concluded that many mental health professionals are ethnocentric because they are insensitive to the beliefs and customs of their clients. The result has been that cross-cultural therapeutic efforts have been less successful than similar efforts where clients and therapist have the same cultural orientation. Earlier, Pinto (1981) identified four cross-cultural consultation styles: self-centered anti-adaptive, technique-centered non-adaptive, client-centered adaptive, and contract-centered adaptive. The first of these, self-centered anti-adaptive, is blatantly racist because the consultant considers the culture of the consultee to be inferior and thus disregards contextual issues in the consultation process. Consultants using the second style, technique-centered non-adaptive, are to some degree culturally sensitive, but because they are unaware of the need to adapt consulting techniques to the culture of the consultee they are ineffective. Consultants who use the third style, client-centered adaptive, are culturally sensitive and gear their consulting strategies to the values and traditions of the consultee. Consultants who use the fourth style, contract-centered adaptive, establish consulting contracts without regard to the unique cultural perspectives of their consultees and are likely to be ineffective because they proceed with the contract as written and may fail to ensure that the consulting process is culturally sensitive. Not surprisingly, Pinto (1981) recommended that consultants engaged in cross-cultural interactions adopt the client-centered adaptive style. In order to implement this consulting style, consultants need to

[1]*Source: Life Values Inventory* by R. K. Crace and D. Brown (1996). Chapel Hill, NC: Life Values Resources. Reprinted by permission of the publisher.

be familiar with the culture of the consultee. Hogan-Garcia (1998) noted that cultures have the following characteristics:

- A distinct history
- Specific intra- and intergroup interaction patterns
- Value orientations
- Distinct factors that determine social status within the culture
- Language and communication patterns
- Family life process including gender roles and marital customs
- Healing beliefs and practices
- Diet and clothing
- Religious beliefs and practices
- Artistic forms of expression
- Preferred recreational activities

Two of the aspects of culture identified by Hogan-Garcia, value orientations and preferred verbal and nonverbal styles, will be discussed in this section. Consultants who expect to be successful in cross-cultural consultation will need to pursue additional information about the customs, traditions, and worldviews of their consultees in books such as *Understanding Diversity* by Okun, Fried, and Okun (1999).

Earlier in this discussion it was asserted that values are primary influences on goals and expected outcomes. Therefore, an important point of departure for understanding people from various cultures is to understand their cultural values. Typically cultural values are classified into categories dealing with social relationships, time, activity, and self-control (Carter, 1991). What follows is a somewhat simplified listing of the values most often associated with each of these categories, a brief definition of each value, and some typical behavior associated with each value. Following this listing, the issue of assessing consultees' values will be addressed.

Social Relationship Values

- Individualism—the individual is the most important social unit. Independent behavior and decision-making is approved and encouraged.
- Collectivism—the group or tribe is the most important social unit. Behavior that is in concert with group expectations is approved and encouraged. Behavior that elevates the individual is discouraged. Expectations are communicated subtly.
- Collectivism: lineal—the group is the most important social unit. Behavior that contributes to the group or tribe is encouraged. In the matter of personal decision-making, individuals are expected to defer to the wishes of persons in status positions such as fathers and mothers. Independent decision-making is discouraged and, in some instances, punished severely. Deference to people in authority is expected and practiced.

Values Regarding Time

- Future orientation—the part of life that is ahead is most important. Goal setting and preparing for the future are encouraged, as is punctuality.
- Present orientation—the present is most important. Live in the moment and the future will take care of itself. Setting future goals is less important. Punctuality is less important.

- Past-present orientation—the lessons and traditions of the past must not be forgotten as the future is planned. Punctuality is important, as is planning for the future. Honoring family and cultural traditions is encouraged.
- Circular orientation—time is recurring and future events are not as important as what is occurring in the present. Keeping track of time mechanically via watches and calendars is not important. Events do not start at a specified time. Rather they begin when all the people involved are present.

Values Regarding Activity

- Doing—the problems that are presented by nature and society are to be addressed and "fixed" as quickly as possible. Problem solving is encouraged.
- Becoming—the problems presented by nature and society can wait. Immediate problem solving and action taking may be unnecessary.

Values Regarding Self-Control

- Self-control is moderately important—it is all right to allow your emotions to show and to discuss your innermost thoughts. Emotions such as joy and sorrow are expressed somewhat openly. Innermost thoughts are self-disclosed with friends, family members, and therapists.
- Self-control is very important—that is, controlling one's feelings and emotions is very important. Emotions such as joy, anger, and sorrow may be masked. Discussing feeling and innermost thoughts is viewed as inappropriate in most situations including therapeutic encounters.

Consultants engaged in cross-cultural consultation must draw accurate conclusions about the values of their consultees. The question is, how can this be done? Sue and Sue (1999) and Ho (1995) warn against using sociodemographic characteristics as the basis of this decision, because this can result in erroneous stereotypes. There are two reasons why using cultural stereotypes based on external features and labels may be problematic. First, there is great variability among people in all cultures. Although the typical values pattern among white European Americans is individualism, future time orientation, a doing activity orientation, and moderate concern for self-control, most consultants could easily identify a number of white European Americans who do not hold all of these values. Second, because of acculturation many members of cultural minorities have adopted some or all of the values of the dominant culture. Certain factors, such as those identified by Hogan-Garcia (1999), may provide clues to the values system of the consultee: the length of time immigrants have been in this country, first language spoken or facility with English, and nature of the community in which they live. Consultees who are relatively new arrivals to this country, maintain their native language, and live in communities with people who are from their country or region of origin or are geographically isolated from the dominant culture are *more likely* to hold the typical values of their culture. Thus among Native Americans, the most diverse of all the minority groups in this country (Herring, 1996), those who live in isolation and retain their native language are more likely to hold a collective social relationships value, have a circular time orientation, value a high level of self-control, and hold a being activity value. Hispanic Americans who are new arrivals, speak Spanish in the home, and live in communities with other newly arrived Hispanic Americans may hold a collective-lineal social value, a being activity value, have a moderate concern about self-control, and a present time orientation (Altarriba & Bauer, 1998; Carter, 1991). Asian Americans may hold a collective-lineal social value, a past-future time orientation, a doing activity orientation, and value a high level of self-control. African Americans may hold a collective social relationship value, a past or present time orientation, have a moderate concern for self-control, and a doing activity orientation (Carter, 1991) or have a values system similar to white, European Americans because of acculturation (or individual variation). As the consulting process evolves, consultants will need to verify whether these are the cultural values of their consultees. This issue will be taken up in more detail later in the chapter.

Space will not permit an extensive discussion of the preferred verbal and nonverbal styles of the major cultural groups in this country. However, Tables 15.1 and 15.2 contain summaries developed by Srebalus and Brown (in press).

What are the implications of the information contained in Tables 15.1 and 15.2? One is that the "therapeutic" communication style often taught to mental health professionals is inappropriate when dealing with many consultees. For example, in the matter of eye contact, nonacculturated Native Americans and Asian Americans may prefer indirect eye contact. The consultant who uses the standard of eye contact preferred by white European Americans runs the risk of being viewed as rude by Native Americans and aggressive by certain groups of Asian Americans such as the Vietnamese. Consultants who insist on using the therapeutic verbal styles that have been found to be effective with white European Americans may also be seen as rude or insensitive. Consultants who use the technique of reflection of feelings, which requires the consultant to identify and verbalize the underlying emotions of the consultee, are likely to alienate Asian Americans and Native Americans, who value a

TABLE 15.1 Preferred Nonverbal Communication Styles of Major Cultural Groups

Group	Handshake	Nods; Facial Expression	Interpersonal Space	Eye Contact
European Americans	firm	smiles & head nods signs of interest	36–42 inches	at least ¾ of the time
American Indians	soft and pliable—firm may be seen as aggressive	smiles and head nods may be seen as foolishness	36–42; closer with peers	indirect
Hispanics	firm for males; soft and pliable for females	initially reserved; animated later	24–36 inches; no desks	indirect, at least at first
African Americans	firm; brother's handshake	expressive nods and facial expression common	36–42 inches	may look away when consultant is talking
Asian Americans	soft and pliable	few smiles; head nods sign of respect	36–42 inches	indirect—look at cheek

Source: Helping in a multicultural society, D. J. Srebalus & D. Brown (in press). Boston: Allyn & Bacon.

TABLE 15.2 Stylistic Differences in Verbal Behavior of Major Cultural Groups

Group	Self-Disclosure	Loudness	Interruptions	Pauses	Directness	Rapidity
European Americans	acceptable; content oriented	moderate	acceptable	yes; may make nervous	direct; task oriented	moderate
American Indians	unacceptable; loss of control	soft; controlled	unacceptable	comfortable	indirect	slow
Hispanics	acceptable	moderate	unacceptable	comfortable	indirect	varies
African Americans	acceptable; affect oriented	moderate	acceptable	yes; may make uncomfortable	indirect initially	moderate
Asian Americans	unacceptable; sign of weakness	soft	unacceptable	comfortable	indirect	slow

Source: Helping in a multicultural society, D. J. Srebalus & D. Brown (in press). Boston: Allyn & Bacon.

high level of self-control. Further, consultants who are accustomed to being interrupted and corrected by their African American and white European American consultees must learn to ask for feedback from their nonacculturated Native American and Asian American consultees after making factual statements or drawing conclusions. They must also learn to be treated as authority figures and not be thwarted in their efforts to establish a coordinate relationship with consultees from these cultures. Obviously, there are many other implications of the information in Table 15.1 for the cross-cultural consultant. Cross-cultural consultants must also be aware of the preferred verbal and nonverbal styles of their consultees, and the information presented in Table 15.2 provides a starting place for the acquisition of this knowledge.

As noted early in this section, the model presented in this chapter has its roots in several sources, including Caplan's theory (1970) of mental health consultation, social learning theory, values theory, systems theory, and the multicultural literature. To recap: Caplan's theory provides some understanding of the consulting process and a set of diagnostic categories that can be useful in the process of assessing both consultees and clients. Social learning theory provides consultants with a basis for developing new behavior and, to some degree, for understanding the motivation of consultees. Values theory provides an important explanation of motivation in that values are the basis of goals. Further, outcome expectation is viewed as a more important source of motivation than is self-efficacy in the model. Consultees are likely to ask themselves, "Are the changes that I need to make worthwhile based on my values?" prior to embarking upon a change process. If the answer to this question is positive then consultees are likely to engage in a process to improve their skills and knowledge. Systems theory provides a useful reminder that consultees, clients, and the consulting process exist in a social context with boundaries, norms, and established communication patterns. Moreover, consultants, consultees, and clients are influenced by the social systems to which they belong, such as their families or communities. Finally, the multicultural literature reminds us that not all cultural groups share the same values and, partially as a result of their values, do not communicate in the same manner. Consultants must take the cultural values and communications styles of their consultees into consideration. Similarly, consultants and consultees who expect to maximize the impact of their work must be sensitive to the cultural values and communication preferences of clients.

The Consulting Process

Earlier it was noted that consultation in mental health settings has the twin foci of improving consultees' ability to provide services and improving the mental health of their clients as result. Thus, two processes are occurring simultaneously. The less formal of these involves efforts to improve consultees' knowledge, skills, self-confidence, and objectivity. The more obvious process, which involves efforts to improve the work of consultees, involves helping the client. Both of these simultaneously occurring processes start with the establishment of the consulting relationship and continue by establishing goals, selecting interventions, intervention implementation, evaluation, and termination.

The following discussion is organized around efforts to assist consultees with their clients, and makes digressions into the processes involved. The stages in the consulting process will be discussed as though they occur in an orderly, linear fashion, but the reality is that they rarely occur in the manner discussed here. Relationship development and maintenance is an ongoing concern in consultation, and problem assessment, goal setting, intervention selection, and implementation may occur several times during a single consultation. The only certainty is that the consulting process begins with relationship development and ends with termination.

Relationship Development

Several issues must be addressed during the relationship-development stage of consultation. These are:

- Who is the consultee?
- Who is the consultant?
- What are the consultee's cultural values?
- What techniques and strategies should be used to develop the relationship?
- What problems should be anticipated?
- What should be done in the first interview?

Identifying the Consultee

In cases involving professionals, identification of consultees poses few problems—with one exception. Outside consultants are often hired by administrators striving to improve the efficiency or effectiveness of personnel within an agency or organization. In order to achieve this goal, consultants may need to provide consultation to personnel within the agency as well as to the administrator. This is a classic example of a dual relationship and should be avoided if possible.

Information gathered during the consultation process is confidential, and thus it is incumbent upon the consultant to clarify what types of information can be disclosed and which must be kept in confidence. For example, information gathered through anonymous surveys about morale, perceptions of the functioning of the organization, suggestions for improvement of the organization, and perceptions about the effectiveness of the leadership should be shared with administrators. Additionally, information collected about administrators during observations may be shared. However, data collected in individual consultations with therapists, case workers, or others should not be shared with administrators. Unless consultants draw these distinctions, they are unlikely to be effective.

Another situation that requires consultants to carefully identify the consultee is when they engage in cross-cultural family consultation (Brown, 1997). In family consultation the parents or other caregivers are consultees and children are excluded. The configuration of families varies across cultures, but they can generally be classified as either nuclear or extended. In nuclear families one or both parents or their surrogates are the consultees. In extended families godparents, grandparents, or other family members may be involved in the consultation. Among some Native American tribes, the family often includes tribal members who have responsibility for the children. The question that must be answered is, "Who are the caregivers?" Once the caregivers are identified, the cultural values of the family become a factor in the selection of the consultee. When family members hold a collective-lineal value they may be either patriarchal or matriarchal. For example, Korean families are often patriarchal and a consultant who assumes that both parents will be involved in making decisions about the children is likely to offend the father. Moreover, the manner in which assistance is provided in these families is crucial. One consultant contradicted a Korean father with the result that the father withdrew from the consultation. She had unwittingly caused him to lose face because he was not accorded proper respect.

In order to identify the consultee, the consultant needs to ascertain the expectations of the person engaging them. In the case of consulting with administrators just discussed, determining the consultee is simply a matter of defining the consultation process, clarifying the role of the consultant, and discussing issues such as confidentiality. When consulting with families, consultants should ask if all important caregivers are present at the first meeting. If there is reason to believe that the family holds a collective-lineal value and that one member of the family is the primary decision-maker (as will be the case in some Asian American and Hispanic American families), observation of the behavior of the people present may reveal this information. If it does not, consultants should ask questions regarding the decision-making process in the family.

Identifying the Consultant

Up to this point, the focus of this discussion has been on the mental health practitioner as consultant. Thomason (1995) pointed out, however, that mental health professionals may have to work in tandem with tribal healers because the parents may not speak English and the beliefs of some Native Americans are not in keeping with current thinking among social workers, psychologists, or mental health counselors. Specifically, some Native Americans attribute mental health problems to supernatural forces and to lack of harmony with nature (Herring, 1996). Tribal healers undergo years of training to deal with these problems and thus may be allies in the consultation process.

As noted above, co-consultation may be required when dealing with Native Americans who do not speak English. Obviously, when the consultant does not speak the language of the consultee someone who does must be involved in the process. If a consultant is available who speaks the language of the consultee, the non-speaker should immediately refer the consultee. If no one is available who is a trained consultant and who speaks the language, consultation can proceed through an interpreter, although finding an interpreter will be difficult at times. Immigrants from many countries such as India and China may speak dozens of variations of the official languages of their countries. Since provincial dialects can vary from each other almost as much as two different languages, it is important to find a speaker who is fluent in the dialect of the consultee.

The Consultee's Values

The matter of determining the consultee's cultural values was discussed in an earlier section of this chapter. However, it is worth reiterating that the consultee's social relationship values, time orientation, activity orientation, and values regarding self-control should dictate many aspects of the consulting process, including scheduling appointments, relationship development strategies, and interventions. Since formal assessment of the consultee is not a part of most consultations, these values will have to be ascertained via clinical observations. Punctuality is one important indicator of time orientation. If the consultee is early or no more that a few minutes late for the first appointment it is likely that they have either a past-future or future time orientation. Consultees who are several minutes to an hour or more late for appointments probably have a present or circular time orientation. Accurate conclusions about time orientation are important, initially because of the need to schedule appointments and later as interventions are designed. Consultees who have a collective social relationship value are likely come to the consultation with other people who are members of their organizations or, in the case of family consultation, their families. They may use "we" more than "I" and make extensive reference to their families or groups. If the consultee holds a collective-lineal value, he or she may be more deferent to the consultant than would be the case with someone who holds an individualism value. This deference may be shown by head nods or bows or the use of titles such as *doctor* or *mister*. Deference may also be demonstrated by subtle references to the expertise of the consultant. (In one encounter with a Native American, I finally gave up on the idea that he should call me by my first name instead of Dr. Brown.)

All consultations involving Asian Americans and Native Americans should begin with the assumption that consultees place great value on self-control, even though this will be erroneous in many instances. This assumption dictates that the data-gathering process be as nonintrusive as possible, that is, that it ask for personal information only on an absolute need-to-know basis. It also dictates that questions about feelings be replaced with questions about thoughts (What do you think? versus How do you feel?) and that reflections of feelings not be used until there is clear clinical evidence that this type of consulting lead would not be offensive. No initial assumptions should be made about the activity values of consultees, but it will be important to ascertain this orientation as the consultation progresses.

Probably the best indicator of activity values is the approaches that consultees have used to solve problems in the past. Consultants who ask consultees to describe their problem-solving behavior are likely to get at least an inkling of their activity orientation.

Techniques and Strategies

The techniques and strategies to be used in establishing a consulting relationship with a consultee will be dependent upon the conclusions drawn about their cultural values. Unfortunately, the processes of assessing cultural values and establishing the consulting relationship occur simultaneously. This is why consultants need to take the approach that is least likely to be offensive to a consultee. For example, consultants may allow themselves to be placed in a superordinate position by some consultees while they assess their social relationships values, and should take care in judging who the decision-maker will be. Further, as noted, consultants should suspend the use of feelings-oriented interviewing strategies until they determine that they are appropriate. They should also be cautious in their selection of other verbal and nonverbal interviewing techniques as they try to ascertain the value structure of their consultees.

Anticipating Problems

The major problems to be anticipated during the relationship-development phase of consultation have already been identified, but a summary will be presented here. First, anticipate that there may be problems identifying the consultee, particularly when consulting with families. Identifying the consultee and establishing role relationships may also be a problem when entering an organization or agency as an external consultant. Determining whether to defer to a tribal healer may also become an issue when dealing with Native Americans. Additionally, the language of the consultee can present the consultee with the choice of making a referral or working with an interpreter. Finally, consultants must be prepared to determine the cultural values of their consultees and to accommodate their values in all phases of consultation, including the scheduling of appointments and the selection of techniques that will be effective in the relationship-development phase of consultation.

The First Interview

Diller (1999) made several suggestions for conducting a first session with culturally different individuals, most of which apply to consultees from all cultures. One of his suggestions is: Do your homework! Culturally competent consultants understand the values, history, customs, and traditions of the cultures of their consultees. During the first meeting, be warm and respectful and focus less on getting down to business and more on the comfort of the consultees. Explain the nature of consultation, including confidentiality issues, using as little jargon as possible. Check with consultees to make sure they understand the consultation process. Then allow consultees to tell why they have come for consultation. Do not be afraid to ask questions or use other means to seek clarification. Once a basic understanding of a consultee's problem is obtained, explain what can be accomplished, the amount of time that it will take to accomplish it, and the roles the consultee, the consultant, and the client will play in attaining the consultee's goals. Explain that additional goals may be established during the consultation process. At the end of this session, establish a time for the second appointment or, if the decision has been made that another consultant needs to be involved, establish a concrete process by which the referral can be made.

Assessment

The questions that must be addressed in the assessment stage of consultation are:

- What is the client's problem?
- In order to address the client's problem, will the consultee need to improve their knowledge, skills, self-confidence, objectivity, or some combination thereof?
- What is the consultee's motivational level?
- Are there systems variables that contribute to the client's or consultee's problems?
- What are the issues that must be anticipated?

The Client's Problem

The assessment of the client begins in the consulting interview and continues as the consultee interacts with the client. Assessment is complete when there is agreement between the consultant and consultee regarding the nature of the client problem. Initially the consultee is asked to describe the client's problem in his or her own words. However, Brown and Schulte (1987) and Bergan and Kratochwill (1990) offered a number of other client-assessment strategies that may be useful. Bergan and Kratochwill, who have a behavioral orientation, suggested the ABC model of assessment. This model is described next:

> A = Antecedents. What situational factors elicit the client's problem behavior, including any interactions between the consultee and the client? Cognitions such as anger are often antecedents to behavior and should be assessed by the consultee as well.
>
> B = Behavior. The consultee should describe the behavior in objective terms. This description should include how often the behavior occurs, where the behavior occurs, with whom the behavior occurs, and the relative intensity and duration of the behavior.
>
> C = Consequences. The consultee should be asked to describe the immediate and long-term consequences (positive and negative) of the behavior.

Bergan and Kratochwill's ABC model is an excellent approach to assessing the client, with two exceptions. One is that they recommend systematic observation that begins with defining the behavior in observable terms, establishing the rate at which the behavior occurs prior to intervention (baseline) through observation and continuing to make systematic observations after the intervention has been implemented. This is a labor-intensive approach that is impractical outside of settings such as schools and correctional institutions. Even in institutions, the amount of time required to gather data about the client using observational approaches might make this approach to data collection unfeasible. The second shortcoming of the Bergan and Kratochwill model is its lack of emphasis on cognitions.

Brown and Schulte (1987) used a social-learning framework (Bandura, 1986) as the basis of their assessment strategies. They suggested that the client's skills, behaviors, knowledge, self-efficacy, and motivation be assessed, as well as environmental variables that may prompt or inhibit certain behaviors. The major difference between Brown and Schulte's model and that of Bergan and Kratochwill (1990) is the former's emphasis on self-regulating cognitions, including self-efficacy expectations and the client's appraisal of the behavior to be performed. Because the assessment of self-efficacy expectations and appraisals is ultimately the responsibility of the consultee, she or he should be taught assessment strategies. Brown and Schulte suggested the use of simple scales to assess the client's self-efficacy and appraisal of the importance of the situation. Other strategies must be used to assess other factors related to the client's problem. For example, a juvenile probation officer supervising a juvenile with a chronic anger problem who must go to school to fulfill the terms of his probation might engage in the following assessment strategies.

Self-efficacy assessment. "How confident are you that you can go to school and, when verbally harassed about your time in jail, keep from fighting? Rate your confidence on a 1 to 10 scale, with 1 meaning that you have no confidence in your ability to refrain from fighting and 10 meaning you are sure you can refrain from fighting."

Appraisal assessment. "How important is it for you to refrain from fighting in school? Rate the importance of avoiding fights using a 1 to 10 scale, with 1 meaning it is of little importance to you to avoid fights and 10 meaning it is very important to you to avoid fighting in school."

Assess other cognitions that may be antecedents to fighting. "What are your thoughts about what is likely to happen when you go to school? Do you ever get angry as you anticipate what other students may say to you? If yes, what are your thoughts?"

Assessing environmental factors. "Are you concerned about the reactions of your peer group if you do not fight when another student makes a remark such as 'jailbird'? Rate how concerned you are about your friends' reactions to your behavior when you are harassed by other students on a 1 to 10 scale, with 1 meaning you are not concerned at all about their reactions and 10 meaning you are very concerned about your friends' reactions to your behavior. What is your family's reaction to your suspension from school after you fight? Rate how concerned you are about your family's reactions to your behavior when you are harassed by other students on a 1 to 10 scale, with 1 meaning you are not concerned at all and 10 meaning you are very concerned about your family's reaction to your fighting."

Assessing behavior. "Describe the last incident that led to a fight. What was the first thing that was said or done by the other student and then what did you do? From that point on describe what happened as though it was a television program, that is, tell me what you and the other student did and said on a scene-by-scene basis." If the consultee is not satisfied with the verbal behavior resulting from the scene-by-scene description of what transpires, he or she can ask the client to role-play the last interchange that they had with another student that resulted in a fight.

Assessing cultural values. What is the client's native language and their facility with English? How long has the client been in this country? Where does the client live? Who are the client's friends? Is their ethnicity the same as his? Are his favorite foods related to his ethnicity? Are his favorite forms of entertainment related to his ethnic background?

Assessing the Consultee

As noted earlier, the assessment of the consultee is less formal than the assessment of the client and begins at the start of the consultation. However, once the client's problem has been identified, the assessment of the consultee must be completed. In the assessment of the consultee's Caplan categories—lack of knowledge, lack of skill, lack of self-confidence, and lack of objectivity—will affect the process. Lack of objectivity is the subtlest of these factors and the hardest to ascertain. Most consultees will admit that they lack the knowledge, skill, or self-confidence needed to work with a particular client, but few will admit that they harbor biases that interfere with their work. In many instances, consultees who are having trouble with their cross-cultural work are practicing inadvertent racism because they are not fully aware of their cultural values and the ethnocentrism that grows out of them. Some mental health professionals (e.g., Diller, 1999; Sue & Sue, 1999) believe that the insensitivity of mental health professionals to the values and worldviews of cultural minorities accounts for the low return rates of these groups to mental health centers. Therefore, if the consultation involves a cross-cultural relationship, consultants should be sensitive to the possibility that a clash of cultural values is responsible for the difficulty.

Assessing objectivity. When assessing professional consultees such as teachers, nurses, parole and probation officers, social services workers, psychologists, and mental health counselors, the first question that must be posed is: Do they have cultural values that differ from those of their clients? If the answer is Yes, the next question is: Is there bias in the relationship? Evidence that bias exists in the consultee–client relationship would include hints from the consultee that the client is not capable of achieving the goals that have been established; criticism of client behavior that is characteristic of his or her group; and lack of motivation because of the feeling that the client is "hopeless."

As Caplan suggested (1970), psychological problems may also result in lack of objectivity, and the consultant needs to determine if this is the case in each consultation. Although transference, countertransference, characterological disorders, and theme interference may result in lack of objectivity, so may common mental health problems such as undiagnosed depression and oppositional personality disorders. Professionals may also have biases regarding individuals who are mentally, physically, and psychologically challenged. Further, it is not uncommon, when dealing with families, to encounter problems such as substance and alcohol abuse, religious fundamentalism, blended family issues, and favoritism among siblings that may trigger lack of objectivity. The presence of some of these problems, such as substance and alcohol abuse and depression, may result in termination of consultation and referral of the consultee for treatment. The consultant's dilemma when there is lack of objectivity is to determine whether to terminate the consultation and refer, or to deal with the problem in the context of consultation without crossing the line into psychotherapy.

Assessing lack of skill, lack of knowledge, and lack of self-confidence. Assessment of lack of knowledge and lack of skill can often be accomplished by asking the consultee to outline the approaches that they have used to deal with clients' problems in the past. Often the descriptions of interventions that have been tried reveal that the consultee has insufficient knowledge or skill to deal with the problem at hand. Professionals who lack knowledge may misdiagnose a client's problems or select inappropriate interventions. In many instances this knowledge deficit results from failure to stay abreast of research regarding new developments in treatment of mental health problems. Parents who come to family consultants often lack the knowledge they need to institute changes in their families. They may also lack the communication skills needed to intervene in their families. Not surprisingly, lack of self-confidence is usually related to lack of knowledge or lack of skill. It may also be the result of too few performance enactments (Bandura, 1986), that is, opportunities to practice a skill or apply knowledge learned in the past. As with client assessment, lack of self-confidence among consultees can be assessed by asking consultees to rate their self-confidence to deal with a client on a 1 to 10 scale, with 1 meaning little or no confidence and 10 meaning that they have a very high level of confidence that they can deal with the client's problem.

Assessing motivation. Lack of objectivity manifests itself in a variety of ways, but the motivational level of the consultee may be an indicator that there is bias in the consultee–client relationship. The assessment of motivation can be assessed, as with clients, by asking consultees to rate their motivational level on a 1 to 10 basis, with 1 meaning very low motivation and 10 meaning a very high motivational level. Consultees are often reluctant to admit that their motivational level is very low, and thus they may rate their motivational level in the midrange of the scale even though their motivation is low. Midrange ratings, that is ratings of 4 to 6, may be clues that motivation is quite low. Other indications that the consultee's motivation is low are a number of failed interventions resulting from failure to follow through, and procrastination in the initiation of interventions. Blaming the client or the client's family may also be an indicator that the consultee's motivation is low. Obviously, lack of motivation can stem from lack of knowledge, lack of skill, lack of self-confidence, and contextual variables such as role overload, and thus it is not a foregone conclusion that low motivation is a result of lack of objectivity.

Assessing systemic variables that may influence consultee. All consultees operate in a context that influences their functioning. If the consultation occurs in the workplace, these variables may include formal policies, supervisor's expectations, peer group expectations, and constraints on functioning growing out of inadequate physical facilities and lack of certain equipment. Consultants who are unfamiliar with the organization should tour the facilities, interview supervisors, and read policy statements prior to initiating the consultation. Further, consultees should be asked to provide their perceptions of the expectations of the people in the organization, the limitations placed on them by physical facilities, and the extent to which the funding of the organization limits their ability to deal with clients.

Issues that Should Be Anticipated

At the end of the assessment phase of consultation, it becomes necessary that the consultee and consultant reach accord on the nature of the client's problem and on what skills, knowledge, and attitudinal changes must be made by the consultee if the client is to be served. Acquisition of knowledge or skills often requires the consultee to spend additional time and energy on work-related problems, which can result in resistance to the consultation process (Brown et al., 2001). The consultant's role at this point is to identify ways that the acquisition of knowledge and skills can be accomplished in the least painful way. Caplan (1970) suggested that if many people in the organization have skills and knowledge deficits, the consultant should attempt to have these deficits addressed through in-service education, as opposed to dealing with them on an individual basis in the context of consultation. Consultants may also provide readings, recommend training experiences, or engage in direct teaching to develop new skills and extend consultees' knowledge.

As noted, the consultee may also lack motivation because of various problems including inadvertent racism, differences in values, psychological problems, and other biases. It is probably too early at the end of the assessment phase to begin addressing these concerns. However, if cultural bias is widespread, a prejudice-reduction workshop should be scheduled that will help all individuals in the organization become aware of their own cultural values, the perceptions growing out of those values, and the potential conflicts that may arise when dealing with people who have different cultural values.

Goal Setting for Client and Consultee

Questions that must be asked in this stage of consultation are:

- If there are multiple concerns, how will goals for the client be prioritized?
- Given the goals that have been set for the client, what are the goals for the consultee?
- How can resistance, particularly that growing out of bias, be ameliorated?
- How can therapy be avoided?

Setting Client Goals

In the matter of setting goals, all consultants agree (e.g., Bergan & Kratochwill, 1990; Wallace & Hall, 1996) that it is imperative that the consultee and the consultant agree on the goals that are to be pursued. Wallace and Hall (1996) also suggested that the goals set should be realistic, specific, simple and straightforward, and measurable. Additionally, target dates should be attached to each goal.

Many clients have multiple problems and thus the consultant and consultee will establish and prioritize multiple goals for the client. Consider again the juvenile probation officer whose client has a chronic anger problem. The client may also have issues such as a poor relationship with parents and dealing with his peer group. Which problem should the consultee and consultant discuss first? The usual answer to this is to address the client's problem that is most likely to result in a successful outcome, particularly if the consultee has motivational concerns or lacks confidence that they can successfully deal with this client. However, if one of the clients' problems places him in jeopardy of being incarcerated if it is not addressed immediately, the decision will likely be to deal with it first. Ultimately the decision regarding where to start should be left to the consultee, although the consultant should make recommendations regarding the priorities that are placed on goals.

The final step in the goal-setting process for the clients is client involvement. Consultants want to make consultees better therapists, case managers, parents, teachers, social workers, and so forth. Most helping processes include clients as active agents in their change processes. The consultee should sit down with the client, identify the problems he or she is experiencing, and establish priorities for coping with those problems. Once this is done, consultants and consultees are ready to proceed to the strategy selection phase of consultation.

Setting Consultee Goals

Setting goals for the consultee is a less formal process than setting goals for the client, and actually occurs across several stages of consultation. Once the goals for the client are established, the consultant may begin the goal-setting process by asking, "Given the goals we have established for the client, what new knowledge or skills do you need to be successful?" This question will be restated later when the specific strategies to be used with the client are selected.

Dealing with Resistance

Resistance occurs when the consultee is opposed to the intervention and can take two general forms, active and passive (Brown et al., 2001; Wallace & Hall, 1996). There are two general forms of resistance and three general sources of reaction. One of these sources is a natural reaction to change when the change threatens an individual's status, requires additional work, or alters an aspect of the individual's functioning that they value highly. The second general source of resistance is psychological deficits such as low self-esteem, oppositional personality disorder, and passive-aggressive personality type. The third source of resistance to change is bias or prejudice; consultees may not believe that change will result in successful outcomes with clients who are culturally different or who have physical, mental, or psychological deficits. Depending on the consultee, one or both types of resistance are likely to emerge as the goal-setting process begins. Some cues that resistance to the change process is beginning are that consultees demonstrate less enthusiasm for consultation, fail to follow through on agreed on tasks such as discussing the goals of consultation with the client, or begin to respond to the consultants' suggestions with Yes, but ("Yes, that is a really good idea, but I tried that last year and it did not work").

Resistance should be expected, and once it occurs the consultants must ask themselves several questions. These are:

1. Is the consulting relationship collegial?
2. Is the change process occurring at a pace acceptable to the consultee?
3. Have I taken steps, such as gaining the supervisor's endorsement for the change process, so that the consultee feels that they will not be disadvantaged by the change process?
4. Does the change process threaten a cherished belief or strategy that the consultee holds or practices?
5. Does the change process increase the workload of the consultee without compensation?
6. Is the change process becoming overly complex?
7. Does the consultee understand the personal benefits of the change process (e.g., ability to deal more successfully with clients, increased approval from supervisor, higher success rate)?
8. Does the change process satisfy one or more of the consultee's basic values, such as Concern for Others, Financial Prosperity, or Responsibility?

9. Does the change process threaten the consultee's place with his or her peer group?
10. Has information about the change process been communicated clearly?

If a consultant can answer in the affirmative to most of these questions and the resistance is mild, it is likely that the source of the resistance is normal psychological reactance. However, if the answer to some of the questions posed above is Yes and the resistance to the changes required by the consultation process is intense, it is likely that psychological deficits are the basis for the resistance. Further, consultants who cannot answer Yes to these questions when they examine their consultation processes are probably raising the anxiety of their clients and increasing their resistance needlessly, and changes in their approach to consultation are required.

As implied in the foregoing paragraph, one way of dealing with normal resistance to change is to make certain that the consultation process is endorsed by supervisors; involves change processes that do not endanger the consultee's status in the organization; is based on a coordinate relationship; is characterized by open communication; and is conducted at a pace acceptable to the consultee. However, when dealing with psychological deficits that lead to resistance or lack of objectivity growing out of bias or prejudice, reducing resistance becomes more complex. Moreover, dealing with psychological deficits or biases and prejudices always poses a threat to the consulting relationship. Nonetheless, it is incumbent on consultants to deal with these issues when they arise because the consultation process is unlikely to yield positive results unless they are identified and their influence on the treatment of the client eliminated.

Normal resistance is dealt with by improving process variables that may be heightening the consultee's anxiety and through the use of information. An example of the latter strategy occurred when a consultant provided a therapist (consultee) who was struggling to shift her focus from individual to group therapy with research summaries comparing individual and group therapy. The use of information is also one approach to dealing with resistance growing out of psychological deficits and bias. Specifically, with regard to cultural or racial stereotypes, information that counteracts the beliefs of the consultee can be presented in written form or through the use of consultant stories. A teacher who believes that African American students do not learn as well as white European American students might provide several examples of African American students who have excelled. The social worker who complains pejoratively about Native Americans being on "Indian time" should be told that Native Americans may hold a different time orientation and be *gently* reminded that the social worker's job is to help the family regardless of the family's orientation to time. If the social worker holds the value Concern for Others, as many social workers do, this new information about time orientation will be incorporated into the desire to be of service to others.

If information does not ameliorate the consultee's lack of objectivity, the next (and often last) step is confrontation. Confrontation by the consultant involves pointing out discrepancies in the consultee's behavior. Discrepancies can occur as follows:

- in verbal behavior — consultee tells two versions of the same story
- between verbal and actual behavior — consultee says one thing and does something different

■ in actual behavior	consultee treats client differently from day to day
■ between verbalizations and body language	consultee agrees verbally but shows discomfort nonverbally

Confrontation can take many forms. It can identify behavior that is indirectly related to the lack of objectivity. It can also involve self-confrontation and direct labeling of sources of the lack of objectivity. Of these three forms of confrontation, direct labeling of the basis of the lack of objectivity is most likely to have a deleterious effect on the consulting relations. However, confrontations of all types should be used as a last resort to deal with lack of objectivity, not only because they may harm the consulting relationship but also because they may damage relationships outside of the consulting relationship.

When confrontation is used to identify discrepancies in behavior that are linked to lack of objectivity, the statements made to the consultee should be presented tentatively rather than as flat statements of fact. The pairs of statements presented below contrast these approaches and represent confrontations dealing with the four types of discrepancies in behavior just described.

1. *Flat Statement:* Based on the information you relayed in the last two sessions, you have two views of Jamarcus. One is that he is bright and can do well academically, and the other is that he isn't capable academically.
   Tentative: You seem to be ambivalent about Jamarcus' academic ability. Correct me if I'm wrong, but in our sessions you have described him both as very capable and as not very capable.
2. *Flat Statement:* On several occasions you told me that you would observe your client's behavior in the treatment unit and to date you have not followed through.
   Tentative: Am I correct in my recollection that you planned to collect observational data on your client on several occasions?
3. *Flat Statement:* It appears to me that although you insist that your oldest child John isn't the favorite child, he receives more attention than the other children do.
   Tentative: Is it possible that you are overlooking the fact that John receives more attention than the other children in the family even though you insist that he is not the favorite?
4. *Flat Statement:* You get visibly uncomfortable when you discuss Xue even though you profess to be as concerned about her as you are the other people with whom you work.
   Tentative: I'm wondering if there aren't some things about Xue that make you uncomfortable, though you insist that you view her just as you do other students.

The second type of confrontation that can be used to make the consultee aware of discrepancies in their own behavior is self-confrontation. Self-confrontation can be used when the overall pattern of the consultees' behavior will not allow them to achieve their goals. Several examples of the use of consultee self-confrontation follow:

Vignette 1. Consultee is a parent who wants her children to grow up responsible and organized, but because of her guilt over her failed marriage is inconsistent with her children. She "lays down the law," then feels bad and picks up the children's clothes, makes their beds, and generally pampers them. They have become increasingly unmanageable at home and at school, but she has failed to follow through with any of the agreements that have been reached to date.

Self-Confrontation. "Mrs. Brown, you have said that your guilt results in some inconsistent behavior when it comes to disciplining your children, but you have also said that you want your children to grow up to be mature, responsible adults. Given what your children are learning at home, what type of adults do you think they will be?"

Vignette 2. Mr. Jones is a teacher in a training school. He appears to stereotype some of the minority students in his class, particularly the African American students, as being less able than the other students are. The result has been that his classroom is in chaos and students have complained bitterly to the superintendent of the school. He faces dismissal if the situation in his class does not change quickly. He is motivated yet unwilling to deal with his racism.

Self-Confrontation. "You're hoping to get your classroom under control soon, but to this point we haven't made much progress toward getting a handle on the problem. You insist that some of your students are incorrigible, but the fact is that they are the types of students that you will have to deal with within this institution. If you were in their place and had yourself as a teacher, how would you view you?"

The third type of confrontation involves direct labeling of the basis for resistance to the consultation process. The statements that follow illustrate this approach:

- We have met several times, and it seems to me that we have made little progress. You seem downright oppositional, in that every suggestion that I have made has been rejected. I'm wondering if we shouldn't terminate the consultation.
- It is clear to me that you treat people of color differently than you do white people, and that is partially the reason that we are not progressing.
- You have said that your self-esteem is at low ebb right now, and I wonder if that isn't getting in the way of our progress.
- You seem to have an aversion to severely handicapped people, and I think this is blocking our progress.

Avoiding Therapy

Consultation, like therapy, involves an interpersonal relationship and a great deal of very personal self-disclosure. Throughout the consultation process there is thus always the danger that the consultation process will be subverted and turn to addressing the psychological problems of the consultee. As noted earlier, this is to be avoided. All changes in the consultee's attitudes and behavior should take place in the context of enhancing her or his functioning *with the client* (Caplan, 1970; 1985). Randolph (1985) suggested that, in order to avoid altering the focus of the consulting relationship , consultants should master a technique he called the *supportive refocus.* Consider what might happen when the consultee with low self-esteem is confronted with the statement from the foregoing paragraph and responds as follows:

CONSULTANT: You have said that your self-esteem is at low ebb right now, and I wonder if that isn't getting in the way of our progress.

CONSULTEE: (Sigh.) You're right. I just can't seem to get things right. I'm very shaky right now. I'd like to be more effective, but I'm afraid of making more mistakes.

CONSULTANT: It is clear that your self-esteem is at an all-time low, and one way to raise it is to make you more effective with your client. However, if you wish to work on the problem with a therapist I'd be glad to make a recommendation.

The consultant has (1) shown her or his support for the consultee; (2) returned the focus to the goal of the consulting contract, which is to improve the consultee's ability to deal with the client; and (3) offered to identify a therapist who can focus on the consultee's problem exclusively. The question that sometimes arises is, What if the consultee's mental state precludes meaningful involvement in consultation? If this is the case, two courses of action are available: termination of the consultation process and referral, or renegotiation of the contract with the consultee to terminate the consultation and begin therapy. If the consultant is internal, that is, works in the same organization or agency as the consultee, engaging in therapy with the consultee should be avoided because it establishes a dual relationship.

Selection and Implementation of Interventions

The major questions to be answered at this stage of the consulting process are:

- What is the most appropriate intervention for the client, given his or her cultural background, the problem that has been identified, the preferences of the consultee, and the contextual variables in which the client and consultee function?
- What steps must be taken to prepare the consultee to implement the intervention?
- What preliminary steps must be taken to evaluate the process and outcomes of the intervention?

Selecting the Most Appropriate Intervention for the Client

In a general sense, the most appropriate interventions are those that are easily communicated, require the least amount of work to learn and implement, and are acceptable within the consultee's organization. Interventions should be acceptable to consultees and in keeping with their personal values (Conoley, Conoley, Ivey, & Scheel, 1991). Additionally, the intervention should be appropriate given the client's cultural values. For example, interventions that bring special attention to clients are inappropriate in cultures that value humility. In this same vein, interventions that require clients to make independent decisions are inappropriate for individuals with collective social values, and certain forms of psychotherapy are inappropriate for clients who value a high level of self-control (Sue & Sue, 1999). In fact, all of the commonly used interventions, from behavioral contracts to psychoanalysis, are rooted in Eurocentric values. Therefore, they should either not be used or modified with clients who have differing values and worldviews. Consultants who work in mental health clinics should expect to encounter a number of practitioners who are using inappropriate interventions with their minority clients. Some guidelines for selecting interventions based on the cultural values of the client can be found in Table 15.3.

TABLE 15.3 Guidelines for Selecting Culturally Sensitive Interventions

Values	Examples of Acceptable Interventions	Examples of Unacceptable Interventions
Social Relationships Values		
Individualism	Traditional interventions used by mental health professionals such as rational-emotive behavior therapy (REBT) (Ellis, 1994) and assertiveness training	Most interventions accepted to some degree
Collective	Group contracts, synergistic therapy (Herring, 1996; Thomas, 1996); person-centered approaches; family therapy and consultation- and community-based interventions; cooperative learning in the classroom	Individual behavioral contracts; assertiveness training because of concern for harmony (simpatico); individual approaches to therapy may be less acceptable than group approaches
Collective-Lineal	Family consultation with the primary decision-maker; group contracts; community interventions	Adlerian family education, therapy, or any approach that emphasizes democracy in the family; assertiveness training
Time Orientation		
Future	Behavioral contracts; setting long- and short-term goals, traditional approaches to therapy	Few traditional interventions are unacceptable if the individual has an individualism value and a doing orientation
Present	Family therapy; contextualist approaches to therapy (Thomas, 1996); informal contracts	Formal behavioral contracts based on specific dates
Past–Present	Behavioral interventions	Formal behavioral contracts based on specific dates
Circular	Informal contracts with events as suggested guidelines, instead of dates; network (Attneave, 1969), and contextualist (Thomas, 1996) approaches to therapy. Use of native healers or traditional native activities such as the talking circle, storytelling, and synergistic therapy (Herring, 1996)	Behavioral contracts; traditional approaches to therapy such as psychoanalysis, rational-emotive therapy (RET), person-centered. Any intervention that requires an orientation to mechanically kept time is inappropriate
Activity Orientation		
Doing	All traditional interventions	None excluded based on this value alone
Being	All traditional interventions; family interventions preferred	None excluded based on this value alone
Value Placed on Self-Control		
Highly Important	All behavioral approaches	Any intervention that requires independent decision making or in-depth self-disclosure of feelings or thoughts including most approaches to psychotherapy; assertiveness training
Moderately Important	All traditional approaches	None precluded on the basis of this value alone

Preparing the Consultee for Implementation

The role of consultants at this point in the consultation process is to ascertain that the consultees have the knowledge, skills, self-confidence, and objectivity needed to implement the interventions that have been selected. This may be accomplished through direct teaching, the provision of materials such as books and videotapes, or through linking consultees to people who have mastered the intervention to be implemented. (This type of linking is more problematic in parent consultation.) As noted, Bandura (1986) believed that one of the most powerful ways to develop new skills is via vicarious modeling, which involves consultees in the observation of models similar to themselves performing the task they must learn. Consultants cannot be fully conversant with all the interventions that consultees need in their work with their clients; however, they can be expected to locate people and resources that can be used to develop these skills.

Preparing for Evaluation

In one sense, this section is misplaced. Preparation for evaluation of consultation outcomes begins with the assessment phase. At the end of the assessment process, clients' problems are identified and goals are established. Whether these goals are attained is the focus of the evaluation. Prior to intervention, the consultant should simply review the nature of the client's problems, the goals that have been established, and how the intervention should impact the problem.

Follow-Up and Evaluation

The questions to be answered at this stage of consultation are:

- How should the implementation process be monitored?
- How will the consultation process be evaluated?
- Is it time to terminate the consultation?

Is the Intervention Working? Monitoring the Process

After the intervention is implemented, the consultant and consultee will continue to meet to monitor the consultee's progress, redesign the intervention as necessary, and evaluate the outcome of the consultation. Consultees may be asked to bring tapes of therapy sessions, but typically the consultee is asked to make verbal reports regarding the client's progress and his or her problems or successes with the intervention. In addition to the obvious task of helping the consultee determine the progress that is being made, the consultant should serve as a source of social support for the consultee. Change can be stressful and frustrating, and thus the consultee will need support in many instances. During the intervention process, resistance may once again manifest itself (or in some instances arise for the first time). If this is the case, the strategies presented earlier should be utilized. As the consultee's success becomes obvious, the consultant may wish to conduct some of the follow-up sessions by telephone or through the use of e-mail.

If it becomes apparent that the intervention being implemented is not working, the consultant needs to review the consultee's knowledge of the interview and her or his skill and self-confidence regarding the intervention.

Evaluation of Outcomes

Probably the single most important issue regarding the outcome of consultation, once the client's problem is identified, is what criteria should be used to determine the success or failure of the process. Behavioral consultants such as Bergan and Kratochwill (1990) have developed elaborate schemes to evaluate the outcomes of their work. These schemes involve establishing a baseline using an observational system and then, once the intervention is put into place, continuing to make observations periodically. Their designs are usually referred to as *single-subject* designs (Heppner, Kivlighan, & Wampold, 1999). Once the target behavior is reached, the intervention is withdrawn and the consultation terminated. The result of the single-subject approach to consultation is a numerical description of what transpired during the consultation process.

Unfortunately, many types of consultation outcome do not lend themselves to the type of quantification called for in single-subject evaluation designs. Another and quite different group of approaches to evaluating consultation is the *qualitative* approaches. "Qualitative research involves understanding the complexity of people's lives by examining individual perspectives in context" (Heppner, Kivlighan, & Wampold, 1999). Qualitative research is typically not concerned about cause-and-effect relationships. Rather, it focuses on reality as it is constructed by the consultant and consultee, and may involve strategies that ask the consultant and consultee to write a narrative description of their views of the consultation process. Qualitative research results in a verbal description of the process and outcomes of consultation. The recommendation here is that the consultee's perspective on the success or failure of the enterprise be the primary criterion used in the evaluation process. Consultants may want to pose questions similar to those that follow.

To the Consultee:

1. Have the goals set for the client been attained?
2. Was the intervention selected responsible for the change, or were other factors responsible for the outcome?
3. Do you feel that you would be able to use the intervention that you are using with this client with other clients in the future?
4. What have been the client's personal reactions to the intervention?
5. What suggestions do you have for improving the consultation process?
6. Would you recommend that colleagues (or parents) seek consultation based on your experiences?
7. Were there organizational factors that limited your ability to take advantage of the consultation process?

To the Client:

1. How have you changed since you began work with the consultee?
2. What were the factors that helped you make the changes you identified?

Consultants and consultees may use several other approaches to evaluate the process and outcomes of consultation. For example, they may use a formative evaluation checklist (Wallace & Hall, 1996) to track the process at each stage in the consultation. Additionally, a number of rating scales have been developed that can be used by the consultant and consultee to evaluate the impact of the consultation on the consultee and client as well as the consultation process (Brown et al., 2001).

Terminating the Consultation Process

Termination of the consultation process should occur (1) when it is clear that consultees' mental health precludes them from being reliable collaborators in the consultation process; (2) when resistance makes it impossible to move ahead in the consultation process; or (3) when the goals of consultation have been attained. In situations (1) and (2), the decision to terminate consultation is largely the consultant's responsibility. In situation (3), that is, when the goals of consultation have been attained, the decision to terminate may be initiated by either the consultant or the consultee.

Ethics and Cross-Cultural Consultation

All of the major groups of mental heath professionals have codes of ethics designed to guide the decision making of their members. Recently Pedersen (1997) raised questions about the adequacy of these codes of ethics as they pertain to minority groups. His discussion focused primarily on the American Counseling Association's code of ethics (ACA, 1997), but applies equally well to other codes such as that of the American Psychological Association (APA, 1992). One of Pedersen's major criticisms of the codes of ethics governing mental health practitioners had to do with their individualistic perspective. Both the APA and the ACA codes of ethics contain statements pertaining to promoting the welfare of the individual, recognizing the uniqueness of every individual, encouraging freedom of choice, and avoiding dual relationships that would preclude dealing with clients and their families simultaneously. As Pedersen noted, the use of language that focuses on individualism may lead mental health practitioners to overlook the perspective of clients who hold a collective value. Promoting the welfare of these clients requires mental health practitioners to recognize and respect their relationships to their families, groups, and tribes, and not to promote individualism.

Pedersen (1997) also pointed out that the codes of ethics of mental health professionals require that they be aware of their own values, and that they avoid imposing their beliefs on the people that they serve. He also suggested that mental health practitioners may not be fully aware of their cultural values (National Advisory Mental Health Council, 1996). Earlier in this chapter it was suggested that cross-cultural consultants need to familiarize themselves with the values and worldviews of their consultees and their clients. Clearly, cross-cultural consultants must also become aware of their own values and worldviews as well.

Finally, until recently ethical guidelines for consultants were all but missing from the codes of the major groups of mental health practitioners (Brown et al., 2001). Some progress has been made in this area, but no code of ethics can provide a set of decision-making rules that covers all situations. Perhaps the APA code (1992) has the clearest statement in this area.

After admonishing psychologists to follow ethical standards, legal guidelines, and psychological licensing board rules, the code makes this statement: "If neither the law nor the Ethics Code resolves an issue, psychologists should consider other material and the dictates of their conscience, as well as seek consultation with others when this is practical" (p. 1958; see Chapter 1 for more detail). The implications of this statement and similar statements in other codes of ethics are twofold. Clearly psychologists and other mental health professionals must recognize that their codes of ethics have limitations such as those pointed out by Pedersen (1997), and are expected to identify material that can help them resolve issues not covered by the usual guidelines. Moreover, consultation is recognized as one means by which psychologists and other mental health professionals can gain the skills they need to deliver services to their clients. Cross-cultural consultants may themselves need consultation.

REFERENCES

ACA. (1997). *Code of ethics and standards of practice.* Alexandria, VA: American Counseling Association.

Altarriba, J., & Bauer, L. M. (1998). Counseling the Hispanic client: Cuban Americans, Mexican Americans, and Puerto Ricans. *Journal of Counseling and Development, 76,* 389–396.

APA. (1992). Ethical principles of psychologists and code of conduct. *American Psychologist, 47,* 1597–1611.

Attneave, C. (1969). Therapy in tribal settings and urban networks. *Family Process, 8,* 192–210.

Bandura, A. (1971). *Social learning theory.* Englewood Cliffs, NJ: Prentice-Hall.

Bandura, A. (1986). *Social foundations of thought and action: A social–cognitive theory.* Englewood Cliffs, NJ: Prentice-Hall.

Bergan, J. R. (1977). *Behavioral consultation.* Columbus, OH: Merrill.

Bergan, J. R., & Kratochwill, T. R. (1990). *Behavioral consultation and therapy.* New York: Plenum Press.

Brown, D. (1997). Implications of cultural values for cross-cultural consultation with families. *Journal of Counseling and Development, 76,* 29–35.

Brown, D., Pryzwansky, W. B., & Schulte, A. C. (1998). *Psychological consultation: Introduction to theory and practice* (4th ed.). Boston: Allyn & Bacon.

Brown, D., Pryzwansky, W. B, & Schulte, A. C. (2001). *Psychological consultation: Introduction to theory and practice* (5th ed.). Boston: Allyn & Bacon.

Brown, D., & Schulte, A. C. (1987). A social learning model of consultation. *Professional Psychology: Research and Practice, 18,* 283–287.

Caplan, G. (1970). *The theory and practice of mental health consultation.* New York: Basic Books.

Caplan, G., & Caplan, R. B. (1993). *Mental health consultation and collaboration.* San Francisco: Jossey-Bass.

Carter, R. T. (1991). Cultural values: A review of the empirical research and implications for counseling. *Journal of Counseling and Development, 70,* 164–173.

Conoley, C., Conoley, J. C., Ivey, D., & Scheel, M. (1991). Enhancing consultation by matching the consultee's perspective. *Journal of Counseling and Development, 69,* 546–549.

Crace, R. K., & Brown, D. (1996). Life values inventory. Chapel Hill, NC: Life Values Resources.

Diller, J. V. (1999). *Cultural diversity: A primer for the human services.* Pacific Grove, CA: Brooks/Cole.

Ellis, A. (1994). Rational emotive behavior therapy approaches to obsessive-compulsive disorder (OCD). *Journal of Rational-Emotive & Cognitive Behavior Therapy, 12*(2), 121–141.

Feather, N. T. (1988). Values, valences, and course enrollments: Testing the role of personal values within an expectancy-valence framework. *Journal of Educational Psychology, 80,* 381–391.

Gallessich, J. (1982). *The profession and practice of consultation.* San Francisco: Jossey-Bass.

Heppner, P. P., Kivlighan, D. M., & Wampold, B. E. (1999). *Research design in counseling.* Pacific Grove, CA: Brooks/Cole.

Herring, R. D. (1996). Synergistic counseling and Native Americans Indian students. *Journal of Counseling and Development, 74,* 542–547.

Ho, D. Y. F. (1995). Internal culture, culturocentrism, and transcendence. *The Counseling Psychologist, 23,* 4–24.

Hogan-Garcia, M. (1998). *The four skills of cultural diversity competence: A process for understanding and practice.* Pacific Grove, CA: Brooks/Cole.

National Advisory Mental Health Council. (1996). Basic behavioral science task force of the National Advisory

Mental Health Council: Basic behavioral science research for mental health: Sociocultural and environmental processes. *American Psychologist, 51,* 722–731.

Okun, B. F., Fried, J., & Okun, M. L. (1999). *Understanding diversity: A learning-as-practice primer.* Pacific Grove, CA: Brooks/Cole.

Pedersen, P. B. (1997). The cultural context of the American Counseling Association Code of Ethics. *Journal of Counseling and Development, 76,* 23–28.

Pinto, R. F. (1981). Consultant orientations and client system perceptions: Styles of cross-cultural consultation. In R. Lippitt & G. Lippitt (Eds.), *Systems thinking: A resource for organization diagnosis and intervention* (pp. 143–178). Washington, DC: International Consultants Foundation.

Poindexter, C. C., Valentine, D., & Conway, P. (1999). *Essential skills for human services.* Pacific Grove, CA: Brooks/Cole.

Randolph, D. L. (1985). *Microconsulting: Basic psychological consulting skills for helping professionals.* Johnson City, TN: Institute of Social Science and Art.

Rokeach, M. (1973). *The nature of human values.* New York: Free Press.

Srebalus, D. J., & Brown, D. (In Press). *Helping in a multicultural society.* Boston: Allyn & Bacon.

Sue, D. W., & Sue, D. (1990). *Counseling the culturally different* (2nd ed.). New York: Wiley.

Sue, D. W., & Sue, D. (1999). *Counseling the culturally different* (3rd ed.). New York: Wiley.

Thomas, S. T. (1996). A sociological perspective on contextualism. *Journal of Counseling and Development 74,* 529–536.

Thomason, T. C. (1995). *Introduction to counseling American Indians.* Flagstaff, AZ: American Indian Rehabilitation Research and Training Center.

Wallace, W. A., & Hall, D. L. (1996). *Psychological consultation: Perspectives and applications.* Pacific Grove, CA: Brooks/Cole.

FOR FURTHER READING

Brown, D., Pryzwansky, W. B., & Schulte, A. C. (2001). *Psychological consultation: Introduction to theory and practice* (5th ed.). Boston: Allyn & Bacon.

Summarizes the major models of consultation and provides suggestions for consulting with teachers and parents.

Caplan, G., & Caplan, R. B. (1993). *Mental health consultation and collaboration.* San Francisco: Jossey-Bass.

An updated version of Caplan's ideas about consultation in mental health settings.

Caplan, G., Caplan, R. B., & Erchul, W. P. (1994). Caplanian mental health consultation: Historical background and current status. *Consulting Psychology Journal, 46,* 2–12.

Another article on Caplan's idea that provides a good historical basis.

Dougherty, A. M. (1990). *Consultation: Practices and perspectives.* Pacific Grove, CA: Brooks/Cole.

A readable book that provides a number of concrete suggestions to the novice consultant.

Wallace, W. A. (1996). *Psychological consultation: Perspectives and applications.* Pacific Grove, CA: Brooks/Cole.

Another basic book that discusses a single model of consultation.

ABOUT THE CONTRIBUTORS

Duane Brown, Ph.D., is Professor of Education at the University of North Carolina–Chapel Hill. He has authored or co-authored over 100 books, research studies, and articles, many of which focus on consultation. Currently he and his co-authors are preparing the fifth edition of their book, *Psychological Consultation: Introduction to Theory and Practice.*

Brian Cade practices in Sydney, Australia. For over 25 years, he has developed the use of the brief approaches. Registered as a family therapist with the United Kingdom Council for Psychotherapy, he is primary author of *A Brief Guide to Brief Therapy,* published in 1993.

Salvatore Cullari is a Professor and Chairperson of the Psychology Department at Lebanon Valley College. In addition to consulting, he maintains a small private practice, specializing in eating disorders and severe mental illness. Dr. Cullari is the author of *Treatment Resistance: A Guide for Practitioners* (1996) and Editor of *Foundations of Clinical Psychology* (1998). Both of these books are published by Allyn and Bacon.

Dr. **Patricia A. Farrell,** a licensed psychologist, police surgeon, and private practitioner, has more than two decades of experience in the mental health field. While at Mt. Sinai Medical Center in New York City, she was the national clinical monitor for a treatment for Alzhemier's disease. Her biography in *Who's Who in America* lists her work as medical consultant to the Division of Disability Determination and to various pharmaceutical corporations.

David M. Gonzalez is a Professor and Director of Training for Counseling Psychology at the University of Northern Colorado. He received his doctorate from the University of Colorado, Boulder in 1988 in clinical psychology and is a licensed psychologist. He co-authored the text *Helping Relationships: Basic Concepts for the Helping Professions* with Art Combs and co-authored the text *The Process of Counseling and Psychotherapy: Matters of Skill* along with I. David Welch.

Alan R. Graham, Ph.D., is a licensed clinical psychologist in Illinois and is president of Associated Clinical Psychologists Consultants. After receiving his Ph.D. from Northwestern University in 1976, Dr. Graham has lectured and written extensively on clinical and business of practice topics. An active member of both the state and national psychological associations, Dr. Graham is the Illinois Psychological Association Health Care Reimbursement Chair and Chair of the Steering Committee of the American Psychological Association Business of Practice Network.

James P. Guinee received his Ph.D. in counseling from the University of Illinois at Urbana–Champaign in 1994. He is a licensed psychologist and training director at the University of Central Arkansas Counseling Center and an Adjunct Professor in the Department of Health Sciences and the Department of Psychology and Counseling. His research interests include supervision and training, ethics, religious issues in counseling, and dream interpretation.

He is a member of the American Psychological Association and the American College Counseling Association. He is also president of the Arkansas College Counseling Association. He has published several articles on supervision and training, and currently serves on the editorial boards of the *Journal of Counseling Psychology* and *The Counseling Psychologist.*

Dale L. Johnson, Ph.D., is Professor of Psychology at the University of Houston. His Ph.D. in clinical psychology was from the University of Kansas. He is a past president of NAMI and chairs the APA Task Force on Serious Mental Illness. He is on the National Institute of Mental Health National Advisory Council.

Samuel Knapp has been the Director of Professional Affairs for the Pennsylvania Psychological Association since 1987. (The views presented in his chapter do not necessarily represent those of the Pennsylvania Psychological Association.) He has written 15 books, more than 70 articles or book chapters, and made numerous professional presentations on ethics, law, and other professional practice issues.

Dr. **Clifford N. Lazarus** is a licensed psychologist currently in full-time practice in Princeton, New Jersey, where he directs Comprehensive Psychological Services. From 1989 to 1994, he was the Associate Director of Princeton Biomedical Research, P.A., a leading facility dedicated to evaluating new generation psychiatric medications for pharmaceutical companies and the Food and Drug Administration.

Dr. Lazarus has published numerous professional papers, articles, and book chapters, and has co-authored two popular books: *Don't Believe It for a Minute—Forty Toxic Ideas That Are Driving You Crazy;* and *The 60-Second Shrink—101 Strategies for Staying Sane in a Crazy World.*

Janet P. Moursund received her B.A. from Knox College and her Ph.D. from the University of Wisconsin, where she worked with Dr. Carl Rogers in his research on variables affecting psychotherapeutic outcome. She has taught at Michigan State University and at the University of Oregon. She is currently Associate Professor Emerita in the Counseling Psychology Department at the University of Oregon. Dr. Moursund is author or co-author of eight books in the field of psychology and counseling, including *The Process of Counseling and Therapy, Integrative Psychotherapy in Action,* and *Beyond Empathy.* Dr. Moursund lives in Eugene, Oregon, and can be contacted at <jmour@oregon.uoregon.edu>.

Dr. **Teresa B. Moyers** received her Ph.D. in clinical psychology from the University of New Mexico in 1991 with a specialty in addictive behaviors. She currently works at the Substance Abuse Treatment Program at the VA Medical Center in Albuquerque, New Mexico, and as an Assistant Professor at the University of New Mexico Psychology Department. She is a founding member of the International Association of Trainers for Motivational Interviewing. Her research interests focus on the impact of therapist beliefs and attitudes in the treatment of addictive behaviors and the use of motivational interviewing for health problems.

David C. Speer, Ph.D., is currently an Associate Professor in the Department of Aging and Mental Health, Louis de la Parte Florida Mental Health Institute, University of South

Florida, Tampa, Florida. He has worked in community-based mental health service delivery settings as a clinician, evaluator, researcher, and CEO for over 20 years.

Dr. **Robert Walrath** received his PsyD. from Nova Southeastern University in 1984 and practices in New Hampshire as both a licensed psychologist and a certified school psychologist. He is a consulting psychologist to the Merrimack, NH school district and is an Adjunct Facility member at Notre Dame College in Manchester, New Hampshire, teaching courses in psychological and special education assessment. He is a managing partner of Manchester Counseling Services, PLLC in Manchester, New Hampshire, where he practices primarily with children and adolescents. Dr. Walrath lives in Manchester, New Hampshire, with his wife and two daughters.

Ira David Welch, Ed.D., ABPP, is a Professor and Director of Training of the Ph.D. program in Counseling Psychology at Gannon University in Erie, Pennsylvania. He received his doctorate from the University of Florida in 1970. He is a licensed psychologist in Pennsylvania. In his practice, he has specialized in working with adult individuals around issues of chronic illness, grief, bereavement, and death and dying. Dr. Welch has published widely in the fields of education, psychotherapy, and counseling. His latest books are *The Path of Psychotherapy* (1998) and *The Process of Counseling and Psychotherapy* (1999) with David M. Gonzalez.

INDEX